RETURN
TICKET HOME

PHILIP MORRELL

To The Memory of The Lady Upstairs

RETURN
TICKET HOME

© 2014, Philip Morrell
ISBN: 978-0-9928652-07

Published by Magna Carta S.C. Limited (publishing)
136 Hamilton Terrace,
London NW8 9UX

www.returntickethome.com

Design by John Amy at promo-design.co.uk
Front cover illustration by Robert Scurrah

REVIEWS

Martin Bell, OBE is a British UNICEF Ambassador, a former broadcast war reporter and former independent politician. He was the Member of Parliament for Tatton from 1997 to 2001:

"The book is a treasure. It offers delightful memories at every turn of the page. I especially like the chapters about being a Barnardo's Boy and about the buccaneering days in the travel industry."

Bruce Oldfield, OBE is a British fashion designer, best known for his couture occasion wear. He dresses Hollywood actresses, British and International royalty and European aristocracy; famous clients have included Sienna Miller, Barbra Streisand, Catherine Zeta-Jones, Diana Ross, Rihanna, Kelly Brook, Taylor Swift, Elizabeth McGovern, Rosamund Pike, Anjelica Huston, Faye Dunaway, Jacqueline Jossa, Melanie Griffith, Charlotte Rampling, Jerry Hall, Joan Collins, Queen Noor of Jordan, Queen Rania of Jordan and Diana, Princess of Wales – Bruce Oldfield is an ex Barnardo boy:

"Philip Morrell's journey began in the Doctor Barnardo's Home, Woodford Bridge, in 1950, and, six decades later, ended in triumph on the Thames, when he lent Her Majesty the Queen his boat for the unforgettable 2012 Diamond Jubilee Flotilla. But it's what happened in between that makes this book such a riveting read. The way in which he started out in a Bayswater bedsit, and went on to build up a trail-blazing travel firm which pioneered journeys to all four corners of the world, including the hitherto closed-off People's Republic of China. In 'Return Ticket Home', Philip doesn't just tell the incredible story of how he went from Barnardo's boy to successful businessman. He shows that, however limited your chances at the start of your life, you still have the opportunity to rise above them."

NOT QUITE THE LAST WORD

As with all journeys, this book had to come to an end at some point. That said, some of the storylines within it remain 'live' to this day, as people emerge from the shadows of the past, bringing added colour, illumination and clarification to the events as described. If you visit the website, www.returntickethome.com, you will find not only updates to these ongoing stories, but 'out-take' chapters that didn't make it past the final edit. Along with a whole feast of images and intriguing titbits of research and information. In other words, the book may have been written, but the journey still continues.

CONTENTS

Part Three

Part Four

Part Five

FOREWORD

To paraphrase that titan of travel writing and influencer of me, Peter Fleming: this book is a superficial account of an unsensational journey throughout my life in the business of travel. This warning to the reader justifies, I think, the superficiality of the book. It is easy to be dogmatic at a distance, and I daresay I could have made my half-baked conclusions on the 'major issues' sound convincing. However, it is one thing to bore one's readers and quite another to mislead them; I do not want to run the risk of doing both and thus I have kept major issues in the background.

The book describes what I saw and what I did in some detail, albeit in considerably less detail than what other travellers or people in the travel business might go into. If the book has any value at all, it is in the light it throws on the process of travel – commercial travel – at particular moments in time in parts of the world that, although not always remote, are seldom visited.

I admit that, on occasion, I have seriously attempted to assess various happenings, but only because (a) I thought I knew a smidgen more about those particular situations than anyone else, and (b) if they had not been explained, then certain sections of the book would not have made sense. For the rest, I make no claim to being directly instructive. It is true that one cannot travel through life without finding out something about it, and the reader, following vicariously in my footsteps, may perhaps learn a little, but not that much.

ACKNOWLEDGEMENTS

I owe a debt of gratitude to more people than can conveniently be named, people of all degrees and many nationalities. He who befriends a fellow traveller in life is not easily forgotten, and I am very grateful indeed to everyone who helped me on what turned out to be a very long and interesting journey. Special thanks though goes to Thomas Ovans, Kuoni, Philip Jackson, Christopher Knowles, Robert Scurrah, Voyages Jules Verne, Sister Monica, John Carter, the daughters of Marian Kozuba-Kozubski, David Scutt, David Pattison and Michael Maynard and the contributors to the VJV *Travel Reviews*.

As Fleming so eloquently remarks in *News from Tartary*: "Most journeys begin less abruptly than they end, and to fix the true beginning of this one, in either time or space, is a task which I do not care to undertake. I find it easier to open my account of it at the moment when I first realised, with a small shock of pleasure and surprise that it had actually begun."

Philip Morrell, February 2014

NOTE TO THE READER

I have applied the spellings of the names of places and people as they were known at the time when the event took place; e.g., Leningrad for St. Petersburg and Peking for Beijing, to name but two. Where not directly relevant to the running narrative, background portraits on various people (and places) are collectively assembled under the heading 'Excursions'. All net proceeds for this publication are in aid of Doctor Barnardo's. Elsewhere under 'Stories in Brief' and in no particular order, anecdotes and background information is given.

Part One
THE BALLOON AND
THE SIXPENCE

HAVING been found wandering the streets of London my mother was summoned to collect me from the Church Mission. But on her arrival, she concluded that her circumstances were so dire that the best course of action was to sign me off and let Doctor Barnardo's Homes (as the organisation was then known) look after me instead.

This is how it came about that I and Sister Wright from the Church Mission found ourselves standing outside the imposing entrance to Doctor Barnardo's headquarters on Stepney Causeway, in London's East End, where the sign above the door read: 'No Destitute Child Ever Refused Admission'. I had just turned six, and it would be 35 years before I saw my mother or June again.

A Story in Brief

FORKS IN THE ROAD: (letter from Sister Wright – Church Mission Hammersmith – dated 3rd May 1950) addressed to Doctor Barnardo's Homes in Stepney Causeway, London enclosing my admission form signed by my mother. 'Dear Sir – Reference: Philip Morrell. Thank you so much for accepting this very unwanted boy – I enclose the agreement and a small birth certificate. At present I think it is impossible to do anything about June (my half-sister) – her mother has never been convicted of anything but June is doing very well at School – we shall have to watch the position carefully after Philip gets away. Philip is the kind of little boy one longs to see cared for and well trained otherwise he is a potential criminal – Yours Faithfully – Sister Wright.' Which all just goes to show I suppose that there are many forks in the road ahead and it's only by chance we take the right one.

CHAPTER 1
IT DOESN'T HAVE TO END
LIKE IT BEGAN

In many ways, my mother's journey through life was predestined to be short and sad. But by comparison mine had begun on the banks of the Thames and this is where mine was to end.

N the Barnardo's TV advertisement 'A Life', 30-year-old Michael is seen happily chatting about his stable life: he has a job, a girlfriend and a baby. However, as he moves on to speak about his past, he somehow regresses back in time, and then we see him as an angry and troubled teenager. Finally, as Michael continues to get younger still, we see how he suffered abuse as a child and we get a glimpse of the support he received from the charity. The advertisement ends with the line: 'It doesn't have to end like it began. Join us to fight for a child's future.'

The poignancy of the piece is heightened when you know that Jaysson James, who plays the part of Michael, was himself in care for much of his life. How this advertisement came about is also an interesting story. It so happens that Jaysson overheard the film crew as they partook in a brainstorming session in a local café and he volunteered the information that his own story mirrored that of the fictional character, Michael. He had no acting experience whatsoever, but what immediately became clear was that he was the real deal: a rounded, together and very genuine young man who had overcome a heart-breaking childhood and was now running his own company.

For many an ex-Barnardo's child, this advertisement struck a deep chord, and I too can identify with much of Michael's passage through life, perhaps with the exception of the angry and troubled teenage period. In my case, I coped by re-inventing myself – you see, I was always on the move, forever being shunted between different orphanages and different foster parents. Each time I was presented with a new set of circumstances, I would adapt my outer self in order to accommodate my new situation: my innermost thoughts and emotions were kept firmly tucked away.

Some people might consider my life before Barnardo's to have been one of abuse, but that was not how I saw it at the time. I knew instinctively, for example, that my plight was indelibly intertwined with that of my mother's and, even at the age of five, I understood that her lot was not an easy one.

Nowadays it has become quite acceptable to wear one's past at Barnardo's as a badge of honour, as a symbol of a rags-to-riches story. However, my overriding emotion back then was not pride, but shame: shame that I did not know who my father was, shame in the manner in which my mother was living and shame that, as a Barnardo's boy, I was somehow different from my contemporaries.

To explain my situation was painful: when quizzed, I would simply say that my parents had died in the war. It was pretence, yes, but it was an effective form of emotional insurance that I invoked for many years. When I reached the age of 40, overcome with guilt, I decided to confront my past and go off in search of my mother and half-sister, June.

The bare facts were as follows: my mother, Ivy May Merry, had married Alfred Morrell at Fulham Registry Office on 10 January 1931; they were both just 19 years old. On the marriage certificate Alfred was described as a builder's labourer and Ivy as a cleaner for the Aerated Water Company, with their address given as 14 Chelmsford Street, Fulham. Over the next eight years they were to have three children – Kenneth, Alfred and June – but their lives would be changed forever by the outbreak of war in 1939. When German bombers appeared in the skies over London, during the afternoon of 7 September 1940, it heralded a tactical shift in Germany's attempt to subdue Great Britain and marked the start of the Blitz. For the next 57 days, London was bombed day and night. Fires consumed large parts of the city, forcing people to seek shelter wherever they could, often in the city's overcrowded Underground stations, which were soon fitted out with bunk beds for 20,000 people.

First-aid facilities, chemical toilets and communal canteens opened up all over the Underground system, under the supervision of specially designated shelter marshalls. The authorities provided stoves and bathrooms, and trains were pressed into service as mobile food dispensers. It wasn't just a random free-for-all, either: in order to maintain order and minimise queuing times in the larger shelters, special tickets were issued. Committees quickly formed to take charge, and bodies such as the British Red Cross, YMCA and Salvation Army did their best to improve conditions underground. Some organisations laid on concerts, films and plays; others lent out books from local libraries.

In these enforced, confined spaces, some personal relationships blossomed, while others inevitably withered; the latter is what happened to the marriage of Ivy and Alfred Morrell. At the start of the war, it had been decided that Ivy and the three children should escape the privations and dangers of wartime London by going to live with an aunt in Devon.

The idea was, when Alfred could spare the time, he would come down and visit them. In the meantime, he would carry on working as a factory labourer and go home each night to the house in Fulham. This is what he did until 19 September 1940, when, along with thousands of other Londoners, he decided to ignore government advice and seek shelter from the bombing in the nearest deep Underground station on Gloucester Road. It was a journey he was to make on many subsequent occasions.

Meanwhile, down in Devon, Ivy hadn't heard from Alfred in months, and was getting worried that he'd been killed. Since telephoning was out of the question, she decided to leave the children with her aunt in Devon and take the train up to London, in order to find out why Alfred had not been in touch. It was a journey that ended badly. On turning the corner into Chelmsford Street, Ivy was confronted by a scene that was to change the direction of her life and cause untold damage to her long-term mental health.

By a cruel coincidence, she arrived at the family home just in time to see the family furniture being moved out. Alfred had fallen in love with another woman, Ada, whom he had met whilst sheltering from the Blitz in the Underground station on Gloucester Road. As a result, the furniture from Chelmsford Street was being shipped out to the new house he now shared with Ada.

This revelation came as a hammer blow to my poor mother. Returning to Devon to be reunited with her children, she fell into a deep depression from which she never really recovered. It got so bad that other members of the family decided she was in no state, either emotionally or financially, to look after the children. Henceforth it was decided that the two boys (Kenneth and Alfie) would go and live with their father, at his new home in Hastings, while June would live with her mother before eventually moving in with her aunt.

It was during this interim period that Ivy and June moved into a basement flat at number 56 Brackenbury Road, Hammersmith, west London. It was not a happy time. Ivy sought solace wherever she could find it, mostly in drink, and she then had the misfortune to fall pregnant through a chance encounter. This is how I, Philip Morrell, came to be born at Hammersmith Hospital on 1 April 1944.

Unfortunately, the arrangements for June's adoption by her aunt had fallen through, as a result of which she ended up acting as my surrogate mother. What little money there was, my mother spent on drink, which meant that food and clothing were in permanently short supply. During the five years I lived at Brackenbury Road, I can't remember having a single hot or cooked meal; each night, before going off to the pub, my mother would leave out for us slices of bread on which she had sprinkled sugar. The only supplements to this diet were bits of crackling that we scavenged from Hart's fish and chip shop, plus broken biscuits from the dairy next door: the shopkeeper would only let us have these once the 'closed' sign went up.

Every so often June and I would be sent off to call on relatives, to beg a few coppers for coal or food. Almost invariably the curtains would remain drawn, the door unanswered, and we would come away empty handed. When all else failed, we would have to make do with discarded fruit from Hammersmith Market.

Come night-time, June and I shared a bed covered not with sheets, but with an old army overcoat. As for shoes, June had a solitary pair of plimsolls and I had a pair of plastic wellington boots. Sadly, even my boots were problematic, in that they were felt not to be acceptable indoor footwear. This meant that, while June was allowed inside friends' houses in her plimsolls, I had to wait outside in my boots, in all weathers.

As my mother was hardly ever at home, I spent my days, at the age of five, touring round London, hopping on and off trains and buses. None of this escaped the attention of our neighbours, who lost little time in informing the authorities about my mother's wayward behaviour, including the fact that she had started bringing men home from the pub, one of whom had turned violent and broken a window. Inspectors were dispatched from the local authority and interviews conducted, but, somehow, things continued much as they had always done.

However, disaster struck one day when I was dangling my legs over the banks of the Thames: one of my boots fell off. Afraid to go home with just one boot on, I decided instead to continue my tour of London's public transport system, until I found myself being collared by a bus conductor at the Albert Memorial for having not paid the fare. Next thing I knew, I was being handed over to police and, by them, delivered to the Church Mission, which I recall as being close to the Lyric Theatre in Hammersmith.

In due course my mother was summoned to collect me. But on her arrival, she concluded that her circumstances were so dire that the best course of action was to sign me off and let Doctor Barnardo's Homes (as the organisation was then known) look after me instead. This is how it came about that I and Sister Wright from the Church Mission found ourselves standing outside the imposing entrance to Doctor Barnardo's headquarters on Stepney Causeway, in London's East End, where the sign above the door read: 'No Destitute Child Ever Refused

A Story in Brief

'Dear Sir, I have come to a decision with myself that I want to go in the Merchant Navy. I have thought about this question for a long time and I do not hope you think that I have been disregarding your advice as I have treated it with due respect. I know that I am turning in a good trade and I do not think for one minute that I could stick this job much longer so I have come to the decision that I must leave. Well sir, that is all for now and hopefully it is the right decision and hoping to hear from you in the very near future. I am Sir – Yours Sincerely Philip Morrell.' I wrote this letter to my aftercare superintendent on 27 March 1960 – I was eventually turned down for the Merchant Navy on account that I had broken my stonemason's apprenticeship indentures – I was 16. Extract taken from my Barnardo's records.

IMAGE COURTESY: BARNARDOS.

Admission'. I had just turned six, and it would be 35 years before I saw my mother or June again.

Unsurprisingly, June was beside herself when she came back from school and couldn't find me for our routine afternoon food-gathering mission. Having searched for me in all the usual places, she went to find my mother in the pub. "I can't find Philip anywhere," said June, sounding just like Nancy in *Oliver Twist*. To which my mother replied: "I just didn't have the money to clothe and feed the boy, so I signed him over to Barnardo's."

Distraught, June went back home alone. Shortly afterwards, she too was put into care, in a local authority home in Sidcup, Kent. There is a passage in Leslie Thomas' book *This Time Next Week*, an account of his time in Barnardo's: "A strange word. 'Home'. Say it one way – just 'home' – and it is the warmest syllable in the language: deep as a hearthrug, satisfying as dinner, assured as love." I gulped when I read this, since it concisely and emotionally summed up how I felt during the 10 years I was under the jurisdiction of Doctor Barnardo's Homes.

As for Ivy, the truth is she never really recovered from her depression and died well before her time. I can see now that she never really had a chance: her own mother had died at the age of just 39, in the great influenza pandemic of 1918, and her father, William, had brought up all seven children himself, never marrying again. In short, Ivy had not been dealt a fair hand in life, and by the end she seemed to have given up the will to live. Right up until her death, there were many personal emotional boxes that she chose to keep firmly closed, including the one with my name on it – to have opened it up would, I believe, have brought her not just great pain, but unbearable shame.

In many ways, my mother's journey through life was predestined to be short and sad. But by comparison mine had begun on the banks of the Thames and took me, via various orphanages and foster parents, to lonely Bayswater bedsits and then to St Paul's Cathedral and St George's Chapel, Windsor Castle, where I left my mark as a stonemason's apprentice. From there, I went on to work in the old Covent Garden Flower Market, at the Theatre Royal in Drury Lane (on its original production of *My Fair Lady*) and for the earliest incarnation of what is now Thomson Holidays. I formed the pioneering travel company Voyages Jules Verne, travelled the world, staged great events and opened up borders. I stood and spoke on the podium of the Great Hall of the People in Peking, and I built some unique ships – among them the *Spirit of Chartwell*, the royal barge that carried the Queen and her family along the Thames, in front of millions of onlookers, on the occasion of the Diamond Jubilee Pageant.

It feels like I have been on a circular journey in life, which has ended as it began: on the Thames.

TEA FOR TWO

My half-sister, June, trained briefly as a 'nippy' (waitress) with J. Lyons & Co., which operated a chain of Teashops and Corner Houses (large, food-oriented department stores) throughout London. Here are her recollections of that experience, along with her reflections on our shared childhood:

"I was only 15 or so when I trained as a nippy. They were quite strict about appearance: your hair had to be neat and tidy, you weren't allowed to wear nail polish and, before you went out on the floor, you would be inspected by an overseer, who made sure that you looked all right. I worked at the Tea Shop in Hammersmith Broadway, close to King Street market, where I used to go as a little girl to see if I could get any food for me and Philip. Sometimes, the stallholders might give me a couple of apples; if we got a banana that was wonderful.

Right from when we were very small, my mother couldn't really cope. She'd had a bit of a nervous breakdown; I'd say she never really recovered from the time when she went round to our old house and found my dad – her husband – winching all the furniture out on pulleys. She loved him, she really did, but he'd met someone else, you see. He moved down to Hastings, which, strangely enough, is where I live now. He had three children with this other woman too, but never married her.

As a result, Philip and I were always hungry. Occasionally we'd have a slice of bread, sprinkled with sugar. (The brand of the bread was Neville's, the first sliced bread there'd been.) We used to go through the bins looking for food; the lady upstairs would sometimes look out of her window and see us. Every so often, when I was out on the road looking for food, Philip would come with me. We'd sit on the step in Brackenbury Road, by the fish and chip shop, and see if we might get something to eat.

Quite often, Philip would go off on his own, even though he was very small. He only had one pair of shoes, a pair of wellington boots, so he used to wear them in summer and winter alike. When I think of him as a little boy and how we used to live in that little, dark basement, it amazes me how well he did in later life. I suppose that with the kind of upbringing we had, he developed some kind of fortitude. He's a fighter and I am too – otherwise you just give up, don't you?

Eventually, of course, Philip ended up in Barnardo's and I went into a care home in Sidcup. What was it like? It was heaven, because I got food. Though I always wondered why Philip and I had been split up and hadn't both gone to Barnardo's. I suppose it was just the policy at the time.

One thing my mum did tell me, a very long time ago, was that she thought Philip's dad was a man with the surname Howe, and one thing about my mum was that she never told a lie: she was as honest as the day is long. I do actually remember the chap; he was quite a dark-headed fellow. He used to knock her about, as usual. I know it sounds strange, because my mother came from a nice family, but I don't think she ever really had a fair chance in life.

The fact is, I was her mum; I used to call her Ivy and, when I had children of my own, I would walk all the way from where I lived in Battersea to where my mum lived in Hammersmith, pushing my children in a big bassinet pram. My mum's own mother died when she was just four, and I don't think she ever had the love a child should have. 'They used to bath me last out of all the children,' I remember her complaining, 'because I was the skinniest.'

There was so much sadness in our lives, in those early days, for Philip and me, and you never quite get rid of it; somehow it stays with you and never quite goes away. All I can say for certain, looking back over our childhood, is that being part of a family, having a mum and dad who love you and look after you, is the most important thing in the whole world."

CHAPTER 2
THE BALLOON AND
THE SIXPENCE

When Sister Wright came bearing an envelope with my name on it,
I was only allowed to open it on the condition that I ate everything put
before me – inside was a birthday card with a big '6' on it.

I remained at the Church Mission in Hammersmith, just a few hundred yards from my home, until arrangements were made to transfer me to Doctor Barnardo's. It was while I was still at the mission that I reached my sixth birthday, an event that remains indelibly etched in my emotions.

As I recall, I had completely lost my appetite and was having to be coaxed into eating. It had gotten to the point that, when Sister Wright came bearing an envelope with my name on it, I was only allowed to open the envelope on the condition that I ate everything put before me – even the custard, which I hated. Inside the envelope was a birthday card with a big '6' on it; attached to the card was a balloon, and inside the neck of the balloon was a solitary sixpence.

For some reason, I took this as a sign that my stay at the Church Mission was to be a temporary one, and that I would soon be reunited with my mother and June. Alas, this proved to be a forlorn hope: it would be 35 years before I saw either of them again. Nevertheless, I kept the birthday card and balloon for many years, as if, somehow, they were my return ticket home.

For the journey to Doctor Barnardo's, Sister Wright and I travelled by Underground to Stepney Causeway, the organisation's headquarters. It was raining heavily as we came out of the station; the roads were glistening with a wet sheen and the tyres of the cars made a swishing sound as they went past.

The Barnardo's building was a sort of industrial wharf, the kind of place that could easily have been a Victorian workhouse. Once we were inside, my personal details were noted down and all my documents handed over, including my birth certificate and proof that I had been baptised in the Church of England. With the taking of my photograph, my Barnardo's registration was complete. Sister Wright was told to take me to the 'Ever Open Door', the name by which the Dr Barnardo's Garden City Home for Boys, at Woodford Bridge, Essex, was then known.

Based around Gwynne House on 39 acres of land, the Boys' Garden City was opened by Dr Barnardo's in 1909. Over the ensuing 20 years, some 30 small detached cottages were built onsite. Each individually named cottage was home to 30 boys, under the supervision of a house matron, and contained two dormitories each sleeping 15 boys.

Meanwhile, other facilities were gradually added, including a swimming pool, chapel and 75-bed hospital serving what was, by the 1930s, a population of around 750 boys. Woodford Bridge became a receiving house for children aged up to 15 in 1948, and in 1949 it was designated an 'Ever Open Door', meaning literally that no child would ever be turned away.

An average day would begin at 6.30am with general household duties, including polishing the dormitories and landings and cleaning the bathroom. Boys were then required to make their beds, wash and get ready for a daily inspection, before being marched to breakfast and finally school. The building known as Canada Hall served as the communal dining room, while the bakery not only produced loaves (5,000 per week) for us boys, but also for our female counterparts at the nearby Village Home in Barkingside.

Of course, I knew nothing about all this on 26 May 1950, the day I arrived at the gates of the Garden City home. To tell the truth, I had not a clue what lay ahead of me; I was in a permanent state of childlike wonderment, which only intensified when I was directed to the Quartermaster's stores, a series of huge rooms containing rack upon rack of clothes. And not just hand-me-downs, as you might expect: all the trousers, shirts, shoes and three-piece suits bore respectable brand names and were brand new.

I must have looked like a typical street urchin, clad in tattered and worn-out clothes. No doubt this is why, before being allowed to try anything on, I was whisked off for the first hot bath of my life and a quick bout of DDT-ing, while my rags were presumably burnt in the communal incinerator. Once cleaned and fully kitted-out, I was put in Angus Cottage, joining the 29-or-so boys who were already resident there.

Today, I expect Angus Cottage has been converted into a lovely, middle-class detached home and sold for a handsome sum; the thing I recall most fondly about it is the way the cherry trees fringed the frontage and how I used to jump up and

A Story in Brief

THE BOYS DID GOOD: Two famous ex-Barnardo's boys look back at how the organisation treated them:

Fashion designer **Bruce Oldfield**, who joined the Barnardo's nursery when he was just one year old: "I think there were some very bad things about the way we were brought up and the way they looked at child care in the 50s and 60s. In my time, there were 25 boys under one roof, 3 to 17 years old, all slightly disturbed. It was very institutionalised and it was bound to be rough justice."

Writer **Leslie Thomas**, author of *The Virgin Soldiers*, drew on memories of his childhood in Barnardo's in his autobiographical first book *This Time Next Week*: "The home I lived in, at Kingston, was a rough, old dump. We called it a mouldy, old shack. The place put terror into your heart. There was a great big tower and it looked like a prison. But it grew on you." IMAGES COURTESY: BARNARDOS.

try to reach their fruit (never once succeeding!).

Suffice it to say that compared to 56 Brackenbury Road, my new living conditions were idyllic. I was getting three meals a day and was both well clothed and properly scrubbed. It was as if a light had gone out in one room and been turned on in another; I cannot remember ever feeling any sense of remorse at being separated from my mother and June. There was no crying myself to sleep or anything like that. I suppose that, at such a young age, there was just too much for me to take in and get used to.

Unquestionably, the conditions at Barnardo's were infinitely superior to those experienced by some children who were living with their families. Rationing had only just been lifted, and quite often boys from outside our village would come knocking at the gates, begging for food. At the same time, though, the high walls and gates that confined us (we were never allowed out unaccompanied) were a constant reminder that, although we yearned to be the same as everyone else, we were different.

Of course, things have moved on in child psychology since then. At the time, you weren't just an orphan or foundling: you were an indelibly branded Barnardo's boy. The fact was even advertised on your school uniform, in some instances. Although I was too young to articulate the reasons why, I knew that I hated the stigma; it never came as any surprise to us when one of our number turned their back on the comforts of the Garden City and ran off in search of some tenuous familial bond, as indeed I eventually did.

There were treats, especially around Christmas time. We were always given free tickets to see the Bertram Mills Circus, the best British circus of the day, perform at Olympia. There would also be Christmas parties at Woodford Bridge, both to please the cameras and to prick the public conscience during the yuletide season. I remember one such occasion, when the BBC had set up their cameras to film a mock party in one of the halls. We boys were sat around circular tables, each of which accommodated a well-known celebrity. When it was my turn to have the microphone thrust before me, I was asked if I knew whom I was sitting next to – and I did: it was Peter May, the England cricket captain!

Despite these high points, there were plenty of moments that I still remember with a sense of dread. One of these stands out in particular. We all slept in shared dormitories, and the rule was: when the light was switched off, the talking had to stop. One night, the house matron became more-than-usually annoyed that we were disobeying this rule and stormed into our dormitory to warn us that, if the talk didn't stop, an unspecified punishment would follow.

To her evident fury, the chatter continued, at which point she made us all get out of bed and sit in the playroom. Then, having found some sticking plaster, she taped up our mouths so tightly we could barely breathe, let alone speak. She left us like that for several hours, before letting us go back to bed. We were 6 years old. After this, we never talked again after lights out.

It wasn't long before I was on the move again. I had been at the Garden City home for just six months when I got the exciting news that I was to be 'boarded out', which in Barnardo's parlance meant I was to be fostered. Accompanied by a uniformed matron, I boarded a steam train at King's Cross Station, en route to a remote and distant northern destination somewhere, I believe, near Aberdeen. The date was 7 December 1950 and I was six-and-a-half years old. By the time we had made our way up the snow-covered hill to my new home, it was already getting dark. The matron knocked at the door and we waited for an age, before it slowly creaked open.

Standing in the doorway was a very startled woman. Straight away, she and the matron launched into a tense and rather hushed conversation, in the middle of which the woman asked, rather worryingly, "Didn't you get my letter?" At this point, I realised that she was not expecting us: not to put too fine a point on it, she had cancelled the order that was me. The problem was, it was getting late; not only was there no way we could get back to the train station, but also the matron needed to contact Barnardo's for instructions, and there wasn't a telephone in the house.

Seeing that we were in a bit of a pickle, the woman agreed that I could stay until the matter had been resolved, which probably made this the shortest-ever fostering on record: within two weeks, I was making the return trek to Woodford Bridge. I arrived back on 22 December 1950, just in time for Christmas and the annual visit to the Bertram Mills Circus.

So, it was back to the familiar Garden City routine, the high point of each week being the film show. A particular favourite of ours was *Boys Town*, not least because it mirrored our own lives. It is a dramatised biography of a real-life priest, Father Edward J. Flanagan (played by Spencer Tracy), who helped a group of underprivileged children at his Boys Town home in Omaha, Nebraska, USA. In the film, Father Flanagan takes the troublesome Whitey Marsh (played by Mickey Rooney) to Boys Town and, even though the young man runs away on three separate occasions, the priest manages to rescue him and bring him back, before Whitey ultimately falls into a life of crime.

In many ways, these films provided us with glimpses of what life was like, or at least was supposed to be like, in the outside world. Without doubt, *Boys Town* had strong resonances for us, in terms of both the subject matter and the characters portrayed. It served as a reminder that there were many forks in the road ahead and that, sometimes, it is only by chance that we choose the right one.

MEET DR BARNARDO

Thomas John Barnardo was born in Dublin in 1845, to Abigail and John Barnardo. His father was a Hamburg-born furrier, possibly of Jewish extraction. At the age of 16, after converting to Protestant evangelicalism, young Thomas decided to become a medical missionary.

As a child Barnardo was not always in the best of health, and he never grew above 5ft 6in (170cm). He came to London in 1866, to train as a doctor – he never formally qualified, but adopted the title of 'Doctor' anyway. In 1867, he set up a ragged school in the East End where poor children could receive a basic education. One evening, a young boy attending the school, Jim Jarvis, took Barnardo on a tour of the streets and showed him homeless children sleeping on roofs and in gutters.

Determined to help these destitute youngsters, Barnardo opened his first home for boys on Stepney Causeway. One night, an 11-year-old boy named John Somers was turned away because the shelter was full. He was found dead two days later, from malnutrition and exposure. From that point on, the sign over the front entrance at Stepney read: 'No Destitute Child Ever Refused Admission'.

From an early age Barnardo preached the evils of alcohol, and as a result he was not always welcomed in pubs. On one occasion he suffered two broken ribs, when drinkers placed an upturned table on top of him and started dancing on it. Nevertheless, some of his earliest followers were people he had helped to give up drink.

Barnardo's unorthodox methods often landed him in trouble – sometimes, even, in court. He freely admitted that he removed children from parents he deemed incapable of looking after them. In 1872 he bought a well-known gin palace in Limehouse, the Edinburgh Castle, close to the docks in the East End of London. He turned it into his mission headquarters and a coffee house.

The site for the Village Home at Barkingside was given to Barnardo as a wedding present, on the occasion of his marriage to Sarah Louise (Syrie) in 1873. The first three cottages were built there in 1875, at a cost of £500. The village was constructed, in a horseshoe shape, around a green and was originally just for girls (eventually 1,500 girls lived there).

Most of the children at Barkingside were there because their parents either didn't want them or couldn't afford to look after them; only 15 per cent had been orphaned. Initially, boys were housed exclusively at nearby Woodford Bridge. There was a reciprocal arrangement whereby the boys baked bread for the girls, who in turn did the boys' laundry. It was only after the Second World War that boys began moving into Barkingside as well.

The cottages at Barkingside all had floral names, such as Heather, Woodbine, Craven, Daisy, Forget-Me-Not, Honeythorn, Jessamine, Primrose, Myrtle and May. There was a babies' bungalow, a hospital wing and special cottages for children with TB, polio and vitamin deficiencies. The church at Barkingside was built in 1892 and is the only specially designated children's church in Britain. The pianos in the church today were donated by Elton John and Mike Oldfield, composer of *Tubular Bells*.

Doctor Barnardo worked at an ingeniously designed desk equipped with vertical wings that could be folded out. Called the Wooton, it was popularly known as the 'King of Desks'. The doctor and his wife, Syrie, had seven children of their own. Three of them died young and one, Marjorie, was born with Down's syndrome. Doctor Barnardo's appointments were regulated by a specially made clock called the Davison: at the beginning of an appointment, he inserted into it a small tablet that would cause a bell to ring when the allotted time was up.

By the time Dr Barnardo died, on 19 September 1905, his charity ran 96 homes caring for some 8,500 children. His funeral was as big a public event as Winston Churchill's, lining the streets with mourners all the way from Liverpool Street to Stepney. His body lay in state at the old Edinburgh Castle, the former pub that he had turned into his mission headquarters.

THE FUNERAL OF THOMAS JOHN BARNARDO IN THE EAST END OF LONDON

CHAPTER 3
BAKED BEANS IN AN ENVELOPE

Of course, preparations had to be made for our journey (to run-away from Barnardo's), so it was decided that the contents of the preceding evening's meal should be saved.

THE Italian phrase 'la dolce vita' (the sweet life) became popular in the English-speaking world following the success of the 1960 film of the same name, directed by Federico Fellini and starring Marcello Mastroianni, Anita Ekberg and Anouk Aimée. Previously commonplace only in Italy, within a short space of time the phrase was adopted by restaurants all over the UK – for example, the La Dolce Vita restaurant on Clarence Street, Swindon, which today occupies the site of the magnificent old Empire Theatre, through whose doors all kinds of well-known entertainers once passed. The list of stars is long and distinguished: Laurel and Hardy; Leslie Philips; Frankie Howerd; George Formby; Tommy Trinder; Charlie Chester; Max Miller; Norman Wisdom; Gracie Fields; Arthur Lucan (in character, in drag, as Old Mother Riley); a very young Julie Andrews. Plus, I might add, a seven-year-old boy by the name of Philip Morrell.

I had been sent from the home in Woodford Bridge to go and live with my new foster parents, Mr and Mrs Collet, and their son, Michael, in Swindon. The Collets lived almost next-door to the Empire, and Mrs Collet worked there in various capacities: her jobs included those of usherette, box-office clerk and barmaid. In the evenings she would take me along to the Empire, so that I was never alone at home. It was, I suppose, an economical form of babysitting. What's more, sitting up in 'the gods' (the cheapest seats) night after night, I got to know all the different routines, in addition to getting free drinks.

I had been transported, seemingly in the blink of an eye, from putting on make-believe shows – as I did back in the Garden City home, using a shoebox and torch as a projector – to actually being in a real, live theatre. Not merely as a

A Story in Brief

THE LOST BOY ON THE TITANIC: It seemed like the perfect opportunity when, in 1912, 17-year-old Barnardo's boy Frederick Humby landed a job as plate steward onboard the SS Titanic's inaugural voyage to New York. Prior to this posting, he had been to the Watts Naval Training School, the forerunner of the Parkstone Sea Training School, in Dorset, where I myself was sent in 1957. A stained glass window was created, in Frederick's memory, bearing the inscription: 'To the Glory of God and in memory of Frederick Humby, a boy hero, who perished on board SS Titanic – 15 April 1912. Last seen at the Barnardo's Boys' Garden City Home at Woodford Bridge, in Essex; the window has since disappeared.

punter, either, but on the business side of things, and it was all rather exciting. For the first time ever, life really did taste sweet.

With my mother now a locked-away memory, I was in my element at the Collets' home; I loved Mr and Mrs Collet and considered them my mum and dad. Best of all, their son, Michael, was the same age as me, and we would spend endless days together during the long, hot summer of 1951, wandering the fields, bird-nesting (collecting eggs) and picking blackberries.

One day, in the Collets' garden, I came across a fruit I had never seen before – a gooseberry, as it turned out – and I was not sure if it needed to be peeled before being eaten. So, I presented the berry to Michael with the question, "How do you eat this?" Whereupon he promptly popped it in his mouth. Even today, I still feel somehow cheated and embarrassed by this incident.

I remember episodes of scrumping for fruit and sneaking under the corrugated iron fencing at Swindon Town Football Club for a free view – something only us small ones could manage. At other times we would go into Swindon town centre, lying in wait for the American GIs who had a base nearby and who, we had heard, were generous dispensers of candy and chewing gum to the local kids. The accepted technique (though it rarely worked in our case) was to match the GIs stride for stride, and then come out with the line: "Any gum, chum?"

Before long, Michael had accepted me as an equal brother and was looking out for me with a real sense of care. Unfortunately, however, the dolce vita that I had been enjoying, for the first time in my life, at Clarence Street was to last barely longer than six months. As the weeks went by, I came to understand – or at least sense – that Mr Collet was ill and that the burden of looking after him, holding down a job at the Empire and bringing up two boys was proving too much for his wife. Although I hardly suspected it at the time, I feel sure that a plan was being hatched by those in charge of me whereby I would be returned to Barnardo's without having to be told outright, so I could instead be let down slowly and quietly, over a period of time.

In the end, it was a sore throat that gave the Collets the opportunity they had been looking for. Back in those days, it was not uncommon for the slightest inflammation to be interpreted as tonsillitis, at which point one would be whisked off for a tonsillectomy. This was the diagnosis in my case, and it was decreed that I should immediately be admitted to hospital. Afterwards I would not be returning to Clarence Street, but to the 'recovery unit' of the Village Home in Barkingside.

I remember being plied with jelly and ice cream – in those days a luxury, but in this case a necessity as a throat lubricant – following my operation. At Barkingside I stayed; every time I asked when I would be going back to Swindon, I got the same answer: "Soon." But after three weeks, it was clear even to me that

I was not going back to the Collets'. This became a certainty when I was transferred to Honeythorn, one of the cottages on the green at Barkingside.

The routine in Honeythorn was not much different than it had been in Angus Cottage, at the Garden City. I vividly recall the day King George VI died, on 6 February 1952, paving the way for his daughter, Princess Elizabeth, to accede to the throne. We Barnardo's children always had a great affinity to the Royal Family and were all saddened at the King's death.

It was around this time that I became aware that some of my fellow Barnardo's boys were to be sent to new homes in Australia and Canada, a trip that was to involve a journey on a great ocean liner. It was a source of resentment to me that I had not been chosen to join them. (Although years later that feeling abated, when a haunting BBC television series, *Barnardo's Children*, showed that not all of these children had enjoyed happy experiences.) So, there was to be no overseas adventure for me; instead, on 2 April 1952, the day after my eighth birthday, I was transferred, for some unknown reason, to another Barnardo's Home: New Lodge, in Windsor. This chopping and changing of both homes and schools was certainly not doing my education, not to mention my confidence, any good.

Things weren't helped by the fact that, back in those days of pen and ink, I was left-handed and could never quite get the hang of writing without smudging what I had already written. As for being able to copy from the blackboard, I was simply unable to get anything down on paper. Thus it wasn't long before I fell hopelessly behind my contemporaries. (Only much later did I come to the realisation that I was, and still am, severely dyslexic). An additional problem was that the school I now attended was not part of Barnardo's. At both the Garden City and Village homes, lessons had been given onsite. At New Lodge, however, we went to a local school a short distance away from Windsor Castle.

The building that housed us was incongruously grand. It had taken three years to build and was designed in Tudor-Gothic style, complete with Delft tiles and stained-glass windows bearing quotations from Shakespeare's *Hamlet*. Its first occupants had been the Belgian ambassador Silvain Van der Weyer (1802-74) and his wife, Elizabeth; the place had been built as a wedding present by the bride's father, on land granted to the Van der Weyers by, it was believed, Queen Victoria, who later came from nearby Windsor Castle to visit the couple for tea. By the time New Lodge was purchased by Dr Barnardo's Homes, in 1942 for £24,000, most of its original treasures had been stowed away.

Despite the richness of its décor, New Lodge was, by Barnardo's standards, quite small: it housed just 150 boys and lacked a church as well as a school. On weekdays, life revolved around the coach ride into school, and on Sundays, around the walk through the countryside to church. The grounds at New Lodge were vast and thus perfect for sport, at which many of the boys excelled.

Yet even though conditions within the Barnardo's homes – especially New Lodge – were far better than those experienced by many a child in the outside world, it is an inescapable fact that many ex-Barnardo's children were left feeling ambivalent or even hostile to the institution. Much of this was due to the way in which Barnardo's was founded and administered, in line with Church of England doctrines. This religious zeal resulted in a form of branding, both of the institution and of the children in its care. Little attention was paid to child psychology (admittedly a failing not just limited to Barnardo's): what the organisation did not take into consideration was that we children longed to be treated just like any child on the outside, rather than being branded and stigmatised. On many occasions boys would write letters with the 'Dr Barnardo's Homes' letterhead cut off, only for the internal censor to insist that they reinstitute it.

Another thing we hated about New Lodge was the fact that we were dressed in a different uniform than the other children at the local school: we had to wear clearly identifiable, gold-taped collars, lapels and cuffs. We also loathed the events known as 'showcases', whereby us Barnardo's boys were invited to mingle with would-be Saturday-afternoon parental escorts, who, having surveyed and selected their preferred child, would deign to offer him their company at a later date.

It was against this background, at the age of eight, that I and another boy hatched a plan to run away – 'to do the bunk', in Barnardo's parlance. The idea was to follow the Thames all the way to London, since that was where we believed 'home' was, or at least should be. During my time at Barnardo's, there were hundreds, if not thousands, of similar planned escapes. Though most ended in failure, any attempt earned status among the rest of the boys. No surprise, then, that wartime escape films were so popular with us.

Of course, preparations had to be made for our journey, so it was decided that the contents of the preceding evening's meal should be saved, an operation that involved stuffing baked beans along with a knife and fork – for the sake of completeness, if nothing else – into an envelope. Our provisions in place, we bided our time until the end of the school day and, instead of getting on the bus back to New Lodge with the others, we set off for London.

For a short while, everything went well. However, it wasn't long before the road began separating from the river and, lost, cold and with all our provisions eaten, we wandered into a farm. We found that raw turnips were not as easy to eat or as tasty as we had hoped. Continuing our journey, we were spotted by a police car at around midnight and taken to the local station for interrogation. In due course, representatives from New Lodge arrived at the police station and we two runaways were brought back home, in disgrace. As my partner-in-crime was a few months older than me, he was held to have led me astray and punished with several lashes of the cane.

I was to stay at New Lodge until 20 February 1954: a period of just under two years, the longest stretch of time that I had spent anywhere apart from 56 Brackenbury Road. My next port of call was Cheshire and another set of foster parents. As for the Empire Theatre in Swindon, it closed down in 1955 and, after lying idle for a few years, was eventually demolished, making way for the aforesaid La Dolce Vita restaurant. The last show the Empire staged was the Christmas pantomime *Robinson Crusoe*, 57 years after its first production, *Dick Whittington and His Cat*. And as for myself, in 2012, a full 60 years after failing to complete my Dick Whittington-esque journey to London as an eight-year-old, I finally made it into London along the Thames, to City Hall – not to become the Mayor of London but to listen to him. That, though, is a story for later.

DR THOMAS JOHN BARNARDO

A Story in Brief:

IMAGE COURTESY: BARNARDOS.

SYRIE MAUGHAM: (Dr Barnardo's daughter) having earlier divorced Henry Wellcome of the Wellcome Trust, married Somerset Maugham at a time before Maugham had openly declared himself as being 'gay', later becoming an interior designer in her own right and credited for having designed the first all-white room. In the early 1910s, she established an interior decorating business in London, and as her reputation grew, opened showrooms in New York and Chicago. She is best-remembered though for the music room at her house on King's Road, London and the salon at her villa at Le Touquet. The music room was actually the only room designed in all white. Syrie's daughter Liza married in 1936, and the London house Syrie decorated for her was among her best work. Later Syrie travelled to India with Elsie de Wolfe to paint the Black Hole of Calcutta white. Amongst the long list of high society clients Syrie could count on was Wallis Simpson.

CHAPTER 4
THE PAST IS ANOTHER COUNTRY

*Looking now at that copy of the 'Reader's Digest' publication
'Yesterday's Britain', with its photograph of my hop-picking relatives,
I am struck by the relevance — to me, at any rate — of its sentiments.*

O N 22 September 1951, the front cover of *Picture Post*, the leading photo-graphic publication of the day, carried the image of the young Princess Elizabeth on horseback, saluting the Grenadier Guards at the conclusion of the Trooping the Colour ceremony on Horse Guards Parade. She was deputis-ing for her father, George VI, who was unable to be there because of ill health. Inside the magazine were a further four colour pages devoted to the event and the preparations for it, along with the caption: 'An able deputy takes over her father's duties.'

The remainder of the issue consisted of various articles and photographs, including features on a Mr Universe competition (and two women's views on it), 'Music Hall Under the Arches' (a piece on the Players' Theatre in London) and 'Sex and the Citizen (What to Tell Your Children)'; a travel article on 'St Francis and the Pilgrims' Way to Assisi'; coverage of the assassination of King Abdullah of Jordan and its perpetrators' execution; and a celebrity profile of the West End actress Tallulah Bankhead. But the article that was flagged up most prominently on the front cover, and which ran for six pages inside, was about the annual East Enders' exodus to Kent. Under the headline 'Hopping Holiday', this piece des-cribed the annual three-week hop-picking vacation enjoyed by the sun-starved inhabitants of the East End, in countryside 50 miles outside the capital.

Back then, every September some 40,000 Londoners would escape the smoke and grime of the city for the fresh air and open fields of hop-country. The majority headed for Kent, but one-in-10 went to work in hop gardens on the East Sussex side of the 'Kent Ditch' (as the river separating the two counties is colloquially known), where they were put up in special camps around the small village of Bodiam. While their services were undoubtedly needed, the hop-pickers themselves were not exactly greeted with open arms: they were required to arrive just one day before the hop-picking was due to start and expected to depart as soon as it had ended.

Pubs were equally unwelcoming. To their customary 'Everyone is Welcome' signs, landlords would add little supplementary messages, such as 'No – no coaches, no gypsies and no hop-pickers.' Classier establishments might add the qualification, '… due to lack of room.' As a result, pickers preferred to travel direct to their camps, by lorry, without stopping on the way, bringing everything they needed for their stay, apart from firewood.

Most of those camped at Bodiam were from east or southeast London, while a thousand came from nearby Hastings. Among the latter were my mother's husband, Alfred, accompanied by Ada, the lady he had met while sheltering in the Underground during the Blitz, and their three children.

The huts everyone occupied were corrugated iron sheds, arranged in long lines, and were windowless except for a space above the door. These structures were not designed for anything other than a short, three-week stay. None of them were equipped with toilets or running water; instead, the hop-pickers had to use communal latrines and water standpipes. Luxuries were non-existent, although, of an evening, there would be a knees-up. These took place either outdoors, around a campfire, or indoors if they could find a pub that would let them in. "We only go down hopping," they would sing, "to earn a pound or two." But while the money certainly came in handy – traditionally, it was spent on winter clothes for the children – the truth was, most people went hop-picking because they enjoyed it.

There were snootier sections of society who saw hop-picking as the kind of activity suitable only for the lower classes. Not that this bothered Bert Hardy, the famed *Picture Post* photographer who, in September 1951, came to join Alfred and the other pickers at Bodiam, for he too had begun life in humble inner-city surroundings, in Blackfriars. The eldest of seven children, Bert left school at 14 to work for a chemist who, as a side-line, developed photographs for customers. Soon, Bert began taking photographs himself. His first success was capturing, in 1936, King George V and Queen Mary passing in a carriage, which resulted in him selling 200 postcard prints of the picture. Next he began freelancing for *Bicycle Magazine*, and used his income to buy a small-format Leica 35mm camera.

After a stint with the General Photographic Agency, in 1941 Bert was hired by Tom Hopkinson to work on *Picture Post*. He got his first credit in the magazine that same year, with a photo-essay chronicling the work of the Blitz firefighters. It was the start of an illustrous career. Despite being completely self-taught

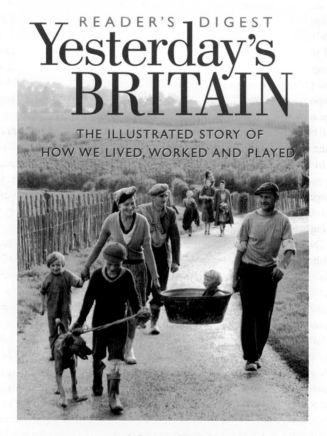

READER'S DIGEST

Yesterday's BRITAIN

THE ILLUSTRATED STORY OF HOW WE LIVED, WORKED AND PLAYED

A Story in Brief

THE PAST IS ANOTHER COUNTRY/READER'S DIGEST: The book *Yesterday's Britain* poses – and answers – the question "What was it like?" What was it like to sleep in an Anderson shelter as the bombs rained down? To eat snoek? To hear rock'n'roll for the first time? To sit the 11-plus? To later generations, who didn't have those experiences, this volume serves as a sort of travel guide to the last 100 years. It highlights some of the things which would strike a visitor from present day as bizarre or downright alien. Did television really stop broadcasting for an hour every evening, so that parents could get the children to bed? Did men actually sit on the beach in their heavy suits with a knotted handkerchief on their heads? Was there truly a time when motorways were as empty as the open seas?

and the fact that he used a Leica camera (an unconventional choice at the time), Bert went on to become the *Picture Post*'s chief photographer. It was his belief that you didn't need to own an expensive camera in order to take good pictures; to prove this, he wrote an article in a magazine for amateur photographers for which he took, using a cheap Box Brownie camera, a carefully posed photograph of two young women sitting on railings above a breezy Blackpool promenade. The picture, taken in 1951, has since become an iconic image of post-war Britain, and it epitomises Bert's ability to capture the essence of the country's working classes, which presumably is why he was sent to cover the annual hop-picking holiday in Bodiam.

Indeed, Bert Hardy's pictures vividly convey the hop-picking experience: the long morning trudge to the hop fields, the hop measurers and their horse carriages, the arduous work involved in stripping the 'bines' (shoots), the primitive living conditions and the dancing and singing around the campfire in the evenings.

There was one particular image that, for some reason, *Picture Post* did not publish in 1951 and which did not see the light of day for some years. It was finally published in 1998, on the front cover of a *Reader's Digest* publication entitled *Yesterday's Britain*. This book covers the eight decades leading up to 1980 and is full of evocative photographs, images, incidents and anecdotes from the 20th century.

Sumptuously illustrated throughout, *Yesterday's Britain* required a memorable image for the front cover, an image that would sum up the whole period, and it was Bert Hardy who supplied it. In the background of his photograph you can see the hop fields, with just the hint of a distant river fringed by mature trees. In the foreground is a rather charming family scene: a man and woman carrying either end of an unfilled zinc bath tub in which a young girl sits, accompanied by two older children (one boy, one girl) and a dog, straining at its leash. They, and those following behind them, are clearly making the long trek back to the hop-pickers' camp after a hard day's graft. This isn't just any family, however: the man in the picture is Alfred Morrell, my mother's husband, and the woman is his new partner, Ada. The boy is Johnny Morrell, the little girl in the zinc bath is Vicki Morrell, and the older girl is Sheila Morrell.

It is not the only significant Morrell family photograph to have come to light. In July 1938 an unknown photographer took a picture, in Margate, of my grandfather, William Morrell; his daughter, Amy (my aunt); and Amy's son, John Humphreys. The happy holiday snap was taken a year after Amy's husband, Jack, had been killed in an explosion, at Fullers Brewery in Fulham. No doubt my grandfather was lending his daughter some emotional support: he had himself lost his wife at the young age of 38, in the great influenza pandemic of 1918, and brought up all seven of their children by himself.

John Humphreys, my cousin, joined the Army when he was older, but was medically discharged on the grounds of shell shock. He became such a recluse that Amy was ashamed to let him out of the house, in case the neighbours saw his state. Sadly, after Amy died there was no one to look after John, whose life spiralled downwards to such an extent that he ended up living as a vagrant on the streets, where he eventually died. The poignancy of this story was only brought home to me many years later, when I was told that a representative from a company named Hoopers had called at my home and that I was to ring them back.

Hoopers are a firm of genealogists who specialise in tracing relatives when someone dies without leaving a will. They had called to tell me that John had lived and died rough on the streets without knowing, or perhaps without understanding, that Amy had left him an inheritance. Looking at that photograph of John in happier times, I felt I simply could not bear to benefit from his misfortune, so I signed my portion of the inheritance over to June, who, unlike me, had actually known him – indeed, it was to Aunty Amy's house that June was supposed to have gone when her father, Alfred, left the family home.

Looking now at that copy of the *Reader's Digest* publication, with its photograph of my hop-picking relatives, I am struck by the relevance – to me, at any rate – of the sentiments expressed in the introduction: "The past, it has been said, is another country. If so, it is a place in which all of us have travelled. We remember its customs; we recognise its highways and byways. We all know people there. If the past is another country, then each of us is a passport citizen of that land."

I may have only been seven years old at the time when Hardy took that picture, but I could already then have testified to the truth of those words.

CHAPTER 5
ANY PORT IN A STORM

When Mrs Kipling urged me to call her 'Mum' and Mr Kipling
'Dad', I found myself quite unable to do so; the words simply
refused to come out.

ON 20 May 1954, I travelled up by train from Windsor to Chester, accompanied by a Barnardo's matron. I was 10 years old and heading for the house of my new foster parents, in rural Cheshire. From Chester we took a local bus to the place that was to be my home: it went by the name of Kipling's Nurseries and was close to the little village of Neston.

It was already dark by the time we got there, and I can still remember the illuminated fuzzy shapes materialising behind the opaque-glass front door. Next thing the door opened, and there, standing before us, were the Kipling family: Mr and Mrs Kipling and their three children, John, Sylvia and Janet. They had been playing a board game called Ludo on the carpet, in front of an open fire, and straight away I was invited to join in. It was a friendly enough gesture, yet I felt awkward accepting their invitation – as I was to learn over time, it's never easy to make an immediate commitment to liking, let alone loving, someone when you're starting from cold.

The fact is, I arrived at the Kiplings' house with complexes: I had been damaged by committing myself emotionally to my former foster family, the Collets of Swindon, and then finding myself back at square one, in a Barnardo's home. Nervous of repeating that experience here in Neston, I was understandably reticent about displaying my feelings.

Next morning, when Mrs Kipling urged me to call her 'Mum' and Mr Kipling 'Dad', I found myself quite unable to do so; the words simply refused to come out, and, as a result, throughout the rest of my stay I steadfastly called them Mr and Mrs Kipling. It was a snub, I sensed, that rankled with them both, and one can understand why – after all, they just wanted to do the right thing. At the same time, though, I can't help thinking that they weren't properly briefed beforehand as to what to expect. The minute I declined their invitation to call them 'Mum' and 'Dad', I felt the seeds were sown and the inevitable conclusion of this fostering would be failure. And so it proved to be, although confirmation of this was not immediate.

I was immediately enrolled at the primary school in Neston Village a couple of miles away, where, among the teachers and my fellow pupils, I found sanctuary from 'the people who lived up on the hill', as the villagers called the Kiplings. Each day I walked to and from school, whatever the weather. I wore shorts, which was not just cold but embarrassing: I was the only boy in my class not to have progressed into long trousers. My mind was always elsewhere as I made my way down those country lanes and across the fields; in my imagination I travelled to exotic locations, picturing myself as a stowaway on a rickety galleon, in search of pieces of eight on some far-off treasure island. Sundays, of course, were church days, it being one of the conditions imposed by Barnardo's on foster parents that children placed in care should attend a Church of England service at least once a week.

It was a 'penny-halfpenny' bus ride from the Kiplings' house to All Saints Church in Thornton Hough, and so, before I left the house, Mrs Kipling would give me three pennies for the return bus fare and three pennies for the church collection. It wasn't long before I worked out that I could walk all the way to Thornton Hough and back, thus saving three pennies each week for myself. Unfortunately I came unstuck one Sunday, when Mrs Kipling didn't have the appropriate change and, instead of giving me six pennies, gave me one whole sixpenny bit. In church, when the collection bag was winging its way towards me, I realised that I had no loose change. On the basis that only three pence out of the sixpence piece belonged to God and the other three pence was mine, I reached my hand deep into the bag and, having grabbed an assortment of coins, selected three individual pennies for myself before depositing my sixpence bit.

Little did I know that all this had been observed by my fellow-church-goers and become the talk of many a local dinner table in the surrounding villages thereafter. Blissfully unaware, I carried on with my Sunday moneymaking activities. I even boosted my church-related earnings with pocket money given by the church for singing in the All Saints choir (plus we got extra for performing at weddings).

At school, nearing the end of my primary education, I was fast approaching the preparation phase for the 11-plus examination, which would determine whether I would go to the soon-to-be-opened Neston Comprehensive School or

A Story in Brief

LADIES DAY: As a boy of 10, I was fostered out for a couple of years to a family at Neston, in Cheshire, where the highlight of the year is the traditional Ladies' Day Walk. This takes place on the first Thursday in June, and in the early days of the last century, the day would sometimes end in near riot, with policemen being called from neighbouring villages to help maintain order. These days, though, Ladies' Day is very peaceful. The children parade wearing white dresses and carry staffs decorated with flowers to match their dresses. The procession walks through the village to the Parish Church. The procession continues to Neston Cross to listen to the 'National Anthem' and 'Abide with Me'. The children retire to the Civic Hall for tea. Ladies' Day was also when the funfair came to town – I remember the £5 challenge to get into the boxing ring – I'm still glad I ducked out.

be elevated to the lofty heights of a grammar school, such as the one my foster brother, John Kipling, attended in West Kirby. If the truth be known, I was never in the running: there wasn't the slightest possibility that I could have passed the exam, a fact not lost on the Kiplings, who considered it a total waste of money to buy textbooks for me. And so they didn't.

However, the fact that I was the only bookless child at the entire school did not escape the attention of the staff. One teacher, Jack Davies, decided to try to beat the odds and volunteered to give me private tuition, sometimes at his home – incredibly valiant and charitable of him, but alas I was a hopeless case.

In my first school report, the deputy headmistress, Mrs Llewellyn, wrote, 'Philip greatly overestimates his abilities,' an observation which I found immensely insulting, since at this point I wasn't aware of my shortcomings. While I struggled with the written word, I found I had a firmer grasp of concepts than other children when it came to more pictorial subjects, such as history and geography.

As my life situation became common knowledge, I began to get mothered by the other boys' parents, which you might think would have been a positive development, yet I absolutely hated it. All I ever wanted was to be the same as the other boys, but everything that happened to me seemed to emphasise the fact I was different. For years afterwards, I had an utter trepidation of visiting or having a meal in other people's houses, and I put this down to these early, uncomfortable experiences of being invited round to other children's homes for tea.

Nevertheless, during my time at Neston I did make plenty of friends among the boys in the village and spent as much of my time with them as I could. We fished, scrumped (stole fruit in other people's gardens) and played football, and for us the annual Neston highlight was Ladies' Day, when the funfair came to town.

All this changed, of course, following the 11-plus, when most of my friends went off to grammar school or other non-local schools. Meanwhile, I waited to be transferred to the local comprehensive, which was still being built. It was during this period that I noticed an envelope on the mantelpiece, behind the clock. Seeing that it was from Barnardo's and curious that it might concern me, I opened it and, to my astonishment, found a payment made out to the Kiplings.

The discovery had a big effect on me. I can't be sure if it was the trigger that set other things within me in motion, but my outlook on life certainly changed at this point. It came as a profound shock to me that my foster parents might be receiving funds to look after me; from that point on I believed, unfairly, that the foster care I was receiving was not being dispensed altruistically, from the kindness of their hearts, but for financial reward.

How or why I can't remember, but I became aware of brochures advertising Barnardo's Parkstone Sea Training School, and the idea was mooted that this might be a better option for me than the Neston Comprehensive

On top of this, I have now a dim recollection of a meeting with someone from Barnardo's at which the possibility of my going to the Sea Training School had been raised.

Quizzing myself now, I can't be sure exactly whose decision it was to leave the Kiplings. Was it actually mine, or was I merely steered into believing this was the best course of action for me? It is a difficult question to answer, given that I was actually quite happy when out playing with my friends in the village. In that respect, I would have been happy to stay in Neston. Yet at the same time, I remember being intoxicated by the thought of wearing a sailor's uniform. Before I knew it, I was undertaking all kinds of medicals in preparation for a life at sea.

News of my impending departure from Neston soon reached my friends and teachers and created a strange air of melancholy. Clearly, the school staff and my friends' parents felt sorry for me, which made me wonder whether I was making a serious mistake in leaving. I felt like an uncertain bridegroom, on realising that the wedding presents had arrived and that there was no way out. Even now, I choke up when thinking about my last day at school. The headmaster, Mr Llewellyn, had summoned all the children and the teachers to the main hall, as if for morning prayers. The words he spoke that day were as follows:

"Some of you might be aware that Philip is about to embark on a very long journey – on which we, of course, all wish him good luck. But, before he goes, we thought he should take something with him from us. With this in mind, all the teachers arranged a collection and bought this leather wallet, which, although now empty, we are sure that, when he returns, will be stuffed full."

I was called forward to receive the wallet, and in that emotionally charged moment I realised that I was among friends, making me wonder why on earth I was leaving them. By then, though, it was too late. I said goodbye to the Kiplings, without any sense of remorse, on 15 May 1957. I had lived with them for three years. I was now 13, and much was to happen when I reached my next port of call: Barnado's Sea Training School, near Poole in Dorset.

CHAPTER 6
THE SAILOR'S HORNPIPE

My earlier, storybook enthusiasm for being a sailor boy quickly wore off. Almost as soon as I got to the Doctor Barnardo's sea training school, I realised that the whole thing had been a ghastly mistake.

A hornpipe replicates, in dance, the life of a working mariner. It shows a range of duties that must be performed aboard a ship – rowing, saluting, climbing the rigging and hauling in the ropes. It requires very little space, no female partner and needs only to be accompanied by a simple tin whistle or, as per the 19th century, a squeezebox. Seafarers have been dancing hornpipes – the best-known version is to a tune known as the 'Sailor's Hornpipe' – for centuries.

In his diaries, Samuel Pepys refers to the hornpipe as 'the jig of the ship', while Captain James Cook instructed his men to perform the dance in order to maintain health and fitness. It became less popular when the practice of hiring ship fiddlers fell into disuse, but I have to say that it serves as the perfect metaphor for my life at Parkstone, which opened as the Russell Coats Nautical School in 1919. When I arrived there, on 15 May 1957, it had been given its new name and a new role: to prepare us Barnardo's boys, through proper naval discipline and training, for a healthy, open-air life at sea.

We were accommodated in five separate houses: Broughton, Johnston, Howard, Lady Russell Coats and my own house, Arranmore, where I quickly had to forget about being called Philip and get used to answering to '56' instead. Uniform was the standard Royal Navy 'square rig' – round hat, blue collar and bell-bottom trousers – while blue serge jumpers and shorts served as our everyday working attire.

There were about 36 boys in each house, divided into two dormitories, with ages ranging from 12 to 16. Meals were taken in a central 'mess' (dining room) just off the parade ground; nearby were the chapel and the gymnasium, which

A Story in Brief

NAMES ON A STONE: At the age of 15, I spent a short spell as an apprentice stone-mason, at Whitehead and Son, in Kennington. This was the firm which had created the monument to the 33 members of the engine room who died in the Titanic disaster: a bronze statue of Nike, the Greek Winged Goddess of Victory, sculpted by Trieste-born Romeo Rathmann, flanked by carvings of the doomed officers. The memorial was unveiled in front of 100,000 people, at Andrews Park, in Southampton, by Sir Archibald Denny, in 1914. "By the manner of their deaths, the engineers carried out one of the finest traditions of our race," he declared. "They must have known that pumping could do no more than delay the final catastrophe, yet they stuck pluckily to their duty. Driven back from boiler-room to boiler-room, fighting for every inch of draft to give time for the launching of the boats, not one of those brave officers was saved." IMAGE COURTESY:'PSTS.

doubled as the band's practice area and as the venue for the weekly film shows – my personal favourite was *Yangtse Incident: The Story of HMS Amethyst*.

The school itself, a 10-minute walk away, consisted of a series of temporary structures built around a parade ground, as well as a sick bay and swimming pool. In addition to being taught all the usual academic subjects, we received instruction in a number of nautical skills, including knot tying, Morse code and signals – if you wanted to avoid seamanship lessons (which I most certainly did), then you could join the band instead, under the tutelage of 'Bandy' Joyce, an ex-Royal Marine bandmaster.

My earlier, storybook enthusiasm for being a sailor boy quickly wore off. Almost as soon as I got to Parkstone, I realised that the whole thing had been a ghastly mistake; I felt that I had not just been misled but let down, and the longer I stayed there, the stronger this feeling grew. The way the various streams worked at the school was the boys were divided up into those who, at 15, would enter the Royal Navy (through the *HMS St Vincent* and *HMS Ganges* training establishments) and those who, at 16, would join the Merchant Navy (usually with the Union-Castle Line or the Cunard Line).

There was a final group of boys who had decided that a life at sea was not for them and who, at 15, would leave to find a job in 'civvy street'. The way I saw it, working on one of the great Union-Castle or Cunard ocean liners was an exciting prospect but out of the question, since that would mean staying on at Parkstone until I was 16, and there was no way I was going to put myself through that. Somehow, I needed to find a way to survive the next two years, and that wasn't going to be easy.

It soon became apparent that there would be no help from anyone outside. Not long after arriving at Parkstone, we were invited to write to relatives (if we had any) to find out if we could lodge with them during the school holidays. The nearest thing to relatives I could think of was the Kiplings, but, having written to them and gotten no reply, I realised that I was going to be one of the 20-or-so boys with nowhere else to go.

The worst thing for us holiday 'stay-behinds' was how the school authorities chalked up on the mess blackboard, beside the dishes of the day, the number of days left until the holidays. They tried to make it better for us by serving us fried eggs (a real treat) on the day the others left for their holidays, but we still had to clean the place up once the meal was over. We also awaited, with some trepidation, the dubious pleasures of the institutionalised holiday camp at St Mary's Bay.

Being one of the younger boys at Parkstone was no fun. Until then, I had mostly spent time with children of my own age, in children's homes, or had at least tasted a softer life with foster families. At Parkstone, though, there were significant differences in ages between the boys and, in an atmosphere of militaristic discipline, these differences translated into a rigid hierarchy, whereby older boys received not just greater privileges but, in some cases, a licence to bully too.

For example, if a boy's relatives sent him a parcel, then he might use its contents as a tradable currency, either in exchange for something else or to curry favour with other boys. Once or twice a week, the housemaster would call us together; he would be clutching the latest delivery of mail – freshly passed by the internal censor – and the names of the recipients would be called out, one by one. Without fail my hopes would be high at the start of one of these sessions, and without fail they would be dashed by the end: not once at Parkstone did I receive a letter or a parcel. The regime at the school was harsh anyway, but I felt this even more acutely because I was depressed and didn't want to be there.

A normal day would follow the same monotonous routine. The bugle would sound at 6.00am, this being the signal for us to leap up, get washed and make our beds so that the creases in the sheets and blankets lined up in perfect symmetry. Then came the floor-cleaning. First, the heavy iron beds would be moved to one section of the room and the exposed hardwood floor polished with Ronuk wax by teams of boys on their knees, rubbing in a rhythmic 'left, right, move back, rub' drill; this would continue, section by section, until the whole floor was a perfect mirror. The same treatment would then be given to the brass fittings on the windows.

The next bugle call was the signal to go to breakfast in the mess. The mess was by far the largest covered space in the school, and, like the dormitories, it had a hardwood floor, which meant that, if you were detailed to do so, you would have to stay behind and polish it once the meal was over. The rule was that all meals were to be eaten in silence until permission to speak was given by the officer. You collected your food from a large, open hatch, where there also stood a large urn full of hot water into which was dangled a tea bag the size of a cushion; this would occasionally be stirred, not with a spoon but with a boat oar. The brew was known as 'grog', the same word used to refer to the daily naval ration of rum, but the one significant difference was that the liquid inside the urn tasted neither of rum nor, for that matter, tea. Once you had collected your tea, you would use a mug to scoop cornflakes, or some other cereal, out of giant boxes and into your bowl, and then ladle milk on top.

After breakfast, 'defaulters', as boys who had broken any of the numerous Parkstone rules were known, would report for a hearing followed by a punishment administered by one of the senior officers. The rest of the boys would assemble and wait for the bugle that would call us to line up, in formation, on the parade ground. As a member of the band, I would collect my drum and join the rest of the band in front of the flagstaff; we would play the national anthem while the colours were raised. At this point we marched off, still in formation, to our lessons.

Without doubt, I hated Morse code classes the most. I was hopeless at writing things down, and had no chance of being able to transcribe all those dots and dashes. The lessons were conducted by Mr Busby, who seemed to take a perverse delight in tapping out code at impossible speeds. I soon gave up even attempting to decipher his signals and just put any old rubbish down on my pad. Having done my worst, I would sit there, staring into space and reciting in my mind the embroidered message hanging on Mr Busby's classroom wall. It read:

> *For when the One Great Scorer comes,*
> *To mark against your name,*
> *He writes not that you won or lost,*
> *But how you played the Game.*

I well remember one day, during Mr Busby's lesson, when the radio was switched on. It was 7 February 1958, the day after the Munich air crash involving the Manchester United football team and their manager, Matt Busby, who shared our teacher's surname. As we anxiously listened for news of survivors, I had no idea that in later life I would meet some of the players who had been caught up in the crash, and would even end up organising football specials for United fans.

Aside from football, our main interest was girls – by now we were all 13 or 14 years old and well into puberty. The unfortunate officer given the task of imparting sex education was Commander Woolven. Basically, he bumbled, we giggled and, in the end, we learnt more about sex from photographs of bare-chested African women in the National Geographic magazine than we did from the Commander.

At lunchtime we would all duly return to the mess, as we would again for dinner. All too frequently for my liking, these meals featured pilchards, sardines, haddock, spam or luncheon meat, none of which I could stand. I thus got by on eating nothing but bread and jam and, consequently, was as thin as a rake. After dinner there would be a period of relaxation, either in the grounds, the playroom (for table tennis) or out on the playing fields (for cricket, football, and athletics in the evening. Bedtime was 8.00pm and lights-out was at 9.30pm; sometimes the radio would be playing up until then.

Our housemaster in Arranmore was Mr Butcher, and he was a real stickler for tidiness. So much so that he insisted our clothes be stowed each night in open, numbered lockers on the ground floor, so that he could tell, at a glance, if everything was in order. If it wasn't, he wouldn't say anything at bedtime, but would wait until four in the morning, empty the contents of all the lockers onto the floor and stride into the dormitories shouting, 'Cocktail!' This was the signal for us all to jump out of bed, find our clothes, fold them up neatly and put them back in our respective lockers. The only problem being, we all had identical clothes and the only way to tell who owned a piece of clothing was to inspect the tiny label for the school number inscribed on it (in my case, 56). As a result, the whole process took ages.

There were other jobs that required doing within the house. Some were a lot cushier than others, and it seemed to me that being chosen for these was dependent on Mr Butcher's daughter, Dawn, taking a shine to you. By far the best job that Mr Butcher could bestow was working in his family kitchen, which offered the twin benefits of warmth and getting something nice to eat. Unfortunately, however, I was not on Dawn's list of favourites and spent most of my time polishing floors. Mercifully, weekends brought some respite from the drudgery: there was no school and no seamanship lessons and, on Saturday and Sunday afternoons, we were even allowed off the premises.

I remember well the drill on Saturday mornings, when Mr Butcher would sit at a table in the shower and washing area and hand out pocket money. I would be given a shilling, enough to buy a ticket for a matinée screening at the local cinema. I rarely got to see a film, however, as generally I was in debt, having traded my expected shilling for a share of the contents of another boy's parcel earlier in the week.

Without money, my afternoon-off options were particularly limited: it was compulsory for us to wear naval uniform, so we were extremely conspicuous should we stray into areas that were out of bounds – that is, most of the places us boys wanted to go. One such forbidden zone was Poole Harbour and quayside; there were usually a few Dutch coasters moored there, and the crews would always be willing to let us on board, once they saw our naval uniforms.

I suspect one of the reasons why the harbour was out of bounds was that it was a source of contraband smokes and, even though we had no money to pay for them, the sailors would often give us the odd cigarette or two, out of kindness. Indeed, the quest for tobacco was responsible for my one and only inclusion on the defaulters list: I agreed to hide a cigarette on behalf of another boy which was subsequently discovered in one of my inside pockets. At Parkstone it was unwise to try and save one's hide by explaining what had happened, so I had to take six of the best, energetically administered by the cane-wielding Commander as I lay bent across his desk, trousers-down.

I found that a less risky way to spend my weekend was to walk to the top of nearby Constitution Hill and idle amongst the pine trees, observing the tour coaches that would stop there for views across Poole Harbour. From this vantage point I could clearly make out privately owned Brownsea Island and, to the right, a row of flying boats that had been mothballed after the war. Completing this idyllic scene was a colourful collection of sailing boats of different shapes and sizes, all bobbing around picturesquely in the placid waters.

Not only did I find this panorama entrancing to look at; it also gave me an idea as to what I was going to do when I left Parkstone: become a coach courier, escorting tour parties and managing their travel arrangements. This is exactly what happened. In fact, not only did I go on to become a coach courier, but also I had dealings with the National Trust, which today owns Brownsea Island and has opened it up to tourists. I even renewed my acquaintance with the flying boats, when I tried to re-create the famed Cape-to-Cairo route many years later.

On reflection, I believe that my happiest moments at Parkstone were spent playing in the band, which was modelled on a full-scale Royal Marines Band, complete with various drums, cymbals, drum majors, trombones, cornets, euphoniums and sousaphones. My 'speciality' was percussion, so I had the full range of instruments at my disposal: side drums, bass drums, cymbals, Chinese drums and timpani. We certainly had our fair share of public performances, sometimes during the half-time interval at the Poole Speedway Track and at Armistice commemoration services in local churches.

The highlight of our band calendar was always the school's Open Day, which involved us roaming the area in advance, knocking on people's front doors and selling tickets. (It was while on ticket-selling duty that I made friends with a local couple who subsequently invited me round most weekends to watch black-and-white films on their TV and have a piece of cake. This proved a welcome port of call, given that I mostly had no money to go to the cinema.) As for the Open Day itself, the event was always well attended and we would all put on a magnificent show incorporating displays of seamanship, flag signals and knot tying, plus gymnastics, marching music and a rendition of the 'Sailor's Hornpipe' performed by six cadets.

Not long after the 1958 Open Day we had a celebrity visitor to the school: the entertainer Max Bygraves was invited by the Commander to come and inspect the home in between shows – to which we were later invited – at the Bournemouth Winter Gardens, where he was performing with Petula Clark. Until then Max had been exclusively affiliated with the BBC, but he was now in the throes of changing to ITV, which wanted to launch its new hot property via a Christmas special. This gave him an idea: as it was the season of good cheer, why not have the Barnardo's band and hornpipe team perform on the show?

Why not indeed? This is how it came to be that several coach-loads of us found ourselves being ferried up to the bright lights of London town. It was all very exciting: parked outside the theatre was a solitary Rolls Royce with the number plate MAX 1. At rehearsals, however, our excitement turned to terror as we learnt that the show was going to be filmed live, in front of an audience. What's more, the producer went berserk when all 50 of us trundled onstage with our boots on. We made such a racket that we were told to go off and remove our footwear, before repeating the exercise in total silence.

Eventually, I and five other boys did get to perform the hornpipe on Max Bygrave's 1958 ITV Christmas special, for which we were paid a fee of 10 shillings. No sooner had I made my television debut than my thoughts began turning to my imminent departure from Parkstone. I felt confident that, as soon as I was in the outside world, I would get a job, find somewhere to live and start earning some real money.

In 1959, Easter came early. It was decided that I should leave Parkstone at the end of term, on 15 March, two weeks before my 15th birthday. It was the moment I had spent two long years waiting for. I remember luxuriating in the warm glow of freedom as the steam train took me out of Poole, passing along the waterfront en route to Waterloo Station in London. It seemed like we passed within touching distance of the great ocean liners moored on the Southampton quayside: this was a scene right out of the Golden Age of travel, and I wanted some of it.

Although I did not enjoy my time at Parkstone, there is no doubt in my mind that it was a fine institution of which Barnardo's can be justly proud. Many boys went on to achieve high rankings at sea, while many others made their mark in business and in life generally. In short, the Parkstone experience instilled in them both a sense of self-reliance and of wonderment – a combination not readily available in the outside world. In the end, the dance had proved worthwhile.

CHAPTER 7
THE HOLIDAY CAMP

In August 1958 it was announced that we would be having a
two-week stay at the seaside, at a place called St Mary's Bay in Kent.
I didn't know exactly what to expect – Butlins it certainly wasn't.

THERE were 140 boys living at the Barnardo's home in Parkstone, Dorset, and for the 20 of us that did not have relatives to whom we could go during the summer holidays, the last few weeks of term were an emotional roller-coaster ride, mostly of the downhill kind. First we had to endure the build-up of excitement amongst those boys who were lucky enough to be going away. Then we had to watch as, one by one, they headed off to the Poole railway station to embark on their summer break. Finally, as if to rub salt into the wound, we were required to clean the entire place from top to bottom, once the other boys had left. Only after this did those of us who were left behind get a holiday – of sorts.

In August 1958 it was announced that we would be having a two-week stay at the seaside, at a place called St Mary's Bay in Kent. We set off in the back of a canvas-covered ex-army truck for the five-hour drive; I didn't know exactly what to expect, but I had heard of Butlins and seen their brochures, so I was hoping for the best. As it turned out, Butlins it certainly wasn't.

The site, originally a disused aerodrome, was bought in 1924 by a local entrepreneur and used as a holiday camp during the summer months – and as a turkey farm in winter! St Mary's Bay Holiday Camp, as it came to be known, extended over a vast area and accommodated in excess of 1,000 children, plus helpers. Its stated purpose was to provide a safe environment where children from different backgrounds could be brought together to mix and make friends, overcoming the class differences that might otherwise have divided them. A noble enough aim, but the buildings were forlorn in the extreme and did not look like they had been given a lick of paint in all the 34 years of the camp's operation.

A Story in Brief

BUTLINS IT WASN'T: In 1958 I was staying at the St Mary's Bay Holiday Camp, and I can assure you, it was nothing like the kind of place run by Billy Butlin. That said, we did get taken out on the odd excursion, and one day we went on a trip to nearby Folkestone, to see the the joint Daily Mail-Butlins English Channel swimming challenge, which was won that year by an Asian. His name was Brojen Das; he was from East Pakistan, and he arrived in Britain fresh from swimming across the Mediterranean, from Capri to Naples. Mind you, a year earlier, he wouldn't have had the chance of the Channel swim; it was the time of the Suez crisis, and Butlins had amongst others banned Egyptians (then considered the best swimmers) from participating, on the basis that they had the Canal, so they weren't going to be given the English Channel as well. **IMAGE COURTESY: PSTS.**

Accommodation was a series of basic Nissen huts where up to 50 children would sleep, under a cylindrical roof of corrugated steel, on straw mattresses. Meals were served in one huge, central dining hall in which all of us of would congregate at once: I can still recall the deafening noise and the towering mountains of sliced bread spread with margarine.

Within a day there would be nothing left of the shilling-a-week pocket money we were given; it was either spent straightaway or used to settle a debt with another boy. I needed to come up with another source of income, and decided to generate this by collecting empty fizzy-pop bottles and returning them to the shop to claim a three-pence per bottle deposit. I wasn't the only boy to go into this line of business: each day, hundreds of St Mary's kids could be found scouring the beach for bottles. As a result, the pickings were thin and the competition fierce.

One day, however, while walking behind a restaurant with another boy, I caught sight of row-upon-row of stacked boxes containing dozens of already-returned bottles. Our eyes lit up as we glimpsed the solution to all our financial problems, but before we could enact our plan two people from the restaurant jumped out and nabbed us. Obviously other boys had tried this before, and it was assumed, quite wrongly, that we were the culprits. We protested our innocence, but to no avail: the police were called and they took us back to the camp, where a black mark was unfairly registered against our names.

Although the accommodation at St Mary's was fairly spartan, there were plenty of sports to take part in – on one occasion the camp even hosted an international children's football match, England versus Germany (we lost, but not on penalties at least). Among the facilities was an outdoor boxing ring, and I was encouraged by some of the other, less courageous, boys to sign up for a bout, which proved a big mistake: I ended up with a broken nose.

We were also taken on excursions to local places of interest. One day we were on a cliff near Folkestone, overlooking the English Channel, when Billy Butlin (of holiday camp fame) landed nearby in a Heath Robinson-looking contraption of a helicopter: I think he was sponsoring a cross-Channel swim. His arrival was ironic, because back at St Mary's, every time you made a complaint or put in a request that the organisers felt was unreasonable, they would reply: "What do think this is, Butlins?" Having spied the man himself somehow gave me that extra bit of confidence in my complaining.

My experiences at St Mary's did leave a lasting mark on me, as I discovered many years later while on jury service at Southwark Crown Court. One of the cases involved a lady who, disappointed by the size of her benefit cheque, had manually altered the amount on the cheque to the substantially larger sum to which she felt entitled. Then, in response to criticism from her partner, she changed the number back to the original amount. The cashier at the post office took one look at the disfigured cheque and refused to hand over any cash at all, even though the woman had explained the circumstances.

There was no doubt in my mind that if the teller had given her the exaggerated amount, then the lady would probably have kept it. Crucially, though, this could not be proven. It was late in the afternoon when we retired to the jury room, at which point we had a quick show of hands: everyone thought the woman guilty, with the exception of myself. Thus I recounted, to my fellow jury members, my decades-ago St Mary's Bay experience of being accused of purloining empty bottles, not because I had actually done so but because I was in a state of mind that inclined me towards that course of action. Was this not also the case here, I pleaded to my fellow-jurors?

The ensuing discussions went on for some time, and the judge became agitated over how long we were spending on what he might have considered a piddling little case. Finally, to break the deadlock, we sent a message to the judge asking if someone could be found guilty for a state of mind, as opposed to an actual deed. The answer came back in the negative.

It was seven in the evening when we finally re-entered the courtroom, to record a unanimous verdict of not guilty. I must say it's something I am glad I did and something I still often think about. Thinking bad things is one thing; doing them is quite another.

CHAPTER 8
THE AFTERCARE OFFICER

On arrival in London I was met by my aftercare officer. He was an ex-policeman and clearly saw little difference between me and the juvenile delinquents he had encountered in his previous career.

ON arrival at Waterloo Station I was met by my aftercare officer. He was an ex-policeman and clearly saw little difference between me and the juvenile delinquents he had encountered in his previous career. He wore a trilby hat and a full-length, fawn-coloured raincoat and drove an Austin 10 motorcar that was clearly his pride and joy. It was his responsibility to find me a job and a place to live, but in the meantime I was to stay at the Barnardo's home in Kingston Hill, Surrey.

Leslie Thomas, author of *The Virgin Soldiers*, also spent some time at this home. In *This Time Next Week*, his first book, Leslie describes how he was eight years old when World War II broke out and attending an elementary school in Newport, Gwent, where he was good at English but not much else. His happy childhood came to an abrupt end, however, at the age of 12, in 1943, when his father drowned after his ship was torpedoed. Six months later his mother died, upon which Leslie and his younger brother, Roy, were sent to Kingston.

Initially, the Barnardo's staff sent Leslie out to train as a bricklayer. However, most of his walls ended up collapsing, so he took up writing instead and went on to become one of Britain's foremost authors, with 30 titles and an OBE (awarded in 2004) to his name. The title of his Barnardo's memoir alludes to a song of hope often sung at the home, as follows:

This time next week,
Where shall I be?
Sitting by the fireside,
Scoffing my tea.
Plenty of comics,
Lots of books,
No more matrons' dirty looks...

Rather uncannily, it was suggested that I too should become a bricklayer – at the time, Barnardo's were fixated with the idea that boys should progress, via an apprenticeship, to a profession. I didn't stay long at Kingston, but during the short time I was there, I was rather happy. The place was arranged on a much more human scale than the Village Home or Garden homes; also, I was glad to be away from the monotonous routine at Parkstone and to have the chance just to laze around. Not that this period of leisure lasted: my time at Kingston turned out to be a period of calm before the storm. Having been on an emotional rollercoaster involving various sets of foster parents, I was now about to enter a tunnel of horrors.

On 27 April 1959 my aftercare officer came to collect me, the plan being that we would go to the lodgings he had found for me and then on to the Youth Employment Office. My new home was to be with a family who lived at 119 Fordell Road, in Catford, south London; the man of the house was a sous-chef at the Savoy Hotel, on the Strand.

After being shown my room, I was driven to the Youth Employment Office in nearby Lewisham, to see what job openings there were for me. Sure enough, the first vacancy on the list was for a bricklayer; but instead of signing up for this, I went for the more artistic-sounding position of stonemason, even though this meant committing to a lengthy, seven-year apprenticeship.

In due course I was taken to the premises of Messrs Whitehead & Sons, opposite the Kennington Oval Cricket Ground. There I met Mr Whitehead and signed my indentures, and it was agreed that I would start at 8.00am sharp the following Monday. My wages were to be two pounds, four shillings and four pence per week, all of which would be paid to my Catford landlord – all, that is, except for two shillings' pocket money, a sum that would have hardly covered my bus fare. It was just as well that, while I was in Kingston, I had swapped some of my possessions for a bike: I now faced a 15-mile round trip to work and had no other means of getting there.

However, I had a problem in that if I tried to tighten the nut at the point where the handlebars met the frame and jerked too hard on the handlebars, then only the handlebars would turn, rather than the bike itself. This made riding the contraption a bit of a hair-raising experience.

My digs were also proving less than ideal. It was then standard practice for Barnardo's aftercare officers to use landlords or accommodation they had used in the past, which was how I ended up in Catford with the Longmead family. The big problem with this system, from my point of view, was that the people who were putting you up were all-too-aware of their 'Good Samaritan' status: many a night I would go to bed early and cry my eyes out in despair, with the words, "If it weren't for people like us, where would boys like you be?" ringing in my ears. It was a question I did not feel inclined to answer. With no friends and no money to speak of, I spent most of my time alone in the local parks whenever I wasn't working.

My employers, Whitehead & Sons, were a family-owned business that had been going for several generations and had quarry interests in Galway, Ireland, and Carrara, Italy. Their marble factory in Kennington was spread over a huge area and housed stonemasons, marble-cutting machinery and gigantic grinding and polishing beds, all of which created a huge din and massive amounts of slurry. Elsewhere there were long lines of marble blocks, between which apprentices who knew their way around could find refuge from the Dickensian mayhem outside.

As for myself, I was assigned to the stonemasons' shed, alongside 10-or-so Italian craftsmen who had learnt their craft at their forefathers' knees and were not about to impart their secrets to a nobody like me. This meant that I spent most of my time performing menial tasks in the factory.

Soon enough I and another apprentice got our own back at the Italians, thanks to the thick layer of dust that had settled on the fluorescent light-diffusers hanging from the workshop roof. By throwing bits of marble at those diffusers, we could dislodge several years' worth of thick dust onto the heads of our reluctant mentors, who became incandescent with rage and more determined than ever not to teach us any of their trade secrets.

Back in those days, Whiteheads were the company of choice when it came to supplying upmarket marble, stone and granite sculptures. During my time with them, I worked on St Paul's Cathedral, St George's Chapel in Windsor and many a Greek ship-owner's apartment in Eaton Square. Staff safety was not even a consideration, let alone a concern, as I discovered when working on the entrance of a new office block in Southwark. My Italian supervisor, or 'fixer', had gone to lunch and left me alone as I drilled holes into a wall; all of a sudden the drill bit got caught in my shirt sleeve and started drilling along the length of my arm.

Later, when Mr Whitehead came to visit me in the hospital, I got the distinct impression he was more worried about his liability insurance than my health. As

A Story in Brief

A BUDDING MICHAELANGELO: 'I took Philip along and we saw Mr Square (White-heads), the firm's General Manager. He explained that the firm had been in existence for over 150 years and there was certainly no shortage of work in their direction. The firm are engaged on stonework on several historical buildings in London and had the contract for St Paul's renovation and the Festival Hall. I feel sure from what I saw when we were conducted over the works and seeing the different processes of handling and carving stone, that Philip will be with good employers. The inter-view was most satisfactory one from all points of view and it was agreed that the lad could commence on Monday the 27th of April 1959 at commencing wage of one quarter of the craftman's rate which at the moment stands at 4 shillings, ten and half pence an hour'. Extract from the Barnardo's aftercare superinten-dent's report.

compensation, I received not a hefty payout, but two of Mr Whitehead's old shirts.

It was around this time that Juan Garro arrived in the factory. With his tanned complexion and dandified clothes, he stood out from the rest of us pasty-faced and pallid young men, and I soon gravitated towards him. He said he was Spanish, but in fact he was from Gibraltar. Juan did not just stand out physically: in terms of attitude he was the complete opposite of everyone else – a real free spirit, not hemmed in by convention or rules.

When I told him I had signed up for a seven-year apprenticeship, his reaction was that I shouldn't in any way let that stop me from upping and leaving if I felt like it. And I certainly did feel like it. I was thoroughly unhappy living with the Longmead family and the money I was earning at Whiteheads was never going to allow me to be independent, so I contacted my aftercare officer, who agreed to ask Whiteheads to release me from my indentures. They duly did so, thanks to no small amount of obsequiousness on my part.

I was now in need of a new job, and two came along in quick succession. The first was with a second-hand office equipment company in Essex, while the second was with an ice cream company and involved me pushing a cart around the streets, selling ice cream door-to-door and occasionally at the Valley, Charlton Athletics' football ground. (Regrettably, I was prone to eating most of my stock, though this taught me a business lesson I would never forget.) I had by then left the Longmead family of Catford and moved in with the Martins of Goodmayes, who turned out to be devout Plymouth Brethren. This meant that no televisions or radios were allowed in the house and, everywhere you looked, there were quotations from the scriptures – all rather unnerving and a little creepy.

I was subsequently employed as a trainee barber by an ex-Barnardo's boy who had set up business outside the gates of the Ford Motor Factory in Dagenham. It was not so much a barber's shop as a hair-cutting factory: there were about 30 chairs and the emphasis was not on the coiffeur's skill, but his speed. The car workers wanted a cheap haircut and they wanted it quick, which meant that the peak times for business were around seven in the morning and four in the afternoon, either just before or just after a shift. Each haircut took no more than five minutes; one barber, nicknamed 'The Fly', regularly trimmed up to three minutes off this time. In a kindly, if ill-advised, fit of generosity, the business owner offered to let me practice on him. The haircutting went all right, but, unfortunately, blood began to flow when I set about his face with the open razor!

Meanwhile, life with the Martins was not going well. They had found out that I had got an evening job working in a pub, and this was such anathema to them that I was told to pack my bags and leave. I contacted Juan Garro with a view to taking up his offer of going to live with him and his family. There was, however, a small difficulty in that I was still only 16 (about to turn 17). As I was officially under the jurisdiction of Barnardo's until the age of 18, I needed my aftercare officer's permission to move home, which I knew would not be forthcoming. I thus decided that I would move in with Juan regardless.

Juan, his brother, Ernest, and his sister, Isabel, all lived with their mother. The Garro residence consisted of two rooms and a small kitchen, in a tenement building on Colville Terrace, just off the Portobello Road; Peter Rachman, a notorious west-London landlord whose name has become synonymous with exploiting tenants, owned the building. When Juan took me round there for the first time, I could sense his mother's mixed feelings: her maternal instincts prompted her to recognise me as a needy stray, but her survival instincts cast me as just another mouth to feed. She spoke no English, but there was no mistaking the message in her eyes, and it wasn't welcoming.

It wasn't long before the aftercare officer tracked me down to my new address. Juan spotted him first and whisked me down from their third-floor flat to a hiding place below the basement steps, where I crouched until I saw the officer leave. As it turned out, he never returned, and that was that: at just 17 years old, I was out in the big wide world and, as I saw it, free at last. What I could not have envisaged, though, was the level of hardship that freedom would bring.

CHAPTER 9
THE RENT COLLECTOR

I understood from Mrs Garro's manner that she hoped my presence
would be brief. Having burnt my bridges with Barnardo's having run
away, I was left in a rather invidious position.

I reached the age of 17 in 1961, not long after my arrival at the Garro's rooms on Colville Terrace ('apartment' or 'flat' would be too-grand terms to describe their humble abode). Much of the time between then and my 18th birthday, on 1 April 1962, was spent dodging the 'tick man' who would come knocking on the door to be paid for clothes bought on the never-never (in my case, 'never' meant just that!).

Even more of my time was taken up trying to find a job, so that I could make a contribution to the Garros for rent and my general upkeep. Juan, who had brought me to Colville Terrace in the first place, to the evident disdain of his mother, had got a job laying telephone cables somewhere in the wilds of Hertfordshire and suggested that I do the same. It paid well, he said, and there was the prospect of lots of overtime.

That was how I came to be working for the British Cable Company somewhere in rural England, my job being to assist an operative in soldering copper telephone cables with a blowtorch. This particular individual, I have to say, was rough in the extreme, and I can only assume that I said something that disturbed him because, at one point, he dragged me through some bushes into a nearby field and started threatening me with his ignited blowtorch, which singed my face in a distinctly worrying way.

Although Mrs Garro did not speak a word of English – our means of communication were our eyes and gestures – I understood from her manner that she hoped my presence would be brief. Having burnt my bridges with Barnardo's, I was thus in a rather invidious position: in order to survive, or at least navigate a

A Story in Brief

THE GOLDEN EGG: 'I called there (at Philip's new lodgings) at 8.00pm last Friday evening. The property is situated in a very cosmopolitan area of west London inhabited by many races. The Garro family themselves are Gibraltarians and Ernest, who answered my ring at the doorbell, said Philip had been employed with him at the Golden Egg, Parker Street, Holborn, as a trainee chef for the past two weeks. He said that he and his family, consisting of Mother, a brother age 19 and a sister age 16, would be happy to accommodate Philip. I made the request to to be shown the sleeping accommodation and found that Philip will be expected to share a large bedroom – he occupying one bed, Ernest another and the older brother a bed settee. The rooms occupied by the family are one living room in which the family eat, and a double bed settee is pulled down for the mother and daughter.' Extract from the Barnardo's aftercare superintendent's report. I, meanwhile was crouching and hiding with Juan behind the basement steps below. **IMAGE COURTESY: TOM VAGUE.**

safe passage to somewhere else, I needed to hang-on to Juan's coattails. This meant that, whatever job he got, I got, and whatever exploration he made, I made. Given that he went everywhere and tasted all the fruits, even the forbidden ones – as I say, he was a completely free spirit – any concerns his mother might have had at his bringing this stray home were, in a Spanish flourish, simply brushed aside.

All the while I lived at Colville Terrace, I can only ever remember meeting one English person, and that was the lady living upstairs with a Jamaican: something decidedly avant-garde in those days, given that it was such a liaison that had in 1958 sparked the Notting Hill race riots. The remainder of the habitués of Colville Terrace and the surrounding streets originated from either the Caribbean or the ex-British colonies in South-East Asia, which meant that the Garros and me, and the lady upstairs, were a bit of a rarity.

Just 200 feet away was Portobello Road, which really came alive on Saturday mornings, both for tourists and for residents from more prosperous parts of London seeking bric-a-brac, jewellery and Swinging London paraphernalia. In fact, in many ways, Portobello Road rivalled Carnaby Street in this regard, at the same time as heralding a new set of social mores that would make easy game of naive new arrivals.

I remember, once, someone calling at the Garro's home, claiming to be from the television licence surveillance team. Even though nobody else in Colville Terrace would have bothered to get a TV licence – or, indeed, had the money for a TV licence – the impostor demanded, and was given, cash in lieu. It was an obvious ruse.

I was not immune from this naivety, either. Once, when I was living in a bedsit in Shepherd's Bush in west London, I spotted an advertisement in a newsagent's window: it held out the prospect of untold riches that could be earned as a travelling salesman, with all expenses paid and training given. I duly turned up at some rooms above a pub, where both the induction and training took place, and found 30 others who, just like me, very sincerely wanted to be rich.

We all listened intently to our American instructor as he delivered his messianic spiel, worried that we might miss the secret of how to become rich. Trouble was, the job turned out to be nothing more than door-to-door magazine-subscription selling, albeit with a North American twist: we were supposed to pose as struggling students urgently in need of funds to pursue our studies. For our doorstep spiel, we were required to choose a subject that we were meant to be studying, and I rather stupidly chose acting. Ridiculous, really, as I was so self-conscious at the time: I couldn't even walk past a bus without thinking all the people on it were looking at me.

Undeterred, I joined the get-rich-quick scheme. Our first sortie entailed being piled into a convoy of vans and driven into the wilds of 'Middle England'. Once there, we were allotted sales pitches and told to start knocking on doors and selling subscriptions. In my case, however, stage fright soon caught hold. I knocked on my first door, which was opened by a real battle-axe of a lady. Hesitatingly, I launched into my prepared script: I said I was raising funds to help pay for my studies and that, with each magazine subscription I sold, I would earn points (rather than cash) that would go towards my tuition, etc. The lady asked me what I was studying and I replied, "Acting."

"Well," she said, "with projection like that, you'll never be an actor," and then slammed the door in my face.

Needless to say my confidence was shot to pieces, and in the end I only ever sold one single, solitary subscription for *Time* magazine before coming to the conclusion that the lady was quite right in her observation that I would never make an actor. Nor, for that matter, did I fancy being a salesman, which meant that, once again, I was on the lookout for a new job.

Looking back now, I can see that the five years between leaving Barnardo's at 15 and finally reaching the age of 20 were the hardest to endure: I was living entirely on my wits and without any form of emotional safety net. That said, I do think this period was the making of me, due to my experience of the unforgettable sights and sounds of Colville Terrace, the place where all different classes and races collided.

Eventually I left the Garro's home on Colville Terrace for a series of bedsits that stretched, in an arc, between Shepherds Bush, Lisson Grove, Westbourne Grove and the Queensway area of Bayswater. It seemed, in an uncanny way, that I had followed in the footsteps of Peter Rachman. For while I used the coffee bars of Queensway as a substitute front room, both for company and to escape the privations of my bedsit, Peter Rachman (in one of whose many houses the Garro's and myself were then living) was down the road in another coffee bar, running his property portfolio with the aid of a local phone box.

CHAPTER 10
THE LUNCHEON VOUCHER

*I hesitated for a moment, unsure not only whether it was right
to take this last, remaining morsel from her, but also of how it would
help me get to work.*

I T was in a cloud of marble dust and uncertainty that Juan Garro had moved centre-stage in my life. He was forever getting involved in mad schemes. One time, we went on 'safari' in Hatfield. The idea was to go visit Juan's girlfriend, Cindy, but in order to add a bit of excitement to the whole operation, he suggested we – i.e., I, Juan and his brother – spend the night in a wood close to where his girlfriend lived. It is testimony to Juan's powers of persuasion that we agreed to go along with this scheme, setting off together on the train with spare clothes dangling behind our backs from coat hangers. We duly found our way to the wood that Juan had identified and hung our clothes on the branches of a tree; however, come nightfall, we found that the ground was frozen and sleep was impossible. To make matters worse, we were then picked up by the police and taken to the station for questioning.

On another occasion Juan came up with an alternative solution, which was to sneak on board a stationary train at Hatfield Station and sleep the night there, rather than outdoors. Later, during the small hours, the train suddenly moved off, and it was ages before the blasted thing stopped and we could get off.

Juan's crazy ideas weren't just limited to finding unsuitable sleeping places. One day, he decided that he and I both needed a smart suit of clothes and he alighted upon the John Collier store, at the junction of Colville Terrace and Portobello Road, as the place that would provide us with our outfits. Juan chose a black pinstriped suit design, put down a £1 deposit, and signed an agreement to pay the same amount in instalments, once a month, for the next few months. It took three weeks for our suits to arrive but, once we had put them on, we never took them off. We would walk around the area like black-clad twins, taking care not to walk past that particular branch of John Collier's, whose staff might not have appreciated seeing us wearing their suits, given that we had found ourselves strangely and suddenly unable to make any of the repayments.

After the telephone-cable laying job in Hertfordshire, which I gave up on the strength of my experience on the receiving end of a blowtorch, I was taken on as an omelette cook at the Golden Egg cafe in Kingsway, following which I became a butcher's assistant in Westbourne Grove (and was soon fired for no apparent reason); a cleaner at Lawrence's department store in Bayswater; an assistant at Barker's delicatessen counter on Kensington High Street; a sales assistant in a travel goods store in Paddington; and a member of staff in a paint company off Pall Mall, not to mention my two-week spell as a door-to-door salesman. My key requirements from all these jobs was that I should get (a) a few free meals and (b) advancement up the salary ladder. As for ready money, that was invariably in painfully short supply.

One morning, things had got so bad that I couldn't even muster the bus fare to work, in Pall Mall, so I decided to ask the lady who lived with the Jamaican man above the Garros for some money. When I climbed the stairs, however, I found her sitting forlorn and distressed on an unmade bed: it seemed her lover had walked out on her. This rather threw me, as the reason for my visit was anything but to hear her tale of woe. Seeing her distress, I wondered whether this was the most appropriate moment to ask for money, but I took a deep breath and asked anyway. To my relief she did not turn on me for having made such a callous request; instead, she told me she didn't have any money herself, but did have a three-and-sixpenny luncheon voucher that she had been keeping in reserve. I hesitated for a moment, unsure not only whether it was right to take this last, remaining morsel from her, but also of how it would help me get to work. Temporarily turning my back on human sentiment, I bit my lip and took the luncheon voucher.

I was never to see the lady again, but my more immediate concern was how to convert this bit of paper into cash. The trouble with luncheon vouchers was that you never got any change: you either had to consume the full value in food or forfeit the balance. Knowing this, I went into the Wimpy Bar opposite Paddington Station and ordered the cheapest item on the menu, in the hope of getting the maximum amount of change. Of course, when I handed the voucher to the counter assistant, I was told, in no uncertain terms, that there would be no cash forthcoming in change.

It was time for some amateur dramatics. I pleaded my case with the manager, explaining my predicament and leaving him in no doubt that my job depended

A Story in Brief

HE HATED BUSKERS: From my office window in Tottenham Court Road, I watched both Centre Point and the Post Office Tower being built. In between times, though, my duties consisted of running chores for Sir Isaac Wolfson, the boss of Great Universal Stores, who had an enormous office on the ground floor. About once a week, a ragamuffin troupe of singers, looking the worse for drink, would parade in single file down Tottenham Court Road belting out all kinds of Italian arias; one of them was actually rather good, and passers-by would stop to listen. To Sir Isaac, though, they were an infernal nuisance, and interfered with his board meetings. I would therefore be given five pounds (an enormous sum at the time) which I would hand to the lead singer, on condition that the group move one. Not surprisingly, this encouraged the singers to come back week after week, in pursuit of this hefty pay-off.
IMAGE COURTESY: PRESS IMAGE.

on my getting to work that morning. To my huge relief, he announced that even though it was strictly against company policy, he would make an exception and give me my change of three shillings.

Rushing out into the street clasping those precious coins, I was all set to catch the bus when I spotted an office employment bureau in a nearby basement and popped in to see if they might have a suitable job vacancy for me. And indeed, they did. So, instead of buying me a bus fare to my job in Pall Mall, the loose change from the luncheon voucher took me to Tottenham Court Road, for a job interview at Sir Isaac Wolfson's Great Universal Stores. The vacancy was for an accounts clerk and, because the interview was perfunctory in the extreme, with no awkward questions being asked about my academic or professional qualifications, I was simply told to report the next week, ready for work. Later, however, I began to feel anxious: I could hardly read or write, and I was sure it wouldn't be long before I was found out.

When I turned up the following week, I discovered that I was to share an office with just one other clerk. As for my responsibilities, I was to record, in handwriting, details of all the refurbishment work being carried out in the company's high-street shops – including some occupied by John Collier's, whose (still unpaid-for) suit I was wearing. There was nothing for it but to come clean to my new office companion, and admit that I had obtained the job under false pretences. To my astonishment and eternal gratitude, he told me that he was quite happy to fill in all the ledgers himself, while at the same time teaching me how to write properly.

At that time, Great Universal Stores was a large conglomerate of companies including a travel firm called Global Overland Tours, based in Holborn, where I would often be sent to collect travel tickets for Sir Isaac. I would like to say that I truly met him, but whenever I delivered a package to his enormous, ground floor office, he would simply say, "Just put it down there" without ever looking up.

It was around this time that Sir Isaac agreed to be the main financial supporter of John Bloom, another well-known Jewish businessman who was starting up his discount washing-machine business, Electromatic. I was to eventually come across John when he later went into the travel business, selling holidays to Bulgaria, but at that time I was still struggling to climb even the lowest rungs of the career ladder. Yes, I had improved my status – office clerk, rather than manual labourer – and I was receiving a free education from my colleague, but financially I was still experiencing difficulties, despite the free kosher lunch that all Great Universal employees received.

Sometimes I had so little money that it wouldn't last the week, which made for an excruciatingly embarrassing visit to the manager's office to ask for an advance. Eventually, I reached the point where the amount I owed in advances exceeded the amount I was due to get in my wage packet the next week.

Something radical had to be done, and so I got a job with the company that came to clean our offices early each morning. It was, in effect, a fool proof plan: I would have two jobs yet only have to pay one bus fare. Every day, before the normal working day began, I would report at the tradesmen's entrance with the rest of the cleaners and proceed to clean all the offices, including my own. The tricky part was always the moment when I had to change out of my cleaner's overalls and into my John Collier suit and walk through the main entrance at 9.00am, with all the other office workers.

As far as I know, I was never found out, and what's more, the £5 I earned each week was enough to clear my debts. While for many years I was ashamed to admit to this desperate moonlighting, today I view it as a coming-of-business-age.

The merry-go-round of bedsits that I lived in after moving out of the Garros' changed almost as regularly as I changed jobs. They were expensive, too, swallowing as much as 50 per cent of my earnings, so I was constantly on the lookout for something cheaper. A 'room at the top' might sound like an elevation in personal status and living standards, but for me the reality was quite the reverse: a cramped little area right up in the roof, usually with an inconveniently slanted ceiling.

Often one could only afford a place if prepared to share it with a complete stranger, and I wonder now how I managed to pilot a course through all this upheaval and still come out the other side in reasonable shape. After leaving Colville Terrace I spent three years living this twilight existence, completely alone and often hungry and cold, with absolutely no safety net. I now find it quite strange that, even in moments of despair, it did not occur to me to try tracking down members of my family – I think I felt that it might have somehow broken the spell, sucking me back to I-don't-know-where.

Constantly short of money, which even the jobs at Great Universal stores couldn't satisfy, I found a job at a barber's shop in Bayswater, opposite the bedsit where I was living – if nothing else, the cash tips came in handy. During the brief time I worked there I met a man who would steer my life in yet another new direction. He was the main understudy for Professor Higgins in the Drury Lane production of *My Fair Lady*, and through this connection I entered the theatre, not as an actor, but as a dresser for the male chorus.

Once again I took on two jobs to make ends meet. By night, I was at the theatre. By day, I worked for a florist accessory supplier in Covent Garden Flower Market, making up the lettering for funeral wreaths; these would be dipped in glitter before being placed on the graves of the deceased.

Always on the lookout for other work, once I'd packed in my job at the flower market I found employment with World Wide Pictures on Chancery Lane. My job was to handle the logistics for the supply of theatrical props for use in government information films as well as the TV show *Dixon of Dock Green*. It wasn't a bad job, yet I only stayed for a while. Having learnt Spanish, after a fashion, through living with Juan's family, I felt I should put this one asset to some use and so applied for a job with a travel company. My mentors at World Wide Pictures were aware of my intentions and urged me to stay, even when I had handed in my notice, but it was to no avail. I felt bad to be leaving them, but the prospect of travelling abroad, perhaps to Spain, was too tempting to turn my back on.

At the same time, I couldn't help but think back to that kind lady in Colville Terrace. With her last luncheon voucher, she had unwittingly helped in changing the course of my life.

CHAPTER 11
COMING IN FROM THE COLD

The absolute worst time in bedsit land, though, was Christmas – not for any sentimental reason, but because all the coffee bars on Queensway, and everywhere else, were closed.

JOHN Warner, owner of the La Siesta coffee bar on Queensway, was a person who worked to live, rather than the other way round. Whatever profits he made would invariably be channelled to finance his one abiding passion, travel – specifically, travel to Spain, hence the name of his business. Year in, year out, the annual rhythm was the same: John would work all the hours that God sent during the busy summer months and then, when winter came, he would leave someone trustworthy in charge and take off to Spain. Given that the Mediterranean sunshine was at a premium during the chilly UK months of December and January, John's destination of choice was the sub-tropical island of Tenerife, where he stayed at the colonial-style Hotel Monopole in the old quarter of Puerto de la Cruz.

By 1963, John was one of Ted Langton's earliest and most loyal customers, making full use of Ted's Euravia Airlines (the forerunner to Britannia Airways) and its weekly winter charter flight service, on a Lockheed Constellation, from Luton to Los Rodeos airport, Santa Cruz de Tenerife. Returning to a dank and grey Queensway, in London's Bayswater, after two weeks soaking up the warm and invigorating sunshine on the 'Island of Eternal Spring', was always a painful process for John. Nonetheless, like countless tourists before and since, he would bring back the obligatory flowers and toreador posters, which would then be deployed around La Siesta's tables and walls with a view to enhancing the 'Spanishness' of the establishment. John was not the only bar or café owner on Queensway who sought to evoke a theme of some distant and warmer idyll:

A Story in Brief

AN EVENING JOB: In 1960 I obtained a position with a hairdressing business (more like a hair-cutting factory actually) with premises outside the gates of the Ford Motorcar factory in Dagenham owned by an ex-Barnardo's boy. I lived in digs close by in Goodmayes. The Barnardo's records contain this rather alarming letter from my landlady at the time and addressed to Barnardo's: 'Dear Sir, Ref: Philip Morrell – enclosed please find my account for the past four weeks. Confirming my telephone message will you please find other accommodation for Philip. We are finding the strain too much for us. Therefore must ask you to take steps at once please. Yours Sincerely.' During the telephone conversation she had alluded that my required removal had something to do with my external activities but refused to say what – something that foxed Barnardo's completely. The problem was the family were Plymouth Brethren and I had gotten an evening job in a pub which was apparently unacceptable to them – so I was moved on. **IMAGE COURTESY: S.MANTEGAZZA.**

there was also the Brasil, La Margherita, Il Barino, Bertorelli's, the Magyars and the Danube.

Customers were an eclectic mix – after all, this was the Swinging Sixties, when anything and everything supposedly went. Had it been invented, customer profiling would no doubt have revealed that a good thirty per cent of La Siesta's customers originated from nearby bedsits. Most were Spanish or Italian, the remainder of the clientele being made up of spivs, chancers, tarts, gays and actors – plus, every now and again, the occasional unsuspecting 'normal' punter.

From La Siesta's split-level seating area, the whole world of human eccentricity – both the customers inside and the passers-by outside – could be observed. As for us bedsit folk, we were there principally to keep warm. We treated La Siesta and its ilk as our lounge, front room and meeting place combined, and the aim was to spend as much time as humanly possible idling over one cup of coffee. This didn't go down too well with the owners of the coffee bars, who viewed our presence as incompatible with making a profit and did their level best to discourage lingering. Thus if you didn't want to get noticed, you had to keep rotating your custom, on a day to day basis, across the whole range of Queensway coffee bars.

As already mentioned, the vast majority of La Siesta's customers were Spanish or Italian and only passing through London. They were there to learn English, and the moment they achieved the very minimum English language proficiency certification, the Lower Cambridge, they would be gone. I, meanwhile, was an oddity, but a useful oddity: I was probably the only real, live Englishman my fellow bedsitters would ever get to know, since most English people disappeared off into the suburbs at the end of the day. As a result, my foreign friends took every opportunity they could to practise their English language skills on me – so much so that I ended up speaking English with a Spanish accent and people kept asking which part of the Continent I came from. Many a time I wished I could return to some sun-kissed homeland, just like my Spanish and Italian peers were forever doing.

Life in the Bayswater bedsits was rudimentary if not rough. Cooking and washing facilities were basic, and in winter the only way you could keep warm was by incessantly feeding coins into the gas meter, to keep the gas fire going – even then, you only got the benefit if you stood directly over the flickering flames. Trying to plug in an electric fire didn't work either: landlords not only forbade this, but also actively thwarted you by sealing over the sockets so that you couldn't run up an electricity bill that they would have to pay. Nonetheless, this didn't stop the more resourceful among us from running surreptitious cables under the carpet and out into the communal hallway. We also found ways of bypassing the meter that the landlords rigged up to TV sets (two shillings to watch an hour's worth of programmes): a quick thump or two on the side of the TV, plus a bit of cable re-jigging, allowed us to watch as much TV as we wanted, without further coins having to be put in the slot.

The absolute worst time in bedsit land, though, was Christmas – not for any sentimental reason, but because all the coffee bars on Queensway, and everywhere else, were closed. All of a sudden we room-renters had no lounge or front room, so we would stock up on goodies and huddle in each other's bedsits for both company and warmth.

As a rule, no one stayed long in any one bedsit. On one occasion I found myself short of funds and, unable to pay the rent, decided upon a moonlight flit. I waited until I was sure the landlady was asleep – she occupied the room next to the front door – and negotiated the creaking stairs down from my room. Little did I know that she had been lying in wait: just as I opened the front door, she burst screaming out of her room and grabbed my suitcase. I scarpered off at full pelt down Inverness Terrace, only too happy to let her have my suitcase, as I knew full well that its contents nowhere near reached the value of the rent.

As well as foreigners, of course, Bayswater also attracted gay people. Back in the 1960s it was still illegal to be openly homosexual, but this was a law that did not seem to apply in Queensway; indeed, this was the location of the Harlequin Club, where male guests performed Madison line dances that would have put the professionals of *Strictly Come Dancing* to shame. On nearby Inverness Terrace was the lesbian venue Robin Hood, which might more appropriately have been called the Maid Marian. Aside from all other considerations, the great attraction of both clubs to us bedsitters was that they stayed open until at least midnight, whereas the coffee bars shut at 10.00pm. Likewise, earlier in the evening, La Siesta served as something of a holding area for bona fide gays waiting for the clubs to open, and it was also a place where people could have a cup of coffee before crossing the road to the Irish dance hall.

Every weekend, noisy ceilidhs would be held in the dance hall, in the course of which unlimited numbers of couples would either advance in a long line or proceed round a circle, performing traditional dances with names like 'The Walls of Limerick', 'The Waves of Tory', 'The High Cauled Cap', 'Cross Reel' and 'Bonfire Dance'. This being the 60s, some attendees would lapse into jive movements instead, which would provoke the master of ceremonies to halt the music and deliver the stern warning: "No jiving, or you're out!" It wasn't long before the Irish Dance Hall was out, too: it could not keep up with the fads and fashions of the era, and nor could it escape the attention of one Frixos Demetriou.

How to describe this larger-than-life character? Born in Cyprus, Frixos had an unsmiling countenance, wore sunglasses in all weathers and, with his funereal dark suits, looked like he belonged to the world of Hollywood movie thrillers, rather than the genteel British business world. At Frixos' insistence, the time-warp facades of the Irish dance hall were stripped away and replaced by an altogether smarter and more discreet exterior. Look a little closer, and you could make out the words 'Olympic Casino & Gaming Club', printed in a discreet font presumably so as not to draw attention to the fact that a dance venue had been replaced by a gambling joint. Without question, obtaining a gaming licence for these premises must have been hard work, but one way or another Frixos had managed to secure one, much to the dismay of many locals, who lamented that the area was 'going to the dogs'.

The opening of the casino was good news for La Siesta, since it not only brought in extra custom, but also gave us hard-up bedsit folk, gazing out through the window at the arriving gamblers, a glimpse of how the other half lived. We were now joined by lots of posh kids, who drank milk shakes as they waited, with their skates around their necks, to go to the Queensway Ice Rink. There was the occasional celebrity, too, such as Dusty Springfield or Harry H. Corbett, of Steptoe and Son fame. Another personality who passed through the portals of La Siesta was the fashion designer John Stephen, the so-called 'King of Carnaby Street', who later opened one of his emporiums next door.

Although Frixos had a valid gaming licence, by 1967 he was worried that his casino might be affected by forthcoming legislation, and so resolved to find an alternative business venture. He happened to be in Milan, on a diverted flight to Athens, when he saw a strange little car parked near the airport. Enquiries revealed that it was a Vignale Gamine, a humorous little 'Belle Époque' roadster based on the Fiat 500 chassis. Straightaway this set his businessman's brain ticking, and Frixos determined, there and then, to secure the world rights to market the car.

On the return journey from Athens, he diverted to Turin, where coach-building firm Vignale was based, in order to view the company's products. Four days later, he returned with his German-Swiss legal adviser, Ernest Huppert, to make a rather unusual business proposition. Not accustomed to thinking small, the pair asked if Vignale would be prepared to sell them a run of some of their Fiat-based models. The reply was "yes", and so Frixos bought 200 cars on the spot, in cash; what's more, he guaranteed to buy the rest of the next six months' production, as long as Vignale would build the cars right-hand drive.

Before long, full of optimism, the pair signed a similar deal with another Turin coachbuilder, Francis Lombardi, to import Lombardi's pretty little Fiat 850-based coupé, the Grand Prix. There was, explained Frixos, some logic behind his seemingly profligate spending spree: "I wanted to be able to force [the manufacturers] to incorporate special equipment for my market." It wasn't long before his Queensway base was bulging with literally hundreds of cars, parked in a specially cleared zone beside his casino. He had invested a fortune – some estimates put the total sum at over £500,000 (almost £8 million today) – without so much as a single order to offset what he had paid out.

One thing everyone did agree upon was that the Gamine two-seater was great fun. It became known as the 'Noddy Car' and acquired fashionable status among the Chelsea set; even nightclub owner Peter Stringfellow had one. What's more, the car came in all sorts of gaudy colours, like 'Portobello Yellow' and 'Hollywood Green' (a sort of peppermint hue). However, it was underpowered, dubiously manufactured and worryingly prone to rust. Sales were sluggish, to say the least.

For most people in the car import business, this would have meant curtains. Luckily, Frixos was rich enough for this not to bother him too much. His gaming licence was renewed and, all of a sudden, he didn't need the car business any more. To avoid hefty UK customs duty, in 1970 he decided to re-export some of the unsold Gamines to his native Cyprus, where they sold better. Frixos' own story didn't end happily, though: that same year, back in Cyprus, he was sat in his own, parked Noddy Car when a runaway army tank squashed both him and the car flat.

Back in Queensway circa 1963, the restaurant world was increasingly dominated by the expatriate Italian and Spanish communities. These were tight-knit circles and, as an Englishman, I found myself on the outside, unable to get employment as a waiter in one of their eateries or banqueting venues. Things suddenly changed, however: forget chilly west London – casinos were now opening up in the sunny Bahamas and required croupiers who could speak English. The casino operators came and recruited large numbers of Spanish and Italian Bayswater bedsit-folk, and it wasn't long before La Siesta began to lose customers and I began to lose my coffee-bar companions.

It was at this point that Rafael Fuentes arrived on the scene, as La Siesta's new head waiter. In looks he resembled El Cordobés, the raffishly handsome, intrepid matador whose poster hung on the wall, alongside the jukebox that seemed forever to be playing 'Cuando Calienta El Sol'. Rafael had that quality which females seem to find irresistible – namely, conducting himself as if he was quite unaware of how attractive he was. His effect enhanced by a certain little-boy look, a slight lisp and a gentle, golden tan. Straight away, he garnered the admiration of the girls – and some of the boys too, for that matter.

Rafael needed a place to stay, and it so happened that I was in need of a lodger for my bedsit at 11 Warrington Crescent, Maida Vale. His presence was, I have to confess, a mixed blessing. Each night he enacted a sort of horizontal El Cordobés performance with the English girls he brought home. There may not have been any sounding of trumpets; he may not have turned full circle and doffed his hat to the crowd; but there were plenty of muffled "olés" as he went in for the kill! The thin sheets on my bed were incapable of masking the noise and even less effective at dispelling the envy. I was stuck at the 'just-holding-hands' stage with my girlfriend Carmen, who was Spanish, like Rafael, but who, when it came to men, remained true to her strict Catholic upbringing.

Others, too, were feeling that there had to be more to life than the Bayswater bedsits. In the winter of 1965, John Warner decided he was tired of eking out a living from La Siesta and resolved to sell up and move to Paris. Together, Rafael and I accompanied him to Victoria Station, to give him a proper send-off on the Golden Arrow train. It was, I have to say, a sad affair. We stood there, the three of us, under the arched platform entrance bearing the words 'Golden Arrow'. Prosperous-looking passengers swarmed past our shabby little group, all of them dressed to the nines, for this was not a mere trip: it was the beginning of a journey to what, in those days, was the faraway, magical city of Paris. Little did I realise, as I waved the train off into the distance, that my journey, too, was about to begin.

Tucked away in my garage today is one of Frixos' Noddy Cars; I bought it at auction for no other reason than to maintain a link with this part of my past.

CHAPTER 12
THE TROUBLESHOOTER WHO WOULDN'T SHOOT

The occasion was a group job interview, in which we applicants had only one question to answer: could we multiply the sum of 39-and-a-half guineas by five? Everyone guessed and everyone gave a different answer.

T HE year was 1963 and the occasion was a group job interview, in which we applicants had only one question to answer: could we multiply the sum of 39-and-a-half guineas by five? Everyone guessed, everyone gave a different answer, and we all passed! We were instructed to report next day at 9.00am sharp, to begin our jobs as reservation clerks for newly formed coach-operators Cosmos Tours. Our offices were in a converted car showroom on Vauxhall Bridge Road, Victoria, which had been transformed (superficially, at least) into a call centre.

Cosmos offered not just conventional coach tours, but new-fangled 'fly-coach' tours to the Continent as well. These were all priced in guineas, generally featured capital cities separated by impossible distances and had enticing titles such as 'The Grand Tour of Spain, Portugal and Morocco', 'Five Countries and Paris', 'A Leisurely Tour of Central Europe' and 'A Leisurely Tour of France and the Costa Brava'. Indeed, the word 'leisurely' featured in most of the tour names, despite the fact there was nothing leisurely about them: without exception, they involved getting up with the lark each morning for a whistle-stop drive, at breakneck speed, along the autobahns of Belgium, Holland and Germany and the minor roads of southern Europe.

That said, seats on those tours sold in the tens of thousands. Most of the journeys involved a quick trip to Paris, and before long it became commonplace to see a dozen-or-so Cosmos coaches each day in the French capital, alongside those of its sister company, Globus Gateway. There was no question as to which of the firms was held to be superior, though: then, as now, Globus was considered the 'Blue Riband' of coach-tour companies, due not only to the higher category of hotel at which its passengers stayed, but also to the fact that the person in charge on a Globus vehicle was referred to as the 'Tour Director', while Cosmos only had a common-or-garden 'Coach Courier'. Globus had not always been so grand: the firm started out in Switzerland in the late 1920s, at a time when Swiss tourism had just started to recover some of its pre-World War I popularity. Everywhere there were local travel agents happy to arrange hotel and railway reservations, together with excursion options and obligatory boat trips across the country's many beautiful lakes.

Nowhere in Switzerland was there more demand for this kind of service, especially during the summer, than at the resort of Lugano, and it was here, in 1928, that Antonio Mantegazza set up a small firm named Globus Viaggi. Far from a fleet of modern coaches, all Antonio had at his disposal was a rowing boat, with which he ferried both tourists and cargo across Lake Lugano. It was from these humble beginnings, nonetheless, that Antonio's two sons, Sergio and Geo, were to build up one of the biggest travel businesses in the world.

Today, the company comprises some 30 different firms, including Globus Gateway, Cosmos, Avalon Cruises and Monarch Airlines. Even in the 1950s, Globus Viaggi was operating 33 different tour coaches across a range of routes, itineraries and destinations, including Rome, Venice, the Dolomites and the French Riviera. It wasn't long before the network expanded still further, under the ever-capable management of Werner Albek, Antonio's business partner.

It would be no exaggeration to say that the origins of the modern 'Grand European Tour' can be traced back to Antonio and Werner and the shores of Lake Lugano.

In these modern times, the history of travel might be seen through the narrow prism of the ubiquitous package-tour operators offering nothing more than the basic return flights and hotel accommodation. Yet before these came the likes of Antonio Mantegazza, who first laid down the foundations and then perfected the art and organisation of travel, and whose name is up there with the 'greats'.

I remember Antonio's young son Sergio well. I first saw him from a distance, standing (as was his wont) at the back of the Cosmos Tours reservation hall with his UK associate, Mr Jackman. Sergio was enigmatic and slim, seldom spoke and always wore polo-necked jumpers, which was not quite the done thing in those days: if you were a manager, at least in the UK, you were supposed to wear a collar and tie. How he must have marvelled at the success of his new baby. Here were cluster upon cluster of desks, each cluster consisting of six busy reservation clerks, all connected up, via headphones, to their own 'key-and-lamp' telephone switch-board, with each blinking light representing yet another coach tour sale.

If you were on the answering end of those phones, there was hardly time to catch your breath. The calls came in non-stop; no sooner had one series of tours sold out, than several relief tours were laid on. The secret of this success lay not in the exciting-sounding tour names, but in the way in which the itineraries were presented in the brochure. First, the whole thing was printed in colour, a novelty in those days; second, each tour description was adorned with eye-catching photographs, maps and graphics – again, a near first within the travel industry. The brochure was designed and written in the Globus offices, in Lugano, but printed in Turin, taking full advantage of the latest colour-printing processes.

Interestingly, in years to come, those same Turin print works (there were two) were to become embroiled in a bitter dispute between Thomson Holidays and Clarksons, with accusations flying around that either company could gain access to the print works to get sight of the other's plans and to undercut their prices. For the moment, though, the tours offered by Cosmos were mostly of 10 nights' duration and would sell for 39 guineas (£40.95). So, for under £5 a day (around £70 today), a Cosmos customer got full board, all coach travel, return ferry crossings and the services of a coach courier.

It was cut-price travel, of course, and was dependent on a high degree of efficiency on our part in order to make a profit. It was essential that as one coach party left a hotel, the next would arrive, thus ensuring continual occupancy – simple enough if you're only dealing with one hotel, but Globus had hundreds, if not thousands, of hotels across Europe on their books, not to mention venues for en route meal stops.

Remember, there were no computers or email at that time, and telex was still in its infancy. This meant that all arrangements had to be made face-to-face with each supplier – who, more often than not, wanted to be paid in cash on departure – on the basis of which head office would come up with an intricately-detailed, idiot-proof 'technical itinerary' for the coach couriers to follow.

As for myself, I had taken the job as reservation clerk, with a view to one day getting a job as an overseas coach courier or, failing that, a hotel receptionist. The issue was, as always in those days, my age: it was a hard-and-fast rule that you had to be 21 to be a coach courier and I was only 19 (and looked even younger). The job of vetting and training coach couriers was then the exclusive domain of a gentleman from Lugano, John Bacannello. John was of mixed English and Italian parentage, which meant that, in addition to having a phlegmatic Anglo-Saxon manner and smoking a pipe, he was also prone to gesticulations and a sense of theatricality that spoke of his Latin roots.

Before and after the war, John had worked as a guide and resort representative for the legendary Harry Chandler's Travel Club of Upminster in both Austria and Switzerland, before eventually settling down with his family in Lugano. This was how he had come to be employed by Globus, first as a tour director himself, and then as trainer of the firm's tour directors and coach couriers. Each winter, John was summoned to the Cosmos offices in London, in order to supervise the selection and training process. Having reduced the applicants to a manageable number, he would run a series of training courses in a room above a pub in Victoria, the idea being not just to pass on the requisite coach-courier skills, but, more importantly, to vet the applicants close up.

Once the course was over, John would decide which candidates would make it through to the final test, which was a face-to-face interview with gruff, chain-smoking Herbert Harrison, the man who had the ultimate say on who would be taken on. Candidates who got the nod from Herbert would be taken on as a Cosmos courier, a job that, in those pre-internet, pre-email, pre-long-distance phone days, was extremely sought-after. Once on the road, out of reach of head office, the courier was quite literally king, on top of which there was plenty of opportunity for extra earnings, via commissions, shop kickbacks and tips.

The requirements were simple: you had to be over 21, speak a Continental European language and, ideally, have prior overseas work experience; unfortunately, at that time, I could satisfy only one of those three requirements, but that didn't stop me dreaming. Throughout the winter I attended every single one of John Baccanello's 20-or-so training courses – the venue was close to the office and the courses were held after working hours, so it was no chore. One was well aware of being a pupil at the feet of a master craftsman in the art of travel; what's more, John had written a manual covering all the different aspects of a courier's work which he would take us through section-by-section. He viewed the tour director/coach courier role very much in theatrical terms; it was his philosophy that a tour was a bit like a play: it should have an impressive beginning, a substantial middle and, most importantly, an uplifting ending. The latter, he stressed, was of key importance if you wanted to orchestrate the tipping moment to your advantage.

John's particular bête noire was clumsy or lazy microphone technique, and this is something that has stayed with me all my life: it still grates when I hear badly executed announcements on an aircraft or in a terminal. By the time I had attended all of John's courses, I knew his thoughts not just on microphones but on every aspect of the tour director's craft; all I needed was a chance to put this wisdom into action.

In the meantime, I carried on working alongside my reservation-clerk colleagues: it was our job to make up the seating charts for each coach (44

A Story in Brief

THE LUNCHEON VOUCHER: This humble meal ticket was introduced in 1946, when food rationing was still in force, following the end of the war. The government granted an extra-statutory tax concession to the value of three shillings a day, believing that this would help citizens afford healthy meals. Prior to that, companies had to have their own meal vouchers printed, and make arrangements with local restaurants to accept them. In 1954, however, businessman John Hack realised that a single standardised voucher, acceptable across the UK, would be more logical and convenient. In 1955 he started the Luncheon Vouchers Company, and just one year later, a conglomerate of nine large catering companies bought the company, with Hack staying on as managing director. The vouchers were even used as a form of payment in Cynthia Payne's brothel in London during the 1970s, though I doubt change was ever given. IMAGE COURTESY: S.MANTEGAZZA.

passengers per coach). The first seats to be snapped up were always the four behind the driver and the courier; invariably these were occupied by busybodies who thought they could do the job better than you. By contrast, the four banquette seats that ran along the back of the coach were usually favoured, for some reason, by nurses, who saw Cosmos Tours as a cheap and convenient way to see Europe, especially if they came from the Commonwealth countries.

Once we had taken the initial reservation over the phone, we would receive a booking form and deposit from the travel agent (no bookings came in direct from customers). The next task was rather more complicated, as it involved converting the quoted prices from guineas into pounds, shillings and pence, then multiplying that figure by the number of passengers, deducting 10-per-cent commission for the travel agent and, finally, deducting the deposit, thereby leaving the balance to pay (hence our initial interview test, which we had all got wrong). The paperwork would then be handed over to our army of typists and the invoice eventually sent out.

It was monotonous work, but at least I felt close to the action. There was one tour in particular that took my fancy: 'The Grand Tour of Spain, Portugal and Morocco'. So openly desperate was I to escort this tour, and so often had I been rebuffed by Herbert Harrison, that my work mates would teasingly call me 'Mister Grand Tour', as if I was on a fool's errand. Little did they know, though, that I had a plan up my sleeve. I had observed that Cosmos were not interested in organising one-off tours, on the grounds that these did not offer the same kinds of economies-of-scale as their regular, scheduled operations. However, as the demand for more ad-hoc arrangements intensified, the firm took on a Polish ex-RAF pilot named Eddie in order to set them up. Realising that Eddie was going to need new couriers for his coach tours, I started cosying up to him.

At that time I was still sharing the third-floor bedsit at 11 Warrington Crescent, Maida Vale, with Rafael from the La Siesta café. Being a kindly soul and, in addition to helping me with my spoken Spanish, Rafael provided me with invaluable help in sending off job applications to Spanish hotels. Sadly, though, it proved all to no avail: I never got any replies to my letters and came to the conclusion that my best chance of getting to Spain was to stick it out at Cosmos and see if anything turned up.

Nothing came through Herbert Harrison, though; he left Cosmos and the last I heard of him was in an article headlined 'The Troubleshooter Who Would Not Shoot'. Herbert had joined another travel company as a kind of trouble-shooter, sorting out local issues and complaints. Apparently, though, he became so unhappy with his working conditions that, on one assignment, he refused to 'shoot', got the sack and lost his claim for compensation. Strangely enough, I did have indirect contact with Herbert, via his son, John. For some reason that I could never quite fathom, John seemed to detest his father, which is perhaps why he agreed to help on a certain matter sometime later.

The matter in question involved a Swiss girl, Helen Struele, who worked alongside me on the Cosmos reservation desk. Helen's parents ran a hardware store in Goldach, near St Gallen, and, after working for Globus in Lugano, she had been seconded to Cosmos for the winter season, which was how came to I meet her. After six months in London, she moved back to Lugano and, once there, invited me over.

My problem, as always, was that I had no money, but John Harrison, who was working for British Air Ferries, operating car-carrying flights out of Southend Airport to Geneva, offered me one of the complimentary return flight tickets that he received as part of his salary package. The only catch was, I had to travel under his name. Well, the flight out from Southend passed off without problems, but on the return journey things went awry: I had completely forgotten that I was travelling under an alias, so when the Tannoy announcements at Geneva Airport kept requesting a 'Mr John Harrison' to report urgently to the check-in desk, I remained calmly anchored to my seat, and duly the plane departed without me.

A BRIEF AUDIENCE WITH – SERGIO MANTEGAZZA

I had waited several months to interview Sergio Mantegazza, under the impression that I was to join him somewhere convenient in the Med, on board his mega yacht *Lady Marina*, the very same vessel on which Tina Turner had stayed on the year before. Imagine my disappointment, then, when this idea was quashed in favour of an alternative venue and date in either Monte Carlo or Lugano.

To be honest, I had been surprised that he had even agreed to see me in the first place, it being well known that he declined all publicity, and interviews were usually completely out of the question – not surprising, really, given that in 1995 Sergio had briefly been kidnapped from his Lugano offices. When the appointed time came for the interview and I was intending to send a writer in my place, an immediate riposte came flying back, making it clear that he would only be interviewed by me.

It was, then, with some trepidation that I made my way to Sergio Mantegazza's Lugano offices, which were in a nondescript, commercial part of Lugano: a million miles, in scenic terms, from the idyllic headquarters of his that I remembered from years gone by, at Piazza Luini, close to Lake Lugano.

Outside was Sergio's £300,000 Mercedes Maybach, with his chauffer standing nearby. Still wondering how best to greet, and then put questions to, one of the richest men on the planet, I navigated the building's security system, was escorted through some pretty ordinary business premises and finally reached the office, via that of his personal assistant, of Mr. Mantegazza himself. Given his reputed net worth of $3 billion, this room struck me as small and frugal in the extreme.

Straight away, Sergio rose graciously to greet me; even at the age of 86, he still looks extremely fit and has a fine shock of white hair. I made a mental note that I needn't have worn the suit and tie I had kept so carefully un-creased for this meeting. Instead of the polo-neck jumper I always recall him wearing, he was in a jacket and an open-neck shirt. His mood was relaxed, too, and it wasn't long before I came to the realisation that he was actually more interested in hearing my story than telling me his.

I had earlier sent him a piece I had written about the time when I first joined Cosmos Tours in 1963/4 as travel clerk; I got the feeling that this article had in some way reminded him of how he felt when he first entered the travel business, and that this was why he had agreed to see me. I was, if you like, a child from one of his creations who had gone on to other things, and he was interested to hear how I had fared.

Upon prompting, Sergio told me a small part of the story of Globus Gateway and Cosmos Tours. He explained that before and in the years after the war, the majority of international tourists arrived in Lugano by train, until he began selling – to overseas travel firms – his locally organised excursions and coach tours, both within Switzerland and in the surrounding countries.

During the war years, too, it seemed the company had not been entirely bereft of business; it had ticked over, thanks to travellers from the German part of Switzerland, who, having been effectively 'locked in', had nowhere else to go on holiday.

Before long, though, it became clear that by attaching their own names to Sergio's tours, overseas tour operators were in a position to cut him out entirely. With this in mind, he joined up with Simmons-Gateway in the early 1950s, a New York-based operator, to market the Globus coach tours to potential customers in the United States.

It proved an immediate success, and over time Sergio bought out Simmons-Gateway, and thus Globus and Gateway tours was born. The operation then just continued to grow and grow, even in the face of stiff competition from rival US outfit Caravan Tours. What's more, it remains something of a triumph, and is now mainly managed by the Albek side of the partnership, a relationship that goes back to the very beginnings of Globus Viaggi.

As for the British market, which was the source of most of his passengers, Sergio decided to start his own company from scratch in 1962. For this, he sought the assistance of George Jackman, who had come from Hotelplan, and Wilf Jones, who came from the Workers' Travel Association.

The name he chose for the company was Cosmos Tours. There had been much discussion beforehand as to whether this should be spelt with a 'C' or 'K', but given that there was already a company in Yugoslavia called Kosmos, they had decided upon Cosmos with a 'C'. Again, the company just got bigger and bigger, and came in time to have both its own airline, Monarch, and its own riverboat company, Avalon.

As he told me his story, I couldn't help reflecting how incongruous it was, that so much of the pre- and post-war travel business had been built on the patronage of the Workers' Travel Association, which in 1921 had grown out of the British Labour Party and the Trade Union Movement.

Amid all the glories, though, there have been dark moments for Sergio: the sadness when his eldest son took his own life, and then, of course, the trauma of the kidnapping.

Today, his other son, Fabio, runs the business; Sergio only becomes involved in strategic decisions, and busies himself, along with his daughter, in looking after his many investments. Plus, of course, there is the helicopter and the huge yacht.

The night before our meeting I had tossed and turned, uncertain as to how I should comport myself in his presence. As I say, though, he was more interested in hearing my story than in telling me his, and as a result the conversation flowed easily.

However, as I left his small office, I couldn't help feeling this had been a kind of Citizen Kane moment. There sat Sergio, inscrutable with all his billions, now in the autumn of his years. As I emerged into the streets of Lugano, I sensed I had barely scratched the surface: there was still much untold and unrevealed – wrapped perhaps in a 'rosebud'-like enigma.

CHAPTER 13
THE DEBUTANTES

I think what really concerned the organisers was what 30 wild young debutantes might get up to once let off the leash in Paris. To that end, I had been ordered to keep them busy at all times.

I T was at 11 Warrington Crescent that my lifelong dislike of banks began. Things first went wrong when Cosmos started to pay my wages directly into my bank account, instead of paying me in cash. I was lying in bed one morning when my landlady knocked on the door clutching my rent cheque, which in her words had 'bounced'. Even though I had spent my life hovering around the breadline, I was pretty certain that I had enough money in my account to cover the amount, but my pleas were to no avail.

My landlady made it clear, in no uncertain terms, that I was to pack my bags – or bag, in my case – and be gone by the following morning. Not a good start to the day at all, but a few hours later things took a distinct turn for the better, when I got a telegram from Eddie, Cosmos' new bespoke-tours manager, asking me to go to the office at once. It turned out that one of his tour escorts had phoned in sick, and a replacement was needed.

I wasn't feeling particularly well, but I wasn't going to let feverish flu and aching limbs get in the way of this heaven-sent opportunity. The tour I would be leading consisted of a breakneck, three-and-a-half-day dash down to the Costa Brava, followed by a week in Lloret de Mar and then another three-and-a-half-day scramble back to London. This typical tightly stretched Cosmos schedule may well have been the reason why the original courier had bailed out.

Aside from the punishing schedule and my flu, two other things bothered me: first, the fact that I had hardly been abroad before; and second, that I didn't speak French. Not that there was anything I could do about these drawbacks at this late stage, of course. So, drawing on all the lessons I had learned in John Baccanello's classes, I picked up my 'uniform' (a Cosmos Tours badge and an

A Story in Brief

LOVE ME WITH ALL OF YOUR HEART: Anyone who has ever been on holiday to Spain, or sat in a coffee bar in the 1960s, will have heard this song. It's based on the Spanish language ballad 'Cuando calienta el sol' (When the sun warms up), written by Nicaraguan bandleader Rafael Gaston Perez, and made famous first by the Rigual Brothers. The English lyrics are sometimes credited to Michael Vaughn (or Maurice Vaughn) and sometimes to Sunny Skylar. The song was published in 1961, and although both the Spanish and the English versions are love songs, the lyrics are not translations of each other. A version recorded by The Ray Charles Singers went to number three on the Billboard Hot 100 and spent four weeks at number one on the Pop-Standard singles chart in June 1964. The Spanish version was for ever blasting out of the La Siesta's jukebox in Bayswater, which was sandwiched between posters of El Cordobés and Manolete.

armband bearing the word 'Courier') and, feeling important all of a sudden, rushed back to my bedsit to swot up on the technical itinerary and prepare myself for the trip ahead.

At this point, my biggest worries were my health and how I was going to wake up at 5.00am next morning, in order to get to Victoria Station by 6.30am to meet my party. It was then that someone told me a sure-fire way to cure the flu: find an Indian restaurant – no easy task in London back then – and order a Vindaloo curry. The nearest place I could find was the Star of Bombay, at the junction of Portobello Road and Notting Hill Gate. It was early afternoon and the place was empty; I sat down and asked for the menu.

There was a special 'Vindaloo' menu, listing various strengths from mild to positively explosive, and I went for the fiercest, explaining to the waiter that I was there for medicinal reasons. Unfortunately, though, this being my first Indian meal, I didn't quite know what to expect, and no sooner had the dish arrived in front of me I scooped the burning mush into my mouth as quickly as possible. I was back out on the street in minutes.

Mission accomplished, I returned to my bedsit to ponder how I was going to overcome the getting-up-in-the-morning issue. I then had a bright idea, which entailed gathering all the pots and pans in the bedsit and laying them on the floor beside my bed, having first placed my alarm clock inside the biggest pot of all, so that, when it went off, the ring would be amplified. I could do no more. With my bag packed and my uniform laid out at the bottom of my bed, I drifted off to sleep, albeit with a strange burning sensation in my throat.

At 5.00am the alarm went off as scheduled, making the same kind of metallic din as if someone had just dropped a bunch of cutlery on the floor. In one bound I was up and dressed, badge proudly pinned to my lapel and Gestapo-like armband around my sleeve. As I strode authoritatively down to Warwick Avenue Underground station, I made sure that everyone who passed was aware of my new importance.

To my horror, though, when I got to the ticket booth I found that, instead of uttering intelligible words, I could only manage the hoarsest, barely audible whisper. In that I wasn't aching any more, the Vindaloo had clearly done its job – the bad news was that I had completely lost my voice. A bit of an impediment, one would have thought, for a budding tour guide, but in fact my inability to speak proved to be a bit of unlooked-for good luck.

By the time I arrived at coach bay 7 in Victoria Coach Station, my unsuspecting charges were already there and waiting for me, all dressed to the nines and with suitcases lined up beside the East Kent coach that was to take us to the Channel ferry at Folkestone. After a few painful croaks, it dawned on me that eliciting customer sympathy was going to be my best bet, in terms of deflecting attention from my lack of experience. The passengers' response to the few words I tried to utter was to take me under their collective wing and mother me – fine by me, since it meant no commentary was given or expected.

According to the itinerary, we were to be picked up on the other side of the Channel by one of the West Belgium Coach Company's vehicles and driven down to Spain. It has to be said, at this point, that the drivers of these coaches were a motley bunch. Most of them owned the vehicles they drove, and when it came to cutting corners, they knew every trick in the book. In order to take advantage of the cheaper fuel prices in Belgium, many of them had built secondary fuel tanks beneath the floor. Not only was this illegal, but it was also dangerous: we were, in effect, being conveyed aboard a mobile bomb, albeit a bomb with seats.

The next dodge involved the no-man's land border area between Belgium and France, where drivers would make an unscheduled stop to buy vast quantities of duty-free cigarettes and booze. Instead of just using their own individual allowance, they would buy an amount equating to the total allowance for everyone on board – i.e., 44 passengers. The cartons of fags and booze would be surreptitiously placed in the luggage racks above each passenger's seat and retrieved once we had passed through the border area, to be sold, at a vast profit, to hotels and restaurants along the route.

Of course, the French customs officers were well aware of these shenanigans and were forever diving under coaches in an attempt to find hidden fuel tanks. Rarely did they find what they were looking for, though, and the drivers made a small fortune. I soon came to realise that, while nominally the courier was in charge, it was actually the drivers who called the shots. Apart from anything else, there were two of them and only one of me.

These drivers never stopped to change over: as one driver got out of the driving seat, the other would slide in and take his place, without the coach ever coming to an actual halt. On my particular coach the illicit diesel was swilling around in a secret tank just under the central passageway; the smell was so strong that it could only be masked by vast amounts of deodorising spray. The full extent of my powerlessness was brought home to me when I had a disagreement with the drivers about some matter or other and, as a result, they threatened to withhold the deodorising spray. As far as they were concerned, it was their coach, not the company's, and that was the end of it.

The upside of the trip was the fact that, at long last, I was abroad – in Spain, no less. I had never before felt that kind of warm sunshine on my back or seen a sea as blue as it was here; it was such a delight to stand in the main square, in front of the Lloret de Mar town hall, and watch local girls dance the slow, rhythmic

'Sardana' in their colourful dresses. The square and the beach were separated by the main coast road, down which the teeming French and German tourists drove, lining their cars, sardine-like, along the seafront for a couple of miles or more.

Our hotel – or, more accurately, pension – was tucked away in the old part of the town, into which it was impossible for coaches to pass. At the beginning of the journey home, the coach had to stop on the main coast road so that we could load up the luggage. As a driver and I hauled the bags up onto the roof, the nurses who occupied the back banquette seats boarded the coach in floods of tears, after saying their farewells to their holiday romances.

It was during this procedure that disaster struck. Since we did not have credit facilities with the hotels at which we were scheduled to stay, I had been issued with a brown envelope full of cash, with which to settle up on departure. Up until this point, I had guarded the envelope with my life; however, needing to free both my hands in order to throw the luggage up to the driver, I had unwisely placed the envelope on the boot of a nearby parked car. Totally forgetting that I had done so, I blithely got on the coach and we set off for London, via Carcassonne, Limoges and Paris.

After we had been driving for a few miles, I went through my mental checklist and suddenly realised, to my absolute horror that I had left the money behind. In that terrible moment, I saw my courier career coming to an abrupt and very final end. Quietly, without divulging the real reason to the passengers, I asked the coach driver to turn back and head for the spot where we had loaded up.

When we got there, though, I was confronted by a vast mass of identical-looking cars and found myself unable to pinpoint on which car boot I had left the package. Now panic really set in. I began running frantically up and down the beachfront, and it was only after I had repeated this process several times that, to my delight and sheer relief, I found the money, unmoved from where I had left it an hour ago.

Exhausted, we headed back into France. Not long after passing through Limoges, at a small crossroads where we had right of way, a battered Citroën 'Deux Chevaux' crossed right in front of us without its driver looking. In an instant our coach crashed directly into the car, mangling it beyond recognition and killing the two elderly occupants outright. It was an ugly sight, and, not surprisingly, a number of my passengers were pretty shaken up by the experience. The coach driver was taken to the local police station for blood tests and to provide a witness statement, while I ferried my charges to a nearby café to settle them down, arrange a meal and organise a replacement coach – all in pidgin French.

Our problems did not stop there. Understandably, the driver who had been in control at the time of the accident was spooked, and felt unconfident in getting behind the wheel again so soon – so unconfident that he drove behind the replacement coach, in his own empty, battered vehicle, and it was in this convoy-type formation that we finally reached Ostend. The adventure had started unpromisingly, and ended eventfully.

Nevertheless, in the company's eyes at least, I had earned my spurs, and it was felt that I might be able to help out with another potentially tricky situation. The tour party in question involved some 30 well-brought-up young women, who were travelling to London from Australia and New Zealand in order to take part in an updated version of what used to be the London debutante season.

Traditionally, the season began after Easter, ended on the 'Glorious Twelfth' (12 August, the start of the shooting season for red grouse) and incorporated a number of social-cum-sporting events, such as Royal Ascot and the Henley Royal Regatta. Although the formal presentation of debutantes at court had been abolished in 1958 by Queen Elizabeth, the events that had made up the season continued, albeit under the sponsorship of large companies rather than wealthy parents. Meanwhile, in the farthest flung corners of the Commonwealth – the Antipodes, in particular – the tradition of 'coming out' persisted into the 1960s, and large groups of young girls would gravitate to London, the weeks before their trip having been taken up with instruction in grooming and the appointment of a suitable chaperone.

Usually the itinerary would consist of a voyage on one of the great ocean liners, beginning in Australia or New Zealand and sailing, via Hong Kong, India and Suez, to Genoa, where the young ladies would disembark. They would then undertake a version of the old-style Grand Tour, before moving on to London, where the fun would really begin. It just so happened, though, that this year the fun had begun early – and got rather out of hand.

Once out at sea, intoxicated by their first taste of freedom, the young women had decided to make the most of their new-found liberty. By the time the liner docked at Genoa, they had already become acquainted with the good life, and once the good-looking male courier assigned as their escort around Italy had, shall we say, 'seized the moment' with some of the debutantes , what was supposed to be a sedate introduction to good taste became unconstrained mayhem on wheels.

A counsel of war had been duly convened between the tour organiser, Eddie, and the debutantes' chaperone, Lady Mackworth. The conclusion was reached that a new courier should be assigned for their post-London Season tour, in the course of which they would be visiting Champagne country, Paris, Madrid and Barcelona, before eventually setting sail for home. This time a courier would be allocated who could be counted upon to not only keep his hands to himself, but also ensure the girls did the same.

I can only assume that at this point, mindful of my earlier exploits and youthful looks, Eddie must have said to Lady Mackworth, "I have the very person in mind." Either way, I was duly briefed and then dispatched, in a coach, to meet 'Lady M' and the girls at Bailey's Hotel, South Kensington. That day we would be travelling to Dover, for the Ostend ferry, and onwards, to an evening function in the cellars of Moët et Chandon, in Epernay, and finally Paris. Having had the full background story from Eddie, I was determined not to blot my copybook by appearing in any way interested in the girls.

As I walked down the aisle of the coach, I made a point of looking straight ahead, indifferent to the flirtatious glances coming my way. To be honest, though, I think what really concerned the organisers was what 30 wild young debutantes might get up to once let off the leash in Paris. To that end, I had been ordered to keep them busy at all times and was entrusted with large amounts of cash to spend on educational and cultural evenings at such places as the Comédie-Française.

All I can say is, I did my best. In the event, however, large numbers of my charges managed to evade my watchful gaze and ended up partying in the fleshpots of the Quartier Pigalle. Nevertheless, it struck me that I could get to enjoy this kind of specialised tourism business, which made it rather disappointing when a woman, built along the lines of Hattie Jacques, turned up at the hotel in Paris and told me she was taking over as courier. Instead of accompanying the girls to Madrid, I was to return immediately to London.

Mortified, I wondered if I had been found out, since at one point I too had weakened and partaken of the debutante fruit. Once again fearful for my future as a courier, I bid sad farewells to the girls and to Lady Mackworth, who handed me a letter to be delivered to my employers in London.

Naturally, I was now plagued by the question: what had Lady M written in her letter? During an idle moment on the flight from Le Bourget, I fumbled in my inside jacket pocket for the letter, wondering whether it revealed anything untoward or damaging. I noticed that the envelope was only lightly sealed, and so, after gingerly opening it, I began reading her missive.

She started off by going through the events of the tour: its origins in Australia and New Zealand, the ocean voyage, the Italian tour, the London season and all the problems she had experienced when it came to controlling not just the girls, but the guides and couriers as well. She concluded, however, by declaring that once Philip Morrell had been put in charge, everything had been sweetness and light. She even implied that, since Philip's relationship with the girls was so proper and upright, perhaps he might be gay.

Back in the early 1960s, that kind of talk was tantamount to questioning one's manhood. For a while, I seriously debated whether I should ditch the letter, but in the end, and purely for career motives, I decided to deliver it as instructed. Probably the sentiments expressed by Lady M in the letter caused some amusement among those who read it, but then again, who knows? And besides, had 'Hattie Jacques' not come between me and temptation, I might well have ended up running not a travel company, but a six-million-strong sheep farm in the Australian Outback.

At the end of the day, what my two tour experiences had demonstrated to me was that I could do a lot better for myself than just being a reservation clerk and occasional stand-in courier. Thus I left Cosmos and took a job on Bond Street with Inghams, the ski-holiday company founded by Walter Ingham.

My new job paid more, the bus fare was lower and there was plenty of overtime on offer. I had also sent off letters to all the other tour operators, applying for a resort representative job, and was hopeful of success. I even got my old room back at 11 Warrington Crescent – the landlady said she would take me, provided I did not pay my rent by cheque, but with good old, reliable cash, up-front.

A Story in Brief

SHOWBIZ TIES: It's thanks to Juan Garcia-Roady (Thomson's agent in Tenerife) that I still have a cupboard full of expensive Versace neckties; he gave me one each time we met. In 1976, Juan married Hollywood film actress Jacqueline Beer who had featured in various blockbuster films alongside Rock Hudson, Doris Day, Tony Curtis and Clint Eastwood, and who had played glamorous receptionist Suzanne in the long-running American TV series *77 Sunset Strip*. Her marriage to Juan ended, however, when she fell in love with the celebrated Norwegian adventurer Thor Heyerdah of *Kon-Tiki* fame – the raft used in his 1947 expedition across the Pacific Ocean from South America to the Polynesian islands. It was named after the Inca sun god, Viracocha, for whom 'Kon-Tiki' was said to be an old name. Her new husband died in 2002, by which time Juan (we fondly called him 'Juan of these days') had succumbed, some years earlier, to a heart attack.

Part Two

A VIEW FROM THE QUARTERDECK

AT this point, perhaps, I should remind my reader (and myself) that my story is told from the point-of-view of the underling that I was: a Baldrick, not a Blackadder. Thus my observations were made very much from the chaos of the quarterdeck, rather than the lofty overview of the captain's bridge. All around us, it seemed that travel companies were rising and falling in dramatic fashion, with a whole host of different characters taking centre stage.

In the interests of brevity, I have not sought to chronicle all the comings and goings, but rather to try and explain how the Thomson organisation came to buy a collection of travel companies for under £2 million in 1965/6 and and eventually, in 1998, float the group of those same companies for nearly £1.7 billion some 35-odd-years later, despite what I can only describe as a baffling level of incompetence. Ask what made the difference, and I point to the skill and perseverance of a small handful of individuals, who resisted the heavy hand of corporate interference and made the company Thomson the unassailable edifice we know today.

CHAPTER 14
BOND STREET TO BENIDORM

There are characters you meet, without whom your life would have taken an entirely different turn; for me, Trevor Davies was one of these people.

IT was the beginning of 1965. John, the former owner of La Siesta, had gone to live in Paris and Rafael had found a new job working in the Brasil coffee bar up the road, opposite the Queensway Ice Rink. Meanwhile, I had moved up a notch in the travel business, rising from my lowly status as a reservation clerk, working out of a converted car showroom in Victoria, to my new position as a 'travel planner' in the altogether more salubrious surroundings of Old Bond Street.

Today, travel companies would be hard pressed to pay Old Bond Street rents, especially up at the northern end, where Inghams had set up shop. Back in those days, though, the area was something of a mini-hub for travel companies, with Universal Skytours around the corner on Piccadilly, Thomas Cook & Sons just off Oxford Street and Horizon Holidays close by on Hanover Square.

Why Old Bond Street? Well, its northern end was, and still is, home to one of the world's greatest concentrations of upmarket jewellery shops. With skiing most definitely considered a pursuit of the middle and upper classes, this must have been uppermost in the mind of Walter Ingham in 1948 when, fresh out of the army having risen to the rank of major, he decided to locate his pre-war business on Bond Street.

Before long, Rafael, who had been living with me at 11 Warrington Crescent, returned to his home in Pontevedra, northern Spain, once more leaving me with the tedious task of finding a roommate. Indeed, it was this prospect that spurred me on to escape the London bedsit scene altogether and get a job overseas, as a resort representative. This was easier said than done: I sent off dozens of applications to the many different travel companies that were starting up all around. As for the minimum age requirement for such a position, 21, I got round this by the simple expedient of adding a year to my age – a deception that boomeranged back on me many years later, when Thomson Holidays started paying my pension a year early.

By and large, I received nothing but rejections: from the myriad applications I sent off, only three resulted in face-to-face interviews. Two of the firms, Horizon and Global Overland, gave me the thumbs-down, but Trevor Davies, the overseas director of Universal Skytours, saw something in me and let it be known that there might be a position available in either Yugoslavia, Italy or Spain. He could not give me a definite answer there and then, and made it clear that he would only know for certain in around six months' time, closer to the start of the summer season. Thus I ended up, towards the end of 1965, working for Inghams in Old Bond Street and rubbing shoulders with my betters in this 'crème de la crème' of shopping areas.

What attracted me to the resort representative job, as opposed to the arguably more prestigious role of coach tour manager/courier, was the range of perks that came with it: free and secure accommodation, three meals a day and a tax-free salary topped up by commission fees and tips. For the first time in my life, I would have the chance to accumulate some capital.

For the moment, though, I had to content myself with my position at Inghams. It was, as I have said, a prestigious set-up, befitting the prosperity of the area and our clientele. The reception area was full of Alpine travel posters, globes of the world, timetables, scores of reference books and, of course, comfortable wing chairs deployed around an enormous, circular coffee table piled high with glossy brochures.

At that time, the firm's core business was the running of its twice-weekly ski train services to the Austrian and Swiss Alps. However, the job didn't begin and end when people got on and off the train. Hotels, and the room allocations held by Inghams' guests within them, were unavoidably small and frequently in remote Alpine locations, and this called for intricate station-to-hotel transfers. Furthermore, once our skiers had arrived at their destination, we still needed to hire them their ski equipment and secure their access to ski lifts. Just as today, this was an extremely labour-intensive business from our point-of-view, especially when we were operating under the glare of a knowledgeable and critical clientele, who knew every bit as much about skiing as us, maybe more.

In addition to being intensive, the ski season was short, starting just before Christmas and ending by Easter. This left hotels bereft of guests during the long summer months, as Inghams had been singularly unsuccessful in developing a complementary 'Lakes and Mountains' programme for the long months when there was no snow. Instead, and quite inexplicably, the company launched an overnight-coach tour programme to the French Riviera, Italy and Spain – the absolute antithesis of what Inghams stood for. Bad news for the business, but good news for me: when I was given the job of working on these tours, it provided me with experience that would come in useful later on.

Meanwhile, in my personal life, my girlfriend Carmen had likewise gone up in the world, and was driving a spanking brand new white Mini. The combination was quite a show-stopper for the lads at the office, who would press their noses up against the window to gaze at this tanned goddess, her long, flowing black hair contrasted with a white mini skirt and white knee-length boots, when she came to pick me up from work. To much blush-inducing ribaldry from my male colleagues, I would be driven back in the white Mini to Warrington Crescent. When it came to inviting her in, though, I would glance anxiously up towards the third-floor bedsit, my ardour dampened not only by the knowledge that my fellow bedsit sharer would most likely be in residence, but also by the shameful prospect of having to reveal to Carmen the unimpressive nature of my actual living circumstances.

Not that I wasn't trying to improve my situation: I was doing as much overtime as I could, working all hours under the sun – or rain, as it often turned out to be – taking advantage of the fact that Inghams' new Swiss owners, Hotelplan (the Major had sold out to them in 1962 and retired to Elba), had not yet really got their feet under the table. Instead of whiling away my time and money in the coffee houses of Queensway, I accumulated cash instead. By the end of my six-month stint at Inghams, I had managed to save £70, the largest sum of money to have ever graced my pocket. Financially, the sun was starting to peep over the horizon; yet emotionally, things still felt bleak. It was bad enough living in a '60s bedsit, having to pay more than half one's earnings to unfeeling landlords in exchange for cramped and often bitterly cold accommodation, but the financial and physical discomfort was nothing compared to the emptiness of either living on your own or sharing with one other transient occupant.

Fortunately, my professional life was about to crank out of first gear. Step forward Trevor Davies, operations manager of Universal Skytours, a man whom I hardly knew but who had identified some faintly discernible spark in me, albeit if only through my completed job application form. There are characters you come in contact with, without whom your life would have taken an entirely different turn; for me, Trevor Davies was one of these people. Towards the end of my time at Inghams, Trevor confirmed that he needed a resort representative in Benidorm commencing April 1966, and that a flight would be arranged for me if I reported to the Skytours office. I, meanwhile, had other ideas about how I was going to get out there.

It so happened that I had been asked by Cosmos to work as assistant courier on the 'Grand Tour of Spain, Portugal and Morocco'. Not only would I fulfil a long-cherished dream by going on this tour, but also, towards the end of it, in Granada, I would separate from the group and make my own way, by train and bus, to Benidorm, in order to reach the resort, as requested, by 11 April 1966.

Or at least that was my cunning plan. The aforesaid 'Grand Tour' duly commenced at Lympne, a less-than-grand old RAF airfield in Kent. There the passengers were individually weighed before embarking on a three-hour flight, aboard a rickety ex-Berlin Airlift plane, to Perpignan, in the heart of the French Pyrenees. To say the members of the tour party were nervous about this was a bit of an understatement. Since 1949 there had been at least nine well-publicised air crashes either on or near Mt Canigou, a peak lying on the airport's approach route that was rumoured to give off a magnetic pull, interfering with aircraft navigational aids.

Fortunately we landed without mishap, and waiting for us outside the terminal building was a Leyland Tiger, then the preferred coach for all tour couriers. It was reputed to be the best in the business at ascending steep inclines with a full load of passengers plus luggage (there were no motorways in those days); nonetheless, it would be remiss not to mention its radiator boil-over issues.

Anyway, the 'Grand Tour of Spain, Portugal and Morocco' was considered the blue-ribbon tour in Cosmos, employing only the very best couriers who had served their time on the likes of the whistle-stop 'Seven Countries And Paris' and other, similarly back-breaking, European tours. In those days, witnessing first-hand Franco's Spain and Salazar's Portugal, not to mention the exotic souks and kasbahs of Morocco, still carried an element of Hemingway-esque adventure – as in *Death in the Afternoon* and *The Sun Also Rises* – and the unknown. In short, it was the tour all couriers wanted to escort.

The senior courier for the tour's first departure (and my boss) was James Adams, a man who had seemingly done it all before. He had been everywhere, knew everybody and took complete control of any situation, commanding the respect of guests and hoteliers alike, who instinctively understood that this was a person to whom they should defer. Yet this aura of authority did not emanate from any stridency of voice or manner: James made use not so much of words as of elegant hand movements. He had impeccable sartorial taste, too; clothes hung elegantly on his upright physique, giving him a more-than-passing resemblance to James Bond.

The ability to create an authoritative persona was essential, given that in those days there were always guests, usually located in the front of the coach, who thought they knew more than the courier and were just itching to get hold of the microphone, given the first sign of any courier weakness. Conscious of this, and as per John Baccanello's instructions, James organised his tours as if they were cameo theatrical pieces – to him, guests were mere bit players and potential sources of income, obliged to follow his every cue. Likewise, the coach driver received detailed, orchestrated instructions from James when it came to moving off or slowing down, all carried out in perfect synchronisation with his microphone commentary.

Frankly, I was in awe of the man. Although I had been on numerous courier courses, in addition to meeting other couriers and observing them at work, I had never seen such a skilled exponent of the guiding craft as James Adams. I, too, was cast in the role he wanted me to play, as the runner of his errands – checking passports, helping the driver load the luggage on top of the coach and then lash it down, etc. This left the way clear for James to take centre stage, though of course he still had plenty of work to do behind the scenes. The three-week 'Grand Tour' had to be organised right down to the last minute: back in those pre-motorway days, enormous distances had to be travelled and numerous en-route stops arranged, which meant starting out at the crack of dawn and rarely reaching one's destination during daylight hours.

From Perpignan, the itinerary wound its way along the Mediterranean coastline to Barcelona, across the central plain to Madrid, Avila and Salamanca, and then on to the Portuguese border at Fuentes de Onoro before continuing, via Coimbra, to Lisbon. After Lisbon came Seville, La Linea de la Concepcion and Gibraltar, for the ferry to Tangier. In Morocco there was a mini tour, which included visits to Casablanca, Rabat, Fez and Meknes. The homeward journey took guests back across the water to Granada and then up the entire length of Spain to Perpignan, for the flight back to the UK.

It was, even by today's standards, an almost impossible feat of motoring. The tour certainly opened my eyes, and not just in terms of the geographical distance covered: every bit as amazing was the way in which James conducted himself, organising each and every detail in advance. To me, his example represented both a coming of age and a loss of innocence: for the first time in my life, I realised that it was possible to be in control of events rather than merely subject to them, as I had been before. I was certainly hoping that some of James's stardust personality would rub off on me.

However, James was not impressed by my taste in women. When the tour reached Madrid, I contacted Carmen (who had now returned home) and asked her to come meet me at the Hotel Ronda, on the outskirts of the city. My purpose,

A Story in Brief

MANUEL BENITEZ PEREZ: He was better known as El Cordobés, the famous Spanish matador who, in the 1960s and 70s, brought to the bullring his own unorthodox and theatrical style. He was born into poverty, reared in an orphanage, and began his adult life as a construction-worker and petty criminal, while dreaming of being a bullfighter. On 20 May 1964, while making his first appearance at Las Ventas, in Madrid, he received a near-fatal goring. Seven years later El Cordobés was the highest-paid matador in history. He retired in 1971, and returned to the bullring in 1979, but came in for criticism in 1983, when a bull that he was about to fight, killed a person who had illegally jumped into the ring. After he finally retired in 2000, he acted in several films, and today lives in seclusion near Córdoba. Of course, if naming rights had existed in his heyday, he would have made another fortune from the sale of posters.

I confess, was to demonstrate my prowess in being able to capture such a beauty. But having met her, James took me aside and counselled: "Whatever else we do in life, we should only mix with people from whom we might learn something, or else who might advance our progress in life." He viewed Carmen, despite her lustrous outer appearance, as a member of the great unwashed. Almost in an instant, so greatly was I in awe of James, she was dispatched from my life, never to be seen again.

Perhaps as a form of consolation, or maybe initiation, James introduced me to the notorious pleasures of the Bar Filadelfia in the dock area of Lisbon, home of fine coffee and beautiful mixed-raced Brazilian girls; later, too, he showed me the erotic belly-dancing clubs beside the railway line that fronted the beach in Tangier. The latter was a city that had recently, albeit only partially, shaken off its complicated 'Free Port' status when seemingly everything was still permissible, and its very name conjured up the exoticness of an Arabian Nights adventure. This was an environment in which writers, actors, spies and gays felt inspired and at home – another Bayswater, really, except with sunshine and a Berber twist.

We stayed at the Hotel Continental, located right in the heart of the Kasbah. Since this whole area was inaccessible to motor vehicles, James led us (and our porters) in a single, snake-like file through the tortuous, winding alleyways. For our first night in Morocco, he had arranged the programme in such a way that guests would be free to explore Tangier's abundant nightlife by themselves – James was not going to allow valuable Tangier hours to be taken up attending to guests, determined as he was to give himself up to the city's many and varied intoxications. He told me that our evening was to be reserved for a visit to the Casino Municipal de Tanger and that I should dig into my battered old bedsit-dweller's suitcase and select appropriate attire for the occasion.

At the appointed rendezvous time, I descended the hotel's wooden staircase to the marble-floored reception where James, always punctual, was waiting. Looking at what he was wearing, I couldn't help feeling that some of my Inghams savings might better have been invested on some new kit, rather than being kept in reserve in case things in Benidorm did not work out.

Somehow, James had spirited from his luggage a gold lamé evening jacket, silk waistcoat and neckerchief, plus a pair of slick, jet-black lined trousers, which were complemented by elegant, black patent-leather shoes. To complete the picture, James was puffing on a cigarette fixed to an ivory cigarette holder, while a flunky brushed imagined Kasbah dust from his shoulders. Taking in my outfit, he mumbled something along the lines of, "Is that the best you could do?"

Not long after, this gentleman and his vagabond sidekick ascended the 'members-only', first-floor section of the Casino Municipal de Tanger, where the scene that met them could have come straight out of Ian Fleming's Casino Royale: deep plush carpeting; lots of green and burgundy surfaces; Tiffany-style lace lighting; mahogany hardwood finishes; croupiers and specially imported, attractive Egyptian ladies. Fortunately, there were plenty of pillars in the salon behind which I could discreetly hover without causing embarrassment either to myself or, more importantly, to James. Suitably concealed, I could watch my boss working the tables with the aplomb of a professional. Once he had collected his winnings from the cashier's window, protected by ornate brass grilles, it was off to the belly-dancing clubs, before returning to the charms of the Hotel Continental.

Even in March, the humidity in Tangier was practically unbearable, particularly in the airless Kasbah. To make matters worse, when I got back to my room at 2.00am and turned on the light, I saw that my bed was covered in langoustine-size cockroaches. The creatures fled for cover when the light came on, only to scuttle back the minute I switched it off. There was nothing for it, then, but to go to bed with the light still on, accompanied by the uneasy sensation of being crawled over by armies of imagined insects.

I had a fitful night's sleep to say the least – short-lived, too, for at sunrise next morning we embarked on our whistle-stop tour of Casablanca, Rabat, Meknes and Fez, before taking the ferry from Tangier back to Gibraltar. This ferry trip, as it turned out, provided James's principal source of income.

At that time the duty on alcohol and tobacco was extremely high in both Spain and Morocco, whereas on the Gibraltar ferry such items could be bought at a fraction of the normal price. So, what James would do, much like the Cosmos coach drivers between France and Belgium, was purchase the full allowance on behalf of the whole, up to 48-strong, tour party, both on the journey to Tangier and on the journey back. He would then sell his booty to barkeepers and hoteliers in each destination, thereby augmenting the commissions paid by those shops he included in the itinerary and the end-of-tour tips paid by our exhausted guests.

As with everything else concerned with the courier's job, James had conducted an in-depth investigation into the science of tipping. Choosing the right 'tipping moment', he explained, was critical. If you left it too late, guests would get together to make a hurried collection, giving them carte blanche to bung any leftover loose change (usually pesetas and dirhams) into the hat. If there was one sound the courier and driver didn't want to hear, it was the jingling of low-value coins, as opposed to the reassuring rustling of notes.

It was even worse, though, if you staged the tipping moment too early, as this gave the guests time to consult with one another and agree on a less-than-expected or hoped-for amount per person. Thus the tipping moment needed to be orchestrated in such a way as to minimise guests' thinking time while also, via an uplifting microphone commentary, giving them the opportunity to reflect on the happenings of the tour. Mixed in was a reminder that, while tipping was in no way compulsory, all monies would be gratefully received and split equally with the drivers. As for a suitable amount, this perhaps could be calculated as a per diem sum, multiplied according to the duration of the tour.

Providing the timing was right, James said, the technique never failed. As a result, he wasn't just wealthy when it came to worldly experience, but in terms of hard cash too. Not that I would be witnessing his expertise for much longer: when the 'Grand Tour' got to the Moorish city of Granada, I took my leave of the group and headed to Benidorm, so that I would make my 11 April appointment as instructed. I was never to see or hear of James again (nor, for that matter, Carmen), but his strictures and guidance were to remain with me throughout my travel career.

Unfortunately, my solo trip didn't start that auspiciously. Having taken a 14-hour train journey to Murcia, I arrived too late to make the bus connection to Benidorm and had to rent an overnight room from one of the station hawkers. Just like Phileas Fogg, I was now one day behind schedule. There was nothing for it, then, but to make a dent in my £70 savings and hire a car to drive all the way to Benidorm.

My instructions were to report to the Hotel Alameda, in the old town. There, my pre-arranged accommodation was a cubbyhole directly above the hotel's wood-burning ovens. The tiled floor of my room was so hot, you couldn't walk across it in bare feet: you had to launch yourself out of bed and into your shoes.

Nevertheless, I had arrived. The journey that had begun in the salubrious surroundings of Old Bond Street and the chilly bedsits of Bayswater had brought me here to my quaint new home on the Spanish coast. Wherever you went in town, the advertising posters carried the slogan 'En Invierno el Sol y En Verano la Brisa', which translates as 'In winter the sun and in summer the breeze.' For me, summer was about to begin, in more ways than one.

CHAPTER 15
MY TIME IN THE SUN

At first, it all seemed too good to be true. When my first pay cheque arrived, I was struck by the sudden, fearful sensation that I was going to get found out. Truth is, I would have willingly done the job for nothing.

NOW that I was safely installed in Benidorm, my main sources of guidance were Miguel Bayona, the owner of the Alameda, with José, the head waiter, and, most importantly, the resident contingent of fellow resort representatives who could be found at their local watering hole of choice, the Bar Hampshire.

The good news, from my point of view, was that Universal Skytours had become an immensely successful travel company. The publication of the new Skytours summer brochure could be likened to the arrival of Nouveau Beaujolais: long lines of customers would form queues outside travel agents, in order to bag their hotel and holiday date of choice. On the day it came out, the front page of the brochure featured a right-hand corner slash announcing, '60,000 Holidays Already Sold!' – and it was true!

In the 1960s, Benidorm was completely unlike the caricature unkindly bestowed on it now. It had very few hotels and was considered something of an upmarket resort, the one that sold out first each year. As mentioned, the Hotel Alameda was located in the old town, where the sweeping Levante and Poniente beaches are intercepted by a charming maze of narrow, whitewashed alleyways decorated with Moorish styled ironwork and complemented by flower-bedecked troughs.

The hotel itself was almost entirely made from carved hardwoods, designed in the traditional Spanish Colonial style and built by Miguel's father many decades earlier. It was entirely devoid of en-suite facilities, air-conditioning or a bar, but what it lacked in creature comforts was more than matched by its immense charm,

A Story in Brief

A SENSE OF OCCASION: Back in the 1950s and 60s, no one would have boarded a flight to the sun in anything other than their Sunday best – and certainly not in shorts, as many do nowadays. Apart from anything else, it would have been considered an insult to the crew. Every flight, no matter how short, included an in-flight meal or snack. As a cost-saving measure, Court Line introduced a system whereby one meal was stowed in the back of the seat in front out for outbound passengers, and another for returning passengers. They abandoned this system, however, when outbound passengers began consuming both meals. In the days of Independent Air Transport, Captain Marian Kozuba-Kozubski would buy the ingredients from local shops, and bring them home for his wife and three daughters to pack in picnic boxes (in those days, there were no fold-down tables). He would then ferry the picnic boxes to the aircraft, in his car.

and there was hardly ever an empty room. The sheer prestige and popularity of this establishment meant that Miguel was one of the most important personages in all of Benidorm (he later became Mayor); his only rivals being the owners of the Hotel Avenida, whom for some unknown reason we were advised to steer clear of.

The nearest airport to Benidorm was located in Valencia, a three to four-hour coach journey away. Flights were then operated by Britannia Airways, Skytours' sister company, from Luton and Manchester. Each of the Bristol Britannias that touched down at Valencia would be carrying 117 passengers, half of them destined for Benidorm and half for the San Juan, the hotel financed by the company's founder, 'Captain' Ted Langton, at Playa San Juan, four long, bumpy hours away by coach.

Flight times in those days were 'indicative', which meant a three-hour delay was quite usual and up to six hours' delay was not an infrequent occurrence. From a resort representative's point of view, this meant that a typical day comprised a long journey to Valencia with outgoing guests, a habitual three-hour (or longer) wait at the airport, and then another long journey back to Benidorm with newly arrived guests; the total length of the working day was seldom less than 12 hours. Worse still, a company edict stipulated that at least one of the representatives (usually me) had to remain at the airport for two hours after the aircraft had departed, just in case it should unexpectedly return.

This was the most tedious and monotonous task imaginable, except for on one occasion when I was sitting in the airport's upper-level bar and something unusual caught my eye. Instead of moving along the runway, in preparation for take-off, the fully loaded Bristol Britannia aircraft was taxiing in front of the terminal building with smoke and flames billowing out of a port-side engine. Passengers were scrambling frantically out of the emergency exits and clambering all over the wings.

Suddenly I was having to deal with the fallout from a full-scale emergency, all on my own. Thankfully, no one was injured in the fire, and everyone was safely brought back to the terminal building with their luggage. The fire was put out and the aircraft discreetly towed to another part of the airfield. There was a long wait until the replacement aircraft arrived; unsurprisingly, when it finally did, some passengers required a great deal of persuasion to board.

The locals certainly couldn't accuse us British tour representatives of not putting money into the local economy, much of it at the Bar Hampshire, which was hidden away in the heart of the old town, far from tourists' prying eyes. This little piece of the UK was owned and run by John and Rosa Hampshire, a couple who had come to Benidorm a few years earlier. On its walls were black-and-white signed photos of celebrities, such as the actor Albert Finney and the actress Susan Hampshire (John's sister), and the food was traditional English away-from-home fare: roast beef, roast lamb and non-stop full English breakfast.

We tour representatives did not go to Bar Hampshire for the food, as we got our meals free of charge in the hotels. What drew us there, rather, was the chance to idle over a gin and tonic and engage in a little shop talk. Most of the crowd were old hands who had come to Benidorm to escape the rat race and soak up a bit of sun at the same time as a lot of alcohol; I remember that quite a few of them had previously worked in the Indian Civil Service.

I was there not to booze – I still hated the taste of alcohol – but to schmooze; to network with my fellow tour representatives and pick up the tricks of the trade. A fruitless mission, as it turned out: the inhabitants of the Hampshire Bar were not at all commercially minded, and it became clear to me early on that I was going to have to tread carefully when it came to implementing the kind of sales techniques I had learnt from John Bacannello and James Adams.

On the plus side, I had, for the first time, a place to live where I did not have to pay weekly rent. Three meals a day were also provided free of charge, and rather than having to traipse to the local launderette, a weekly wash service was provided by the Alameda's helpful chambermaids. As for the kind of shivering that I was used to in my Bayswater bedsit, that too was a thing of the past – indeed, if anything, living above hotels' kitchens meant there was now perhaps too much heat.

At first, it all seemed too good to be true. When my first monthly Banco de Bilbao pay cheque arrived, I was struck by the sudden, fearful sensation that I was going to get found out. Truth is, I would have willingly done the job for nothing and got by on tips and commissions: it felt like the company was doing far more for me than I was for them.

I soon got to know my way around Benidorm, thanks to José, the Alameda's head waiter, who showed me the resort's numerous nightclub venues and encouraged me on various excursions. One particular place that caught my eye was a 'sala de fiestas', a kind of live music-act venue seemingly reserved for local young couples, on the outskirts of town. It was a place where an element of formality persisted, but where people went to get that little bit closer, romantically speaking, free from the watchful eyes of chaperones and parents. Their unlit corners were the favoured spots.

Stage shows consisted of traditional regional dances such as the Jota Arago-nesa, Zambra, Fandango, Sevillana and Flamenco – all authentic dances, for this locale was very much off the beaten tourist track. The climax to the evening was always the same: a sort of re-enactment of the flower-seller scene from Charlie

Chaplin's film *City Lights*. The title song, 'La Violatera' (the Violet Seller), would be sung by a young and beautiful member of the troupe dressed in the typical polka-dot, multi-layered frock and who would coquettishly distribute blooms from her basket to selected members of the audience.

One evening, I became hugely over-excited when the lady gave me a flower, convincing myself that she was attracted to me (as I most definitely was to her). From that point on, I did not miss a single show until the troupe had finished its engagement in Benidorm. Using my initiative, I extracted, from the venue owner, a contact address for the girl. José agreed to help me renew my acquaintance with her.

The address we had been given turned out to be a building on the palm tree-lined Main Boulevard in Alicante, only when we got there, it looked more like an office than a normal residence. We climbed the stairs to the first-floor reception and knocked on an enormous door. A matronly lady appeared and beckoned to us to sit in front of her desk. We said we had come to speak to Isabel, at which the matron nodded and asked, in a firm voice, how old I was. At this point, José roughly grabbed me by the arm and removed me from the premises, explaining that he had spied cubicles along the corridor – the place, he informed me, was a brothel!

It was, I have to confess, a disappointment, but the feeling was not so much of unrequited love as of feeling somehow duped. I decided there and then that, henceforth, I would skip romance and concentrate on accumulating some capital. From that point on, members of the opposite sex were relegated to the workaday status of secretaries, useful for completing my tiresome reports to Trevor Davies at head office, but for nothing more.

Of course, there were compensations. One day, I discovered that tickets had become available for a bullfight in Alicante featuring the legendary El Cordobés, last seen on a poster back at La Siesta in Bayswater. This was an event not to be missed, as well as a chance to package up a coach trip down the coast to Alicante, taking in an obligatory call at the leather shop on the way, the bullfight at the impressive Plaza de Toros and a quick snack, followed by the return trip to Benidorm, all with accompanying commentary.

In due course, the big day came around. By three in the afternoon, the sun was high in the sky, crowds were assembling around the high brick walls of the bullring and the air was full of electricity and excitement. After all, this was the day the famed El Cordobés, a sort of George Best of the bullring, was to appear.

It was swelteringly hot and, in retrospect, I was glad I had gone for the more expensive 'sombra' (shade) tickets. I sipped my ice-cold Coca-Cola and waited for the afternoon's action to begin. No sooner had the fanfare of trumpets heralded the entrance of the warm-up act – a novillero (trainee matador) and accompanying picadors – than a cold wind kicked up from nowhere, and I began to wonder if the sombra seats and ice-cold Coke were such good ideas after all. Suddenly, too, I began to experience excruciating stomach pains. Although I wanted to leave the bullring, I stayed in my place, aware of the convention that dictates that patrons should only move from their seats in between fights.

The novillero prancing around the ring was taking an age to kill his bull, to hoots and whistles of derision from the crowd. At long and agonising last, the messy end to the contest came and, with this, I rushed to the exit and collapsed against the outer walls of the bullring. As the food and drink hawkers gathered around me, no doubt suspecting a heart attack, I was picked up off the ground and bundled into a nearby car, upon which there followed an Inspector Clouseau-like interlude as the driver hee-hawed incessantly on the car's horn on the way to hospital.

In a moment of lucidity before lapsing into unconsciousness, I told one of my kind rescuers that I had left my charges behind in the bullring and, having deposited me at the hospital, they promptly raced back to the Plaza de Toros to find my tour party and let them know what had happened. I underwent a variety of tests and was told that I was suffering from acute colic. My thoughts began to turn to how I was going to get back to the bullring to collect my guests and get them back to Benidorm, given that the bullfight was over long since.

I needn't have worried. Sitting right outside the main entrance to the hospital was the coach, complete with all the passengers. As I was conveyed back to Benidorm, lying flat on the floor of the bus, I couldn't help fretting over how this would diminish my status with guests, but was pleasantly surprised to discover that customer sympathy was again working in my favour, especially later, when it came to tipping time.

This whole episode put me off bullfighting for life. (The stomach pains did not relent completely until I returned to London a year later and found their cause to be not colic, but an allergy to peanuts, which I had been consuming in vast quantities.) Nonetheless I kept thinking about how to expand the programme we offered our guests, getting them out and about, so to speak. This was certainly something the hotels were keen on, too, since it gave staff a chance to have a good clean – and a quiet siesta. The solution? Well, it was obvious to anyone who had been schooled at John Baccanello's guide courses or come under the influence of James Adams: the resort representative simply needed to organise a structured programme of events throughout the holiday, in exactly the same way as if it were a coach tour.

This is what I set about doing. In addition to giving guests plenty of free time in the resort, I balanced this out with escorted tours into the hinterland, with donkey treks and trips to fishing villages. The emphasis was on seeing the 'real' Spain during the day and, in the evening, perhaps going out to a soirée at a local nightclub (where the real money was to be made).

Straight away my plan paid dividends. To begin with, I earned commission on the sale of the tour tickets and also got a fee for guiding the tour. But what really brought the pesetas rolling in was the fact that I now had all the guests congregated on one coach. This made it so much simpler to direct them to the 'preferred' leather and embroidery shops (i.e., those that paid me commission) and to sell them tickets to the 'salas de fiestas'.

When selling these tickets, I paid attention to the golden rule that James Adams had taught me: start from the back of the coach and work forwards. If you started at the front, the first 'no' you got would encourage people further back to follow suit. When you started at the back, though, and worked your way to the front while jangling a few coins, all you had to say was, "I suppose you will be coming too?" and, lo and behold, people did.

The most expensive outing by far was the donkey ride. It began with a drive into the mountains to the village of Callosa de Ensaria, where up to 100 gaily-decorated burros (donkeys), plus their equally folklorifically attired owners, would be gathered outside the entrance to the cemetery. In my sales pitch, I described the trek as a thrilling journey along tortuous mountain paths culminating at a cascading waterfall, where it was possible to pause for a while and bathe in a hollow, dreamlike pool.

I have to confess that, in reality, there was seldom enough water in the 'pool' to get completely wet. There was also an adjoining shack, from which came the endless, amplified loud strains of 'Juanita Banana', an irritating and popular ditty that was popular all over the Spanish-speaking world at the time. The event would usually come to a close with the donkey owners putting on an impromptu musical show, as some of them would have brought their guitars with them. Today, the tour would not survive even a cursory inspection from gimlet-eyed weights-and-measures men, but my recollections are that all who attended seemed to have a jolly good time.

Crucial to the tour's success were the organisational prowess of Francisco, who owned the local estanco (tobacconist and newsagent). He was the gangmaster on whose shoulders rested the job of dealing with the donkey owners, many of whom looked upon this caper as a sort of pension – this was still Franco's Spain, after all, and state benefits were in short supply. Sadly, in years to come newspaper articles began appearing about cruelty to donkeys, as a result of which the animals were left to run wild and their owners left without a source of income.

By contrast, the tour to the fishing village of Calpe was a lot simpler, comprising an hour's drive north (with appropriate commentary), up to where the fishing boats were moored on the quayside and the fishermen, by prior arrangement, were tending their nets, with a few boxes of wriggling fish for the guests to look into. Overlooking this scene of timeless marine tranquillity was the Bar Calpe, a building with a somewhat down-at-heel appearance but all the potential of a tourist gold mine. As far as I could glean, it was being run by the family's grown-up daughter, who, despite being a little on the plump side and having a fiery look in her eyes that the Spanish described as loca (crazy), was undeniably a stunner. Such as stunner, in fact, that I entertained the fantasy of running the Bar Calpe with her, once the season was over. Our romantic partnership was not to be, but the platonic relationship we struck up did have unexpected, and not entirely welcome, consequences later on.

As for the night-time venues, there were three main 'salas de fiestas' that had sprung up during the days when Benidorm was a favourite summer retreat for residents of Madrid. The first of these to re-open and cater for a non-Spanish audience was the Granada, having fine-tuned its offerings to make it less 'flamenco' in content and therefore more accessible to tourists. Run by a rather elegant and kind German couple, Arno and Lisa, the Granada was quite swish, décor-wise, by the standards of the day.

It was clear from the outset that it was Lisa who wore the lederhosen. She cut a dramatic figure, with her flowing blond hair and penchant for red, tight-fitting dresses. You never caught her without her make-up, and she moved around the club like a sort of Lilli Marlene; the men might gawk, but they knew instinctively that there was a barrier beyond which they could not go.

The most popular of the musical acts at the Granada was a trio that went by the name of Los Trio Paraguayos. While they had no connection with the original act of that name, they were very talented performers: at a given point in the act, one of them would somehow toss the guitar behind his back and continue playing, while at other times he would replace a broken string without missing a chord. Not only was the venue popular, but it paid well too: Lisa and Arno gave me a hefty 30-per-cent commission on every ticket I sold.

In addition to the Granada, soon my services were in demand from the two other Salas in town: Bobby's Bar and the Alhambra. Not everything went smoothly, though. I discovered that the alcohol at Bobby's Bar did not originate from the usual branded bottles and actually made the guests unwell. And as for re-opening night at the Alhambra, it was a disaster. They had just redecorated, and the green paint on the seats hadn't dried properly. As a result, my guests ended up looking like blotchy emerald pandas and, once the show was over, putting in big dry cleaning bills.

Thereafter I re-concentrated my efforts on the Granada, a fact not missed by the other resort representatives as they gazed, in some amazement and not a little envy, at the pied-piper line of customers following me along the winding path to the club. It wasn't long, in fact, before outright jealousy started to make its presence felt among my colleagues: chit-chat around the bars hinted that the local taxman might be showing some interest in my extra-curricular activities.

(Sadly, too, Lisa eventually succumbed to the admiring glances of the lead singer of Los Trio Paraguayos, whereupon Granada was suddenly no more.)

But in the meantime, my most pressing requirement was to make use of my hard-gotten gains. First I bought a complete new wardrobe at the tailor's shop next to the Hotel Alameda, and then I set about completing the picture of new-found affluence by buying a car. The only drawback was that I didn't have a driving licence. I resolved to take some driving lessons, which consisted of driving up and down some isolated lanes between the old town and Poniente Beach, followed by a quick bit of parking practice.

There were two parts to the driving test. First was the theory section, which took the form of multiple-choice questions in response to familiar, comic strip-type situations. Next came the practical section, which was held in a field outside Alicante. Cones were set out in different configurations, and you could arrive early in order to practice negotiating them. Unfortunately, on the day of my test it was raining heavily, and the whole area quickly turned into a quagmire. A marquee had been erected in the field for the theory test; placed on tables inside it were samples of the comic-strip illustrations, along with a pencil for placing a tick beside your chosen answer. As the skies continued to open, people crowded round the tables and the whole event descended into a bit of a musical-chairs farce, not helped by the fact that, after conferring on the theory section, I discovered that I had got every single answer wrong.

At this point, in walked the main tester. "Todos approbados!" (All approved!), he shouted, thus announcing the welcome news that we had all sailed through the exam with flying colours – even me, who had not only got every question wrong, but hadn't even been asked to demonstrate my driving ability. So, after a small contribution towards the main tester's birthday present, I got my hands on a real-life driving licence.

Next came the car: a Morris Minor, which I bought from a fellow tour repre-sentative and promptly re-sprayed turquoise. The car drank more oil than petrol, but boy, it looked good. The only cloud on the horizon was the worry about what I was going to do when the season ended. The August thunderstorms were already heralding the onset of autumn and, faced with the prospect of returning to a freezing Bayswater bedsit, I decided that my only solution was to stay put in Benidorm and hope to get the same job back the following season.

The fantasy of running the Bar Calpe had evaporated, I just couldn't see myself serving Fanta and Coca-Cola for the rest of my life, but an alternative and rather more practical plan suggested itself. It came via Francisco, the donkey gangmaster, who told me that all the young people in his village were mad keen to get into the tourist scene in Benidorm, but were required to learn English first. Why, then, did I not live in the village during the winter and provide English lessons, thereby covering all my expenses? It sounded like a good idea, so, once the last transfer coach of the season had made its run to Valencia Airport, I promptly piloted my Morris Minor up into the mountains.

Francisco had already printed posters and leaflets announcing that 'El Inglés' would be offering English classes three times a week, at his flat overlooking the public washing troughs on the edge of the village. Everything seemed pretty much set up, until it became clear that, in addition to being completely ill-equipped to teach English, I could make neither head nor tail of the grammar books that Francisco had obliged his pupils to buy. On top of which, my flat was freezing cold.

The temperature suddenly rose, metaphorically at least, when I received a visit from Margarita from the Bar Calpe. She turned up in the middle of one of my English lessons and went what I can only describe as berserk – the word loca just didn't do her performance justice. She told me of her great displeasure in learning that I had chosen to spend my winter in the mountains instead of her family's bar – a suggestion admittedly I made much earlier in a rash moment of passion, that had now come back to haunt me. I think it was when she started muttering dire threats about setting her brothers onto me that I decided I should probably get out of town altogether.

I switched hurriedly to Plan B: drive north to Barcelona and catch a flight to Stuttgart, to stay with some German guests I had met during the summer at the Hotel Alameda. I would leave my Morris Minor at the short-term car park in front of the terminal building, for retrieval at some point in the future.

And so my first Benidorm summer was over. Already, though, things were starting to change in this once-sleepy part of the world: plans were being made to knock down the Alameda Hotel and replace its elegant colonial lines with a purpose-built concrete monstrosity, replete with air-conditioning and en-suite facilities, but with no character.

As for me, well, I didn't know it, but my future was now written on my forehead, in letters that were as invisible as they were indelible. I was destined for a life in the business of travel.

CHAPTER 16
SUMMER HOLIDAY

In April 1967, a group of 30 aspiring guides, of mixed nationalities and genders, and I set off from Victoria Coach Station on what proved to be an eventful journey.

I readied myself to leave Benidorm. As soon as the doors of the local Banco de Vizcaya branch opened, I went in and withdrew all my hard-earned pesetas. The hotels had all closed for the season and the shops had their shutters up; the town looked forlorn in the driving rain.

I called in, for the last time, at the Hotel Alameda, which was now a pile of rubble, and found the hotel's night-watchman, who, in a previous life, had thwarted every attempt of mine to smuggle young ladies up to my cubby-hole above the kitchens. He had a letter for me from head office: my guardian angel, Trevor Davies, had read one of my weekly reports regarding the Eastern European travel operation run by the washing machine entrepreneur John Bloom and wondered if, on my eventual return to London, I might call in for a chat.

I had always been fascinated by John Bloom's business methods. He had started out working as a door-to-door salesman for a Dutch washing machine company and then gone into business in his own right, selling twin-tub Electromatic machines for about half the price of an equivalent model in the shops.

John's success was due in no small part to the way he sold his machines through full-page newspaper advertisements: a device now known as 'off the page' marketing, whereby the whole deal is explained and there is no further need for promotional support. In those days there were no call centres or credit cards, so the whole enterprise depended on people completing coupons (cut from the advertisement) and sending them, with a cheque, to Bloom's offices, situated at Gallows Corner in Essex. The business only unravelled due to a postal strike, which lasted for nine weeks and thus dried up John's cash flow.

In addition to washing machines, Bloom had also dipped a toe into the holiday market, and it was this that Trevor wanted to talk to me about. For the moment, though, he had more pressing matters on his mind: a terrible air crash in Yugoslavia. It had occurred just after midnight on 2 September 1966. Britannia Airways flight 105 was on its final approach to Ljubljana airport, but the aircraft's altimeters had been incorrectly set, which meant that the Bristol Britannia was flying 1,000 feet lower than it should have been. At 0.54am the aircraft crashed into trees, killing 98 of the 117 people on board. Trevor now had the unenviable task of both caring for the survivors and comforting the bereaved, all against a background of intense publicity highlighting the seemingly lamentable safety record of charter airlines at the time.

As for myself, it was as much as I and my failing Morris Minor could do to get to Barcelona Airport, from where I was to take the flight to Stuttgart to stay with my friends. I had met Inge and her brother at the Hotel Alameda; they had driven down to Benidorm in their battered Volkswagen Beetle for a break in the sun and had stood out from the crowd, as they were the only non-Skytours passengers in the entire hotel. They were probably a bit surprised that I had taken up their invitation to come and see them in Germany: earlier that summer, on a grainy TV in Benidorm, I had watched England beat Germany in the 1966 World Cup Final and, on seeing Bobby Moore lift the cup to an exalted crowd, wished I was in London to soak up the sense of pride and optimism.

Now, though, looking at the UK from a very comfortable village house in Germany, I wondered if I would ever go back to Britain, so bleak did the economic outlook seem. Suddenly enthused by all things German, I engaged a private tutor, with the aim of learning the language, and although my German vocabulary never extended beyond a few hundred words, it was to be very useful, later in life, in my role as a self-appointed German expert (I always sought to make a little go a long way).

Life in Germany was extremely comfortable – apart from the time spent discussing socialist politics with disaffected and over-indulged German youth – but it was also, I have to say, extremely boring, which is why I decided to return to London and take up Trevor Davies' offer of a chat and, possibly, a job.

I arrived at Heathrow in early December 1966 and went straight to the head office of Universal Skytours, which had extremely grand premises on South Audley Street, just behind Park Lane, in the building that was later to be occupied by Asil Nadir and his Polly Peck organisation. Strangely enough, I had never actually met Trevor Davies in person – my actual face to face interview for the rep's job at Skytours had been undertaken by his assistant. And against a grey London backdrop, he cut a dandified figure with his neckerchief, sharp suit and

A Story in Brief

FLIGHT TO THE SUN: There is no doubt that General Franco did much to promote the influx of British tourists to Spain. What is less well known, is the part played by Captain Cecil Bebb. Who was he? The British pilot who, in July 1936, flew from Croydon Airport to pick up General Franco from exile in the Canaries and fly him secretly to Tetuan, in the part of Morocco owned by Spain. From here, Franco planned and implemented his attack on the Republican regime in Spain, which resulted in the Spanish Civil War. At the end of World War Two, the aircraft flown by Bebb was presented to Franco, and the pilot was awarded an array of medals. Interviewed in 1983, Bebb said he had been asked to "go to the Canary islands to get a Rif leader to start an insurrection in Spanish Morocco. I thought, what a delightful idea, what a great adventure." IMAGE COURTESY: DOUG GOODMAN.

pink shirt with white collar. It was immediately apparent that he was still overwhelmed with the aftermath of the air crash, yet he found time to have a chat and to explain that he had a project in mind for me. What's more, he also arranged lodgings for me, on the company's account, at a bed-and-breakfast in Sussex Gardens, near Paddington Station. He asked his colleague, Norman Lewis, to take me across the road to an Italian restaurant and buy me lunch.

As we ate, I discovered that Norman Lewis was the son of the famous travel writer, also named Norman Lewis, whom Graham Greene had declared the greatest travel writer of all time. I can testify that Norman Junior was one of the best negotiators and most charming people that I ever met, and he was to have a big influence on my life over the next 12 years.

So, I was back in London once more, but in altogether better circumstances than when I had left. The journey that had begun at La Siesta in 1965 had taken me through Spain, Portugal and Morocco, to Benidorm and Stuttgart and then back to London. During those 18 months, I had metamorphosed from bedsitter to travel clerk, assistant courier and, finally, resort representative; now, at the age of just 22, I seemed to have landed a plum job with the travel elite. I couldn't help wondering if I was worthy to be among such august company, or whether I would be unmasked as the imposter I really was.

These were exciting, if volatile, times. In rapid succession, the travel industry had to cope with various pound-sterling crises, the imposition of the £50 foreign currency allowance and the Regime of the Colonels in Greece. Closer to home, too, there were substantial corporate troubles.

In order to gain a better understanding of the latter situation, we need to go back to 1965 and early 1966, when Gordon Brunton – on behalf of the media mogul Roy Thomson, 1st Baron Thomson of Fleet – bought an assortment of travel companies, including Gaytours, Luxitours, Riviera and Universal Skytours, the firm I had now joined. The hope was that each firm would prosper separately in its own right, while at the same time benefiting from being part of the Thomson Travel Group.

The truth was, however, that each of those individual companies had been created by risk-taking business buccaneers with strong opinions as to what would work and what would not – for them, decision-making needed to be immediate and without consultation. No one embodied this spirit more completely than 'Captain' Ted Langton, the founding father of Universal Skytours, who had created not only the travel company itself, but had also added its own, in-house airline (Euravia/Britannia Airways) and hotel group.

Ted was even a favoured Western capitalist of Marshal Tito of Yugoslavia. But whereas communist leaders might be able to get away with that degree of dictatorial independence, it is anathema to your average board of directors. And so, the swashbuckling Captain one day returned to his offices to find that all the locks had been changed and that he was now on the outside, ousted in a bloodless coup.

With the Captain gone, there were just 18 people working in the South Audley Street office, four of whom were to help make the company the most important travel firm there had ever been. These were Trevor Davies, Norman Lewis, Andreas Sawicki and the irrepressible Lionel Steinberg (of whom, more anon).

The Captain's departure presented some problems. Like all self-made men, he had been blessed with the ability to keep a number of balls in the air at the same time, his philosophy being that if one ball fell to the ground, then plenty of others would still be up there. So, when Skytours lost the Captain, it lost the only man who knew exactly how many balls there were, along with the secret of how each was kept aloft. The ship really was now without its Captain, and those who remained on board – in addition to those who had just joined, such as myself – had to quickly learn not just how to navigate, but how to take evasive action.

No sooner had I arrived at Universal Skytours than I encountered the results of Ted's individual business style. It turned out that, on a flying trip to inspect his interests in The States, his eye had been caught by the sleek, silver and robust Greyhound coaches criss-crossing the length and breadth of the US. He would never have travelled on one himself, of course, but he decided to buy six Greyhounds and promptly arranged to have them shipped, via an agent, to Belgium, at that time the gateway for the European coach-tour business. There was no consultation or democracy involved in his decision: he just brought the coaches over, and that was that. The first anyone else in the company knew about it was when George Fisher was instructed to dream up a collection of intensive cross-Europe itineraries that could work the coaches around the clock, under the title of 'Universal Coach Tours'.

So ambitious did George Fisher's itineraries turn out to be, that the distances proved impossible to achieve in the allotted times. Furthermore, no one had worked out how the coach drivers and guides could be safely rotated over such long journeys. Time was running out fast: not only had the tours been launched and publicised, they were so attractively priced that they had already sold out. By the time I arrived for my first day of work at South Audley Street, it was clear that this unwelcome musical-chairs parcel had been passed around everyone in the office and was sitting there, waiting for me.

It was then that I realised why Trevor Davies had called me back from Benidorm. The key Universal Coach Tours itineraries would be to the resorts of

Loutraki, in Greece, and Sunny Beach, in Bulgaria. So, I was to be an instant Bulgarian expert, on the strength of having mentioned the country in one of my reports to Trevor. There was nothing for it but to roll up my sleeves: I might never have been anywhere near Bulgaria, but that didn't stop me from learning about it.

What I discovered was that Bulgaria, then a hard-line communist nation, had some fine beaches and a desperate need for Western currency. This was something that had already been spotted by washing-machine man John Bloom, who, just a few years earlier, had negotiated an exclusive deal to sell two-week, all-inclusive Bulgaria holidays for as little as £59.

Naturally, Captain Langton had been eager to get in on the act, but in order to match Bloom's rock-bottom prices, the coaches would have to be worked mercilessly around the clock. This would mean operating non-stop for three-and-a-half days and nights in each direction, making a total of seven nights' travelling time and seven nights' stay at the chosen resorts.

There were, in those days, no safety regulations to be taken into consideration, which was just as well, since each coach carried two Belgian drivers who would change places while actually at the wheel. As for the number of stops en route, these were kept to an absolute minimum. But even so, the schedule was impossible to achieve, which was a bit of a disaster. Nevertheless, out of this dark cloud I was at least able to conjure a silver lining, with a little help from Cliff Richards.

One of the big movie hits of 1963 had been 'Summer Holiday', in which Cliff and friends play bus mechanics who persuade London Transport to lend them a double-decker bus. They convert this into a mobile hotel and drive across Europe to Athens. I loved the thought of travelling across Europe with a bus full of friends, and managed to convince my bosses that our prospective tour guides would benefit hugely from a similar journey, in terms of familiarising themselves both with the route and the new Greyhound buses.

So, in April 1967, a group of 30 aspiring guides, of mixed nationalities and genders, and I set off from Victoria Coach Station on what proved to be an eventful journey. It was possibly the longest and most enjoyable audition in history, since the aim for the participants was to convince me of their suitability for employment.

We spent most of a very pleasant April trundling happily across Europe, but soon after leaving Bulgaria's Black Sea coast, disturbing news came through from Greece, our next stop and final destination. On 21 April 1967, a group of Colonels (some of whom I met years later, in the company of Lord Thomson) had seized power in Athens following a swift coup d'état. Nobody knew what the implications of this revolution might be, but the decision was made to proceed nonetheless to the border, to see whether our coach would be allowed to cross. Thus, on 23 April, the occupants of a gleaming Greyhound bus were among the first foreigners to enter a country that was now in the hands of a military junta. We made our way from Salonika to Athens along empty roads that bisected eerily lifeless streets: the country seemed deserted. In a way, it was wonderful to have the country to ourselves. And as for work experience, the situation was hardly typical, but at least I got a chance to see how potential tour escorts might work under pressure.

My guide selections made, we began the long trek back to Ostend, for the Channel Airways Golden Viscount service to Southend. One of the party, whose documents were not in order, had to make several attempts at entry into the UK (and endure several return trips to Ostend), an episode reported in the newspapers as 'The Affair of the Yo-Yo Yugoslav'.

It had been a memorable trip for all of us, but when it came to paying punters, the coach tours never really got going. The fact is, absolutely nothing was simple about this venture. I spent months trying to find ways to make the insane itineraries work – finding drivers, identifying rest stops, making hotel reservations, etc. There were even problems with the coach windows, which were sealed shut in order to stop hot air coming in. That would have been fine, except the air-conditioning hardly ever worked. But what really did it for this ill-judged enterprise were the changing costs of travel: almost overnight, coach tour operators found themselves unable to compete with the advent of the passenger jet.

Originally, the coach tours were supposed to begin at Victoria Coach Station and connect with the Greyhounds at a ferry port on the other side of the Channel. In the end, however, I had to ditch this plan (given that the distances were just too great to be covered exclusively by coach, despite the fact there were no en-route overnight hotel stops) and instead fly passengers from Southend to Maastricht, where they would meet up with the coaches. After just one, short summer season these tours were abandoned, as were the gleaming Greyhound coaches, which were quietly sold off and forgotten.

CHAPTER 17
A VIEW FROM
THE QUARTERDECK

I once found Lord Thomson in the lounge area of the Hotel Atlantis, in Tenerife. Placed in front of him was a pile of newspapers sent by special courier from all over the globe; at first I thought he was reading them.

IT was now five months since I had left the Morris Minor at Barcelona Airport, and rescuing it could be put off no longer. Great upheavals were taking place at work and home, and besides, I could do with the money I would make from selling the car. So, in late April 1967, I found myself on a BEA Trident flying to Barcelona, wondering (a) whether my car would still be there and (b) how long it might take to get it fixed. I had booked two nights at a hotel, just in case.

The good news was that there was no charge for parking. The bad news was that I couldn't find the car where I'd left it. Not panicking quite yet, I started a section-by-section search of the whole of the airport perimeter and suddenly, there it was, tucked behind one of the outbuildings. What's more, it looked sparkling clean and cared-for. Not only did the engine start with the first turn of the key, but also the tank was full of petrol and the windscreen wipers in perfect working order. Clearly my little Morris Minor had been adopted in my absence, and so as to avoid any possible upset to the surrogate parent, I decided that, instead of overnighting in Barcelona, it might be prudent if I drove straight out of town and headed for Calais.

The car behaved itself impeccably right up until the time I sold it, and even afterwards it continued to make a positive contribution to my life: the money I got for it formed a good chunk of my deposit on the tiny, end-of-terrace house I bought in Bromley. At last, Philip Morrell was on the property ladder.

Speaking of being upwardly mobile, the travel business was on the move too

A Story in Brief

THE MAN WITH IMPECCABLE MANNERS: It would be hard to find a more polite pilot than Group Captain John 'Cat's Eyes' Cunningham CBE. During World War Two, he was an RAF night fighter ace, credited with 20 kills, of which 19 were claimed at night. And when his HS125 executive jet touched down on runway 26 at Luton Airport, in 1972, with no landing gear down, he was the first to apologise to the tower. "I am awfully sorry," he said. "I seem to have made a mess of your runway." The plane had been chartered by Thomson Holidays to bring the Spanish Minister of Tourism, accompanied by Norman Lewis, for discussions in London on Spanish hotel developments. The following Monday, 'Cats Eyes' called his pilots into his office and explained that the landing gear horn had been annoying him, so he had pulled the circuit breaker. On no account, he urged, were his fellow pilots to repeat this ill-advised action. **IMAGE COURTESY: DOUG GOODMAN.**

– in some cases, it was out of control. As the summer wore on, my coach-tour programme became more and more problematic. Because of the unplanned, but now necessary, air-flight component, the company was losing a tidy sum on every ticket sold, and it became increasingly clear to me that once the season was over, the whole thing would be scrapped. I needed a new role, and quick. Yet everything around me was in turmoil and confusion. The lease on South Audley Street had expired, as a result of which we were temporarily relocated into cramped offices in Kings Cross (where Captain Langton had his Luton Airport coach terminal), before being found more salubrious offices on Oxford Street, in the former first-floor showrooms of furniture-makers Waring & Gillow.

In contrast with our previous premises, our new accommodation offered vast amounts of open-plan space, plus intricately inlaid, handcrafted parquet flooring. The effect was somewhat spoiled, however, by the way in which the flooring was now cross-sectioned with soft steel partitions and the elegant plasterwork above our heads obscured by suspended ceilings (which later housed the computer-system cables). Still, the delights of Oxford Street were just a canter down one flight of steps, a fact not lost on a number of the female staff.

Perhaps even less helpful to the efficient running of the office was the presence of a nearby cartoon cinema, in whose plush, red seats we could spend an afternoon of respite from the chaos. At this point, perhaps, I should remind my reader (and myself) that my story is told from the point-of-view of the underling that I was: a Baldrick, not a Blackadder. Thus my observations were made very much from the chaos of the quarterdeck, rather than the lofty overview of the captain's bridge.

All around us, it seemed that travel companies were rising and falling in dramatic fashion, with a whole host of different characters taking centre stage. In the interests of brevity, I have not sought to chronicle all the comings and goings, but rather to try and explain how the Thomson organisation came to buy a collection of travel companies for under £2 million in 1965/6 and eventually, in 1998, float the group for £1.7 billion, despite what I can only describe as a baffling level of incompetence. Ask what made the difference, and I point to the skill and perseverance of a small handful of individuals who resisted the heavy hand of corporate interference and made Thomason the unassailable edifice we know today.

Take Gordon Brunton, for example. He was an old school friend of Vladimir Raitz, the co-founder of Horizon Holidays, and both were from publishing backgrounds. Raitz had worked for United Press and Reuters before branching out in 1950 by marketing package holidays to Corsica, with charter flights in-cluded; assisted later by his business associate, Len Koven, he then went on to form the respectable, if not downright conservative, Horizon Holidays. Brunton, meanwhile, had worked his way up to become right-hand man to Lord Thomson of Fleet, who owned an empire of radio stations, TV stations and newspapers (flagship titles being *The Times* and *The Sunday Times*).

It was Brunton's masterstroke to suggest going into the travel business. Why was it such a perfect fit? Well, in publishing, all the expenditure was incurred up front, while the advertising receipts only came in later. The travel business worked the other way round, in that you took customer deposits and balance payments in advance.

It was only natural then, that, when Brunton came up with this neat idea, he should first turn to his old friend Raitz, who then introduced him to Captain Langton (Skytours), Aubrey Morris (Riviera Holidays) and Norman Corkhill (Gaytours/Luxitours). It is not known why Raitz had not offered up his own Horizon Holidays instead, but this meeting of travel minds set in motion a series of events that would change the face of tourism, as well as the demise of Raitz's own company.

All of a sudden, people in the travel industry started to look at the business in a different way, with holidays increasingly viewed as commodities. In Brian Warne's brilliant and sadly now out-of-print book, *The Genghis Khan Guide to Business*, the humble barrow boy is held up as the market trader par excellence. At any moment of the day, he knows exactly what he can get and what he needs to get for his fruit and veg. What's more, this amount is always changing: it may be different on a Tuesday from what it is on a Monday; it may change between the second week of December and the third week in January.

The barrow boy may not write much down, but he carries, in his mind's eye, an exact understanding and perception of his business from day to day, hour to hour and minute to minute. All the information he requires could be written on the back of an envelope – it has to be brief because he needs it quickly, to guide his every move. Speed is the issue here: even the largest organisation favours instant approximate accuracy over 100 per cent precision several weeks after the event.

On top of which, one must remember that the barrow boy is in the tricky business of selling perishable goods. He has to get up early, buy from trusted suppliers and then arrange his goods on his barrow in such a way as to give the impression that his range of fruit and veg is not only diverse, but also includes a reassuring mixture of workaday staples (e.g., potatoes) as well as more visually pleasing products (e.g., grapes and melons).

As to the exact composition of his display, this will have been fashioned over time, through trial and error, taking into account the social profile of his customers and the offerings of his rival barrow boys.

With his finger continually on the pulse, the barrow boy has an intuitive sense of the value of any given product, enabling him to rearrange his display and alter his prices, as necessary, throughout the day. He makes his profit not by adhering to fixed and absolute margins, but by providing a mix of products and being left, at the end of the day, with as few perished or unsellable products as possible. Instinctively, the barrow boy knows that unsold products are an inevitable evil, but he permits them only to be profit leakages and to never amount to an actual loss. The precept he follows is that of buying at the right price and selling at the right price too. The parallel with the travel business is striking.

I once found Lord Thomson in the lounge area of the Hotel Atlantis, in Tenerife. Placed in front of him was a pile of newspapers sent by special courier from all over the globe; at first I thought he was reading the various editorials, only to discover that he was actually measuring the column inches of advertising that his papers had achieved. It was quite an eye-opener for me, I confess: compared to the fledgling travel industry, the newspaper business might have seemed well ordered and well documented, but they were both based on the same principles as those that guided the barrow boy.

Unfortunately, this was a lesson that had still to be learnt at Thomson House. The stated aim was to achieve something called 'synergy', by merging the various independent barrow boy-type operations (Captain Langton et al) into one. This would be achieved in three ways: first, by bringing all the different companies under one roof; second, by installing a computer system to replace the old manual charts; by replacing the barrow boys with a succession of managing directors, ending up with a certain Hilary Scott, who seemed to know little about travel beyond his annual skiing holiday in Gstaad (which, unfortunately, I was charged with arranging).

Of course, anyone who knows the first thing about market trading would appreciate that it is not that simple to increase the size of a stall or, for that matter, to make that stallholder work with other stallholders, all of whom have tailored their businesses to fit a particular geographic location and specific target audience. The analogy holds for travel.

The worst aspect of the Thomson merging operation was that all the firms within the company now had to buy their raw materials (i.e., flights) from the in-house airline, Britannia Airways, rather than using their own, often cheaper suppliers. No surprise, then, that there was great resistance to these changes. Indeed, many brave souls chose to lie down in front of the corporate steamroller, and it was just as well they did: it wasn't long before the hoped-for synergies proved illusionary.

The computer system proved unable to cope, the full extent of its short-comings being exposed when planes started reaching their destinations with insufficient seats for the returning passengers. The whole thing was a mess and was soon exploited by others. It is perhaps no coincidence that Thomson bought Skytours at the same time as Clarksons Travel Group carried its first air passengers to the Med and yet, within a couple of years, Clarksons had overtaken us, relegating us to a poor second in the league table.

There was no secret as to why this happened: the building of one big, un-wieldy Thomson barrow had not only halted our momentum, but had made us look stale and hopelessly over-priced. From my lowly position, however, I was not aware of the tectonic plates that were now shifting around me; I was more concerned about the completion of the coach tour programme and whether there would be a job for me afterwards.

This was a time when I heard Prime Minister Harold Wilson talking about the 'pound in your pocket' not being devalued. Yet before I knew it, I was dispatched on a whistle-stop tour around hundreds of Mediterranean hotels, my unenviable task being to renegotiate room rates to compensate for the pound Sterling's 14 per cent devaluation. It might not have been so bad if we weren't already, in some cases, paying hoteliers barely a pound for full board.

CHAPTER 18
WHEN THE BURGLARS
CAME TO CALL

I had gone out of my way to get my passport stamped at Timbuktu Police
Station. Stupidly, I had left it in the inside pocket of my jacket, which had
been hanging on a back of a chair at home when the burglars came.

I N February 1968, I found myself in Las Palmas with Ernesto Garcia-Roady,
the local agent for Skytours. He was the brother of a certain Juan Garcia-Roady,
who had married the actress who played the girlfriend of 'Cookie' in the 1960s
American hit series *77 Sunset Strip*. Juan was also the Skytours agent in Tenerife,
and he was to go on to build the Hotel Atlantis in Puerto de la Cruz.

I had been invited by the two brothers to join a cruise ship that was operating
seven-night voyages from Las Palmas, calling in at ports along the West African
coast. Operated and owned by a Yugoslavian company, the vessel was on the whole
quite cosy, despite looking more like a tramp steamer than an ocean liner.

We sailed non-stop from Las Palmas to Bathurst (present-day Banjul) in The
Gambia, after which we toured the country and continued our West African
voyage into the Gambia River. Later turning north, we called in at the Senegalese
capital, Dakar, and visited Kayar, a truly amazing fishing beach. Not long after we
had set sail from Dakar, I was asked by the captain to come up to the bridge, where
he said the office in Las Palmas had received an urgent message from headquarters, instructing me to return to London immediately.

By this time, the ship was already well out to sea. Studying the map, I
identified a place called Villa Cisneros, the capital of Spanish Sahara, as the likeliest
place for me to disembark. The captain obligingly agreed to call in there, hoping
perhaps that I might put some extra cruise custom his way if he did so. Pulling
into that harbour was a memorable experience: its waters were teeming with

A Story in Brief

TO TIMBUKTU AND BACK AGAIN: This picture, taken in 1974, shows me with some local children outside the house in Timbuktu where the French explorer René Caillié had stayed. He had gone there in 1828, because the Société de Géographie had offered a 10,000 franc prize to the first European to visit Timbuktu and come back alive (Europeans were not welcome). In preparation for his trip, Caillié spent years learning Arabic, studying local customs and the Islamic religion. Having saved £80 he joined a Mandingo caravan going inland, dressed as a Muslim, and declared he was an Egyptian Arab who had been carried off by the French to Senegal and now wanted to return to his native land. After spending a fortnight (20 April – 4 May, 1828) in Timbuktu, he joined a caravan crossing the Sahara to Morocco, and returned, via Fez, to France, were he claimed his 10,000 francs. He died at the age of 38, however, from tuberculosis. **IMAGE COURTESY: GIANNI ANTOGNINI**

jumping silver fish, which glinted in the hot sun. The setting was everything you would expect of a Spanish Foreign Legion outpost: a prison, a Catholic church, a sand-coloured castellated fort and, of course, lots of soldiers.

Fortunately, General Franco had shown admirable foresight in building an airport that was regularly served by military aircraft flying in supplies for the garrison from Las Palmas. It turned out that my luck was in, too: not only was there a flight that very morning, but the local commandant, having explained my plight, was kind enough to offer me a seat. On landing in Las Palmas, I took an inter-island flight to Santa Cruz de Tenerife, where I knew I could hitch a lift on the next day's charter flight. Back in the UK, I travelled from Luton Airport to the old Waring & Gillow offices at Oxford Street. I soon found out why they needed me back so urgently, though it wasn't for any of the reasons I had expected.

Before leaving on the West African jaunt, I had been asked by Hilary Scott, the latest of Gordon Brunton's appointees as managing director, to fix up his annual skiing holiday in Gstaad: he was a habitué of a certain hotel there and always stayed in the same room. It emerged that, although I had booked the accommodation, the hotel had been unable to confirm the exact room number.

As a result, all hell had broken loose in my absence, and on my return Mr Scott informed me that I would be lucky to keep my job after letting him down so badly. But it turned out that the boot was on the other foot: the story of my emergency recall soon got around and, in the process, did Scott's standing amongst the staff no good at all. We never knew if his departure was due to this particular incident, or to the fact that he had been 'found out' more generally, but it was the managing director who happened to be the doomed employee, not me.

The episode summed up, for me, the failure of the powers-that-be at Thomson House in understanding how to make this disparate outfit function.

WHEN THE BURGLARS CAME TO CALL

My West Africa trip of 1968 proved useful some years later, when the company was looking for a show-stopping way to launch a winter brochure. I suggested using the Canary Islands flight service to link with an onward flight to Mali, stopping first in Bamako and then Timbuktu. It was an idea that got us a lot of publicity at the time, although I must say that the hotel in Timbuktu was the worst I had ever stayed in – airless and windowless, not unlike the prison in the film *Papillon*.

At one stage, I began to wonder if we would ever get out of Timbuktu: not only had we picked up an injured Polisario Front guerrilla fighter, but it was also debatable whether, because of the soaring temperatures, the aircraft's engines had the strength to get us back off the ground. Luckily, the plane did manage to become airborne, which helped lessen my disappointment at the theft of my passport (I had gone out of my way to get it stamped at Timbuktu Police Station). Stupidly, I had left it in the inside pocket of my jacket, which had been hanging on a back of a chair at home when the burglars came to call.

SID SILVER (LEFT) WITH RIVIERA AGENTS c1965 AND ROGER LAMBERT (RIGHT)

A Story in Brief

A MAN OF MANY TALENTS/A SINGULAR MAN: "Sidney Silver was a grammar school boy, who, over the years, had gathered a singular cultural knowledge. An excellent mimic, a singer of original Cockney songs, he had this fantastic ability to reach out to people. His knowledge of football, theatre and films served him in good stead, but most importantly, it also served our company. He became without doubt the most successful sales agent in the business, and served as the front man for both Riviera and Thomson. If he had one fault, though, it was his inability to make decisions, both at work and in his love life. There were several times when he was a step away from marriage, only to cry off at the last minute. Yet he valued the company of the ladies and his successes in this area were many. He also became a lover of good food, something he was unable to resist". Aubrey Morris.

IMAGE COURTESY: ROGER LAMBERT.

CHAPTER 19
FERNANDO'S HIDEAWAY

Both Peter's first and second barbecue excursions turned out to be dismal failures – as he later realised, people had been put off by him naming them 'Fernando's Hideaway' and 'Johnny & the Sky Rockets'.

THE Thomson computer system suffered from the fatal flaw of being unable to accommodate human error. In essence, the system was a data-processing operation that made use of punch cards: one card represented outward flights, another return flights and a third hotel rooms. The idea being that, as the reservation department received a booking request for a particular holiday, a typical booking-for-two would result in five punched data cards (four for flights and one for the room) being placed in an envelope, on which would be written the names of the passengers, their home address and the details of the agent.

The contents of such envelope would then be processed in order to produce invoices, flight lists and hotel room lists. Using our previous system (a large chart), it had been easy to check availability at a single glance. With the cards, however, it was a nightmare: staff purposely kept cards out of the system to protect their own holiday entitlement and, worse still, cards rarely found their way back into the trays once a cancellation had been made.

Rather than increasing efficiency, the punched-card system had quite the opposite effect, a situation that was not to be remedied until a 'real-time' computer system was installed a couple of years later. All the while, our deadly rivals, Clarksons, were making further inroads into our business, and prospects for the future looked dire. Although Riviera Holidays had joined Skytours under one roof in London, Manchester-based Gaytours and Luxitours steadfastly resisted any moves towards integration, as did Britannia Airways, who were based in Luton.

All in all, it was a truly half-baked attempt at creating the 'synergy' we were all urged to strive towards. Given that Skytours was already an integrated company, with its own airline, hotels and regional offices, it was difficult to understand what could have possessed Brunton to complicate the issue by purchasing Riviera Holidays and the two Manchester-based companies as well. For some time, the Skytours operation had been concentrated on bucket-and-spade destinations in Spain, Italy and Yugoslavia, whereas Riviera Holidays were that bit more adventurous, venturing into what then seemed far-off Greece and Morocco. As for Gaytours and Luxitours, they were a combination of both, albeit with much of their business coming from Blackpool landladies and football specials.

What saved Thomson from extinction was the original Skytours 'gang of four', from South Audley Street, being joined by some talented staff from Riviera Holidays, in particular Aubrey Morris and Roger Lambert, whose job involved keeping the travel agents – who generated 90 per cent of our sales – onside during this difficult period. In 1969 this small-but-select band was joined by Brian Gurnett, a rarity in those days: a marketing man with coalface experience in the travel business. At long last, new thinking – and new lifeblood – was being injected into the company.

Change was on the way at Britannia Airways too. The airline needed to get rid of its piston aircraft: not only did they look old-fashioned, but they were more expensive to run than the jet planes our competitors, Clarksons, were already using. The job of choosing replacement aircraft fell to a Mr Swift and J.E.D. Williams, who, having studied all the alternatives, came down in favour of the Boeing 737. Today, of course, the 737 is the short-to-medium-haul workhorse of choice for most airlines, but Britannia and Lufthansa were the first two companies in Europe to put their faith in it.

The 737 proved an inspired choice, more efficient and nimble than the BAC 1-11s and Lockheed L-1011 TriStars operated by Clarksons' Court Line. It was the Spanish Armada all over again, with the great Clarkson galleons being outmanoeuvred by our Britannia frigates. And it was a real battle, make no mistake – those of us in the Waring & Gillow building certainly considered ourselves to be fighting a war in which there would be only one winner. No matter how divided we were by internal politics, we were stuck together like glue in our determination to see off Clarksons.

As this titanic struggle raged overhead, humble foot soldiers such as myself were required to carry on with day-to-day troubleshooting on the ground. By the start of 1969, there were issues to be resolved in the Italian resort of Rimini, where small, family-run hotels were hosting thousands of British tourists each year and trying to make a living on the £1 a day we paid them for providing accommodation plus three meals. Unsurprisingly, the cuisine was not of the

A Story in Brief

HERNANDO'S HIDEAWAY: 'Hernando's Hideaway' is a tune from the musical *The Pajama Game*, set in a sleazy, dark 1950s nightclub in Cedar Rapids, Iowa. In real life, though, Hernando's Hideaway was a raunchy dive in Illinois, perched on a cliff overlooking the highway between Dubuque and Galena. To this day, a number of places around the world are also called Hernando's Hideaway; indeed, it became the nickname for the MP's smoking room in the House of Commons. The Labour Member of Parliament, Stephen Pound, told the House during a smoking debate on 14 February 2006: "I refer the House to the dystopic hell – 'Hernando's Hideaway' – that is the Smoking Room on the Library Corridor. It is like the Raft of the Medusa most nights, with great groups of people crammed into it." In similar vein, the Sky-tours representative in Rimini, Peter Van den Graff, named his venue 'Fernando's Hideaway', on the grounds that British holidaymakers found it easier to pronounce the 'F' than the 'H'. **IMAGES COURTESY: MICHAEL MAYNARD/ROGER LAMBERT**

standard for which Italy is renowned, and many guests either ate out at restaurants or simply went without. It was just as well that the sun was lovely and warm and expectations were not high.

I should explain that in those pre-email days, when even a telex was a novelty, resort head representatives were pretty much left to their own devices – if the customers didn't complain when they got home, then the head rep was understood to be doing his job. And it is fair to say that Peter Van Den Graff, the head representative in Rimini, very much had ideas of his own. The way he saw it, the guests were in his charge, they belonged to him, and he was jolly well going to give them what they wanted. Naturally, too, he was determined to keep the fruits of his endeavours: an attitude that did not endear him to the local agent, whose living depended on revenue from excursions and airport transfers.

Peter's guests tended to be older, rather than younger; the war was by no means a distant memory, and even fresher in their minds were recollections of recent holidays in Spain, where, in their estimation, the arrangements had been infinitely superior to those they were now encountering in Italy. There was nothing for it, thought Peter. Not only was he going to have to cater to British wartime nostalgia, he was going to have to make Italy more like Spain, while improving the food at the same time.

He therefore alighted upon the Operation Olive, the Allied offensive on Germany's 'Gothic Line' of defence launched during the autumn of 1944. Although not as well-known as the Normandy D-Day landings, it was the biggest battle fought in Italy and one of the turning points of the war. The aim, Churchill declared, was to destroy the German army in Italy, thereby allowing the Allies to reach the Balkans before the arrival of the Red Army. Thousands died in the fighting, and it turned out that many were laid to rest at Coriano Ridge War Cemetery, close to Rimini.

For Peter, this revelation was a godsend. He organised an excursion that turned out to be hugely popular: a respectful and moving narrative accompanied by dramatic lighting and sound effects, including growling tanks and exploding mortar shells. In comparison with this blockbuster outing, the trips offered by the local agent, to tourist markets and San Marino, seemed tame and tawdry.

Peter's wife, Karin, arrived with a new-fangled, mobile chip-making machine from Holland and did a roaring trade, moving from hotel to hotel selling her wares to hungry Brits. Meanwhile Peter, determined to ensure his guests enjoyed Italy as much as Spain, decided to introduce the kind of barbecue that was currently all the rage in Spanish resorts, and he called on all his experience to create not just a meal, but an occasion too. His requirements were precise: a rustic farmhouse under no circumstances too close to the resort, since the whole event needed to be packaged as an excursion, which was where the real money was to be made. He soon found the perfect venue, a farmhouse with a lovely forecourt in a mountain setting 10 kilometres outside Rimini.

Both Peter's first and second barbecue excursions turned out to be dismal failures – as he later realised, people had been put off by him having named the venues 'Fernando's Hideaway' and 'Johnny & the Sky Rockets'. They just didn't sound Spanish enough. He then had a brainwave, renaming the venue 'The Spanish Inn'. Guests now arrived in droves.

When I appeared on the scene, in response to angry communications from the local agent, it was clear to me that Peter had hit on a winning formula. With a kind of calypso band playing in the background, Peter would front the whole occasion, cigar in hand, urging the barbecue audience to dance one minute and to answer quiz questions the next. By turns he would jump behind the bar, to help serve drinks, and position himself in front of the roasting meat, turning the barbecue spit. The man was in his element: in control and making a fistful of money.

One of Peter's most successful cash-generating sideshows was a baby lion owned by one of the locals which, for a price, would be placed on ladies' laps for a holiday souvenir snap. All right, so the little cub did occasionally nibble the odd British thigh, but these were the days before 'health and safety' had been invented.

Having witnessed Peter in action, it didn't take me long to realise that it would be impossible to tame such a free spirit – or the lion. Indeed, with all his energy and enterprise, Peter was making the rest of the organisation look better than we actually were. Wisely, I concluded to leave things just as they were, even if the local agent didn't like it.

The story didn't end there, however. During the winter months, Peter had the plum job of head representative in Tenerife. After he eulogised the Atlantic island to his Spanish Inn confederates, they asked him to take them along for a season, to see if they could repeat the winning formula of Rimini. Thus Peter, Karin, the barman and the baby lion-handler set off for Hispanic paradise.

By January, however, reports were getting back to London that all was not well in Tenerife. Hoteliers were complaining of unpaid bills, and resort representatives all around the island were contacting us with tales of discontent. It seemed that Peter and his crew were treading on some well-established toes, and by the time I arrived there, in my capacity as trouble-shooter, Peter and his pals had scattered throughout the island, with the police in hot pursuit. What's more, the baby lion had now grown into a rather bigger lion and was inflicting serious bites, rather than playful nibbles, on the holidaymakers. Not that I was ever able to deliver my reprimands in person: I never managed to catch up with Peter and, the last I heard, he had disappeared and gone to live in Ian Smith's Rhodesia, where, I believe, he was to remain.

Peter was, nevertheless, a unique individual, not dissimilar to another larger-than-life character I encountered, John Smith. When I met John, he was working for Skytours in Ibiza. In a previous life he had been a door-to-door butcher, operating out of a van in Sheffield, and he was certainly the housewife's choice, with his good looks and quick patter. In Ibiza, however, he was employed as entertainment manager at Los Tres Carabelas, a group of hotels comprising three giant blocks and housing 2,000 guests, most of them British but with a sizeable smattering of Germans as well.

Once again, complaints came in to head office from the local agent, who was miffed that so many guests were preferring to stay within the confines of the hotel, under John's entertainment spell, while the agent's excursion coaches lay idle. The key to John's success was his ability to cater for the children, who made up a quarter of the guests (the hotels were marketed as 'family-friendly'). He had worked out that if he came up with a programme of events that would take the kids off their parents' hands, then those mums and dads would be free to participate in his other organised activities.

Every day, John would organise what he called his 'Pied Piper' run, which involved him leading some 150 kids behind him in single file. They would start at the hotel and proceed through the centre of Ibiza Town, singing 'Knick-Knack Paddy-Whack, Give the Dog a Bone (This Old Man)' in David Lean's *Bridge on the River Kwai* fashion, and the kids loved it. At a charge of 25 pesetas per child, which included a packet of crisps and a Coke, the venture was a resounding success by any standard. In the afternoons and evenings he also organised a full programme of entertainment, but the real moneymaking events were his multi-lingual bingo sessions. These too were a big hit, largely because he had the personality to pull it off, annoying serious bingo aficionados with his calls – "Two fat ladies: *ein-und-zwanzig!*" – but providing a textbook lesson in how British and German holidaymakers could cohabit happily under the same roof.

Of course, with bingo there has to be prizes, and these came in the form of teddy bears, which John was importing by the container-load from the mainland, as well as cash. It was the latter element that brought the enterprise to the attention of the killjoys in London, who didn't like the idea of guests playing for money. John, typically, found a way of getting around this. When the lucky bingo winner went up to collect their cash prize, John would have a quiet whisper in their ear and then announce: "Ladies and gentlemen, our lucky and most generous winner has kindly donated half his [or her] winnings to the Children's Fund!" Invariably this earned a huge round of applause, but I never did get to the bottom of the matter, with regards to where those funds ended up or whether any children in fact benefitted. Later, the company tried to replicate John's formula without him and, needless to say, failed miserably.

Meanwhile, back in London, rumours had begun to circulate that we would be moving to new offices at the beginning of 1970. I just hoped I would finally get my own office, rather than the desk I was currently occupying in the corridor.

AT LAST! – REAL-TIME COMPUTING THAT WORKED – GLH 1971

A Story in Brief

THE GOOD DIE YOUNG: Once all the companies at Thomson Holidays had been fused together, under Bryan Llewellyn, a healthy friction developed between those on the buying side of things (i.e., those working on overseas operations) and the marketing department (the selling side of things). There were, however, a few brave souls that could straddle the divide, one such person being the much-liked Jim McCluskey, from Management Accounts. When Thomson began operations in the States, they also acquired Arthur's Travel, in Philadelphia, and Club Universe, in Los Angeles, and Jim was to work for them both. When those companies closed, he found employment with a variety of American travel companies, and then decided to become an English teacher, which is why he found himself in Southern China. Sadly, it was here that he was mugged and stabbed to death. A poignant reminder to me at any rate that, earlier, I had asked Jim to manage our China sales office in New York. **IMAGE COURTESY: DOUG GOODMAN.**

CHAPTER 20
GOODBYE TO OXFORD STREET

The day of the big move was close at hand. Bryan Llewellyn had been appointed managing director in September 1969 and we hoped it would herald an improvement in the company's fortunes – and it did.

SID Silver had grown up in the East End of London and, like his mentor Aubrey Morris of Riviera Holidays, started out as a black cab driver (some say carpet salesman); indeed, this was how the two men had reputedly met. Sid was, without question, a 'big picture' man: I can't recall him ever sitting behind a desk or, for that matter, with his jacket off. He saw his role as being the public face of the company, and he put on a first-class show. Listening to Sid, you were convinced that our motley bunch of companies was doing just fine – it lifted our spirits no end whenever he declared, sotto voce, "Who are these Clarksons upstarts, anyway?" For us, Sid was the man with his finger in the dyke; we needed characters like him and Lionel Steinberg to keep up our own morale and to boost confidence throughout the industry.

When it came to contacts within the trade, Sid knew just about everyone and went to so many cocktail parties and product launches that I never saw a photograph of him without a drink in hand. One such bash, to which he invited me, took place in a rather grand apartment overlooking Regents Park, where I met the legendary big band leader Joe Loss.

It was common knowledge that Sid loved mixing with celebrities, especially those from the football world. I don't think he ever watched a match; it was enough for him to be in the company of people within the game, especially if they were involved with Tottenham Hotspur or England. At one point, we all had to go around wearing ties from a tie shop on Tottenham High Road run by Spurs captain and defender Dave Mackay. We were, it seemed, in a kind of friendly, informal sponsorship situation, which is how I came to meet Bobby Moore, the England football captain, and fix up a holiday – at Sid's behest, of course – for him and his wife, Tina.

Sid really came into his own when it came to public speaking, especially when he was talking to travel agents or fronting up football specials (and there were plenty of those). When the English national team was in Madrid to play Spain at the Santiago Bernabéu Stadium, Sid managed to secure several thousand tickets to the game through his contacts at the Football Association. I was accor-dingly summoned and told to book several thousand beds in the Spanish capital, for the nights before and after the game.

By the end, I was really scraping the barrel, using any and every hotel we could find. Suddenly I remembered the Hotel Ronda, on the outskirts of town, where I had stayed with James Adams a few years earlier and had reacquainted myself with Carmen. It was there that the last 200 beds were finally secured.

As for getting the supporters to and from the game, it was clear that tying up all our aircraft for one-off flights to and from Madrid was a somewhat uneconomic proposition. Consequently I was given the task of organising excursions that could be sold to the fans while they were in Madrid, thereby boosting our wafer-thin profit margins. I came up with a sightseeing tour of Madrid for the morning before the game and an evening dinner-cum-show once the match was over.

With his usual panache and spare-no-expense attitude, Sid had booked the Presidential Suite at the very grand Grand Hotel Melia, undoubtedly the best hotel in Madrid. Also, lest he be without company, he had arranged for all the support staff to arrive in Madrid one full day in advance of the invading English hordes. He may have started out as a cab driver (or carpet salesman), but he certainly knew a thing or two about high living.

Once Sid had assembled us troops in the lounge section of his suite, he treated us to one of his stirring, Field Marshal Montgomery-type speeches, describing how the morrow's battle was to be won. No sooner was it over than the suite doors swung open, and in strode a whole team of smartly liveried waiters wheeling trolleys laden with large silver salvers. It was a veritable feast; without further ado, we tucked into vast quantities of sandwiches and canapés and a matching amount of wine. Even as I ate and drank, I couldn't help wondering if I had been a bit too frugal in the past when putting in my expenses claims.

Next morning, of course, the action started in earnest, as charter flights started to arrive from all over the UK and the disembarking fans were first distri-buted around their various hotels, then given a sightseeing tour and deposited at the stadium. Even before the game the fans were in buoyant spirits, and the mood of euphoria went up a notch when the final whistle went, with the score 2-1 in

England's favour. The plan then was for a quick run-around in the coaches, both to take in further highlights of the city and to kill a bit of time before arriving at El Retiro Park for the post-match dinner and show.

At first, all went well: the coaches arrived, unloading the fans at El Retiro's theatre-cum-dance hall, which was the venue for the dinner, and drinks were duly served. However, as the minutes ticked by, it became clear there was something seriously wrong: there was no sign of any catering and even less of the promised floor show. It wasn't long before the fans (and Sid) started to get anxious and I started to get harangued as to what was going on, to a back chorus of "Why are we waiting?"

After a couple of hours of nothing appearing, something had to be done to quell the increasingly mutinous fans, and it was resolved that I, having made the cock-up in the first place, should get up onstage and make some kind of announcement. It was an unnerving prospect, to say the least. As I paced anxiously to and fro around the empty kitchen, wondering what to say, I noticed that, although there was no food, there was still a vast amount of wine left. Stepping out into the smoke-filled hall, I explained the unfortunate situation to the baying multitude, but explained that there was a silver lining, in that drinks were going to be on the house and everyone could have as much as they liked.

As introductions to public speaking go, it was a baptism of fire; but as things turned out, I needn't have worried. My words were met with a mighty roar of approval from the collected throng, who weren't really in a mood to eat anyway. There was, however, a slight drawback to this unlimited free-booze policy, in that many of the fans never made it back to their hotels – some even missed the flight back to the UK as well.

All in all, then, it was a pretty eventful trip, the tone of which had been set by Sid's let's-push-the-boat-out approach. Sid, however, wasn't the only larger-than-life character in the company. There was Lionel Steinberg too.

I always had the impression that Lionel and Sid somehow consumed each other's oxygen – with each, so to speak, wanting to be the ringmaster rather than a mere functionary. Both were true and endearing eccentrics, but Lionel had a real flamboyance about him and dressed nattily, whereas everyone else wore rather stuffy and conservative clothes. Perhaps this was because he had been brought up in South Africa, where he had been a successful lawyer, and was unconstrained by British notions of convention. Either way, he had the ability to sweep into a room, be the centre of attention and then sweep out again before you quite knew what had happened. It was his job to take on our great commercial foe, Clarksons, in addition to bodies such as the Civil Aviation Authority and the Board of Trade, from whom approval was required to do just about anything.

As for me, I was spending more than half the year on the road, a million miles away from the ebb and flow of politics at the Oxford Street offices. I was quite glad of it, too; indeed, I adopted a conscious policy of keeping my head down and of being abroad as much as possible. Much of my time was spent in Yugoslavia, traditionally seen as a 'hardship posting', due both to the complexity of the geography and the way you had to secure approval from the various worker committees each time you wanted to do a deal.

Even there, though, company politics still reared its ugly head, such as on the occasion when Dubrovnik was chosen as the destination for the inaugural flight of our newly acquired Boeing 737 and I was 'missed' off the invite list. I felt sure that dark forces were behind the decision to keep me behind the scenes, handling instead the VIPs' arrival arrangements at the nearby coastal resort of Budva.

It was during this period that my boss, Norman Lewis, penned some eloquent prose following his visit to a little-known part of Portugal called the Algarve, which, according to Norman, meant 'garden' in Moorish Arabic. Not only did almond trees blossom there as early as February, he said, but there was a huge plot of coastal land, just perfect for a hotel, at a place called Olhos de Agua.

For us the Algarve was virgin territory, but such was Norman's inspirational charm and energy that we followed up his idea immediately. In next to no time, he, Brian Gurnett and I were touching down at the newly opened Faro Airport and hiring a car, with a view to inspecting this little piece of Portuguese paradise. The trouble was, Norman couldn't actually remember where this plot of land was; we went to one location after another, clambering around almond trees and trudging over ploughed fields. When we did finally find a spot that Norman felt probably was his 'Olhos de Agua', the would-be developer had given up and gone home.

In terms of pinning down this once-in-a-lifetime development opportunity, then, the trip was a total washout. However, it lingers in our memories thanks to something that happened the next morning, at the wonderful Hotel Praia da Rocha, a byword for service of the impeccable, old-fashioned kind. We each had separate rooms on the same floor, but had agreed to meet in my room for breakfast. At the appointed time, everyone assembled and I proceeded to take the various room-service orders for breakfast, which I recall consisted of various selections of juices, yoghurts, toast and boiled eggs, respectively boiled for three, five and, in my case, seven minutes. There were also Danish pastries, coffee and tea. I gave my room number (325) and was told that the order should be with us in 30 minutes.

Three-quarters of an hour later, breakfast had still not arrived, which seemed strange, given the fine hotel we were in. I phoned room service, slightly irked, and,

A Story in Brief

BEHIND THE FAÇADE – WARING AND GILLOW: In 1968, those of us working for Thomson Travel found ourselves inside a building with an impressive history: the former headquarters of furniture firm Waring and Gillow, at 176 Oxford Street. This was a company formed in 1897, by the merger of two firms: Gillow (of Lancaster) and Waring (of Liverpool). Both businesses had an distinguished pedigree; Gillow's was founded in 1730 by Robert Gillow, who started out as an apprentice joiner. Later, on running into financial difficulty, the company joined up with the firm founded by John Waring, when he came over from Belfast in 1835 and established a wholesale cabinet-making business. Waring Senior was succeeded by his son Samuel, who supervised the furnishing of hotels and public buildings throughout Europe, and built both Selfridge's department store and the Ritz Hotel. Gillow's, meanwhile, fitted out the royal yacht *Victoria and Albert*, the liners *Lusitania*, *Heliopolis* and *Cairo*, and both *Queen Mary* (1936) and *Queen Elizabeth* (1940) for Cunard. IMAGE COURTESY: DOUG GOODMAN.

after being given an apology, was asked to repeat the order, as something had obviously gone awry. I placed the order again; we waited another 30 minutes, and still no breakfast. After I repeated the order one final time, still without success, Norman decided to take matters into his own hands and picked up the phone. He made it clear that he was not going to put up with this appalling lack of service any longer and rang room service to complain about the lack of breakfast in Room 325, only to look at the telephone dial and see that we were actually in room 326! Sure enough, when we popped our heads out into the corridor, we saw that outside the room next door was a fleet of food-laden trolleys, while inside was an irate occupant fed up with being disturbed and unable to get out of his room because of this breakfast barricade.

Discretion being the better part of valour, we decided to leave, not least because it was nearly lunchtime. Not only had we ran out of time, we also didn't want to get landed with an enormous bill for three breakfasts we hadn't eaten. So, the great Algarve hotel development never happened. But what was about to happen, back in London, was a move to new offices. On our return from Portugal, tea chests were piling up at our Oxford Street headquarters and the day of the big move was close at hand. Bryan Llewellyn had been appointed managing director in September 1969 and hoped it would herald an improvement in the company's fortunes – and it did.

CUBA LIBRE

I was once on a flight bound for Montego Bay, Jamaica, together with the flamboyant Lionel Steinberg and Elis Evans, the then marketing director at Thomson. Britannia Airways had bought one solitary Boeing 707 to fulfil our long-haul flying commitments to the Ministry of Defence and 'affinity group' (closed group travel for, say, teachers or farmers where minimum holiday prices were not imposed) charters. However, this was not enough to keep the aircraft fully utilised, and as a solution Lionel had suggested flying it to Jamaica.

Lionel had previously visited the island and made preliminary arrangements with three hotels; these deals now needed wrapping up, which was to be my job. This proved a more difficult task than anticipated: Jamaican hoteliers had existed quite comfortably, thank you very much, on $100-a-day tourists from the United States, but all Thomson were offering was a meagre $15, which was to include an evening meal as well.

Naturally, the hotels initially scoffed at this trifling sum, but the main issue they had at the time was a hotel occupancy level that seldom rose above 40 per cent, plus as soon as there was any hint of violence on the island, the Americans stayed away in their droves. This was a 'devil and the deep blue sea' conundrum for them and, not surprisingly, only three hotels agreed to our propositions. One hotelier in particular embraced the idea of not having to suffer the ups and downs that resulted from over-reliance on US tourists, and his name was Hugh Maitland-Walker.

Hugh – or 'Huge' Maitland-Walker, as we later referred to him, due to his more than ample size – wholeheartedly embraced the concept, which is how his Shaw Park Beach Hotel, located on the beguilingly named, palm-fringed Cutlass Bay, came to be the first to sign up with us. 'Huge' was the spitting image of Lord Lucan, and it was no surprise that he was the subject of many a Lucan 'sighting' – he had even been taken in for questioning by the police. He was certainly no slouch when it came to livening things up, either. On the island, he would drive around in an enormous, pink-coloured classic American convertible and, in London, he would have a Rolls-Royce and engage a uniformed chauffeur, so as to create what he thought was the right image.

He was also very finely attuned as to which direction the Jamaican political winds happened to be blowing. When Michael Manley was elected Jamaican Prime Minister in 1972, most local hotel operators and Americans were dismayed at his policy of rapprochement with Castro's Cuba. By contrast, Huge became an overnight convert to Manley's new Cuban policy.

As befitting his lofty status as general manager of Shaw Park, Huge had been allocated his own private house, located in secluded grounds behind the hotel itself. I shall never forget meeting him there one memorable evening, during the 'Cuban' period, together with Peter Robertson, the local Thomson representative (and an ex-member of the Yardbirds rock group). It became clear that our host was high on something – he was certainly not smoking Woodbines – as he proceeded to conduct a classical orchestral piece coming out of the hi-fi system. At appropriately high points in the symphony, he would fall onto his knees, still conducting, in a performance that would have put Simon Rattle to shame.

Suddenly, the telephone rang. It was the hotel reception, calling to say that the Jamaican Minister for Tourism, accompanied by his Cuban counterpart, was on his way up to the house. On hearing this unwelcome news, frantic efforts had to be made to clean the place, occasioning much shouting and wafting of newspapers, to disperse the lingering smell of the concoction that Huge had been smoking.

This was to little avail – the air was still pungent in the extreme when our guests arrived – but they did not let on that they had noticed anything untoward, and joined us on the terrace outside. For Peter and me, it was both comical and impressive to watch the ease and solemnity with which Huge switched from invisible-orchestra conducting to a diplomatic charm-offensive. Thankfully, the ministers only stayed for half an hour, at which point we tried to encourage Huge to continue with his earlier, interrupted performance, but he was now spooked and having none of it.

I was also intent on launching my own Cuban initiative. I had been to the Cuban embassy in Kingston, to see if I could get a visa, but this proved difficult because there was only a fortnightly flight that linked the two islands. Not wanting to spend two weeks there, I bought a one-way ticket instead, hoping that, once I had arrived, I could find an alternative way off the island after a few days.

From the minute I got to Havana, I was given the VIP treatment. I was not only shown around the island, but also given accommodation in the hotel formerly owned by 'Long Legs' Diamond. The Cubans were very keen to get Thomson into Cuba and even keener on the hard currency that this would bring. A banquet was held on my behalf at the El Floridita cocktail bar and fish restaurant, said to have been frequented by Ernest Hemingway. All the while, I was concerned about how I was going to get off the island – there seemed few possibilities other than to wait for the next flight to Kingston in 10 days' time.

After huddling together to discuss the matter, my hosts said that they might have a solution to my problem and that I should be ready to leave the hotel after breakfast the next morning. A 'Cubatur' car duly picked me up, as arranged, and drove me, with my escort, to a remote section of Havana Airport. The car came to halt before a troop-carrying flight to Luanda, in Angola, that was just about to depart – it turned out that the plane would be making a refuelling stop on the island of Barbados.

On boarding the aircraft, I noticed that the main compartment was full of Cuban soldiers holding their rifles upright. I, however, was sat in a special, curtained-off section at the rear of the aircraft, from where I disembarked at Bridgetown Airport, Barbados, in a somewhat cloak-and-dagger operation. I later found out the reason why: both countries were denying this kind of co-operation and that air traffic even existed.

What of my two companions on this Caribbean trip? Elis Evans eventually left Thomson for South Wales where he founded his own newspaper, which proved so successful that it began challenging Thomson Newspapers' Western Mail and was bought out by the bigger company. As for Lionel Steinberg, the last time I saw him was when he, Adele Biss, Roger Davies and Bryan Llewellyn came to the opening of my emporium of travel in 1979. By then, Lionel had opened his own aircraft seat-broking company across the road from me, in Marylebone. Lionel later sold the business and took up residence in Mallorca. Sadly, though, he never quite succeeded in managing his personal demons, and while some people say he fell to his death from his villa, others say he jumped.

As for Huge, the last I saw of him was in Jamaica; the hotel had been sold and he had bought a large, abandoned plantation where he intended to pass the remainder of his days, free at last from being apprehended as the fugitive earl he wasn't.

RICHARD DAY (UNITOURS) MEETING POPE JOHN PAUL II

A Story in Brief

THE ORPHAN KNIGHT: Born in Vienna, in 1935, Erich Reich was one of thousands of small children deported by Nazi Germany to Poland. In August 1939, at the age of four, he arrived in the UK under the Kindertransport agreement. He never saw his parents again; they were murdered in Auschwitz. After the war, in 1948, he emigrated to the newly-formed state of Israel, but returned to London in 1967 and joined Thomson Holidays. By 1970, he had been promoted to operations director, after which he left to join Thomas Cook, where he became managing director of tour operations. In 1987 he set up Classic Tours, a charity fundraising company which specialises in activity-based global travel, and which has generated some £75m for more than 300 UK charities. He was knighted in the 2010 New Year honours list. **IMAGE COURTESY: UNITOURS NEW YORK.**

CHAPTER 21
BLACK CAT, WHITE CAT

Greater London House had once been a distinctive building sporting
an array of Egyptian-style ornamentation, including a solar disc
dedicated to the sun god Ra and two gigantic black cats.

GOSSIP grew into rumour and, eventually, rumour hardened into fact. The location for our new offices would be the slightly down-at-heel, not-yet-fashionable Camden Town. We were to be based in Greater London House, known to all as 'GLH' and which had, in its previous life, been the factory where the Carreras Tobacco Company had made its premium Craven 'A' cigarettes.

This had once been a distinctive building sporting an array of Egyptian-style ornamentation, including a solar disc dedicated to the sun god Ra and two gigantic black cats (Carreras' logo was a black cat) that crouched on top of the columns flanking the front entrance. The structure had been designed in 1926, just four years after archaeologist Howard Carter's discovery of the tomb of Tutankhamen, an event that popularised Egyptian themes in the minds of architects and the general public alike. What's more, the appetite for Egyptian art deco had been further stimulated by architectural displays at the 1925 Paris Exposition and by exhibitions of Egyptian archaeological discoveries at the British Museum.

However, by the time we arrived at the 'Black Cat' building, as it was known, and started unpacking our tea chests, there was not a hint of the place's illustrious past. All the exterior Egyptian ornamentation had been removed by the developers, who had painted the facade a soporifically bland shade of battleship grey. Inside was not much better: instead of the hoped-for custom-built office suites, we got a repeat of the Waring & Gillow steel-and-glass partition experience. The partitioning was not merely tangible, either: one section of the building was reserved for directors (we dubbed it 'Directors' Row'), and in front of each office was stationed a sentry box, occupied by officious secretaries whose job it was to

A Story in Brief

JOHN BRUNO, THE MAN IN THE BACK ROOM: It always puzzled me why Captain Langton sold Skytours when he did, for the price he did. He wasn't, it is fair to say, particularly interested in corporate structure; his style of operating was to present himself as being pretty much synonymous with the whole company. It was both the firm's strength, and its weakness. Nevertheless, every 'seat of the pants' operation needs a back office person, someone who runs behind and picks up the pieces: a confidant who knows both where the skeletons are hidden, and where the crown jewels are kept. For Langton, that person was Italian-born John (Gianni) Bruno. How depressing it must have been, then, for Langton, when Tom Gullick, of rivals Clarksons, lured Bruno away. At exactly the same time as Clarksons launched their own holidays to the Costas, in competition with Skytours in 1965.

IMAGE COURTESY: PAUL DIGGINS.

prevent us lesser beings from drifting in without making a prior appointment.

There was no question in my mind at the time that Hilary Scott's haughty fingerprints must have been all over the planning of this set-up, as well as the rules regarding who could use the directors' loo (strictly key-holders only). Mere underlings, such as myself, had to share offices. There were two other colleagues sitting in the same room as me; one of them was to eventually run the homeless charity Centre Point, the other his own Italian specialist tour company.

Once installed in GLH, the idea was that we were to be galvanised into a fighting force, with a structure that generated a healthy friction between buying and selling. (I was most definitely on the buying side.) And boy, did we need it. By 1970, just five years after having started operations, Clarksons were not just selling standard holidays to beach resorts in Spain, Italy and Yugoslavia; they were offering a whole pick-and-mix selection, including cruises, ski breaks, stays at lake and mountain resorts and short breaks to places like Bruges and the Dutch bulb fields.

We at GLH were flogging products that looked tired and unimaginative in comparison. Mercifully, however, Hilary Scott had gone and the original Skytours 'gang of four' Andy Sawicki, Norman Lewis, Trevor Davies and Lionel Steinberg from South Audley Street were now joined by Bryan Llewellyn, Roger Lambert, Aubrey Morris, David Walker, Norman Corkhill, Brian Gurnett and Elis Evans.

A SINGLE SPARK CAN CAUSE A PRAIRIE FIRE

In his book *The Tipping Point: How Little Things Can Make a Big Difference*, Malcolm Gladwell defines a 'tipping point' as the moment of critical mass, the threshold, the boiling point when major change happens. He argues that ideas, products, messages and behaviour are spread like viruses, thanks to what economists call the 80/20 principle, whereby 80 per cent of the spreading is done by 20 per cent of the participants.

He could also have cited the famous Mao Zedong quote, "A single spark can cause a prairie fire." There were certainly individuals around me at Thomson whose sparks set all kinds of travel 'prairies' on fire. I can't say I was a leading light in any of this, but I can claim to have witnessed, with my own eyes, the events that turned out to be tipping points when it came to making our company into a fighting force that could take on all comers.

The first of these, without question, was Peter Swift and J.E.D. Williams' inspired decision to choose the American-made Boeing 737, despite internal and governmental pressure to buy British aircraft. The second event occurred in June 1970: I was sitting in Andy Sawicki's GLH office with Norman Lewis when, all of a sudden, Trevor Davies, Elis Evans and Lionel Steinberg burst into the room, demanding to know the answer to one question: could we secure full-board winter accommodation in Mallorca for as little as £1 per night?

Despite the startling nature of this intrusion, we were able to confirm that, yes, it could be done – possibly for even less. Having confirmed this, our three excited colleagues announced that Thomson was to be the first tour operator to challenge both the Board of Trade's minimum holiday-price directives and the strength of its resolve to maintain them.

At this juncture, a little bit of background information needs to be supplied. As things stood in those days, the only way to make Britannia Airway's gleaming new fleet of Boeing 737s pay, during the idle winter months, was to dispatch them not on holiday flights – apart from one weekly trip to Mallorca and Tenerife – but on occasional jobs for the Ministry of Defence and, if things were really slack, on flights for Canadian travel companies, whose high season was our low season.

Even worse, if there was simply no work around, then these expensive airliners would be mothballed in draughty hangars until the start of the UK holiday season – all because of ridiculous, government-imposed minimum-price regulations that put winter, and some summer, holidays beyond the reach of large numbers of the British population. It fell to the flamboyant Lionel Steinberg, along with Peter Swift, to present the company's case to the Board of Trade. In order to achieve maximum impact, they needed to demonstrate the absurdity of the minimum holiday-price regulation.

They came up with the idea of dividing the flight operations week into two shorter segments, one of three nights and the other of four nights, instead of the conventional seven- or 14-night duration. The four-night holiday would start on a Monday and end on a Friday, while the three-night holiday would begin on a Friday and end on a Monday. This gave us the chance to utilise our aircraft in the hitherto slack midweek period.

In terms of price, we could now offer a three-night holiday to Mallorca for just £18, as opposed to £150, the unsaleable minimum price laid down by the Board of Trade directives. Lionel's appearance in front of the Air Transport Licensing Board was reported in the July 1970 edition of *Flight Magazine*. Under a headline reading 'Majorcan Diversion?' BEA representatives voiced strong objections to Britannia's proposed £18 winter package holidays in Mallorca.

In front of the Board's members was a proposal from Britannia Airways to operate 40 return flights from Luton to Palma, as part of the three- and four-night package holidays featured in Skytours' winter programme. Opposing the granting of a licence, Arnold Heard, BEA's route-licensing superintendent, said that the short-duration holidays were a dangerous threat to BEA and that Britannia, in unfairly undercutting its competitors, could ruin the business of other airlines.

He went on to declare: "This case is as damaging as any in the tour-operating business can be to an airline."

In reply, Peter Swift said that the deal represented 170 hours of flying and would fill a void in mid-week winter utilisation. Lionel Steinberg then assured the board that there was a tremendous demand for this type of holiday and therefore no question of making a profit at the expense of scheduled airlines. That was it. There was nothing more to be done but await the outcome of the Board's deliberations, which were due in September. In the meantime, the possibility of a breakthrough needed to be kept under wraps, in case Clarksons got wind of it and queered our pitch, especially since we intended to add a whole raft of other destinations including Portugal and Tunisia to this formula.

At the same time as all this was going on, the third tipping point occurred: the arrival of Bryan Llewellyn (the previous September) as managing director. Previously Bryan had worked as managing director of Thomson Publications, and although (as far as I know) he had no background in travel, he brought with him a wealth of talented people from the wider world of business, including firms such as Yellow Pages, Unilever and Lyons (of Corner House and Jam Tea Cake fame). Yes, we now had our shiny Boeing 737s, and yes, we would soon boast a glossy brochure offering our breakthrough £18 short-break holidays, but it was Bryan and his team who moulded the company's various disparate parts into a single, coherent body.

They achieved this in a dynamic and unconventional way. Normally, when a company is losing money and over-trading relative to its capacity, the solution is to reduce the company's overheads. The genius of Llewellyn, however, was to transform the companies not by contraction, but by growth. And grow we did, sometimes by as much as 100 per cent per year. Achieving this kind of growth, while at the same time re-calibrating the company from within, is a balancing act that few have managed before or since, either in business or in government. Without a doubt, Bryan's presence boosted my morale.

With the departure of Hilary Scott, along with his directors' loo and sentry-box secretaries, the boss's door was now open to all, no matter how lowly you were. What's more, Bryan had an instinctive understanding of commercial essentials, not least the market-stall rules of buying right and selling right.

Over a period of time, the four separate brands would be brought together under one name. Of course, choosing what that name should be was a tricky and contentious business. The boys at Thomson House preferred to keep at arm's length from the troublesome, loss-making subsidiary travel companies, not least since secretive moves were still being made to sell them. Thus there was initially some resistance to using 'Thomson' as an over-arching brand name. Once these objections had been overcome, however, new brochures began to appear under the names 'Thomson Skytours', 'Thomson Riviera Holidays', etc.

And so the process evolved in stages. Bit by bit, the word 'Thomson' grew in size, gradually replacing the name of the original brand until, eventually, all that remained was the prominent 'Thomson Holidays'. This was accompanied by the image of an albatross-cum-seagull travelling across a tangerine sun, the company logo and the catchphrase: 'We take the care and you are free to enjoy yourself.'

Physically, too, the company coalesced. The offices in Manchester were closed and, at long last, all the different sections were brought under one roof, at Greater London House, with only Britannia Airways retaining their base in Luton. Ironically, there would come a time when both the airline and the travel company would share the same headquarters at Luton, but that was still some years hence. As for myself, I was given the task, along with others, of travelling the world in search of possible new areas of activity: skiing, lakes and mountains and even our old friends, coach tours.

It was a frenetic time. I would forever be flying off hither and thither, hiring a car, stopping in front of likely looking hotels in Norway, Austria and Switzerland and making a deal, wherever possible, on the spot. Although my choices were impromptu, they seem to have stood the test of time: 42 years later, some of these randomly selected hotels and resorts still feature in the company's brochures.

Meanwhile, the boys in Spain were building hotels by the dozen; other minds within the company were applying themselves to the task of matching Clarksons' newly launched cruise-ship programme; and back at GLH, Bryan Llewellyn, our new managing director, was busy restructuring the company so that we now had focused brands and proper recruitment and training for resort representatives and resort managers.

Bryan introduced a legal department, a press office, a computer system that worked and a photographic and brochure-design department, in addition to setting up sales, reservations and marketing sections and a passenger relations department. It also emerged that we would be providing for family holidaymakers too, with 'baby patrollers' stationed at various resorts. The way Bryan dealt with unsold tickets – our perishable stock, to use that old fruit-and-veg-stall metaphor – was to introduce cleverly targeted offers with names such as 'Square Deal' and 'Wanderer', thereby ensuring full airplanes and full hotels all year round.

It was around this time that the BBC's *Holiday* programme appeared (its first airing was in 1969). At first, the travel trade turned up its collective nose at this upstart, dismissing it as showbiz candyfloss. Soon, though, with the help of the show's authoritative presenter, Cliff Michelmore, the programme grew in influence; before long, it transpired that a positive mention on the *Holiday* programme would lead to big increases in sales. We were to discover this when our new three- and four-night packages, at the unheard-of price of £18, formed the main item in the first episode of the 1970 autumn series. We had geared up the office with extra reservation staff in expectation of a big response and, even before the programme had finished, the phones were ringing off the hook.

Within weeks we had sold tens of thousands of these holidays and, what's more, caught our competitors completely off guard. Travel agents, who took most of the bookings, began concentrating their efforts on Thomson rather than Clarksons holidays, thereby boosting the amount of money coming in. Not only that, but our airline was booked up all year, as were the hotels; as a result, we were able to negotiate even cheaper rates, thereby reducing our outgoings – a veritable virtuous circle made perfect.

Clearly, the three- and four-day idea was a hit. The following season saw a whole range of places getting the same short-break treatment, including Iron Curtain destinations such as Moscow and Leningrad. The great thing about this was that it introduced tens of thousands of new passengers to Thomson who could then be persuaded to choose us again for their main summer holiday. Suddenly we looked sexy, and sexy is how we wanted to look. The short-break concept was quite simple and small, as corporate strategies go, and yet it changed the fortunes of our company as well as the entire British travel industry. Indeed, far from being a threat to airlines, as suggested by BEA, these holidays not only increased the overall number of passengers, but also boosted interest in winter holidays generally. Everyone prospered.

We didn't just sit back and congratulate ourselves. In late 1970 I was asked to attend a meeting in the boardroom, which was unusual as I was not a director. Underway was a tactical exercise called 'War Games', and pretty much all the company top brass were present. It turned out that this was a council of war, with the strategic aim of deciding how to hit Clarksons where it would hurt them most.

Only later did I discover the reason I had been invited to attend. Apparently it was known that I had spent some time in Germany, and now, with my 300-word German vocabulary, I was to be the instant in-house German travel-market expert. German-based tour operators were eating up available hotel stock by paying far more than we were, and it was wondered whether we could form a mutually beneficial alliance, whereby they might get access to our cheaper hotel rates and we might open up an extra source of hotel beds.

Now in charge of forming this alliance, I was dispatched to Hanover and the headquarters of travel operators Touristic Union International (TUI). There I met a very stern Dr Fischer, the company's chief executive; straight away there was something about his demeanour that suggested he saw no mileage in my idea of an alliance. I remember the meeting for two main reasons: first, the Doctor's intimidating presence, lent added menace by his black-gloved prosthetic hand (he had lost the real one in the war); second, and rather more pleasantly, I invited his extremely helpful secretary back for a drink at the bar of the Hotel Inter-Continental.

While there, I suggested that she might wish to inspect the fine features of my room, an undertaking which required a carefully thought-out path to the lift, avoiding the receptionist's unwanted gaze. I sent her ahead and, after what I took to be a decent interval, followed, but on exiting the lift I immediately became aware of a frock-coated gentleman standing outside my room. Spotting my hesitation, he enquired as to whether this was indeed my room; upon my replying in the affirmative, he flung open the door with his pass key to reveal my *Deutscher mädel* lying snugly in wait for me, on top of the bed. I had only booked and paid for a single room, and my protestation that she was just inspecting the room cut no ice. With much blushing, the secretary left the room and I never saw her or Dr Fischer again. Ironically, in 2000, TUI's parent company acquired the Thomson Travel Group – from what I hear, they are still looking, in vain, for those elusive synergies.

CHAPTER 22
THE NOBLE SAVAGE

*However, one thing I have learned is, when a project is
as successful as theirs was, there is often disagreement as to
who deserves the credit.*

FIFTEEN years after the St Mary's Bay Holiday Camp experience with Dr
Barnardo's, I had a holiday camp experience of a completely different and
more upmarket kind, only this time I was working for Thomson Holidays.
I was given the job of trying to work out why the Club Méditerannée (Club Med)
concept had been successful in America but hadn't really caught on in the UK.

At the time, Club Med had just one small office in London and, from
what I could see, were doing very little business over here. It took me a while,
but eventually I made contact with their headquarters, which were in a swanky
building on the Place de la Bourse in Paris.

I immediately formed the impression that the people who worked for Club
Med were pretty full of themselves, pumped up by the organisation's huge popularity and fashionable image in France, plus its portfolio of venues in such exotic
locations as Tahiti, Guadeloupe and St Moritz. In short, they seemed to be on a
roll, not just pleased with themselves but positively pouting.

However, one thing I have learned is, when a project is as successful as theirs
was, there is often disagreement as to who deserves the credit. Should it be Gérard
Blitz, the former Belgian water polo champion who had co-founded the company
in 1950 (note: his uncle of same name won the Olympic medals) based on his
experience operating transit camps for returning Belgian soldiers, or his business
partner Gilbert Trigano, from whose family's factory Blitz had sourced materials
for his post-war camps and whose idea it (reputedly) had been to go into the
holiday camp business? Opinions were divided.

There was, of course, nothing new about holiday camps. But Club Med scored over the cheap-and-cheerful Butlins brand with the promise of sunshine and warm seas, along with what Gérard Blitz called 'an antidote to civilisation'. Blitz saw no need for the holiday 'villages' (as he called them) to make money beyond covering their costs. What mattered to him was that people could be briefly liberated from their workday lives to exist as noble savages, perhaps even doing some cooking and a bit of washing-up, should they feel like it. Whereas it was Trigano who, by creating a less primitive environment – he substituted exotic thatched huts for the old canvas tents – turned Club Med into a profitable business.

Before encountering Trigano in person, Norman Lewis and I had a meeting with two of his colleagues at which we soon discovered the reason why Club Med holidays weren't popular with Brits: most of the venues were only open for a short, intensive summer season (June, July and August), meaning that there wasn't much leeway when it came to offering discounts to us travel companies. On top of this, the shortness of the season meant we would have to use expensive scheduled airlines instead of charter planes, thereby pushing up the price of what Brits essentially saw as a cheap, holiday camp-style break.

In essence, Club Med were offering holidays in huts where you had to make your own bed and help with the washing-up – at twice the price of a Thomson holiday in a hotel. Even when you threw in sunshine, good food and non-stop beach and water sports, it still didn't look that attractive a deal from our side of the Channel. As we trudged up the stairs to see Monsieur Trigano, we were aware of just how hard a sell Club Med was going to be back home. Still, we consoled ourselves with the thought that an association with Club Med might result in a little bit of the chic rubbing off on Thomson Holidays.

We certainly got an eye-opener when we walked into Monsieur Trigano's office and found that it was more like a presidential suite. Talk about how the other half lived: sumptuous sofas, expensive carpets, and original works of art on the walls and a hi-fi playing gentle classical music. Meanwhile, a general laissez-faire atmosphere prevailed, with people seemingly coming and going as they pleased. Presiding over all this, from behind the grandest of desks, was Gilbert Trigano.

We exchanged a few pleasantries; he asked if we would care for some lunch and we proceeded downstairs, to what we had assumed would be a restaurant but which in fact turned out to be a health club. What's more, the Club Med boys (Trigano wisely stayed behind) suggested that we should join them for a workout in the gym. Now, Norman and I were in Paris for one reason, and one reason only: to make a good impression. This left us with no option but to accept their unexpected invitation.

Neither of us, I have to say, was in peak condition: Norman was a 30-cigarette-a-day man and I was a chain-smoker of cigars. Unfortunately, it took

A Story in Brief

HUGHIE GREEN: In the late '50s and '60s, tour operators often used celebrities to promote their holidays. On the front cover of the 1959 Skytours brochure, for example, you will find a picture of TV's 'Double Your Money' host Hughie Green. No surprise, because Skytours boss Captain Langton owned a nightclub (Winston's, on Clifford Street), where Green was a regular. A little-known fact about Green is that he served as a pilot in the Canadian Air Force during World War Two. Rather more widely publicised was the occasion when he was flying a plane in the Berlin air corridor, at the end of the war, and found himself being buzzed by Russian jets, who felt he had strayed out of his allotted airspace. Even more newsworthy, was the revelation that he was the father of TV presenter Paula Yates, who had travelled with husband Bob Geldof on Voyages Jules Verne's 'Red Arrow Express', and who died in the year 2000.

our hosts no time at all to find us tracksuits and swimming trunks, upon which they threw themselves into their exercise routine. At first we more than kept up with them, keen as we were to fly the British flag. Before long, however, we found ourselves running on empty, at which point we rolled over onto on our backs in submission, completely done for.

Our French counterparts clearly thought this a compete hoot and suggested that we should retire to the sauna, which I confess was a new experience to me and none too appealing either, given that I was going to have to take all my clothes off. But I sensed the pride of our nation was at stake, not to mention Thomson's pride, so we joined our French hosts in the very uppermost level of the sauna, where the temperature was at its fiercest and most unbearable. Having endured only a few moments of this ordeal, I duly fainted, and found myself being thrown into the pool as a means of reviving me (a somewhat dangerous manoeuvre, I later reflected). Our reward, at the end of all this, was to lunch on fruit juice and a few lettuce leaves.

Mercifully, though, the Club Med people did accept Lord Thomson's invitation of a meeting and presentation, which took place a week later, in London. This was my first visit to the Thomson Organisation's London head office, on Gray's Inn Road, as well as the first occasion I had met Lord Thomson. The boys in marketing had been hard at work, making a promotional film about all the ways in which we were going to raise Club Med's UK profile, and clearly our guests were impressed. As indeed was I, though not so much by the film as by the fact I was in the presence of all the Thomson top brass, including the main man himself. During the splendid lunch that followed, it was agreed that I should make a tour of some of the Club Med venues, starting, since it was winter, with their place in St Moritz.

The St Moritz Club Med turned out to be a converted infirmary on the outskirts of the town; to my eye, it still looked and felt more like a hospital than a holiday resort. To Club Med, though, cosmetic appearances were far less important than the quality of the food, plus the non-stop activities and general 'animation'. I was struck straight away by some intriguing aspects of Club Med life: you paid for things not with cash, but with beads, and no one locked their rooms, since guests weren't given door keys.

It was a confusing arrangement, but one which provided unexpected benefits, in my case, when I went in search of my room. After walking down endless identical-looking corridors, I found I had completely forgotten my room number, so I pushed on the door I happened to be standing next to and discovered a gorgeous-looking French ice-maiden – I never did find my room.

Next morning, coming down for breakfast, I and all the other guests were required to approach the dining room via a hallway lined with distorting mirrors, the idea being to get us into a good mood by laughing at ourselves. On top of which, we had to cook our own eggs and were made to sit next to each other, whether we liked it or not: each table-for-10 had to be filled up before another table could be occupied.

The philosophy was that, even at that early hour, some social interaction with strangers would do us good. It was all very un-British, leading me to form the opinion that this Club Med concept was only going to appeal to a small number of people in the UK, as indeed it proved. We marketed a few Club Med places for a couple of seasons and then quietly dropped the programme altogether. As for Gilbert Trigano and, later, his son Serge, they did eventually scale up to more purpose-built structures, such as hotels, and for decades Club Med prospered. However, after three successive years of losses during the 1990s, the Club Med management was to suffer the indignity of being the subject of a cautionary case study for the Harvard Business School, entitled *Death of a Brand*.

Salvation did eventually arrive in 1997, though, in the form of Philippe Bourguignon, the man who had rescued the Euro Disney enterprise, and perhaps Harvard should re-appraise their case study now that Club Med, with help from Saatchi & Saatchi, are once again reaching out as a very successful global brand.

For us, though, this Continental-style holiday camp was never really a starter.

CHAPTER 23
THE CAVIAR WARS

My visit to Moscow in 1971 followed the expulsion from the UK,
earlier that year, of some 105 Soviet diplomats on the grounds of
'behaviour unbecoming of a diplomat'.

I T was New Year's Day, 1971. I was still only 26 and yet there I was, with the highfalutin' title of 'Regional Controller – Rest of the World', sat atop a corporate pyramid of managers, sub-managers and, below them, dozens of local representatives, couriers, baby patrollers and entertainers.

Geographically, my domain now stretched to most corners of Europe and North Africa, as well as a little bit of the Caribbean. Across it was deployed a team of hotel negotiators whose job was to sign up hotels and make arrangements for the receiving of guests. It was a highly complex operation, especially when it came to skiing holidays (I'm thinking equipment hire and ski-lifts) or trips to parts of the world where visas were required.

In a previous life, working on the delicatessen counter at Barkers of Kensington, I had learnt that the duty of the buyer was to choose a mix of products that would not only make money, but also bring a dash of colour and excitement to the food hall display. In many ways, my job now was no different. It seemed to me that our principal role in 'Rest of the World' (ROW) was to work alongside the marketing department as innovators, and between 1971 and 1974 we did more than our fair share of innovating, initially in Russia.

My visit to Moscow in 1971 followed the expulsion from the UK, earlier that year, of some 105 Soviet diplomats on the grounds of 'behaviour unbecoming of a diplomat', which most people assumed meant 'spying'. The terms of the expulsion had been spelt out in a tersely worded Foreign Office memo, which required the 105 to leave Britain within two weeks and thereafter limited the number of UK-based Soviet officials to around 460, equivalent to the number left behind. Perhaps predictably, it was the Soviet visa and consular offices at Kensington Gardens that bore the brunt of the reduction in personnel, thereby preserving of the status quo (which exists to this day): obtaining a Russian visa takes an inordinate amount of time.

The departure scene was captured on the front page of the *Daily Express*, which carried a photograph of Ivan Zavorin, London station head of Intourist, the Soviet Union's official travel agency, standing on the Tilbury quayside and waving his colleagues farewell as their ship bore them back home.

These weren't the only people heading out from the UK to distant lands. By the early 1970s, many of us in the travel industry were keen to open up the hitherto forbidden lands that lay beyond the Iron and Bamboo curtains. Working against this possibility was the fact that the Soviet Union and the West were still very much immersed in the Cold War, as well as the upheavals taking place in the People's Republic of China, which was undergoing another of its great internal convulsions in the form of the Cultural Revolution. Elsewhere, Albania was still in the Stalinist grip of Enver Hohxa, while Yugoslavia and Romania expertly played the politics of 'my enemy's enemy is my friend.'

The summer 1972 edition of Thomson's in-house newspaper, *Holiday Maker*, had the word 'MOCKBA' (i.e., 'Moscow' in Cyrillic script) as its headline, before going on to explain not only that I had dreamt up the mad idea of short breaks behind the Iron Curtain in the depths of a Russian winter, but also that, within a week of these holidays going on sale, some 5,000 had been sold. Really, though, that had been the easy part. The hard work, rather, had been obtaining the requisite visas and getting the Soviets to agree, for the first time, to let a Western charter airline (Britannia) enter Soviet airspace.

These negotiations were tense and fraught: the Soviets certainly wanted the visitors and the foreign currency, but they also wanted the passengers to be carried by the state-owned airline, Aeroflot, and, although eventually unsuccessful in this, they held out for as long as possible. All the while, I was convinced that private discussions among my delegation were being bugged.

Nonetheless, I must say I had some interesting encounters, particularly with Ivan Zavorin, who was now back in Moscow, with personal reputation enhanced and an office right on Red Square, overlooking the Kremlin. One day he invited me from London to Moscow for a short-notice meeting, which I was happy to attend, except that it was now taking up to two weeks to obtain a visa, the Russian embassy in London was so short-staffed.

When I informed Zavorin of this, he told me to board a flight to Moscow and that he would arrange for my visa to be issued on arrival. In those days, even if you arrived with a perfectly valid visa, it was an intimidating experience to have

A Story in Brief

A GAME OF LIFE AND DEATH: Hollywood star Gig Young won Best Supporting Actor for *They Shoot Horses, Don't They?*, and appeared in films like *Sergeant York, The Three Musketeers*, and *Teacher's Pet*. He married his fifth wife, 31-year-old German-born Kim Schmidt, at the age of 64, but just three weeks after their marriage, the couple were found dead in their Manhattan apartment. According to the police, Young first shot Schmidt, and then turned the gun on himself. The pair had met while Kim was a script girl on what turned out to be Young's last film, *The Game of Death*. Before that, she had worked for Thomson Holidays, both in Moscow, and in the Alps. IMAGE COURTESY: DOUG GOODMAN.

to confront the young Red Army soldiers that masqueraded as border officials. Arriving in Moscow with the smallest infraction as to the details – or, worse still, without a visa at all – was to invite being marched off to some windowless room, interrogated for hours on end and then put on the first plane back to London.

As it turned out, even getting onto the Moscow-bound flight in London without a visa was a feat in itself, requiring much sleight of hand and holding of nerve. Once on board, genuine fear began to overcome me. What if Zavorin did not turn up? What would happen then?

Many a time I had made that knee-trembling walk off the plane and towards the Moscow Airport passport booth, but always with the correct documents. Sure enough, when it was my turn to present my passport, there was no sign of Zavorin. This was at a time when you were required to slide your passport (including visa) through a small gap in the elevated glass booth that the officials occupied. I did so and, following the mandatory flicking of passport pages, I heard the words '*Visum! Visum!*' bellowed at me. Perhaps unwisely, I tried to engage the official in some kind of conversation, in order to explain that a Mr Zavorin had told me a visa would be waiting on my arrival.

Within seconds, buttons were being pushed and bells were ringing, and it wasn't long before the booth was swarming with severe-looking, uniformed gentlemen, all wearing the same over-sized military caps. Then, as reality rapidly turned into a nightmare, I was taken to a windowless room and interrogated, during the course of which I attempted to explain the role of this elusive Mr Zavorin. This was to no avail. As anyone who has ever fallen foul of the Soviet system knows, there was no leeway allowed for front-line officials. Preparations were already being made for my confinement in the secure area at the nearby airport hotel, in preparation for my deportation, when my absent host finally decided to put in an appearance.

In an instant, the atmosphere changed. Recognising that they were in the presence of a higher authority, the airport officials went into apologetic mode, with much kowtowing and obsequious pronouncements of unfortunate misunderstandings, etc. The net result was that I was released, without further ado, into the care of Ivan Zavorin, who, despite my disquiet, proceeded to laugh the whole thing off as something of little consequence. Discussions duly went ahead that very day, at a secluded Aeroflot venue somewhere on the perimeter of Sheremetyevo International Airport, and an agreement was reached to let our planes enter Soviet airspace.

From these unpromising beginnings, I like to think, began the thaw in Soviet-UK relations, resulting in not just a trickle of passengers arriving at Moscow and Leningrad airports, but a flood of some 1,000 visitors per week. Once there, they were escorted by a team of UK representatives shadowed by their Intourist counterparts.

Naturally, most guests were content to leave excursion arrangements to these local representatives, not least since this was the only way of getting tickets to the Bolshoi and Kirov ballets. Sales of these tickets were enormous, as were the commissions being earned, but this presented a problem for our representatives: owing to strict currency regulations, roubles could not be exported. Sizeable sums were thus being built up, and some of the representatives found an ingenious way of getting around the currency restrictions.

The way they did this was to buy huge quantities of tinned caviar and fur coats which was sourced from overseas students attending Moscow and Leningrad universities, having paid for them in non-convertible roubles. The resulting booty would then be transported, via the company's aircraft, and put up for sale in the UK. Eventually this little capitalist-trade enterprise came to the notice of Mr Zavorin, who not only demanded its immediate cessation, but also saw that the culprits were expelled.

Although the 'Caviar Wars' were over, it seemed that nothing could stop the advance of tours into the farther reaches of the Soviet Union. The short breaks to Moscow and Leningrad were extended to cover most of the country, stretching from the Caucasus in the south to Archangel in the Soviet Arctic, Siberia in the east and, eventually, into Outer Mongolia. In all, some 250,000 Britons got their first glimpses of life behind the Iron Curtain during this time.

CHAPTER 24
GARDEN OF THE GODS

I visited the Roda Beach Hotel site in February 1972, to find that, while construction was indeed underway, the hotel was being built in the wrong place.

U P until the early 20th century, visitors to Corfu were mainly of royal or aristocratic descent. The island was a playground for the elite of Europe, among them Emperor Wilhelm II of Germany and Empress Elisabeth of Austria; indeed, it was at the Mon Repos Palace that Prince Philip, the future Duke of Edinburgh, was born to Princess Alice of Battenberg in 1921. It wasn't until 1956 and the publication of the naturalist Gerald Durrell's best-selling autobiography *My Family and Other Animals*, chronicling the foibles of his family (especially his elder brother, Lawrence), that Corfu came to the attention of the wider British public.

In his book, Durrell paints a vivid and affectionate picture of life on the island between 1935 and 1939, offering detailed descriptions of the fauna and flora and promoting Corfu, albeit unconsciously, as a holiday destination for the cultured and upwardly-mobile middle classes. Getting there, however, was no easy matter; it either involved a long drive from Athens followed by a ferry journey, or else having to pay a hefty sum for a seat on one of the infrequent scheduled flights.

Effectively, then, a stay on Corfu was limited to the fortunate few who had both the time and the money. Two things changed all this: first, the abolition of minimum holiday-price controls in 1970; and second, the decision by the Greek military junta to offer attractively subsidised hotel construction loans.

In a short space of time, this modestly-sized Ionian island went from being an exclusive reserve of the privileged to the hugely popular holiday resort it is today. It had it all, especially for Brits: not only was the flight time from the UK relatively short, but also, once you were there, you had sunshine, safe and sandy

A Story in Brief

IT'LL BE NICE WHEN IT'S FINISHED: In 1920, Charles-Edouard Jeanneret adopted Le Corbusier (his maternal grandfather's name), as a pseudonym, reflecting his belief that anyone could reinvent himself. The practice of adopting a single name to identify oneself was adopted by many different artists during that era – Cassandre being but one; it wasn't that controversial a move. The same cannot be said for Le Corbusier's work, though; ever since his death, the value of his contribution has been fiercely debated. For instance, the public housing projects influenced by his ideas are seen as having isolated poor communities in monolithic high-rises, and broken the social ties that are integral to a community's development. Certainly the guests at the Roda Beach Hotel, in Corfu, felt that the raw concrete finishes would have benefited from a lick of paint. **IMAGE COURTESY: DAVID BUCKLAND/DOUG GOODMAN.**

beaches, Venetian architecture and distant echoes of the former British occupation of the island (e.g., cricket on the green). In brief, Corfu was, and is, the perfect mass-market destination, though it should be noted that it remains popular with the global jet set, especially on the north-east coast, where homeowners include members of the Rothschild family and several wealthy Russian oligarchs.

We at Thomson were not the first of the large tour operators to venture into this hitherto upmarket territory. That honour went to Clarksons, who, in 1971, started up a weekly BAC 1-11 charter flight from Luton, having first snapped up all available accommodation on the island. It was clear that if Thomson wanted a piece of the action, then we would have to get someone to build a hotel for us. Enter constructor of hotels Dinos Arvanitis, whom I met for the first time in the lobby of the Athenée Palace hotel in Athens, towards the back end of summer 1970.

The purpose of the meeting was to see if any of Dinos' various Greek hotel schemes might be of interest to Thomson, and the answer was that none were. For want of anything better, I then showed Dinos a dog-eared postcard that I had been keeping in my inside jacket pocket for some time. It depicted a row of colourful washing dangling in a narrow alleyway, in what appeared to be the historic old part of Corfu Town. Shoving this picture across the table, I told Dinos that this was where Thomson would ideally like to have a hotel.

I presumed that Dinos must have grown up and gone to school in France: he loved all things French, spoke the language fluently, smoked endless Gitane cigarettes and had a French wife, too. He and his architect brother, Rigas, also shared a fondness for Charles-Édouard Jeanneret, better known as the visionary French architect Le Corbusier.

When it came to doing business, though, I sensed that Dinos was troubled by his political conscience; he was very left of centre, yet here he was, up to his ears in the capitalist hotel-development business and, what's more, dealing with a right-wing military junta that was dishing out low-interest building loans. Then again, this peculiarly Greek variant of schizophrenia was not uncommon in those days. Dinos' main business was his travel agency in Athens, but he also owned and operated a hotel on the Peloponnese aimed at the French-speaking market. We parted on the understanding that if something in Corfu did eventually turn up, he would let me know.

Soon after, he rang to tell me he had found the most wonderful site in Corfu and would like me to see it as soon as possible. We agreed to meet at the Hotel Cavalieri, in Corfu Town, and the idea was that I should travel with him from there to the north of the island, where this heavenly hotel site was to be found. Our plans were initially thwarted, though, by the weather.

As I arrived in Corfu Town, the Sirocco wind kicked up from nowhere and, with the rain lashing down, it proved impossible to venture beyond the hotel's front door, let alone get to the north of the island. We therefore remained marooned in the Hotel Cavalieri for some days, until the wind and the rain had finally abated. It came as no surprise to me when I later read that in Corfu the Sirocco was responsible for depression and suicides – having spent days cooped up indoors, I could well appreciate why.

Eventually we made it to the northern coastline, near a place called Roda, where we looked out at the snow-capped mountains of Albania, just across the water. Dinos was right, the site more than matched the build-up he had given it: two beautiful sandy coves, divided by a raised, olive tree-rimmed promontory, where the main hotel reception area would be located.

On arriving there, we met the landowner, an expatriate Greek now living in Paris, and together we scrambled up and down the site, which thanks to the rain and the Sirocco had become a swamp. Despite the sogginess of the ground, we could see at once that this was the perfect location for our hotel. We agreed then and there to proceed with the project, and once the paperwork had been completed a schedule of advance payments was agreed, following which Dinos and his architect brother began to draw up plans for what would become known as the Roda Beach Hotel.

The project they came up with was for a 260-room hotel. The construction work was to be carried out in two separate phases: the first 130 rooms would come on stream in June 1972, while the next 130 rooms would be ready in May 1973. Our marketing department got to work on producing text that would do justice to this seaside paradise, while artists started producing colourful visualisations of the finished hotel for inclusion in the 1972 summer brochure.

Straight away, the Roda Beach was a roaring success; virtually as soon as it had been launched, all the rooms were booked. All that was needed now was to build the place. Construction had been due to start in August 1971, with guests arriving in early June 1972, but Dinos found himself beset by planning issues; instead of having nine months to complete the first phase, he now only had six.

To say I was concerned at this turn of events was an understatement. I visited the site in February 1972, to find that, while construction was indeed underway, the hotel was being built in the wrong place. Instead of the plot we had agreed on, as illustrated in the brochure, the construction was happening on a different and altogether-less-attractive site nearby.

When asked why the hotel had moved, Dinos told me that the landowner had decided to hang on to the pretty bit of the land, in order to build his own private villa, and had offered up this less lovely location as an alternative. This was, I soon realised, a pretty much take-it-or-leave-it scenario, and given that the hotel had already sold out, I was obliged to accept the change of plan without a murmur. As a company, then, there was nothing we could do, but the switch of location presented us with a few prickly issues, especially since the UK newspapers were at the time full of stories about unfinished hotels and tour operators were very much on the back foot.

You didn't have to be a genius to realise that the media would have a field day if they were to get wind of the fact that the hotel was not only late, but wasn't even in the place where it was supposed to be. Sure enough, the Daily Mirror got hold of a story that the hotel was behind schedule and was unlikely to open on time; this information was emblazoned across a double-page spread sporting the headline 'Heartbreak Hotel' and a photograph of a forlorn-looking parent and child, dangling their feet over the empty concrete shell of a swimming pool.

We were now under pressure and in the spotlight, too. On the day of my visit, the Sirocco was so strong, you could hardly stand up, on top of which the rain was pelting down and the site was awash with mud. Somehow, Dinos had encountered a group of Australian backpackers in Athens and recruited them to work as builders on the Roda Beach site. Bizarrely, they had built themselves a series of tree-houses – to be above mud level – and were now living out a sort of Robinson Crusoe existence: quite a departure from their original plan, which had been to work their way overland from Australia to London. Once the place was built, many of them would metamorphose from construction workers into water ski instructors, boutique shop attendants and barmen.

For the moment, however, the place hadn't actually been built. In April, it became clear to me that the hotel was going to be seriously delayed, so I set about trying to find alternative accommodation for 260 guests: no easy task, as there was a real shortage of hotel rooms on the island at that time. The only available hotel was in Corfu Town itself, and even then it would only be able to accommodate guests up until the end of July, after which Italian holidaymakers had booked it out solidly. The one hope we had to hold on to was that the Roda Beach would be ready by then.

However, it wasn't. The only course of action available to us was to embark upon a campaign of undisguised bribery: we set about offering free car hire, free excursions and free booze to guests staying in Corfu Town hotels, on the basis that they would give up their accommodation and go stay at the unfinished Roda Beach instead, thereby allowing us to put our arriving Thomson guests into their newly vacated rooms.

For this plan to succeed we needed a 100-per-cent conversion rate, and by a miraculous stroke of luck – plus, of course, the offer of free booze – we managed to achieve it. What's more, we repeated the same exercise again and again for several weeks, until we could finally claim the Roda Beach was finished (though not everyone agreed it was ever finished).

I will never forget the day the first convoy of coaches arrived. Ten minutes before they were due to pull up, the site foreman blew his whistle, signalling that everyone should stop working instantly and vacate the site. The bedlam and noise came to a sudden, merciful halt, to be replaced by an atmosphere of complete and utter calm; you could even hear the birds singing. Even as the coaches proceeded, in a dust cloud, down the unfinished driveway, air freshener was being sprayed in an attempt to counteract the overpowering smell of wet paint. As I helped the guests off the coach, I asked one of them what he thought of the place, to which he replied: "It'll be nice when it's finished."

As it happens, this guest wasn't referring to the state of the building, but to its brutal, battleship-grey Le Corbusier-style external finishes, which wouldn't have been out of place on a Glasgow or Peckham council estate. I didn't have the heart to tell him that this was how the place was meant to look.

LEO ROUPIOZ AND RICHARD DAY WERE GIVEN $10,000 BY CAPTAIN LANGTON

A Story in Brief:

IMAGE COURTESY: UNITOURS NEW YORK.

PROMISE CUT SHORT / A NIGHT TO FORGET:
When Captain Langton spotted Leo Roupioz, working as a waiter in a pre-war Parisian hotel, he reckoned he had unearthed a promising find. Not only did he sponsor Leo through hotel school, but he gave him $10,000 to open Universal Tours, in Paris, which made Leo's fortune and enabled him to buy the Grand Hotel in Saint-Quentin, Northern France. However, on the morning of 20 January 1997, the police were called to the hotel to witness a gruesome scene. The receptionist had been shot dead and a valet held captive. Upstairs, still in bed, were the bodies of Leo Roupioz (72) and his wife Gisele (66), first shot and then killed with an axe. On each body was left a handwritten note from the perpetrator, night-watchman Jean-Baptiste-Hennequin, decrying his lack of recognition. When the police arrested Hennequin in Paris, they found a stash of weapons and newspaper clippings. He immediately confessed to the murders, and was sentenced to 22 years.

CHAPTER 25
THE BANANA FLAMBE INCIDENT

The place the exiled Saudi king chose for his many wives and 105 children was the Kavouri Hotel. At a stroke Andreas had not only been blessed with a full hotel, but a hotel full of guests well catered for in the cash department.

I spent a lot of time in Greece during the early '70s and, gathering my thoughts now, I realise the full extent of the changes that had taken place between then and my first visit, in April 1967. In the early days, I still entertained somewhat naïve and charming images of the country which had been planted in my mind by films such as *Summer Holiday* and *Never on Sunday*, starring Cliff Richard and Melina Mercouri respectively. To an extent, that Greece persisted, especially in Athens' Plaka district, where you could still while away the night-time hours under the stars, to the strains of bouzouki music and the sound of smashing plates as diners got up and performed, to huge encouragement from the rest of us, their own impromptu interpretations of the Syrtarki dance.

However, some killjoy, most probably in the Mayor's office, started worrying about the safety issues presented by the smashing plates, not to mention the moral dangers posed by the many colourful ladies of the night. The end result being that Plaka received an official clean-up, which destroyed the very essence of its Greek spirit and substituted an empty tourist cliché. Small wonder, then, that the tourists eventually abandoned Athens and headed straight to the Greek Islands, where the old simple, Hellenic charm lived on. Before that happened, though, there were evenings to be had just like the particularly terrifying one I spent in the company of one of our hoteliers.

In later years, when democracy was restored after the rule of the Colonels, my companion went on to become an MP, but this particular occasion pre-dated his political aspirations. On the night in question, he and I had soaked up the best that Plaka could offer, smashed all the plates in the taverna and been ushered out into the empty streets to find that dawn was breaking. Reluctant for the festivities to stop, my hotelier host insisted we go to an all-night restaurant on Syngrou Avenue. The place specialised in one signature dish and nothing else: kokoretsi, consisting of seasoned offal (sweetbreads, hearts, lungs or kidneys) wrapped with lamb or goat intestines. This was washed down with soup containing the same foul-smelling ingredients.

Why was the restaurant open at this unearthly hour? There was one specific purpose, it being the widely held belief amongst the locals that kokoretsi was the best antidote to a night of boozing. It was, they maintained, imbued with magical detoxification properties – especially useful if you happened to be driving. Since my hotelier friend had the car, I was left with no choice but to accompany him.

It was not an enjoyable meal. As someone who, at the time, considered avocado a touch too exotic, I can honestly say that kokoretsi was the most repulsive dish I have tasted in my entire life. But whereas I shuffled the stuff listlessly around my plate, my host just could not get enough of it.

His belief that this delicacy would improve his driving proved to be a mistake, however. What followed next would prove altogether more stomach-churning than mere offal-wrapped intestines. We left the restaurant as the sun came up and slumped into his very grand Mercedes. Now, Syngrou is a long avenue that extends downhill from the Arch of Hadrian to the sea – a distance of some three miles – and all the way it is criss-crossed by other main avenues, each guarded by traffic lights. Thinking back now, it is clear to me that the testosterone surging through my host's veins had not been diminished, as hoped. This meant that, instead of a leisurely passage back to my hotel, I was to endure something much more terrifying: a game of Russian roulette with the traffic lights.

The rules were simple: my host would purposely wait until the lights turned red and then drive across each and every intersection, with the inevitable screeching of tyres and expletives from other drivers. This dance with death was repeated about 20 times until, a trembling wreck, I was finally allowed out of the car at the forecourt of my hotel. I never did see my host again, who as mentioned later became a Greek MP – all I can say is my experiences that night rather summed up, for me, the hopelessness of the Greek democratic endeavour.

There were many such characters in Greece in those days, such as Andreas Lazaris, who had migrated to Athens with his father from Romania, after they had been persecuted for being Jewish. A trained architect, Andreas decided to build a hotel in Kavouri, an up-market Athenian suburb on the sea. If truth be known, Andreas did not have a clue how to run a hotel, but no sooner had the building work finished than he had an amazing stroke of luck, in the shape of an exiled Saudi king.

A Story in Brief

THE TWO NORMAN LEWIS-ES: The author Norman Lewis, who died in 2003, aged 95, was considered by many (including Graham Greene) to be the most under-rated travel writer of the 20th century. He didn't just pass through a country, he lived there, blended in, and shared the life of its inhabitants. He wrote: "I am looking for the people who have always been there, and belong to the places they live". He wrote his first book in 1935 (on Spain), and went on to write many more, including *A Dragon Apparent* (about Vietnam, in 1951) and *Golden Earth* (a year later, on Burma). His son, also called Norman, was my immediate boss at Thomson Travel, and took me once to meet his father, at his home in Finchingfield, Essex, on a hot summer's day (we got bitten to death by midges). I also worked with Norman Junior's brother Gareth, who helped me get into China, on the Romanian airline Tarom.

The story goes that King Saud of Saudi Arabia had been exiled, in 1964, by his half-brother and successor, King Faisal, and had ended up in Egypt as a guest of President Nasser, who allowed him to run a propaganda campaign with the aim of regaining his throne. After the Arab-Israeli War, however, everything changed; Saud was no longer welcome in Egypt and had to find, at short notice, somewhere that could accommodate his many wives and 115 children.

The place he chose was the newly-built Kavouri Hotel. At a stroke, then, Andreas found himself not only with a full hotel, but a hotel full of guests who were well catered for in the cash department. Among the things for which King Saud had been exiled was his propensity for lavish spending (using predominantly State funds). He continued this policy of high living at the Kavouri, handing out tips in the form of gold Rolex watches or fistfuls of dollars, and it wasn't long before people from miles around were clamouring to get a job in Andreas's hotel.

Sadly, this state of affairs couldn't last forever. One day, the King felt ill and summoned his doctor from Austria to examine him. Before the physician could get there, however, the monarch suffered a heart attack in his sleep, and died. His body was taken to Mecca and laid to rest at the Al Oud cemetery in Riyadh. There was much lamentation, not least on the part of Andreas.

The fact that Andreas was now without a tenant was not lost on us. Initially I contacted him with a view to leasing his hotel, but, having been spoilt by the King's largesse, he was deaf to our humble propositions. We didn't give up, though, and as part of the wooing process I got one of my assistants to take him on a tour of our hotels in Puerto de la Cruz, Tenerife, the idea being to show him that our standards were every bit as 'kingly' as those to which he was accustomed.

The visit concluded with a meal at Puerto's finest restaurant, which once occupied a wonderful position overlooking the harbour walls close to the Old Town and was renowned for its speciality dessert, banana flambé. This was served up in the usual spectacular fashion: a kerosene burner was stationed beside the table and then large quantities of brandy were poured, with a flamboyant flourish, on top of a mass of sizzling bananas, resulting first in a loud bang and then an enormous shooting flame.

Andreas had never witnessed such a theatrical display; thrilled by what he had seen, asked that it be repeated. Now, at this juncture, I should explain that Andreas was not blessed in terms of hand to eye coordination – indeed, it was a mystery to me how he had managed to become an architect, when he couldn't even draw a straight line. Unfortunately, at the critical moment when the lashings of brandy hit the pan, he got far too close to proceedings and managed, with his bumbling hand movements, to confuse and disorientate the waiter. The result being that next minute, the pan, kerosene burner and banana flambé had toppled into Andreas's lap, transforming him from a diner into a human torch. He had to be whisked straight out into the street and sprayed from top to toe with a fire extinguisher.

Eventually, though, our courting of Andreas did pay off, and he agreed to our proposal to lease his hotel. What's more, when it came into our hands, it did so with a newly-installed sewage disposal system, as insisted upon by the authorities, who had felt there could be significant improvements on the original method: a long pipe, emptying straight out into the sea.

Convinced he could satisfy the authorities without having to hook up to (and pay for) the municipal sewage network, Andreas had initially opted for a new German system that involved feeding sewage solids into a series of settling tanks. The remaining liquid content was then channelled around the hotel garden, which he planted with a specific type of bush-like tree, designed to gobble up this unwanted residue. Only in principle was it a good system. The first sign that all was not well was the way the swimming pool water kept turning green, no matter how much chlorine was added. Next, instead of thriving on their sewage-enriched soil, the trees first drooped, then toppled over and died. Andreas was thus obliged to hook up and pay for mains utilities, just like everyone else.

Meanwhile, I had been called to another hotel emergency 10 miles away, close to the ancient city of Marathon. There were two hotels there, one occupied by Clarksons guests and the other, the Costa Rica, contracted to Thomson. Prior to our taking it on, the Costa Rica had been empty, but I saw an opportunity to undermine our rivals by tying it to Thomson. The owner was one Nicholas Kalamaras, who had chosen the name for his hotel on the grounds that he was also the consul general for the aforementioned Central American country. I can only conclude that Nicholas's appointment had been made in absentia, given that he was completely nuts. He was also incapable of running a hotel, a fact, alas, I had not been aware of when I signed him up for a bargain price. It wasn't long before I discovered the full extent of his ineptitude, when I got a call telling me that a guest riot was effectively in progress.

The holidaymakers had banded together to complain about the poor food, the un-made-up rooms and the non-functioning swimming pool. So united were they in their campaign that they had formed into one cohesive unit, with a committee and spokesman even. Now they were demanding that someone from the company should come and address them.

The minute I got there the spokesman and his committee launched at me, demanding to know (a) what I would be doing to improve the situation and (b) how much compensation they would be getting. Rather brushing this aside, I issued a request that all the guests assemble in the lounge. About 80 of them turned up, and it soon became clear they were not impressed by my presentation.

Before long, they started to heckle and shout; everyone had a particular aspect of the hotel that they hated. The haranguing only stopped when the guests eventually got tired and dispersed, leaving me exhausted, embarrassed and vowing that never again would I take the lowest price without considering the value of what I was getting in return. Too late, I called to mind Elis Evans' simple dictum, stated all those years ago in the Thomson promotional film: 'Value for money is a two-way equation' – i.e., what you pay and what you get.

However, bad news wasn't just coming from mainland Greece. That September, I was back in London when I heard that the infamous Sirocco wind had returned to Corfu, backed up by rain that hadn't stopped for days. Things had got so bad that guests at the Roda Beach were now holed up inside the hotel and, due to landslips, cut off from the rest of Corfu (and the outside world).

Telephone connections with Corfu were not good at the best of times, which was good in one respect, in that the press had not got wind of the story. However, this also meant that our response had been too slow, which is why I was immediately dispatched to try and sort things out. So bad was the weather situation that it was not until late the next day that I made it through all the flooding and debris and arrived at the Roda Beach. The most pressing problem became clear straight away: rainwater was pouring through the ceiling and into the open-plan reception area. Apparently Dinos had not asphalted the hotel's numerous flat roofs, nor had he completed the planting that would have bound the surrounding soil that fringed the boundaries of the ground floor rooms; as a result, earth was now being washed into some of the bedrooms.

The walk through the reception was made all the more disconcerting by the squelching noise of the sodden carpet under foot. Even more disconcerting, though, was the presence of another angry-guest committee, plus spokesman. This time, it was they who were demanding a mass meeting, to which I replied that, as all the hotel guests had booked their arrangements individually with Thomson, this was how I intended to engage with them now – individually. Without further ado, I announced that I would set up a desk in reception from which I would explain, on a one-to-one basis, our planned course of action. The simplest solution, of course, would have been to move all the guests into another hotel, except that option was not actually available to us: everywhere else on the island was full.

This left me in a difficult situation. I had to offer guests the alternative of moving to another hotel, so they could not later file a legal complaint that they had been marooned. At the same time, however, I had to offer a package of goodies that would make it more attractive to stay put. What did this package consist of?

Free booze, of course, plus a 50-per-cent refund of the price they had paid for their holiday, provided they remained at the Roda Beach.

I set up my desk in the reception area, and before long a lengthy, snake-like queue had formed. I duly explained the deal to the first couple who sat in front of me, then to several dozen others. As time wore on, the number of people in the queue dwindled to just a handful; most had got tired of waiting and had anyway found out from their fellow-guests the terms of the deal that we were offering.

Fortunately, everyone agreed to stay on at the now-sodden Roda Beach and I was able to congratulate myself that, through a combination of doggedness, determination and delaying tactics, I had loosened the grip of the dreaded committee and their appointed spokesperson. The rain might have been coming in through the roof, but we, the company, were back in control and the press didn't get to hear of it.

PHILIP MORRELL PASSPORT PHOTO AGE 28

A Story in Brief:

TO BE A NIPPY: A 'nippy' was a waitress who worked in J. Lyons & Co tea shops and cafés in the UK. Originally, the term for a Lyons waitress was a 'Gladys' but from about 1926, because the waitresses nipped around the tea shops, the term 'nippy' came into use. Nippies wore a distinctive maid-like uniform with a matching hat, and, as my half-sister June recalls, from her days as a 15-year-old nippy at the Lyons café in Hammersmith Broadway, your supervisor made sure your hair and fingernails were in order before you were allowed out on the floor. Just round the corner was Cadby Hall, the factory where Lyons made large numbers of their products, including jam tarts. Not only did my half-sister work there for a while, but so did several of the original Thomson marketing team – but not I suppose having made jam tarts.

CHAPTER 26
ME AND MICK MCMANUS

The delegation was led by the legendary Mick McManus. He was the wrestler the grapple fans loved to hate, a seasoned bender of the rules famed for his trademark black trunks and forearm jabs.

BY the mid-1970s, the demand from tour operators for hotel rooms in Mediterranean coastal resorts had become insatiable. Beds were needed, and quickly, if we were to cope with the sheer volume of passengers arriving on evermore frequent flights, in ever-larger aeroplanes. In many instances, the suitability of the destination was less important than the availability of land and a suitable builder. Sometimes there would be obstacles; for example, a local official worried about the effect one of our schemes might have on their community. While in normal circumstances this might have been enough to make us look elsewhere, these were far from normal circumstances. Nothing was allowed to get in the way of our quest for increased hotel capacity.

The mayor of Magaluf, in Mallorca, had come to the conclusion that enough was enough. Over an incredibly short period of time, he had seen his idyllically quiet fishing village transformed into a bustling tourist resort packed with high-rise hotels, bars and restaurants, some claiming their cuisine to be 'every bit as good as what Mum makes at home.' The last thing he wanted was another hotel.

Our particular location had been chosen due to its proximity to the Mallorcan capital, Palma, and its airport. Initially, the idea of developing Magaluf had been put forward to us by an eccentric German architect named Hans Bott, who had moved to Alicante after World War Two, during which he had served as a test pilot on the rocket-powered Messerschmitt Me 163 Komet. He was a man preoccupied with – nay, obsessed by – the need to minimise wasted space. To him, a corridor was a crime, which meant that his designs were not only simple but also cheap to build, hence our interest in him.

Bott's plans for Magaluf were big and bold. He envisaged a vast water-park, made up of inter-connected swimming pools dotted with bridges and artificial islands and topped with palm trees. Rising up from the middle would be three gigantic accommodation units housing 2,100 holidaymakers between them. There would also be a profusion of bars, restaurants, nightclubs and lounges, while facilities would include crèches, tennis and badminton courts, giant chess boards, horse rides and even a children's zoo.

The overall design theme was to be Central and South American 'Indian', with Aztec, Mayan and Inca murals covering the exterior of the accommodation blocks. There would be strictly no air-conditioning inside, since this was thought to be something only fussy Americans would want. I can only imagine the Mayor must have choked on his chorizo when he looked at Hans's plans; I later heard how appalled he had been both by the appearance and the sheer overwhelming scale of the project, rejecting it out of hand.

At the time, I was in Tunisia, pleading a rise in the price of olive oil and local labour as an excuse not to increase our payments to hoteliers for the coming season. One night I got a call in my room at the Hotel El Hana, in Sousse. It was Norman Lewis, ringing from London to tell me that the mayor of Magaluf had turned down Hans's scheme and that there was no chance of us winning an appeal against the decision. It was late, the call had woken me up and, in my drowsy state, I mentioned that the day before, in the taxi from Monastir Airport to Sousse, I had passed a plot of scrubland with a large beach frontage. "Could the Magaluf hotel project possibly be built there instead?" I ventured.

I had only meant this as a sort of aside, but, an hour later, the phone went again. It was Norman; he had clearly been mulling over this notion of relocating Hans Bott's South American hotel from Magaluf to the edge of the Sahara Desert. He asked if I knew of a local 'leading light' who could make this happen and, as it happened, I did: Aziz Milad, the local Thomson handling agent.

There were a few issues to be addressed before taking this idea any further: first, the land was just a stone's throw from the Tunisian Presidential Palace; secondly, it was renowned for its mosquitoes; and third, it lay directly under the Monastir Airport flight path. I was told not to worry about the latter two – there weren't that many flights in and out of Monastir, and as for the mosquitoes, a bit of spray would soon put paid to them.

Within weeks, Hans Bott, Norman Lewis and I were summoned to Tunis for an urgent planning meeting with local officials and for fundraising discussions with the Tunisian Central Bank. This was attended by World Bank representatives, whose brief was to raise the required capital on the back of a guarantee from us. The scheme was to be built in exactly the same way as had been proposed at

A Story in Brief

NOT THE DETERGENT TYPE: I often quote these lines from the 1959 film *I'm All Right, Jack*: Lecturer: "To market a commodity, it is necessary to exploit – and that costs money. Currently, we are giving away a set of electro-plated teaspoons for every four packets of Detto purchased". Windrush: "Excuse me sir, but has the firm considered the alternative?" Lecturer: "What alternative?" Windrush: "It has just occurred to me, sir; sell the teaspoons and give away the Detto". The exchange ends with the lecturer telling Windrush "not only is there no future for us, there is no future for you – remarking – you are not the detergent type!. A master of this craft (turning things upside down to see if they would work better) was Thomson marketing man Brian Gurnett, who had worked for Lord Leverhulme, at Unilever, marketing not Detto or Frisko, but Persil. In fact, a surprising number of Thomson marketers came from jobs either with Unilever, or Joe Lyons, of jam tart fame.

Magaluf, only the South American murals would be dropped. This meant that despite the desert location, there was still to be no air-conditioning.

The time allocated for construction was 18 months, and building work began at once. Soon, the site was swarming with thousands of Tunisian workers, working furiously around the clock amid clouds of smoke and showers of sparks that were more reminiscent of 18th-century, Industrial-Revolution Great Britain than North Africa in the 20th century.

It wasn't long before metaphorical sparks began to fly, too. The main source of friction was the relationship between the local architects and our own Hans Bott. At the root of the problem was Hans's somewhat direct, Teutonic approach to site management, which meant that all hell broke loose every time the Tunisian architects tried to alter his designs.

It wasn't just the other architects that Hans had differences with. Aziz Milad, the man who was going to be operating the hotel, also put his two pennyworth into the design process, and it was him that the Tunisian builders took notice of, not Hans. One particular flashpoint was over the choice of carpeting for the new hotel. On one of his frequent trips to Paris, Aziz had been offered a huge quantity of moquette-style, woven-pile fabric carpeting at a low price, and so he had bought the lot. There turned out to be so much of the stuff that Aziz ordered it to be laid not just on the floors, but on the walls too, even though this was going to make the rooms even hotter.

But things got worse. First, we discovered that the hotel fronted an extremely busy industrial shipping lane. Then, ugly black smears started appearing all over the carpet, thanks to workmen inadvertently walking into the building with tar on their feet. Hotel staff members were instructed to change into different shoes each time they came in and went out of the hotel, but to no avail: the smears just multiplied.

The hotel, at least, was scheduled to open on time, but not all of the promised facilities would be ready. Managing guest expectations was therefore going to be tricky, especially given the range of different nationalities involved: 1,900 from the UK (via Thomson) and another 200 via French, Italian and Scandinavian tour operators. With such a large concentration of guests from different countries all stuck in one isolated, mosquito-ridden hotel where workmen were still finishing off most of the surrounding infrastructure, it was clear we were going have to pull out all the stops in order to avert a full-scale guest uprising. The only solution was to put on a programme of non-stop entertainment and hope that, by keeping the holidaymakers occupied, we would get away with it.

When President Bourguiba and his entourage arrived for the official in-auguration of the Sahara Beach Hotel (as it was to be called), the place was fully booked. Seated on a throne that had been erected in the reception area, His Excellency sat and received all and sundry, including me. In eager attendance was an obsequious rent-a-crowd clad in Arabic garb. Veiled women ululated while kowtowing staff swore oaths of lifelong obedience to their president.

Unfortunately, though, Bourguiba's presence coincided with the daily buffet lunch, a cost-saving arrangement that involved 2,100 guests not so much approaching the 50-metre-long buffet table as attacking it from all sides. Usually there would be waiters and table-clearers to clear up the carnage left by the guests, but, this being Inauguration Day, they were all lined up in reception, rather than manning their posts in the dining room.

It wasn't long, then, before a near-riot situation developed in the eating area as guests cleared their own tables, ferrying dirty plates and cutlery to the kitchens, only to return and find their places had been taken by later arrivals. Sensing imminent disaster, I rounded up every available representative, baby patroller and entertainment manager and led them to the front line. Even with these reinforcements in charge of table clearing, the place was like a battlefield. Instead of displaying due respect and reverence to the person of President Bourguiba, large numbers of British guests wanted to tell him what they thought of him for disrupting their sojourn in the sun.

Not a triumph, I confess. All the more important, then, to get the entertainment side of things right, which was going to involve something a bit more professional than the typical French approach (loud singer playing a loud synthesiser). To this end I had engaged not only an entertainments manager and a UK disc jockey, but also a house band and a children's entertainer named 'Mr Popcorn' (whom we later had to let go, when his hands started wandering up the kiddies' T-shirts).

Furthermore, in addition to booking these live 'showcase' acts from the cruise-line circuit, I came up with the idea of offering free family holidays to professional artistes and entertainers, throwing in a bit of pocket money (usually £50) in exchange for a couple of performances at the Sahara Beach Nightclub. It was a roaring success: we attracted a whole host of established and up-and-coming stars, including Marty Wilde, Paul Daniels, the Rubettes, David Berglas, Charlie Williams, Jim Bowen and many others. Ticket sales from these shows more than offset the cost of the free holidays – and, more importantly, took the punters' attention away from the builders still working in the grounds.

While the nightclub acts went down well with the guests, it wasn't always the case with the locals. One evening, Aziz Milad was in the audience for the performance by our burlesque drag act, Guys in Disguise, who started cracking jokes about tummy bugs and the Sahara Beach buffet and then about the fact that we were sharing the resort with so many mosquitoes. Talk about a sense-of-humour failure: Aziz promptly stopped the show and threw the 'Guys' out (though they were later to work for us in Malta and The Gambia).

It wasn't as if I hadn't been trying to get on top of the mosquito problem, either. I had bought 1,200 electronic mosquito-killing machines, which were at that moment sitting in customs at Monastir Airport. No matter what I did, no matter what lengths I went to, I was unable to extricate these machines from the iron grip of the customs officers, as a result of which the Sahara Beach guests continued to be feasted on by the impertinent insects.

The success of the nightclub (Guys in Disguise apart) helped boost holiday sales and encouraged us to try out some new promotional activities. We came up with the idea of inviting six lower-league English football teams, and their fans, to the Sahara Beach for a holiday-cum-football tournament. To give a bit of gravitas to the proceedings, we extended the invitation to a few well-known ex-footballers (e.g., Gordon Banks), as well as the World Cup referee Jack Taylor.

The initiative achieved its twin 'goals' – that is, a full hotel and happy guests. This encouraged us to take our winning entertainment formula one step further, moving from one sport into another. Back in the late '60s and early '70s, 'all-in' professional wrestling dominated ITV's Saturday afternoon viewing schedule, and it occurred to us that it would be simple to build a ring at the Sahara Beach and invite a few wrestlers to come and have a free holiday, with £50 appearance money thrown in.

Hence the arrival, in my Camden office, of a delegation led by the legendary Mick McManus. He was the wrestler the grapple fans loved to hate, a seasoned bender of the rules famed for his trademark black trunks, forearm jabs and catchphrase, 'Not the ears, not the ears' (a reference to his cauliflower ears). He cut a fearsome sight as he sat opposite me, across a rather worryingly narrow table.

Aware that, even then, McManus must have been on about £1,000 per bout, I hedged around for a while, when it came to spelling out the financial details of our offer. In the end, there was nothing for it but to state that the deal was £50 plus a free holiday, at which point McManus rose slowly from his chair and declared, rather menacingly, that he wouldn't even take his jacket off for £50. With this, he promptly put his jacket back on and left the building. There was, then, to be no all-in wrestling at the Sahara Beach – not, I suspect, that this was a cause of undue regret to its owner, Aziz Milad, who later bought out our share in the hotel and duly went on to wealth and fame.

Born in Kairouan, one of the holiest sites in Islam, Aziz learnt about the hospi-tality business at a hotel school in Nice before returning to Tunisia, first to run the State-owned hotel group Société hôtelière et touristique de Tunisie in 1960 and then to set up his own firm, Tunisian Travel Service, which expanded into a major hotel group and airline business, with interests in the UK.

By the time of the Tunisian Revolution of 2010-11, Aziz was probably the most significant businessman in all of Tunisia. Shortly before that, however, his name had achieved a certain amount of international notoriety, when it was revealed that the French foreign minister, Michèle Alliot-Marie, had twice visited Tunisia for a holiday on a private jet belonging to him. It also transpired that on one of these trips her parents had signed a property deal with Mr Milad, who had close links to the recently ousted Tunisian leader, President Zine al-Abidine Ben Ali.

It was the end for the French minister, who was forced to resign. It was also the beginning of the end for Aziz, who, following the overthrow of the ruling elite, discovered that his assets had been frozen by the new Tunisian government. Later those assets were to be unfrozen, but by that time Aziz was already unwell, and it wasn't long before he died.

CHAPTER 27
A CONVEYOR OF BAD NEWS

I started slowly, with the sister translating everything I said into French. Eventually I got to the real reason for my call.

IN the outside world, it wasn't just the UK government's incomes policy that was causing Thomson problems. There was also the Miners' Strike of 1973, which brought on the Three-Day Week and put pressure on the pound, followed soon after by the Arab-Israeli Yom Kippur War and the subsequent fuel shortages and price hikes. In short, this was an inauspicious time to be a tour operator, and I couldn't help wondering whether we at Thomson would be able to shelter from the storm, let alone Clarksons, who, having been taken over by their main aviation provider, Court Line, seemed now to be holed below the waterline.

Court Line had also taken over Vladimir Raitz's Horizon group of companies, which meant they were now saddled with the consequences of having to fly a leased pair of Lockheed L-1011 TriStar aircraft, with their much higher seat capacity, in addition to the smaller and humbler BAC 1-11. To make matters worse, the company had also bought LIAT, a Caribbean inter-island airline that was eating up Court Line's now-dwindling cash reserves. The pressure was now on Clarksons to fill up all 400 seats on their TriStars, as opposed to just 119 on their 'One-Elevens'.

The only option open to them was to start offering holidays at hefty discounts. By contrast, we at Thomson were looking at a much healthier situation: not only were we operating smaller, 130-seat Boeing 737s, but we had also negotiated much more flexible leasing contracts. On top of which, as a means of maintaining the public's confidence in an uncertain holiday-booking climate, we were now offering the option of free cancellation, plus guarantees that there would be no fuel or currency surcharges.

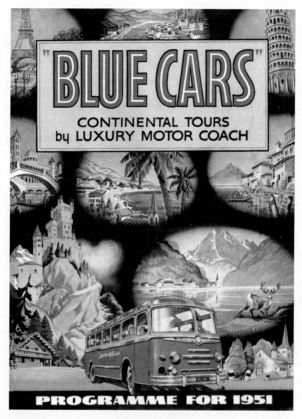

A Story in Brief

THE GREAT AMERICAN COACH ADVENTURE: Captain Ted Langton was not a man who did things by halves, as noted by the UK trade journal *Coaching and Bus Review*. In its November 1950 issue, the magazine featured Langton's latest audacious undertaking, which was to take one of his re-designed 'Blue Cars' Leyland Royal Tiger coaches on a promotional trip around the United States and Canada. "The scheme is a bold one", the Review observed. "By mid-January, when the coach is expected back in this country, it will have done something like 12,000 miles criss-crossing the States and Canada on visits, by prior arrangements with agents, to the principal cities between the Atlantic and the Pacific. Culminating with the coach's arrival in Washington, in time for the American Society of Travel Agents convention. Driver throughout will be Mr A.R.V. Rogers (lucky man!), the company's foreman driver, who has already clocked up over 200,000 miles on Blue Car tours on the Continent."

Poor old Clarksons, of course, were obliged to follow suit. So desperate were they to fill their planes and hotels that they began selling holiday packages below cost, charging as little as £50 for a fortnight's all-inclusive holiday to Mallorca. Straight away, travel agents started to suspect that all was not well at Clarksons HQ, on London City's Sun Street, and began holding back customers' holiday payments, thereby deepening Clarksons' cash crisis. Yet worse was to come.

In mid-April 1974, I was in Lisbon for a meeting with the local agent who was to drive me to Estoril and Cascais, where Thomson had a sizeable number of holidaymakers. The route took us through a wretched favela-type slum district on the outskirts of Lisbon, and I asked the agent whether the members of the current regime were not worried these people might rise up against them one day. "Not at all," came the reply: a more likely scenario was that President Marcello Caetano's liberal policies would result in a right-wing military coup, as opposed to a popular uprising.

A few days later, on the morning of 25 April, I was back in London and heard on the radio that, during the course of the night, a group of low-ranking Portuguese army officers had taken control of the country, in a coup which had distinctly – and surprisingly – communist overtones. I immediately called the agent, who was staying at the Hotel Carlos I in Lisbon; not only was he asleep, but he was completely unaware that he was now in the middle of a revolution, albeit not of the political persuasion he had predicted. The uprising was given the name 'Carnation Revolution', because not only were no shots fired, but also, when the people spilled out into the streets to join the revolutionary soldiers and celebrate the end of the dictatorship, they placed (red) carnations in the soldiers' lapels and down the muzzles of their rifles.

All very well, we thought, but what was worrying was the way in which workers' committees had taken over a large number of hotels, including some we were involved with. The airport remained closed for a number of days, and it took some effort to persuade the Portuguese military to let our aircraft into the country, in order to evacuate our holidaymakers. Eventually, they gave us the green light and it fell to me to travel on the first of the evacuation flights out of the country, as part of a process whereby, for a short time anyway, we withdrew all our holidaymakers from Portugal.

This reminded me that I had been present at the start of another coup several years earlier: on 21 April 1967, I had crossed into Greece from Yugoslavia just a couple of days after the Greek colonels had taken over the country. They were to remain in power for another seven years, until July 1974, when, following the brutal put-down of student demonstrations and the ill-advised invasion of Cyprus, the junta collapsed. What really undermined the colonels was their disastrous attempt to recruit men for the Cyprus invasion. More than anything else, this revealed their weakness, encouraging rival officers to depose them and hand over power to a civilian government.

At that time, Thomson had thousands of holidaymakers both in the Athens area and across the Greek islands. Telephones were down and the Foreign Office, via the British Embassy, was giving out useless and contradictory advice, as usual; in the end we ignored it and arranged the evacuation ourselves. Fortunately, the political situation in Greece soon stabilised and we were able to re-commence operations.

There is, of course, a limit to the amount of protection any tour company can offer. Take the 1973 attack at Athens Airport, in which 24 Thomson holiday-makers were caught up. Thankfully they escaped unharmed, but three people were killed and 55 wounded when two Arab gunmen first opened fire and then started throwing grenades into a crowded passenger lounge. At the time, the terminal building at Athens had a split-level departure hall and passengers waiting to fly out were exposed to any kind of attack from the bar area above. The shooting began as passengers were about to be searched before boarding a flight for Tel Aviv (the gunmen had intended to hijack the plane, but were thwarted by the police).

In all, there were about 1,500 people packed into the departure hall when the first grenades were thrown, sparking panic among the crowd. As chandeliers fell from the ceiling, the gunmen, who said they belonged to the Palestinian militant group Black September (also responsible for the kidnap and massacre of Israeli athletes at the 1972 Summer Olympics in Munich), opened fire with sub-machine guns, shooting indiscriminately into the crowd. Even after the shooting was over, the gunmen held 35 passengers hostage at gunpoint for more than two hours, before finally surrendering to police.

I witnessed an entirely less violent, but still vivid, event at Corfu Airport a year later. On 15 August 1974, I was surprised to see how few passengers disembarked from the huge Court Line TriStar that had just arrived. Next day I went back to the airport and bought an English newspaper, which carried a story announcing that Court Line and Clarksons had gone bust. But even though they had been our deadly rivals, none of us Thomson staff felt any elation at this news. All 1,150 employees had lost their jobs, and we knew that it could so easily have been us.

The Department of Trade and Industry's final report into the Court Line / Clarksons collapse concluded as follows:

"The short answer is that there was no single reason for the collapse, which was caused by a number of contributory factors. Court Line expanded rapidly in many directions, some of which were both logical and justifiable, others not. The overall management was throughout inadequate, and it was, in any event, never supported by the necessary financial control. This meant that, as Court Line expanded, it became progressively vulnerable to any substantial setback in any of its areas of activities. When a serious setback occurred, triggered off by the oil crisis of autumn 1973, it immediately affected the shipping, aviation and leisure divisions. The group was so highly geared, so structured, and having such inadequate financial control, that it might well have been brought down by a substantial reverse in any of its major activities."

For me, above all, the year 1974 will be remembered for what occurred on 3 March. I was at my home, near Hampton Court, when a newsflash interrupted the TV programme I was watching, reporting that a Turkish Airlines aircraft, a McDonnell-Douglas DC-10 performing Flight 981, had disappeared from the radar screens and was thought to have crashed. Moments later, another bulletin confirmed that this was the case. As the crash had happened while the plane was en route from Paris to London, the importance of the event did not immediately dawn on me; only when further coverage revealed that the flight had originated from Istanbul did I realise, with a sickening feeling in the pit of my stomach, that there had been 30 Thomson passengers on that crashed plane.

What's more, there were another 30 Thomson passengers now waiting at London Heathrow, to board the return flight to Istanbul. The minute I realised this, I leapt into the car and drove straight to Heathrow. There, I found our Istanbul-bound passengers, among them the boxer Billy Walker and his brother George. I explained the facts, as I knew them, to the passengers and suggested that they go home and wait for our office to contact them. They left the terminal in what I can only describe as fatalistic relief.

There had as yet been no airline or airport announcement regarding the crash, but rumours were already beginning to circulate. People waiting for friends and relatives to arrive on the flight had seen me explaining matters to the would-be outgoing Thomson passengers, and they sensed that I had reliable information to impart. It wasn't long before I found myself surrounded by a number of very distressed people. They were clinging to the hope that the aircraft's disappearance from radar had been due to a mechanical malfunction, and I found myself skirting uncomfortably around the facts, not wanting to let them know the full horror of the event. I was only saved from having to break the terrible news by an announcement over the public address system, requesting that all people waiting for passengers off Turkish Airlines Flight 981 go to the airport chapel.

The facts, it turned out, were as follows: the aircraft had flown from Istanbul that morning, landing at Paris's Orly Airport just after 11.00am local time. Just

167 passengers, together with 13 crew-members, were on board, and 50 of these disembarked at Paris. Flight 981's second leg, from Paris to London, was normally under-booked, but due to a strike by BEA employees, many London-bound travellers who had been stranded at Orly were rebooked onto it. Among them were 17 British amateur rugby players who had been to watch a France-England match the previous day; the flight also carried six British fashion models and 48 Japanese bank-management trainees on their way to London, in addition to passengers from a dozen other countries and, of course, the 30 passengers from Thomson Holidays.

The aircraft left Orly at around 12.30pm for its flight to Heathrow. It took off in an easterly direction and then turned to the north, in order to avoid flying directly over Paris. Shortly thereafter, the aircraft was cleared to flight level 230 and began turning west, for London. Just after it passed over the town of Meaux, controllers picked up a distorted transmission from the plane: the aircraft's pressurisation and over-speed warnings were heard over the pilots' words in Turkish, including the co-pilot's exclamation: "The fuselage has burst!" (The cargo hatch, owing to a faulty locking mechanism, had failed, causing an explosive depressurisation.) The flight disappeared from radar shortly afterwards and its wreckage was later found in the Ermenonville Forest, 25 miles northeast of Paris. The aircraft had disintegrated. Of the 346 on board, only 40 bodies were visually identifiable. Nine people were never identified.

Now that our outbound passengers had left for their homes and waiting friends and relatives were gathered in the airport chapel, the office booked me on the next flight to Paris Orly, to liaise with the authorities and Turkish Airlines. Meanwhile, our London office began the task of contacting next-of-kin.

At Orly, I checked in at the airport Hilton Hotel and found a message waiting for me from the office. They had contacted the next-of-kin of all except two of the passengers, who had given a booking address in Sheffield. One of them, it emerged, was a French national, and the office wanted me to contact her relatives. Neither my French nor my nerves were up to this task; instead, I went to the hotel's telephone switchboard and explained my problem, and they agreed to call the number I had been given, to find out if anyone in the household spoke English.

By the time I got back to my room the telephone was already ringing: there was indeed someone in the household who spoke English, and this turned out to be the crash victim's sister. Having never been given any kind of training in how to cope with this sort of situation, I asked her if she was sitting down, as I had some bad news to impart, and then drew her attention to the Turkish Airlines flight that had crashed the day before. The room she was speaking from had a chilling echo, and sitting alongside her were other family members. I started slowly, with the sister translating everything I said into French. Eventually I got to the real reason for my call, and as I did so, the whole room erupted in harrowing screams.

I explained the facts to the girl as simply as I could: her sister, who had been living in Sheffield with her English boyfriend, had bought a short-break holiday to Istanbul and, sadly, the two of them had been returning on the crashed flight. Clinging to every scrap of hope, the poor woman asked if there was perhaps a possibility that her sister and boyfriend had disembarked at Orly. There was, I said, a slim chance – sadly, though, the Turkish Airlines office confirmed that the couple had not disembarked in Paris.

Looking back, those 12 months, beginning in October 1973 and ending in November 1974, were undoubtedly the worst that the travel business had been through. Clarksons had disappeared, and although many other travel companies had started up in its stead, nonetheless a large number of them either vanished or were eventually merged with others during the succeeding years. Thomson would still go on to expand in terms of both volume and geographical reach, stretching as far as Cairo, Tel Aviv, Damascus, Baghdad, Amman and even Peking, but it had been the most turbulent and, in some respects, saddest year any of us could remember.

Fortunately, Bryan Llewellyn's nerve as our helmsman had held, and thanks in no small measure to his steady hand on the tiller, we were clear of the storm.

CHAPTER 28
A GLIMPSE INTO THE MIDDLE KINGDOM

I found myself on the border between Hong Kong and the People's Republic of China. I was intrigued by the prospect of a peek behind the Bamboo Curtain. I could just make out the tiny border station of Lo Wu.

I N November 1974, I found myself on the border between Hong Kong and the People's Republic of China. Along with a number of other tourists, I was intrigued by the prospect of a peek behind the Bamboo Curtain, into this most mysterious of lands. We were taken to a hill with spectacular views across the Pearl River and into the Chinese hinterland. To our left, I could just make out the tiny, remote border station of Lo Wu, which was the northern terminus of the Kowloon-Canton Railway and, effectively, the border between the People's Republic of China and the territory of Hong Kong.

This was an area that only came to life during the twice-yearly Canton Trade Fair, when selected Hong Kong businesspeople were allowed to cross the frontier in order to trade with their Mainland Chinese counterparts. For the rest of the time it was mostly deserted, since there were no through trains between Hong Kong and Canton – even visitors with visas had to get off at Lo Wu and change onto the Chinese train that ran onwards to Canton.

As I gazed across to Lo Wu station, screening out the strident commentary of our local guide, I allowed my mind to drift to a future time when I would be able to operate a train service all the way from London's Victoria Station, continuing through China and finishing up in Hong Kong. It was with a head full of such plans that I browsed the bookstall in the departure lounge of Hong Kong's Kai Tak Airport and picked up a copy of Edgar Snow's *Red Star over China*. I read it from cover to cover during the long flight back to London, and by the time the

A Story in Brief

CENTREPOINT: Today, the charity Centrepoint is well-known as a provider of support for homeless young people, offering not just accommodation, but specialist support to help young people back into education, training or employment. It was founded in December 1969, by the Reverend Kenneth Leech, who set up the charity's first shelter in a Soho church, and in 1970, Nick Fenton, who shared an office with me at Greater London House, left Thomson to become the organisation's first full time director. Its most famous patron was, of course, Diana, Princess of Wales; her work is carried on by Centrepoint's current royal patron, her son Prince William, the Duke of Cambridge.

plane touched down I was completely hooked: somehow, I just had to make contact with the Chinese.

Little did I know that it would take another three years before I could turn this vision – or more accurately, this obsession – into a reality. Or that it would transform my life, requiring me to open up an office in Hong Kong from where I would run the 'Central Kingdom Express', a weekly train service travelling all the way back and forth between London and Hong Kong.

For years had I imagined that, somewhere in Peking, there must have been an official incinerator into which they consigned all requests for entry into China from Western tour operators. What I had failed to appreciate, though, was that no Chinese official then would dare expose themselves to the kind of criticism that might result from direct dealings with Western capitalist organisations. The only type of contacts sanctioned by the authorities were with so-called 'Old Friends of China', a title bestowed only on certain diplomats, trade unions and countries (such as Albania) that were signed-up adherents to the thoughts of Chairman Mao Zedong.

This brings me to another powerful leader, Lord Thomson. Though far from a communist, he did profess to be a man of the people, and his frugal tastes certainly backed this up. Not only did he travel to and from work on the Underground, while his executives drove posh cars or were ferried by chauffeurs, but he always flew economy class on a plane, even if his directors were seated up front on the same flight.

When it came to food, his requirements were similarly down to earth: his favourite dish was chopped tomatoes and onions, washed down with lashings of orange juice (he was a teetotaller). His lack of extravagance, I sensed, was born not out of any meanness, but from the fact that he got no pleasure from spending money on himself – a trait that I noticed had passed on to his son, Kenneth. At the same time, he did not take issue with, or pass any kind of judgment on, those people who did spend lavishly on themselves, if that was what they chose to do.

In 1971 I spent a week alone with Lord Thomson in Tenerife, where I was able to observe his down-to-earth nature at close quarters. There was nothing he liked better than to recall the days when he first started out, as a radio-set salesman in the small Canadian town of Timmins, Ontario. The problem he faced in those days was that, no sooner had he sold his customers their shiny new radio sets than they wanted to return them: due to the remoteness of the location, all they could pick up was a lot of crackling. 'Needs must', then, he decided to start his own radio station in the back of a cinema – and the rest, as they say, is history.

He had arrived in Tenerife on the inaugural Britannia Airways Boeing 707 to find that his luggage had gone missing, having been put on a flight to Singapore.

As was typical, he didn't make a fuss; we just bought him a few essentials at a local shop and he was perfectly happy. During the course of his stay, Lord Thomson helped me negotiate a couple of tricky hotel contracts, and clearly enjoyed being back in the thick of things again.

He was flattered that I had read everything that had been printed about him, right back to his earliest beginnings. I think it is fair to say that he took a bit of a shine to me, as demonstrated by the time I was in Bryan Llewellyn's office and 'Lord T' (as we called him) rang to say how much he had enjoyed his stay in Tenerife, while also lavishing praise on me. The only reservation he had was that he thought I was too thin and should see the company doctor – this was my passport to free private health cover for some years to come, all paid for by the company.

Basically, Lord T was a man of few words, yet you felt every word counted. He spoke in a characteristically soft, non-threatening Canadian drawl that, together with his lack of airs and graces, immediately endeared him to me and to everyone else in the company. Those lines of Kipling's, 'If you can talk with crowds and keep your virtue, or walk with Kings – nor lose the common touch,' rather summed him up. Given his power over the media, he was courted by royals, politicians and junta leaders alike, yet he was equally comfortable down in the gutter, with the rest of us.

The same affection was not always felt for Gordon Brunton, Lord T's appointed man in charge of the travel companies, who, from what I could make out, had come from a typical British establishment background. He had worked in publishing most of his life and knew precious little about travel, and his style was the complete opposite of Lord T's. Two or three times a year we'd be asked to lay on a special Brunton resort visit, so that he could meet representatives and local managers at the sharp end of the business. This would normally conclude with him hosting a grand farewell meal, at which he would ask the various representatives, "What are your real problems?" thereby inviting them to speak 'out of school' about any gripes they might have, regarding the deficiencies of management back at HQ.

Far from being kept confidential, the juiciest bits of criticism would then be directed back to the relevant people at Greater London House, in the manner of a hand grenade being tossed into a room. We soon put paid to this, however. Before a Brunton visit I would coach the local resort managers on the answers they should give, and after that the hand grenades stopped.

My last recollections of being with Gordon Brunton were at the lunch-table at the Roda Beach Hotel on 4 August 1976. I had been called to the reception to receive a call from Thomson House, informing me that Lord Thomson had died earlier that day and was asked to pass on the news to Gordon Brunton – it was a sad moment.

Typical of Lord T's no-fuss approach was the occasion at Athens Airport when I arranged for a special VIP coach to meet him as he disembarked the plane – completely unnecessary, as it turned out, since he made it clear he preferred to take the normal passenger coach to the terminal. We had arranged for him to stay at the company-run Kavouri Hotel, on the outskirts of Athens, but before checking in he wanted to be reassured that he was not displacing a bona fide, full-fare-paying customer: we assured him he wasn't.

It was during this stay that he told me he was shortly to meet up with the top Chinese leadership. The meeting was to take place at the Conghua Hot Springs resort, 75 kilometres north of Canton, where many of the country's politicians went during the summer, when their residential compound in Peking became unbearably hot and stifling.

During the 1950s, Premier Zhou Enlai had developed the site, also known as the Liuxi River Springs, as a rest and recreation area for the Communist Party elite, and also as a place where visiting heads of state could be entertained. Various Chinese leaders stayed here, including Chairman Mao himself, Liu Shaoqi, Zhou Enlai, Zhu De, Deng Xiaoping, Hu Yaobang and Hua Guofeng, as did many foreign heads of state, including President Richard Nixon, Chairman Ho Chi Minh, King Sihanouk of Cambodia and many others. It was also the place where I was to be entertained a few years later, once I had worked out how to get into the country. For the moment, though, tourism to China proved to be a total non-starter.

Before Lord T set off, I urged him to ask if Thomson Holidays might send in a few tourist groups, remembering my tantalising glimpse across the border in 1974. When he returned, he told me the Chinese weren't interested, although secretly I reckoned he had been too embarrassed to ask for something for his own account. The last time I saw Lord T was a year later in Athens, where he had been invited by the Greek Junta and gone somewhat reluctantly, as he did not want his visit to be seen as an endorsement for the regime.

In Athens, he told me that he had received a repeat invitation from Zhou Enlai; however, the idea of us sending tour groups there just did not get off the ground. Instead, I had to console myself with reading everything I could on the country and building up my resolve to get behind the Bamboo Curtain. Everything came to a head one day in Jamaica sometime later, when I suddenly had a big idea and couldn't wait to get back to London, to put it into action.

CHAPTER 29
FACE-TO-FACE AT LAST

I found someone in London's Chinatown who had a Chinese typewriter and would be able to translate a letter I had written referring to Lord Thomson as an 'old friend of the Chinese people'.

MIANZI is the word the Chinese use when talking about 'losing face', 'saving face' and even 'giving face'. In light of the severe consequences that stem from losing face, the majority of Chinese people strive to save it, for both themselves and others: they suppress negative opinions and emotions in order to avoid causing disrespect, shame or dishonour.

In China, open criticism, directed either at oneself or others, is considered extremely damaging. One may lose face not just by personal displays of anger or bad temperedness, but also by publicly revealing flaws and failings in others. Yet it is by no means a simple system; for example, while being exposed to criticism at work almost certainly leads to loss of face, being exposed to too much praise can have the effect of disrupting team harmony. So, how do Chinese officials solve this dilemma? By giving neither criticism nor praise. Extremely confusing for outsiders, but the fact remains, if you want to do business with Chinese people, then you have to find your way through this maze of unwritten rules and social expectations. During Mao's Cultural Revolution and shortly thereafter, the avoidance of 'risk-taking', especially with foreigners, became an obsession among Chinese people desperate to avoid loss-of-face situations.

At the time in question, the guide to 'official' thinking in China was the People's Daily. This was far more than a newspaper: leading cadres were required to study it each morning, in order to gauge the prevailing correct political line and to understand not only which Chinese people were in and which were out, but also which foreigners were considered to be bona fide 'old friends of the Chinese people'. Being seen with the Premier, in this case Zhou, was key to being

A Story in Brief

SWINGING LONDON: In late 1966, I was living near Stuttgart, in Germany; the World Cup had just been won by England, and *Time* magazine, had identified the phenomenon of 'Swinging London' describing it thus: "In this century, every decade has had its city. The fin de siècle belonged to the dreamlike round of Vienna, capital of the inbred Habsburgs and the waltz. In the changing '20s, Paris provided a moveable feast for Hemingway, Picasso, Fitzgerald and Joyce, while in the chaos after the Great Crash, Berlin briefly erupted with the savage iconoclasm of Brecht and the Bauhaus. During the shell-shocked 1940s, thrusting New York led the way, and in the uneasy 1950s it was the easy Rome of La Dolce Vita. Today, it is London in the 1960s". And no one personified 'Swinging London' more than John Stephens, the so-called 'King of Carnaby Street', whom I met once in the La Siesta Café, on Queensway, west London. **IMAGE COURTESY: MR LI TIE FEI -CHINA.**

recognised as such a friend, and from 1949 to 2010 only 601 people were bestowed with the accolade. This explains why, for so long, Western attempts to get tourists into China fell on stony ground. Foreigners were far too tricky a commodity to handle, especially if they had not been formally identified as 'old friends'. As a result, we at Thomson and most other travel companies never received any replies to our requests.

Then, two significant events occurred: Zhou Enlai died in January 1976, followed by Mao in September of the same year. A confusing interim period followed, only ending when Deng Xiaoping came to power in 1977 and began to make obscure yet, to my ears, foreigner-friendly pronouncements to the effect that China should now 'learn from the West'. Another of his sayings, with regard to competing economic ideologies, was: "It doesn't matter if a cat is black or white, so long as it catches mice."

Encouraged, if still crossing my fingers, I took this as my cue to have another go at getting tourists into China. As soon as I had flown into London from Montego Bay, Jamaica, I asked Gareth Lewis (Norman's brother) to go out and buy a map of Asia. When Gareth returned, we spread the map out on the meeting table in my office and, over the course of the next few days, pored over it, pointing knowledgeably to Peking. Every so often we would come out with phrases such as, "There must be a way for us to get in."

It wasn't just talk, either. I had come up with a plan: to find someone in London's Chinatown who had a Chinese typewriter and would be able to translate a letter I had written referring to Lord Thomson as an 'old friend of the Chinese people' and alluding to his links with the revered late premier, Zhou Enlai. I admit that my scheme was a touch audacious, but I felt I was on reasonably safe ground, given that Lord Thomson had died the previous August.

My more immediate problem, though, was not so much composing the letter as ensuring it got delivered and did not suffer the same fate as all my previous written requests. The question was, how to go about it? There weren't that many conduits into the People's Republic, apart from the Chinese state airline, which operated just one fortnightly flight into Europe. This flew from Peking, not into Britain or France, but into 'friendly' Albania, ruled by communist leader Enver Hoxha. Officially, Albania, like China, was closed to 'open' tourism, but it occurred to me that we might have a chance if we could smuggle one of our people into the country with a trade union delegation and get my letter delivered from there.

I also began working on another possible angle, this time using a map of the Chinese capital. My strategy centred on Chang'an Avenue, the main thoroughfare that runs through the heart of Peking, and in particular on the point just before it meets Tiananmen Square. This is the spot where the Peking Hotel stands, opposite the offices of Luxingshe (the official Chinese tourist agency). The Peking Hotel was where foreign airline representatives used to stay and also locate their offices, including those who worked for the Romanian outfit, TAROM.

It hadn't escaped my notice that Romania and its Ceausescu regime were, along with Albania, considered firm 'old friends of the Chinese people'; hence TAROM's weekly flight service from Bucharest, via Karachi, to Peking. This being the case, it was reasonable to conclude that there must be regular communication between TAROM's head office in Bucharest and their station manager in China, who would, of course, be based in the Peking Hotel. As airlines always use their own aircraft to transport company mail, I concluded that it might just be possible to get my letter delivered by a TAROM plane to the airline's Peking office, and from there have it make the short journey across the street to the Luxingshe offices.

Armed with this idea, I called on TAROM's manager in London, a Mr Ungureanu, in order to put a proposition to him. In exchange for ensuring the safe delivery of my letter and there being a positive result from the Chinese authorities, TAROM would earn the right to carry our guests to China. It was an idea that clearly appealed to Mr Ungureanu and his airline, not least because their flights to Peking were largely empty. In addition, he personally knew the TAROM station manager in Peking and was certain his colleague would be able to deliver my letter to Luxingshe.

I was not confident of success; nonetheless I handed Mr Ungureanu the letter, on the basis that it was worth a try. I thought little more of it until a month later, when I was sitting at my desk in Greater London House and was called to reception to sign for a telegram. This was unusual, as everyone was using telex by then. Even more unusual was the message waiting for me when I opened the envelope; it was from China and simply read: 'You may organise four groups of 50 guests to come to China to visit Peking and Shanghai in November 1977 for one week, signed Luxingshe.'

With trembling hands, I took the telegram back to my desk and sat there for some time, reading it again and again, luxuriating in what it said. I had done it, I told myself; it seemed impossible that my plan had worked, and yet here was the proof. This was the telegram that would change my life. I only wish I still had it: it would be framed and hanging in pride of place on my office wall.

That said, the news did present me with a problem that I was not sure how to resolve. I hadn't told anyone else at Thomson about my China venture, and although I was ecstatic about getting the go-ahead from Luxingshe, other people in the building might not feel the same way, given that I had chosen to operate outside my corporate brief.

It became clear that whatever my next steps were, I was going to have to tread very carefully indeed. The way I went about things was as follows: first of all, I replied to the Chinese, graciously accepting their kind invitation, and then gradually introduced the subject to my marketing counterparts at Thomson. Initially they were bit miffed and responded to this new venture in a distinctly lukewarm way; only after a while did they agree to print a two-colour, four-page leaflet for distribution to travel agents.

The public, however, went overboard for the whole thing. In no time at all, the seven-night, £495 packages were sold out. Our press department got to work and, before long, I was appearing on the BBC early evening news programme, alongside Isabel Hilton, who had written a series of articles in the Sunday Times about her experiences as a student in Peking and Shanghai (she went on to present the BBC's The World Tonight radio programme).

It was in October 1977 that I set foot in China for the first time. I went with Roger Davies, who had been placed in charge of Thomson Holidays after Bryan Llewellyn moved to the publishing division. To get there, we first travelled to Iran, which was still under the control of the Shah (and would have some issues a couple of years later, when the Ayatollah Khomeini came to power). From the capital, Teheran, we flew with Iran Air on their Tokyo-bound flight, which was scheduled to make an intermediate stop in Peking. The thrill of finally arriving in China was made even keener by the fact that Roger and I were the only two passengers in possession of a Chinese visa, and thus allowed to disembark at Peking.

Our first impression was of an eerily empty terminal building. Our second impression, as we were driven into town by our escort, was of a population living under very real hardships. It was bitterly cold, yet hundreds of thousands of people were camped out, in makeshift shelters, on open ground in front of their dwelling places – a result of the terrible earthquake that had devastated the nearby city of Tangshan on 28 July 1976, killing at least 240,000 people (some say up to 650,000) and causing damage to buildings all the way to Peking, 140km to the west. China had spurned all outside offers of assistance, and more than a year later the population were still clearly traumatised.

When we arrived at the Peking Hotel, a big sign in English greeted us: 'We have friends all over the world.' It made me feel that I had somehow scaled the dizzy heights and was now an 'old friend' myself. Nonetheless, there was still plenty of work to be done. The producer of the BBC Programme Holiday, Tom Savage, had given me a so-called 'near broadcast-quality' camera to use during the trip, so I set about visiting and filming all the usual sites: the Great Wall, Ming Tombs, Summer Palace, Peking Zoo, Forbidden City and Great Hall of the People, to see Mao lying in state. Then there was the obligatory outing to an agricultural commune, with its 'barefoot doctors'. We even visited the Peking Opera (on our first evening – we were all suffering from jetlag and nodded off!).

It wasn't until a little later in the visit that we finally met the Luxingshe officials, which was my introduction to the concept of a 'side-on' business meeting. Unlike us Westerners, who are used to having face-to-face meetings across a table, the Chinese view meetings as a much more orchestrated affair. Participants are usually seated in a semi-circle of stuffed, antimacassar-covered armchairs, with seats allocated according to seniority (I found myself next to a certain Comrade Wan Fu).

The meeting ritual would commence with the circulation of a kettle and the drinking of green tea, followed by a lengthy interlude of pleasantries, usually aimed at massaging the cadre's top official's ego by recounting stories of his glorious revolutionary past. Said official would then read out a previously agreed script, the main purpose of which, from what I could gather, was to take up as much of the meeting as possible, in order to reduce the amount of time left for any unanticipated questions that might embarrass the top man because he wouldn't have a pre-agreed, pre-prepared answer at the ready. I soon came to understand that these meetings were not business discussions as we understood them, but rather rituals that one had to go through so as to 'give face'. This was followed by a splendid Peking-duck banquet in the evening, with frequent toasts to 'old friends', etc.

As nothing of substance would ever be agreed or discussed during the meetings or banquets, it was necessary to first engage with lower-ranking cadre members, in order to reach agreements that could be included in the senior official's speech. There were times, however, when one would leave a formal meeting and discuss for hours afterwards whether perhaps some coded message had been secreted in the scripted speech.

There was a point on which the Chinese were very clear: there should be no Americans in our tour groups. That much we understood. What we failed to achieve, though, was an agreement from Luxingshe that we could bring in some more tourist groups after the four initial parties they had agreed to. It would take another visit from me before this could be arranged.

In November 1977, I had the pleasure of accompanying our first-ever groups into China. As stated, we used TAROM to fly them there, which proved not to be a totally unproblematic arrangement: on the return trip, a protracted delay at Karachi resulted in a number of guests refusing to re-board the plane. The guests themselves presented challenges, too. Many of them had been waiting nearly all their lives for the opportunity to visit China, and some took up the Chinese offer to accommodate 'special requests' rather too literally. One man in particular, an abattoir owner, insisted that the only reason he had come to China was to see how a local slaughterhouse operated. Despite the fact that our hosts were never going to agree to this, he never let up throughout the trip and caused unbelievable hassle and loss of face, both for our Chinese hosts and myself.

On the plus side, we stayed at the famous Peace Hotel in Shanghai, situated on Nanjing Road, facing the Bund. This beautiful building had been constructed by Sir (Ellice) Victor Sassoon in the late 1930s, when it was known as the Cathay. To our astonishment, a jazz band was still playing in the first-floor bar, having survived the purges of the Cultural Revolution.

I was in the Peace Hotel bar when I received a most unwelcome phone call from the office in London. There had been a fire in my apartment block, caused by Christmas tree lights overloading an electrical socket, and the blaze had spread right up to my flat on the top floor. To make matters worse, the conflagration had coincided with a firemen's strike, which made it clear what my priority would be when I got back to the UK: I was going to have to find somewhere else to live.

CHAPTER 30
BROKEN STRINGS

I had been trying to tune this rather poorly made instrument
and the neck had snapped off, leaving me with an unsightly bundle
of wood and strings.

I N reality, the Bedford 'Green Goddesses' weren't fire engines at all, but self-propelled pumps, designed to suck up huge quantities of water from lakes, rivers and canals and transfer it where required. Thus they were not so much front-line extinguishers of flames as auxiliary vehicles that might prove useful backup in the event of, say, a nuclear attack. With no radio, no cutting equipment and only a single ladder, they were singularly ill equipped to cope with a fire in an apartment block like mine. Nonetheless, because of the UK firemen's strike that began on 14 November 1977 and lasted until January 1978, it was a squadron of Green Goddesses (driven by armed servicemen) that was dispatched to try and quell the flames at my apartment block, opposite Lords' Cricket Ground in St John's Wood.

How had the fire occurred? It turned out that the janitor had installed an enormous Christmas tree in the reception area, where the galaxy of fairy lights with which it was festooned had overloaded the socket, thereby leading to the blaze. Once started, the fire spread quickly and soon found its way, via the lift shafts, to my small apartment at the top of the building.

On first learning of my burnt-out flat, over the phone in Shanghai, I did consider returning to London immediately, but decided there was little point. Besides, it was easier to close my mind off to this piece of bad news in Shanghai, rather than rush straight back to Britain and confront it.

When I eventually got back to the UK, I saw for myself how extensive the damage was. It was going to take a full-scale repair and refurbishment programme to put things right, which was particularly frustrating, since my apartment had been redecorated just a couple of months before the fire. It wasn't much of a comfort when the owners of the block offered me a temporary flat in the basement of the burnt-out building: the iron bars on its windows merely added to the gloom, as did the wrangling with the insurers, who were proving less than helpful.

Meanwhile, I had invited some of the officials I had met in China to come and visit the UK on a study tour, planned for May 1978, during which I hoped to obtain a longer-term and more secure supply of those sought-after Chinese visas. At this time, the Chinese were particularly interested in what life was like in Hong Kong, so I arranged for them to visit the colony before flying to London. They arrived wearing ill-fitting Western clothes – no doubt supplied by 'central casting' in Peking – rather than the customary Mao suits, and we put them up at the Portland Hotel.

During their stay the Chinese officials took part in a series of meetings and visits, including a memorable trip to the House of Commons, where they were hosted by Clement Freud, MP, and the chairman of the House's China Committee. We had always skirted around potentially embarrassing, loss-of-face issues with our Chinese guests, but Clement Freud immediately launched straight into subjects we had hitherto considered taboo, such as human rights in China and why he and other MPs couldn't visit China when they wanted.

To our surprise, the Chinese were well able to handle this kind of situation and avoided being put on the spot by channelling every question through an interpreter, even though they all spoke perfect English. The interpreter would go through the motions of relaying the MP's questions while the rest of the party formulated a response, usually in the form of platitudes or outright gibberish. Even the astute Mr Freud found himself outwitted and outmanoeuvred.

As we were returning our Chinese delegates to their hotel, I spotted someone sitting in the lobby whom I thought I recognised. Once the Chinese were settled in their rooms, I went back to check and, sure enough, there was Ernest Garro, brother of Juan Garro, the young man who had hidden me from the Barnardo's aftercare officer all those years ago, when I was just 17.

It turned out that Juan had married a Dutch lady and was living in the Netherlands, while Ernest was working as a chauffeur, which was why he was waiting in the hotel lobby. I could not help but compare my present circumstance to his: there I was, jetting all around the world and hosting a high-level delegation from China, and there was Ernest, working as a chauffeur. To spare both my own and Ernest's feelings, I didn't explain the reason for my being in the hotel that day, or tell him about my position within the Thomson organisation. I was spared from any more awkwardness when he was called to his car by reception, but I regret not asking for his contact details – as it was, I never did see him or his brother

A Story in Brief

THE VANISHED GIANTS: At one time, Lunn Poly was the largest chain of travel agents in the United Kingdom. The company had grown out of two successful travel agencies established in the 1890s: The Polytechnic Touring Association and Sir Henry Lunn Travel. Both firms were acquired in the '50s by Harold Bamberg's airline group British Eagle, and the names were joined together to produce Lunn Poly, which became a nationalised company in 1971. Next, Harry Goodman's Sunair bought the firm for £175,000 and, a year later, Thomson bought both Sunair and Lunn Poly from Cunard. Though 'bought' is probably not the operative word, since Cunard were required to pay Thomson a sizeable sum to take the companies off their hands. No doubt, though, that Lunn Poly was the jewel in the crown. What a pity, then, that with all that history, names such as Lunn Poly and Britannia Airways should now have disappeared, sacrificed apparently on the anvil of corporate branding. **TOP IMAGE COURTESY: DOUG GOODMAN.**

again. It was a reminder, if ever I needed one, that my course through life could easily have been so different.

Looking after our Chinese guests kept me very busy. Following a round of meetings and a tour of Greater London House, I personally drove the delegation across the length and breadth of the UK, taking them on a tour first of the West Country and then of Scotland, before eventually delivering them back to London and the airport.

It was, I have to say, a revealing trip. Being in such close proximity to my guests over an extended period gave me an insight into how things in China were determined, as well as a better understanding of the etiquette one needed to observe when dealing with the Chinese. Armed with this inside knowledge, I used every available opportunity to work on the guests, with a view to getting as many entry visas as I could – by the time they left I had secured several thousand, with validity extending right into the following year.

In addition, the Chinese invited me to make a reciprocal visit to China, to visit some hitherto closed-off parts of the country: Chungking; the Three Gorges, on the Yangste River; Wanxian City; Wuhan; Wuxi; Suzhou; the Conghua Hot Springs and Canton. Naturally I accepted, and by mid-July I was back in China, flying on an old Russian-made Antonov aircraft from Peking to Chungking, the second city of Sichuan province. The flight itself was uneventful, save for the usual in-flight delight of green tea, served by a stewardess pouring hot water from a kettle. At one point my colleague couldn't find his seatbelt, so the stewardess suggested he hold onto the table instead.

It became clear straight away that Chungking was a very different city to Peking. It stands on a series of steep hills, overlooking the confluence of the Yangtse and Jialing rivers, and a walk through the old part of town left me in no doubt that I was now in the 'real' China. The place was literally teeming with people going about their clearly less-than-easy lives, many of them carrying back-breaking loads up and down the steep banks that led to the river. Meals were taken in the steaming noodle houses that dotted the narrow alleyways and, unlike Peking, no one rode a bike: the hills are far too steep.

Ambling down the main Chungking drag one day, in search of mementos to take home, I found myself surrounded by thousands of onlookers. The crowd was so overwhelming, it had to be held back by baton-wielding militia. The locals found the sight of a 'big-nose' (as they referred to Westerners) utterly fascinating and, for some reason which I never quite fathomed, they found my footwear the most spellbinding sight of all. For my stay in Chungking, I was accorded the special accolade of being accommodated at the State Guest House, located on an elevated position outside the oppressive hustle and bustle of Chungking itself.

Also staying there was a woman called Han Suyin, who, coincidentally, was the subject of an article I had read on the flight from Peking. She was a woman of mixed Belgian-Chinese parentage and, as well as being something of a celebrity in China, had come to the attention of the Western world through her best-selling love story, *A Many-Splendoured Thing*. First published in 1952, it is an account of Han Suyin's affair with the distinguished Times foreign correspondent Ian Morrison, which she wrote in an attempt to cope with her grief after he was killed while reporting the Korean War. In 1955 it was made into a Hollywood film, *Love is a Many-Splendoured Thing*, that the author herself disowned as gross and inappropriate.

Han Suyin's real name was Elizabeth Kuanghu Chow, and she had trained as a doctor in Peking and at the Royal Free Hospital in London. ('Science was our god,' she wrote in her first book, *Destination Chungking*, 'a beneficent god to make China a rich and happy nation.') By the time I met her, she had published two biographies of Mao Zedong and was most certainly considered an 'old friend' of China. I got the impression that she was not only aware of her exalted status, but a teeny bit vain, too: she couldn't wait to get hold of the magazine featuring the article about her, and came running to my room for my copy.

Unfortunately, at this point I received some very disturbing news from London. My office called to inform me that, due to contractual difficulties (with the vessel which had formed the centrepiece of the Thomson cruising programme), the company had decided to pull out of cruising altogether and, since it was the cruising department that was handling all of the reservations for the China programme, tours to China would suffer the same fate.

I knew, as soon as I put the phone down, that I was in an extremely difficult situation. There I was, on a kind of State visit, in the company of high-ranking Chinese officials whose arms I had twisted to secure thousands of extra entry visas, and there were still another 10 days to go until we reached Hong Kong. I sat down to consider my options, and came to the inescapable conclusion that I should leave Thomson and start up my own China tourist business. First, though, I had to explain to my hosts, in a sufficiently gentle manner that they would not lose face, that although Thomson were no longer interested in China, I had come up with the idea of starting my own tourist business instead.

I decided the best thing to do would be to take some of the lower-ranking officials aside and explain my dilemma. On hearing my news they were understandably shell-shocked, as well as being worried about the loss of face that the top leadership – and, by extension, they themselves – would suffer. For the moment, though, our tour continued, in the form of a trip from Chungking down the Yangtse River on board one of the regular passenger steamship services, via Wanxian and the Three Gorges, to Wuhan. It was a fascinating journey, but my mind couldn't help straying to thoughts of how my hosts might react – first, to the loss-of-face, and second, to the as yet half-formed idea of me starting up my own business.

For my part, I felt both embarrassed and vulnerable, but there was no hint whatsoever as to my hosts' attitude; they remained as inscrutable as ever. So, my grand tour continued. We flew from Wuhan to Shanghai and then drove to scenic Wuxi, for a cruise on a launch across Lake Tai Hu, to the garden city of Suzhou. Finally, we took a train south to the Conghua Hot Springs, near Canton, which had a particularly poignant resonance moment for me, since it was here, some four years earlier, that Zhou Enlai had invited Lord Thomson to come and stay. Somehow, being in the same spot completed a physical and emotional circle.

It was in Canton that my visit reached its climax, with a banquet at the East is Red Hotel. My Chinese hosts and I assembled in one of the hotel's private dining rooms, around an enormous, circular dining table adorned with both the Chinese and Union flags. My seat was to the right of the leading official, Mr Wan Fu, and, as the evening wore on, we drank endless mao-tai (a potent liquor made from sorghum) toasts to 'old friends', while enjoying a multiple-course dinner in which the star turn was, once again, the Peking duck.

Delicious though the food was, I was anxious to find out what my hosts thought of my new proposal, being desperate not to leave China without getting a response. Throughout the entire evening, they had given me not a hint of what they were thinking, so, at what I considered to be an appropriate moment towards the end of the meal, I asked, via the interpreter, if Mr Wan had had time to consider my request. After an interminable pause, and with the table now silent in anticipation, he responded quietly and deliberately: "Out of 10,000 happenings, the most difficult is the beginning." It was the Chinese-coded way of letting me know that they would indeed help me with my new endeavour.

The next morning, elated, I took the Lo Wu train bound for the border, where I changed onto the Hong Kong-bound train. I took a deep breath as I remembered that this was the very spot, in 1974, from where I had gazed across into the forbidden and mysterious land of China.

I knew that it couldn't all have been just been a dream, because of the guitar – or at least, the pieces of guitar – I was carrying with me which I had bought in Peking at the Friendship Store, a Chinese version of the Soviet Berioska, or foreign-currency shop. I say 'pieces' because, during my stay in Wuxi, I had been trying to tune this rather poorly made instrument and the neck had snapped off, leaving me with an unsightly bundle of wood and strings which I decided to leave behind, in my hotel wardrobe.

My Chinese hosts, however, would not hear of me discarding this valuable item, so it first re-appeared with my luggage at Suzhou, where I again tried to dispose of it, this time in a dustbin. It resurfaced after Canton, even though I had hidden it under my bed. And as I rummaged through my things en route to the Lo Wu border station, there was that confounded guitar again, now inter-mingled with my luggage. At the time, I naively thought that this episode epitomised the simple and heartfelt honesty of the Chinese people. It was only much later that I came to understand that they were motivated solely by the fear that, if the guitar got thrown away, then someone might accuse them of stealing it.

THOMSON HOLIDAYS REACHING ITS FIRST MILLIONTH PASSENGER 1974

A Story in Brief

UNFINISHED BUSINESS: In 1972, there was a lot of bad publicity about unfinished hotels, and, to be fair, a good proportion of the hotels in our brochure were illustrated not with photographs, but with artists' impressions of what the hotels would look like when finished. Fortunately, Brian Gurnett and I found a gentleman who could turn architectural drawings into visualisations so realistic, it was hard to tell whether the image was a photograph or an artist's impression. Not that clients were fooled once they reached the resort; as a result, I found myself defending numerous trades-description cases all over the country. In Manchester, our legal counsel put forward the plea of autrefois convict, which means a defendant cannot be indicted for a crime for which he has been formerly tried and convicted. It cut no ice with the judge – we still lost. Sole consolation was that George Best had a boutique across from the Court House, and I got his autograph.
IMAGE COURTESY: DOUG GOODMAN.

CHAPTER 31
SHOULD I GO OR SHOULD I STAY?

Like most corporate animals, I preferred to straddle, hoping that I could develop a business opportunity on the side, while maintaining my current security of employment. In reality, though, straddling seldom works.

I had joined Skytours (later Thomson Holidays) on 11 April 1966, at the age of 22, and in the intervening 12 years had risen from humble Benidorm resort rep to the grandly titled position of 'Regional Controller – Rest of the World'. I was travelling the world, all expenses paid, and had regional managers, resort managers and hundreds of resort representatives reporting to me. I was responsible for the contracting of hundreds of hotels worldwide and was in charge not just of hiring local agents, but also of handling logistics once passengers arrived at their destination airport.

At head office we had pretty much written the manual for the efficient running of a tour operating business and, as a result, I suppose I had acquired a heady sense of power and importance that was going to be hard to give up.

I had thought about leaving Thomson on at least two previous occasions – looking back now, I'm glad I didn't. One of my ideas had been to set up a coach-tour service around the main cities of Europe, on a hop-on, hop-off basis. Another involved organising a consortium of hoteliers and UK travel agents in a sort of grand coalition, code-named 'Spectrum', but despite substantial capital commitments from some of the would-be participants, the enterprise had failed to get off the ground.

The end result, then, was I stayed put at Thomson. Like most corporate animals, I preferred to straddle rather than jump, hoping that I could develop a business opportunity on the side, while maintaining my current security of employment. In reality, though, straddling seldom works: the pressing demands of the corporate body nearly always leave you without the energy to pursue your parallel plans.

In some respects, I felt I had delegated so many of my responsibilities at Thomson to the tier below that I was now bored. All the frontier-busting exercises of the past were now over, and with competition from Clarksons now a thing of the past, the company was intent on 'vertical expansion' – i.e., increasing capacity in the bucket-and-spade destinations on the Spanish costas – rather than introducing new products and destinations onto the market.

It had reached the point where the prospect of performing another round of contract-renewing felt akin to painting the proverbial Forth Bridge. I now saw myself as a ground-breaking innovator, rather than a plodding corporate functionary. Forget beach holidays – I wanted to create journeys. At the time, however, I didn't quite know what this ambition would entail, or how long it would take to realise. On the plus side, I had the support, albeit tenuous, of the Chinese, in terms of any new venture on which I might wish to embark. On the negative side, although I had sufficient financial reserves to last six months without a salary, I had no actual capital saved.

Furthermore, I did not have any premises and this was a problem: to become a member of the all-powerful Association of British Travel Agents (ABTA), you were required to have an ABTA-approved place of business, a financial bond and to have been operating for at least three months. To many people this seemed like a bit of a cartel arrangement, not least because ABTA travel agency members were only allowed to sell products from ABTA member tour operators. Any start-up business was going to have great difficulty meeting the entry requirements, and, like many others in my situation, I wondered how I was going to break into the industry with no capital, no premises, no ABTA membership and only a sketchy idea of what I was going to sell.

The solution to this conundrum came from a couple of unusual directions. My first stroke of luck was bumping into a visiting lecturer from the Ball State University of Muncie, Indiana. Every year, Ball State organised European coach tours for its graduating students, and the lecturer needed to find a travel company that could make the necessary arrangements. Initially I thought the best plan would be to take on the task myself, but closer examination of the margins revealed that any profits were likely to be slim, certainly below the £10,000 I reckoned I needed as start-up capital.

It thus occurred to me to go back to the various suppliers for this series of coach tours – i.e., the hotels and the coach company – to see if I could negotiate even better terms. Marko Milasevic (who hailed from Yugoslavia and more latterly worked under me on the Thomson 'City Breaks' programme) offered to help me and, with his negotiating skills, was extremely instrumental in the setting-up of my new company. At some personal risk (he was still employed by Thomson), Marko succeeded in securing substantially better rates on both coach and hotel prices for the Ball State tour, resulting in a much-improved profit margin of £8,000, just £2,000 short of my target.

So far, so good, and it was around this time that my second piece of good fortune materialised: our handling agent in Istanbul was relocating to London, in order to access better medical treatment for his disabled son. Not only that, but he had also bought Sunquest Holidays, a firm of tour operators dating back to the days of John Bloom and his vacations to the Black Sea resorts of Bulgaria and Romania. This meant that the handling agent would be able to assist me with various aspects of starting up my company – namely, approved premises, ABTA accreditation and an ABTA financial bond.

At last, my plan was taking shape. I would piggy-back my intended tour operation, using a conflation of my company name with that of Sunquest Holidays, thereby overcoming the issues of accreditation, bonding and premises. Throw into the mix my £8,000 Ball State profit, and I now had all the basics required to start up a business; the only thing left to do was to decide what products to market and when. Unfortunately, I got both of these elements horribly wrong. This I put down to my rather romantic and idealistic view of China, no doubt stemming from the fact that the version of the country I had seen was the one the authorities had wanted me to see, as opposed to the relentless daily grind that was the reality for the majority of the population in the immediate post-Cultural Revolution period.

The crucial mistake I made (and which I never made again) was to assume that my customers would buy into the same enthusiasm and idealism. I gave my tours fancifully revolutionary and folksy names, such as 'The Barefoot Doctor', 'Every Journey of a Thousand Li' and 'Learn from Tachai'. What's more, I compounded these errors by targeting specialist groups – e.g., farmers and doctors – through their specialist publications. The result was that most of these tours failed miserably.

A WALK IN THE PARK

I launched my 12-page, two-colour brochure in September 1978, distributing a limited supply to local agents and specialist publications, but by the end of October I had not received one solitary booking. By the end of November I had spent half of my capital, on a press launch, printing and distributing the brochures and the salary of my as-yet-unoccupied reservation clerk.

It was now abundantly clear that trying to sell these Chinese tours through the usual High Street travel agencies and specialised publications was simply not going to work. I needed to subject my marketing strategy to a radical rethink, and came to the conclusion that my offerings were too obscure, too esoteric. What people wanted was a more straight-forward, up-and-down description of the arrangements I was selling.

Looking at the range of holidays I was offering, it seemed that the most enticing was the 'Central Kingdom Express', a 42-day rail journey that ran all the way from London (Victoria), via Paris, to Warsaw, Moscow, Ulan Bator, Peking and Canton, selling for an all-inclusive price of £1,795, which covered a stay in Hong Kong and the return flight home. The first of these train excursions was due to depart on the morning of 28 February 1979, and the grim reality was that, as of November 1978, not only did we have no bookings for this once-in-a-lifetime adventure, but funds were running so low that only £4,000 was left in the pot.

It was time for decisive action. I decided that the only option left open to me was to ditch the rest of the China tours and put all my funds and efforts behind the promotion of the Central Kingdom Express'. I sent out press releases and placed a couple of small advertisements in the *Daily Telegraph* – no easy task in itself, since newspapers were now reluctant to accept travel ads, after a number of tour operators had gone out of business and left readers out of pocket.

I remember the figures very clearly: each advertisement cost £600 and I could afford just two. The first of these appeared in the *Daily Telegraph* on the first Saturday of November; it measured just six-by-three inches and the centrepiece was an etching of a steam locomotive, beneath the words 'The Direction of the Company is Proud to Announce the 'Central Kingdom Express' – something I had lifted from Tsar Nicholas II's original guide to the Trans-Siberian Railway.

The night before the paper came out I could hardly sleep, thinking how much rested upon that single advertisement. As soon as the news stand across the road opened up, at 5.00am, I headed over and bought a copy. There is always something special about seeing one's own words in a newspaper for the first time, and that morning I felt like I was engaged in some kind of communion with destiny, while at the same time keeping my fingers crossed and hoping there weren't any spelling mistakes.

The reality, of course, was rather less dramatic. Having opened the newspaper, it took me a long time to find my small advertisement – so long, in fact, that I wondered if it had been left out. Eventually I spotted it in the bottom left-hand corner, looking rather smudged. And so I headed for my office, in the hope that the phones would soon be ringing off the hook with enquiries and bookings. I waited all day, during the course of which I received one single request for a brochure, to an address that (coincidentally) is across the street from where I now live. I delivered the brochure personally that very evening and now pass the same house every single day, recalling those first moments when my hopes were raised, only to be swiftly dashed again.

The following week a few more enquiries did come in, but most calls concerned something other than bookings. Apparently, the steam locomotive depicted in my advertisement was a shunting engine that had never even made its way out of King's Cross, which meant that it was not remotely associated with an 'express' of any type, especially not one going to China. It seemed that every steam-engine anorak in the land had seen my little advertisement and been offended by it, and now wanted to let me know.

The following week we repeated the advertisement in the *Daily Telegraph*, albeit without much enthusiasm. And then, suddenly, it happened: we opened the post and there, on the desk, was a completed booking form, with a £300 cheque as deposit – our first booking! However, no sooner had I begun showing off this prize than the phone rang and the caller informed me, somewhat abruptly, that I might be receiving a booking form and cheque in the post, but that I was to return them both, since they had decided not to proceed.

At the time, this seemed the cruellest cut imaginable, but I was wrong: worse was to follow. During the weeks leading up to Christmas, we did manage to scrape together 22 reservations for the inaugural run of the 'Central Kingdom Express'. Not as good as the 40 we had hoped for, but at least it was a start. During the Christmas holidays, however, disturbing news began to filter through, to the effect that the Chinese had begun amassing thousands of troops on their southern border with Vietnam and even begun shelling a number of Vietnamese positions. The reasons cited for the attack were the mistreatment of Vietnam's ethnic Chinese minority and the Vietnamese occupation of the Spratly Islands, in the South China Sea.

In order to prevent Russian intervention on Vietnam's behalf, Deng Xiaoping warned Moscow, the next day, that China was prepared for a full-scale war against the Soviet Union. In preparation for this conflict, China placed all its troops along the Sino-Soviet border on an emergency war alert, set up a new military command in Xinjiang and evacuated 300,000 civilians from the conflict zone.

At first, I was not particularly concerned by this news, being under the illusion that the Sino-Vietnamese border was a long way from our intended route. However, by 17 February things had taken a more serious turn: Chinese troops had now actually entered Vietnamese territory and the story was dominating the news agenda, with both sides making bellicose noises regarding the imminent prospect of all-out war – hardly a re-assuring situation for my 22 passengers on the 'Central Kingdom Express'. Unsurprisingly, they were talking about pulling out of the journey if hostilities continued.

For me, it was a desperate situation. So precious were these few passengers

A Story in Brief

AN OLD FRIEND OF CHINA: Felix Greene was a British-American journalist who first visited China for the BBC in 1957, and who later produced documentary films depicting life in a number of Communist countries and areas, including Tibet, Cuba and North Vietnam. His critics accused him of giving a very rosy and one-sided view of life in these places, and purposely suppressing information about the extent of starvation in China. I know that when I appeared on the BBC in 1977, following the Thomson breakthrough into China, I felt that the clips shown, of Greene's film *One Man's China*, did present a flattering picture of life in the People's Republic. In 1985, ailing and close to death, Felix (he was the cousin of the author Graham Greene) expressed a wish to visit China one more time. The Chinese authorities asked me to make the travel arrangements for this old friend of China, and we were privileged to do so. IMAGE COURTESY: ROBERT SCURRAH/VOYAGES JULES VERNE.

for my intended new business that I invited them, individually, to a 'reassurance briefing' in my apartment, now partly restored following the fire. This was only a partial success: four of the guests pulled out, citing the fact that they had relatives living in the conflict zone. So I was left with 18 passengers plus a tour escort and the likelihood that, if the Chinese shelling intensified, I would be left with no passengers and no business at all. Cue yet another sleepless night.

Next morning at dawn, as soon as the gates of Regent's Park opened, I went for a long walk to clear my head and to work out what to do next. As if things weren't bad enough, I had paid the Soviets, Mongolians and Chinese in advance for their services, on top of which the train tickets had already been issued, meaning that I wasn't even in a position to give the passengers a refund, should they cancel.

In short, I was on the verge of bankruptcy before my business had even begun. As I wandered around wistfully in the early dawn light, I could see all too clearly that I was going to have to get down on my knees and beg for my job back at Thomson. My new endeavour was turning out to be anything but a simple walk in the park.

CENTRAL KINGDOM EXPRESS PASSENGERS ARRIVING HONG KONG, APRIL 1979

PartThree
ON MY OWN ACCOUNT

THE trouble about journeys nowadays is that they are easy to make but difficult to justify. The earth, which once danced and spun before us as alluringly as a celluloid ball on top of a fountain in a rifle range, is now a dull and vulnerable target. Nor do we get, for hitting it in the right place, the manicure set or packet of Edinburgh rock which formerly rewarded good marksmanship.

All along the line, we have been forestalled, and forestalled by better men than we. Only the born tourist – happy, goggling ruminant – can follow in their tracks with the conviction that he is not wasting his time.

These words ring even truer today than they did in 1935, when the great adventurer Peter Fleming penned them. Is it not a fact that budget airlines and open borders have, like an inexpert belly dancer, revealed too much to us too quickly, with the result that the spinning celluloid ball is a much duller and less alluring object than it once was?

I well recall the occasion when the Huddersfield Town football team visited the Great Wall of China. Asked for his impressions, a player replied: "Once you've seen one wall, you've seen them all." Which neatly sums up, I believe, what happens when overseas travel comes pre-packaged, effort-free and ready-to-consume.

By contrast, Peter Fleming set out in 1935 on a 3,500-mile journey across the roof of the world, travelling from Peking to Kashmir, the exotic 'Venice of the East'. His was an epic expedition to one of the remotest parts of the planet, yet even he ended up uncertain whether, having merely followed in footsteps of others, he deserved the degree of satisfaction he had been hoping for. Furthermore, he lamented that it is only the born tourist, unburdened by lofty

A Story in Brief

AN AMERICAN QUEEN: In October 1993 the *Voyages Jules Verne's Travel Review* interviewed Her Majesty Queen Noor of the Royal Hashemite Kingdom of Jordan. "The story of Queen Noor is well known. An American with Arab blood, and a graduate of Princeton, she found herself working in Jordan, where she met King Hussein. They married and she became Queen of a troubled Middle Eastern kingdom. She has been described as 'preppy' which as far as I understand the term implies a sort of athletic blue-stocking, American style. Perhaps because they both begin with 'pr' there seems to be an inference of primness in the word, too. But I detected no trace of that, although she is clearly a diplomat. Poised, yes, handsome, articulate, a sense of humour as well as a sense of propriety and a certain robustness of manner that is unmistakably American".

expectations of discovery, who can follow in the tracks of others without being afflicted by the notion that he is wasting his time.

It is a point of view with which I have some sympathy. After all, having myself travelled to many of the farthest-flung parts of the world, it seems to me that, very often, one makes a journey as much in the mind as in the flesh. Even so, I'm sure that if Peter Fleming had been around to walk in my own shoes, he would have had no trouble recognising those same remote areas, beyond the Pamirs and Hindu Kush, through which he had travelled some 40 years previously. Somehow, the veil of Communism had cocooned them in a time warp.

That veil was soon to wear thin, however. And so, when I ceased to be an employee within Thomson Holidays and started running my own travel business, Voyages Jules Verne, my goal was to keep that wonderful, celluloid ball permanently aloft and spinning. In short, my intent was not so much to arrange holidays as to create journeys, and in this endeavour, the writings of Peter Fleming, Paul Theroux and Sir Fitzroy Maclean were my inspirations...

CHAPTER 32
MY VISIT TO THE KREMLIN

The building in question was the Great Central Hotel (today
The Landmark) first proposed by Sir Edward Watkin, the director of the
Great Central Railway. The British Railway staff called it the Kremlin.

UNABLE to afford the services of an established public relations company, I was obliged to contract with a start-up company (like mine). Going by the name of PACT, it operated out of a shared suite of open-plan, communal offices called the Barley Mow Centre, in Chiswick.

The company was not exactly overburdened with staff; in fact, PACT was just one person. His name was David Moore and he had organised my earlier China press launch. Sadly, though, these proposed trips had not been a success, as a result of which I now had just £2,000 to spend on a final, last-ditch attempt to drum up interest in my 'Central Kingdom Express' journey.

David clearly doubted there was any news value in this venture for either the travel trade publications or the national press, especially given the meagre amount of money I was putting in. If we were going to get the kind of coverage we wanted, then we needed to piggy-back onto someone else's campaign. After racking his brains for some time, David announced that he had a glimmer of an idea, but that he needed to find the right person to make contact with at the British Railways Board (BRB).

It was early 1979, and the state-owned BRB was receiving a lot of stick from the press with regards to the punctuality of its services, union issues and appalling levels of customer satisfaction. There was a chance, then, that they might welcome a 'good-news' story such as ours, in order to deflect the negative publicity they were getting.

The BRB was housed in what had clearly once been a very fine building opposite Marylebone Station. Interestingly, the building had a connection with

A Story in Brief

ALADDIN'S LAMP: Almost certainly, the Aladdin Lamp Company (where I had started the business) owes its continued existence to Aladdin Industries UK, at Greenford, in west London. The UK manufacturing plant, which opened in 1932, was built to make Aladdin kerosene heaters, lamps and other products for sale within the Empire; the government in this country had imposed strict import tariffs during the Great Depression, in order to protect British industry and jobs. Before then, all Aladdin lamps sold within the Empire had been of American manufacture, even if the wick adjuster knob said London. However, had it not been for the British factory, Aladdin lamps would most likely have gone out of production altogether sometime between the mid 1960s and '70s. A flood which swept through the US factory, in 1954, meant that some of the tooling work was transferred to Greenford. Thereby keeping the Aladdin flame alight. **IMAGE COURTESY: VJV.**

the design of my vessel *Spirit of Chartwell* (the same interior designer Jonathan Peters was engaged), which became the Royal Barge for the Queen's Thames Diamond Jubilee Pageant some 32 years later. It was also just across the road from Dorset Square, where I would later locate the headquarters of my travel company, Voyages Jules Verne.

The building in question was the Great Central Hotel (today the Landmark London). It was first proposed by Sir Edward Watkin, a railway entrepreneur who championed the idea of Marylebone Station (which the hotel was to serve) as the hub of an international railway network, which would run through a tunnel under the Channel and thence spread out, à la the 'Central Kingdom Express', to every corner of Eurasia.

As things turned out, Sir Edward's notion proved a touch over-ambitious (not unlike his proposal for the colossal, never-to-be-completed Watkin's Tower, which he envisaged as a rival for the Eiffel Tower in Paris). When the scheme ran into financial difficulties, the site of the hotel was sold to Sir John Blundell Maple, of the celebrated Maples furniture company. He succeeded where Sir Edward had failed, and oversaw the hotel's opening in 1899.

By the time David and I found ourselves climbing the elegant staircase to the BRB press office, the original stupendous marble facades lay hidden behind plasterboard walls and workaday office partitions. Similarly, the delicate architraves and friezes lay imprisoned behind suspended ceilings. It seemed to me that the state-owned company, in systematically obliterating any traces of its headquarters' previous grandeur, British Railways could not have done a better job of protecting itself against accusations of opulence. No wonder it was referred to as 'The Kremlin' by the people who worked there. Tea was served to us in paper cups by John Smith, the BRB press officer, as we sat in his humble cubicle. Clearly, appearances of austerity needed to be kept up, even in the upper echelons of power.

One thing soon became obvious, as we looked round John's office: the whole room was littered with less-than-flattering press cuttings and you didn't need to be a PR expert to guess that he might be well-disposed to a good-news story, for a change. No sooner had we explained about the 'Central Kingdom Express' than he set about formulating plans for a joint press release, to mark the train's departure on 28 February. Fortunately, John displayed no signs of knowing that the Chinese and Vietnamese were currently shelling each other. For us, it was perfect: not only was the press release being sent out on British Railways paper, but it was also being distributed (at their expense) to their extensive mailing list, thereby lending immediate credibility both to the journey and to my company. That I only had 18 paying passengers was something I felt I had better not reveal.

We agreed on a headline for the press release – 'From London to Hong Kong for 22 pence a mile' – following which I set about arranging the departure ceremony for Victoria Station. With the money I had saved on advertising costs, I splashed out on a buffet at the Grosvenor Hotel for the media and departing passengers, who would be led out to the train by a troop of Scottish pipers.

For the big departure-day bash, I booked a lounge on the hotel's mezzanine floor. There was one thing still bothering me; namely, that the media might realise how few passengers I actually had. The BRB press release was already taking effect: pieces had appeared in the newspapers, and interest was building up to such a point that there was a question of TV crews turning up to cover the event. If I was going to make it feel like I had a complete trainload of passengers, I was going to need a lot more than 18 bodies; in fact, I reckoned I needed at least 150 people on the day. It was with this target in mind that I issued invitations to practically everyone I knew and, in turn, everyone they knew, the aim being to make the room seem so full that the reporters would (a) not realise there were just 18 passengers and (b) be unable to tell a genuine passenger from a mere rent-a-crowd invitee.

Along with some helpers, David Moore and I arrived at the Grosvenor Hotel nice and early on the morning of 28 February. We knew for certain that we could count on our 18 passengers turning up, but we were not sure how many of my rent-a-crowd invitees would show. On top of which, I had no idea if any reporters would make an appearance, with the media perhaps being less reliable than anyone. All we could be sure of was that we had laid on press packs and a sparkling-wine buffet for 150 people.

The event was due to start at 9.00am and finish in time for my passengers to catch the regular boat train that would take them to Folkestone for Calais. I had booked the Band of the Coldstream Guards and found them somewhere to change into their uniforms. I also distributed posters and bunting all around the station and, having sorted out a place for the pipers to stand and play, returned to the reception to find that chaos had broken out, though of the most welcome kind.

The mezzanine lounge was jam-packed with guests, passengers, invitees, print journalists from around the globe and radio hosts and TV crews, all vying for position. The place was one almighty, heaving scrum and, in such a dense crowd, I couldn't even identify my 18 passengers.

The buffet was devoured in next to no time and the sparkling wine downed; my lasting memory is of Kate Adie, the BBC news anchor, picking through the remains of the food. As for the number of interviews I gave that day, I lost count. All I do know is that somehow I managed to con the lot into thinking that they were sharing the room with a whole trainload of passengers about to set off from Victoria Station, London, to Kowloon Station, Hong Kong. Before long, the crush in the lounge became so intense that I decided to get my passengers out to the station platform much earlier than planned.

The morning commuters didn't know what to think as pipers led my 18 passengers, surrounded by hundreds of journalists and various freeloaders, down the main hotel staircase and out through the rear entrance, onto the station concourse. Best of all, I had arranged for the station announcer to read out: "The train about to leave Platform Eight is the 'Central Kingdom Express', calling at Paris; Berlin; Warsaw; Moscow; Irkutsk; Ulan Bator; Datong; Peking; Canton and Hong Kong."

It was a PR triumph, if I do say so myself. Over the next 24 hours, the announcement would be carried on newscasts across the world. As the pipers approached platform eight, the Band of the Coldstream Guards played some roaring tunes, concluding with 'Rule Britannia'. As my dozen-and-a-half passengers, some basking in the unexpected attention more than others, began to board the train, the throng was so great that no one noticed the drabness of the less-than-express-looking British Railways carriage.

It was at that moment, I recall, that I had my first Mel-Brooks-in-*The-Producers* moment: against all expectations and all the odds, I now had an enormous hit on my hands. As the crowds gradually drifted away and the media frenzy slowly died down, I could not again help thinking back to the time in 1974 when I had gazed across, from Hong Kong, into China.

I had dreamed of a train service from London to China and now, at last, it was a reality.

POSTSCRIPT: Over the years, the 'Central Kingdom Express' and its derivatives have carried luminaries such as Germaine Greer, Dennis Waterman, Rula Lenska, Sir Bob Geldof, Paula Yates and Paul Theroux, the latter of whom went on to write a book about the journey, entitled *Riding the Iron Rooster*.

Germaine Greer was not our only famous feminist passenger. Indeed, one of our earliest complaints came from Marilyn French, author of *The Women's Room*. (French is mentioned in the lyrics of Abba's song *The Day Before You Came*, in the line: 'must have read a while / the latest one by Marilyn French / or something in that style'.) Her name meant nothing to me at the time, but I could see that she knew how to compile a good complaint letter: I battled with her for months before she was satisfied.

Of all the complaints I received, I shall never forget my first, from a certain Doctor Shackleton Bailey. The principal cause of his discontent was that the journey was too rushed, with too many early starts. There was, he lamented, not even time for a leisurely bowel movement.

CHAPTER 33
ALADDIN'S MAGICAL LAMP

As I sat in the forlorn silence of my borrowed premises and
contemplated a phone that refused to ring, I couldn't understand
why I had no customers.

TO be fair to Ali, the handling agent who had relocated to London from Istanbul, he did agree to allow me to use his office and Association of British Travel Agents (ABTA) licence at a time when I still had some authority in Thomson. I expect he thought his offer would never actually be taken up and that, once I had considered the full consequences of leaving Thomson, I wouldn't actually go through with it. Now that I had left my employers and arrived at his headquarters, in the former Aladdin Lamp factory in west London, I sensed he regretted having ever made the offer, which explained both why he was being evasive and why my 'Central Kingdom Express' receipts were not being released from his account.

Secretly, he must have calculated that if my venture went belly-up, then he would need some form of insurance, in the form of my takings. That these seemed to be under lock and key in his vaults was both frustrating and disappointing. At the same time, I could not afford to lose sight of the fact that Ali was the only person I knew who was both able – and prepared – to help me.

It was true that, while at Thomson, I had been considered something of a big shot by agents like Ali. After all, he had done well out of the contracts I had given him, in arranging transfers, excursions, local guides and hotel accommodation for the thousands of tourists we sent to Turkey each year. However, I wasn't at Thomson any more, as I was all too aware. It seemed that I had made the mistake of confusing Oriental largesse for genuine friendship and, all of a sudden, the tables were turned. I was now reduced to the status of a paper tiger.

"As a matter of fact, I'm going right through to Hongkong!"

A Story in Brief

A TICKET TO RIDE: Meet Vic Allan, the ex-Thomson man who worked out how to write a train ticket all the way from London to Hong Kong: "In February 1979, while I was at the ABTA Convention in Los Angeles, I turned on the television in my hotel room, and saw, to my amazement, the departure of the inaugural 'Central Kingdom Express'. The passengers were crossing the concourse at Victoria Station, led by the Band of the Coldstream Guards – a brilliant piece of PR arranged by Philip. I helped a little, designing the posters and providing reference photographs from which Robert Scurrah produced great artwork for the brochures (witness 'The Raj Express', and 'The Cape to Cairo' etc). My own company Trainseurope Ltd. had the honour of providing much of the rail ticketing for the journey. In fact we still do, although nothing quite matches the excitement of that first departure all those years ago."

It was with a great show of magnanimity that Ali had placed a small office at my disposal and assured me that until I had my own place and ABTA licence, all I would have to pay was the telephone bill. Since then, however, all my attempts to gain Ali's attention, in order to spell out the terms of our understanding on paper, had proved fruitless. Suddenly, the undertakings on which I had based my decision to leave Thomson were starting to look a bit fragile – in short, it felt like payback time.

In the blink of an eye, the roles had been reversed and now it was I who was vulnerable and required Ali's assistance. There was no doubt that, with the 'Central Kingdom Express', I had a potential hit, but my elation was tempered by the realisation that I was now dependent, to a rather uncomfortable degree, on Ali. I had hoped that, after all the hoopla at Victoria Station, I would be swamped with bookings, but I wasn't. I and my passengers may have been splashed all across the newspapers and the airwaves, but this had not translated into actual business.

As I sat in the forlorn silence of my borrowed premises and contemplated a phone that refused to ring, I couldn't understand why I had no customers. After all, the 'Central Kingdom Express' story had been covered by the world's media, among them the *Los Angeles Times*, *The New York Times* and T*he Christian Science Monitor*. The coverage that gave me the most pleasure was a cartoon by 'JAK' (Raymond Jackson) in the *London Evening Standard*; it showed some rather posh-looking passengers sipping champagne and caviar in a sumptuous railway carriage, with a route map of the 'Central Kingdom Express' on the carriage wall and a Chinese peasant trying to get into the compartment, telling the horrified occupants of the compartment: "As a matter of fact, I'm going all the way to Hong Kong". This was all good publicity, of course, but it was not backed up by any kind of commercial success.

Meanwhile I had earned that ultimate media accolade, coverage in China's *People's Daily*. This being the political mouthpiece of the People's Republic, I felt sure that my backer, Wan Fu in Peking, would have read the article and that its publication conveyed official approval for my venture. At that time, articles in the *People's Daily* were read not so much for what they said, as for what they implied. If a large number of articles appeared in the paper devoted to a particular political idea or figure, then this was taken as a sign that the idea or official was on the way up. I thus knew that my mention in the *People's Daily* would have given 'face' to my old friend Wan Fu, and done me no harm either.

Thankfully, too, things began to change on the sales front. The first sign of this was when a letter arrived from Los Angeles, simply addressed 'Central Kingdom Express, London'. While the British public and travel trade seemed unimpressed by my trans-continental railway venture, it emerged that Americans were positively beating a path to the door of US tour operators, who, in turn, wanted to represent me in their market.

In addition to wanting to book places on the 'Central Kingdom Express', these transatlantic travellers also offered me a way out of my situation with Ali. Although I could not trade in the UK on my own account, since I was not an ABTA member, the Americans couldn't give a proverbial damn about my ABTA membership, or lack thereof: they just wanted to book places on my train.

It was just the break I needed. In next to no time, I appointed two US sales agents – one on the West Coast, in California, and the other on the East Coast, in Philadelphia – whereupon the bookings started to roll in so fast, I could hardly meet the demand. Rather than having the money paid into Ali's ABTA-registered account, I asked my American agents to hold on to any payments until I had found my own premises, formed my own company and opened my own bank account. Already, I was envisaging what my new shop display might look like. It had to be something that evoked a theme: an image of great journeys and the 'golden age' of travel, rather than just bog-standard bucket-and-spade holidays.

That, however, was for the future. In the real world, a shortage of cash was the more pressing issue: in order to secure my new premises, I had to pay three months' rent up front, give personal guarantees (i.e., my apartment), decorate my new headquarters and print and distribute a new brochure. As the last of the available capital had been used up in promoting the 'Central Kingdom Express', I was left with no option but to borrow money from a friend in return for shares in the new company. (I was able to pay him back after three months.)

It was only once all this was in place that the time came to reveal to Ali how I would be extricating myself from his domain. To be fair, he made no fuss; I presumed his ambitious 'Turkish delight' emporium idea (which he intended running alongside his holiday company in the Aladdin Lamp factory) had bombed and that everyone was going to be vacating the factory; and indeed, he did subsequently relocate his company, Sunquest Holidays, to Bond Street. Meanwhile, we moved to our new London premises on Glentworth Street, close to Baker Street – a handsome Art Deco building, which came with a lovely roof-top garden.

Many years later, I had cause to wonder what happened to all Ali's unused and expensive-looking confectionery-making equipment, when the Aladdin Lamp factory building got taken over by DIY chain B&Q. As things worked out, I only saw him once more, on a visit to his fashion boutique (where he had now based Sunquest Holidays) in Bond Street when I tried, yet again, to retrieve the money of mine that was still sitting in his account. This attempt, like all the others, ended in failure; in response to my request for the sum of money I felt I was owed, he presented me with a bill for telephone calls which, miraculously, came to the same amount!

As far as I know, following the demise of his Turkish delight project, Ali's fashion business suffered the same fate and Sunquest was duly sold. One of his favourite spots, the Playboy Club, on London's Park Lane, was closed down, and Ali eventually returned to Turkey, where he later died. Despite our differences, I was sad to hear the news of his death. My dealings with him had provided me with useful experience at a crucial crossroads in my life. It had marked the point where I had started on the way up and he had, sadly, begun to travel in the opposite, downwards direction.

DEMOCRACY WALL: 1979 VJV ORGANISED VOGUE MAGAZINE PHOTO-SHOOT

A Story in Brief

THE FIRE GOD SYMPHONY: In October 1978, the Chinese poet Huang Xiang decided to take out of concealment some political poems he had written during the Mao years. Furthermore, he resolved to go to Peking to show them off, despite the dangers of expressing anti-Mao sentiments. Soon, word of his plan got around, and three friends decided to accompany him on the 1,500-mile trip to the capital. On 11 October 1978, with a bucket of flour paste, they proceeded to an alley off Wangfujing (East Wind Street) and began pasting hundreds of Huang Xiang's poems, including his epic work 'The Fire God Symphony.' A curious crowd soon gathered, spilling out onto the avenue. Sympathisers linked arms to protect the four from the surge of the crowd. Huang Xiang, now encouraged, recited all of his poems from memory (some six hundred lines). That night people crowded the alley trying to read the poems by torchlight – and so was born Democracy Wall.

IMAGE COURTESY: VOGUE MAGAZINE.

CHAPTER 34
RENDEZVOUS IN CHRISTIANIA

While people may be pleasantly thrilled by dangerous escapades performed by someone else, what they really aspire to is adventure that might, in the right circumstances, be within their reach.

WHEN wondering what name to choose for my company, the first idea that came into my head was 'Bradshaw's'. On reflection, I didn't think that many of my potential customers would make the connection with the man who invented railway timetables (George Bradshaw), so in the end I went for 'Jules Verne' instead. Before ruling out 'Bradshaw's' altogether, however, I conducted some research, in order to find who owned the title or copyright of the name. It turned out, according to John Price, then the compiler of the Thomas Cook European Rail Timetable, that it was owned by the confidential printing (i.e., for the Royal Mint and government) company McCorquodale and that the McCorquodale logo had even incorporated the Bradshaw imprint.

At the time, I was trying to sweet-talk John into listing my 'Central Kingdom Express' in the Timetable, which I was convinced would ensure its success. Alas, my train service got only a passing mention and I had to wait to seize one of the few advertising slots instead. You may remember that I had swiped a copy of Thomas Cook's famous timetable from Herbert Harrison's desk in 1965 and had carried it with me ever since. That book meant a lot to me and, in the hope of getting my rail service included in it, I contacted McCorquodale and made two interesting discoveries.

First, they had been trying for years, unsuccessfully, to protect their copyright in India, where Bradshaw's Continental Railway Guide – for decades a rival to the Thomas Cook publication – was being published by someone else entirely. Second, and more relevant to me, they would have no objection to me keeping the Bradshaw name alive.

Many years later, the journalist and former MP Michael Portillo did just that, with a series of excellent television programmes on Bradshaw's work. This led me to reflect on the strange coincidence whereby, in the same period of time, in the small town of Christiania (Oslo today), both George Bradshaw and Jules Verne chanced to use the services of the 19th-century travel guru Thomas Bennett.

While in a philosophical frame of mind, I can't help reflecting on the nature of travel itself. It seems to me that, once we have decided to go somewhere, everything about the journey is thereafter subject to constraints that are completely beyond our control. Time, holiday allocations, other people, money, aeroplanes, trains – all have to be harnessed to meet our individual requirements. Once we have secured the time, the money and the permission to make the journey, we fully expect to be able to reach our destination, whether by road, air or rail.

To find out what is available today, we almost inevitably consult the internet. However, before computers, what did we do? We consulted a timetable – well, we might have made a telephone call, but the person at the other end of the line would be consulting a timetable. The reality is, no mass transport system can function without the complex considerations of time and space. Obvious enough, yet we overlook the fact that, behind every aeroplane on a runway and every train at a platform, there is an intricate organisation at work, tasked with achieving maximum mobility at minimal risk.

Imagine, then, the effect that the introduction of a railway timetable must have had on the psyche of the nation. In the beginning, the whole point of railways had been to transport goods more quickly between the port of Liverpool and the mills of Manchester. Out of this had arisen the unexpected and hugely lucrative phenomenon of passenger travel – the Liverpool and Manchester Railway (L&MR), inaugurated in 1830, was the world's first inter-city passenger railway in which all the trains were timetabled and hauled, for the most part, by steam engines – which soon spread down to London and Birmingham. By 1839, when Bradshaw published his first guide, train services were beginning to criss-cross the UK; by 1855, there were over 8,000 miles of railway track between all the major cities.

All of a sudden, there was a nationwide rush towards rail travel, engineered by a mass of competing interests and looking ever more messy and chaotic. What was needed, and fast, was a unifying, controlling element – this turned out to be Bradshaw's Railway Guide.

George Bradshaw (1801–53), English cartographer, printer and publisher, was born near Salford, in Lancashire. On leaving school, he was apprenticed to an engraver, after which, in 1820, he set up his own engraving business in Belfast, returning in 1822 to Manchester, where he again set up as an engraver and printer, principally of maps. His first published work was a map of his native county, followed in 1830 by Bradshaw's Maps of Inland Navigation, a work detailing the canals of Lancashire and Yorkshire.

At the time, no one had the slightest inkling that the canal system was about to be superseded, save for Bradshaw. Early on, he realised that the railway system was an unstoppable force, and so, on 19 October 1839, he published, in Manchester, the world's first compilation of railway timetables. This cloth-bound tome cost sixpence to buy and was titled Bradshaw's Railway Time Tables and Assistant to Railway Travelling. The next year, the title was abridged to the more digestible Bradshaw's Railway Companion and the price doubled (i.e., to one shilling).

This was the start of a thriving business. Before long, new volumes were being published at regular intervals, together with special seasonal supplements. It is interesting to note that the first Bradshaws were published before the introduction of 'railway time' in November 1840. Prior to this regional standardisation of time, based on the time in London (i.e., Greenwich Mean Time), local time was used across the country, as if following a sundial.

Once out of the sidings, there was no stopping the Bradshaw express. In December 1841, in response to a suggestion from his London agent, William Jones Adams, Bradshaw reduced the price of his timetables to the original sixpence and began to issue them monthly, under the title Bradshaw's Monthly Railway Guide. Many railway companies, who produced their own timetables, were unhappy with this development, to which Bradshaw responded by becoming a railway shareholder and by putting his case before the various companies' annual general meetings. Before long, the guides, in their familiar yellow wrappers, became so strongly linked with their publisher that, for Victorians and Edwardians, the term 'railway timetable' became almost universally supplanted by 'Bradshaw' (in the same way as one might call a raincoat a Mackintosh, a vacuum cleaner a Hoover or, today, a smartphone an iPhone).

By 1845, the eight-page edition of 1841 had grown to 32 pages; by 1898, it was a fulsome 946 pages long. Curiously, in April 1845, the issue number suddenly jumped from 40 to 141, and while Bradshaw maintained that this was a simple error, others have wondered if he might have been trying to attract more advertisers by making the publication seem more venerable. Either way, the new numbering remained in place.

The next step was to go international. With the realisation that travel through continental Europe was now within easy reach, the year 1847 saw the publication of Bradshaw's Continental Railway Guide, which eventually grew to over 1,000 pages and included not just timetables, but also guidebook information and a hotel directory. The publication eventually achieved immortality through its appearance in Around the World in Eighty Days (1873), in which Verne writes of his protagonist, Phileas Fogg: "Under his arm might have been observed a red-bound copy of Bradshaw's Continental Rail and Steam Transport and General Guide, with its timetable showing the arrival and departure of steamers and railways."

By the time of Bradshaw's death, in 1853, his railway guides had become a national institution, quoted in contemporary novels and on the music-hall stage, as in the chorus of an 1876 hit by Fred Albert & Henry S. Leigh:

> *Birmingham and Sandringham, Ulverton and Wolverton,*
> *Dorchester and Porchester, Rochester and Ryde;*
> *Arlington and Darlington, Torrington and Warrington,*
> *She said she'd sure to find it in my Bradshaw's Guide.*

Even after Bradshaw's death, his timetables went from strength to strength. In 1865, Punch magazine heaped praise upon his publications, pro-claiming: "Seldom has the gigantic intellect of man been employed upon a work of greater utility."

And still the guides kept getting bigger. As the railway system expanded and some 150 different railway companies began offering routes across the country, every single change was recorded in the 'Bradshaw', which became the standard manual for rail travel well into the 20th century.

It wasn't until 1923 that the guide began to decline, not so much in quality as in usefulness. In this year, in excess of 100 railway companies were amalgamated into the so-called 'Big Four' railways: the Great Western; the London, Midland and Scottish; the London and North Eastern; and the Southern. Thus there were fewer individual company timetables, on top of which three of the Big Four transferred their timetable production to Bradshaw's publisher, Henry Blacklock & Co., between 1923 and 1939. The presentation and style of the Bradshaw did not adapt to changing tastes, retaining its florid Victorian formality well into the Edwardian era and beyond. As Sherlock Holmes observed, "the vocabulary of Bradshaw is nervous and terse, but limited'".

By the 1950s, it was clear that the Bradshaw's diminishing effectiveness, together with its dated presentation – a style, ironically, that was later to become fashionable again, when everything 'retro' became chic – meant that its survival was beginning to look increasingly unlikely. The final nail in the coffin came when the Big Four were nationalised in 1948 and became British Railways, whose six regions initially likewise used Henry Blacklock & Co. to produce their own timetables, before moving on to other publishing houses.

Attempts to restyle the Bradshaw were made from 1955, but never came to fruition. In the end, it cost more to buy a single Bradshaw than to buy a complete set of British Railways regional timetables. The writing was on the wall, and May 1961 saw the publication of the last-ever edition, No. 1521. (Its Continental counterpart had ceased even earlier, in 1939.)

It is more than half a century since the Bradshaw's guide was laid to rest and yet, in a strange way, it lives on, if only as a nostalgic symbol of the excitement associated with travel. Somehow, its accuracy and reliability did not in any way detract from the sense of adventure that comes with the discovery of new places. With a comforting anonymity and a beguiling authority, it served to reassure, never lecturing, hectoring or selling. Its legendary precision is commemorated even today in India, where the main timetable for Indian Railways is still known as Newman's Indian Bradshaw.

The fact was that everybody – simply everybody – used a Bradshaw. In Daphne du Maurier's *Rebecca*, the second Mrs de Winter remarks: "Some people have a vice of reading Bradshaw's. They plan innumerable journeys across the country for the fun of linking up impossible connections." And in G. K. Chesterton's *The Man Who Was Thursday,* Gabriel Syme declaims: "No, take your books of mere poetry and prose; let me read a timetable, with tears of pride. Take your Byron, who commemorates the defeats of man; give me Bradshaw, who commemorates his victories. Give me Bradshaw, I say! Without a Bradshaw, where in the world would we be?" Even Bram Stoker's *Count Dracula* reads an 'English Bradshaw's Guide' when planning his voyage to England.

Of course, if Bradshaw was the patron saint of Voyages Jules Verne, its founding father was the author of *Around the World in Eighty Days*. Everyone knows the name of the great French writer, which made it a commercially sound choice for a travel company. Even though Jules Verne's books are relatively little read today, in the face of competition from Captain Kirk or Luke Skywalker, his reputation, and the titles of his books, still have the power to conjure up a little magic in the hearts and minds of modern-day travellers.

What of the man himself? Born in 1828 to lawyer Pierre Verne and his wife, Sophie Allote de la Fuÿe, who came from a family of shipbuilders and sea captains, the young Jules Verne was brought up in Nantes. The family spent summers in a country house in Brains, just outside the city, on the banks of the Loire. As he describes in his autobiographical short story, *Souvenirs d'Enfance et de Jeunesse*, the sight of ships navigating the river was the beginning of a lifelong infatuation with travel and exploration.

It is thought that these early leanings may have been fostered by one of Jules'

A Story in Brief

THE FIRST FLIGHT: On what day exactly, was civil aviation born? According to Peter Jackson, author of The Sky Tramps, the first daily international passenger service, operated over a sustained period, began on 25 August 1919. That was the date on which Lieutenant Bill Lawford flew one passenger – plus cargo of newspapers, leather, grouse and Devonshire cream - from London to Paris. Mind you, the charter flight phenomenon had already got off the ground six months earlier, when Sir Woodman Burbidge, of Harrods, hired an ex-World War I bomber to fly him from Hendon to Brussels, for a business meeting. Technically, this flight was illegal, since it contravened a wartime ban on civil flying that was still in force; that said, it established, early on, the aviation industry's disdain for bureaucracy. Rather less grandly, my first flight was a 30-minute trip over London in 1956. It cost ten shillings – and everyone was sick.

teachers at boarding school: the inventor Brutus de Villeroi, who later became famous for creating the US Navy's first submarine, the Alligator. It is even possible that De Villeroi inspired Verne's conceptual design for the Nautilus in *Twenty Thousand Leagues under the Sea*, although no direct exchanges between the two men have been recorded. Such was Verne's fascination with adventure that there is an apocryphal tale about him stowing away on a ship bound for the West Indies, only for his voyage to be cut short when he found his father awaiting him at the first port of call.

What is beyond dispute, however, is that Jules and his brother would often hire a boat on the river and that, on one of these outings, found themselves stranded downstream when a plank came loose and the boat sank. Stuck on a small islet, they were forced to wait until low tide to wade across to the mainland and walk home. It is far more likely that Verne's genius sprang from this kind of childhood drama, rather than from anything that happened to him in adulthood.

Having survived his ordeal on the island, Jules went from school to university in Paris, in order to study law. His first forays into literature were libretti for operettas, but his contributions to the literary magazine *Musée des Familles* demonstrated that his peculiar gift was for adventure stories involving extra-ordinary voyages, which, for all their originality and fantastical nature, were based on hard scientific and geographical fact.

However, when his father discovered what he was doing, he promptly withdrew all financial support and Verne was forced to become a stockbroker, although he continued to pursue his literary ambitions, helped by advice from fellow authors Victor Hugo and Alexandre Dumas. In 1857, Verne married Honorine de Viane Morel (note the name), a widow with two daughters, with whose encouragement he continued both to write and seek out a publisher.

Verne's first novel was *Five Weeks in a Balloon*, which came out in 1863. He knew nothing about ballooning, nor had he ever been to Africa, but is thought instead to have drawn on the works of others, in particular two pieces of writing by Edgar Allan Poe: 'The Balloon-Hoax', a fake account, originally published by Poe in a New York newspaper, of an Englishman accidentally crossing the Atlantic in a balloon; and 'The Unparalleled Adventures of One Hans Pfaall', a short story, again published as if fact, about a trip to the moon in a balloon. It is interesting that, rather than Frenchmen, many of Verne's protagonists are Englishmen, a reflection of their reputation as explorers and imperialists.

Verne's publisher was Pierre-Jules Hetzel; having been introduced by the writer Alfred de Bréhat, the pair enjoyed a professional partnership that lasted most of their lives. Hetzel's editing skills undoubtedly played a part in Verne's success, and it was Hetzel who introduced Verne to Nadar (Gaspard-Félix

Tournachon), founder of the Society for Encouragement of Aerial Locomotion by Means of Heavier-Than-Air Craft and from whom Verne gleaned much of the information that would give his writings their secure scientific foundation.

The reality was, Verne was neither a scientist nor a globetrotter: he was far more interested in stories and their power to amaze and inspire than he was in technological detail or in geographical or anthropological authenticity. His genius emanated from the power of his imagination, which he employed in order to create a marriage of fiction and ideas. Much of the research for his works was accomplished through reading about and discussing the scientific breakthroughs of the day with knowledgeable people. He wrote about the general more than the particular and, although he correctly foresaw space exploration and other scientific advances, a great deal of what he predicted never came to pass.

In the decade after 1863, Verne wrote many of the classic novels for which he is best remembered. He followed *Five Weeks in a Balloon* with two books – *The English at the North Pole* and *The Desert of Ice* – featuring Captain Hatteras. Then came *Journey to the Centre of the Earth*, one of his best-loved works, and perhaps the only one that can still take us into genuinely uncharted territory, given that the earth's core remains unbreached by man.

(There is also a 'lost' novel from this period: *Paris in the Twentieth Century*, a dystopian tale written in 1863 and set in a world of skyscrapers, high-speed trains, cars, computers and a global communication network. Hertzel refused to publish the novel, deeming it too pessimistic and scarcely credible; the result was that the manuscript lay undisturbed in a safe until its rediscovery, in 1989, by Verne's great-grandson.)

Undoubtedly, the imagination of readers in Verne's lifetime was most actively stimulated by *Around the World in Eighty Days*, written in 1872. This is the story that is most relevant to the genesis of Voyages Jules Verne just over a century later, demonstrating that, while people may be pleasantly thrilled by dangerous escapades performed by someone else, what they really aspire to is adventure that might just, given the right circumstances, be within their reach.

The story begins in London, on 2 October 1872. Phileas Fogg, a wealthy English gentleman and bachelor of London, and his newly employed French valet, Passepartout, are about to attempt to go around the world on a 20,000 pounds wager, an enormous amount at the time and equal to half of Fogg's fortune. The challenge has been set by Fogg's friends at the Reform Club, following a discussion over a newspaper article claiming that, with the construction of a new railway line in India, a circumnavigation of the globe is now possible in 80 days.

The two bold adventurers decide from the outset to travel light. When they depart on their journey, they carry only a carpet bag holding for each of them two shirts and three pairs of stockings, a raincoat, a travelling cloak, a spare pair of shoes, 20,000 pounds in cash and, of course, most importantly, Bradshaw's Continental Railway, Steam Transit, and General Guide.

The name 'Phileas Fogg' is a play on words, alluding to England's famously overcast climate; it is also thought to refer to an American traveller and author, William Perry Fogg, who went around the world and described his tour in a series of letters to the newspaper *The Cleveland Leader*.

In terms of character, certainly Fogg is the typical (one might say stereo-typical) Englishman, with a facial expression described as "repose in action" and a modest, mathematically precise approach to life. One can detect, in Verne's writing, the ever-present Gallic ambivalence towards the English, expressed both through amusement at Fogg's detachment and admiration for his sanguineness. Overall, Fogg comes across as an unquestionably heroic figure, as does his faithful retainer, Passepartout, with whose help he prevents the woman he eventually marries – Fogg does have feelings, you see – from performing the ritual of self-immolation in India.

From start to finish, the story is punctuated with one extraordinary event after another: mutinies; attacks by Sioux Indians in America; the purchase of an elephant to make up for the absence of a railway connection, etc. There is even a point at which the London detective, Fix, tries to arrest Fogg on suspicion of being an international bank robber. There are countless other escapades, too, although these do not include travel by air-balloon: Fogg considers the idea at one point, but rejects it. All of which means that, when they return to London, just past the deadline, it seems that the bet is lost and poverty (comparatively speaking) beckons. However, Passepartout realises that, by crossing the International Date Line, they gained a full day and so are the victors.

In contrast with many of Verne's other books, *Around the World in Eighty Days* is not really about the future. It is far more about the possibilities of travel in reasonable comfort, which 19th-century technological innovation and con-struction – trans-continental railways and the opening of the Suez Canal – have made possible. Verne is heralding the dawn of international travel for the middle classes, rather than just for explorers and aristocrats; indeed, some claim the book was inspired by a Thomas Cook advertisement in 1872, for a real-life, seven-month journey around the world.

Ironically, despite all his exciting visions for the future, Verne does not seem to have been an optimist himself and was circumspect, to say the least, about the benefits of modern technology. Indeed, many of the happy endings in his books result from the pleas of his publisher, Hetzel, who knew that stories that ended well would sell better.

An interesting postscript to the story is the fact that the bank from which Fogg had withdrawn the 20,000 pounds was Barings, the institution that, a century later, the broker Nick Leeson was to help bring down. It is also worth pointing out that Mike Todd's 1956 film adaptation of Verne's story includes a memorable journey by hot-air balloon, which never happened in the book.

THE SEND OFF: THE LONDON-PEKING MOTOR CHALLENGE – HYDE PARK 1990

A Story in Brief

GRAHAM ROCK: One Challenger who deserves special mention, is the journalist Graham Rock, driving a Times-sponsored Mercedes, and accompanied by his wife Joan. Graham sent regular, amusing pieces back, and his charming company was enjoyed by everyone. Soon afterwards, though, he died at the young age of 56, from cancer. As the founding editor of the *Racing Post* in the 1980s, Graham had inspired a new generation of racing journalists. He was a betting expert, and paddock commentator for BBC television, as well as a jockeys' agent, guiding the South African Michael Roberts to the British jockeys' title in 1992. At the end, he wrote these poignant words: "I drove home with Joan. The sun was inching towards the horizon. We cruised through the flat East Anglian landscape, fields and trees brushed with scarlet and gold. The magic of the moment flashed before my eyes every few minutes. I remember thinking that I could die a happy man. Nothing has changed since."

CHAPTER 35
THE EMPORIUM OF TRAVEL

Would it be fanciful to liken the threshold of a travel company office with a frontier? Passing from a wind-scoured London street into a room of palms, Chesterfield sofas, and travel posters from the golden age of travel.

I N business, the distinction between genuine innovation and clever marketing is sometimes a fine one. In the travel industry, that distinction is finer still, due to the intangible nature of the product. Customers buy experiences, which in turn become memories. By the late 20th century, of course, there was little left to discover in the world. Pretty much all paths were well-trodden, in one way or another. However, to me, travel means far more than just reaching a destination: I feel that the manner of departure and arrival is at least as important as the actual being there and it was my belief, when I started up Voyages Jules Verne, that this aspect had been overlooked, amid the rush for cheap, competitive travel in the '50s and '60s.

A week of cheap sun on the Costa Brava was all very well, but, in the end, where was the excitement and the adventure? Sure, for those people with the inclination, time and money, it was always possible to hitch a ride on a cargo ship or canoe the length of the Zambezi. Most of us, however, don't get that kind of opportunity; furthermore, when it comes to danger, we would probably prefer to experience it vicariously, through the pages of a book. Nonetheless, it was clear that people who weren't up to paddling a dugout down an African river still craved adventure of a sort. Which is why, back in the 1970s, the most important development for the travel industry entrepreneur was the rediscovery of the 'journey'.

Having served my apprenticeship in this business, I had come to the conclusion that in order to survive, let alone thrive, you needed to adapt and innovate. Nothing demonstrated this more clearly than the way in which Thomson had

A Story in Brief

HO CHI MINH'S TRAIL: In 1992, Alexander Frater was the chief travel correspondent for the *Observer*, and author of *Beyond the Blue Horizon*, the story of the Imperial Airways route to Australia. On returning from a VJV trip to Vietnam, he was asked, "Would you go back?", to which he responded, "Like a shot". Before his visit he had the pre-conceived notions – common, as he put it, to anyone of his age – "of war, violence, deforestation, defoliation... then total poverty... a nation that had won theoretically and in fact lost." To his surprise and pleasure, the scars of war had all but vanished under a carpet of dense tropical lushness. As for the former American airfields, they had been preserved by the Vietnamese, he reckoned, as an ironic commentary on the conflict. The war itself, though, was a distant thunder. "One of the most beautiful countries I have ever seen," he concluded.

turned down the opportunities presented to them in China. Maybe my unusual upbringing stood me in good stead, too. I viewed things from the point of view of an onlooker, rather than as an active participant, and could see that change was in the air and that the travel industry needed to respond to people's secret desire for adventure.

From the outset, the object of setting up Voyages Jules Verne was to create 'journeys', rather than holidays or tours. What's more, the way in which these journeys were presented had to have a bit of theatre about it, a bit of music hall song-and-dance (although none of the cheap, end-of-pier stuff). This was one of the reasons why getting the right company name was so important. I had to come up with something that evoked exotic travel while also suggesting that this was an organisation with pedigree: the kind of institution that would be a byword for reliability and discretion.

Furthermore, the name had to appeal to the thinking traveller, rather than just the mass of holidaymakers; it needed to convey a hint of one-upmanship. For me, 'Jules Verne' had a whiff of excitement and sulphur about it, the drawback being that it sounded rather banal when used in tandem with the English words 'travel' or 'journeys'. Thus, the altogether more cosmopolitan, French-sounding 'voyages' was chosen. This is how Voyages Jules Verne (VJV) was born.

It should be mentioned at this point that Jules Verne's *Les Voyages Extraordinaires* is a series of 54 novels – including all his most famous ones – published between 1863 and 1905. According to Verne's editor, Pierre-Jules Hetzel, the aim was "to outline all the geographical, geological, physical and astronomical knowledge amassed by modern science and to recount, in an entertaining and picturesque format... the history of the universe". That the books succeeded in this aim was due to Verne's meticulous attention to detail, coupled with his sense of wonder and exploration: a matter of science joining up with a rattling good yarn.

Verne's stories formed a rich pool of inspiration from which we at Voyages Jules Verne drew. In addition, the company name readily lent itself to a design theme. Out of late Victorian and Art Deco, it was the latter style that eventually won, with its modernist lines and its echoes of the golden age of travel in the 1920s and '30s. This was reflected not just in our brochures and poster designs, but in the look of our offices as well.

Our address was 10 Glentworth Street, near Baker Street, and we had moved there in October 1978, after a brief spell at Ali's Aladdin Lamp factory in Greenford. This distinctive building was to be our home for the next few years. A tour escort, who worked as a VJV guide for many years, describes his initial impressions of it in his book *A Million Miles*:

'Would it be fanciful to liken the threshold of a travel company office to a frontier? By passing from a wind-scoured London street, in the winter of 1980, into a room of palms, Chesterfield sofas, model locomotives in glass cases and seductive travel posters from the golden age of travel, before the internet, mobile phones and last-minute travel had reconfigured notions of time and distance, I seemed, with a single step, to move from one world to another.

This was no run-of-the-mill travel agent. A painted placard, like a pub sign, depicting an ocean liner and a steam locomotive, swung above the entrance to an anonymous office. No garish stickers featuring cheap fares to the Costas or to Florida; just an opulent waiting room to an exotic emporium, hinting at romance and exploration. It was stagecraft; a brilliant piece of theatre that enchanted me, like a child in a toyshop. Like a child, I saw only adventure and a foxed album of faded, tantalising images: a steam locomotive and its train unfurled along the platform and a long, long journey east, around the globe to China.'

In a piece of good fortune, the Glentworth Street office was located in Berkeley Court, a residential block that had been built during the 1930s in the urban Art Deco style of the period, with a blend of strong straight lines, broken curves, geometric ironwork and bold colours (in this case, red brick and granite). From the street, a covered driveway discreetly tunnelled into the building, described a parabola past the porter's office, and re-emerged further down the street, with office premises, including those of VJV, in its embrace.

The interior of our office had the same period look, an effect that was heightened by a pair of venerable leather Chesterfields, some antique Louis Vuitton travelling trunks doubling as coffee tables, four antique desks, a selection of potted palm trees and a pair of working model locomotives, the Hussar and the Gladstone, in the shop window. The jet-black marble fascia carried the words 'VOYAGES JULES VERNE', etched in stainless steel in the sans-serif font favoured by the great French poster artist A.M. Cassandre. This was echoed in the overhanging sign, which depicted a variation on Cassandre's most famous poster, an advertisement for the French ocean liner *Normandie*, its bow cleaving through the ocean as it bears down on the viewer in a show of power and confidence.

All things considered, the Art Deco design was the perfect motif for the travel philosophy of Voyages Jules Verne. The movement began in Paris in the 1920s, and by the 1930s it had become popular throughout the world. Its artistic sources included Greco-Roman, Ancient Egyptian, Aztec and, perhaps most notably, African. These influences, plus a popular fascination with aviation, railways, steamships, electricity, radio and the general advancement of technology, informed the movement's evolution.

Artists of the time, unlike their predecessors, could travel with comparative ease and expose themselves to a wide variety of cultures and styles. Travel was no longer the prerogative of the few. The design of Art Deco travel posters usually followed a commission by a patron who had a corporate name and a railway, steamship or aeroplane service to promote. It reflected the service in question, as well as the way in which it would be seen by an observer either on the move or in a travel agent's office.

Immediate impact was everything: the observer had to be gripped by the essential elements of name, service and destination, and Cassandre's poster of the SS *Normandie* was perhaps the single greatest example of the Art Deco fascination with technology and transportation. Cassandre himself noted: "The poster artist is an operator; he does not issue a message, he merely passes it on. No one asks for his opinion. He is only expected to establish a connection – clear, powerful, accurate." True enough, when the intention is to stimulate emotions, particularly nostalgic ones, and the objective is to entice travellers to embark on a voyage across continents, photographs are less fitted to the task than posters, which carry the added power of alchemy.

The task of a poster, from the Voyages Jules Verne point of view, was to distil into a single image the allure of 'going on a journey', and it worked. While the journeys themselves had to conform to certain, pre-defined expectations, it was the poster art that provided the element of magic. Just as Cassandre's originals had played upon my fantasies, so our new generation of posters cast their spell over our customers. As the great travel writer Eric Newby commented, after looking through our 'Great Journeys of the World' portfolio: "To read through them, one might wonder whether a commission from the Royal Geographical Society might be appropriate." This was exactly what we had intended: Voyages Jules Verne was taking its customers to places where, up until now, only explorers had trodden.

The success of our distinctive 'Great Journeys' posters encouraged us to expand the use of art as a selling tool. If the vivid acrylic colours and bold lines of Art Deco had been perfect for pan-continental voyages, the pastoral curves and subtle washes of watercolour would be suited to other destinations, in particular those of the Classical world.

Indeed, when Voyages Jules Verne first started out, in 1978, our visual identity pre-dated any actual product; in a reversal of the traditional modus operandi, the company had a proprietor and a poster design concept, but no railway, steamship or aeroplane service to promote. We used the posters to capture the essence and the theme of the proposed journey, before the details of that journey had been finalised. The aim was to give the impression of a service, or style of journey, that had survived from an earlier, more elegant era, and it was no accident that our first major destination was China, which for many people carried strong associations with the pre-Revolutionary period, when cities like Shanghai flourished in all their plutocratic glory.

We wanted the journeys to be enhanced not just by the places themselves, but by the way in which our passengers reached them. In the case of China, it was aboard the extraordinary 'Central Kingdom Express', which over a period of six weeks followed a route from London to Hong Kong via France, Germany (both East and West), Poland, the USSR, Mongolia and China.

This was just the first in our 'Great Journeys' series. There was also 'The Cape to Cairo Express'; 'The Raj Express'; 'Around the World in Eighty Days'; 'The London to Peking Motor Challenge'; 'The London to Saigon Motor Challenge'; 'The Patagonian Express'; 'Tibet and the Roof of the World'; 'The Karakoram Highway'; 'The Silk Road Revisited'; 'The Centenary Orient Express'; 'The Kyle of Lochalsh Highland Line'; 'The Great Indian Pacific Railroad'; 'On the Tracks of Marco Polo'; 'News from Tartary'; 'The London to New York Motor Challenge'; and 'Albania'. More recently, too, under the banner of the Magna Carta Steamship Company, there has been 'Heart of the Highlands' and the 'Spirit of Chartwell'.

The Voyages Jules Verne design process, whether in airbrush or watercolour style, has always remained the same. I would outline a very rough sketch of the intended subject – be it art history, painting, walking, opera, bird-watching, natural history, houses and gardens, science or inland or ocean cruising – and suggest text, and this would then be given to the artists (Robert Scurrah, Sir Hugh Casson, Alison Musker and others), who had free rein to interpret the guidelines in their own way.

It was rare for the finished works to become full-size posters, but they were used otherwise to provide a focal point for advertisements, to add zest to headlines and captions in brochures, or to serve as letterheads, business cards or labels. There was, of course, one other compelling reason for developing an in-house art style: it was far cheaper than paying large royalties to photographic agencies. Over the years, our artwork migrated from billboards to brochures to web pages, where the intensity of colour and form could be shown to great effect. As we expanded, we opened branches in New York, Peking and Hong Kong in addition to London, and we appointed general sales agents in locations all over the world, including Paris, where our artwork accompanied the headline 'L'art du Voyage Retrouvé' ('The Art of Travel Rediscovered').

CHAPTER 36
THE GARDEN ISLE

Digging deep into pockets to reveal vast quantities of banknotes, diamonds, silver and gold, all given to him by his associate and first namesake Cecil Rhodes, the legendary mining magnate and railway builder.

WHEN it came to sheer, knee-trembling trepidation, few experiences in life could match that of approaching, through the skyscrapers and mountains, and landing at the old Kai Tak airport in Hong Kong. There was, however, one journey which surpassed this in terms of scariness, for both passengers and pilots alike. In the late '60s and early '70s, before the extension of the runway at Funchal, there was only one reliable way to get to the island of Madeira. This involved taking a domestic flight from Lisbon to the neighbouring island of Porto Santo and then making the two-hour ferry voyage across to Funchal. Having made that stomach-churning crossing myself, I can well understand how they came to choose this particularly restless bit of sea as the location for the film Moby Dick. It was only in later years that they came up with more comfortable ways to reach the island, especially if you were a well-heeled traveller.

In the early days for those in a hurry, there was always the Southampton to Funchal (via Lisbon) flying boat service, but this was subject to prevailing sea conditions. Whereas for those with a bit more time on their hands, nothing could beat a passage on one of the Union Castle liners, which stopped off at Funchal en route to the Cape.

The hotel de rigueur in Madeira was Reid's, which at that time was still owned by the family of the same name. There, the cream of British society, having fled the British winter, was to be found whiling away the time on the hotel's many verandas – for example, George Bernard Shaw and Winston Churchill, who could be seen at his board and easel, painting the lush surroundings.

For me, starry-eyed and coming from a cold, grey London, this was real travel: an experience which brought back memories of my unsanctioned passage aboard the Train Bleu in 1965 and which encapsulated the golden age of travel, where the getting-there was every bit as alluring as the destination itself.

When I worked at Thomson, I had attempted to convince the foot-dragging guys and girls in the marketing department that Madeira ought to be one of our destinations. Thus, in 1969, I took it upon myself to travel over there, despite the fact that the operations department of Britannia Airways was unwilling even to contemplate the idea of flying to Funchal. Not least, they didn't have the equipment to do so: there was only one jet plane, the Boeing 727, that had a strong enough reverse-thrust braking system to land there safely.

From what I recall, there was only one airline in the UK at the time which did have 727s and that was Dan Air, whom we nicknamed 'Dan Dare', after the cartoon character, because they seemed prepared to fly to places other airlines wouldn't consider. Thus, it was Dan Air I had in mind for Funchal. Such was the difficulty of landing on the runway, it was akin to touching down on an aircraft carrier, but without the wire to bring the plane to a halt. What's more, due to the complete lack of flat ground on the island, the runway at Funchal had been cut into the side of a mountain. It was extremely short, with sea at both ends, and had barely 200 metres of wing clearance.

To complicate matters even further, the runway was built on a pronounced upward slope at one end and was prone to that most fearsome aspect of flying, wind shear. Before attempting to land, the pilot would usually indulge in a bit of a fly-past, which felt as if he was trying to ensure that we passengers understood the utter precariousness of what he was about to attempt. We, meanwhile, clung on to our seat rests for dear life.

Once down on the ground, I was put up by the Madeiran tourist authorities at the Santa Isabel Hotel, which, before it was demolished, used to stand opposite the Sheraton and close to the Savoy. It was owned by a certain Jaime Enrique Welsh, known as "Jimmy", who revealed to me, over a drink in the hotel bar, that the length of time the average Santa Isabel guest stayed at the hotel was three months.

Most of these, he told me, still arrived in Madeira by passenger liner from Southampton, hoping to pass their winter in more moderate climes. The bad news, from his point of view, was (a) that airplanes were starting to take over from ocean liners, and (b) that his elderly guests were – quite literally – dying out. Given that Jimmy could no longer count on his traditional, long-stay guests to fill his hotel, he was keen to meet me and explore the ways in which Thomson might bring in guests during the summer, when his and most of the other hotels were empty.

But first, a little about the island. It turned out that there were two main

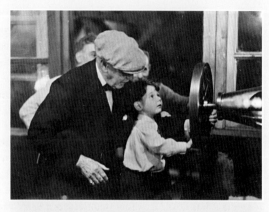

A Story in Brief

THE TALE OF WILLIAM REID: He arrived on Madeira aged 14, and with just £5 in his pocket, having been sent by his father, to seek his fortune After working in Lisbon, he made his way to Funchal, where he found a job in a bakery, before joining W.Wilkinson in a business devoted to the letting and management of 'quintas', or estates, on behalf of Madeiran and foreign owners. In due course, he turned the Quinta dao Fontes into the Royal Edinburgh Hotel, and later added the Hotel do Carmo and Hotel Santa Clara to his chain. He dreamt, however, of building a luxury hotel that would attract the rich and famous, and would establish a reputation around the world. So he bought a piece of land across the Ribeiro Seco (a ravine to the west of Funchal) and started building. He died in 1888, at the age of 66, but his legacy lives on, in the form of the magnificent Reid's Hotel.

IMAGE COURTESY: OTILIA WELSH/DOUG GOODMAN.

competing family businesses: the Blandy family controlled most of the shipping and wine, in addition to Reid's Hotel, while the Hinton family (Jimmy's forebears) oversaw the sugar industry and much else. There existed an intense state of rivalry between all these enterprises, and the conflict was often more than just commercial.

This rivalry went back a long way. Though William Hinton was born in Naples in 1817, really he hailed from the Hinton family's country seat in Wiltshire. In 1837, after graduating from Oxford, he went to Madeira, where he met and married Mary Wallas, the daughter of wealthy merchant and sugar mill-owner Robert Wallas. William Hinton made his fortune on the back of the island's then burgeoning sugar industry, and it was at his sugar cane mill in Funchal that his younger son, Harry, pioneered a steam-driven production process that soon outperformed all the competition.

Before long, the Hinton brothers, Harry and Cecil, controlled practically the whole of the island's sugar industry. Harry started importing automobiles and fuel into Madeira, in addition to acquiring vast tracts of savannah land in Angola and Mozambique for yet more sugar plantations and factories. The younger Hinton was more than just an industrialist; he was a buccaneering adventurer. Even when the first Boer War was at its height, he agreed to accompany a friend on his steam yacht for a six-month voyage around the South African coastline. On arriving at his hotel in Cape Town, Harry found a dishevelled old man with a long white beard relaxing on the veranda. "Cecil," exclaimed Harry, in a rather Livingstone-meets-Stanley moment, "I'm Harry, your brother." Cecil, however, was gruff and reluctant to engage in any kind of conversation.

The last time Harry had seen Cecil was 40 years ago, when he had left the family home and gone off to seek his fortune in Africa. Seeing how down-at-heel his brother looked, Harry asked if he was in need of any money, to which Cecil took great exception. "Who do you think I am?" he retorted, digging deep into pockets to reveal vast quantities of banknotes, diamonds, silver and gold, all given to him by his associate and first namesake Cecil Rhodes, the legendary mining magnate, railway builder and politician.

This was the last time Harry ever saw Cecil and, shortly after his return to Madeira, word reached him that his brother had died. Harry, meanwhile, continued to prosper: as well as his interests in Madeira, he invested in the construction of the Benguela Railway that ran from Lobito, on the Angolan Atlantic coast, right up to the point where it joined the Zambian railway system. He was an influential figure in sport, too, especially in Portugal, to which he introduced football in 1875 (thereby paving the way for stars such as Cristiano Ronaldo, who not only hails from Madeira but also once very kindly gave up his seat on a plane so that I could sit next to my son). Harry also brought the first motor car (a Wolsey) to the island in 1904 and, in later years, could be seen driving around the island in an impressive convertible Mercedes, one of only 10 ever made and frequently requisitioned by the state for the carriage of visiting heads of state.

In Angola, Harry even owned a private railway carriage to take him and his family into the interior, where his vast sugar plantations lay. It was along this route, so Jimmy told me, that he had been taken for his 21st birthday, at which point Harry had informed Jimmy that he was to eventually inherit it all. I could never quite work out why Jimmy's surname was not Hinton and was always too shy to ask, but there was no doubt that he had the finest education money could buy: Eton, Cambridge and, finally, the Sorbonne in Paris, where he studied architecture. Designing and building the Santa Isabel Hotel had been his first project.

I couldn't help secretly comparing my own, more humble background with Jimmy's rather privileged upbringing and education, yet he wore his wealth and status so lightly, I wondered whether he was perhaps embarrassed by it. In my mind, I had the image of a picture I had once seen, in which a couple of young ruffians were standing next to some top-hatted and dress-suited Eton boys – something I had done myself in real-life, while at the Barnardo's home in Windsor. Instead of gazing at the boys in wonderment, however, I recall offering up taunts and jeers. Our backgrounds were very different, Jimmy's and mine, although this never got in the way of our friendship.

In 1969, when I first visited Madeira, the island's sugar factories were in full production, yet they were losing money by the bucket load and dependent on government subsidies; otherwise, thousands of the island's cane growers would have been put out of business. That said, it was many years before Jimmy received a penny in subsidies, and when he eventually did, the authorities promptly requisitioned his remaining factory. As a result, where the Wallas/Hinton sugar mill once stood in the centre of Funchal, you will now find nothing but a community garden.

Perhaps sensing the further decline of the sugar business, Jimmy wanted to get more involved in his first love, tourism. By now, his parents had retired and were living at their lovely Quinta do Palmeira residence, while Jimmy was left to run the family business on his own. He was about to get a lot busier, as he went on to represent the whole Thomson operation throughout Portugal and, later, after I had formed Voyages Jules Verne, to represent me as well, especially when I started up flights to Madeira, the 'Garden Isle'. Guests who booked this trip could take garden tours and listen to lectures in the grounds of Quinta do Palmeira, where Columbus had twice stayed, before guests moved on to Marrakech, perhaps then to take our High Atlas tour.

Among his possessions, Jimmy had a valuable collection of first-edition travel books, mainly relating to the ancient Silk Route and Tibet. One day he gave me his favourite, to read on the flight home; it was a 1953 first edition of Heinrich Harrer's *Seven Years in Tibet*, with a glowing introduction by Peter Fleming (of whom more later). I could not put that book down and, to my lasting shame, never gave it back. I mention all of this in order to show how, when forming Voyages Jules Verne, my head was full of different ideas and influences and never more so than when returning from that first meeting with Jimmy.

There was, of course, a significant difference between Jimmy and myself when it came to formative travel experiences. While I had longed to be a passenger aboard Union Castle liners and flying boats, observing them from afar while I was at Barnardo's, these had been no more than Jimmy's regular means of commuting between home and Eton. I remember Jimmy telling the story of how, on one of these voyages from Funchal to Southampton, he and the other boys were royally and kindly entertained by Lady Clementine Churchill and her entourage in her private suite of cabins. He thought nothing of it; but for me, that kind of thing was part of the rich tapestry of journeying, rather than holidaying, that I wanted to create.

While at Thomson, I had opened up the Central Asian Silk Road cities of Samarkand, Bukhara and Khiva, so now, with my access into China, it was natural that I should be dreaming up journeys across the Tian Shan (Heavenly Mountains), Hindu Kush, High Pamirs and Tibetan Plateau to Lhasa. Indeed, I did try, unsuccessfully as it turned out, to get in touch with Herr Heinrich Harrer and ask if he would escort one of these journeys, given that he was a consultant for Neckermann, who were now marketing my products in Germany. However, it was my friend Jimmy whom I turned to for a loan, when I needed to put up £50,000 to satisfy the requirements of the Civil Aviation Authority's Air Travel Organisers' Licence (ATOL), without which I couldn't trade. He didn't let me down.

With the cash in place and my bond application duly submitted, I was unexpectedly summoned to a full hearing, for which I was asked to bring along my legal representatives and accountants. When I got to the Civil Aviation Authority's Kingsway offices, I was directed to a large room full of booths, in which sat reel-to-reel tape recorder operatives. Before the proceedings commenced, I was cautioned that everything that I said would be noted down and recorded. It was a bewildering experience; all I wanted was a licence, a bit of paper covered by Jimmy's loan. Yet there I was, facing my very own version of the Nuremberg Trials, and for no reason, it seemed to me, other than to intimidate an aspiring entrant into the business of travel – in other words, just the kind of tussle with small-minded British bureaucracy that was to dog and irk me throughout my career.

CHAPTER 37
THE GREAT TRAIN BAZAAR

The classic Paul Theroux book 'Great Railway Bazaar', is an account of the author's four-month journey, in 1972, from London to Japan – the original inspiration for the Central Kingdom Express.

PEOPLE often thought that, as most of the Voyages Jules Verne 'Great Journeys' involved trains, I was some kind of closet railway buff, but nothing could have been further from the truth. Nor was I, by nature, the intrepid explorer type. I did, however, have an experience that brought my Barnardo's diet to mind – baked beans, boiled potatoes, pilchards and luncheon meat – in a rather remote location. It happened on a trip I made to Nepal, with the aim of becoming the first foreigner to trek across the Himalayan foothills to Tibet.

I had flown from London, via Delhi, to Kathmandu and travelled by car as close to the Nepalese/Tibetan border as I could get. Once there, I found the road had been washed away in a landslip, leaving me no option but to clamber up the hillside to the town of Zhangmu, where the Chinese had built a very basic hotel. As I was crawling up that steep and muddy incline, past local Tibetans who paid little heed to the existence of the official border, I observed a lone Japanese man coming in the opposite direction. This was particularly disappointing for me, since I had only made this long and tortuous journey in order to claim that I was the first foreigner to have done so. Now I had that sick-to-the-pit-of-the-stomach feeling that Scott must have had, on discovering that Amundsen had beaten him to the South Pole.

From Zhangmu I travelled by car, on the unmade roads skirting Mount Everest, as far as Xigatse, where I spent the night in easily the worst hotel I had stayed in since Timbuktu. The worst thing was using the outside latrines at night, which involved perching on a high wall, dropping your pants and directing your rear end towards the valley below.

As we followed the high mountain passes leading to Lhasa, I began to suffer the first sign of altitude sickness: a thumping headache, which no amount of paracetamol could dispel. Once in Lhasa and having visited the Potala Palace, I retired to my hotel room, where I treated my local Tibetan guide to the Western culinary delights that I took with me everywhere, despite ribbing from my colleagues – not just Mars Bars, but also packets of Batchelors cup-a-soup in every flavour imaginable. For my Tibetan guide, raised on a diet of rancid butter and tsampa (dumplings made from roasted flour), the latter constituted an absolute banquet. No wonder he insisted I should leave him my last packets: I may not have been the first foreigner to cross that particular border, but I was certainly the first to introduce cup-a-soup.

A further idea I had, upon starting up Voyage Jules Verne, was to invite well-known personalities to be an escort or a guest lecturer on my tours. I first wrote to the broadcaster James Cameron and the politician Shirley Williams, who was chairing some China-related committee in the House of Commons at the time, but neither could make it. Nor, at first, could the author Paul Theroux. I think my approach must have had some impact, however, because a few months later I received a request from *National Geographic Magazine* in Washington, D.C., asking if I could arrange a photographic and journalistic visit around China, to be undertaken by Paul Theroux.

Fitzroy Maclean's *Eastern Approaches* was one of the inspirations behind the Voyages Jules Verne approach to travel, but another big influence was the classic Theroux book *The Great Railway Bazaar: By Train Through Asia*, an account of the author's four-month journey, in 1973, from London to Japan, via Europe, the Middle East, the Indian subcontinent and Southeast Asia, and back again, via the Trans-Siberian Railway.

The reason that so many people love trains is the romance and glamour associated with long-distance rail travel, be it the Orient Express, which was the inspiration for so many novels and films (*Murder on the Orient Express, Stamboul Train*), or the Trans-Siberian, which ploughed (and still ploughs) through remote and snow-bound forests alive with the echoes of Imperial Russia, Doctor Zhivago and the Cold War.

In deciding to travel by train, Theroux claimed he had found the perfect medium for lazy travellers who want "to stay in motion, straddling the tracks and never arrive or feel they ought to". To Theroux, the denial of adventure is almost the whole point of his journey; he sits in the corner of his compartment and waits not so much for sensation and excitement, as for passengers – the characters that populate his book – to come to him. It's a wonderfully original idea and it set the tone for a whole new generation of travel books. Travel writing became a genre of its own, featuring the solipsistic musings and wanderings of individuals who were undertaking journeys based on an over-arching theme or idea and who had both the time and the desire to put it into practice.

Unlike in *Eastern Approaches* or *News from Tartary*, the risks you ran were less from threats to your personal safety than from running out of money and reputation. *The Great Railway Bazaar* demonstrated that exotic travel did not just concern geographical places and that the emotional and cultural core of travelling was within the reach of anyone with the determination to get up and go. People had been doing this independently for years, along the 'hippie trail', and the organised train journey was the catalyst for a new type of packaged travel experience.

The first Voyages Jules Verne train departure from London for Hong Kong occurred just four years after the publication of *The Great Railway Bazaar*. Eight years later, in 1987, Theroux was persuaded to join a Voyages Jules Verne tour as writer-in-residence. The outcome was *Riding the Iron Rooster,* of which the first 50 pages are devoted to Theroux's experiences on the Central Kingdom Express. The rest of the book, in which he recounts his impressions of China, are apparently dedicated to challenging the Chinese maxim, 'You can always fool a foreigner.' It is this resolve not to be fooled which colours Theroux's attitude to everyone and everything that he encounters throughout the book.

Ambitious writers are dangerous creatures. It is not in their nature to accept things for what they are: would have little to say if they did. There is a tendency to dramatise the insignificant details of everyday life; furthermore, when strangers are forced into unnatural and intimate cohabitation, their tics and eccentricities, which might go unremarked in a domestic setting, are very easily thrown into high relief, especially against the background of a series of trains lumbering through the Soviet Union, the Mongolian People's Republic and China during the Cold War.

Typically, Theroux kept his distance, observed and wrote, but as far as the group of people in the party was concerned, the end result turned out to be an entertaining but distorted view of his fellow travellers. The group in question was a remarkably varied collection of individuals from America, Britain and France. One of the more elderly Britons made it as far as Irkutsk, but fell ill and had to return home. Another Briton spent several days in a Mongolian hospital, where he was treated with something normally prescribed by vets for horses.

Two of the Americans were ex-servicemen who, haunted by experiences in some hellhole or other where the US had taken a stand, ran through the train at the Russian border shouting, "They've taken our boys!" One broiling night on the train from Shanghai to Canton, the four French people in the party, who were

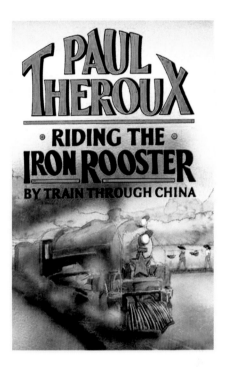

A Story in Brief

POETRY IN MOTION: In 1980, I hired the King George V steam engine, for a short West Country press trip, to launch our 'Kyle of Lochalsh Highland Line' great journey. This was a locomotive with some pedigree, too: in 1971 it had become the very first train to break the mainline steam ban, which had been in place since 1969. It was based at the Bulmer's Railway Centre, in Hereford, and its restoration to main line service and subsequent operation is said to have opened the door for the return of steam trains to UK mainline railways. In later years, I paid a return visit to the railway centre; I went there with a view to buying a number of original Pullman carriages, then being used by Bulmer's (the cider firm) for entertainment. In the end I decided against the idea; I guess that operating the vessel *Spirit of Chartwell* fulfilled my ambition to run my own luxury train.

sharing a compartment, began arguing with each other about whether the window should remain open and the light on, the upshot of which was an attempt by the husband of the married couple from Marseille to throttle the girl from Paris, who spent the remainder of the journey sleeping on the floor of the corridor.

On another evening, as the train lingered interminably and inexplicably, as it always did, at the border between Mongolia and China, Theroux, who had been listening to the news on his radio, announced that there had been an explosion at the Chernobyl nuclear plant. In other words, he had plenty to write about. However, he did not care to be part of an organised group, which is hardly surprising for a writer who is used to travelling at his own speed. Theroux's time on the train formed a convenient and useful prelude to the rest of his own journey around China (he left the group in Peking, before re-joining it in Shanghai). I thought it odd that he should have agreed to travel with us in the first place.

What Theroux produced was a sketch in words that was, I felt, cartoonish in its glibness; his characterisations of his fellow passengers were not just sour and Dickensian, but all rather similar. By contrast, his encounters with people in *The Great Railway Bazaar* were spontaneous and entertaining. The writing in the earlier book is terse and to the point and, occasionally, in its spare style, offers casual insights into the world as it was at the time.

From the point of view of Voyages Jules Verne, it is the final chapter of *The Great Railway Bazaar*, devoted to Theroux's return through Russia, that is the most interesting. Although much of what Theroux describes of Russia seemed to have changed by the time of the first 'Central Kingdom Express' in 1979, many of the details of the train journey were very similar. Things like the beetroot soup, slopping from side to side in the restaurant car's metal bowls; the sun slanting pink and gold across the snow in early spring; the odour of unwashed Russia in the carriage corridors; the gilded cupolas on neglected churches – that strange, other-worldly atmosphere pervading this great country which, even in its untouchable vastness, always seemed to behave as if it were under siege.

There were also the encounters with Russians who would demonstrate their desire for world peace, no doubt sincerely felt, but conveyed to you through the gift of a postcard featuring a ground-to-air missile. In addition, there was a sense of time passing, or rather of it not passing, as you spent days bouncing and rollicking across a landscape which, as the new day dawned, was almost indistinguishable from the one over which darkness had fallen the night before.

As for the passengers, they spent their time engaged in a state of permanent physical inactivity and poor digestion, interrupted by fitful and unrefreshing bouts of sleep. Look out of the train window, and time and place were interchangeable. Without doubt, a rail journey across Siberia was the best possible insight into the mass of contradictions that was Russia, a country utterly absorbed in its arrogance and its neuroses.

'All travel is circular,' writes Theroux, as he makes his way back to London, and that's something for which most of us are glad. It seems to me, on reading his book, that Theroux does not like much of what he sees; nevertheless, what he did, in writing *The Great Railway Bazaar*, was to give others the chance to make their minds up for themselves. It certainly made the geography more familiar to people like me and alerted me to the joined-up nature of the Eurasian railway network, the realisation of which was the inspiration for the 'Central Kingdom Express'.

Paul Theroux later wrote the novel *The Mosquito Coast*, which was made into a movie in 1986 starring Harrison Ford, who later said: "It's the only film I have done that hasn't made its money back. I'm still glad I did it. If there was a fault with the film, it was that it didn't fully enough embrace the language of the book. It may have more properly been a literary, rather than a cinematic, exercise. But I think it's full of powerful emotions."

Maybe so, but I thought it a pity that *The Great Train Bazaar* was not made into a movie instead; I think it would have been far more successful. Also – I know it's not entirely relevant, but I mention it anyway – the house where I then lived had, for a while, been rented by Harrison Ford.

THE TRAVELLER'S ALMANAC COVER BY ROBERT SCURRAH

A Story in Brief:

IMAGE COURTESY: VJV.

ERROL FLYNN: In 1953, the Xamena family moved from Palma to the remote area of Illetas, just 8 kms from the capital, and decided to take in paying guests, at the Hotel Bon Sol. At that time, Mallorca was popular with wealthy Europeans, but because it had no international airport, guests arrived by sea, some in their own yachts, and taxi drivers were paid by the few hotels there were, to 'persuade' visitors to choose their establishment. So when, in 1953, the screen star Errol Flynn arrived in his yacht, plus followers, he took over the tiny Bon Sol. There's no doubting the heavy drinking and games that went on. Later Flynn returned to the hotel with Patrick Wymark and had a villa built close by (now demolished). His visits are commemorated on a stone just a short swashbuckle away from the hotel.

CHAPTER 38
NEWS FROM TARTARY

Fleming conforms to the stereotypical image of the Briton unable to travel
without his marmalade. But to read 'News From Tartary' is to instantly want
to be Fleming, to be doing what Fleming did and when he did it.

A few days after my Glentworth Street emporium of travel opened, a very
frail old lady walked in. She explained that, due to our connections with
the People's Republic of China, we might be interested in creating a
particular journey that she had in mind. It turned out that the lady was anxious
to keep the name of her friend, Gladys Aylward, alive and was proposing that we
organise a group trip from London by train to Manchuria, then on through China
to Hong Kong, before ending up at Taiwan, where Gladys was buried.

At that time, there were only about a dozen Chinese towns and cities open
to foreign visitors and, when I had a look at this lady's suggested itinerary, I
realised straight away that it wouldn't be possible. The Chinese had made it clear
that they forbade entry into China to missionaries, which is what the lady in my
office was (and Gladys Aylward had been).

Their tale was, however, intriguing in the extreme. It transpired that Gladys
had been born in lowly circumstances, in Edmonton, north London, in 1902. At
an early age she had taken work as a scullery maid, but all the time harboured
ambitions to travel overseas as a missionary. She embarked upon a determined
programme of study in preparation for this calling, only to be turned down by the
China Inland Mission, who felt she did not have sufficient academic qualifications.
Undeterred by this setback, Gladys decided, in 1932, to spend her life savings on
a railway passage from London to Yangcheng in Shanxi province, China.

It was, to say the least, a perilous trip, and at one point, in Siberia, Gladys
was forced to get off the train and find an alternative means of getting to China.
She eventually reached her destination and, on arrival, was put to work alongside

A Story in Brief

SPECIAL CORRESPONDENT: Before becoming a full-time author, Peter Hopkirk was an ITN reporter and newscaster, then the New York correspondent for Lord Beaverbrook's *Daily Express*. He then worked for nearly 20 years on *The Times*; first as chief reporter, then as a Middle East and Far East specialist. In the 1950s, he edited the West African news magazine *Drum*, sister paper to its legendary South African namesake. Before entering Fleet Street, he served in the same battalion as Lance-Corporal Idi Amin, later to emerge as the Ugandan tyrant. No stranger to mis-adventure, he has twice been held in secret-police cells – in Cuba and the Middle East – and has also been hijacked by Arab terrorists. His works have been translated into 14 languages, and unofficial versions in local languages frequently appear in the bazaars of Central Asia. In the early years of Voyages Jules Verne, he provided not just inspiration, through his books, but a great deal of assistance in person.
IMAGE COURTESY: ROBERT SCURRAH/VOYAGES JULES VERNE.

a more senior missionary, Jeannie Lawson. Together, they went on to set up what became known as 'The Inn of the Eight Happinesses'. For a time, Gladys also worked for the Chinese government as a 'foot inspector', which involved touring the Chinese countryside in order to enforce a new law outlawing the old-fashioned, feudal practice of binding young Chinese girls' feet. Her presence was by no means always welcome, since there was much resistance, frequently violent, to this new edict. Nevertheless, Gladys successfully settled into her work and, five years after leaving England, decided to give up her British citizenship and officially become Chinese.

By this time, Gladys was widely revered among the local populace, due to the way in which she had not only taken orphans into care, but in some cases adopted them as well. Her disregard for her own safety was legendary; once, she intervened personally in a volatile prison riot, as part of her campaign (successful, as it turned out) for prison reform.

In 1938, the region was overrun with invading Japanese forces, at which point an unbowed Gladys led more than 100 of her orphan charges across the mountains to safety, despite having been wounded herself. She never married and returned to Britain in 1948, when the Communists took over China; she was never to return, because, when she tried to do so, she was denied entry by the authorities, no doubt because of her missionary background.

Instead, Gladys settled in Taiwan and, in 1958, founded the Gladys Aylward Orphanage, where she worked until her death in 1970. The publicity that came as a result of the 1958 film based on her life, *The Inn of the Sixth Happiness*, made her uncomfortable, not least due to the liberties the producers had taken with the storyline. She was played in the film by the Swedish actress Ingrid Bergman, who was tall and blonde and looked nothing like Gladys, who was small and had dark hair and a Cockney accent. Nor, sadly, was I able to bring about a happy ending to her story: this was a 'Great Journey' I was unable to arrange (although, with the changing attitudes in China today, it is something I would certainly attempt now, if I still owned Voyages Jules Verne).

Still, with a name like Voyages Jules Verne to live up to, I felt compelled to offer journeys that involved an element of derring-do and had set my sights on the border areas around China, which were, for the most part, various sections of the old Silk Road. Opening up these long-closed borders proved to be a long and tedious business. Although I could count on my Chinese connections for help, it was a lot harder securing co-operation from neighbouring countries, such as the USSR, Pakistan, Vietnam and Nepal, who were openly suspicious of China's motives.

The section of the Karakoram Highway, from Pakistan to Tashgurgan and onwards to Kashgar, in what was once Chinese Turkestan, was a particularly difficult nut to crack. I had already obtained permission from the Chinese to cross the border, but my Pakistani agent in Rawalpindi was getting nowhere with the Pakistani Army, who effectively controlled the area, because of its close proximity to Afghanistan and disputed Kashmir. This did not prevent me from advertising the intended expedition, and I had a long list of soft-adventure expeditionaries who could not wait to be the first to travel with me along the famed Karakoram Highway.

This meant that I was under a certain amount of pressure to deliver. In an attempt to get the Pakistanis to relent, I flew to Islamabad for a meeting with our local agents and a tour of the local government ministries. I also arranged for the Chinese to meet me on their side of the border, which involved them making a two-day trek from Kashgar.

Things got off to a poor start. I spent a fruitless and frustrating week going from ministry to ministry, from army barracks to army barracks – each time there seemed to be the tiniest glimmer of hope, it was almost immediately snuffed out. Having spent a week getting nowhere, I decided there was nothing for it but to tell the Chinese I would not be coming. So, I flew back to London, in order to re-think my strategy, in the meantime instructing my Pakistani agent to continue his rounds of the government ministries and the military authorities. Finally, a month later, a special exit permit was issued and I immediately flew back to Islamabad.

Once I arrived, I took a dramatic flight across the Pamirs to Gilgit. From there, I began my journey along the Karakoram Highway, which more or less follows the course of one of the tributaries of the Indus River, as far as Karimabad, where the privations of my tiny inn – and there were many, including mud floors – were more than compensated for by the breath-taking scenery.

From Karimabad we gradually climbed upwards, passing endless military convoys as we did so. Finally we reached the Pakistan/China border at the Khunjerab Pass, where our Chinese escorts were waiting to take us, by jeep, to Tashgurgan. In my personal rankings of sheer hotel terribleness, while the gold medal goes to the place I stayed in in Timbuktu and the silver to the place in Xiagaste, Tibet, third place most definitely goes to our overnight residence in Tashgurgan, where we were obliged to share the outside latrines with farm animals. And if the term 'hotel' was a misnomer when applied to the hovel in Tashgurgan, then the term 'highway' gives the wrong idea about the Karakoram, which, for most of the way to Kashgar, was little more than a track. What's more, a half-built track, since there were tens of thousands of People's Liberation Army conscripts still constructing it.

Nevertheless, to arrive in Kashgar, having crossed the Tian Shan, Kunlun and Pamir mountain ranges, and experience all the wonderful sights, sounds and smells was, for me, as memorable as my first visit to old Istanbul. The Turkish comparison was apt, too, since there was a sizeable Turkic population living there: a minority people who eked out a living on the edge of the Taklamakan desert (one of the driest places on earth, its name is reputed to mean 'he who goes in does not come out') and who could be seen trading horses, camels and jade in the exotic Sunday bazaar.

Their presence served as a reminder that China is not just populated by Han Chinese. Just as this area had been an ancient crossroads on the Silk Road, so too had it played an important role in the strategies of the British and Russian colonial powers, as they sought to gain influence over the area in what became known as the 'Great Game'. This was the title of a book by Peter Hopkirk, author also of *Foreign Devils on the Silk Road*, the story of the trans-Asian highway linking those two great ancient super-powers, Imperial Rome and China.

In later years, Peter helped us out with a number of pre-expedition preparation lectures, but there was one book in particular that I am sure gave him inspiration. Written by Peter Fleming, the brother of James Bond creator Ian Fleming, it was called *News from Tartary*. An account of an adventure in 1930s China, in the region then known as Chinese Turkestan, it is, in my opinion, not just a marvellous story, but a literary masterpiece.

Today, of course, pure adventure is not what it was. The world is not only a smaller place, but also sometimes a more violent, less compassionate, less reasonable one. The British Empire, of course, is no more, although memories of its power still live on even in 20th-century China, a country that never came under British rule. To a certain extent, men like Peter Fleming, Peter Hopkirk and Fitzroy Maclean, though undoubtedly possessed of an innate force of will, owed their boldness to a sense that, whatever they did and wherever they went, they were ultimately protected by their nationality (unlike they would be today).

For although China was not part of the British Empire, it was adjacent to countries that most definitely were. Back in the 1930s, when India was still Britain's proudest imperial possession, China, by comparison, was a broiling, seething mess. The Japanese were in control of the north-east of the country and were eager to take more, the Nationalists and Communists were at each other's throats and warlords fought viciously to establish petty states for themselves. On the fringes of the old imperial empire, Xinjiang, then known to westerners as Chinese Turkestan or Tartary, veered between restlessness and utter ungovernability.

This was a part of the world which was constantly vulnerable to exploitation by those who, like the Russians, sought to export revolution by sowing discord among the discontented. Xinjiang itself was not only a volatile mix of different religions and ethnic groups; it stood on the edge of a region made up of nomadic peoples and ever-shifting borders – a spectacular meeting point of desert, mountain and empire which had for so long been a playground in the Great Game. As Fleming so succinctly pointed out, in his foreword: "Nobody could get in. Nobody could get out."

It is worth, at this point, investigating the origins of the Great Game, or 'Tournament of Shadows', as the Russians called it. These terms were coined in the 19th century to describe the struggle between the British and Russian Empires for strategic supremacy in Central Asia. This cat-and-mouse contest is usually regarded as beginning in 1813 with the Treaty of Gulistan between Russia and Persia, and ending with the Anglo-Russian Convention of 1907, although there was a second, milder phase after the Bolshevik Revolution of 1917, when the new Soviet government summarily annulled all treaties signed by its predecessor.

Throughout the 19th century, the British had been concerned that Russian expansion into Central Asia would intrude into their sphere of influence and threaten, in particular, their sovereignty over India. The convention of 1907 brought an official close to hostilities between the two empires, but these were rekindled with the establishment of the USSR, when Soviet agitators resumed their activities in the region, fomenting trouble in Xinjiang with a view, according to the British, to doing the same in India.

At the same time, the USSR opened consulates in Urumchi, the capital of Xinjiang, and in Kashgar, the oasis town at the far western end of the Taklamakan Desert. This was with a view, it seemed, of uniting Xinjiang and Gansu, the neighbouring province to the east, in a 'red republic' that was to be called Kashgaria and would be ruled by Feng Yuxiang, a one-time Christian warlord turned communist sympathiser.

All of a sudden, then, India had become vulnerable to communist infiltration, with much of it suspected to be coming from the Soviet consulate in Kashgar, close to the border with the USSR. Mikhail Borodin, a senior Comintern agent, was busy stirring up trouble among the 'toilers of the East' – i.e., China. He was receiving assistance in this from the left wing of the Chinese Nationalist Party (KMT), and this was an alliance that lasted right up until the defeat of the last remaining Chinese warlords in 1927, at which point Chiang Kai-shek, then the KMT's military leader, took violently and suddenly against both Borodin and communism.

With civil war between the KMT and the Communist Party of China (CPC) now inevitable, Stalin turned his attention to India, seeking to cause as much disruption and industrial unrest as he could manufacture. The perfect base from which to operate was Xinjiang, now about to enter a five-year-long period of chaos and conflict, both political and religious, following the assassination of its governor. It was no surprise, then, when a Soviet-backed governor was appointed, and he invited in Soviet troops who promptly took control of large parts of the province, including Yarkand, the gateway to India. The British, who had no influence beyond Kashgar, understandably became anxious, and it was against this background of uncertainty that Fleming was sent out to Xinjiang on behalf of *The Times* newspaper, in order to establish exactly what was happening there.

To read *News from Tartary* is instantly to wish to be Fleming – to be doing what he did, when he did it, and to be able to write about it with his effortless elegance. The spell is cast with his opening words: 'Most journeys begin less abruptly than they end, and to fix the true beginning of this one, in either time or space, is a task which I do not care to undertake. I find it easier to open my account of it at the moment when I first realised, with a small shock of pleasure and surprise, that it had actually begun.'

If there is a finer passage to herald a tale of adventure, then it has yet to be written; it sets the tone for a remarkable tale that is brilliantly told. Superficially, Fleming conforms to the stereotypical image of the Briton unable to travel without his marmalade; yet in reality, he is anything but the insensitive, thick-skinned imperialist. Late in the book, when he devotes, reluctantly (because he does not wish to bore the reader), a few pages to explaining the politics of the region, he notes: 'We still find it impossible to be deeply stirred by things that happen to those fellow-beings whose skin is a different colour from our own.' That, I would suggest, is not the remark of a man observing the world from the safety of a lofty tower.

There are those who prefer the account of the journey written by Fleming's travelling companion, the Swiss woman Ella 'Kini' Maillart, which is said by some to be more poetic (and by others, more turgid). Personally, I feel that although Fleming is a realist, his writing is far from unpoetic – on the contrary, his descriptions of encounters with both people and landscapes are rich in imagery and powerfully expressed. He is certainly a master of the telling word and, in addition to being a pithy analyst of the facts, has a distinct flair for comic understatement when describing scenes such as the following: 'As we arrived at the inn, the building next to it – an eating-house where we had breakfasted – quietly and rather sadly collapsed, crumbling into rubble in a cloud of dust. It was one of those days.'

Not that this for one second undermines Fleming's dedication to the undertaking at hand. His writing is skilful and unpretentious: honest appraisal, dressed in elegant English, and respect for his surroundings is what he does so well. He is never, as he puts it himself, 'unscrupulously imaginative.' Fleming remains clear-eyed when it comes to the utopian visions of others. He treats people as he finds them, provided they are honest and well-meaning; but when it comes to revolutionary remedies, he is a sceptic. When he says, 'I have travelled fairly widely in 'Communist' Russia (where they supplied me with the inverted commas),' you detect not so much prejudice as a certain sense of disappointment.

Indeed, a large part of Fleming's book deals with the journey itself: the period of optimism as arrangements are being made; the frustrating delays when there are no camels available for hire; the boredom when the travellers are stranded in benighted, windswept outposts on the Tibetan plateau, as they follow their deliberately indirect route to Xinjiang. Even when it seems impossible that there is anything of interest to say about long marches across featureless terrain, Fleming finds ways of making his narrative fascinating. He makes little of the discomforts, too, although it is clear that the journey is an arduous one for both him and his companion. They find themselves, on various occasions, utterly exhausted; their clothes, diaries and typewriters soaked through due to the incompetence of their guides.

Yet even in these extremes, they still apply themselves assiduously to the job of record keeping. Apart from the few pages where Fleming summarises the complicated political circumstances prevailing in Xinjiang, he writes hardly at all of the main purpose of the expedition. He does not need to, as the chaotic and impenetrable nature of the place is all too evident from the details of their slow progress from Lanzhou to Kashgar. The point of the enterprise lies in the journey itself, then, rather than in its notional aim, a fact that Fleming recognises when he writes: 'The trouble about journeys nowadays is that they are easy to make, but difficult to justify... only the born tourist – happy, goggling ruminant – can follow in their tracks with the conviction that he is not wasting his time.'

When access to Xinjiang was finally granted to Voyages Jules Verne in the 1980s, I was still imagining that it must have been a far more exciting place in Fleming's time. Yet to my surprise, I soon discovered that apart from the absence of civil war and open rebellion, the region had hardly changed in the intervening half century.

Just as they are about to leave Kashgar for India, Fleming and Kini Maillart are invited to a banquet given by the local officials. A General, Liu Pin, gives an expansive speech, "which comes to an end with the disarming admission that he had not the faintest recollection of what he had been saying or why he had said it. Whereupon, with a loud cry of 'Y.M.C.A.!' he started to dance, uncertainly but with great vigour, and, in this impromptu exhibition, Kini was soon persuaded to join him. Nobody was assassinated."

This last description sums up the Fleming attitude: debonair on the surface, fatalistic at heart, philosophically ready to accept the inevitability of failure. In his view, 'all serious subjects, and particularly anything to do with myself, seem, almost as soon as they have been broached, to be not worth discussing after all.'

This is not to say that Fleming is incapable of shrewd analysis; he has a clear understanding of the events taking place in that obscure, war-torn corner of Central Asia. With just as much perspicacity, however, he also understands that outcomes are ultimately predicated on the unknowable and the unexpected and that, in the end, the journey is the thing.

In 1984 we invited Peter Fleming's grandson to undertake a commemorative re-enactment of the journey described in *News from Tartary*. We announced the event with a specially commissioned Robert Scurrah poster featuring sand dunes, camels and a mirage-like destination meant to be Kashgar. As for Peter Fleming himself, he retired after the war to squiredom in Nettlebed, Oxfordshire. He is buried in Nettlebed churchyard and his gravestone bears his own apt and poignant words:

He travelled widely in far places;
Wrote, and was widely read.
Soldiered, saw some of danger's faces,
Came home to Nettlebed.
The squire lies here, his journeys ended –
Dust and a name on a stone –
Content, amid the lands he tended,
To keep this rendezvous alone.

CHAPTER 39
EASTERN APPROACHES

The name of Fitzroy Maclean no longer means much, if anything, to anyone not brought up in the era of the Cold War; in 'Eastern Approaches', he wrote an account of his experiences while a diplomat in Moscow.

DUE to the absence of a genuine national press in the US, there is little option but to advertise in what are essentially regional newspapers with a limited geographical reach. Thus, when you are a small travel company trying to reach an upmarket audience, you have to find some other way to advertise than via the papers. It doesn't help either that, unlike in the UK, there is not much of a tradition of travel agencies operating on the High Street. As a result, finding your customers is a bit of a needle-in-a-haystack affair and can take up vast amounts of energy and cash.

One way to advertise is to approach the various alumni associations that abound in the US, each of them concerned with raising money for a particular school, museum or place of learning. In contrast to Europe, there is much more of a philanthropic tradition in the US, and these fund-raising bodies have large databases of well-heeled and, usually, well-educated supporters: the kind of people who might be interested in broadening their minds through travel.

The way it works is that alumni associations invite proposals from a number of travel companies, and these have a much greater chance of success if their proposal is presented as unique, exclusive and with a well-known personality attached, usually from the world of academia. The travel firm is expected to produce the promotional literature, be responsible for all operational risks, cover mailing and administration costs and make a pre-determined contribution to the association's coffers.

On the plus side, this is a low-cost and highly targeted strategy; on the down side, the associations guard their databases like gold dust, which means that not only are your profit margins pretty small, but you also have no chance of following up and tapping into accumulated goodwill from your customers. I thought I'd try it out first in the UK, and managed to do a deal with both the National Trust and the Royal Geographical Society which involved me publishing, for their members, a version of the *Voyages Jules Verne Travel Review*, which came in a tabloid newspaper format and contained a range of different articles relating to our tours and adventures.

The initiative proved an abject failure. Our offerings for the genteel folk of the National Trust seemed to them too much like hard work, and as for the members of the Royal Geographical Society, I came to the conclusion that they preferred the armchair variety of travel to the real thing. The only bright spot was that when I came to sign the deal with the Royal Geographical Society, they insisted this should be done on David Livingstone's desk (which had been donated to the society), and it was on this occasion that I met one of my literary travel heroes, Fitzroy Maclean. At that time, he was running a hotel up in the Scottish Highlands, so I took the opportunity to get him to agree to an interview for our *Travel Review;* the article as it appeared read as follows:

'The name of Fitzroy Maclean no longer means much, if anything, to anyone not brought up in the era of the Cold War. Yet he was one of a handful of men on whom Ian Fleming was thought to have modelled the character of James Bond; in *Eastern Approaches*, he wrote a best-selling account of his experiences while a diplomat in Moscow in the 1930s: an account that is a masterpiece of inter-war derring-do and which is still in print. He was also instrumental in arguing for Tito, a communist partisan who later became leader of Yugoslavia, as the man most likely to be of use to the Allied cause against Hitler in World War II, when many would have chosen another candidate simply for not being a communist.'

Above all, it is Maclean's book *Eastern Approaches* that is relevant to our purpose. It is not a travel book in the modern sense of the term: Maclean did not set off on a jaunt to write purple prose, as if on a glorified holiday. On the contrary, his journeys were not without risk, and were genuine Tintin-like adventures. Most of us wouldn't have done what he did – but we are happy that he did it. Along the way, he inspired a certain spirit of travel that was to surface decades later, when the world was opening up to travellers at large.

In some respects, given his background, Maclean's story is a bit of a surprise. In 1933, after an education at Eton and Cambridge, where he read Classics and History (graduating with first-class honours), he joined the Diplomatic Service. In 1934 he was posted to the British Embassy in Paris, where he soon tired of the undemanding routine and requested, in 1937, a posting to Moscow. 'As a young man at the embassy, one was asked to every party and I couldn't have enjoyed myself more,' he explains of his move. 'But then I felt I was getting a bit set in my ways. I had met a lot of fascinating Russians in Paris... so I thought I would like to go to Russia.'

In those days, Paris was almost the pick of the foreign postings for a young diplomat. The Foreign Office responded by implying that he must be out of his mind – he could be posted to Rome, Berlin or any exotic, comfortable place he chose, but if he insisted on going to Moscow, then no obstacle would be placed in his path, as nobody else wanted to go there. Maclean writes: 'The years which I had spent in Paris, with its essentially Continental political atmosphere, had convinced me that, without first-hand knowledge of the Soviet Union and its political system, any picture that one might form of the international situation would inevitably be incomplete.'

He was also aware of an incipient smugness, which 'if prolonged unduly, seemed bound to lead to chronic liver trouble, if to nothing worse.' So, he did insist on going to Moscow and found himself living through what turned out to be a momentous period of 20th-century history. It also transformed his own life: from those two years in Moscow, the rest of his career flowed.

1930s Moscow was the fulcrum of a vast empire. The Soviet Union was a confederation of unlikely bedfellows that extended from the Polish border in the west to the border with China and the Pacific Ocean in the east. Revolution in 1917 had quickly turned into totalitarianism exercised by one party, the Communist Party, which throughout the 1930s was effectively in the hands of Joseph Stalin, who, aided by the secret police, ran the USSR with ruthless, maniacal thoroughness. It was not long after Maclean's arrival that sudden mysterious changes in government, accompanied by wild accusations of treachery, signalled the beginning of Stalin's so-called purges.

For a man of his background, it would have been natural for Maclean to be unequivocally opposed to communism. Yet there were many well-educated and thoughtful people in the West who had high hopes for the success of communism and were prepared to turn a blind eye to the stories of mass starvation caused by ill-thought-out agricultural policies and the persecution of countless people for imagined crimes against the state.

Maclean, however, went to Russia with a reasonably open mind – until, that is, he saw that 'everybody was terrified of everybody else.' Yet even though personal contact with the man in the street was pretty much out of the question, he learned to love Russia and the Russians, observing: 'I think one thing about them is that they are enormously human and, of course, the one thing that communism or state socialism does not allow for is human nature." Indeed, it was the natural adventurer in him and, perhaps, that British tendency to disrespect

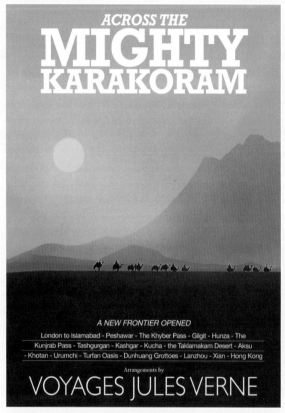

A Story in Brief

MAN OF ACTION: In later life, Sir Fitzroy Maclean and his wife Veronica managed the Creggan Inn at Strachur, on beautiful Loch Fyne. He commissioned his wartime friend and yacht designer Alfred Mylne II to build the motor yacht *Judi of Bute*, for cruising around the West Coast of Scotland. Among his extensive library, was a full set of early editions of James Bond novels, which sold in September 2008 for £26,000; many said he was the man on whom Ian Fleming had based Bond's character. Maclean also bought Palazzo Boschi villa, on the Adriatic island of Korčula, in present-day Croatia, where he spent much of each year. Legislation barred foreigners from buying property, but Tito intervened on behalf of the man who has been his ally during World War II. During the Croatian War of Independence, Maclean and his wife delivered medical supplies to Korčula, and he was posthumously awarded one of Croatia's highest honours, the Order of Prince Branimir.

IMAGE COURTESY: ROBERT SCURRAH/VOYAGES JULES VERNE.

pomposity and absurd rules, even to the point of foolhardiness, that resolved him to break out of his diplomatic cage and to see what lay in the furthest reaches of the USSR, the far-flung and forbidden former khanates of Central Asia.

Even now, that part of the world exudes an air of mystique – it is, after all, easy to romanticise the unknown. The old tribal lands of Uzbekistan and Kazakhstan and their associations with the Silk Road and Bukhara and Samarkand, cities of legendary beauty and enchantment, were impossibly enticing: they lay in what was, to foreigners, a forbidden zone, theoretically impenetrable. For Maclean, then, they offered a suitable target and it is his attempts to reach them that form the first, and most fascinating, third of *Eastern Approaches*.

Bearing in mind that it was only in the early 1990s that independent travel become possible in the Soviet Union, the magnitude of what Maclean attempted, against the background of one of the most despotic regimes in history, is remarkable. Soviet citizens at the time were disappearing at an alarming rate, often for the unforgivable sin of being seen in the company of a foreigner. His first attempts to penetrate the forbidden corners of the Soviet Union arose initially out of curiosity about the places themselves, together with a disinclination to believe that the Soviet state, in the form of its citizens, would entertain any serious interest in where he, an insignificant junior diplomat, might wander.

In a way, Maclean was right, for, once he left the confines of Moscow's remit, he found that patience and a kind of brazen guilelessness got him pretty far and that the officers of the NKVD, the secret-police forerunners of the KGB, performed their duties with less-than-energetic zeal. Nonetheless, it took four attempts to get where he wanted; and furthermore, in the one case where he had a definite and authorised diplomatic objective, he failed. Not that it mattered, for what counted was the adventure itself, during the course of which he witnessed the casual cruelty that is the inevitable consequence of power vested in ideology and its proponents.

For his first foray eastwards, Maclean decided that a route via Baku, which was open to foreigners, might be the least obtrusive. From the Azerbaijani capital, he expected to cross the Caspian and so find a way to Soviet Central Asia. However, in Baku he made his first mistake by informing the representative of Intourist, the state travel agency for foreigners, of his plans, after which he retreated to the nearest restaurant for a late breakfast of caviar and vodka, to reconsider them. On this occasion he was compelled to return to Moscow, although not without a sojourn in Tiflis, the capital of Georgia, where he ran into an eccentric Englishwoman, Miss Fellows, who had arrived as a governess in 1912 and never left.

On his second attempt, Maclean booked a berth on the Trans-Siberian

Railway, absconding at a point well before his stated destination, in order to make his way to Alma-Ata, the capital of Kazakhstan. One of the vivid images he describes is that of the assistant stationmaster at Alma-Ata suckling a baby while the stationmaster lay 'unconscious face downwards on the floor, where he remained throughout the interview.' From there, Maclean reached Tashkent and then, to his amazement and without too much ado, Tamerlane's fabled capital, Samarkand.

The third attempt was a more serious affair, at least in the sense that it was sanctioned by Maclean's employer, the British government. On this occasion, the aim was to try to reach Xinjiang, the Chinese province known then in the West as Chinese Turkestan, which for many decades throughout the 19th century had witnessed a tussle for the balance of power between the British and Russian empires.

After the Bolshevik Revolution of 1917, Russian interest in the area had declined, only to be revived in the 1930s as Stalin decided that growing unrest in China in general, and in Xinjiang in particular, presented an opportunity for the expansion of Soviet influence. Concern over Soviet activity there had been growing in the West for some time: Peter Fleming, on behalf of the *London Times*, had explored the region for similar reasons three years before, approaching it from within China. Maclean was hoping to reach Urumchi, the capital of Xinjiang, from within the USSR, in order to plead with the local authorities for better treatment of Indian traders and British citizens who, it seemed, were subject to discrimination in favour of all things Russian.

Armed with official passes (one Russian and one Chinese, in which his name was rendered as 'Ma-ke-ling' or 'the horse that corrupts the morals'), it looked like Maclean would achieve his objective. But having made it to the Chinese side of the border, he was thwarted from progressing further, either by Chinese bureaucratic obstructiveness or by a change of heart on the part of the Russians, whose influence in Xinjiang was perhaps greater than had been imagined.

That border was to remain all but closed to Westerners for several decades, until a group of Voyages Jules Verne passengers, celebrating '2,100 Years of the Silk Road', made the crossing in 1986. Maclean's final journey was to Afghanistan, via Tajikistan and the River Oxus. Once again, with surprising ease, he reached Bukhara, where the red Soviet flag flew from the crown of the magnificent 'Tower of Death' a minaret from which, as recently as 1920, traitors and other miscreants had been thrown to their deaths by the Emir of Bukhara's henchmen. Maclean then crossed the Oxus by means of an old boat propelled by a tractor engine and made his way into India, via a corner of Afghanistan.

Apart from the debonair tone in which he recounts these journeys, the most striking thing about Maclean's descriptions to anyone who visited Russia and Soviet Central Asia in the late Soviet era is how little it had changed since the events recorded in *Eastern Approaches*. Samarkand and Bukhara still seemed like distant outposts, both of more illustrious times and from Moscow's reach, while the whole rickety edifice that was the USSR seemed permanently stuck, mentally and physically, in about 1940, as if it had made it to the Second World War and then simply stagnated.

Maclean's book illustrates very well the schizophrenic nature of the country. In Moscow, he is witness to Stalin's show trials, those charades of breath-taking inhumanity, and elsewhere to the wholesale imposition of state policy on the hapless population by mindless ideologues. On the other hand, he observes the almost comic manifestations of state security in the form of NKVD officers, who, on the whole, were simply content to tag along wherever he went.

TRAVELLING SOFT CLASS: 1979 VJV ORGANISED VOGUE MAGAZINE PHOTO-SHOOT

CHAPTER 40
WHERE MAO ONCE STOOD

I found myself on Mao's rostrum in the Great Auditorium, in front of an
assembled multitude of European tour operators and flanked by the
BBC's Magnus Magnusson, who had been engaged as moderator.

O NCE I had worked out the general outline of a 'Great Journey' – or, for
that matter, a more ordinary journey – I would set myself certain tests
before going ahead with it. The way I saw it, if I couldn't capture the
essence of the thing within a five-by-three-inch advertisement, it probably wasn't
going to appeal to anyone else. If the combination of words and images seemed
to work, then I would have it sketched up as a rough poster.

Early on, I came to the realisation that concepts could be more evocatively
communicated through artwork than photography. It was also cheaper. However,
as well as a strong image and a few well-crafted words, you needed a sympathetic
font, and luckily I knew someone who could supply this vital third ingredient. His
name was Robert Scurrah and he used to be the art editor at Thomson. During
the mid-'70s he had worked in London at the Saward Baker advertising agency,
who had sent him, on day release, to the London College of Printing in order to
study Art Deco design influences including Cassandre, Roger Broders and Tamara
de Lempicka.

After a spell as an art director in Bermuda, Scurrah moved to Thomson
Holidays and eventually left to go freelance, having got tired of designing signs
for hotels and labels for luggage. His partner, Barry, was largely responsible for
designing the magnificent window displays at the John Lewis store in Oxford
Street, so I hired the two of them to transform the Glentworth Street offices into
my travel emporium.

Right from the start, I used poster artwork in all our promotional material:
advertisements, brochures and business cards alike. I confess, I had visions of

the 'VJV' logo becoming my own personal marque, much like the Cassandre-designed Yves Saint Laurent 'YSL' logo; in my mind's eye, I imagined a whole range of VJV-branded clothes, perfumes and travel paraphernalia, which was why I had registered 'Voyages Jules Verne', 'Phileas Fogg' and 'Maison Jules Verne' as business names.

The posters also performed another important, more down-to-earth function when it came to managing operational risk. I was acutely aware that having 100 per cent of my business activity based in China was a risky strategy and that the company really ought to be offering a whole range of different 'Great Journeys' in other parts of the world. That, however, was easier said than done: it is actually very difficult to come up with three good product ideas, let alone hundreds; launch too many products in one go, and you risk not just a high failure rate but economic disaster.

My approach was thus to 'float', or trial, various tour and travel ideas in the form of advertisements, but not actually make any hard-and-fast arrangements until we got some actual feedback – i.e., bookings. By and large, this plan of action paid off. Admittedly, there would sometimes be a few operational somersaults required on our behalf, but the alternative was just too risky: all too easily, you could spend large amounts of money on setting up and marketing an arrangement, only to find that no one was interested and that all your outlay had been in vain.

Visually, it did no harm to include in your brochure – we used to call them catalogues or 'travel almanacs' – an arrangement that was illustrated by a good-looking poster but which you knew no one would book. The way I saw it, these unwanted journeys were like a backdrop of sand, in which your genuinely popular and successful journeys could sparkle and shine like diamonds.

The marketing and selling of these arrangements was one thing, but the logistics were quite another. As far as I was aware, no one had ever before attempted multi-lingual and multi-variable tour-joining and tour-leaving points. Nor had anyone tried to write out a rail ticket from London to Hong Kong, let alone arrange the buying and issuing of airline tickets at the point of overseas departure. The more international the enterprise became, the more complicated the pre-tour arrangements.

One major stumbling block was the way in which visas could only be obtained upon presentation of the traveller's actual, physical passport in London. Furthermore, once the passport had arrived, visas would only be issued in rigid sequential order, which meant that if you were travelling on board the 'Central Kingdom Express', for instance, you got the Polish visa first, followed by the Soviet visa, the Mongolian visa and, finally, the Chinese visa. All of this involved passports being couriered to London from all over the globe, then around London and, once fully processed, returned to their holders. Without doubt, these were critically weak points in the operation and, every so often, we had to call upon the dexterity of a contortionist to get out of the situations in which we found ourselves.

Each tour would contain passengers from a variety of different countries and agents, all of them paying different tariffs, in different currencies, for a variation of the same thing. The best thing about this arrangement was that with business coming from many different sources I could now guarantee, 100 per cent, that each advertised journey would take place.

Somehow, with just eight full-time members of staff, in an era pre-dating telex, the internet, emails and computers, I had created every tour operator's dream: the perfect, virtuous circle. A result of which was that – irony upon ironies – when Thomson Holidays decided they wanted to re-enter China, the person they had to go through was me.

All this confirmed to me that I had become a truly international tour operator, handling not just British travellers beginning and ending their journey in the UK, but people who might start out in Sydney and end up in London, Frankfurt, Zurich, Rome, New York, Los Angeles, Hawaii or even Oslo. What's more, I was being paid in overseas currencies: US dollars, Hong Kong dollars, German deutschmarks, French and Swiss francs, etc.

Of course, all these different nationalities required multi-lingual escorting, which meant that I now had to hire tour directors with the appropriate language skills. There was no shortage of applicants; indeed, I found myself inundated with replies, and who should the first person lining up outside my door be but Hugo, the former proprietor of the Brasil café on Queensway, who had on so many occasions, during my bedsitting days 14 years previously, urged me to down my cappuccino and be on my way. How poignant, then, to find him coming and asking me for a job – especially when, for reasons I can no longer remember, I turned him down.

The reason that Hugo and a lot of other would-be tour directors were lining up was that we were in the Italian market in a big way, thanks to the efforts of one Stefano Pattaconi. Back in the early '70s, while working for Thomson Holidays in the Soviet Union, I had noticed that Italians had a fascination for socialist countries. Furthermore, because Italian travel agents could not gain entry into the People's Republic of China, that country in particular had for them acquired the status of a sort of travellers' holy grail.

Hence the call I received from Stefano, the Thomson local handling agent in Rimini, a tourist resort on the Italian Adriatic Coast of recently diminished

A Story in Brief

MAO'S STATE TRAIN AND BOAT: By 1991, we at VJV were making frequent use of Mao's State Train, to travel across the Chinese section of the Silk Route, from Urumchi to Xian. Built in East Germany, in 1955, to original Pullman standards, the train was usually reserved for use by visiting heads of state. It consisted of six sleeping cars, two dining cars and a lounge car. Each sleeping car had eight compartments, each one fitted with walnut panelling, fine lace curtains and polished brass fittings. During the day, each compartment became a sitting room, complete with writing table and armchair. We and Lindblad also used Mao's own Yangtse river steamer, the *Kunlun*, named after the Chinese mountain range. Back then, it was a glorious vessel; now it's a forgotten, rotting hulk.

popularity, thanks to the unsightly green algae that had invaded its beaches. Up until now, back in the mid-seventies, Stefano's firm, Viaggi Condor, had been responsible for nothing more complicated than airport transfers, mainly on behalf of British tour operators. However, due to the algae, these companies were now favouring the Spanish Costas and the Balearic Islands and Rimini was becoming a tourist-free zone. In short, Stefano needed to diversify, and quickly, and his chosen new area of activity was the extremely competitive 'incentive travel' market, very popular in Italy at the time.

The way incentive travel worked was that large companies, usually banks, would reward their staff with holidays rather than (taxable) cash bonuses. Stefano had immediately recognised that no other Italian company would be able to offer China as an incentive, and this was why he was now beating a path to my door. I don't believe for a moment that my contacts in China were expecting me to arrange anything more than a few tour groups each year; yet suddenly there I was, pressing for ever-larger allocations, as a result of which Peking had run out of hotel rooms! Indeed, demand had become so intense that I was having to visit Peking practically every month, and always for the same reason: to get more space and more entry visas. This was always a bit nerve-racking, as I had already sold most of the space I was now asking for.

The only place I could find accommodation for Stefano's tour groups was in the city of Tianjin, a four-hour drive from Peking. Not that Stefano cared: all he wanted was something exclusive to offer the banks, and he went on to sell my China arrangements in their hundreds. Though he was not always as prompt as we would have liked when it came to paying us, the business he generated at our very beginnings was one of the pillars on which the company was built.

The best way I could describe Stefano is as a lovable rogue – he reminded me, both in looks and hand gestures, of a certain ex-Sunderland football manager, also Italian (step forward Paolo Di Canio). If I said to Stefano that I wanted to tread with caution, he would proceed to steamroller over any and every obstacle in his path. Although he succeeded in expanding Viaggi Condor from a small, local company into an important player in the Italian outbound tourist market, that was never ever going to be enough; he always needed to aim higher and achieved this, literally, when he founded his own airline.

Alas, things started to go wrong, due to a mixture of bad luck and unforeseen fluctuations in the market. One morning, Stefano visited his usual Rimini café for his morning cup of coffee, returned to his car and, seeing no end to his financial troubles, chose to drive not to the office but to the waterfront, where he accelerated his car into the Adriatic and drowned.

In an industry that survives on little more than ideas wrapped up in a bit of poetry and a lot of hocus-pocus, the formula for success is jealously guarded and, in normal circumstances, rivals are kept at arm's length. I felt that I possessed the two magic ingredients: (a) access to China, and (b) a fair understanding of the operational complexity surrounding it. I was prepared to let other companies in on my secret, provided they didn't get too successful, which meant that I was about to take a very big risk indeed.

First, let me take you back to 1977, when I first climbed the long flight of steps up from Tiananmen Square into the Great Hall of the People. For the past 10 months, Mao Zedong's body had been lying in state within these hallowed portals – it was later moved to a specially built mausoleum, also on the square – and still the queues to file past the Great Helmsman were more than a mile long, zigzagging in all weathers across the square, in a display of reverence that was no doubt genuinely felt by the awestruck country folk for whom this was their first trip to Peking.

At the same time, there must have been many people who were secretly delighted at the final passing of the old dictator, whose rule had reduced the country to a state of abjectness unequalled in the modern era. Not that they would have dared to show it, however, for deeply instilled within them was the (wholly justifiable) fear of recrimination, along with the lifelong habits of patience and conformity. As the mourners shuffled past Mao's body, displayed in a crystal coffin housed in the newly constructed mausoleum, they were all too aware that what was required of them was a show of quiet and uniform respect. It was as if a god had expired.

For many years, the average Chinese citizen never got the opportunity to enter the Great Hall of the People, the nearest thing to a parliament in the People's Republic of China (PRC). The Communist Party leaders made sure of that, investing themselves with the same kind of untouchable mystique as the emperors whom they had supplanted. By the time 1977 came around, however, change was in the air, and unprecedented levels of hospitality were being extended to visitors, like myself, who were making tentative overtures to the Chinese people's natural trading instincts.

The Great Hall of the People was one of the 'Ten Great Constructions' announced by Premier Zhou Enlai in August 1958, during the period of the Great Leap Forward. All situated in Peking, they were to be completed in 10 months' time, in order to commemorate the 10th anniversary of the founding of PRC. Many thousands of 'volunteers' (a highly questionable term in Mao's China) were engaged on the Great Hall's construction between November 1958 and October 1959 and, although the overweeningly Stalinist 'Socialist Realist' architecture speaks only of power, it was, at the same time, a considerable engineering accomplishment. Certainly the immensity of the building, with its myriad halls and meeting rooms, is impressive.

It consists of three sections. First is the central part, incorporating the Great Auditorium, the Main Auditorium, the Congress Hall (where the Standing Committee of the Chinese Communist Party meets in conference), the Central Hall, the Golden Hall and a host of other large halls. Then there is the northern section, consisting of the State Banquet Hall, the Salute State Guest Hall, the North Hall, the East Hall and the West Hall. Finally there is the southern section, which is the office building of the Standing Committee of the People's Congress of China. Each province, special administrative region and autonomous region has its own hall within the complex, each furnished in traditional decorative style.

The Great Auditorium can accommodate some 10,000 delegates, seated beneath the inevitable red star gleaming at the centre of a whorl of lights uncoiling across the ceiling. It was, without doubt, the epicentre of Chinese communism. Yet by 1980, the avowedly capitalist Voyages Jules Verne was already well established as the principal operator of arrangements to China, with offices in London, New York, Hong Kong and Peking itself, in addition to a large number of general agents around the world.

Furthermore, our programmes were to be found in the brochures of some of the most important travel operators in the world, be they in the UK, continental Europe, North America or Australasia – for no other reason, it should be stressed, than I had access to that essential, virtually unobtainable ingredient: entry visas into China.

It was normally unheard of for tour operators to feature the arrangements of a rival, but in this case my rivals had little choice but to comply, if they wanted to include China as part of their offerings. I retained control of every last detail: the visa process, flights, hotels, excursions and the provision of guides. That they featured my arrangements in their brochures was a useful, not to say inexpensive, marketing arrangement, and I was now keen to expand. Nevertheless, organising the itineraries was no easy business; our customers came from a wide range of different countries and sources, and all of them had to dovetail into the same core itinerary on arrival, not least because this was a period when almost all tourists to China were obliged to travel on a group visa.

In addition, as the state-run tourist infrastructure was poor, with insufficient hotels and transportation, there were no guarantees that the itinerary would always be adhered to, or that single travellers would not have to share a room with a stranger. It was by no means uncommon on a Yangtse cruise for up to 16 passengers, male and female and all speaking different languages, to end up sharing with each other. This was made worse by the fact that, in this pre-fax-machine, pre-email era, just about every arrangement with the Chinese had to be made first by cable and, subsequently, by telex.

There was then the question of the relationship between the customers and their Chinese guides, most of whom had no real understanding of the Western mentality, especially when that mentality manifested itself in the form of several nationalities, each with its own tics, traits and sensibilities, all in the same group. Perhaps the most demanding of our tasks, then, was to find sufficient numbers of tour directors. These people did not just point out interesting landmarks; they were also full-time mediators. Firstly, between the group members, some of them awkward customers who were both frightening and baffling to the Chinese, and, secondly, between the group and the representatives of the Chinese state. And they had to do that in up to four different languages.

Back in those early days, the air of disorganisation that characterised travel in China was in stark contrast to the baronial splendour of institutions like the Great Hall of the People. Speaking of seemingly unreachable goals, I made the momentous decision in 1980, three years after my initial visit to China, to try and bring off something of a coup. This was to persuade, albeit through gritted teeth, the authorities to open up the Great Auditorium in the Great Hall of the People for a travel conference involving the various overseas companies that were working with Voyages Jules Verne. To my utter astonishment, the Chinese agreed.

So, on 8 December 1980, I found myself on Mao's rostrum in the Great Auditorium, in front of an assembled multitude of European tour operators and agents. I was flanked by Magnus Magnusson, the British-Icelandic scholar and presenter of TV's *Mastermind*, who had been engaged as moderator, yet was not as moderate as I had tried to persuade him to be when it came to lecturing the Chinese, in their own parliament, on their treatment of the Tibetans.

An enthusiastic drinker of Coke and maotai, Magnus was, nonetheless, immensely kind to me, understanding straight away that I was but a lowly David among these travel giants. Bizarrely, the first announcement that day concerned the murder of John Lennon, which had taken place only hours before in New York; no doubt this meant precious little to the Chinese, but to many of the Western conference-goers, to whom Lennon was as much a champion as Mao had been to his people, there was a fine irony that the news should be broken in a building symbolising the dictatorship of the proletariat.

Once this initial shock had been weathered, the various speeches seemed to go down quite well, as did the huge banquet and the visits to Peking's historic sites. All of this helped to achieve my main aim, which was to cement my precarious and eccentric intermediary role between the Chinese and my would-be competitors.

There was, however, a quid pro quo. In exchange for opening the Great Hall of the People, the Chinese had asked me to organise a training course for their own Chinese guides. To this end, UK-based city guides, resort representatives and guide-trainers were brought to Peking, to steer their Chinese counterparts through such matters as explaining to jet-lagged Western tourists that they would be sharing a room with a complete stranger. This, I assure you, was a far more challenging job than it sounded, due to the fact that Chinese people will do anything to avoid direct confrontation and the loss of face it brings. Being made to look and feel foolish in front of one's peers in China constitutes far more than just having embarrassment inflicted upon oneself; it is perceived as a mortal insult.

This being the case, our Chinese guides were not only incapable of remonstrating with clients, but also had no idea how to defuse outbursts of anger by making use of subtlety and humour. Luckily, I had taken along a selection of training films made by John Cleese, of *Fawlty Towers* and Monty Python fame, including the classic episode 'Difficult Customers', and I am pleased to say that this went down a storm with both the guides and the tourism officials alike, who insisted that the films remain in China once the workshop was over.

There may be copies that are even now being used as teaching aids in China, but only in remote corners of the country. To the urban Chinese, who in a short span of years have become unrecognisably confident and sophisticated, Western ways are no longer as mysterious as they once were.

CHAPTER 41
INCIDENT ON THE YANGTSE

Bewildered, I wondered who this celebrity sitting next to me could
possibly be, since he looked quite unremarkable. Once the aircraft had
taken off, my curiosity got the better of me.

FOR us Barnardo's children, motion pictures were our window to the world
outside, just as they had been, I suppose, for those hapless souls trapped
behind the Iron Curtain. With regards to the kind of films we would be
shown, this was dependent on the generosity of local film distributors and whether
the movies were deemed suitable by our internal censors. For instance, one film
we never saw was *Lord Jeff* (as it was called in the US), or *The Boy from Barnardo's*
(its UK title). At the time, it was thought that the film portrayed the homes in a
bad light, but having now seen the film for myself, I fail to see how they reached
that conclusion.

The producers had meticulously researched and re-created, down to the
last detail, the Barnardo's Sea Training School, in Parkstone, Dorset, that I had
attended. The film starred Freddie Bartholomew and a young Mickey Rooney,
who, in the same year, had starred in the uncannily similar *Boys Town*. For some
reason, we did get to see *Boys Town*, even though the storyline was practically the
same as *Lord Jeff*: orphaned boy runs away from institution, is returned and is
presented with a fork in the road, one route leading to a life of crime and the other
to a happy ending (which, in the case of *Lord Jeff*, was a job as an able seaman on
board the legendary Cunard liner RMS *Queen Mary*).

Our cinema nights at Parkstone followed pretty much the same pattern each
week. Every Wednesday, a projector was set up in the band room and, through a
glow of dust-filled light, the flickering images appeared on the screen – or, rather,
on the large white sheet that served as our screen. We boys would gather, in a state
of some excitement, to watch films that were mainly in black-and-white. From

A Story in Brief

HMS AMETHYST: This is a Belgian poster for the 1957 film *Yangtse Incident*, in which the ship at the centre of the drama, HMS *Amethyst*, was brought out of storage to play the starring role – as herself. At least in most of the shots; as *Amethyst*'s engines were no longer operational, her sister ship *Magpie* was used in scenes where the the ship was moving. No sooner had the film been released, though, than *Amethyst* was broken up, at the Barbican in Plymouth in 1957. Overlooking the site of *Amethyst*'s demise today, is a 17th century warehouse, converted into a large public house and restaurant. Appropriately, this venue goes under the name of The China House. Richard Todd, who played the lead role in the film, was Ian Fleming's absolute first choice for James Bond in *Dr. No* but a conflict of filming schedules in the end meant Sean Connery got the role instead.

what I can remember, most had been produced by the Rank Organisation and, in the opening credits, a Mr Universe-type muscle man would take a swing with a large mallet at an extremely large gong; at this, we boys, for some unknown reason, would shout: "Sock it to 'em, Charlie!"

The films we were shown were mostly of the classic, patriotic, action kind, such as *The Wooden Horse* and, particularly relevant here, *Yangtse Incident: The Story of HMS Amethyst*. The latter movie, made in 1957, was based upon the book by Lawrence Earl and was known in the US by a number of other titles, such as *Battle Hell, Escape of the Amethyst* and *Their Greatest Glory*. It starred Richard Todd and told how, on 19 April 1949, the Royal Navy frigate HMS *Amethyst* sailed up the Yangtse and was fired upon, without warning, by shore batteries of the Chinese People's Liberation Army (PLA). After a heavy engagement, the *Amethyst* ends up lying badly damaged and grounded in the mud. With 54 crew members either dead, dying or seriously wounded and others expiring from the tropical heat and lack of essential medicines, the local Communist Party official, Colonel Peng, instructs the ship's captain that he must accept responsibility for the entire incident, or else the *Amethyst* will remain his prisoner.

After a failed attempt by HMS *Consort* to tow the *Amethyst* off the mud banks, the lieutenant commander-in-charge decides to risk steaming down the Yangtse at night, without a pilot or navigation charts. After some subtle alterations to the ship's outline, to try to disguise her, the *Amethyst* slips her mooring and heads down river in the dark, following a local merchant ship through the treacherous shoals. Having finally broken through the boom at the mouth of the river, she sends a signal to HMS *Concord*: 'Have re-joined the fleet south of Woosung. No major damage. No casualties. God save the King.' You simply couldn't get more patriotic.

In similar fashion to the *Amethyst*, Voyages Jules Verne was sailing along just nicely in 1982. I was practically controlling the whole of the European travel business into China, in addition to having a sizeable share of the American market. However, this left me vulnerable to the Chinese changing their tourism policy and to my competitors realising that getting into China was not quite as daunting as they had previously thought. I clearly needed to tie the Chinese into an arrangement that would secure the status quo and the best way of doing this, I decided, was to enter into a joint venture with them, with the rewards to be split between us. This was not going to be easy, as the Chinese had never before entered into such a deal with a Western company.

My idea was to separate the China business and place it into the newly formed joint venture vehicle, leaving Voyages Jules Verne to continue promoting its 'Great Journeys of the World'. On the face of it, I would be giving up 50 per cent of my revenues and profits in exchange for no tangible consideration, but I felt it would be a worthwhile insurance policy in securing our long-term future.

There then followed a period of tortuous exchanges and negotiations, at the end of which I received an invitation to visit China for an official signing ceremony. Thus, on 20 September 1982, I found myself boarding an Air China (or CAAC, as it was then) flight bound for Peking from Hong Kong. Taking my seat at the front of what was most definitely a one-class aircraft, I was suddenly joined by a gentleman who was being mobbed by such a scrum of camera-clicking photographers and microphone-thrusting reporters that they had to be ushered away by the Chinese stewardesses.

Bewildered, I wondered who this celebrity could possibly be, since he looked quite unremarkable. Once the aircraft had taken off, my curiosity got the better of me and it turned out I was sitting next to one of my boyhood heroes: Sir Edward Youde, of Yangtse Incident fame, who was now the Governor of Hong Kong and on his way to Peking to meet Mrs Thatcher, who was making her first visit to China as Prime Minister. The tone of her relationship with the Chinese had already been set by a previous visit in 1977, while still leader of the opposition, when she had apparently described China as "rather an unpleasant place and governed by unpleasant people".

This ill feeling was reciprocated. Thatcher's visit as Prime Minister was listed as the fourth item on Peking's main radio news that evening, after a commentary on the Communist Party's recent national congress, a report on reactions to the congress among miners in Henan province and the arrival in Xian of another foreign leader, Kim Il Sung of North Korea. In view of the coolness between the two governments, it was not surprising that the Chinese had afforded Sir Edward none of the courtesies that reflected his office, which was why he found himself jammed into a standard seat next to me. That said, the discomfort of the journey was nothing compared to what he had experienced in 1949, on HMS *Amethyst*. The purpose of the ship's trip up the Yangtse had been to replace HMS *Consort*, which had been guarding the British Embassy during the civil war between the Kuomintang nationalists (led by Chiang Kai-shek) and the Communist Party (led by Mao Zedong).

After the *Amethyst* had become stranded in the middle of the river, following the shelling from the Communist forces, Youde used his knowledge of Mandarin to negotiate with the PLA commander, in an attempt to secure the ship's release. He was later awarded an MBE for his part in the escape and went on to pursue a distinguished peacetime career. He is best remembered today for being the Governor of Hong Kong at the time of the signing, in Peking in 1984, of the Sino-British Joint Declaration, which made it clear that, after 156 years of colonial rule, the British would leave Hong Kong in 1997. Youde was the only Welsh Governor of Hong Kong and the only one to die in office, while visiting the British Embassy in Peking in December 1986. He was greatly respected by the Chinese population in Hong Kong, and thousands lined the streets for his state funeral. As he was sat next to me on the aircraft and unable to escape my questions, I asked him to recount his days in revolutionary China and, in particular, the events surrounding the Yangtse Incident and his days as emissary to Peking.

This wasn't just a one-way conversation, either: he was very interested to hear about my joint-venture dealings with the Chinese and the imminent signing ceremony. On our arrival in Peking, Sir Edward was duly chauffeured to the British Embassy in Peking, while I was taken to the Diaoyutai State Guesthouse. Diaoyutai actually means 'angling platform', and the guesthouse is so named because the site was a favourite fishing spot of Zhangzong, Emperor of Jin China from 1189-1208 AD. It is also one of the 'Ten Great Constructions' finished in 1959 to commemorate the 10th anniversary of the founding of the People's Republic.

Originally used to house visiting foreign dignitaries and provincial government officials during the Cultural Revolution, the guesthouse had for a time been the permanent residence of Jiang Qing, Mao Zedong's last wife, known in the West as 'Madame Mao'. After a night spent sleeping in the very same bed occupied by President Nixon during his historic visit to China in 1972, I duly attended the signing ceremony the next day and took part, together with all the leading officials of Luxingshe, in a lavish banquet at which much maotai was knocked back.

From this great high, however, I was soon brought back down to earth, when I returned to London and found Laker Airways and Laker Holidays (who were now featuring my China arrangements in America) had gone bust, having operated its last flight in February 1982. Not only did this put paid to my US-brochure carrying facility (its no luggage allowance policy enabled us to ship all our brochures in numerous suitcases from London to New York free of extra charge), but it also left me out of pocket, as I was still owed money.

Unfortunately, things got worse. Having found an office for the joint venture with China just a couple of shops down from my Glentworth Street headquarters, I soon realised that this co-operative notion was not going to work, upon discovering that my three new Chinese colleagues were entering into commercial agreements with my competitors – at my expense. Rather than securing my future, I had allowed a Chinese cuckoo into my nest, and it wasn't long before I concluded that this simply would not do. I gave up my interest in the joint venture and suggested that my erstwhile colleagues should turn themselves instead into a Chinese tourist office, which is what they eventually did.

CHAPTER 42
AROUND THE WORLD
IN 80 DAYS

I was contacted by Vogue magazine, enquiring if a writer could come along and write up the journey. The writer in question turned out to be Michael Palin.

N 1980 I was still counting the pennies and, given the lack of UK travel agency support, came to the conclusion that the best way to attract attention was to dream up ideas that would generate the same kind of publicity as the 'Central Kingdom Express' had done a year earlier; hence my notion of re-enacting Jules Verne's *Around the World in Eighty Days*. My version would be 57 days long, however, as I didn't think anyone would want to be away for the full 80. My intention was to preserve some of the theatre and authenticity of the original enterprise by using the same modes of transport as in the book. The first step was to contact Hardy Amies, the Queen's couturier, who owned the building on Savile Row where, according to Verne, the fictional Phileas Fogg had lived. I wanted to use this location for my press launch and Amies not only gave me his permission, he didn't even charge me a hire fee.

For heightened dramatic effect, I decided that I would arrive in a horse-drawn buggy and would be met by an actor playing Fogg, in period dress. I needed to clear this with the police, which proved harder than I might have imagined. The sergeant at Savile Row Police Station seemed both uncertain as to whether to take my request seriously and anxious that my stunt might inconvenience well-to-do customers visiting their tailors. Thankfully, I was eventually given the go-ahead for my grand production, which I augmented by booking a string quartet (again in period dress) and inviting, as per the launch of the 'Central Kingdom Express', absolutely everyone I knew. The next morning, I was interviewed on the BBC's

Today programme by presenters John Timpson, David Stephenson and Brian Redhead. The broadcast went as follows:

John Timpson: The 75th anniversary of the death of Jules Verne is to be marked by a package tour with a difference: around the world not in 80 days but in a mere 57, thanks to the invention of the aeroplane. It's the latest idea of a company which has devised other exotic journeys like a passage to China on the 'Central Kingdom Express', a train journey of 9,331.6 miles, give or take a sleeper. David Stephenson has been examining their latest offering in the steps of Phileas Fogg. First, a reminder of that film version in which David Niven played the intrepid traveller.

[Cue a short audio clip featuring the wager at the Reform Club.]

David Stephenson: The two dozen or so intrepid travellers who decide to follow in the fictional footsteps of Phileas Fogg will find quite a few concessions to modern times, although the route is based on the 1870 Bradshaw's Continental Railway and Steamship Timetable, which it's thought provided some of Verne's inspiration. The managing director of Voyages Jules Verne, Philip Morrell, told me travel will be by horse-drawn carriage, train, ship and aeroplane.

Philip Morrell: Lengthy trans-Atlantic and trans-Pacific sectors we're carrying out by aeroplane, principally because there are no scheduled services still operating on those sectors at this moment, and also to get the duration down from 80 days to a more manageable 57 days, so that it brings it within the scope of more people.

David Stephenson: Ballooning is ruled out because, although liberty was taken in the film, it doesn't appear in Verne's story. The route goes via first-class hotels in Paris and Milan, to India, the Far East, China, Japan and America, returning through Dublin and Liverpool, and travellers will be accompanied throughout by Mr Fogg's personal valet, Passepartout.

[Cue another excerpt from the film, in which Fogg interviews Passepartout.]

David Stephenson: The first tour's 'Passepartout' will be chosen from applicants to an advertisement appearing in the personal column of today's *London Times*. He's likely to be over 45 and working in a top London hotel; he may also need to exercise some facility with elephants, which will be providing authentic transport for part of the Indian stage of the tour.

Philip Morrell: That's one of the simple parts of the itinerary in so much as the Indian Tourist Board have a herd of elephants currently in position for us; in

A Story in Brief

NUMBER 14 SAVILE ROW: The picture here shows me meeting the legendary adventurer Phileas Fogg (or at least an actor pretending to be him), as part of a 1980 publicity stunt promoting my round-the-world tour. What catches my eye, though, is not the two figures in the foreground, but the plaque on the wall above the door. This bears witness to the fact that Irish playwright Richard Sheridan, author of *The Rivals*, once lived here. What is the significance of that? Well, in his book *Around The World In Eighty Days*, Jules Verne makes it clear that Phileas Fogg's residence in Mayfair had been Sheridan's old house, back in the 18th century. At the time of this photo, however, it was the headquarters of high-class couturier Hardy Amies, who was kind enough not to charge us for using his front doorstep nor his catwalk for the location.

fact, we are using government elephants, even though they cost a little bit more – perhaps because they are a bit better fed with more straw, say, but that's all laid on in Allahabad.

David Stephenson: And what about the Red Indian ambush? Now that's going to be quite a problem to arrange, isn't it?

Philip Morrell: Well, in fact, the ambush took place in Wyoming and we've arranged with the Wyoming State Tourist Board to lay on stagecoaches between Borie and Cheyenne, and, hopefully, also on that sector we're hoping to get out of mothballs the world's largest steam engine, the *Big Boy.*

David Stephenson: Times may have changed but, even today, an around-the-world trip is not for the faint-hearted. The official brochure describes the programme as extensive and physically demanding; you'll also require resources of a more tangible kind, amounting to £6,600, to cover the basic cost. Well, I wonder, would Phileas Fogg really have approved of all this?

Philip Morrell: Avid readers of Jules Verne will note that he was a past master at improvisation, and that's what we have done.

[Cue the song 'Around the World (in Eighty Days)'.]

John Timpson: I bet you guessed we'd play that. You'll have noticed, incidentally, that Jules Verne's character in the book has been referred to throughout in that report as Phileas with an 'L'. Before you reach for your phone to tell us it was Phineas with an 'N', let me quote from the company's brochure. It seems that two spellings were possible: they say Phineas or Phileas, and we have adhered to Verne's choice of Phileas.

Brian Redhead: So you'll just have to ring Jules Verne if you don't like it.

This was the kind of publicity you just couldn't buy, and following the broadcast we were inundated with people applying to be our Passepartout. The thing that really sticks in my mind is diving into the first shop to buy a suit and shoes that I thought would be appropriate for the launch. I bought the first pair of shoes I tried on – unfortunately, as it turned out, for once the event was underway and I found myself under the arc lights on Hardy Amies' catwalk, delivering my spiel, my feet suddenly began to swell up. I was in such agony that, to this day, I consider it one of the high points of my career that I managed to carry on.

Of course, while I made much of them for publicity purposes, the most complicated parts of the 'Around the World in 80 Days' itinerary were not the theatrical, stagecoach and elephant excursions, but rather the sea crossing from

Basra, in Iraq, to Bombay, which we were intending to make on board an Arab dhow (more of this later).

For the moment, however, we were more concerned with creating an aura of old-fashioned adventure and mystery around our journey; and of course, the yardstick by which all exotic train travel is measured is the *Orient Express*. Though it was seen as the last word in rail luxury, the *Orient Express* passed through some of the wilder corners of Europe, a fact that served to ignite the imaginations of writers like Agatha Christie and Graham Greene, who glimpsed dramatic dynamite in this mixture of ostentatious wealth with banditry and espionage. In short, a legend was created.

Although most people associate the *Orient Express* with that uneasy, glamorous period between the two World Wars, the story actually goes back much further, almost to the beginning of train travel. In the railway almanac, there was one date that always stood out from all others: 4 October 1883, this being the day when George Nagelmackers, the son of a Belgian banker, assembled a splendid rake of deluxe carriages belonging to his own, grandiosely-named Compagnie Internationale des Wagons-Lits et des Grands Express Européens.

The occasion was the inaugural run of what the local press quickly dubbed 'L'Orient Express', and what captured the imagination of the press and public alike was the sheer sumptuousness of the carriages, along with the lavish, indulgent level of service. Just as remarkable was the nature of the journey itself. Before Nagelmackers came along, the notion of 'through trains' linking the great cities of Europe had been almost beyond conjecture, as if they would be tantamount to a threat to national sovereignty. Instead, passengers had been obliged to change from one train to another at each frontier, a tedious and pointless irritant that, not unnaturally, had put off the would-be continental traveller.

To his eternal credit, Nagelmackers succeeded in demonstrating to the various authorities the futility of that procedure and persuaded them to accept his service. What he could do nothing about, however, was the absence of a railway track that reached Constantinople (modern-day Istanbul). True to the spirit of entrepreneurship, he turned a potential pitfall to his advantage, with the help of a steamship service from the Black Sea town of Varna.

The centenary of that first departure fell on 4 October 1983 – clearly, this was an opportunity not to be missed. I had long reserved the same slot on the same platform at the same Paris station, Gare de l'Est, from which the first *Orient Express* had departed. I had also set about making arrangements with the help of Wagons-Lits, as Nagelmacker's company (incorporated into the state French state railway company, SNCF) had come to be known. It was they who owned the copyright of the marque 'Orient Express' and, to use the name, I needed the permission of SNCF, who granted it on the condition that I prefixed it with 'Centenary'. This did not go unnoticed by the recently formed operators of the 'Venice Simplon-Orient-Express' (VSOE), who wrote me a stern letter suggesting that I might like to reconsider my intention to use the title 'Centenary Orient Express'. I was thankful that, for once in my career, I had taken the precaution of following due process and was therefore able to respond with a firm riposte.

The press, who relished the potential rivalry, quoted me as saying that the VSOE was a 'show train for hedonists'. By contrast, my intention was to recreate a sense of occasion, rather than simply to ape a bygone era. "We want to create a feeling of travel as an end in itself," I announced, "rather than a succession of plastic airports, plastic chairs and plastic cups."

Of course, our journey was something of a celebration, which meant that, from Paris to Vienna, passengers travelled in vintage rolling stock of the type that Monsieur Poirot would have known, with Lalique glass fittings and a silver-service dinner (served by authentically inebriated waiters), drawn by a steam locomotive. From Vienna, we travelled on Hungarian rolling stock to Budapest and then in Romanian carriages, first to Bucharest and on through Bulgaria, to the Black Sea coast at Varna. While the nature of true authenticity is always debatable, what you have to remember is that this was happening well before the collapse of communism in the Eastern Bloc, which meant we had to contend with the ever-present uncertainties of the Cold War. Luxury in Paris, I assure you, was not the same as luxury in Bucharest.

Although the trains from Vienna onwards could not compare with the antique Wagons-Lits rolling stock, they were the best that the countries of Eastern Europe could manage at the time, and they added a frisson to the enterprise that no amount of plushly appointed Pullman cars from the 1920s could ever have achieved.

The best word to describe the relationship between Hungary, Romania and Bulgaria at the time was 'fraught'. Nominally united in socialist brotherhood, their alliances were only skin-deep, papering over age-old differences. The question in Budapest, according to the Hungarians (who regarded their neighbours with suspicion bordering on contempt), was whether the rolling stock chartered from CFR, Romania's state railway company, would materialise; and if so, what sort of condition it would it be in. Among all the countries of Eastern Europe, Romania was one of the most impoverished – nobody, it seemed, would have been surprised if the Romanian train had failed to draw into Budapest's elegant Keleti station.

In the event, there was no need to worry. Late in the night, preceding departure for Bucharest, a call came through with the information that the train had arrived. The news prompted a rapid scramble in the darkness to the siding where it had been parked. All was well: the dining car was spotless and had already been prepared for a welcoming breakfast; the staff members were enthusiastic and personable. The 'Centenary Orient Express' would make it to the coast.

Indeed, the Romanian leg turned out to be one of the highlights of the whole journey. When a Southern European temperament combines with a sense of occasion, celebration is the natural result, especially when the national drink, Țuică, is served at breakfast, lunch and dinner. The atmosphere on the train, as it bowled along the Hungarian plains and grazed the Danube at the Iron Gates, the name given to the steepling gorges at the frontier of Romania and Serbia, was jubilant.

All of a sudden, then, the journey had acquired an independent momentum. When a group of folk musicians unexpectedly boarded the train in order to supplement their day's earnings after performing at a local wedding, just as their ancestors had done on the original *Orient Express* a century before, it was entirely in keeping with the festive spirit of what had become a party on wheels. Much of this was attributable to the Romanians, whose exuberance and genuine enthusiasm, in the context of – or perhaps because of – the terrifyingly repressive regime under which they lived, was astounding.

From Bucharest, a steam locomotive hauled the train to Sinaia, from where there were visits to Bran Castle (allegedly Dracula's) and, courtesy of the Communist Party of Romania, to Peleș Castle, which had been built from 1873-1914 by King Carol I and closed in 1975 by Nicolai Ceausescu as a 'State Protocol Interest Area'. Then it was back to Bucharest and the Athénée Palace Hotel, a notorious den of spies in the years leading up to World War II and which had continued to live up to its reputation during the Cold War.

In 1938, A. L. Easterman of London's *Daily Express* had referred to the hotel's 'heavily ornate furnishings, marble and gold pillars, great glittering chandeliers and the deep settees placed well back in the recesses of the lounge, as if inviting conspiracy.' He might well have said the same in 1983, with the insertion of the word 'faded' at the beginning of the sentence. He had also described the hotel as the 'most notorious caravanserai in all Europe, the meeting place of Continental spies, political conspirators, adventurers, concession hunters, and financial manipulators.' Once again, little had changed by the time we got there: infamous though the Ceaușescu government already was, it would be several years before its true odiousness became apparent. All the staff in the hotel, it transpired, and all the seemingly genial locals one met in the bar, were effectively spies of one sort or another.

Then it was across Bulgaria to the coast, where a Bulgarian chartered ocean liner awaited, to transport the passengers to Istanbul. The ship left early in the morning and sailed along the Bosphorus into Istanbul as the setting sun burned the minaret-lined skyline a vivid tangerine (just like the poster I had commissioned for the event) and the distorted, amplified voices of the muezzins summoned the faithful to prayer.

It was almost theatrical, in the best traditions of the original Orient Express, and of course it was fitting that the passengers should stay in George Naglemacker's Pera Palace Hotel. The whole journey had been something of a triumph and it was clear that I would be running subsequent trips along the same lines, although I was now obliged to change the name of the journey to 'Stamboul Train', since it was no longer a one-off service.

It was on one of these subsequent journeys that I was contacted by *Vogue* magazine, enquiring if a journalist could come along and write up the journey. The journalist turned out to be Monty Python's Michael Palin, whom I was not too familiar with at the time. Having met him as the band played and the steam train was being coupled on the Gare de l'Est station platform, I escorted him to one of the train's exclusive 'coupés', which we were to share up until Vienna. On sinking into our 1929 'Riviera' armchairs, I asked him if he would like a drink and, without hesitation, he replied "champagne", which rather took me aback and meant I had to run the whole length of the train in order to rustle up a bottle of bubbly. Having done my hostly duties, I left Palin and the train at Vienna, having exchanged contact details.

Encouraged by the success of this venture, I decided, a few months later, to launch another 'Great Journey'. Called '2,100 Years of the Silk Road', it comprised about 10 different chartered trains, linking London with the ancient terminus of the Silk Road at Xian, in China. The idea caught the attention of the BBC, and I was invited by Clem Vallance and another BBC producer to lunch at an Italian restaurant on Kensington High Street. During the course of the lunch, they posed the question as to who could possibly front the series and, having recently come back from the 'Stamboul' train run, I suggested Michael Palin and duly offered up his contact details, which I had held on to since Vienna.

In the end, the producers decided to make the documentary *Around the World in 80 Days*, instead of covering the Silk Road trip; and as we all know, it was Michael Palin who stood in for Phileas Fogg. The BBC researchers later contacted me to assist on some technical details, particularly in regard to the complicated Arab dhow sequence, but that was pretty much the full extent of my involvement in the series – apart, that is, from putting forward the perfect presenter.

CHAPTER 43
REPAIR TO THE REFORM

Then, out of nowhere, the Falklands War occurred. Following the
Argentinian invasion, commercial craft were drafted in to supplement the
Royal Navy, including 'Queen Elizabeth II', 'Canberra' and the 'Uganda'.

ONE of the first charter travel pioneers in the UK was Vladimir Gavrilovich
Raitz who founded the Horizon Holiday Group in 1949. Before this there
had been the Workers' Travel Association, Sir Henry Lunn, the Polytechnic Touring Association, Viaggi Globus, 'Captain' Ted Langton's Blue Cars,
Thomas Cook, the redoubtable Harry Chandler of Travel of Club Upminster and
let us not forget Thomas Bennett, who probably pre-dated them all. However, as
far as the press were concerned, it was Raitz who was the trailblazer when it came
to the idea of chartering an entire aeroplane. His family were White Russian Jews
who had left the Soviet Union and eventually made their way to London, where
Vladimir worked as a journalist in the 1940s, first for the British arm of United
Press and then for Reuters.

Raitz's story mirrors the great upheavals of the 20th twentieth century that
provoked the flight of persecuted peoples, first from the Soviet Union and then
from the Third Reich. Those who found sanctuary in countries not run by knaves
and dictators still had to make a living; the poor among them might succeed
through sheer determination and perseverance, while others, like Raitz, born in
Moscow to a doctor and dentist, could console themselves with a good education
and a cosmopolitan outlook.

However, the path down which Raitz travelled was far from straightforward.
It began in 1927, when his mother took him from Moscow to join her parents,
who had fled to Berlin after the 1917 Bolshevik Revolution. He never saw
his father again. However, given the rise of Hitler, their choice of destination
was hardly felicitous, and following his mother's remarriage to a Pole (later

murdered by the Russians at Katyn) they moved to Warsaw, where Raitz attended the French lycée.

With war looming, the family finally made their way to London, where Raitz, fluent in Russian, German, Polish and French but with no English, attended Mill Hill School (where he mastered English in the first term) and then the London School of Economics. He became a journalist, a trade which no doubt honed his eye for the main chance. That chance came in 1949. At the age of 27, he had taken his first holiday since the war, in Corsica. A fellow Russian, one Baron Nicholas Steinheil, was staying in Calvi, where he had helped set up a water polo club-cum-holiday camp run by another Russian, Dmitri Filipoff, heir to the largest bakery fortune in Imperial Russia. The 'Club Olympique' consisted of little more than a group of tents on a beautiful beach, but the bar and dance-floor functioned well and Raitz, ever the proud Muscovite with a fondness for vodka, wine and song, spent a carefree fortnight away from impoverished and rationed England.

Just as Raitz was about to take his leave, Steinheil made a suggestion to him. It so happened that Steinheil's father and Tao Khan, a former member of a Cossack riding and dancing team and now the owner of the Chez Tao bar in Calvi (still in existence and trading on its legendary reputation), had some influence with the local mayor. What's more, said mayor could be persuaded to lease a good parcel of land on the beach, where a new club, tentatively named the 'Club Franco-Britannique', might be established, in order to attract British customers.

The idea was seductive, but the problem was how to get people there in less than the 48 hours it had taken Raitz. At that time, Calvi had what Steinheil described as "not exactly an airport": a landing strip built by the Americans during the war. Nevertheless, Raitz invested most of a £3,000 legacy from his grand-mother into the business, presuming that back in London the process of chartering a plane and attracting customers would be straightforward. In fact, Britain, allegedly a country of entrepreneurs, had other ideas, in that state-run British European Airways (BEA) held a monopoly over commercial flights.

In the end, the only way Raitz could get a licence to fly to Calvi – a destination ignored by BEA – was on the condition that his passengers consisted entirely of teachers and students. Horizon Holidays was thus born. On the firm's first trip to Corsica, in 1950, holidaymakers endured a six-hour flight in an unpressurised DC3 Dakota (including a re-fuelling stop in Lyon) and, once they had arrived, slept in tents by the beach equipped with what can only be described as primitive sanitary arrangements. They loved it. What made it even better was that, for travel there and back plus an entire fortnight of sunshine, fresh food and wine, they had paid an all-inclusive price of £32.10, which was roughly half the cost of a return flight to Nice, the closest airport served by BEA.

Slowly but surely, then, a loyal Horizon clientele was cultivated, new destinations were added and standards of accommodation improved, all of which meant that Horizon Holidays grew into one of the largest travel companies in the UK. By the late 1960s, with Raitz still the only shareholder, the company had become immensely profitable, boasting plush offices in Hanover Street. As for Raitz, he had an endless supply of cigars, plus a house in Chelsea. Or at least he had them until 1974, when, squeezed by the oil crisis and the cost-shredding antics of its competitors, Horizon Holidays folded. That, said Raitz, was "the nadir of my existence".

There were, however, other reasons for the company's failure. Raitz had been confronted with the eternal dilemma that faces all prospering entrepreneurs: whether to simply carry on doing what had brought him success, or branch out and compete with the brash newcomers, who came with new ideas, their own aircraft and low prices. Though he had tried to place Horizon at the more exclusive end of the market, in the end it was perhaps inevitable that he would sell to his great rival, Clarksons. Just a year later, Clarksons also went down, together with its parent company, Court Line, in perhaps the greatest fiasco the British travel industry has ever witnessed.

A few subsidiary companies, including Horizon Midland and Club 18-30, did survive the collapse, although the latter, which became associated exclusively with alcohol and hedonism (advertisements featured tag lines such as 'It's not all sex, sex, sex. There's a bit of sun and sea as well') was eventually bought by Thomas Cook, much to Raitz's relief. In turn, Horizon Midland eventually became Horizon Travel and was bought by Thomson Holidays in 1988 – ironic really, given that, in 1965 Raitz had not offered his own company up for sale to his old school chum Gordon Brunton, who was then heading the Thomson group's expansion into the travel trade. Instead, he made the mistake of advising Brunton to buy Captain Langton's Skytours, upon which Thomson set about creating the new, competitive environment that drove Horizon into the hands of Clarksons.

It was at that point that Raitz left Horizon Holidays and became a travel consultant and broker. He also went on to own the Hickie Borman Group, named after the travel agent who reputedly arranged David Livingstone's journeys to Africa. Inducted into the British Travel Industry Hall of Fame, he also published his memoir, Flight to the Sun, written together with the journalist Roger Bray, in 2001. Much earlier, in 1982, Raitz had contacted me, professing fascination with the development of Voyages Jules Verne. He was a member of the Reform Club on Pall Mall and, given the Around the World in Eighty Days connection (in the book, the wager is made in the club), he offered to propose me as a prospective member, which I duly became.

Of course, Raitz had another motive for the meeting: he had heard on the grapevine that Charles Forte, of Trusthouse Forte, wanted to jettison Swan Hellenic, a travel operator specialising in art and history tours, including cruises along the Nile and, in particular, cruises on a Greek ship, the *Orpheus*. In his guise as a broker, Raitz wondered if I might be interested in the purchase of the company, a suggestion that had some merit since Voyages Jules Verne, which had prospered largely on its business in China, was rather too closely linked with that one destination, a dilemma not dissimilar to that which had confronted Raitz's Horizon company a decade or so before.

Before we got down to discussing business, I took the opportunity to get in some gentle ribbing, regarding the occasion in 1965 when I had visited his opulent Hanover Square offices and been interviewed, and turned down, for a resort representative job. He rather graciously responded by saying that, in retrospect, he wished his company had taken me on, as I might well have been able to help him.

With regards to the Swan Hellenic deal, a meeting was arranged to take place in the no-less-opulent offices of Trusthouse Forte, on Park Lane. There I was briefed by the company accountants, and from the outset it was clear there were two hurdles to overcome: first, the charter contract between Swan Hellenic and the Greek owners of the *Orpheus*; and second, the fiercely protective attitude to the company's reputation held by its founder and managing director, Ken Swan.

With the charter contract in hand, I went to Athens to see if its onerous terms could be renegotiated. The office of George Potamianos, the *Orpheus's* owner, was furnished in the most fashionable style and enjoyed panoramic views out across the port of Piraeus. It was a scene straight out of Citizen Kane and it told me everything I needed to know: Potamianos was onto a good thing and he knew it, an impression reinforced by the way he only turned to face me after having first taken a few, thoughtful puffs on his cigar.

It was clear that my journey had been fruitless, and I returned to London empty-handed. When meetings with Ken Swan also turned out to be less than encouraging, I began having second thoughts about the merger, until something suddenly happened which made up my mind for me.

In 1982, I had an arrangement with the cruise line Peninsular and Oriental Steam Navigation Company (better known as P&O) for the marketing both of my China arrangements and of my 'Great Journeys' portfolio. One part of P&O's cruising programme was aimed at schools and colleges and for this, their ship SS *Uganda* was ideal, as it had long since been written-down in value and had ample accommodation for students, teachers and parents alike. The *Uganda* had previously been the property of the British-India Steam Navigation Company, which had been absorbed into P&O in 1972; uniquely, however, she retained the former company's livery. She was also a bit of a money-spinner: the concept of a floating hotel, enabling students to visit the very places they were studying, had proved a huge success over the years and places sold out quickly on every departure.

Then, out of nowhere, the Falklands War occurred. Following the Argentinian invasion in April 1982, commercial craft were drafted in to supplement the Royal Navy vessels, including RMS *Queen Elizabeth II*, SS *Canberra* and SS *Uganda*. Requisitioned on 10 April for use as a hospital ship, the *Uganda* was converted in Gibraltar in less than three days.

Fitted with a helicopter platform at her stern, she was kitted out with full hospital facilities, together with a satellite communications system, a gantry to facilitate refuelling at sea and two water filtration plants. She left Gibraltar on 19 April, arriving in the Falklands area on 11 May. Following the end of the conflict, having serviced the wounded of both sides, she left the Falklands on 18 July with the Gurkhas of the 5th Infantry Brigade on board, and arrived at Southampton on 9 August.

After a major refit at North Shields, in England's North East, the Uganda functioned again as a cruise ship for a short while – it was said that the games-deck windows never did close properly again after having Sea King helicopters landing on the quoits courts – before resuming military duties as a troop carrier between Ascension Island and the Falklands. Eventually, in 1986, she was scrapped, leaving P&O without a vessel specifically aimed at the education market, an omission that concerned the company greatly and its chairman, Sir Jeffrey Sterling, in particular.

Still undecided about the Swan Hellenic deal, I discussed the matter with the directors of P&O, who began to take an interest themselves, in light of their late-lamented *Uganda* no longer being available. It was with some relish, then, that the next time I turned up for what the Trusthouse Forte executives presumed would be a routine round of negotiations, I arrived – to their surprise – with P&O executives in tow and, having explained my decision, simply got up and left the two parties to complete the deal. As I did so, I noted that these stalwarts of corporate Britain were somewhat taken aback by this unorthodox introduction.

Thus Swan Hellenic, through the interventions of Raitz and myself, found its new home. However, this was just a temporary berth, as the company subsequently passed through a number of hands, including those of its former chairman, Lord Sterling, before coming to anchor in the Leisure Group, founded and run by Roger Allard.

Nonetheless I was acutely disappointed that I could not complete the deal myself, due to the fact that I was concerned about Voyages Jules Verne having

A Story in Brief

LEN KOVEN THE ARTIST: Len Koven was not just one of the pioneering directors of Horizon Holidays (from 1954-74), he was a talented artist in his own right, his work having been influenced by Cezanne, Picasso and Braque. Within the travel industry, everyone knew that he was the main man at Horizon, when it came to products and product design. Even to this day, his paintings still sell holidays, as I discovered when I went to visit his daughter Dominique, who runs a villa company, Dominique's Villas, and uses many of Len's sumptuous watercolours on her website.

IMAGE COURTESY: DOMINQUE WEST.

practically all its eggs in one (Chinese) basket – I had viewed the purchase of Swan Hellenic as a one-stop route to product diversification. What had been of particular interest to me was Swan's Nile cruise business, since they and Bales Tours had mopped up all the available Nile steamer capacity, which was controlled almost exclusively at that time by a certain Mr Gafaar, of Eastmar Tours in Cairo. These cruises weren't just popular; they were sold out for years ahead.

Over time, then, I came to regret not completing the Swan Hellenic deal, especially when, five years later, Raitz came calling again, this time with a proposal to buy Serenissima, another specialist travel company, located in swish Sloane Square and owned by Sir Timothy Sainsbury, later to become a government minister.

The last time I remember meeting Raitz was when he stopped by to claim his sizeable finder's fee; in retrospect, giving it to him feels not so much like taking sugar to help the medicine go down, as swallowing pure poison. Acquiring Serenissima was easily the worst deal that I ever did. Just four years later, in 1991, all of the original Serenissima staff members had left and the brand was quietly put to bed. It seemed I had indeed paid a very heavy price for what I thought was little more than a pig in a poke, and I was left with the feeling that I was most definitely 'not the Serenissima type'.

FOOTNOTE: In Raitz's first year of operation, 1950, he flew 600 passengers to Corsica using Air Transport Charter Limited, a Channel Islands-based airline operator. It should be noted, however, that these closed, 'affinity group' (for groups of farmers, nurses, teachers and the like) charter flights were not, as is often claimed, the first of their kind.

To pinpoint the birth of the air package-tour phenomenon, you probably have to go back at least as far as 1936, that being the year Captain Langton (then of Blue Cars) launched a series of charter flights to northern France using a fleet of de Havilland Dragon Rapides. He was followed by the Workers' Travel Association (later Galleon Travel), who chartered not only aircraft but also, in 1938, an entire ocean-going passenger liner. And in 1949, Air Transport Charter Limited, on behalf of other agents, operated student-and-teacher charter flights to Paris, Zurich and Frankfurt; this in addition to the regular charter flights they operated between various mainland airports and the island of Jersey.

For us foot soldiers, the man who seemed to have done much of the heavy lifting in Horizon was Len Koven, the affable American who eventually parted company with Raitz in 1974. His departure apparently stemmed from, among other issues, Raitz's decision to go ahead with the acquisition or term charter of a Greek passenger liner, a move with which he strongly disagreed. In due course, this ship deal did indeed turn sour, as Koven had predicted, and later Horizon was taken over by Clarksons – who in turn collapsed.

Nevertheless, Len Koven's memory lives on through the company he helped form with his daughter Dominique. "My father helped me start Dominique's Villas and designed our brochures for many years," she recalls. "When he retired, he painted most of the time... By coincidence he died on 28 July 2010, just before Vladimir. I organised an exhibition of his paintings in 2011, and to this day I miss him dearly."

MARIAN KOZUBA-KOZUBSKI'S SUNBEAM TALBOT: 1954 MONTE CARLO RALLY

A Story in Brief

MONTE CARLO OR BUST: In 1954, Marian Kozuba-Kozubski not only established the firm that would become Independent Air Transport, he bought himself a gleaming Sunbeam Talbot 90 sports car. Then with the help of a Bournemouth garage owner, he tuned it up and entered it into that year's 1954 Monte Carlo Rally, alongside the likes of Stirling Moss. He was accompanied by Doctor Denise Kellerher, a local baker, and Eric Birkham, who is believed to have financed the whole venture. Marian considered himself an excellent driver – despite the odd, spectacular crash – and had a remarkable ability to go without sleep, always useful in rallying. One of his IAT engineers, Frank Skinner, says the Captain would think nothing about flying deep into Africa, turning the plane around and coming straight back to England. In the event, his tomato soup-coloured Sunbeam Talbot finished the Monte Carlo course well outside the top 50, but that did nothing to stop the Captain taking part in future rallies. IMAGE COURTESY: JOANNA KOZUBSKA.

CHAPTER 44
TO THE DRAGON DELIVERED

Right up until a month before the scheduled departure date, we were
met with a loud Russian "niet" when it came to getting across the border
at Panfilov. Then I had a brainwave – why not write to Mrs Thatcher?

I T was around this time that I moved out of my flat opposite Lord's Cricket
Ground, so that the Chinese staff members destined for the 'tourist office'
would have somewhere to stay. My new place of residence was in nearby Maida
Vale, but I was hardly ever there: I seemed to be spending my entire life travelling
round China, trying to get the authorities to open up the borders.

At that time, travelling overland, the only way of making the crossing between
the USSR and China was to take the Trans-Siberian Railway through Mongolia
(if you were coming from Russia) or through Harbin (if you were coming
from or into China directly from the USSR). There was, of course, a perfectly good
road connection that ran south for 200 miles from Urumchi, in the extreme
eastern province of Xinjiang, to Yining on the Sino-Soviet Border. However, it
had a history of separatist unrest, and so was deemed a 'no-go' for Chinese and
foreigners alike.

Nevertheless, I was determined not to be beaten. It so happened that I had a
particularly helpful contact at Luxingshe, the Chinese state travel service; his name
was Yao Yuecan (later he became the president of Luxingshe) and he lived in
Peking. Yuecan had managed, in the past, to get me overland from Kathmandu
into Tibet, and I began hounding him to get me into Yining; if I could get there,
I reasoned, I might be able to get across the border too, despite the fact it had been
closed for some 37 years.

On his own initiative, and probably at some personal risk, Yuecan made
contact with various local officials and told me that if we both flew to Urumchi,
then we might then be able to travel south to Yining. And this is what we did,

despite incurring the distinct displeasure of the local Xinjiang officials, who, even in 1984, behaved like warlords and clearly felt it was their writ, not Peking's, that applied in this part of the world.

When Yao Yuecan and I presented ourselves to the 'Mr Big' in Urumchi, he flew into a fit of rage, unable to comprehend how someone from outside could have had the temerity to trespass on his authority. Eventually, though, after a week of waiting around in the God-forsaken place, our visit ended in smiles and a banquet of inedible local Turkic delicacies. Toasts were drunk and grandiose speeches were made about "foreign friends" and "peace among nations", at the end of which we were given a signed chit with numerous official stamps and were made to understand that we could now resume the long, winding trek to Yining.

We set off the next morning towards the Heavenly Mountains, more or less following the route of the abandoned Khrushchev/Mao-inspired railway line, on which work had been halted in the 1950s and not resumed until much later. The journey was utterly spectacular. For two days, we passed through exotic, idyllic landscapes, featuring lakes, verdant pastures and mountains, until eventually we reached the lowlands and Yining. Once again, there were banquets and speeches with local officials, as well as a drive to the border crossing, complete with watchtowers, searchlights and minefields. In the distance I could just make out the Russian town of Panfilov (named, I believe, after a Russian General) and wondered if I could ever convince the Chinese and the Russians to open this border for some arrangements that I then had in mind.

It was hard to over-estimate the importance, from my perspective, of making this happen. The fact was that any journey along the Silk Road would make a whole lot more sense if one could start in the west, from the USSR, and end up in Xian in the east, rather than have to travel in a vast circle centred on Peking. This overland route was crucial if I was going to be able to mount my 'London to Peking' and 'London to Saigon' motor challenges. As things turned out, I had to make that trek from Urumchi on several different occasions before I finally succeeded in getting permission.

In the meantime, I was able to announce to the world the launch of our most daring 'Great Journey' to date. It went under the title of '2,100 Years of the Silk Road' and was a feat of logistical travel planning linking 10 different trains, the first emanating from London's Charing Cross Station and the last terminating in the Chinese city of Xian. It was a down-to-the-wire operation, however: permission from Moscow to run the service came through just two weeks before the departure date and, as in Peking, I needed some inside help from a local contact in Moscow, Elenora Ermoshina. It helped that she was well connected politically (I think on her husband's side), as this meant that she had access to the

A Story in Brief

THE IMPRESSARIO: Joe Morrison was an accountant connected to the auditors of Voyages Jules Verne, and a former time partner in Aubrey Morris's Riviera Holidays (they parted on a not-entirely amicable basis, but both kept in touch). His son formed the Bryan Morrison Agency, which went on to become one the leading London booking agents for R&B and progressive rock groups, as well as organising UK tours for US acts. Eventually Bryan had the exclusive booking rights for clubs like Blaises, the Cromwellian and the Revolution, in Bruton Street, Mayfair. Among the notable bands he represented were Pink Floyd, Fairport Convention, Incredible String Band, Tyrannosaurus Rex, The Pretty Things, the Deviants and the Pink Fairies. In later life, he developed a passion for polo after he learnt to play, and even founded The Royal County of Berkshire Polo Club. It was a sport that killed him, too: he died in September 2008, following a polo accident.

IMAGE COURTESY: ROBERT SCURRAH/VOYAGES JULES VERNE.

very highest levels of government.

Even so, right up until a month before the scheduled departure date, we were met with a loud Russian "niet" when it came to getting across the border at Panfilov. Then I had a brainwave: why not write to Mrs Thatcher, who had been having regular meetings with the newly inaugurated President Gorbachev? Not long after I had done this, I had a call from an excited Elenora in Moscow. "I'm not sure what you have done, but, whatever it was, it has done the trick," she told me. "Everyone has been asked to drop everything and make sure that the border is opened and that the group can cross over."

This accounted for the lavish hospitality afforded to those first VJV travellers to cross the border, in 1985. It was the missing piece of the jigsaw puzzle that I required and it meant that, in years to come, I was able to operate a whole range of different tour programmes in this region. In addition to the motor challenges, I introduced trips based around Mao's state train and his Yangtse steamer, the *Kunlun*. The opening of the Panfilov-Yining border crossing was undoubtedly a significant occasion, as documented at the time by one of our tour party:

'The scene outside the hotel on a cool early morning in October 1985 was a particular one. The air was blue with low-grade petrol fumes that belched from the exhaust pipes of a column of polished red coaches. Each of the drivers was in blue uniforms pressed with unusual care. At their backs, the coaches were filled with passengers wrapped against the morning chill, sitting tight with expectation and gazing down on the scene on the pavement.

There, a stream of suitcases flowed out from the hotel into lockers beneath the coach windows. Watching this performance was a group of onlookers wearing a wonderful variety of expressions, ranging from frustration through amusement to amused detachment.

From time to time, a passenger descended from one of the coaches, spoke briefly with one of those in attendance on the hotel steps and hurried inside. Or, a member of the hotel staff would wander out, carrying a piece of paper bearing figures, to consult with someone wearing a fur hat.

It seemed if this cycle of events could continue forever, but, eventually, the moment came when the buses were filled with passengers and suitcases, the hotel doors were closed and the group on the steps was in agreement. The group broke up as the first coach fired a burst of smoke, the blue light on the car in front began to rotate and the procession eased onto the road'.

All this was taking place in Alma Ata, the capital of the Soviet Republic of Kazakhstan. The coaches, with their police escort and pursued by several other less clearly-identified vehicles, were heading towards the Chinese border, to the province of Xinjiang and the Heavenly Mountains. Drivers of oncoming vehicles, forced off the road by the zealous police escort, looked on in wonderment as this cavalcade of foreigners, throwing up clouds of dust, sped out of the city, towards previously forbidden territory.

More attention would not have been lavished upon a group of foreigners had they been United Nations observers inspecting a nuclear arsenal. Our party was comprised of just tourists, but, that day, we made a little history. After all, the group had been travelling, by then, for four weeks, having set out by train from London and then travelled on a series of different trains across France, Austria, Hungary, Rumania, Bulgaria and Turkey.

From Istanbul, we had set out to follow the old Silk Road, crossing into the Soviet Union and continuing through Armenia, Georgia and Azerbaijan. Between Baku and Alma Ata, the vast desert distances had been covered by train, where possible, and aeroplane, when it wasn't possible to travel by train. Now, the journey would continue by road until it met the railway line at Urumchi. As for the rail link across this border, it was still a long way from completion, having been given barely a thought since 1960, the year of the ideological rift between Russia and China. The frontier therefore had to be crossed by coach, and this, as it happened, turned out to be an event in itself. No Westerner and very few Russians or Chinese had crossed this border for the previous 37 years.

The fact that permission had eventually been granted was a sign of times changing for the better, but it was also due to many months of planning, begging and prayer (mainly on my part). Even as our motorised caravan was belting along a branch of the Silk Road, nobody knew quite what to expect up ahead. The Russians, as was their wont, remained unforthcoming in the extreme, but one got the impression that they wanted to savour the moment as well.

By now, the air was clear enough for us to be able to glimpse in the distance, crowned in white, the Heavenly Mountains, beyond which lay China. The nearer we got, the more tangible the excitement and the greater the eagerness to move on, even among the small group of KGB security men, who had accompanied our party all the way from our entry into the Soviet Union and who must have been relishing an assignment which, for a change, didn't involve them hanging around the Kremlin.

As we neared the crossing point, the road got narrower and began dipping down steeply into deep hollows and valleys, causing the coaches to rock heavily on its springs. The passengers, bleary-eyed and weary from the speeches, music and vodka of the night before, slept or stared out the window as the convoy emerged into a grey, gravelly wasteland interrupted only by the odd gnarled and stunted tree. At one point we descended into a gully, at the bottom of which was a grove of trees and a cluster of Kazakh tents, or yurts. The coaches drew off the road, pulled up, in regimental order, outside the tents and released their passengers.

An extraordinary scene awaited the travellers, as they emerged, bleary-eyed, from the buses. Somehow, in this vast wilderness, lavatories and washing facilities had been erected for both sexes. In addition, preparations had been made for a feast: bowls of fruit, plates full of cakes and flagons brimming with juice and yoghurt had been laid out on the kind of folding table you might find at a country fête. Plumes of smoke crackled up from the pieces of lamb cooking on skewers over a fire. This astonishing sight was greeted with an audible murmur of delight. All of a sudden, constitutions revived and conversation became more lively. Even though there were only a handful of takers for the nips of vodka or whisky that were on sale (for hard currency) at a hastily erected stall, the party's expectations rose once again. Not that we were through the border crossing just yet: it would be another two hours before we got to the Russian town of Panfilov and, once there, we found a lot more awaiting us than just customs and immigration formalities.

This was a huge event for a small, forgotten border town and it was not going to pass unmarked. When we got to Panfilov, a full-blown civic reception awaited. The streets were lined with waving citizens and the mayor, in Kazakh hat and accompanied by his platinum-blonde Russian wife, stood to attention on the steps of the town hall. (There I was presented with the customary Russian bunch of gladioli, but, uncomfortable with parading these blooms around, I asked to take part in a rather earthier and more symbolic friendship ritual, which involved my taking a pinch of salt and a pinch of flour to symbolise welcome and friendship.) Then came lunch, and what a lunch it was. There was a feast, with music and dancing by local performers and speeches in praise of these unprecedented events and their undoubted contribution to world peace.

Even though the banqueting hall was a modern, typically Soviet-style building, the occasion itself felt centuries old, in its spirit of hospitality and grandiloquence. After lunch there was a short tour of the town – a little superfluous, in view of the late hour and everyone's impatience to reach the border, but nonetheless important, given the occasion. Finally, a group photograph was taken, at which point everyone piled back onto the coaches and off we roared, towards the east.

By the time we reached the frontier, the sun was already beginning to sink down in the sky. It was, by any stretch of the imagination, a beautiful natural setting: two majestic mountain ranges closed in on a long tapering valley, its sandy floor baking gently in the last rays of the sun. In contrast, the man-made USSR border post was an unprepossessing concrete barn within a wire enclosure and our progress through it was both slow and painstaking. One by one, each passenger was required to descend from the coach, suitcase in hand, and then proceed through luggage and passport inspection. Meanwhile, the coaches were inspected from below, from a pit, and then parked in a courtyard to await their passengers. Nothing could have prepared the travellers for what greeted them as they emerged from the barn and into no-man's land: the grinning shopkeeper stood behind the same drinks stall we had seen earlier that day and, from loudspeakers positioned at each corner of the wire enclosure, the Beatles sang lustily out into the desert.

Once everyone was back on board the coaches, darkness began to descend. Slowly and gingerly, like trains on a new section of track, the buses rumbled to the point where the USSR stopped and China began, and no further. They stopped to allow everyone to disembark and then reversed discreetly back into the night. At this point the Chinese coaches came forward to be boarded and then, once the transfer had been effected, moved off towards bright arc lights, beneath which a carnival dragon pranced in welcome.

From there, the 100 passengers travelled by road, retracing my well-trodden route to Urumchi, where they boarded a charter train that took them through the Gobi Desert, then on to the sand dunes at Turfan, the grottoes at Dunhuang, the end of the Great Wall at Lanzhou and, finally, to Xian, the ancient terminus of the old Silk Road.

In many ways, this was the most complicated exercise I had ever attempted, incorporating enough drama and cliff-hanging moments to last a lifetime, let alone a film. Nonetheless, a border between two powers, in a forgotten corner of Asia, was open once again. Yes, the deed had been done: the great Russian Bear had delivered its charges to the Chinese Dragon.

CHAPTER 45
THE FLASHING MESSAGE LIGHT

Although I was in New York, I immediately activated the evacuation
plan we had rehearsed, with the aim of getting every one of our
passengers out of China by whatever means possible.

EVERYONE remembers the unknown man who stood in front of a column of Type 59 tanks the morning after the Chinese military forcibly removed protesters from Peking's Tiananmen Square area. Thanks to photographs and TV footage, the image of that lone figure blocking the tanks has come to symbolise what happened in Peking on 3-4 June 1989. Many people consider it one of the iconic images of the 20th century. In 1998, *Time* magazine rated the unknown rebel as one of the century's 100 most internationally important people, and one theory as to why the unidentified hero has never come forward (if he is still alive) is that he himself is unaware of his global profile, given the image's lack of exposure in China itself.

The night before the incident, the Chinese government had launched a crackdown on protesters on Chang'an Avenue, which runs east-west along the south end of the Forbidden City in Peking. The man placed himself, alone, in the middle of the street as the tanks approached, directly in the path of the armoured vehicles. He held two shopping bags, one in each hand. As the tanks came to a stop, the man gestured towards the tanks with his bags. In response, the lead tank attempted to drive around the man, but the man repeatedly stepped into the path of the tank in a show of non-violent resistance.

After repeatedly attempting to go around the man, rather than crush him, the lead tank stopped its engines, and the armoured vehicles behind it seemed to follow suit. There was then a short pause, with man and tanks seeming to have reached an impasse. Then, having successfully brought the column to a halt, the lone protester then climbed onto the hull of the leading tank and, after briefly stopping at the driver's hatch, appeared, in video footage of the incident, to call through various ports in the tank's turret. He then climbed on top of the turret and, after a seemingly short conversation with a crew member at the gunner's hatch, descended from the tank.

The tank commander briefly emerged from his hatch and the tanks re-started their engines, ready to continue their journey. At that point, the man leapt in front of the vehicle once more, quickly re-establishing the man-tank stand-off. The most-used photograph of the event was taken by Jeff Widener of the Associated Press, from a sixth-floor balcony of the Peking Hotel. Although he was concerned that his shots were not good enough, the image was syndicated to a large number of newspapers around the world and was said to have appeared on the front page of all European papers.

Variations of the scene were also recorded by BBC film crews and transmitted across the world. I remember seeing those images on my TV screen, feeling a hollowness in my stomach and numbness in my brain (I had been worrying so much, I hadn't slept properly for weeks). Seeing those pictures on my TV screen spoke to me of a disaster that I was about to share with the Chinese people themselves. This was a strange and emotional time for me; I was well aware that the Chinese people were, as a whole, concerned with the cohesion of the country – indeed, the Chinese word luan, meaning chaos or disorder, was being much more frequently voiced than the word for democracy since most people had experienced luan as recently as the Cultural Revolution. What's more, most TV and newspaper reporters had been generally sympathetic to the plight of the students. I shared those feelings, too, while at the same time being aware that the images being beamed around the world would devastate my business.

A day or two later I joined an anti-Chinese government march, which assembled outside a building I was very familiar with: the Chinese Embassy, on Portland Place. The march wound its way slowly and noisily through the centre of London, until it reached Chinatown. There we were addressed by the journalist and writer Jonathan Mirsky, but I confess to feeling uncomfortable with the one-sided way in which he lambasted the Chinese government, with the aid of a megaphone. Much of my unease stemmed from the fact that Voyages Jules Verne had, through its good offices with the Chinese, facilitated Jonathan Mirsky's entry into the country on several occasions. I had also helped the BBC into China during this period, the result being that their broadcasting of these distressing images now felt like a particularly painful form of self-flagellation.

After the march, I returned to my office emotionally drained, and with every intention of closing the business down. However, others cautioned to me to wait a few days, and I took their advice. A quick assessment of the situation sub-

A Story in Brief

LIGHTS, ACTION!: Before entering the travel business with Cosmos Tours, I worked briefly in the film industry, for World Wide Pictures. The job involved keeping track of theatrical props, for use in public information films and TV programmes such as *Dixon of Dock Green*. Founded in 1942, World Wide Pictures is still going today as a film, television and multimedia production company, but its origins lay in the British Documentary Movement, which was created by John Grierson in the 1930s, and produced propaganda and information films for the government during World War II. After the war, the company moved into sponsored films, advertisements, and industrial and promotional films. Two of its early successes were *The Undefeated* (1950), which publicised state welfare services available to disabled ex-servicemen, and *David* (1951), which served as a promotional film for Wales, at the Festival of Britain. The people were extremely kind to me at the time and to this day I can't understand why I left.

sequently revealed that 99 per cent of the profitable part of my business had now disappeared, not least because the Foreign Office had put out an advisory against all travel to China which would lead to wholesale cancellations.

The damage that had been done, complete as it was sudden, was not wholly unexpected, however. The prospect of an event like this had been worrying me for quite some time. But unfortunately, things were also going wrong on another front. Two years earlier I had been travelling in the Cotswolds, visiting a hotelier who owned The Feathers in Woodstock and also managed a country-house hotel in Stow-on-the-Wold called Wyck Hill House. Originally, the latter establishment had been bought by a couple of Texan ladies, who had been so captivated by the house and its location that they decided to buy it there and then. On the day I visited, the sun was shining, the hotel and grounds looked gorgeous, and yes, you guessed it: I fell into that very same Texan trap and went and bought the damn thing pretty much on the spot. Furthermore, I convinced myself that I could conduct my residential, pre-tour seminars here, rather than in the basement of Glentworth Street.

This was the perfect example of how acting on a whim can come back and bite you. In my defence, I would like to point out that VJV had been making very good profits during the preceding years, mainly on the back of our business in China, yet I was unable to take the cash out of the company, as it was needed to support the Civil Aviation Bond. Even worse, I was having to pay a premium to an insurance company, despite the fact that I was putting up the collateral with my own money. Why not buy the hotel, I reasoned, with some of our reserves and use that to support the bond? After all, money invested in the hotel would serve not just as collateral for the bond, but would also generate income, instead of sitting all locked up and useless and not earning its keep. In my mind's eye, I saw myself as the rural lord of the manor, escaping from London at weekends to recharge my batteries in the hotel's beautiful surroundings.

Not that there was much re-charging, since every time I went to the hotel, I seemed to do nothing but spend large amounts of money on things that needed fixing and things that needed buying. It got to the point that, instead of going to the country each weekend to relax, I stayed in London to avoid the stress. The only plus points were that I did eventually transfer the pre-tour briefing meetings to the hotel and I did manage to put on opera evenings there for our Serenissima guests.

Things came to a head one day, with the news that someone had taken a bulldozer to a stretch of land right out front of the hotel, with the aim of building a road. I knew in an instant that this would make the value of the hotel plummet, so I promptly asked to meet the gentleman responsible for the bulldozer, which, by this time, had scoured large tracks of earth, revealing a rough and rudimentary road. Soon after I had issued this edict, a rather hippie-looking chap presented himself in the hotel's lounge.

The proposal the man put to me was this: he owned 100 acres of land around the hotel, and unless I bought the whole lot from him the road would go ahead. Before coming to any decision, I decided to take a look at the land and had to agree that it was stunningly beautiful. It overlooked the attractive little town of Bourton-on-the-Water, where, in my mind's eye, I could just picture myself building a house one day. Thus I agreed to pay what I considered the extortionate price the man wanted, in order to stop the road being built; this meant that, instead of the hotel sitting in just 36 acres, as before, I now owned an estate of some 136 acres. My hippie friend was insistent that, rather than completing all the legal bits and bobs through a lawyer, we write down the deal there and then, on a rough-looking piece of notepaper.

On the grounds that I didn't have much choice, I signed the agreement, although with a suspicion, in the back of my mind, that this somehow represented Townies 0, Country Bumpkins 1. As all this was going on, I was receiving regular telephone updates from Chen Ziqiang, my station manager in Peking, who, from the vantage point of his high-rise apartment building, was watching the students march from the Peking University campus to Tiananmen Square.

During our exchanges, we would regularly try to gauge the likelihood of violent protest or state crackdown and convince ourselves nothing of the sort was in the offing. After all, the moderate Chinese vice-premier, Zhao Ziyang, was on the students' side, so surely there was nothing to worry about.

I was only too well aware that, at any one time, Voyages Jules Verne had upwards of 600 travellers scattered the length and breadth of China. If something were to happen, it would be both a logistical and financial nightmare. I remember sitting in my car, in the hotel car park, before one of our pre-tour China briefing seminars, listening to the BBC World Service in order to try and gauge the latest state of play. What I heard was not encouraging and, when I finally entered the hotel, I heard a couple of ladies querying out loud whether it was safe to go to China. Nevertheless, business went on as usual, and on 2 June I flew to New York to meet agents who, by this time, had bought Lars-Eric Lindblad's exploration vessel *Lindblad Explorer* and were trading, rather confusingly, as Salen Lindblad.

This was the firm that intended to sell our China and 'Great Journey' products in the US and was launching a new product of its own: an exploration vessel later named the *Caledonian Star*. (This vessel had an interesting past: it had started life as a German deep-sea fishing vessel, the *Marburg*, and then been converted into an exploration vessel named the *Nord Star*, before being impounded by government authorities somewhere in Central America.) Given the dramatic events unfolding in Peking, it took a fair amount of mental agility on my part to be sitting in the US discussing local marketing arrangements for my China products. Having concluded our business, we decided to spend the evening of 3 June at the theatre across the road from the hotel. Although sick with worry, I hoped the show would help take my mind off things.

Appropriately enough, the production was Cameron Mackintosh's *Les Misérables* and I can't, for the life of me, remember anything about it. At about 11.00pm we returned to the hotel; I had this awful premonition that there would be a message waiting for me, and indeed there was. The telephone beside my bed was flashing, alerting me that a message had been left. Taking a deep breath, I sat on the end of the bed and listened to the recording. It was bad news: the Foreign Office had advised all British subjects to leave China, and I knew full well that this was an order we would have to comply with or else be exposed, under the terms of our liability insurance cover.

Although I was in New York, I immediately activated the evacuation plan we had rehearsed, with the aim of getting every one of our passengers out of China by whatever means possible. I spent the whole night calling our London and Peking offices, attempting to orchestrate the operation as best I could.

The next day, I checked-in and boarded at Kennedy Airport, where for some unexplained reason the plane sat motionless on the apron. In view of this delay, the TWA crew decided to serve dinner there and then, at which point the aircraft steps were wheeled up to the plane and the door opened. It was only then that we learned the plane had been delayed not due to a technical fault, but because a connecting flight had been late in arriving and passengers from that plane were now boarding ours.

Thinking nothing more of it, I was just tucking into some chicken supreme when I found myself being told to leave the aircraft – since the flight was over-booked and I was travelling on an agency-discounted ticket, I was the hapless passenger who was to be off-loaded. I was both livid and frustrated; I just couldn't believe this was happening to me. Instead of flying back to London, where I absolutely had to be, I was stuck in an airport hotel room, staring helplessly at the CNN news reports and watching events unfold in Peking. It was one of the most frustrating, bed-kicking nights I have ever spent.

When I finally did get back to London, we started the long and arduous job of evacuating our passengers from various points across China. The Foreign Office had announced that special flights would be laid on from Peking, but, when our people went to check with the British Embassy, they were told this service was only for diplomats and their families. Given that all scheduled flights had been cancelled, we had no option but to get our passengers across China overland and out via Hong Kong, which is what we eventually did. While all this was going on, we also had to cancel the holidays of some 5,000 passengers who were due to travel out to China.

I spent hours sitting at my desk, signing mountains of computerised refund cheques – it was as if my own lifeblood, along with that of the company, was slowly draining away. A survey of our finances that summer showed how extensive and dramatic the damage had been. In the UK, we had some 60 VJV staff members spread over offices on Dorset Square and Glentworth Street, plus 35 at the hotel in the Cotswolds; and then there were our offices in Peking, Hong Kong and New York. Suddenly, in the blink of an eye, all these operations were haemorrhaging cash at an alarming rate.

It was a case of taking emergency measures. The only way to save the company, as I saw it, was to consolidate down to a small rump from which, providing we survived, we might at some point be able to re-grow. For this to happen, I needed, in short order, to: (a) sell the loss-making hotel; (b) dispose of 50 per cent of the office space; (c) close the Peking, Hong Kong and New York offices; and, most painfully of all, (d) let 40 of the 60 London base staff go. This was to be followed by (e), which involved conjuring up some instant new products to replace the ones we had lost, and that was pretty much how it turned out.

By the middle of July I had sold the Cotswolds hotel, disposed of half of the office space, closed the New York, Peking and Hong Kong Offices and reduced the staff to 20. At the same time, I set in motion a process of product replacement, which meant that by September we were able to take back some of our laid-off staff, and within another year were back to our original staff numbers prior to the events of June 1989.

What's more, this pruning process ensured that the company not only survived; it became stronger than ever. I count this as my greatest-ever achievement. What had saved us was the fact that my cash had not been spent, but retained within the company: it was these funds that gave us the wherewithal to go on. We survived, despite rumours spread by our erstwhile competitors to the effect that we were on the brink of going out of business.

Not long after, I was invited by Timothy Sainsbury – whose company, Serenissima, I had previously and unwisely taken over – for lunch at the House of Commons. I thought, rather naively as it turned out, that I might be getting a pat on the back, in the light of recent events. Quite the reverse: towards the end of the meal, Sir Timothy revealed the real reason for his invitation, which was that one of his ex-Serenissima staff members had rung him to complain that, following the collapse of the business, I had cancelled all staff bonuses.

I was both shocked and dumbfounded; I just could not believe how someone could have failed to understand the logic of my decision. I left in disgust, although I am pretty sure he did not know it. My lasting regret of the whole episode is the loss of the 100 acres I'd bought from that hippie. I had been in such a hurry to sell the hotel and the buyer had been so keen to buy, but I couldn't help thinking that had I just sold the hotel and kept the land, I could have built a beautiful house with uninterrupted views across the Cotswolds.

WORLD OF WONDERS POSTER BY ROBERT SCURRAH

A Story in Brief

THE DRUM AND MONKEY: Having once been a dresser for the male chorus on the production of *My Fair Lady*, I went, many years later, to see Cameron Mackintosh's production in the Strand. Partly, this was to renew my emotional link with the show, but it was also because I lived next door to Cameron's parents. His father, Iain, would often come around to our house unannounced on his way to the nearby Drum and Monkey pub, where he played the trumpet. He was a lovely man, and despite the fame of his son, his pleasures were always simple. A local story has it that his wife Diana disapproved of these nocturnal visits to the Drum and Monkey and tried her best to discourage them. One day, though, as Diana was taking her dog out for a walk (Spike was Iain's nickname), the animal dragged her into the Drum and Monkey having picked up Spike's scent. I am not sure what happened next.
IMAGE COURTESY: ROBERT SCURRAH/VOYAGES JULES VERNE.

CHAPTER 46
THE LONDON TO PEKING
MOTOR CHALLENGE

*"What needs to be proved today is that, as long as a man has a car, he
can do anything and go anywhere. Is there anyone who will undertake
to travel this summer from Peking to Paris by motorcar?"*

THESE stirring words constituted the challenge issued by the Parisian
newspaper *Le Matin* on 18 March 1907. Thirty would-be contestants accompanied their application with the required 2,000-franc entry fee. In the end,
only five went on to compete in what, though loosely termed a race, was really a
test – of the capabilities and endurance of petrol-driven motorcars (still a
comparatively new invention), and of the supreme optimism of the men that
drove them.

It took two months to reach Paris, and of the five cars that started – an Italian
Itala, two French De Dion-Boutons, a Dutch Spyker and a three-wheeled French
Contal – only the Contal failed to reach its destination. Like Peter Fleming, who
made his way across Turkestan in the 1930s with the nonchalance that is supposed
to be the hallmark of a certain type of Englishman, the Italian Prince Scipione
Borghese, together with his chauffeur Ettore Guizzardi and the journalist Luigi
Barzini, bumped, slithered, pushed, pulled and crashed his way across China,
Russia and Europe with extraordinary insouciance. This is the impression given
by Barzini in his book *Peking to Paris: Across Two Continents in an Itala*, which
for many years after the event (and rather like a cookbook today) became an
institution in every Italian household.

The race was the precursor to many other similar adventures, not least
the 1908 New York to Paris epic, which provided the inspiration for the 1965
comedy *The Great Race*, starring Tony Curtis and Jack Lemmon. This movie left

everyone with the impression that these early rallies were comically sinister battles between gangsters, idiots and smooth-talking aristocrats, rather than the gentlemanly enterprises they mostly were. For example, in Barzini's book the Itala leads throughout, but the Prince and his crew are at pains to ensure the well-being of the other competitors at all times.

The China they passed through was still four years away from the revolution that would end three millennia of dynastic, imperial governance. Foreign influence over the preceding half century had forced some changes in China's outlook, but only enough to maintain a dignified distance from foreigners while retaining, within the Middle Kingdom, an ancient way of life and a world of timeless customs.

The countries that the Prince and his passengers passed through were very different from how they are today. Mongolia, for example, was a Chinese fiefdom whose inhabitants led the same nomadic existence they had pursued for 2,000 years or more. And while the Russian Empire was slowly starting to modernise, it was happening at too slow a pace to prevent the 1917 Revolution, which would eventually turn it into the Soviet Union.

Meanwhile, Europe, ostensibly the bulwark of the civilised world, was a mere seven years away from the bloodiest war in history. Everywhere that the Prince travelled in his fiery chariot, he encountered the eccentricities of despotic rule, the poverty and ingenuity of the ruled and a surprising mixture of indifference, curiosity and awestruck bafflement. Many, if not most, of the people he met en route had never seen a car or even known of the existence of such a creature, yet their prevailing response to it was casual acceptance, rather than fear. When the car was in trouble, people helped. When it ran well, they tried to outrun it on horseback. They then went home to their felt tent, or crumbling hovel, and forgot all about it. It seemed as if those vehicles were driving along a metaphorical ridge, separating the old order from the new.

Strangely enough, the situation was not so different in 1990. China had recently emerged from decades of isolation and turmoil and was still coming to terms with the realities of dealing with the rest of the world. Meanwhile, Mongolia, the Soviet Union and most of Eastern Europe were about to cast off the communist straitjacket, through mainly bloodless coups.

We weren't the first people to try and re-create the 1907 challenge. Several attempts had been made in previous years, but all had failed. Strangely, the main obstacle – bureaucratic intransigence – was not one that had applied to Borghese and his colleagues; once the usual long-winded formalities had been dealt with, they were able to pass from one country to another with comparative ease.

In 1990, however, hostile relations between the Soviet Union and the People's Republic of China meant that no traveller was permitted to cross their mutual land borders. This dated back to the early 1960s, when, as a result of the abstruse political reasoning that prevails in most totalitarian states, all Russian advisers were expelled from China. Mongolia, whose history was mainly one of enmity towards China, was firmly in the Soviet camp. At the same time, the states of Eastern Europe were in flux. A London to Peking Motor Challenge planned for 1988 had already been cancelled by the organisers because of the intractable nature of Cold War politics.

In 1990, although things were changing, a motor race was not very high on the agenda within either the Kremlin or the Great Hall of the People. The tortuous reasoning of politicians and the risk-averse nature of bureaucrats tends to persist through even the most radical of revolutions. Nonetheless, I was not accustomed to letting small matters like revolutions get in the way of a great journey. On the contrary, I saw the uncertainty as a thrilling, additional ingredient of the enterprise. During my time at Voyages Jules Verne, I had built up some solid relationships with the Soviet, Mongolian and Chinese tourist authorities, all arms of their respective state apparatuses; I saw no reason why, through these connections, an international motor challenge could not now be mounted.

Surely, in a spirit of peaceful coexistence and international brotherhood, a rally would be welcomed? If nothing else, it was an opportunity for free publicity (or propaganda). However, in those days, even as the end of the Cold War approached, it was impossible to underestimate the level of state-induced paranoia that prevailed among the apparatchiks in the countries in question. Accordingly, without all the necessary permits in place but aware that the various authorities tended to yield to circumstances once the wheels were in motion, if only to avoid embarrassment, I launched my version of the motor challenge. The route would not be the same one that Borghese and the others took in 1907, but would instead pass through Central and Southern Europe to Istanbul, across Turkey to the Soviet Union at Batumi, in Georgia, and then through the Central Asian republics to Alma Ata, the capital of Kazakhstan, before entering China at Yining to continue along the Silk Road to Xian, and finally to Peking.

All the berths soon sold out, but it wasn't long before there were a couple of quite large flies in the ointment. First, the brutal suppression of the protesters in Tiananmen Square made several of the entrants uneasy, if only because they depended on sponsorship to meet their expenses. Second, the old favourite: the absence of permission to cross the border from the Soviet Union into China, without which the challenge simply could not go ahead.

There was, of course, a precedent, because in 1985 permission to cross this border had been granted to a party of Voyages Jules Verne travellers celebrating '2,100 Years of the Silk Road'. However, it wasn't the Chinese who were the

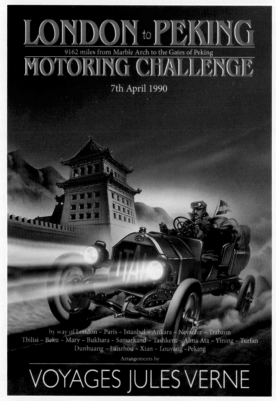

A Story in Brief

THE MAN ON A BIKE: In 1980, after 10 years in investment banking, alongside financial guru George Soros, Jim Rogers decided to travel round the world on his motorbike. I first met him in 1990, when he and his companion entered the VJV London to Peking Motoring Challenge. They drove two top of the range, black BMW motorcycles, which clearly had an effect on the locals; a Chinese cyclist claimed he had been so disorientated by these machines that he had fallen from his bicycle and been injured. Compensation was sought and faces had to be saved – and was provided in the form of a hundred-dollar bill. But the Challenge wasn't the end of Rogers' adventures, by any means. From 1990 to 1992, he travelled around the world, on motorcycle, clocking up 160,000 kilometres and six continents. And in 2002, he and his wife Paige Parker drove a custom-made Mercedes through 116 countries, covering a total of 245,000 kilometres. The trip began in Iceland, and ended outside their home in New York City.

IMAGE COURTESY: DAVID SCUTT/VOYAGES JULES VERNE.

problem: while they had recovered their commercial acumen and were keen to exploit any kind of opportunity, the opposite was the case in the Soviet Union.

So, with the Soviet authorities remaining immovable to the last and steadfastly refusing our requests, it seemed that all was lost. Every conventional approach had been tried, only to be met with obstructiveness or silence. There remained just one final, wildly speculative throw of the dice with which we might just avoid the humiliation of cancelling the whole event. It so happened that the Soviet premier, Mikhail Gorbachev – of whom the British prime minister, Margaret Thatcher, had once declared: "I like Mr Gorbachev. We can do business together" – was due to visit the UK for a meeting at Downing Street, and a banquet was to be hosted in his honour by Queen Elizabeth at Windsor.

This was a major state visit and was part of Gorbachev's attempt to portray the Soviet Union in a more positive light. Recalling the letter I sent to the Chinese in 1977, seeking permission to organise tours for Western travellers, I wrote again – more in despair than hope – to Mrs Thatcher, asking her, as I had done for the Silk Road journey earlier, to take up the matter of the motor challenge with Mr Gorbachev during his visit. It seems that she must have done exactly that, for the elusive permission came through shortly after, thus saving the event from ignominious collapse.

On 7 April 1990, according to schedule, the 'London to Peking Challenge' got underway at Marble Arch. The competitors had been permitted to parade along Whitehall, while the lead car was invited to pose in front of 10 Downing Street. Mrs Thatcher had even written a letter, addressed to all the entrants. It read: 'You are starting on a real adventure. I hope it will be a happy one, bringing the people of many countries closer together.'

Well, the journey certainly wasn't an easy one. You might have romantic notions of what it is like to be bowling along in a modern motor car in the shadow of the Heavenly Mountains, or in the tracks of the Silk Road. However, this doesn't take into account the unexpected, which by definition is unknowable. Organisation, no matter how thorough, can do nothing about geography, or about the limitations imposed by political interference, zealous policemen and local pride. Some things are simply incalculable.

In the end, approximately 60 vehicles set out from London, including a 1939 BSA motorcycle and sidecar, a Morris Minor and a 1912 Lancia, all three of which arrived safely in Peking 56 days later. As far as Istanbul, drivers were able to choose their own routes, provided they arrived in time to start the next leg together. As was to be expected, a handful of cars failed to get that far, including the Lamborghini LM002 four-wheel drive of Baron Guy de Wimnel, the French aristocrat in the Tony Curtis role, who had intended to make the journey in an upgraded London taxi until he discovered, on the eve of departure, that the company doing the work had gone into administration.

In Turkey, the Baron's car was put out of action in an accident, thereby reminding us of the advice of the Turkish tourist authority representative: "In the country, watch for all black things on the roads, as these might be potholes and you will fill them. Red lights are for rather ornamental purposes. Do not expect any common sense from the local drivers." Another crew had left their passports in Paris, necessitating a major retrieval operation before departure from Istanbul. In Ankara, a parking area set aside for the event turned out to have barriers too low for some of the vehicles.

"The roughest thing about the rally," said one participant, "was the deteriorating sanitary conditions as we rolled east. The deal was, we were to have the best available accommodations at each stop. Well, we did have. But the 'best available' got a lot worse as we segued from Europe to Asia. It got pretty grotty."

All this shows that, even in the late 20th century, and even in the form of an organised adventure, great journeys were still possible. For the drivers and their companions, much of the enjoyment sprang not just from what they saw and from what they endured, but from the reactions of onlookers. As with Prince Scipione Borghese some 87 years earlier, they were met with a mixture of indifference, curiosity and, occasionally, wonderment.

In China, a man had cycled over 100 miles just to behold the spectacle of all these fabulous vehicles. Then there was the elderly Russian, brought up on decades of anti-Western hyperbole, unable to restrain the tears of joy that streamed down his cheeks as the cars puffed and blew by. The challenge captured imaginations and inspired an outpouring of international camaraderie.

Perhaps the spirit of the challenge can be summed up in the words of the driver of the oldest car in the rally. When doubters scoffed at his ambition, he replied: "The Lancia will get there because it is agricultural," conjuring up an image that, with its whiff of labour and hardiness and goodness, harmonised perfectly with both the nature and the spirit of the event.

I was to go on to organise two more motor challenges – London to Tibet and London to Saigon – although the planned London to New York challenge never materialised, due to the impossibility of getting cars flown from Eastern Siberia to Prudhoe Bay, Alaska.

CHAPTER 47
THE ENGLISH LADY AWAITS

In a nutshell, my £600,000 had been spent by the Portuguese on a
boat that they didn't own. To put it mildly, this came as a bit of a blow
– in fact, it put me in a blind panic.

M ANY of us, if asked, would struggle to name a river in Spain or Portugal. There is no Rhine or Volga, or even a Thames, to fire the imagination. The Douro, which perhaps is the best known, is the third longest river in the Iberian Peninsula, after the Tagus and Ebro, yet it is the only river that is navigable for large-accommodation river-cruise vessels over any worthwhile distance. The only exceptions to this are the limited navigation from Cadiz to Seville on the Guadalquivir and the even more restricted Guadiana, in Portugal, which for much of its length forms a natural border with Spain.

Traditionally, when people thought of Portugal as a travel destination, they focused not on its rivers but on its capital, Lisbon, and on its resorts in the Algarve, popularly considered a cut above their Spanish equivalents. Nobody considered cruising on the Douro, not least because it had never been physically possible. However, the Douro is an extremely long river: rising in the Sierra de Urbión in Spain, it crosses the Numantian Plateau and flows westward for 556 miles to the Atlantic Ocean, at Foz do Douro. Up until Aranda de Duero, it is a slender waterway and does not widen until it starts to cross the broad plains of Old Castile. Then, beyond Zamora, it narrows again until, at the border with Portugal, just before the splendid city of Salamanca, it plunges 1,000 feet, in a series of gorges and rapids that stretch over a distance of just 30 miles.

Once in Portugal, between Peso da Régua and Oporto, the Douro changes again and becomes a commercial artery, supporting the wine trade from the port-wine growing area as far as Vila Nova de Gaia, where all the great port companies have their offices and warehouses. On the stretch of river from Pedorido to Porto, some coal barges join the wine-carrying traffic too. While originally a sandbar at the river mouth prevented Oporto from developing into a major modern shipping port, that impediment was overcome in 1890, through the building of an artificial port at Leixões, to the north of the estuary.

It's not just the size of the Douro that changes in Portugal, however; it's its character. In Spain, the river is calm and unassuming, and only partly navigable. Across the border, its natural state is chaotic and impetuous. Early on, this made reliable, steady navigation a challenge, to say the least. But in the 1930s the Douro was first harnessed for hydroelectric power and irrigation, and in the 1950s it became the site of one of Europe's biggest energy-production programmes – both these interventions turned the flow of water into something more predictable and manageable.

Strangely, despite this taming of the river, no one had yet emulated the other great scenic rivers of Europe by running overnight-accommodation cruise boats from which the Douro's scenic qualities could be appreciated. As late as 1989, the only company operating on the river was a local firm with a small fleet of vessels, taking passengers up and down the river on day cruises. A prize was there for the taking, and so with this in mind, I paid a visit to Oporto. No sooner had I arrived, however, that I discovered that such a project was already under development: a local company was on the point of purchasing a Rhine vessel, ironically named the *English Lady*, with a view to operating the kind of service I envisaged.

There was, however, one obstacle standing in the way of their project: the *English Lady*, presently based in Holland, needed a substantial sum of money spent on her, in order to bring her up to a presentable standard. Straight away I put in an offer, agreeing to an advance of £600,000 in return for being granted exclusive marketing rights. The deal was done, upon which I devised a seven-night itinerary that is more-or-less being followed to this day.

Demand, as I expected, was instantaneous, and within weeks the entire capacity was sold out. The first sailing was planned for Easter, but a few weeks beforehand I received a somewhat alarming telephone call. It came from a gentleman who said that his name was Fred Woods and who informed me, in a gruff and slightly menacing cockney accent, that, while delighted to see all this money being spent on the refurbishment, the *English Lady* did not actually belong to the Portuguese operators, as they had not yet completed the purchase. What's more, if I did not buy the vessel from him very soon, he had every intention of taking it back, in order to run his own cruises on the Rhine. In a nutshell, my £600,000 had been spent by the Portuguese on a boat they didn't own. To put it mildly, this came as a bit of a blow – in fact, it put me in a blind panic, since

A Story in Brief

OLD STABILITIES: It could be said we make the mistake of looking too far afield for those rare places whose natural beauty is unsullied by commercialism, which have a strong local identity and an element of timelessness. Sometimes such places could be found behind communist curtains, but those old stabilities now hardly hold true and people don't feel inclined, or have the time, to travel to the other side of the world. We have been fortunate to find a place where these qualities have been preserved, hidden away in northern Portugal on the Douro River, which has only recently become navigable to a variety of vessels, revealing magnificent scenery, picturesque riverside ports, quintas and wineries. So in the 1992 edition of the *Travel Review* did VJV herald the opening of the Douro River.

the cruises had all long sold out and there were only six weeks left till the start of the season.

The only thing for it was to charter a plane and fly to a remote airfield in Holland, for a face-to-face meeting with Mr Woods. We went together and inspected the vessel at the shipyard, before deciding on what course of action to take next. What became immediately apparent was that the ship still needed a lot of work before she would be ready to receive visitors; in fact, the 'finish' looked distinctly DIY – more IKEA than John Lewis.

Nevertheless, my decision had to be made there and then, and so I agreed to buy the vessel for £300,000, thereby taking my total investment in the project to £900,000. Plus, I now had to pay the yard to finish off the work and then work out how I was going to get the *English Lady* from Holland, where she was currently lying on the Rhine, to the Douro. A major complication was that she couldn't be sailed on the open sea.

I soon realised there weren't many options left open to me. Indeed, there were just two: (a) have the ship pulled by tugs, for which insurance cover would be hard to find; or (b) have her transported, by dock ship, to Oporto. In the end I went for the more costly plan (b), which meant a further £70,000 on top of £30,000 in finishing-up costs. The net result being, I was now in this project for a cool million. My mood was not exactly lifted when the Portuguese tried to re-assure me with the line: "Don't worry, you will soon get your money back; we are only waiting for the bank to sign the loan deal."

I now unwittingly owned a river-cruise vessel, on top of which I had to work out how to operate the damned thing on the Douro – and fast, since the start of the season was nearly upon us. I had many sleepless nights during this period, wondering how on earth I was going to tie together all these loose ends in time to operate the first cruise.

Finally, I got the call that soothed my jangling nerves. Even as the *English Lady* was being transported across the high seas, my bank rang to say that they had received the funds from the Portuguese operators, but that, before the money could be released, I had to sign a bill of sale. I rushed round and duly did so, emitting a huge sigh of relief once it was all over. I had owned the *English Lady* for four immensely stressful weeks and could now let out a great big, pent-up sigh of relief; henceforth, she was going to be the Portuguese operators' problem, not mine.

By this time I was a nervous wreck, so I convinced myself that I deserved another, this time more leisurely, trip to Oporto, to await the arrival of the *English Lady*. I was sitting at a beachside restaurant table when I saw the dock ship pass; immediately I rushed to the nearby port of Leixões, where she was due to berth. There I was told that she would not be allowed to move onto the Douro River until the harbourmaster had made his inspection. These formalities must have taken all of 30 minutes, upon which the *English Lady* glided towards her new home berth on the Douro, right in the centre of Oporto. News of her arrival was now out and crowds gathered to witness a little bit of history: the first-ever overnight-accommodation cruise vessel on the Douro.

For their part, the Portuguese maritime authorities, who had no regulations of their own regarding inland-waterway hotel vessels, took the view that if the Germans had accepted the *English Lady* on the Rhine, then that was good enough for them.

Three days later, the first Voyages Jules Verne passengers boarded the now-renamed *Alto Douro* for their week-long cruise up and down the Douro. It was the first-ever such cruise on the river and the vessel has been cruising ever since, although it's now a whole lot more John Lewis than IKEA. So successful did this venture prove, in fact, that a couple of years later I introduced a second cruise vessel on the river, again with the assistance of Fred Woods. It was called the *Ivy May* – coincidentally, my mother's name.

Straight away it became clear that these cruises offered a ray of hope on an otherwise-gloomy horizon. After the events in Tiananmen Square, our various other travel products provided colour and range, but contributed little to the bottom-line. It was essential, then, to identify products with potential and scale them up, in terms of volume. Having unsuccessfully tried to replace some of my China capacity with tours to Burma, Thailand and Malaysia, it was clear that my two most promising areas now were (a) river cruising and (b) Egypt.

I had been marketing river cruises worldwide for some time beforehand, so much so that we could consider ourselves pioneers in some respects, especially when it came to the Nile, the Irrawaddy (Burma), the Yangtse, the Rhine, the Elbe, the Rhone, the Mosel and the Danube. To this list we added Lake Nasser (Egypt), the Dnieper (Ukraine), the Lena (Siberia) and the Volga, along with other waterways in the Soviet Union. It was also at this time that another river cruise fell into my lap. Between my initial visit to Oporto and the conclusion of the *English Lady* saga, as just described, I had flown to New York, on my first visit to the city since the Tiananmen Square massacre.

The reason for the trip was to meet up with American tour operators by the name of Intrav, who were facing a tricky situation they thought VJV might be able to help solve. Their problem was that they had made a contractual commitment to chartering and filling a number of Russian riverboat sailings between Leningrad and Moscow, but no one was booking them because Iraq had invaded Kuwait and all-out war now looked likely.

Intrav were prepared to offer 'fire sale' prices on the cruises, which looked pretty appealing anyway: Swiss management and Swiss hotel provisioning, in contrast to the abysmal catering and accommodation generally offered by the Russian state tourist organisation, Intourist. As I saw it, here, in one product, were all the magic ingredients for success: no internal Aeroflot flights, no tiresome unpacking and packing, and the guarantee of Swiss food and Swiss onboard hotel management. Prospective travellers could thus travel in comfort on what had previously been considered something of a hardship posting, and, from the luxurious vantage point of a riverboat, take in the sights and sounds of Moscow and Leningrad, plus all the other cities that make up the 'Golden Ring'.

I couldn't see how it could possibly fail – and it didn't. Backed by the reassuring Swiss imprimatur, the cruises sold first in their dozens, then in their hundreds and thousands. The man behind this extraordinary venture was Ulrich Baur – he too was Swiss, and I later invested a considerable sum in his company, in exchange for UK exclusivity. (The bearer shares I own sit decaying in a long-forgotten bank vault somewhere.) Eventually, Ulrich's company found itself being subsumed by another, but not before Ulrich had left his mark; he was a co-founder of what is now Viking River Cruises.

Although the Gulf War proved beneficial for us, in terms of being able to market these Russian cruises through having bought them at a discount and sold them through direct off-the-page marketing, it had some alarming effects too. Things came to a head in early 1991, soon after the final UN ultimatum for Iraq to get out of Kuwait had expired, on 15 January. At that time, we had scaled up our Egyptian programme to such an extent that we were operating weekly charter flights, with Monarch Airways, to Luxor. The 15 January flight was completely full, with 230 passengers all checked-in and waiting for the flight to be called, when I got a call from Monarch: their insurance company had revoked their war cover and the flight would not be able to operate. It felt like it was going to be another Tiananmen Square moment, and, desperate to avoid another round of financially damaging refunds, I suddenly remembered that there were seats available on a flight to Hong Kong, due to depart a couple of hours later.

Don't ask me how we did it, but, instead of cancelling their trip and going home, most of the passengers jumped at our offer of travelling to Hong Kong. In fact, rather than being yet another curse upon our operations, as had seemed likely at the start, the Gulf War proved instrumental in some of our later successes.

CHAPTER 48
THE WORLD OF WONDERS

*I found myself scouring my well-thumbed
'Times Atlas' for other destinations that might be suited
to the same marketing treatment.*

WHAT makes people with dyslexic tendencies different from non-dyslexics? Well, I suppose it depends on how you define 'different' Consider, for a moment, a person who is primarily a 'picture thinker'. This is someone who has great problem-solving capabilities, who can think 'outside the box', who has the ability to view real-life or imaginary objects in 3D (many famous architects and chefs are dyslexic), who may be highly intuitive and who may also possess the ability to think visually and creatively at lightning speed.

Is that person different? Yes, definitely – indeed, I would go so far as to call them gifted. However, such gifts have a downside. Thinking in pictures and being able to move objects around in your head can blur the boundary between reality and imagination, causing disorientation and confusion. Likewise, the number of options that come from being able to think visually at lightning speed can cause a dyslexic to become overwhelmed and run into difficulties when it comes to remembering instructions, managing time and working out in which order to do things.

Not that dyslexics are born stupid or unintelligent. Far from it: an article entitled 'Secret of the Super Successful... They're Dyslexic' (*Sunday Times*, 5 Oct 2003) explained that 40 per cent of self-made millionaires have been diagnosed with the condition, the majority of them admitting that they did badly at school and that they continue to do badly in aptitude tests. The conclusion, then, is that these people do not succeed despite being dyslexic, but because of it, determinedly rising above the limitations that society has placed upon them.

However, not everyone fares so well: statistics show that over 60 per cent of prisoners and over 80 per cent of young offenders are dyslexic. These are the statistics quoted by Jacqui Fisher in 2007, in her beautifully crafted article for the Berkshire Dyslexia & Autism Advice Centre.

When my son began to show the same dyslexic symptoms as myself, I lost no time in enrolling him at Fairley House, the celebrated London school for dyslexic children, where his mother later became a governor. To me, it seemed that the affliction ran in the family, mainly on the male side and mainly among relatives who were left-handed, such as myself.

As for my difficulty with spelling and syntax, I had put this down to the trouble I had when it came to copying the teacher's comments from the blackboard onto paper. This, I felt, was due not to any deficiency on my part, but to the fact that, as a left-hander, the only way I could avoid smudging the ink was to write out of the back of the hand.

It was only much later in life that I grasped the full extent of my handicap. Well, I say 'handicap' but one thing my dyslexia did do for me was ensure that I was excellent at mental arithmetic. I never learnt my times tables, yet in my first travel job as a reservation clerk, in an era when holiday prices were expressed in guineas, half guineas and multiples thereof, I developed the capacity to carry out the most complicated monetary calculations in my head.

It wasn't just when it came to sums that I had an edge, either. Dyslexics, as Jacqui Fisher points out, have the capacity to approach a problem not in a straight-up-and-down, balance-sheet way, but from a more roundabout, visual perspective. This definitely came in handy when it came to my own, patented idea-testing device, which involved attempting, with the aid of a few paintbrush strokes and a limited number of words, to convey the thoughts and images in my head. If I could do so successfully, then that idea would be progressed, with particular attention being given to names, be they of companies, ships, or great journeys: e.g., Voyages Jules Verne, the *Spirit of Chartwell* and the 'Cape to Cairo Express'.

Even more valuable than this was the dyslexic way of looking at risk management, since in the course of my career I went in for many potentially risky, 'single-throw-of-the-dice' ventures. Conventional wisdom among the travel industry was that tour operators would cover themselves by building an element of wastage into the holiday price. It was usually around 15 per cent, which would be enough to stop them going out of business, but not enough to prevent rival firms siphoning off sales by building in a smaller wastage factor, thereby being able to charge lower prices.

At no time was this kind of price-judgment more crucial than when you were bringing out an unalterable brochure, often published up to nine months in advance. There was a famous case once, when Thomson and their rivals, Clarksons, shared the same Turin-based printer and the Thomson executives mocked up a fake brochure, with incorrect prices, which they left in a location where they thought Clarksons could not possibly miss it. Make no mistake, even small amounts of money could sway the punters one way or the other; success or failure could be determined by a holiday-price differential of no more than £5. With Voyages Jules Verne, I wanted to avoid being tied to this tyranny of locked-in brochure prices, which is why I decided to make use of the periods in between brochures to promote products via advertorials and mail-outs to the customers on our database, which had now grown to half a million.

As for occupancy shortfalls, I shut my eyes to the possibility and proceeded on the basis that our flights and ships would pretty much always operate with full loads. In my dyslexic mind, I pictured occupancy as an ancient rock formation, where layer after layer of eroded earth had been deposited on top of each other and pressed down more and more over time, gradually turning solid. Each layer had its own unique profile, determined by the layer that preceded it.

Thus, for me, each strata of rock came to represent layers of laid-down product, placed one upon another in such a way that, collectively, they would fill an airplane or a ship. The way I viewed things, it was impossible to pre-determine what all the product profiles might be: each would inevitably be shaped by the product profile that had been laid down earlier. I hated the idea of brochures compiled many months in advance, stuffed with large numbers of products that had been shaped not by nature, but by presentation and price.

Instead, I felt it was better to market one product at a time, and, once having understood its profile, then shape the next, this time with an inverse profile. That way, I reasoned, once all the products had been carefully laid one upon the other, the airplane or ship would be full. Otherwise, trying to smooth out the often-chaotic peaks and troughs of demand at the end of the process would inevitably lead to discounting and an undermining of the price integrity of the product. I know this may all sound a bit imprecise and un-business-like, but I can assure you it worked.

Thus by this time our Egyptian programme was extremely well bedded-in, with four weekly Boeing 757 charter flights operating into both Luxor and Aswan, plus an impressive array of enticing, complementary products. Before long, I found myself scouring my well-thumbed *Times Atlas* for other destinations that might be suited to the same marketing treatment. There was no point, I reasoned, in going to those workaday destinations already served by the established operators: not only would they not appeal to our more adventuresome customers, but there was no amount of magic dust that could be sprinkled over them to make them more alluring. No, my new destinations needed to be difficult to get to and not currently serviced by any airline, charter or scheduled. This meant that (a) they would, in the main, have to be outside Europe, and (b) I was going not just to need long-haul aircraft, but also to fill them.

Clearly, it wasn't going to be easy, but it was something I felt we had to do, given that the competition was hotting up from our rivals and the possibility that, as had happened with China, something might go badly wrong in Egypt.

In quick succession, then, I raised my risk level substantially, with direct weekly flights to Agra, in Rajasthan. This had the dual advantage of avoiding the turmoil and chaos of Delhi Airport while delivering travellers straight to the sights they wanted to see, whether it was the Taj Mahal and Red Fort in Agra, the Palace of the Winds in Jaipur, or any of the many other wonders in that part of India. The only drawback was that Agra was a military airport, which meant that each week we needed the blessing of both the military authorities and the state bureaucracy. There was no problem filling up our planes (which were much cheaper than any of the scheduled national airlines), but we never knew, from one week to another, if those planes would be allowed to land.

Direct flights to Tashkent were another challenge, due to the limited amount and poor standard of hotel accommodation, not just in Tashkent but also in the fabled Silk Road cities of Bukhara, Samarkand and Khiva. On top of which, we had our work cut out trying to fit in 230 guests straight after another 230 had just left.

Straight away my mind began whirring, in a Central American way. Costa Rica's national tourist office had already developed a series of evocative posters bearing the slogan 'Land of Wonders', and now I, in turn, started working out flight arrangements along the lines of my 'Great Journeys of the World'. We eventually launched these as 'The World of Wonders', covering Costa Rica as well as Havana in Cuba.

Slightly nearer to home, I managed to convince the Syrians to open up Damascus International Airport to my charters, thereby opening up access to the numerous Roman and Crusader monuments as well as nearby Amman and Aqaba. In addition, there were short-break flights to Leningrad and flights to Funchal in Madeira, which incorporated a bit of winter sun in Madeira with a visit to exotic Marrakech.

Then there was Zimbabwe. Ever since my first visit, in 1979, I had remained in awe of this country's breath-taking beauty, as a result of which I was determined, at the first available opportunity, to incorporate it into my portfolio of destinations. My problem, though, was dealing with Air Zimbabwe, who seemed to operate not as a national carrier but rather as Robert Mugabe's private airline, their planes forever being requisitioned by him for sudden shopping expeditions

A Passage across the African Continent by Railway, Ship and Aeroplane

on the
CAPE
to
CAIRO
express

VOYAGES JULES VERNE

A Story in Brief

TRACKS OF EMPIRE/UNFULFILLED PROMISE: The age of the railway was the age of the Victorian visionary – or at least it was as far as the British Empire was concerned. Nowhere was this truer than in Africa, where the proselytising vision of British 'civilisation' was at its most earnest. Let us not forget that Livingstone was a missionary first, and explorer second. The railways, furthermore, were seen as an indispensable part of bringing the British version of Christianity to the natives – and a useful way of preaching the virtues of free trade. In Africa, the greatest of these visionaries, prophets, entrepreneurs – call them what you will – was Cecil Rhodes, who gave his name to Rhodesia. According to Rhodes, "the railway was my right hand, the telegraph my voice". He dreamed of a railway running the length of Africa, from the Cape of Good Hope to Cairo – hence the VJV Cape-to-Cairo Express, albeit with a few improvisations. **IMAGE COURTESY: ROBERT SCURRAH/VOYAGES JULES VERNE.**

to Europe. The aircraft were allegedly sometimes not serviceable. I recall one flight, when not enough fuel had been taken on in Harare and the plane had to make an unscheduled stop at Marseilles. Since this was the first time an Air Zimbabwe flight had ever landed there, no one was prepared to extend the airline credit for fuel. It became clear that the only acceptable form of payment would be cash or a credit card; since the captain of the plane had neither, he took the only option open to him, which was to make an announcement over the plane's intercom asking for a volunteer to step forward and pay the fuel bill. Luckily, one gentleman did just that, if only to spare himself and the other passengers further delay.

On another occasion, I was trying to arrange direct flights to Victoria Falls, but the Zimbabwe Civil Aviation Authorities would hear none of it: they didn't want some foreign carrier muscling in. In desperation, I explored nearby airports – Kasane in Botswana and Livingstone in Zambia – but they were either inadequate or too small, so I had to think up another possible solution, which was indirectly to involve Mugabe's son, who at the time had an interest in a regional carrier. I decided I would start up a series of direct flights from London to Kilimanjaro, in Tanzania, and from there ferry my passengers by a fleet of smaller Zimbabwean aircraft to Victoria Falls.

Furthermore, this routing allowed us to start operations elsewhere within Tanzania and to Kenya, Botswana, Zambia, South Africa, Mauritius and the French island of Réunion, as well as running the *Pride of Africa* train, owned by Rohan Vos, between Victoria Falls and Cape Town. Before long, we were operating in Namibia as well. I even took a bit of a liberty, to the extant that I didn't feel 'Zimbabwe' had the right poetic ring, by persisting in calling the country 'Rhodesia' in all my travel literature. As I recall, no one complained.

In a relatively short space of time, then, we increased not just the number of destinations we served, but also the number of passengers we carried. The company had branched out into both Saharan and Sub-Saharan Africa, as well as North, Central and South America; Europe; Asia; and Australasia. We were into river and ocean cruising, painting, wildlife, walking, science, exploration and railways, and it seemed to me this plethora of interests ought to be brought together under one all-encompassing title for our brochure. We alighted upon 'World of Wonders', which continues to this day.

Speaking of which, it's a wonder to me now how I took on and managed such a vast and complex range of risks. I really do believe it was the pictures in my mind that helped me do it.

CHAPTER 49
RADIO TIRANA CALLING

All we had to survive now was the transit through Yugoslavia,
but that's another story. The only question remaining was, exactly who
were the other tourists? Within a week of returning home,
I had the answers for some of them.

I N 1971, I had gazed across the narrow straits separating Roda Beach, on the northern tip of Corfu, and the port of Saranda, in Albania, and wondered whether I would ever get into that most mysterious of lands. On one occasion, two Thomson passengers from the Roda Beach Hotel did try to make the crossing in a pedalo, but were apprehended by the Albanian security police and made to turn back.

As for myself, I had tried, unsuccessfully, to make contact with the Albanians in 1977, on the strength of both their close relationship with China and their fortnightly flight from Peking to Tirana. Undaunted, in 1986 I decided upon an altogether different approach.

At that time, occasional groups were allowed into the country, usually with some kind of trade union connection, so I decided to smuggle one of my trusted tour escorts onto one of those trips. The person I chose was Prue Stern, who had not only escorted the first departure of the 'Central Kingdom Express', but had also previously worked for me in Russia, with Thomson. Her instructions were straightforward: once in Tirana, break away unnoticed from the trade unionists and head directly to the offices of Albturist, the state travel agency, with a view to getting permission for VJV tour groups to visit Albania.

The plan worked: shortly after Prue's return, the Albanians sent me a cable confirming that I could commence operations into the country. This was on the basis that passengers would fly, via Belgrade, from London to Titograd (Podgorica today), and then journey overland across the Albanian border, visiting the towns of Skhodra, Tirana, Durres, Saranda and Girocastra. As there was no Albanian embassy in London, all visas had to be processed via the Albanian embassy in Paris, which meant we had to set up a regular courier service to ferry applications and passports back and forth.

However, I was acutely aware that most of our customers would want no more than a quick peep into the country, dipping their toe in the water, so to speak, rather than allocating a whole stack of valuable vacation time. The only way this was going to be possible was to do what we had done in 1971 with Thomson's 'Moscow and Leningrad' programme, and that was to operate twice-weekly flights to Tirana, thus allowing me to create three- and four-night tour permutations. If I could do that, then I was sure that people would come in their thousands, and it was with this aim that I set off to Tirana for face-to-face discussions. To my surprise, the Albanians agreed to my idea without much hesitation. The next step was to find an airline brave enough to fly to Tirana, which, after much barrel-scraping, I did, in the form of British Air Ferries.

True to form, all the available places soon sold out. One of the first to book was the TV weather forecaster Michael Fish, who, a few hours before the Great Storm of 15-16 October 1987, announced: "Earlier on today, apparently, a woman rang the BBC and said she heard there was a hurricane on the way... well, if you're watching, don't worry: there isn't!" That evening and the following morning, the worst storm to hit South East England since 1703 caused record damage and killed 18 people. It was the very day that my first direct flight to Tirana was due to depart and, with most of the other transport systems badly disrupted, it looked likely that I might have to cancel it. However, the first travellers to fly beyond the 'Raki Curtain' were made of sterner stuff. All of them eventually made it to the airport, and the historic first flight from London to Tirana did indeed take off. What's more, thousands more travellers followed. Many came not knowing what to expect, while others joined the group with intentions of a more cloak-and-dagger kind. The experience of visiting Albania is beautifully described in this piece by Geoff Sarbutt, one of the first passengers:

'The small Balkan state of Albania has long held a mysterious fascination for me. My first encounter with this country was as a teenager at home, when my spare time had been spent turning around the dial on a short-wave radio. At that time, Radio Tirana was the eighth most active international broadcaster in the world, transmitting in numerous languages around the clock on many frequencies. In fact, it was difficult not to receive their unique brand of programming; even my friends were aware of them, as Radio Tirana's powerful medium-wave transmitter blotted out BBC Radio 1 in our area for most of the evening. This was during the height of the Cold War, and the short-wave bands were full of East-versus-West propaganda, but here was a country strongly attacking both Washington and Moscow in the same tone.'

Several years later, Albania came into my life again. A colleague at work asked me to send a telex to Albania and told me a reply was required within hours; I failed even to find the relevant number and, in the process of trying, came to the conclusion that there were only eight telex machines in the country and the person that I was trying to contact was not one of the few, since international contact was still shunned at that time. It became a running joke that I couldn't make contact with a country in Europe; over the next months, every time an article or news item on Albania appeared in the press, someone would cut it out and pass it to me, with the cutting remark about me being an expert.

At this stage, the fascination of the unknown took over; I began to take an active interest and soon decided to go and see for myself. Individual tourism was still not allowed at that time, and so I joined a Voyages Jules Verne group tour. It was October 1986 when I made my way to Heathrow. My mind was full of stories from previous travellers; custom checks on entry were said to be formidable – I had heard stories of people with beards or long hair being refused entry or having to visit a barber, of books and magazines being confiscated, jewellery and watches being held by customs at the border until departure, and the constant feeling of being watched. There was even a story going around that tourists were often attacked by stone throwers in some villages.

A delay in departure from Heathrow provided time for my fellow travellers to exchange scare stories before we boarded an ageing Boeing 707 of JAT to Titograd, in Yugoslavia. Further delays in Titograd meant that it was approaching midnight as our connecting coach made its way on the short journey to the Albanian border at Han i Hotit. The road became narrow and winding as we continued, while our tour escort briefed us on what to expect and what not to do. I wondered if I was alone in having a few doubts as to the wisdom of what I was about to embark upon. Then, out of the darkness, came the bright lights of the Yugoslav border post, beyond which we could just see a dimly lit Albanian customs house.

We had all been told the routine: to walk across no-man's land to the barrier, where we would be called forward, one by one, to be checked against the group visa. For now, all the myths began to collapse – where was the dip of disinfectant that all tourists were once required to walk through? The baggage search was comprehensive, but, other than the border guards, none of the customs officers wore uniforms and their handling of us was completed in an unexpectedly friendly manner.

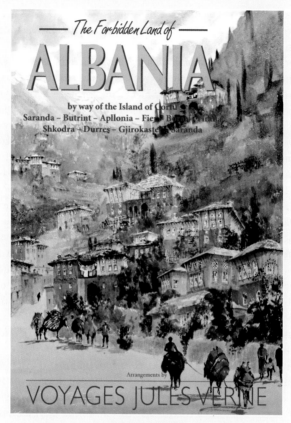

The Forbidden Land of
ALBANIA
by way of the Island of Corfu
Saranda ~ Butrint ~ Apllonia ~ Fier ~ Berat ~ Tirana
Shkodra ~ Durres ~ Gjirokaster ~ Saranda

Arrangements by
VOYAGES JULES VERNE

A Story in Brief

TO TIRANA IN STYLE: I might have considered that it was me who had started charter flights to Albania in 1986 but, someone much earlier had inadvertently beaten me to it. "Independent Air Transport flew out on 31st December 1957, on a mission to bring back Dutch refugees from Indonesia. However, at 13,500 feet, they encountered thick cloud and drifted, by accident, into Albanian air space, where-upon they were forced down by two M.I.G. fighters and made to land at a military airport. Marian Kozubski and the others were interrogated for seven hours, but the Albanians finally accepted that there had been a genuine mistake. As the newspapers and the BBC descended on us back home, Marian and his party were being treated to hotel accommodation, a sightseeing tour that included an ancient castle, and a send-off with a guard of honour supplied by two more M.I.G. fighters. It was publicity you just couldn't buy." Mrs Kozubska, from her unpublished memoirs.
IMAGE COURTESY: ALISON MUSKER/VOYAGES JULES VERNE.

Albania's strongman, Enver Hoxha, had died a year previously and, although most of his legacy was still in place, I wondered just how many tourists' tales were still applicable, even if they were true in the first place. As we ambled onto the awaiting Albturist coach, we exchanged our first impressions and compared stories of what customs had shown interest in. Newspapers and guide books seemed to be the favourites, but we were told that everything would be returned to us on departure from the country; even the man with a beard had no trouble entering.

As the coach made its way to Skhodra, our Albturist guides introduced themselves and briefed us on our itinerary, while members of the tour party exchanged opinions on what little could be seen outside the coach in the midnight darkness. Then came the next surprise. Upon arrival at the Hotel Rosafa, in Shkodra, at 1.00am, we were informed that dinner was about to be served. Where, we asked ourselves, in the Western world would you find a hotel prepared to feed a coach party at one in the morning?

As we continued our tour over the next few days, each of us warmed to the few Albanians who had the courage to speak to us. Generally, we had found the people in the street curious of us, but unwilling to be seen speaking with us in public. Some of us felt let down; none of us had been arrested or accused of spying, despite a late-evening clandestine visit by a couple of train spotters to Tirana Railway Station. Then it happened. As we were returning one evening to Tirana through a village, the conspicuous tour coach was apparently stoned by the locals, causing the windscreen to smash.

Even this didn't live up to earlier tourist tales; only one stone had been thrown and, to our surprise, the local villagers were seen to pursue the culprit – a lone young boy – and hand him over to a policeman, for a stern talking-to. I then recalled that, a few weeks earlier, I had experienced a similar stone-throwing child whilst on a tube train in East Acton; then, the locals didn't rally to apprehend the culprit.

As our tour ended, the members of the party once again exchanged their impressions. Most of us had gained a warmth for the people and for the country, with its stunning natural beauty, particularly in the mountainous areas, but the standard of living was not European and we had seen some of the pollution that outdated heavy industry was causing in some areas.

The customs checks on the way out were less than formal; we were so relaxed that many of us waved or shouted back to our Albturist guides and the border guards as we walked back across no-man's land to Yugoslavia. Our tour escort then felt he had to intervene; the Yugoslav customs officers were asleep and could not tolerate being woken up to such frivolity, but that didn't stop us.

We arrived in Yugoslavia at 4.00am, giggling like a party of schoolchildren.

We had been warned that the Yugoslav customs were likely to confiscate any souvenirs or literature that recognised the Albanian state, to the extent that, on our last full day in Albania, we had all trooped to the post office to air-mail, via Italy, anything that might not get through. On this occasion, however, the one Yugoslav customs officer who made the effort to rise from his slumbers didn't bother with much more than the simplest of passports checks.

After such a visit, my interest in the country grew, so, two-and-a-half years later, when two friends told me they were planning to take the same tour, I jumped at the chance to join them. This time, I had none of the pre-tour apprehension. Once again, an interesting time was had by all, but repeating the same short tour left me wanting more.

In early 1990, I booked myself on the 10-day 'Classical Tour of Albania', but this one turned out to be no ordinary tourist party. On my previous tours, my fellow tourists had mainly consisted of the curious, mainly in couples, but there was always at least one of the party who others had their suspicions about – was he Foreign Office, CIA, or an undercover journalist?

So, in March 1990, I again joined the tour party at Heathrow, but, this time, the mix of travellers was quite different and the couples were reduced to a minority of one pair. The remaining 21 people were a real curious bunch, but then these were not ordinary times; at the time of the closure of the bookings for the tour, the regimes of Eastern Europe were said to be 'falling like dominoes'. The press had long been speculating that, after Romania, Albania would be the last domino. Credence was given to this by several vague reports of demonstrations in Shkodra and Tirana. It soon became apparent that most, if not all, of my fellow travellers had joined the tour to get a ringside seat on what could be the fall of the last Communist state in Europe.

Four of our number were, from the manner of their dress, clearly of the Muslim faith and their motives were confirmed to us when the Albanian customs officers took from them, for 'safe keeping', a large number of Korans, prayer beads and prayer mats. The majority of the rest seemed to come from various walks of life, but all were keen amateur photographers, judging from their array of cameras, while three of them had the latest state-of-the-art video cameras.

The obvious opening line of conversation to most of my fellow travellers was always something like: "Where are you from, what do you do for a living?" I discovered nothing unusual in the mix of declared professions: there was a teacher, a farmer, a hotelier, a builder, a gallery director, a theatrical agent, a railway technician and a fancy goods salesman.

As on my previous tour, the first night was spent in Shkodra. Over breakfast, it became apparent to me that most of the tour party had been up since dawn, to practise their photographic skills. These dawn strolls had not escaped the notice of our Albturist guides; our first visit was to the Ottoman bridge at Mes, where one of our number jokingly asked: "Are we really allowed to take pictures of a bridge?" There was a typically quick reply from our guide: "I don't know what you are worrying about – you have all been up since dawn photographing everything."

The previous tense atmosphere amongst the tour party now started to crumble, and a warm rapport developed between the guides and the party, but, still, many fellow tourists seemed to be holding something back. The railway technician proudly showed off his knowledge of railways, but someone had looked at his so-called staff ID card, which looked remarkably like a photo card for an annual season ticket. The tourists compared notes with each other and speculation was running wild; the railway technician (me) was soon classified as an under-cover train spotter and the only couple were just so good at being tourists that much of the speculation centred on their motives.

The tour guides were puzzled too, particularly when three of the party joined the visit to the remarkable Roman amphitheatre in Durres, while the rest seemed to prefer a stroll in town. Later the same day, while half the party visited the ruins of Apollonia, the other half remained in the town of Fier, to photograph the actions of the Muslim tourists at a disused mosque.

After visiting the beautiful and remarkable atmospheric hillside town of Girocastra, we proceeded to Saranda on the coast, just opposite the Greek island of Corfu. When I mention my visits to Albania, people often say: "Oh yes, I've seen Albania across the water from Corfu." Now I can reply: "Oh yes, Corfu. I've seen it across the water from Albania."

While in Saranda, two of our number took it upon themselves to opt out of the day's visit and hitch a lift on a lorry out of town; they didn't get far before being returned to the hotel. The rest of the party returned to find the two missing and the guides looked increasingly concerned. I retired to my room to enjoy the sunset across the straits of Corfu, whilst noticing from my balcony that, each time one of our number left the hotel for an early evening stroll, a character straight out of spy movies would follow behind, at a not-very-discreet distance.

I eventually went down to the hotel lobby, only to find the errant pair sitting in a corner of the bar. Everyone wanted to hear what had happened to them. Had they been arrested? Had they been thrown in a dungeon? No, they had been swiftly returned to the hotel with no more than a friendly shaking of the head and a waving of the finger by one of the hotel staff. But they hadn't got away with it totally. Over supper, several of my fellow tourists made our views on such a provocative act very clear to them.

There was certainly no opting-out the next day, as we took the long coach journey along the magnificent scenery of the coast road from Saranda to Vlora, which surely must qualify as one of the most scenic and unspoilt areas of Europe. I can only hope that this will not be ruined by an influx of tourist development in the future.

Eventually, near the end of the tour, we arrived in Tirana: I will always remember awaking in my room in the Hotel Tirana, overlooking the main square of a European capital, to the sound, or lack of sound, of people walking or cycling to their work in a near traffic-free environment. Here, we found the first signs of the upheaval that was about to fall on the country: unlike my previous visits, people were now approaching tourists in the streets, stories were heard of small demonstrations and a small black market in foreign currency was appearing. I was witnessing the beginning of the end of an era.

The changes I observed between my three visits were comparatively small but, since my last visit, the events are well known. What I did detect on this last trip was unprecedented openness and realism, in the manner of the genuine friendliness of the Albanian people. While in Tirana, our guides asked if they could assist in arranging ad-hoc visits for the special interests of members of the tour party.

With very little prompting, I was taken on a tour of that first teenage memory of Albania – Radio Tirana. Not only was I allowed into the studios, but met the Director-General. We left Albania on St Patrick's Day, and, as several of our party were of Irish descent, the final meal in Shkodra and the journey to the border were quite memorable occasions. At the border, the Koran and beads were returned and I got back my old copy of the *Guardian*, despite not really wanting it.

All we had to survive now was the transit through Yugoslavia, but that's another story. The only question remaining was, exactly who were the other tourists? Within a week of returning home, I had the answers for some of them. A series of film reports appeared on Sky Television from a reporter looking rather like the fancy goods salesman. I had seen the teacher taking a photograph of a hospital in Saranda and there it was in the *Sunday Times*.

Weeks later, more photographs and an article appeared in the *Observer* colour supplement. The greatest revelation was seen on BBC Two's *The Late Show*: there was the theatrical agent telling the world the whole story, including a photograph of me standing outside Radio Tirana, accompanied by a claim that I wasn't a train-spotter pretending to be a railway technician.

Since this visit, much has changed in Albania, with the fall of the Stalinist government and the mass exodus of refugees. These changes now mean that journalists can enter freely, without having to disguise themselves and join tourist parties. The tours will never be the same again, but then neither will Albania.

CHAPTER 50
THE EGYPTIAN BEAUTY

By the time the party started on the return journey, there was already
a shimmering, mirage-like heat-haze on the road ahead. Passengers
were dozing off. Unfortunately, so was the driver.

THE word 'Coptic' is an adaptation of an Ancient Greek word meaning 'Egyptian', but, after the Muslim conquest, the term became restricted to adherents of the Christian faith. Later, in the 20th century, some Egyptian nationalists and intellectuals revived the term 'Copt' in its historical sense, meaning that all Egyptians were Copts, with some being Muslim Copts and others Christian Copts. Indeed, throughout Egyptian history, there has always been a strong desire within the country to reject the identities that foreign rulers have tried to force upon them and to stress the population's Egyptian identity, regardless of religion.

However, the nine million Christian Copts have always retained their own cultural and religious identity. Whereas Arab invaders routinely practised the subjugation of women, for example, Coptic families apportioned equal rights to members of both sexes. Many Copts gave their children neutral, not overtly Christian names, in order to make life easier in the Muslim-dominated country.

Eastmar was one of the few companies that employed both male and female Copts, and of the latter, the one that rose head and shoulders above all others was Howayda, a tour guide almost exclusively assigned to Voyages Jules Verne groups. I met her for the first time in 1992, at a reception in the Sheraton Hotel, Luxor, to celebrate the launch of one of VJV's chartered Nile steamers. The thing that immediately struck me was her incredible beauty. With her flowing black hair and Nefertari-like big brown eyes, you felt she was a descendant of the Pharaohs themselves; she seemed like a new-born foal, full of the joys of spring and prancing around a paddock full of wildflowers. In my mind, she was an Egyptian version of Gigi, while I played the role of a captivated Maurice Chevalier.

One of the VJV tours that took in Egypt was our eight-day 'Land of Canaan' journey, which included a flight from London to Amman, in Jordan, followed by a visit to that ancient Nabataean stronghold, the 'rose-red' city of Petra. The itinerary then continued to the coastal town of Aqaba, across the newly opened border with Israel to Eilat, then onwards to Taba, in Sinai, Egypt.

Administratively, this was always complex. Such were the political and logistical sensitivities, each traveller required multiple visas. Every time we arrived at a frontier, we were required not just to go through rigorous passport formalities, but also to disembark from the coach and proceed on foot across no-man's land, luggage in hand. Then, having gone through the checkpoint, we had to get onto a different coach, as no single coach was allowed to transit another's territory.

The journey was supposed to have proceeded to Nuweiba, on the Red Sea, which would serve as the base for visiting St Catherine's Monastery, before the party retraced its steps through Jordan, ultimately crossing the Allenby Bridge and heading for Jerusalem. The tour was, as we described it, "a saga of the emergence of this area, where three continents – Asia, Europe and Africa – converge. The formation of the ancient Kingdom of Judah, the laws, legends and teachings passed down and on, played a vital role in the creation and development of three great religions: Christianity, Judaism and Islam."

If there was one point on the map where all three religions met, it was the Taba, on the Red Sea in Egypt, the busiest border crossing between Egypt and Israel. On the October day in question, some 40 Voyages Jules Verne passengers crossed on foot through the no-man's land separating Israel from Taba, where, as scheduled, they found the Eastmar coach and Howayda waiting for them. Suddenly, as they were boarding the bus and the driver was loading the luggage, a storm of biblical proportions blew up from nowhere. Such was the ferocity of the wind and rain that the windows of Taba Hilton Hotel, where the coach was parked, had been completely blown out and passenger boats had overturned in the Red Sea. In view of this onslaught from the elements, the Egyptian border police held the coach at Taba until they considered that it was safe for it to proceed to Nuweiba.

The Taba border stands at the beginning of a road which descends steeply and then hugs the coast, with the Red Sea on the left and the dramatic Sinai Mountains on the right. About a mile out from Taba, where the road runs at around sea level, the coach driver came across a large pool of water in the middle of the road. It looked perfectly fordable, but what the driver didn't know was that under the water there was now a thick layer of wet sand, in which the coach's wheels were now stuck.

A Story in Brief

NEFERTARI: was the Favourite wife of Ramesses I ; she is the only wife of a pharaoh to be depicted on the façade of a temple. No tomb in the whole of Egypt is comparable in artistic superiority and fascination' to that of Nefertari, says Gamal Moukhtar, a former director of the Antiquities Organisation. 'Splendid paintings reflect the genius, the skill of the artist and draftsmen working during Ramesside artistic renaissance.' Art developed on two levels under Ramesside pharaohs of the 13th century BC. Besides excellence of decorative perfection – and nowhere is this more so than in the underground tombs in the Valley of the Kings and Queens at Thebes, site of modern-day Luxor. In the slim figure, delicate profile and elegant posture of Queen Nefertari – her name poignantly means 'most beautiful of them all'.

IMAGE COURTESY: TAREK EL GENDY/HOWAYDA'S SISTER.

The mood on board was relaxed: Howayda had taken charge and hailed the driver of a passing industrial earth mover, who had agreed to return with a tractor to haul the coach free. Things changed dramatically, however, when, after the passengers had sat waiting for half an hour, a huge wall of water burst from a formerly dried-up riverbed and down towards where the coach was now marooned.

When it hit, the water shook the coach violently, and within seconds it wasn't just lapping around the wheels; it had reached the side of the coach and the luggage compartment. Just as people were thinking it was time to wade to high ground, another, fiercer-still wave of water smashed into the side of the coach, at which point everyone's thoughts turned towards getting out of the coach, despite Howayda's warnings that it might be safer to stay put.

Escape turned out to be a hazardous option. The water was now at chest height, so the guides got the passengers to hold hands and make their way through the deluge in a human chain. By now, the current had become unbelievably strong and the footholds so insecure that, when one female member of the party slipped and fell, she was swept out to sea and subsequently drowned. Meanwhile, the rest of the party made it to higher ground.

These were the days before mobile telephones, and news of the disaster reached me only some time later, due, in no small part, to the disruption caused by the storm and the confusion into which it had thrown the police and the rescue services. All I knew was that the passengers – I did not yet know one of them had drowned – and guides had made it back to the Taba Hilton, so the first thing I did was ring the hotel. They put me through to Howayda, who, in a calm and collected manner, explained what had happened. I told her that I had made arrangements with another operator to fly the group home from an Israeli military airport to the west of Eilat. The survivors eventually came back to London, to be met by an onslaught of unwanted press attention. That was the last time I heard Howayda's name mentioned until an even sadder occasion a year later.

Howayda had accompanied our passengers on the Nile steamer *Ra II*, on its voyage from Luxor to Aswan, and on the following morning was woken at 5.00am for the coach journey down the long, monotonous Desert Road to Abu Simbel. The reason for the early departure was to avoid the heat of the day, but on this occasion the coach driver failed to show up, which meant that the coach owner had to stand in at the last moment and drive Howayda and her charges to Abu Simbel himself. By the time the party reached Abu Simbel, the sun was high in the sky and the site was already teeming with thousands of tourists.

Thus, by the time the party started on the return journey, there was already a shimmering, mirage-like heat-haze on the featureless road ahead and the passengers were dozing off in the stifling heat. Unfortunately, so was the driver. Now, there are no halfway houses on the Desert Road, so when it comes to answering the call of nature, coaches tend to pull up beside a rock and let passengers get on with it.

This is exactly what had happened up ahead, with disastrous consequences. One minute, the passengers (from the coach ahead) were standing by the roadside; the next, Howayda's coach had ploughed off the road and into both the stationary coach and its passengers. The scene was one of utter carnage: injured passengers from the first coach were lying on the ground, miles away from medical assistance, while passengers on board the second coach had been badly hurt too. As for Howayda, she had been sitting alongside the driver and as a result, this being in the days before seatbelts, had been thrown through the windscreen and killed instantaneously.

Eventually, all the passengers – the injured and the uninjured – were ferried either by ambulance or by passing coaches to Aswan, whereupon I was informed that there had been an incident on the Desert Road. The first reports indicated that it was terrorist-related, but the full horror only became apparent once our local manager and someone from the British Consulate had made their way to Aswan, to assist with the injured and those that needed to be flown back to London. Many of us mourned the lovely Howayda, who was considered not just Eastmar's but Egypt's best tour guide. Her record said it all: born in 1969, she had graduated in 1990 with full honours, after four years at the Helwan University Faculty of Tourism and Hotel Management, and begun working as a tour guide in 1991.

The loss of Howayda was tragic and painful for her family, friends, colleagues and all those at Eastmar. To this day, I still think of her as she was that first time I met her. Boris Pasternak, the Russian novelist, once lamented: "When a person dies, they die twice – once when they die physically and then when their friends forget them." Well, Howayda had many friends and she will live forever in their memories. Later, meditating on her unlived life – she was just 26 when she died – and on all the other people injured in the crash, I began to wonder what the point of all my striving was. Somehow, this disaster triggered something in my mind that, in the end, led to my selling of the company. Beforehand, I had thought I was responsible for most things; but in the final analysis, it seemed I was in control of very little.

In the aftermath of the crash, I declared that I would return to Cairo and express my thoughts to Howayda's parents. To my shame, this is still a deed left undone, but one day I will honour that promise – I will.

Within two years of this tragic event, I had sold Voyages Jules Verne to the

Swiss company Kuoni, although this was not to be the last I heard of that terrible day on the Desert Road. Like all operators, I had taken out liability insurance to cover for all eventualities, and so had at least been able to console myself with the thought that I would not be burdened by insurance claims. Or rather, that was what I assumed until the insurance company went bust, leaving me facing hundreds of thousands of pounds' worth of claims. It seemed like I had cover for all eventualities except one: the insurance company going out of business itself.

1979 VJV ORGANISED VOGUE MAGAZINE PHOTO-SHOOT IN CHINA

A Story in Brief

FLASH POINT: The most recent 'Yining Incident' was the culmination of protests in 1997, in the city of the same name. The protests were sparked by the news of the execution of 30 Uighur independence activists, as well as the crackdown on attempts to revive elements of traditional Uighur culture, including traditional gatherings known as meshreps. On 5 February 1997, protesters had marched for 'independence for Xinjiang', and were reportedly dispersed by People's Liberation Army gunfire. Official reports put the death toll at nine, while dissident reports estimated the number killed at more than 100. There had also been a much earlier 'Yining Incident' in 1944, when the city was closed off from the rest of the world, following tension between local Uighur people, the Chinese government and the Soviet Union. Which was why, for many years, this border point between the USSR and China had remained firmly closed. **IMAGE COURTESY: VOGUE MAGAZINE.**

Part Four
RETURN TICKET HOME

I N 1985, flushed with my success at Voyages Jules Verne, I had pushed my
unsettled childhood to the back of my mind, on the grounds that making
contact with any of my surviving relatives would only hold me back. Suddenly,
though, I was overcome with guilt and set about finding my flesh-and-blood with
the same vigour that I had applied to all my other challenges. On my sixth
birthday, my mother sent me a birthday card with a big '6' on it; attached was a
balloon and inside the neck a solitary sixpence – I kept it for a long while afterwards, as if it were my return ticket home – now I was about to redeem it.

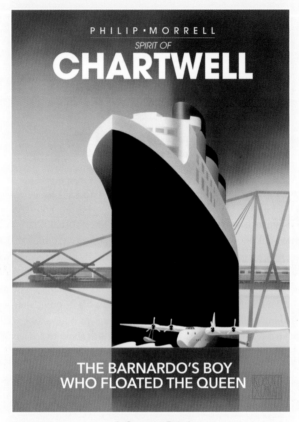

A Story in Brief

THE SILVER TOUCH: Riviera Holidays founder Aubrey Morris, on the early success of his company: "Riviera's growth was outstanding, even within the exceptional travel world we now inhabited. Our representatives in the Italian Adriatic for that first year were provided by Martelli, but we needed a courier to travel with the Smith's party. My thoughts turned to a young man in my Communist Party branch, who had once been on holiday to the Adriatic with Intertours, and being one of the select few who had travelled abroad, could thus be considered almost an expert! Sidney Silver was employed by a company offering discounted white goods and cars to trades unions even though some thought he was a carpet salesman, and despite our disagreements on several aspects of party policy, I respected his intellect and education. Eventually he agreed to take the group, and while he knew no Italian, he spoke French, was adaptable and, most importantly, was the only person we knew we could trust". Sid also helped us very much at the beginnings of VJV.

IMAGE COURTESY: ROBERT SCURRAH/VOYAGES JULES VERNE.

CHAPTER 51
MUTINY ON THE ALGARVE

Nobody, except possibly a Greek oracle, could have foreseen what was
to follow. It is not an easy process buying ships from a Greek. A series
of events ensued that would have tested the nerves of an Onassis.

A NTONIO Pigafetta was an Italian scholar and explorer from the Republic
of Venice. He travelled with the Portuguese explorer Ferdinand Magellan
and his crew on their voyage, by order of King Charles I of Spain, to the
'Spice Islands' in the Indies.

During the voyage, Pigafetta served as Magellan's assistant, keeping an
accurate journal of the expedition, and was one of just 18 men who made it back
to Spain in 1522, out of the 240 who had set out three years earlier. Magellan had
died during the journey and Juan Sebastián Elcano had taken over the captaincy
of the one remaining vessel of the five-ship fleet, the *Victoria*. When she arrived
off the coast at Sanlúcar de Barrameda, near Cadiz, on 6 September 1522, the
Victoria had completed the first-ever circumnavigation of the world. Naturally,
Pigafetta's journal is the source for much of what we know about Magellan and
Elcano's voyages.

One phenomenon baffled the scholar, and, more than three centuries later, it
was seized upon by Jules Verne when he came to write *Around the World in Eighty
Days*. It concerned an incident that happened towards the end of the journey, when
Pigafetta landed on the islands now known as Cape Verde. He wrote:

'On Wednesday 9 July [1522], we arrived at one these islands named Santiago,
where we immediately sent the boat ashore, to obtain provisions. We charged our
men in the boat that, when they were ashore, they should ask what day it was. They
were answered that it was Thursday, at which they were much amazed, for, to us, it
was Wednesday and we knew not how we had fallen into error.

For every day I, being always in health, had written down each day without any intermission. But, as we were told since, there had been no mistake, for we had always made our voyage westward and had returned to the same place of departure as the sun, wherefore the long voyage had brought the gain of twenty-four hours, as is clearly seen.'

Of course, we know now what had happened. Pigafetta had unwittingly discovered the effect of crossing the International Date Line: when you cross it travelling east-to-west, one day is lost, and when you cross it in the other direction, one day is gained. This is the reason why, in Verne's book, Phileas Fogg makes it back to the Reform Club in time to win the wager.

I too had now crossed over a significant frontier in my working life, having sold Voyages Jules Verne, and I soon found that the passing of anything that has been a significant part of one's life, no matter how worrisome, is accompanied not so much by relief as by ambivalence. The release from the prison of responsibility is tempered by both fear of boredom and frustration at the absence of an outlet for one's creativity.

Since the terms of the Kuoni sale prohibited me from entering into direct competition with them, I had to look elsewhere for a challenge. However, it would not be easy to find a project that met the criteria of all my previous enterprises – i.e., something that smacked of adventure while at the same time being manageable, fundamentally safe and commercially viable. Gradually, I realised that cruise ships may be the answer. During my time at the helm of Voyages Jules Verne, there had been all manner of river journeys up and down the great waterways of the world, but almost nothing in Britain.

Of course, the UK has an extensive waterway network, but for the most part it is only navigable by smaller vessels such as light pleasure craft and low-slung barges. This is due to the huge number of roads and railway lines that sprang up during the Industrial Revolution, many of which cross the waterways, resulting in low, arched bridges and narrow locks that are impassable to larger vessels.

However, thanks to the eminent 18th-century engineers Thomas Telford and William Jessop, one British waterway escaped this fate: the magnificent Caledonian Canal, in the Highlands of Scotland, which cuts a dramatic swathe through the Great Glen. This mighty feat of engineering not only boasts more generously-dimensioned locks than its counterparts; it is also unencumbered by height restrictions, due to the provision of swing bridges that can be opened to let large vessels through. It is also largely untouched by commercial shipping, because, almost as soon as it opened in 1822, advances in the construction of even larger vessels rendered the project pretty much redundant.

Commercial success or not, the result was one of the world's most awe-inspiring and beautiful waterways. Indeed, 'canal' is far too utilitarian a word to describe this stretch of water. The truth is that the Caledonian is one of those wonderful confluences of man's genius and nature's bounty: the sections of the canal merely link one inland loch with another, thus providing a continuous flow from Fort William, on the Atlantic, to Inverness, on the North Sea.

Imagine my surprise, then, when I found that despite all its charms, the Caledonian Canal was practically unknown. Perhaps I had stumbled upon the start of a new adventure. First, certain mathematical factors had to be taken into consideration. The Caledonian's physical constraints necessitated a vessel no longer than 150 feet, no wider than 34 feet and with a sea draft (the vertical distance between the waterline and the bottom of the hull) no greater than 11 feet. Also, since the waterway was only 63 miles long, any worthwhile itinerary would also have to include a cruise among the hidden sea lochs around Scotland's western shore.

Taken altogether, the requirement was for a hybrid craft big enough to carry a suitable number of passengers and able to navigate both the inland waters of the Caledonian Canal and the shoreline of the Atlantic. After much fruitless investigative work, I reached the eventual conclusion that no such craft existed. Then, in Greece, a candidate turned up. The *Victoria* (named after Magellan and Elcano's ship) had been found languishing in a harbour after two short seasons in the Aegean. Financial failure meant that the *Victoria*, whose dimensions suited the Caledonian Canal, had been commandeered by her former operators' bank. A purchase was quickly effected, on the basis that she could be brought into service after no more than a quick paint job.

Nobody, except possibly a Greek oracle, could have foreseen what was to follow. It is, I now know, not an easy process buying ships from Greek ship-owners. At the time, though, my knowledge of the shipping world was nugatory. A series of events ensued that would have tested the nerves of an Onassis, never mind a naïve, would-be ship owner such as myself.

Once the *Victoria* had been purchased, we decided to sail her post-haste to Santander, on Spain's north-west coast, to a shipyard operated by Oliver Design, the company that had refurbished the *English Lady*, which l had launched on the Douro in Portugal some years earlier. For certification purposes, it was thought prudent that, for the voyage to Santander, the *Victoria* should be reclassified and reflagged as a personal motor yacht. This immediately attracted the attention of the Greek tax authorities, who, now that the vessel was no longer a commercial craft, demanded extra payments, albeit for just this one voyage.

Long discussions followed before a resolution was found, at which point another obstacle reared its unwelcome head. Under Greek maritime union law, contracted seamen have the right to refuse to join a vessel with a changed flag. In deciding not to serve on the *Victoria* and so leave a vessel which had yet to sail, the seamen were entitled to a month's salary, a point made forcefully by their union, who advised me that a warrant for the vessel to be impounded would be issued in the event of non-compliance. There was nothing for it but to discharge the old crew, who had not yet reported for duty, pay them a month's salary and engage an entirely new crew.

At last the *Victoria* was able to set sail and, having passed through the Corinth Canal, she headed out into the Mediterranean. All was well, or at least it would have been, had it not been for the steel plates welded to the lower windows to make her water-tight, which had become coated in a layer of rust that stretched the length of the superstructure. On the approach to southern Sicily, the Italian maritime police, presuming the *Victoria* to be a rust bucket crammed full of yet another shipment of hapless refugees from Africa, boarded her no less than three times in the course of two days.

Soon afterwards the generator expired, forcing an emergency diversion to Malta for repairs. This was only the first of a few unwanted service stops on the way to Gibraltar: repairs also had to be carried out at Mallorca and Cartagena. The voyage was becoming almost historic – had the *Victoria* been found crewless and rudderless on the high seas, like a latter-day *Mary Celeste*, nobody would have been surprised. All that was missing was a mutinous crew, but not for long. No sooner had the *Victoria* anchored at the small fishing port of Sagres, in Portugal, just shy of Cape St Vincent and the Atlantic rollers that waited beyond, than the crew took one look at the heaving ocean, decided they were Mediterr-anean, not Atlantic, seaman after all, and opted to shelter in the harbour.

That was their first mistake, for Sagres harbour, being close to the open Atlantic, is extremely tidal, and at low tide it dries out – fine for flat-bottomed boats, which can rest on the mud, but not good for ships with tapered hulls such as the *Victoria*. On entering the harbour unannounced, the crew were unceremoniously ejected by the harbourmaster and told to anchor, for the time being, in the lee of a small offshore island. They did this and, after dropping anchor, immediately proceeded to go to sleep. While they slumbered, the un-Mediterranean tide went out, duly causing the vessel to keel to one side.

Worse still, because they had left some lower portholes open, the *Victoria* began to flood. The crew immediately panicked, launched the life rafts and departed for the safety of Sagres Harbour. At the time, I was enjoying dinner in a London restaurant – the very esteemed Ivy. To this day, I can recall vividly these words being spluttered across the table by Vincent Savona, who had taken the call: "What was that, Captain? Abandoned ship?"

Out of a sense of decorum to our fellow diners, we staggered out onto the pavement to hear the whole story. It turned out that the harbourmaster, who had dispatched divers to pump out the water, had soon brought things under control. That was the good news. The bad news was that the crew were now well and truly spooked and, having caught a glimpse of the Atlantic waves, were now seeking the comfort of their own beds back home.

The incident was reminiscent of a similar seagoing nightmare in 1984, when I had bought, in Marseilles, another vessel destined for the sea lochs of Scotland. This time the crew were French, and they had been commissioned to sail the *Rive Guadeloupe* (later *Lord of the Highlands*) around the Iberian Peninsula to the shipyard at Santander, for a makeover. All the way, as the vessel proceeded past Mallorca, Cartagena, Malaga and Gibraltar, the sea conditions were flat and calm. Approaching Sagres, however, the French crew became similarly spooked by the Atlantic rollers and diverted into the port of Portimão, where they all bought tickets on the next plane back to Paris. But before they could leave, they were detained by the harbourmaster and made to hand over the computer key that drove the navigation system (the French crew had taken it to ensure they got paid). Eventually, a fresh crew had to be sent out from the UK to complete the journey to Santander.

In the case of the *Victoria*, a replacement Portuguese crew was duly found. By the time she got to Santander, she was looking in a very sorry state indeed. Nonetheless, since a full survey had been carried out before taking delivery of the vessel, the presumption was that, once in Santander, the repair work would consist of mostly cosmetic refurbishment. The survey had paid particular attention to the *Victoria*'s steel construction, without which UK certification was out of the question. Unfortunately, during the stripping-out process, it became apparent that only the perimeter of the deck was made of steel, with the rest made of wood. Suddenly, the task was no longer embellishment, but wholesale reconstruction. Furthermore, the longer the stripping-out process went on, the more horrors were revealed.

In the end, all that remained of the vessel that had left Greece was the keel and two principal engines. As a result, we now had a new problem: if we were going to reconstruct the ship completely in steel, she would need to be longer and wider, in order to acquire the necessary stability. Thus, the decision was made to make her 23 feet longer by adding a new section forward of the engine space and to increase her width by adding all-round sponsons, in order to create a stabilising skirt. At the same time, we had to ensure that she remained slim enough to navigate the Caledonian Canal's locks, in addition to providing the latest in safety aids and deluxe accommodation.

If, at this point, the fickle *Victoria* had thrown up one last insuperable hurdle, it would have only been in keeping with how she had behaved so far. As it turned out, what emerged from the wreckage was a vessel of truly beautiful proportions, with utterly splendid facilities. The question was: would she fit into the Caledonian Canal? I confess, when I went to Fort William, in August 2000, my heart was in my mouth as to whether the Victoria would be slim enough. To my utter relief, she was – albeit by a matter of inches.

In due course, the *Victoria* became the *Lord of the Glens* and she has operated every season since, rarely falling beneath 99 per cent occupancy. I would suggest that, with her graceful lines, she complements the majestic landscape through which she gently thrums.

KYLE OF LOCHALSH HIGHLAND LINE POSTER BY ROBERT SCURRAH

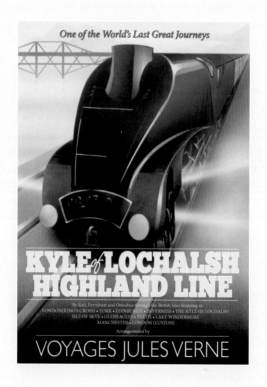

A Story in Brief

RETURN TO PITCAIRN: The mutiny on the *Bounty* took place on 28 April 1789, and the leader of the revolt against Lieutenant William Bligh was an officer by the name of Fletcher Christian. Accounts of what happened relate that the ship's sailors had two rather different motivations. On one hand, they were attracted to the 'idyllic' life and sexual opportunities afforded on the Pacific island of Tahiti. On the other, they were desperate to put a stop to Bligh's harsh treatment of the crew. In the end, some 18 mutineers set Bligh afloat in a small boat, along with 18 of the 22 crew who remained loyal to him. To avoid detection, the mutineers then settled on Pitcairn Island, or on Tahiti, and burned the *Bounty*. In 1992, Voyages Jules Verne organised a voyage across the South Seas, calling at Pitcairn; what's more, we engaged Fletcher Christian's great, great, great, great grandson to escort it.

IMAGE COURTESY: OLIVER DESIGN-SANTANDER.

CHAPTER 52
I SAW A TRAIN

In a way, the story of the 'Spirit of Chartwell' is the story of my infatuation with the adventure of travel and my inability to refuse a challenge.

I think I can claim that, while I was at Voyages Jules Verne (and even after I had left), I helped introduce the British public, in unprecedented numbers, to the rivers of the world. There were cruises along the Rhine, Mosel, Elbe, Danube, Seine, Rhone, Douro, Po, Dnieper, Volga, Lena, Irrawaddy, Yangtse and, latterly, the Caledonian Canal in the Highlands of Scotland, not to mention new projects that were in the pipeline on the Shannon, in Ireland, and the Severn, in the West Country. Yet one of the most celebrated rivers in the world remained stubbornly absent from this list: Old Father Thames, London's conduit and the rippling mirror of English and British history, was not well served by accommodation cruise vessels – in fact, there were none of any meaningful size.

There are numerous reasons why this was so, among them the Thames' physical attributes: unlike many of the rivers mentioned above, the Thames is tidal (with an eight metre tidal range), not just where it meets the North Sea but all the way up to London and beyond, until Teddington. The current is strong and fast and follows a pronounced, curving course. Many of the bridges, already low to begin with, are built over shallow arches, plus there is a marked shortage of pier facilities.

When it comes to the forces of nature, any challenges can usually be met through careful design and the latest technology. It is the obstacles put forward by mankind that tend to be the insuperable ones. Navigation is certainly tricky, especially through central London, where you need the specialist local knowledge of a maritime pilot. Above Teddington Lock the river is non-tidal, but the bridges are low, the river course shallow and the locks increasingly small.

Traditionally, piloting has been in the hands of the Worshipful Company of Watermen and Lightermen, one of the oldest livery companies in the country, dating from the reign of Henry VIII, when the Thames was the hub of a great commercial centre and some 40,000 men earned a living either on or from it. The company was formed in 1555 to control the watermen responsible for the movement of goods and passengers along the river, and it remains the only ancient City Guild to have been formed and controlled by Act of Parliament.

Over the centuries, various agencies and organisations have become mutual custodians of the Thames: the Maritime and Coastguard Agency, the Environment Agency, the Port of London Authority and the Mayor of London (through Transport for London). The result is a complicated regulatory environment, which in my opinion is self-defeating: plenty of rules, but no new-built boats.

This is due, in part, to the accident which took place on the night of 20 August 1989, when the pleasure boat *Marchioness* sank after being run down by the dredger Bowbelle, near Cannon Street Railway Bridge. There were 130 people on the *Marchioness*, including crew members, catering staff and guests at a private birthday party, and 51 of them drowned. Following an investigation, the report by Lord Justice Clarke made safety recommendations that were eventually adopted by both the Maritime and Coastguard Agency and the Port of London Authority. These stringent rules, together with the constraints imposed by the physical nature of the Thames, quickly dampened the enthusiasm of several European operators, notably the Dutch, who had considered introducing their own brand of accommodation vessel to the Thames.

Ironically, too, the imposition of new rules served to discourage the replacement of older vessels with new ones, because of the expense involved in meeting the new regulations and the contrariness with which those rules were applied. For the same reasons, the existing stock of vessels became nigh impossible to sell on – a continuing problem that I believe will only worsen.

As a result, the Thames fleet compares unfavourably with those of any of the other great European rivers. The prospect of river cruises sailing all the way from the Thames estuary up to Oxford remains as elusive as ever.

SCENES FROM A WINDOW CARRIAGE

In a way, the story of the *Spirit of Chartwell* is the story of my infatuation with the adventure of travel and my inability to refuse a challenge. Many of the elements that have influenced my life and have been featured in these chapters find expression in this single vessel.

In 1987, I bought Wyck Hill House Hotel in the Cotswolds, just outside Stow-on-the-Wold. Most weeks, I would make the two-hour train journey from

A Story in Brief

THE NIGHT BEFORE: On 2 June 2012, the *Spirit of Chartwell,* now transformed into the Royal Barge, was moored outside a derelict flour mill in the Royal Docks. After nine months of preparation, everything was ready for the vessel to cast off at one o'clock in the morning, once City Airport had closed and before the Thames Barrier was raised. There was, however, a problem: the wind was gusting up to 30 knots, far in excess of the speed at which it would normally have been prudent to set sail, even without the 10 tonnes of bedding material and floral tributes on the top deck. We steered an eerie course upstream to Cadogan Pier in Chelsea, covered in a black material – a ghostly sight amidst the mist and murk. That night, no one slept; such was the level of anxiety. What happened on the Pageant day itself remains a hazy memory. Did I meet the Queen? I am told I did.

Paddington to Charlbury, on a track that follows the course of the Thames for part of the way. In one of those moments of inspiration that can occur when you're in a bit of trance, it occurred to me that if the river was like a train track, then the vessel could be like a train composed of different sections, capable of being coupled and uncoupled like carriages.

In other words, for the tidal Thames below Teddington, where there were height restrictions but no limits on length, the vessel would be a long, low craft which, upstream of Teddington, would divide into two, in order to pass through the smaller locks and navigate the narrower stretches of river.

With this concept in mind, Oliver Design in Bilbao, who had rebuilt the company's Scottish ships, the *Lord of the Glens* and the *Lord of the Highlands*, was commissioned to draw up plans and a feasibility study. While constructing such a craft presented no insurmountable technical challenges, what scuppered the project were the costs, which would have been twice those of building a conventional vessel, despite the end result being a vessel with only 32 berths. In short, it made no economic sense. The idea of constructing a cruise vessel for the Thames might have sunk there and then, beached before it had left the pier, had it not been for an unexpected request from one of the company's biggest customers.

TULIPS FROM AMSTERDAM

The Magna Carta Steamship Company, which I formed and owned following the sale of Voyages Jules Verne to Kuoni, operated *Lord of the Glens*, a luxury vessel cruising the waterways of the Highlands of Scotland and, uniquely, the Caledonian Canal.

One of our biggest customers, National Geographic, based in Washington, DC, had chartered a vessel in the Netherlands for its tulip-bulb-field cruises, but at the last minute, the company operating the ship had gone out of business and had their vessel impounded by the bank. Straight away, National Geographic turned to me in the hope of being able to charter the *Lord of the Glens* instead, but I was unable to help out, as we were booked up over the period in question.

Given that I was still dreaming about operating a ship on the Thames, I found myself suddenly interested in the fate of this impounded vessel in the Netherlands and decided to try and seek it out. That this proved unexpectedly difficult was due to something that I suppose was quite predictable: disputed ownership.

In due course, it emerged that each of the original partners in the failed enterprise wanted to buy her back, which meant that the last thing they wanted was for a potential purchaser from outside their circle to be aware of her whereabouts. After three months of dogged sleuthing, however, I tracked down the good ship *Charlemagne* to a remote mooring close to Zwijndrecht, in the province of South Holland, where she stood forlornly sandwiched between a number of other seized vessels.

At first glance, she looked in reasonable condition, and it was thought that with a quick daub of paint she could soon be back in service, doing what she had always done. However, there were certain aspects of the vessel that made me think about putting her to a slightly different use. Not only did she have a unique propulsion system, but she was also divided into a series of watertight compartments, in order to comply with German maritime regulations covering coastal operations in the German section of the intertidal Wadden Sea.

These features, together with her unique dimensions, suggested to me that this was a vessel which might be able to travel all the way from Whitstable, in Kent, through Chatham and Rochester and, having passed all the way along the tidal Thames, carry on through to the non-tidal part of the river, as far as Weybridge.

I bought her there and then. My plan was to refurbish her completely, but instead of pursuing the 'floating train' idea, I would achieve the same effect with the aid of a second, smaller day-vessel that would introduce travellers to the upper reaches of the Thames, above Weybridge. I bought the *Noah* from a Dutch operator and changed its name to *Passepartout*, with a view to setting it to work alongside the *Charlemagne*.

Initially, the intention was to replicate a typical European overnight-accommodation river cruiser on the Thames, operating an itinerary from Whitstable to Cliveden. This idea only began to evolve a little later, however – first, I needed to find a shipyard that was able to take on the task of refurbishment, given that most of the likely candidates were already committed to other projects. Meanwhile, I hired the ship's original crew and gave them the job of stripping the vessel. All was going well until someone complained to the police about the work taking place on the Sabbath, as a result of which the crew were arrested and held in a hut for interrogation. Spooked by this turn of events, they duly scarpered, leaving me with no crew and a half-gutted ship.

ENTER MR KOOIMAN

In the end, the only yard that would accept the job of refurbishing the ship was Kooiman, in Zwijndrecht. Unfortunately, being specialist constructors of ocean-going tugs and other working boats, they had never built a passenger vessel before. On the plus side, they were prepared to take on the project and, in the process, perhaps branch out and expand their commercial repertoire. Inevitably, it would seem, concealed defects came to light once the work had started and it soon became evident that we had no choice but to strip the *Charlemagne* back to the bare metal – including all the pipe-work and most of the vital, onboard systems

– if she was to meet the specifications demanded by new Thames regulations.

In essence, we would be building a brand new ship, which is how a £2m project turned into an £8m one. The outcome, once the gutting had taken place, was a space that was strikingly similar to a train carriage, in looks at any rate. The original concept of a marriage between water and railway steel still applied, only now it was more of an interior design than an engineering project. The only question to be resolved was: on what train and what carriage should we base our design? For the answer, I had to go back 27 years to an earlier Voyages Jules Verne train journey, which had recalled what some might call the great age of travel, but what might be better described as the great age of elegant travel.

IN THE TRACKS OF GEORGE NAGELMACKERS

It was 1983, it might be recalled, when I had, to mark the centenary of the first departure of the *Orient Express,* assembled a rake of original *Orient Express* Wagon-Lits carriages at the Gare de l'Est in Paris. The date was 4 October and the purpose of the journey was to carry passengers as far as Vienna, en route to Istanbul.

One of the carriages being the 'Côte d'Azur' designed by the great René Lalique – I recall this with particular clarity, as it was in this carriage that I had shared a coupé with the actor Michael Palin. I decided that my vessel, the *Charlemagne,* was to be designed in its image. In order to redesign the vessel with an appropriate degree of authenticity, it would be necessary to track down the original carriage. Everyone presumed this would be easy: there were few such carriages in existence, perhaps just the one, which would no doubt have been carefully maintained by Wagons-Lits, as a souvenir of an illustrious past.

How wrong could one be? It turned out that the surviving original Wagon-Lits rolling stock, now collectively called the 'Pullman Orient Express', was owned by the hotel group Accor and, although classed by the French government as a National Monument, it was currently residing in a secret, undisclosed location. Eventually, through the good offices of a French railway journalist by the name of Vincent Cuny, the elusive rolling stock was tracked down to a location just south of Paris, in some sidings at Villeneuve.

Now, without a breathing locomotive at its head, a line of carriages in a siding is a depressing vision on a cold January morning, and these carriages wore that air of neglect and gloom reminiscent of coastal resorts out of season. That said, the intricate Lalique marquetry and glass panels were untarnished, as were the wonderful 'Riviera' armchairs with their flared ears; made in 1929, it turned out that only 612 of these magnificent pieces of furniture had ever been manufactured, with an even smaller number still surviving. Straight away, it became clear that we would have to get hold of one of these armchairs as a reference, if we were going to reproduce it.

However, Accor were not interested. Hardly a surprise, I suppose: when you are attempting to source artefacts from historic trains, you are touching upon the rivalries and jealousies that divide owners, collectors and other interested parties alike. We all want these things of beauty, but we know, at the same time, that they are a finite, precious and jealously guarded resource.

THE SPIRIT OF CHARTWELL

It was at this point that Vincent Cuny once again proved his worth. To his astonishment, he had found a number of derelict Wagon-Lits carriages in the middle of the French countryside. Not only that, but one of these carriages contained no less than 33 original Riviera armchairs, several of which were in urgent need of repair. My original intention had been to buy just one of these armchairs, which we would then replicate as required. The vendor, however, refused to play ball and said I was either to buy the whole lot or go away empty handed. There was nothing for it, then, but to buy all 33 chairs and transport them back to Southampton, for an extensive programme of restoration.

In order to comply with the particularly stringent safety regulations governing the Thames, the vessel had to be fully air-conditioned and heated, as well as being equipped with the latest 'HI-FOG' sprinkler systems, a water treatment plant, two 360-degree Schottel propulsion units and two bow-thrusters, for added manoeuvrability as well as back-up in the vent of engine failure.

By the time all this work had been completed, the *Charlemagne* had been transformed into something magnificent. Uniquely for the Thames, she would be a Class IV vessel, which means that she could operate in both coastal and inland waters. (Indeed, she subsequently sailed across the North Sea, from the Netherlands to the Thames Estuary.) To celebrate this achievement, we temporarily re-named her the *Spirit of Chartwell*.

THE RECKONING

When you're in the seafaring business, there is perhaps one hazard even greater than being out on the open sea, and that's when you're trying to get your vessel out of dry dock. The dry-dock operator always holds the whip-hand, and unless you have specified, down to the last detail, the full range of jobs you want done and have paid for them, there is always the possibility they won't let you have your ship back.

Naturally, the owner of a vessel will try and ensure that everything has been agreed upon and accounted for in advance. With the *Charlemagne,* however, this was just not possible: right from day one we were expanding the size of the job, on top of which Kooiman were new to this form of shipbuilding and were learning as they went along.

When the *Charlemagne* first entered Kooiman's yard, I only had a very vague, general idea of what was needed. The yard kept identifying defect after defect, however, and so I found I was left with just the basic shell of the original ship, plus its main engines. Then I had decided to decorate the interior in the style of the 'Côte d'Azur' carriage, which meant the budget for the project had risen from £3m to £6m. Now, just as the ship was due to leave the yard, I was being asked for another, totally unexpected, unbudgeted and unplanned-for amount for additional work. This extra demand left me depressed and somewhat melancholic, as I believed it to be grossly unfair and actually very unlike Mr Kooiman. My oft-repeated refrain was, "How could they do this to me?"

I did what I always did when feeling done-down: I read to myself a John Clare poem entitled 'I Am', and in doing so was struck by a rather good, if odd, idea. My project manager had mentioned in passing that Mr Kooiman, the yard owner, was a religious man – a lay preacher, in fact – and as a result the yard was always closed on Sundays. So, I decided to write Mr Kooiman a letter, expressing disappointment at his unexpected demand for further payment. I also said that I knew that he was a religious man and that I would like to share with him some of John Clare's words, to explain how I felt.

At the end of my letter, I said I would be visiting the yard next day with a colleague (Jonathan Peters, the man who had earlier helped transform the British Railways 'Kremlin' into what is now the fine Landmark London Hotel of today), with a view to discussing the bill.

When morning came, we took the first flight to Rotterdam and drove straight to the yard. Waiting for us on the boardroom table was a mountain of computer printouts, no doubt put there to intimidate us and to justify the demand for more cash. While we waited for yet more print-outs to be delivered, we were invited to inspect the vessel – an invitation I turned down, knowing full well that the *Charlemagne* had been fitted out to a standard that surpassed everyone's expectations; I sensed that to inspect it in advance of the meeting would have undermined my negotiating position.

For his part, Jonathan did an excellent job in explaining away the printouts, dismissing them as historical documents which, having been produced after the event, were as good as meaningless. Having reached this seeming impasse, I decided to ask Mr Kooiman if he had read the poem. He said that he had, but had been able to make neither head nor tail of it. Nor could he understand why I thought him to be religious, since he said he enjoyed nothing more than a drink or two on a Sunday.

I must say, this made me feel a bit of a twit, but I later reasoned that it must have put Mr Kooiman off his guard – after all, no one wants to be considered less than pious. The bottom line is that Mr Kooiman agreed to knock £300,000 off the bill. Meanwhile, the ship-management team, crew members, naval architect and the Maritime and Coastguard Agency were carrying out the final surveys and preparations for the positioning voyage to the Thames. I was feeling quietly pleased with myself for not having inspected the vessel before meeting Mr Kooiman – there was no doubt about it: she was magnificent, way beyond my expectations.

Later, when leafing through the ship's documents, I discovered that the vessel's original name was not *Charlemagne* but *Vincent van Gogh*, and that it had been commissioned some years earlier by David Drier, president of Intrav and the Clipper Cruise Line.

Now, having satisfied the requirements of the Dutch Coastguard, it was time to give the *Charlemagne* its new name. I decided to call her *Spirit of Chartwell* – it was only a temporary name, I told everyone, but it would do for the moment.

JOHN CLARE (1793-1864) THE PEOPLE'S POET

A Story in Brief:

I AM: yet what I am none cares or knows, My friends forsake me like a memory lost; I am the self-consumer of my woes, They rise and vanish in oblivious host, Like shades in love and death's oblivion lost; And yet I am! and live with shadows tost

Into the nothingness of scorn and noise, Into the living sea of waking dreams, Where there is neither sense of life nor joys, But the vast shipwreck of my life's esteems; And e'en the dearest – that I loved the best – Are strange – nay, rather stranger than the rest.

I long for scenes where man has never trod; A place where woman never smil'd or wept; There to abide with my creator, God, And sleep as I in childhood sweetly slept: Untroubling and untroubled where I lie; The grass below – above the vaulted sky.

CHAPTER 53
AN UNWELCOME VISITOR

In May 2010, the 'Spirit of Chartwell' duly glided into the Thames,
but, from the moment we reached Gravesend, there were portents of
what might lie ahead.

I N May 2010, the *Spirit of Chartwell* glided into the Thames; but from the moment we reached Gravesend, there were portents of what might lie ahead. For some reason, the Port of London Authority (PLA) issued an instruction that the vessel should remain at anchor and not venture further up the Thames, despite having received certification from the Maritime and Coastguard Agency (MCA) and despite the fact that we had a pilot on board and were not carrying any passengers. When we warned that the vessel would be dangerously exposed to the elements if she remained in Gravesend, the PLA relented somewhat and decreed that she could proceed to the enclosed waters of the West India Docks.

By this time, we had sold all available places on the series of five-night voyages that were due to start next month. The only formalities to be completed were the risk-assessment river trials, which the PLA and MCA required us to carry out before issuing our passenger certificate. After all the attention we had paid to safety and security, not to say the extraordinary amount of money we had already spent, we imagined that this would be a breeze. The trials were indeed successful, with the exception of one thing: concerns about navigation through Richmond Bridge, particularly in the event of bad weather.

With the PLA now freely quoting from Lord Justice Clarke's *Marchioness* report, this was clearly an issue that was not going to be resolved quickly, and I decided there was nothing for it but to cancel all the planned voyages and think again. The project had foundered, in my opinion, on fundamentally bureaucratic rocks, although we were also beginning to get hassle from Hampton Court Palace and residents in upstream Sunbury, complaining about the lights on the ship.

Yes, I was already getting that same feeling of unwantedness I had experienced in 1994, when I had operated the *Lord of the Glen*'s sister vessel, *Lord of the Highlands*, on the Thames from Tower Pier.

THE LORD OF THE HIGHLANDS

I had bought and reconstructed the *Lord of the Highlands* in early 1994. After an initial cruising season in the Scottish Highlands, I decided to try out a new idea over the three-month period during which the vessel would otherwise be lying idle. The location for my experiment was London, and I was going to see if I could get the public to accept a stay on the ship as an alternative to a stay in a hotel. They would be taken on regular sailing forays up and down the Thames, usually during meal times, and in addition would be afforded the delight of being able to take breakfast on the top deck, overlooking Tower Bridge and the Tower of London.

To my surprise, this venture proved a huge success, particularly among German visitors to London. It was a close-run thing, however: every government body seemed to want a say on what I was up to, and it was only one hour before our first scheduled sailing that I was finally granted the required permission. In addition, the cost of operating on the Thames started to bite, once Transport for London (TFL), who controlled most of the commercial piers on the river, dug out a long-forgotten ruling which said that the agreed daily rate for mooring would henceforth be charged every half-hour, now that passengers were sleeping on board.

Fortunately for me, Sven-Olof Lindblad, founder of Lindblad Expeditions, came to my rescue and took the *Lord of the Highlands* off my hands. She is now happily sailing among the Galápagos Islands, as the *National Geographic Islander*.

IDLE IN WEST INDIA DOCKS

As the *Spirit of Chartwell* sat idle (but still manned) in West India Docks from June 2010 until 10 April 2011, I came up with another plan. This time, the theme was going to be that of a deluxe train on the water: I would create a kind of *Orient Express* on the Thames, providing a setting in which guests could celebrate a special moment in their lives. Attended by liveried stewards, they would glide luxuriously past the great London landmarks, the journey gently punctuated by lunch, high tea, champagne reception and a gala five-course dinner. Cabin accommodation would be available to those wishing to further enhance the experience for a night or two on-board, while our smaller sister vessel, the *Passepartout*, would then convey the passengers on the upstream part of the journey, as far as Cliveden.

Naturally, I assumed that London tour operators, travel agents and hotel

A Story in Brief

THE INSPECTOR COMETH: For nine months, *Spirit of Chartwell* was laid-up with only a skeleton crew. Now, all of a sudden, dozens of workers were preparing the vessel for the Diamond Jubilee. And the officials from London Port Health chose to make an inspection. I complained loudly and bitterly, and of course, they found faults. In advance of the pageant, all moveable furniture had been steam-cleaned, all carpets shampooed, all floors hand polished, every tap and shower-head replaced, every machine deep-cleaned and taken down to its smallest working parts. All fresh water tanks were hyper-chlorinated several times by leading experts in this field. All the crew were rehearsed and trained in food hygiene/handling and all uniforms dry-cleaned and pressed. I doubt there had ever been a cleaner, more hygienic ship anywhere. The inspectors returned, this time in formal uniform with flaring epaulettes. Having rubbed-down the cornices with a wet-wipe, they awarded us two stars– out of five. Thames lesson learnt: don't complain.

concierges alike would be falling over themselves at the prospect of being able to offer something new to their customers. Alas, my faith was misplaced: either they could not, or would not, understand the concept.

It was only when I advertised directly in the press that the public responded, when after having re-started operations they were to make reservations in their thousands. Many guests repeating the journey time and time again over the coming months. However, though this was gratifying, after all the effort and energy we had expended – first putting the original programme together, then cancelling it and starting all over again – a certain amount of disillusionment had set in. Thus, in August 2011, I found myself in Paris, deep in discussion with the famous Bateaux Mouches boat-trip company, who had always wanted to operate in London.

What I discovered was illuminating in the extreme: Bateaux Mouches derived nearly all their sales from hotel concierges, to whom they paid commission. In contrast, I could identify just six measly sales that had come via London hotels throughout the entire season. It became clear to me that visitors to Paris felt a definite connection with the Seine, whereas in London that sense of affinity was absent, and as a result most hotels viewed the Thames as being somehow beneath them. When I told Bateaux Mouches that nearly all our sales came via expensive, upfront newspaper advertising, I could see their interest wane, and with it any chance of them co-operating with me.

Suddenly, in the midst of my talks with Bateaux Mouches, there came a most surprising call. It was from representatives of Queen Elizabeth's Diamond Jubilee team, with a request to use the *Spirit of Chartwell* as the royal barge. Naturally there was no question of lèse-majesté, and I immediately agreed to make the vessel available for six weeks either side of 3 June 2012, during which time she would be adorned with prow sculptures, tapestries, thrones and flowers.

Straight away I abandoned my discussions with Bateaux Mouches and took the next Eurostar train back to London. I guess, as Victor Sassoon might have said, it was a case of: "Well, I tried to give up London, but apparently London won't give me up."

Back home, however, I found we were being moved around the dock from our usual mooring. This was most disconcerting, since it was akin to operating a bus service without having a specific, advertised embarkation and disembarkation point. Also, the 'six-week' allocation period for the Diamond Jubilee turned out to be eight months, after which time we were going to be without a home berth from which to operate our planned 'Memories of London' day voyages (our previous one was to be commandeered for the Olympics, during July and August).

All of this felt incredibly short-sighted. I had, I thought, created something that could have been of long-term benefit for London, which had now been sacrificed on the anvil of a transient event. Enough was enough, I decided. I had done my best, but that the forces ranged against us were both too powerful and too numerous. Once we had fulfilled our immediate obligations post-Jubilee – and we were, I might add, fully booked – we would be turning our backs on the Thames. For good.

MEMORIES OF LONDON VOYAGE – 'SPIRIT OF CHARTWELL'

A Story in Brief

UNDER THE CLOAK OF DARKNESS: At 5.00am on 9 September. I was tracking on my computer screen the *Spirit of Chartwell*'s final Thames voyage to Gravesend – sensing it was only when it arrived there that I could finally be released from the hassles and torments of the river. I would lose millions in the process – but it was as nothing compared to the relief of being free at last. The vessel's destination was the River Douro in northern Portugal, where eighteen years earlier I had operated a cruise vessel without any of the Thames-like hassles. Ironic, really, given that the Douro has many of the physical characteristics of the Thames: it's both tidal and non-tidal; it follows a curvaceous course; and it has areas of shallows and low bridges. Today, the *Spirit of Chartwell* plies happily up and down her new river. Always full, and now with the sun on her back.

CHAPTER 54
THE BUTTERFLY EFFECT

It was with a strange, melancholic chill that I had stepped on board the MV 'Deutschland'. This ship had been Peter's pride and joy, yet, now, it was owned and operated by a financial institution.

I N early August 2012, I found myself on a cruise ship, the MV *Deutschland*, in London's Canary Wharf. The vessel was moored in West India Dock, but she wasn't about to embark on a journey. Instead, her job was to serve as a floating hotel during the London Summer Olympics.

The ship was under charter from a large German tour operator called DER, who had sold a large number of Olympics package holidays that included a berth on the *Deutschland*, plus entrance tickets to various games venues. I don't know exactly how much the guests were paying, but it must have been a fortune – the operators had shelled out £460,000 for the berthing facility alone, and then there were security, tugging, crewing and pilotage charges on top.

I had been invited on board, along with representatives of a number of UK travel companies, to have a look over the ship, with a view to promoting it in this country. After lunch, I was asked to make a short thank you speech on everyone's behalf and I duly rose to my feet. At this point my mind went blank, and I started wittering on about how wonderful it was to be invited on such a fine ship, with so many handsome features that had been fashioned over time by the drive and perseverance of one man, Peter Deilmann.

If I had been braver, or had been given more time to gather my thoughts, I might have said what I really thought, for I personally knew Peter Deilmann and just how perseverant he had been, almost single-handedly building up his cruise company from scratch. The river vessels that he created were not just boats; they were the very finest craft you could imagine, for which he demanded and commanded a very high tariff. Should you find yourself negotiating on the other side of the table from him, he was a nightmare, never budging one iota on price.

It was with a strange, melancholic chill that I had stepped on board the *Deutschland* that day in London. This boat had been Peter's pride and joy, yet now it was owned and operated by a financial institution, and all of a sudden I'd got an overwhelming sense of the terrible events that had led to this change of ownership.

The turning point in the story occurred on 25 July 2000, when the *Deutschland* had been sitting in New York's inner harbour, waiting for the 400-or-so guests who were flying out for a 16-day voyage to Ecuador. It promised to be a lavish trip: 100 of the passengers were coming in on a supersonic Air France Concorde flight which Peter had specially chartered and promoted as a 'once-in-a-lifetime' opportunity. However, tragedy was about to strike.

Usually there would be a runway inspection before every Concorde take-off, but for some reason it didn't take place on that particular day at Paris Charles de Gaulle airport. Lying on the runway was a titanium alloy strip, a piece of debris from a Continental Airlines DC-10 that had taken off five minutes earlier. When the Air France Concorde was approaching maximum take-off speed, one of its tyres ruptured on coming into contact with the strip, striking the underside of the wing and causing one of the fuel tanks to rupture and two of the aircraft's four engines to lose power. At such a late stage in the take-off run, and despite the fire that was now raging below the fuselage, the pilots had no option but to continue with the ascent and then try to re-land the aircraft. There was, however, no time for that: unable to climb above 60 metres, and with fire quickly engulfing it, the Concorde crashed into a nearby hotel, killing 100 passengers, nine crew members and four workers on the ground.

Once the full scale of the disaster had been conveyed to Peter, he had to absorb, understand and immediately deal with its consequences, with regards to bereaved families, the press and the company. He also had to decide what should happen to the 300 guests who were now on board the *Deutschland*.

One can only imagine the physical and emotional strain that was now bearing down on Peter. Not long afterwards, he died too; his death was as unexpected as it was unplanned for and resulted in his two daughters having to take over the company. This was not a success: damaged and without its founding dynamo, the company inevitably began to lose money. The bankers wasted no time in putting all the vessels up for auction, and before you knew it, the Peter Deilmann river cruise operation was no more (only the *Deutschland*, an ocean-going liner, remained).

It seemed incredible that one small strip of metal had caused all this. One piece of titanium alloy had killed 113 people – and probably Peter himself. It had also destroyed his company, the jobs of his employees and the livelihoods of the

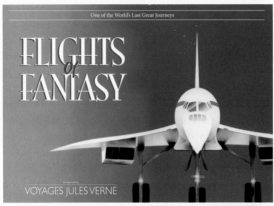

A Story in Brief

BATTLING AGAINST THE QUANGOS: *The Spirit of Chartwell* had been surveyed continuously, before we left Holland for the Thames. Yet the minute we arrived off Gravesend, the Port of London Authority said the vessel could not proceed upstream, despite holding a valid certificate and carrying a PLA pilot. Only after much pleading, in which we pointed out the insecurity of complying with this instruction, were we allowed to berth at West India Dock. I was told that passenger certifications were only issued on a short-term basis after trials and risk assessments; which meant there was no guarantee that we would be able to operate. At one time I complained, but this seemed to make matters worse, since an outstanding complaint meant no progress on certification could be made. I had no option, therefore, but to backtrack. Given that we no longer had our home base in West India Dock, we could never be sure, on any given day, that our voyages would operate. Thames lesson learnt it seems: don't complain. IMAGE COURTESY: ROBERT SCURRAH/MARKO MILASEVIC.

men and women working both on Concorde and in the agencies that specialised in selling supersonic flights. How could the accident have happened? Was it a design fault in the plane? A defective repair job? What if the Concorde had taken off on time and ahead of the DC-10, as it was supposed to? Why hadn't the runway been inspected for debris, in accordance with accepted protocol? These questions remain unanswered. All we know with any certainty is that Peter was responsible for the flight happening and yet, in the final analysis, in control of very little.

In many ways, his plight typifies the travel business, in that survival depends on navigating a safe path through both natural and man-made phenomena: earthquakes in Indonesia; tsunamis in Japan; ash clouds in Iceland; terrorist attacks in the Middle East; strikes in France; rebellions and coup d'états in Africa; revolutions in Portugal; mechanical failure; changes in legislation and, of course, the effects of the weather itself – storms, hurricanes, floods and snow.

And then there is the malign hand of government, which so often gets involved in imposing devaluations and currency restrictions, as well as in introducing new taxes and protectionist legislation, usually with the opposite effect to what's intended. All this gets thrown at travel firms at the same time as they are attempting to perform the high-wire act of meeting fixed commitments, in the form of pre-paid hotels and aircraft. It is no wonder that so many companies either go out of business or end up being absorbed by others.

You only have to go back to the pre-1970 era to find a situation whereby the British government determined the price of holidays, either directly, by its own edict, or indirectly, through the state-run airlines BEA and BOAC. Furthermore, the government had a say in those holidays' duration, location and what they could and couldn't include.

At one point, the government even introduced a rule that said a package holiday could not be cheaper than the published scheduled airline fare. To make matters worse, these scheduled airfares were set by BEA/BOAC in conjunction with other state airlines, who, as well as being equally inefficient, also fixed their fares in a strictly linear manner. This meant that flying to Greece, for example, was much more expensive than flying to Mallorca.

No doubt all this had its origins in well-meaning government attempts to encourage and protect the British aircraft manufacturing industry from unbridled competition from charter airline companies. Nevertheless, because of this artificial manipulation of the market, the general public were paying far too much for their scheduled airfares and, by extension, for their inclusive holidays.

In order to get rid of one type of chaos, the government had created a whole new kind of chaos. Of course, there is now a whole scientific field of study around the notion of chaos theory. This dates back to 1961, when a meteorologist named

Edward Lorenz was using a numerical computer model to re-run a weather prediction. Attempting a shortcut, he entered a very slightly different number into the program and the result was a dramatically different weather scenario to the one determined by the initial run. This accidental discovery led one meteorologist to remark that, if such a small variant could produce such a large discrepancy, then one flap of a seagull's wings could change the course of weather forever.

Following suggestions from colleagues, Lorenz later substituted 'butterfly' for 'seagull', but the point was the same: the tiny atmospherical changes produced by a small set of flapping wings might ultimately, say, alter the path of a tornado or delay, accelerate or even prevent the occurrence of a tornado in another location. In other words, small changes can lead to altogether larger ones.

Lorenz reasoned that in chaos theory only one thing is predictable, which is that, by its very nature, chaos is unpredictable. The same goes for the travel business, too. As I sat down after my speech on board the *Deutschland*, I couldn't help reflecting on how the effects of chaos were impacting me personally.

The West India Docks where the ship was moored had, until recently, been the home base for my own *Spirit of Chartwell* – we had been asked to leave the dock for the duration of the Olympics and were now homeless. A sequence of events had been set in motion that ended with the *Spirit of Chartwell* being sold for a fraction of its true value and sent to the River Douro, in Portugal.

So, which butterfly-wing flap had been responsible? Was it the higher berthing fees in the dock that could be commanded in light of the Olympics, which meant there was no longer any room for vessels, like the *Spirit of Chartwell*, paying a less inflated rate? Or was it Lord Coe applying to have London host the 2012 Summer Olympics in the first place?

CHAPTER 55
TURN AGAIN,
DICK WHITTINGTON

In true Dick Whittington fashion, I thought about how, at the age of nine, I had run away with another boy from a Barnardo's home on the very edge of the Windsor Royal Estate.

I N the run-up to the Diamond Jubilee Thames Pageant, various media events were arranged by the pageant organisers. One was at the impressive Guildhall, while another took place at the Mayor's City Hall, on the South Bank. I had often gazed from afar at this impressive building designed by Norman Foster, admiring its lopsided-jelly structure and wondering what it was like on the inside. Having now seen for myself, I can confirm just how impressive and efficient a structure it is.

The official pageant launch was held in the City Hall auditorium, which I had only ever seen on television. The central concourse had been completely transformed, with a whole array of speakers facing a phalanx of TV cameras. Behind the speaker platform, a screen had been erected from which the Mayor, Boris Johnson, spoke to us, Big Brother-like, in a recorded address.

I did not take much notice of the Mayor's spiel, until he mentioned the wonderful vessel – i.e., the *Spirit of Chartwell* – that was to be transformed into this amazing, floating royal carriage. It was then that my mind drifted back off into the past. In true Dick Whittington fashion, I thought about how, at the age of nine, I had run away with another boy from a Barnardo's home on the very edge of the Windsor Royal Estate (though we'd had no idea that the Queen was our neighbour).

Our intention, until we were caught, had been to follow the course of the Thames all the way to London, in the belief that there we might find happiness, or at least some long-lost members of our families. Listening now to the Mayor, I was asking myself, could this possibly be the self-same gentleman who, in previous months, had failed to answer any of my numerous requests to stage a vessel-naming ceremony with me? There he was, showering praise upon my ship, yet when someone from his office had eventually deigned to reply to us, it had been merely to announce that no time could be found in the Mayor's diary.

Straight after the launch, then, I went to the vessel's fridge and fetched a bottle of champagne, upon which the crew and myself all piled off onto the quayside, swung the damn thing against the hull and named the vessel ourselves.

THE DAY OF THE PAGEANT

According to the original plans for the pageant, the royal party was destined to board the *Spirit of Chartwell* at Chelsea Harbour. However, this idea had to change, in view of our new top-deck structure: with the addition of thrones and canopies, we wouldn't have been able to pass safely under Albert Bridge at high tide. The alternative plan was to use the former Royal Yacht *Britannia*'s tender launch, which had been brought down by truck from Edinburgh, and for the Queen and the Duke of Edinburgh to step off and onto our vessel at Cadogan Pier, on the downstream side of Albert Bridge, where the rest of the royal party would be waiting.

Mercifully, in the end the decision was taken to activate the Thames Barrier, thereby lowering the water level and removing any concerns over other bridge heights and the accessibility of muster stations. And so, as morning broke on 3 June, the covers were finally taken off, revealing the *Spirit of Chartwell*, now transformed into the Royal Barge, in all her splendour. At first the crowds seemed paltry, and I began to wonder whether the weather forecast had put people off, but by 10.00am the river embankment was thronged 10-deep, with every vantage point taken on the surrounding buildings and moored boats on the river packed with what looked like perilously large crowds of people. The sky was overcast but dry, although there was a wind coming upstream from the east that would later bring the rain.

The Queen, together with the Duke of Edinburgh, the Prince of Wales and the Duchess of Cornwall, duly boarded *Britannia*'s tender vessel for the journey downstream, pausing briefly to admire the steam locomotive *Princess Elizabeth* on Battersea Railway Bridge, before joining the *Spirit of Chartwell* at Cadogan Pier. They greeted the invited guests on the top deck, where they were joined by Prince Harry, Prince William and the Duchess of Cambridge.

There was to be no 'crew moment'. (I had imagined the officers lining up to meet the Queen and, perhaps, her going on to sign the ship's visitors' book.) It

A Story in Brief

THE WEIGHT OF EXPECTATION: The requirement was for *Spirit of Chartwell* to be turned into something resembling a coronation carriage. The task called upon the skills of cinematographic producers, set designers, floral experts, sculpture carvers, embroiderers, engineers, awning makers, throne designers, naval architects and a myriad other talented folk. The big issue, though, was weight: most of the extra poundage (largely flowers) was intended for the top deck and it is not without good reason that we have the maritime term 'top heavy'. The total additional top-deck weight was 10 tons, and it was on this basis that naval architects were given the job of re-calculating the vessel's stability. Trouble was, that after eight months, no one could agree. There was nothing for it, then, but for the vessel to go out on the river with 15 tons on the top deck and see what happened. When he came back, the captain reported that, if anything, the vessel felt more stable than before.

IMAGE COURTESY: ADRIAN EVANS.

was not I who was the host, I was told, but the pageant organisers.

Once the royal party had boarded, the flotilla 'float past' began while we remained at our moorings. Many hundreds of unpowered craft – rowers, canoeists, etc – passed by; only when they had moved off did the *Spirit of Chartwell* – Royal Barge ease out into the river, ahead of the main contingent of motorised vessels. Meanwhile, on a specially installed TV screen in the lounge below, the crew were monitoring the movements of both the royal party and the weather, which was not looking good. The wind was picking up again, intermingled with lashing rain, and I was acutely aware that on the top deck there was no protection from the elements.

I had been telling everyone for some time that, even on the calmest day, there is usually a stiff breeze on the Thames, which makes sitting outside not the pleasure you might imagine. It was for this reason that I had spent many months and a small fortune evaluating, designing and constructing a unique all-round glass-screen protection system, which could be erected and collapsed in minutes and even had its own built-in heating and lighting.

In terms of the pageant, it would have required only minimal modification to the Royal Barge specifications to make this protection available. Instead, it had been ruled out of the scheme altogether, so, when the rain and the wind did come, everyone was left unprotected. Stoically, the royal party remained on the top deck, doubtless unwilling to disappoint the millions that had turned out to greet them.

By the time the Royal Barge reached Tower Bridge and moored at HMS *President*, a Royal Naval pier, the weather was at its worst. Waiting there was the vessel *Symphony,* aboard which was the London Philharmonic Orchestra, playing a medley of stirring tunes. Meanwhile the *Havengore*, the vessel that had carried Sir Winston Churchill's coffin in 1964, had drawn up on our inside. For me, it was a doubly poignant moment: the affinity of the *Havengore* with the *Spirit of Chartwell* (Chartwell being the name of Churchill's family home) and the fact that I had spotted the Mayor of London disembarking. I wondered what he thought now, seeing the *Spirit of Chartwell* close-up for the first time.

Once the royal party had disembarked at Tower Bridge, so too did just about everyone else. I had always thought it a crying shame, having put so much effort into transforming the *Spirit of Chartwell*, that the whole get-up was immediately to be de-rigged, thereby denying the public the chance to witness the decorations up close.

On several occasions before the big day, I had contacted the pageant organisers, offering two suggestions as to how we might make this happen. Either I could make the vessel available for public viewing the following day, in Canary Wharf (with the proceeds going to charity), or I could organise, at my expense, a cruise the week after the pageant and auction off tickets in aid of the Help for Heroes charity. Both ideas were turned down, on the grounds that the pageant should be a one-off, one-moment-in-time event.

Maybe so, but I decided, there and then, that in some small way I was going to get my own back. The opportunity arose later that day. Once everyone had disembarked at Tower Bridge, we turned the *Spirit of Chartwell* around and set off downstream through the 'Avenue of Sail' (a flotilla of ships too tall for the city's bridges). In many ways, this was the most pleasurable part of the day for the crew: free of the pageant organisers, we had the vessel completely to ourselves, and as we made our way downstream, thousands upon thousands of people who had not been on the main pageant route came out onto the river banks and their balconies, cheering in response to our hooting.

We were headed for Greenwich Pier, where we would have to wait for the Thames Barrier to be lowered before we could get to the King George V Dock, where the de-rigging was due to take place. As the vessel got closer to Greenwich, the crowds thronged the riverbank, all wanting a closer look at the Royal Barge. Suddenly, in a rash moment, I decided to let a few people come on board, at which point a seemingly never-ending queue formed. Getting them off the ship was harder than getting them on, but what I shall always remember are the heartfelt thanks we received from people who simply couldn't believe that they had been allowed on board.

Eventually we persuaded the last well-wisher to step ashore and made our way to George V Dock. By the next morning, most of the adornments and flowers had been removed and the original *Spirit of Chartwell* was beginning to reveal herself once more. Unfortunately, however, the acrylic film had not come off as easily as expected, removing some of the paint with it, while the rain had left the burgundy carpet in a sorry state of repair. Worse still, it kept on raining. We really were up against it: the pageant organisers needed the vessel out of the King George V Dock in 10 days, and we had now been landed with the job of sanding her down before re-painting her. We also needed to replace the external carpet, which we were only able to do by putting up a huge tent to cover the vessel.

Meanwhile, I had even more pressing concerns, given that the *Spirit of Chartwell* was now homeless on the Thames. We had been told that during July and August, because of the Olympics, we would not be welcome at West India Docks, which we had hitherto considered as our home base.

Ten days later, the *Spirit of Chartwell* sailed from the King George V Dock and, once more, headed for Cadogan Pier, where she had earlier been boarded by the royal party and from where it had been agreed that our 20 remaining sailings would operate. However, just as we were drawing near, the master received a telephone call to the effect that Cadogan Pier would not be able to accommodate us after all, and that we should sail further upstream to Imperial Wharf, in Fulham. The only alternative, we were told, was for the vessel to lie at anchor on the tidal river – so the *Spirit of Chartwell* went, as suggested, to Imperial Wharf.

With this, my disillusionment with the Thames was complete.

'SPIRIT OF CHARTWELL' DIAMOND JUBILEE THAMES PAGEANT 3 JUNE 2012

A Story in Brief

DICK WHITTINGTON AND HIS CAT: We all know the story of the boy who becomes a wealthy 14th century merchant and eventually the Lord Mayor of London, thanks to his cat. What's more, Dick Whittington really did exist, except he didn't come from a poor family and there is no evidence that he had a cat. Interestingly enough, Whittington's statue – with cat – stood at the portals of Newgate Prison at the time of the Great Fire of London in 1666. Today, too, at Whittington Hospital on Highgate Hill, there is a statue of Whittington's legendary cat – this being the very site where, in the story, the distant Bow Bells call young Dick to turn back to London and claim his fortune. **IMAGE COURTESY: ADRIAN EVANS.**

CHAPTER 56
THE LAST FRONTIER

We had already had the honour of floating the Royal Family on the occasion of the Diamond Jubilee. Now also, three astronauts who had soared beyond Earth's confines to land on the lunar surface.

I can remember exactly where I was in July 1968: Torremolinos, in southern Spain, which at the time was considered a very upmarket winter-sunshine destination. Without doubt, the best hotel in town was the Moorish-style Al-Andalus; possibly because of its traditional architecture, it had been chosen as the location for the Hollywood film Hard Contract, starring James Coburn and Lee Remick, which premiered the following April.

The reason I had been sent there was to resolve an over-booking issue, which was nothing new: the manager/owner of the Al-Andalus, Juan Sanchez, had earned a reputation within our company for being a serial over-booker, and I was forever making visits out there, always on the same 'mission impossible'. This time, though, with the movie crew having taken over the whole hotel, Señor Sanchez was so puffed up with self-importance that it was hard even to get him to sit down, let alone apply himself to the over-booking problem. I never got to see the finished film, although I understand that at one point in the shoot the director decided he needed a tourist-coach scene, which ended up featuring our local resort representative.

A year later, on 21 July 1969, I found myself back at the Al-Andalus, once again trying to sort out over-booking issues. The only reason I remember the date so well is that everyone was gathered in the hotel lounge to watch those grainy TV images of Neil Armstrong and Buzz Aldrin, the first humans to step out onto the lunar surface. Memories of these lunar landings played a part when it came to choosing names for my ships.

Originally, I was going to call Spirit of Chartwell 'Columbia' and Passepartout

'Eagle' – in my mind's eye I equated our arrival on the Thames with a lunar expedition, involving a mother ship (*Spirit of Chartwell*) and a smaller landing module (*Passepartout*). Or at least that was my initial concept; I soon discarded it once I realised that no one but me would get the reference.

Next, I alighted upon a Churchillian theme and even opened up a line of communication with Sir Winston's grandson. I had to come up with a name quickly, for the purposes of registering the vessel, and decided to go with *Spirit of Chartwell,* after Churchill's home. It was at this point that fate took a hand, when it turned out that, on the *Spirit of Chartwell*'s very last London voyage, my ship was hired by Olympic sponsors Omega, to carry VIPs from Millbank to Greenwich. Among the passengers were three distinguished astronauts: Thomas P. Stafford, Eugene Cernan and Buzz Aldrin.

Stafford flew aboard two Gemini space flights and, in 1969, was the commander of Apollo 10, the second manned mission to orbit the Moon and the first to fly a lunar module. In 1975, by then a brigadier general in the US Air Force, he commanded the Apollo-Soyuz Test Project, the first of the joint US-Soviet space missions. Cernan went into space three times, as pilot of Gemini 9A in June 1966, lunar module pilot of Apollo 10 in May 1969 and commander of Apollo 17 in December 1972. Apollo 17 was the final lunar landing, and with it Cernan became the 11th person to walk on the Moon and 'the last man on the Moon', since he was the final man to re-enter the lunar module Challenger.

Aldrin, meanwhile, was the lunar module pilot on Apollo 11, the first manned lunar landing in history, and on 21 July 1969 he became the second person to walk on the Moon, following in the footsteps of mission commander Neil Armstrong. These three legendary astronauts signed the *Spirit of Chartwell* visitors' book as follows: 'Thanks for the wonderful hospitality – GREAT! – the only way to go back to the Moon – thank you.'

It was the icing on the cake. On the occasion of the Diamond Jubilee flotilla, we had the honour of transporting the Queen, the Duke of Edinburgh, the Prince of Wales, the Duchess of Cornwall, Prince Harry, Prince William and the Duchess of Cambridge down the Thames. Now we had also carried three astronauts who had soared beyond Earth's atmosphere and landed on the lunar surface.

It was the perfect moment to put a big full stop to my career. The question was, what to do next? My options for the *Spirit of Chartwell* were extremely limited, given that the vessel had been rebuilt specifically for the Thames and would have been unsuitable for other UK waterways. I began to wonder whether I should take her back to the Netherlands or, failing that, to the Douro, in Portugal, where I had sent the *English Lady* all those years before.

By this time I felt thoroughly let down by London and the Thames, and there were dark moments when I would have happily given the vessel away for nothing. It was a hugely frustrating period. Throughout my career, the way I had operated had been to draw a big picture of the challenge ahead and then do my darnedest to make the project work. Usually I had been successful, and I badly wanted to do the same here, on my doorstep, in London – only no one seemed to share my vision for the Thames.

Indeed, it felt to me that the people involved with the river were more interested in failure than success. Contrast this with my earlier experience on the infinitely trickier Caledonian Canal, where it had been a case of "let's see how we can make it happen" – and make it happen we did.

I reckoned we had invested £8 million in the hope of creating something special for the Thames and London, but now, having run out of options, I was going to have to sell the *Spirit of Chartwell* for a fraction of that amount. What's more, I couldn't help feeling that she would be more appreciated in her new home, on the Douro, than she ever was on the Thames.

In the end, however, I decided I would let my loss go quietly and un-noticed. It was telling that, having made the arrangements for the ship's departure, I received an urgent communication from the Thames Pageant people. Their purpose in writing to me was to ensure that their intellectual property rights should not in any way be infringed.

As you can imagine, this did little to brighten my mood. I couldn't help feeling how poignant it was that the *Spirit of Chartwell* should now end its life on the Thames, at the Imperial Wharf in Fulham. For it was near there, in 1950, that I had lost my wellington boot to the river. All I wanted now was for the *Spirit of Chartwell* to slip her moorings in London for the last time, at 5.00am, under the cover of darkness, and sail down the Thames and away from London, unannounced and unremarked.

The Thames was, I feel, the only challenge I did not complete, and my lack of success had not been for want of trying. Typically, even the ship's quiet departure was to be denied me. The river had spoken one last time, and a journalist had been tipped off. Either I made a comment, or they would publish. I let them publish.

BACK TO WHERE IT BEGAN

In 1985, flushed with my success at the helm of Voyages Jules Verne, I had pushed my unsettled childhood to the back of my mind, on the grounds that making contact with any of my surviving relatives would only hold me back. Suddenly, though, I was overcome with guilt and set about finding my flesh-and-blood with the same vigour that I had applied to all my other challenges.

A Story in Brief

THE MAN AND THE MACHINE: Cliff Robertson III was an American actor with a film and television career that spanned half a century. Robertson portrayed a young John F. Kennedy in the 1963 film *PT 109* and won the 1968 Academy Award for best actor for his role in the movie *Charley*. On television, he portrayed astronaut Buzz Aldrin in the 1976 adaptation of Aldrin's autobiographical *Return to Earth*; he played a fictional character based on the Director of Central Intelligence Richard Helms in the 1977 adaptation of John Ehrlichman's Watergate novel *The Company*; and portrayed Henry Ford in the 1987 *Ford: The Man and the Machine*. His last well-known appearances were in 2002 to 2007 as Uncle Ben in the *Spiderman* trilogy. In April 1980, an ESPN sports film crew accompanied the London to Peking Motor Challenge as part of the Hummer car team (together with the car's original designers), who were anxious to test the car for domestic rather than its heretofore militaristic use – the film's anchorman being Cliff Robertson III. **IMAGE COURTESY: ADRIA EVANS/OMEGA.**

Not knowing where to start, I paid a visit to Hammersmith library: Hammersmith being the part of London in which I was born. I was hoping to find out if my mother or sister could be traced via the electoral register, but I spent hours scouring the pages for their names without success.

Next, I went to the General Register Office, to search the national archive of births, deaths and marriages. I trawled through endless handwritten, leather-bound ledgers – it looked again as if I would find no trace, until finally, through an address on a marriage certificate, I secured a possible lead for June, my half-sister. The address I had was in south London, but when I got there, it seemed like every building for miles around had been flattened. It was like a scene from World War II: the only building left standing was a corner pub, while the rest – presumably slums – had been demolished.

I could have given up there and then; but deep inside, something was compelling me to press on, and I decided to investigate further in the pub. Ordering a small ale for myself, I began to make table-to-table enquiries with the regulars. Among their number was one chap who was slightly more lucid than the others, and he pointed me in the direction of some high-rise flats – "those damned high-rise monstrosities over there" – where he believed the previous slum occupants had been re-housed. With that, I headed toward the flats. On reaching the first block, I came face-to-face with endless numbers of floors and passageways. Not really too sure what to do next, I began knocking on each door.

Few people opened their doors, but, when they did, I asked if they knew of anyone called June Morrell. It was only when I had worked my way up to near the top of the building that one lady said yes, she knew June Morrell, but she certainly wasn't going to divulge any further information to a complete stranger. All I could do was leave my name and phone number for her to pass on to June. Two weeks later, to my surprise, June rang and we arranged to meet. I had no idea how I should greet my half-sister after an absence of 35 years. Should I kiss her? Should I embrace her? Should I just shake hands? I had no idea what to do, since in all reality, I did not know her.

When we did meet, I found that she was married to a Maltese garbage collector, and that they were living in down-at-heel rented accommodation. When the conversation came around to the subject of our mother, I discovered, to my astonishment, that she was still alive and living in sheltered accommodation.

June began to pave the way for a meeting. First, she ran the idea past my mother, who agreed to it, and then one day took me to see her. Again, I was not sure how to comport myself. When I encountered her, in her small garden flat, my mother looked very frail. I understood immediately that the meeting was, for her, a painful one: she hardly looked up, and it was evident that in order to cope, she had, like me, blinkered herself to the past.

In short, I was a box not to be opened emotionally. I sensed this and left after perhaps five or ten minutes. It must have been about a month later that June telephoned to say that my mother lay dying in hospital. It was an incredibly sad moment: although frail, she didn't look sick to me, yet it seemed she had given up the will to live. She died shortly afterwards, but it was while she was lying there, unconscious, that June told me the whole, sad story. How Alfred had left her for someone he had met while sheltering in the Underground during the Blitz, and how, unable to cope, my mother had become mentally unstable. This was why I had eventually passed into the care of Dr Barnardo's Homes.

In true pop-star fashion, I helped June buy a decent apartment. When her Maltese husband suffered a stroke, June had to care for him until his death some years later. Strangely enough, the family view was that it was I who had had the harder life. I, however, considered myself to be the more fortunate one.

'SERENISSIMA' COVER BY SIR HUGH CASSON

A Story in Brief:

IMAGE COURTESY: VOYAGES JULES VERNE.

THE IMPRESSIONIST: He's the artist who designed the interior of the royal yacht Britannia; he worked in the camouflage section of the Air Ministry during World War II, and he's said to have been the man who taught Prince Charles to paint in watercolours. For quite some time, too, his paintings adorned the pages of the *Serenissima* brochure, usually commissioned to illustrate particular places and events, such as the celebrations for the bicentenary of French Revolution, in Paris. Most of the original Serenissima artworks were auctioned off for charity, but I couldn't resist keeping one or two back: before, some could be found on board the *Spirit of Chartwell* 'Royal Barge' – which had its own Sir Hugh Casson deck, named after the great man himself –until threatened that is with legal action – when the deck was renamed.

FINIS

I
T may only be a small file-index card that Martine King is holding in her hand, but the words written on it tell the whole story of Philip Morrell's childhood. Martine is the resident archivist for Dr Barnardo's and is based at the charity's headquarters in Barkingside, Essex, on the same site as the residential children's 'village' to which Philip was brought, after being found wandering alone in central London, and to where he has returned today, after an absence of more than six decades.

The typewritten entries on the card record the harsh facts of Philip's early life. Born on 1 April 1944, he was brought from the Church Mission to Barnardo's on 26 May 1950. The latter is a day he still remembers.

For many years, children who had been through the Barnardo's system showed little appetite for coming back to visit or digging out the filing cards that recorded their comings and goings. However, in 1995, a TV documentary series changed all that. "It was in three parts, and was called *Barnardo's Children*," says Martine. "Suddenly, from getting about 150 enquiries a year from children who had been in a Barnardo's home, we went up to 4,000 enquiries overnight."

While former Barnardo's boys and girls are free to view their files, what they find inside them isn't always what they expect. Martine informs:

"We've had boys who come here and say, 'I was in such-and-such a house,' and we tell them, 'You've got a brother – did you know?' Sometimes the answer is, 'No,' especially if they were born in the 1920s or 1930s.

At other times, we have people come here and saying that we prevented their mother or father from having contact with them. They then look into the files and see that the reverse is the case; they come across all this correspondence, which shows we were constantly pleading with their parents to come and visit them. That can be a terrible shock, to have spent your life believing one thing and then to find out, many years later, that it wasn't true.

As a result, when people ask to come and look at their records, we contact our social workers, who then ring and ask the person what they already know, so that we can get an understanding of what issues may arise.

The later a child came here, the more detailed the records. In the 1950s, a child might have a file with just 30-50 pages, but, in the 1960s, that would have grown to 200-300 pages and, by the 1970s, to 2,000-5,000 pages."

It was around the time I was completing this book that I received a telephone call from the Barnardo's social worker: after a nine-month wait, my records were ready. Understandably, the social worker was anxious to understand what I might already know of my childhood, before revealing the 200 documents that made up my file. The hesitancy in his voice indicated that some documents could possibly be upsetting and that, when reading them, I should take into account that the documents were never intended to be seen or read by others. Not only was the language coarse and possibly judgmental in places, but also certain comments had been redacted, for data protection reasons.

This made up my mind for me. I decided there and then that I did not want to see anything other than the original admission form – I just didn't want to burden myself with additional emotional baggage, if it could be avoided. The admission form duly arrived in the mail, along with a note from the social worker stating that he would call again in six weeks' time, to see how I felt about the contents. The admission document read:

SISTER WRIGHT'S DAMNING CONCLUSIONS:

'The mother is a woman of poor moral character and Philip, her illegitimate child, was unwanted and neglected by her. The mother lived in Fulham and was married in 1931, subsequently giving birth to three children by her husband. During the war, she was evacuated to South Devon, and, while she was there, her husband stored the furniture of their home and cohabited with another woman. In November 1941, at West London Court, the mother was given custody of the children of the marriage, and her husband was ordered to pay maintenance at the rate of 10 shillings per week for the mother and 5 shillings per week in respect of each child of the marriage. However, during 1943, her husband returned to her, but two weeks later left her, as they could not get on together and, soon afterwards, in January 1944, the husband took both the half brothers to live with him. Since then, he only paid 10 shillings per week to the mother, in respect of the half sister, June. The mother eventually settled at her present address. She cohabited with the putative father for a short time at her own home, but the man eventually disappeared. The mother was very unreliable in her statements, and reluctant to give information concerning herself. She asked to admit Philip because she was obliged to go out to work. It was known, however, that she lived a very loose moral life, for she was out every night at public houses and entertained men freely in her home. Philip was allowed to wander about the streets alone, and the mother bore no affection for him. Her relatives had nothing good to say of her and the husband's mother stated that the husband had moved to St. Leonards in order to get right away from the mother. Philip is stated to be in good health and clean in his habits. He is of normal mentality but rather backward scholastically, due to his poor environment and the fact he was neglected. He has had measles.'

Dr. Barnado's Homes: National Incorporated Association

OFFICERS REPORT RE APPLICATION FOR ADMISSION OR HELP

PHILIP MORRELL.　　　　　　ADMITTED: 31.5.50.

BORN 1.2.44 AT HAMMERSMITH HOSPITAL
BABTISED: C/E. IN HAMMERSMITH

MOTHER'S RELIGION: C/E.
AGREEABLE N/C.

LAST CONSECUTIVE SIX MONTHS ADDRESS: 56 BRACJENBURY ROAD, W.6.
LAST SCHOOL ATTENDED: BRACKENBURY ROAD SCHOOL.

PAYMENT:	PERIOD:	AGREEMENT:	INFORMATION FROM:
10s. P.W.	PERMANENT.	BY THE MOTHER.	REPORT BAL.

APPLICANT: SISTER WRIGHT, MORAL WELFARE WORKER, 36, GLENTHORNE ROAD, HAMMERSMITH, W.6.

MOTHER: IVY MORRELL NEE MERRY (39) FACTORY HAND, £3 P.W.; FAMILY ALLOWANCE 5s. P.W.;
　　FROM HER HSUBAND 10s. P.W. IN RESPECT OF THE HALF-SISTER JUNE; HEALTH GOOD;
　　GENERAL CHARACTER BAD; RENT 9s.4D P.W. (ARREARS ON 8.4.50. £3.8.0), 56
　　　　　　　　　　　　　　　　　　BRACKENBURY ROAD, W.6.
FATHER (PUTATIVE): HERBERT HOWES (35) WHEREABOUTS NOT KNOWN.
MOTHER'S HUSBAND: ALFRED MORRELL (AGE NOT STATED) SEPARATED FROM THE MOTHER, AND AT W.6.
　　LONDON COURT IN NOVEMBER, 1943, WAS ORDERED TO PAY THE MOTHER 15s.
　　P.W. PLUG 5s, P.P. FOR EACH OF THE THREE CHILDREN OF THE MARRIAGE
　　(SEE BELOW); 16, BUL- (?) ROAD, ST. LEONARD'S. MARRIED THE MOTHER
　　AT FULHAM REGISTER OFFICE ON 10.1.31.
HALF-BROTHERS　　(CHILDREN OF MOTHER'S MARRIAGE): KENNETH (18) AND ALFRED (14) MORRELL;
　　　　　　　　　　　　　　　　　　WITH THE MOTHER'S HUSBAND
HALF-SISTER (CHILDREN OF MOTHER'S MARRIAGE): JUNE MORRELL (11) WITH THE MOTHER.
UNVLE (MAT): MR. M. MERRY, 13, WILLIAM MORRIS ROAD, FULHAM.
AUNTS (MAT): MRS. A. HUMPHRIES, 88, PROTHERO ROAD, FULHAM.
　　MRS. C. HEARD, 88 HOLYPORT ROAD, FULHAM.

THE MOTHER IS A WOMAN OF POOR MORAL CHARACTER AND PHILIP, HER ILLEGITIMATE CHILD,
WAS UNWANTED AND NEGLECTED BY HER. THE MOTHER LIVED IN FULHAM AND WAS MARRIED IN 1931,
SUBSEQUENTLY GIVING BIRTH TO THREE CHILDREN BY HER HUSBAND. DURING THE WAR, SHE WAS EVACUATED
TO SOUTH DEVON, AND, WHILE SHE WAS THERE, HER HUSBAND STORED THE FURNITURE OF THEIR HOME AND
COHABITED WITH ANOTHER WOMAN. IN NOVEMBER 1941, AT WEST LONDON COURT, THE MOTHER WAS GIVEN
CUSTODY OF THE CHILDREN OF THE MARRIAGE, AND HER HUSBAND WAS ORDERED TO PAY MAINTENANCE AT
THE RATE OF 10 SHILLINGS PER WEEK FOR THE MOTHER AND 5 SHILLINGS PER WEEK IN RESPECT OF EACH
CHILD OF THE MARRIAGE. HOWEVER, DURING 1943, HER HUSBAND RETURNED TO HER, BUT TWO WEEKS
LATER LEFT HER, AS THEY COULD NOT GET ON TOGETHER AND, SOON AFTERWARDS, IN JANUARY 1944, THE
HUSBAND TOOK BOTH THE HALF BROTHERS TO LIVE WITH HIM. SINCE THEN, HE ONLY PAID 10 SHIILLINGS
PER WEEK TO THE MOTHER, IN RESPECT OF THE HALF SISTER, JUNE. THE MOTHER EVENTUALLY SETTLED
AT HER PRESENT ADDRESS. SHE COHABITED WITH THE PUTATIVE FATHER FOR A SHORT TIME AT HER OWN
HOME, BUT THE MAN EVENTUALLY DISAPPEARED. THE MOTHER WAS VERY UNRELIABLE IN HER STATEMENTS,
AND RELUCTANT TO GIVE INFORMATION CONCERNING HERSELF. SHE ASKED TO ADMIT PHILIP BECAUSE SHE WAS
OBLIGED TO GO OUT TO WORK. IT WAS KNOWN, HOWEVER, THAT SHE LIVED A VERY LOOSE MORAL LIFE,
FOR SHE WAS OUT EVERY NIGHT AT PUBLIC HOUSES AND ENTERTAINED MEN VERY FREELY IN HER HOME.
PHILIP WAS ALLOWED TO WANDER ABOUT THE STREETS ALONE, AND THE MOTHER BORE NO AFFECTION FOR
HIM. HER RELATIVES HAD NOTHING GOOD TO SAY OF HER AND THE HUSBAND'S MOTHER STATED THAT THE
HUSBAND HAD MOVED TO ST. LEONARDS IN ORDER TO GET RIGHT AWAY FROM THE MOTHER.
　　PHILIP IS STATED TO BE IN GOOD HEALTH AND CLEAN IN HIS HABITS. HE IS OF NORMAL
MENTALITY, BUT RATHER BACKWARD SCHOLASTICALLY, DUE TO HIS POOR ENVIRONMENT AND THE FACT HE WAS
NEGLECTED. HE HAS HAD MEASLES.

A Story in Brief

THE CHALLENGE: By the eve of the event itself, the Challengers had all driven or shipped their vehicles to London, for an exhibition of the cars which I staged in the basement of the Cumberland Hotel. I had chosen this venue because it was close to the start line at Marble Arch, where I had arranged for the Chinese ambassador to cut the ribbon, while the band of Coldstream Guards played, and an enormous Chinese dragon danced. Not that the send-off, on 7 April 1990, passed off without incident. Some several dozen 'anti-China-in-Tibet' protesters staged a demonstration, in an attempt both to shake up the ambassador and disrupt the event. Once the police had restored order, the cars streamed down Park Lane, the Mall and Whitehall and then led above outside Downing Street.

Part Five
EXCURSIONS

If this was a film, rather than a book, then these following passages might be described as 'out-takes'. That is to say, a collection of scenes removed from the final edit. However, I include these 'out-takes' not as comic bloopers, but as a means of providing small, individual cameo portraits, to set alongside the main narrative canvas. Here are the people, places and events that have influenced my thinking processes and my life, both in travel, as well as more generally.

CHAPTER 57
WHERE IS JOHN BLOOM?

The importance of Bloom's offer lay in the revolutionary low price,
which came perhaps to represent something much more – an
emancipation for untold thousands of housewives.

THE first time I became aware of John Bloom was in the early 1960s. The landlady of the digs I was then living in had a copy of the *Daily Mirror* spread out on the kitchen table, opened to an advertisement, which had been taken out by John Bloom, offering twin-tub washing machines at something like half the price you could find in the High Street shops. She was wondering whether to complete the coupon provided and buy one. The importance of the offer lay in the revolutionary low price, which came to represent something much, much more important – an emancipation, if you like, for untold thousands of housewives who could now, in one bound, be free from the drudgery of home boiler washing or, worse still, the weekly trudge down to the launderette.

No surprise, then, that John Bloom came not only to represent the housewife's best friend, but also to be cast in the role of a biblical David slinging shot at the foreheads of industry giants who, with their cosy relationships, could hide behind fixed retail prices, which in those days were still legal. It was a classic situation: on one side, the 'people's champion', breaking down price barriers; on the other, the massed ranks of manufacturers, who viewed Bloom's venture as an open threat – something that, in their eyes, had to be extinguished at all costs.

The way Bloom sold his washing machines was by making the advertisements read just like they were feature articles produced by the newspaper itself. Today, this might be termed 'off-the-page marketing' or 'advertorial'. It wasn't without its complications, however. Even though the whole deal was explained on the page, the sale depended on a coupon being completed and returned, with a cheque, in the mail. The whole enterprise came tumbling down as a result of a nine-week postal strike, during the course of which Bloom's cash flow dried up and backers began to pull the plug.

At the time, Bloom was one of the largest, if not the largest, advertising spenders around, so perhaps it was not unusual for the likes of Lord Thomson, with his myriad newspaper titles, to be seen frequently in his company. I can't help thinking that Lord T must have sensed a kind of kindred spirit in Bloom, thinking back to the time when he, too, was a backwoodsman in Ontario, selling wireless sets.

Incidentally, this completes a curious circle, which involved me being brought back from Benidorm to head office in 1966, when I was just a lowly resort representative. My task was to try and follow in Bloom's wake and run a series of planned coach tours to various parts of Europe. Among the destinations was Bulgaria, a country to which Bloom had earlier organised some pioneering tours, cutting out travel agents by using the same kind of off-the-page marketing techniques he had used to cut out washing-machine manufacturers.

I was entrusted with this task for no reason other than that I had made a casual reference to Bloom's activities in one of my weekly reports to Trevor Davies at head office, as a result of which I became the company's in-house Bulgaria expert, despite having never been anywhere near the place.

Later on, when running Voyages Jules Verne, I utilised Bloom's advertorial approach when it came to promoting my own travel products, and so when I came to write this story, I thought it only right that I should try my utmost to track him down. It seemed as if he had disappeared – both from the public eye and the public consciousness. Even though I had good contacts on Mallorca, the island where he was said to be living with his wife, Anne, I couldn't locate him anywhere.

It wasn't until a year later that I spotted a trailer for a new book on Amazon entitled *Full Bloom*, along with a Twitter account for Kismet, a new company Bloom had set up. I promptly sent off an email, and before I knew it I had John Bloom on the other end of the phone, wanting to know if my enquiry was a prank. I assured him it wasn't, explaining how he had been an original inspiration for much of the marketing that I was to apply in my various ventures. We arranged to meet and he agreed to an interview, as recounted below.

THE RESTLESS SPIRIT

Hackney-born businessman John Bloom left school at the age of 16. By the time he was 30, he had not only made a fortune but also achieved nationwide fame, selling washing machines direct to the British housewife at far lower prices than the established manufacturers could manage.

It wasn't just Bloom's products that captured the public's imagination; it was the buccaneering way in which he sold them. Products were advertised through the medium of 'advertorials': articles that Bloom and his copywriters had penned and which they paid to place in prominent positions in the national newspapers. What struck people straight away was that these advertorials weren't just humourless hard sells.

"There was a bit of jauntiness, a bit of jokiness in there," says Bloom, now 81. "We had stories with headlines such as 'Husband Pockets £30', about how buying a new washing machine had helped cut down the weekly household spend. Elsewhere, we did horoscopes predicting how people with different star signs would save time and money when they bought one of our machines. The idea was to get people's attention. We had headlines such as 'Yours for Nothing' and 'You Are Going to Read the Most Astonishing Advertisement'."

There was also 'How to Succeed in Your Kitchen Without Really Trying' and 'This Book Changed the Lives of over 180,000 Women'. Bloom's approach certainly caught the eye; moreover, it brought in sales. In response to his first newspaper ad, in the *Daily Mirror*, some 8,000 people sent in coupons declaring their interest in buying one of his Electromatic washing machines at a retail price of £40-50.

"There were no credit cards in those days, so, once people had come up with the deposit, they paid the rest on monthly hire purchase," says Bloom. "Four shillings and 11 pence for the cheaper model and seven shillings and 11 pence for the more expensive one, for two years."

Bloom didn't just stop at getting Britain's shirts whiter. He also set about getting its menfolk browner, with a product called Man-Tan (not a great success, he concedes), and then getting the whole family a bit of authentic, overseas sunshine, in the form of holidays to Bulgaria, behind the Iron Curtain.

This wasn't just a pie-in-the-sky notion, either. He went out on a fact-finding tour of the country and met the president, Todor Zhivkov, who agreed to let him have exclusive package-holiday organising rights, provided he sent Brits in sufficient numbers (only 1,500 per year were going there in the early '60s). 'I did not have any experience in the holiday business, but I did not see that as an insuperable problem' Bloom records in his autobiography, *It's No Sin to Make a Profit*. 'I could always buy the know-how.'

It was at this juncture that, like many other tour operators (including Philip Morrell at Thomson Holidays), Bloom came up against a seemingly immovable piece of UK legislation, referred to as 'Provision One', that made it illegal for anyone to charge less for an all-in package holiday than the price of the lowest scheduled return air fare between the two points. His original plan to fly direct from the UK to Bulgaria thus scuppered, the determined Mr Bloom decided to fly his passengers to Ostend, in Belgium, where they would change onto a different plane for the rest of the journey to Bulgaria. This would not be contravening any rules, since Belgium was not bound by British Board of Trade regulations.

Not only did Bloom manage to get the price of a fortnight's holiday down to 45 guineas (£47.25, as against the £70 scheduled return air fare), but he also launched coach-tour holidays to Bulgaria at roughly half that price. In addition, he used those same coaches to take buyers of his washing machines on bargain tours of Europe: a three-day tour of France and Belgium for three guineas, 10 days in the Austrian Tyrol for seven guineas, 10 days in Venice for nine guineas, etc. "One person got the really cheap rate, but I worked on the basis that they would each bring a friend or partner, who would pay the going rate," he recalls. "We didn't make any real money, but it was good promotion."

Although Bloom's involvement with the travel business did not last long, he definitely left his mark. His pioneering of the advertorial concept proved crucial in the promotion of Voyages Jules Verne arrangements. Also, his Bulgarian initiative laid the foundations for that country's success as a tourist destination, with his operation being taken over – at a time, he says, when he was getting several thousand Brits per year to Bulgaria – by Co-Op Travel and, later, Balkan Holidays. Today, some 300,000 British tourists visit Bulgaria each year.

Among the many guests Bloom and his wife entertained in the '60s, in their top-floor Mayfair home, was boss of the Thomson organisation himself, the bespectacled Roy Thomson: not the kind of person you might expect to find at showbiz parties full of celebrities such as Jean Shrimpton and the Beatles. "I think (Lord Thomson) liked the fact that I was a bit of a marketer," says Bloom. "Just as he got started selling radios, he recognised that I was a maverick, like him."

Unfortunately, though, Bloom's trajectory was soon to become a downward one. On 17 July 1964, while he was moored just off the Bulgarian coast on his £330,000 yacht *Ariane III*, news came through to the effect that his business empire had collapsed. As he recalls, "I received a telex which read: 'If you cannot phone by 3.39 British Summer Time this afternoon, irrevocable decisions will have been taken.' By the time I got that message, it was already hours too late."

When his company, Rolls Razor (he loved the word 'Rolls'), went into voluntary liquidation, shares that had been valued at well over £2 nine months earlier fell to just five pence. As well as suffering a spectacular financial fall, Bloom then had to undergo the indignity of a lengthy Board of Trade inquiry, with himself cast as the villain of the piece. He says: "I found myself in a room facing two of the most eminent lawyers of the day, who were backed up by a team of 21 accountants, advisers and whatever. All I had on my side was one lawyer, who wasn't even allowed to take notes. Still, it taught me a lesson, I suppose. I found out that, when I was worth £30 million, I had 30 million best friends, and when I lost all my money, I found I had two or three real friends. You soon learn that, when you're down, people don't just kick you once; they come back for more."

A LIFE IN BUSINESS: JOHN BLOOM

In chronological order, a snapshot of John Bloom's life and achievements:

- ¥ Born 1931 in Nelson Street, east London. His father, Sam, was a tailor.
- ¥ Set up a firework-selling business while still a boy.
- ¥ Left Hackney Downs Grammar School at 16.
- ¥ Got a job as a salesman in Selfridges' domestic appliances department.
- ¥ Clerk in press office, the Board of Deputies of British Jews.
- ¥ Set up coach operator business while doing National Service.
- ¥ Post-demob, ran several small transport businesses.
- ¥ Started selling washing machines from £2 a week on hire purchase deals.
- ¥ Rented HQ in north London and began importing washing machines from firm in Utrecht, Holland, and selling them for £40-50.
- ¥ Reduced overheads by manufacturing machines in UK instead, at Gallows Corner, Romford.
- ¥ Hired opulent summer villa on Riviera and began mixing with stars (among them Terence Stamp, Peter Ustinov, Adam Faith and Lionel Bart).
- ¥ Joined board of Queens Park Rangers Football Club.
- ¥ Moved into trading stamps, TV rentals and mail order.
- ¥ Involved in start of the pirate station Radio Caroline.
- ¥ Helped discover David Bowie.
- ¥ Set up package holidays to Bulgaria.
- ¥ Went into nightclubs after collapse of his washing-machine empire.
- ¥ Ran historical-themed restaurants (in UK and US) entitled 1520 AD.
- ¥ Opened his famous Piano Bar in the middle of Palma, Majorca.
- ¥ Marketed online motor racing game.
- ¥ Currently launching Kismet international skincare range.

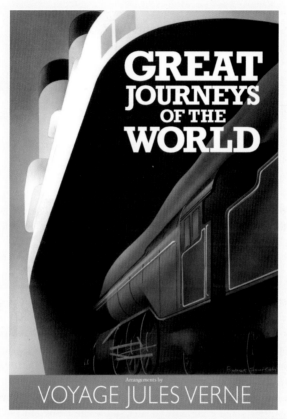

A Story in Brief

TROUBLE ON THE ROCK: Thomson stuck by Gibraltar throughout the difficult years when the border with Spain was closed. Indeed, on the day in 1986 when it reopened, the first vehicle to enter Gibraltar was a Thomson liveried coach. The story made prime-time TV news, but news from the Rock was not always upbeat. Head of PR, Doug Goodman recalls the time the SAS killed three IRA members suspected of planning an explosion near the Governor's Residence. During the shoot-out, one of the bullets ricocheted from a tree, striking a Thomson guest, who in that instant became a witness in the resulting court case. Fearing for his safety, he asked that his identity be kept secret, and all records of his hotel and hospital visit were suppressed. But the minute he returned to Manchester, the Press launched an all-out attempt to find him. Doug was offered a substantial amount of money to reveal the client's identity, but said nothing.

IMAGE COURTESY: ROBERT SCURRAH/VOYAGES JULES VERNE.

CHAPTER 58
MAJOR INGHAM, I PRESUME

As they sailed across the Channel, the Captain decided to properly introduce himself to Harry. "I'm Ingham," he said. "Walter Ingham." "Not Ingham of Ingham's Tours?" asked an astonished Chandler.

THOUGH they would have denied it and certainly did not seek to be, Harry and Rene Chandler were role models for scores of people who created, and struggled to make successful, small tour-operating firms in the years after World War II. These 'husband-and-wife' businesses were based on an enthusiasm for travel – quite often, an enthusiasm concentrated on a single destination – and they struggled to compete with the giants of the industry: the Cooks, the Clarksons, the Thomsons, etc. That Harry and Rene were succeeding with their Travel Club of Upminster was both an example and an inspiration.

At that time – and even more so later, in the late 1950s and 1960s, as the boom in holidays abroad began to manifest – the UK travel industry was an unregulated, sometimes unprincipled and always unpredictable trade. To protect the State-owned British Overseas Airways Corporation (BOAC) and British European Airways (BEA), government regulations ensured that package holiday prices were fixed artificially high, which made them extremely profitable. For practical purposes, only the big tour firms could charter aircraft, so they were the ones who reaped the profits. Everybody else just struggled for the scraps.

So, as they dreamed of building up their niche companies, the people running the little firms saw the Chandlers as an example of what could be achieved against formidable odds. In July 1964, at the peak of the holiday season, the spectacular collapse of a company called Fiesta Tours gave them even more reason to respect Harry Chandler and his standing in their trade. "This industry contains more cowboys than Oklahoma," a senior figure at the Civil Aviation Authority commented at the time, "but I think somebody like Harry Chandler could turn out to be the Sheriff we need to sort them out."

Though this statement was something of an exaggeration, it was indeed Harry, and a few others like him, who dragged the British travel industry from the shadows of those post-war years and into the spotlight of public accountability. They pushed until the industry accepted its responsibilities to the customers who kept it going, and took steps to see off most of the cowboys. By then, Harry had many years of travel trade experience under his belt: unlike most of the small operators who looked up to him, he had not started his business in the late 1940s or early 1950s, but back in 1936, when Europe was unwittingly heading for catastrophe.

The first trip he organised – a fortnight to Bavaria – attracted just five customers, when 15 were needed to break even. (The fact that it coincided with Hitler marching into the Rhineland didn't do him any favours, either.) However, Harry bounced back and, the following year, organised and accompanied five or six groups, none of which numbered less than 30: he had managed to get his sums right.

He ended up with a profit of £100 – the largest sum of money he had ever possessed – and began to build up a mailing list, starting with the former pupils of the East End school he had attended. The next year, 1938, wasn't such a success, but he expanded both his mailing list and his programme of holidays, incorporating Germany and Switzerland. Of course, Hitler's desire to expand his empire by marching into Austria that spring was bad for business, to say the least.

In September of the following year, it was a stroke of luck that Harry was in neutral Switzerland, rather than Germany, on the day that war was declared. He was in the Swiss town of Sarnen, but, after a few days of uncertainty, he left his customers in their hotel and went to visit the British Consul in Geneva, to confirm that arrangements were in hand to get them safely home. On being satisfied that a special train was being organised to transport them from neutral Switzerland, albeit in at least another two weeks' time, he returned with the good news, then turned his attention to getting himself home much earlier.

Giving his group fresh assurances that they were now in the safe hands of the British Consul and that he had passed over their personal and passport details during his meeting, he left them once more. His simple plan – the best plans are the simple ones – was to obtain a visa and passage documents from the French Consul in Geneva and make his way through France, which was not then occupied by the Germans, to one of the Channel ports. He figured there were bound to be ships going to England. Waiting outside the French Consulate for an opportunity to bluff his way in, he got into conversation with a Territorial Army captain who

A Story in Brief

THE WAGES OF FEAR: "After the war, there were quite a lot of medium-sized aircraft left in India. The Americans patched them up and flew them to Europe, but they didn't dare fly the Atlantic with them. Marian (Independent Air Transport), however, agreed to fly these planes to the U.S. According to Vic, his radio officer, the first time Marian stepped into one of these planes, his foot went right through the floor! No wonder that was the only flight Vic took in one of these machines; he said the experience was exactly like the film *Wages of Fear*. It didn't bother Marian, though. He flew these patched-up planes, first to Reykjavik and then onto America. As for a radio officer to replace Vic, he found just the chap he needed: a young man who had been in submarines during the war, when he was only 15 years old." Mrs Kozubska from her unpublished memoirs.

IMAGE COURTESY: DAVID SCUTT/VOYAGES JULES VERNE.

was equally anxious to get back to England, in order to join his regiment.

The two of them manoeuvred their way inside and eventually persuaded the Consul to provide the visas and paperwork. Within a couple of hours they began their journey, driving in the Captain's Lagonda non-stop and at high speed across France, negotiating army checkpoints with a combination of charm, bluster, official documentation and reliance on the Entente Cordiale.

They reached Boulogne but no ship was available, so they went on to Calais, where the Captain found a small vessel whose skipper was about to set off for Dover. A couple of bottles of wine later, along with some patriotic speeches and a bundle of francs, they had secured passage – not only for themselves, but also for the Captain's Lagonda, which was hauled on board by a dockside crane.

As they sailed across the Channel, the Captain decided, finally, to properly introduce himself to Harry. "I'm Ingham," he said. "Walter Ingham." "Not Ingham of Inghams' Tours?" asked an astonished Chandler. "Yes," came the reply, "and I know who you are – we're in the same line of business, aren't we?"

It was an amazing coincidence. Walter Ingham ended the war as a Major, having for a time worked with Harry Chandler in the same unit of the Intelligence Corps, doing Field Security work in Austria. Captain Chandler, meanwhile, ended his war in Singapore, by way of India and Burma, where he was attached to Lord Mountbatten's staff as 'Military Forwarding Officer, Singapore'. His first job was to go to the notorious Changi Prison and arrange passage home for all the British prisoners – some 5,000 in all – interned there, as well as for those in other camps the Japanese had established.

Bearing in mind how important the mailing list from his old school had been when he was struggling to build up his travel company before the war, Harry decided to keep a list of the names and UK addresses of all the men he had helped. It was an inspired decision because, in 1947, he was able to persuade many of them to buy holidays from him as he began to rebuild his business.

His first post-war trip was to Switzerland, to the very same hotel in Sarnen where he had had to leave his clients at the outbreak of war. The owner greeted him like a long-lost son, accepted the payment outstanding since 1939 and assumed that they would continue to do business just as they had done, before being so rudely interrupted!

The post-war travel trade was not for the faint-hearted. As discussed, government directives regulated the prices that could be charged, in order to protect the national airlines. There was also, for several years, a limit to the amount of pounds sterling that could be taken abroad. As if pressure from outside wasn't enough to contend with, the trade itself was a cut-throat business, with consumer protection virtually non-existent.

However, the Travel Club of Upminster survived – indeed, thrived – in the same circumstances that saw the demise of many small operators. Harry Chandler's brochure was unique in that he had no small-print booking conditions; he preferred to rely, as he put it, on 'common law and common sense'. If there were complaints, he preferred to settle them with financial reimbursement and to ensure that the complainant never bought a holiday from him again.

He also sold his holidays direct to the public, at a time when the travel agent was generally perceived to be a middleman who added nothing to the transaction between tour operator and customer, but took a fee all the same. This inevitably led to friction within the ranks of the Association of British Travel Agents (ABTA), the trade's governing body. Harry's genuine desire to work for the good of the industry was often frustrated by such in-fighting.

The great breakthrough for their business, however, was when Harry's wife, Rene, 'discovered' the Algarve, the southern coast of Portugal which, at the time, was virtually undeveloped as far as tourism was concerned. Rene learned of the Algarve in 1960, from an Upminster neighbour who had sold his business and planned to settle in southern Portugal, where he had bought a plot of land and was intending to build some villas. He persuaded Rene to invest £5,000 in his scheme, for which she would get a villa in return.

Harry himself did not visit the area until 1963, although he had sent a handful of clients on holidays there – people, in the main, who were interested in purchasing property. As far as he was concerned, the problem with the Algarve was that it did not have an airport, so holidaymakers had to fly into Lisbon and travel 200 miles south by car, coach or train.

However, the old friend from Upminster informed Harry that Faro would have an airport by 1965, and he was right. As a result, Chandler was able to promote the Algarve as 'Europe's best-kept holiday secret', flying people direct to its little seaside towns and empty beaches. This was an instant success and even more so after a chance meeting in the Algarve with Sidney De Haan, the founder of Saga Holidays.

The meeting took place at the Aldeia Turistica near Albufeira, a purpose-built holiday village with villas, apartments, restaurants and bars. It was October 1966, the sun was shining and the day was pleasantly warm, but there were no holidaymakers.

According to De Haan, the reason for this was that people thought of the region only as a summer destination, so the apartments and villas stood empty. Within half an hour, the two men had struck a deal: Chandler would pay De Haan £5 per person per week for a villa, including maid service, and send his customers there during the winter.

A couple of years before this, the UK travel trade had been shaken by the collapse, at the height of the summer season, of a company called Fiesta Tours. As Fiesta was not a member of ABTA, the industry bore no responsibility for its stranded customers, but Chandler realised what a public relations disaster it would be for the whole industry if nothing was done. He persuaded the then ABTA president, Charles Garner, and other major tour firms to organise a rescue operation and bring home all of Fiesta's customers.

They repeated this action a few weeks later, when a smaller firm named Omar Khayyam Tours failed, leaving a legacy of ruined holidays and angry customers. It was obvious that the industry could not continue unregulated. Harry and a few others realised that, if the trade could not control itself, then the government would step in and enforce a code of conduct, in order to protect customers.

To prevent this happening, Harry came up with a plan he called 'reciprocal booking'. Briefly, it meant that ABTA tour firms would sell their holidays only through ABTA travel agents. The agents, in turn, would only deal with ABTA operators. It was perilously close to being an illegal 'closed shop', but under the circumstances it was a risk worth taking. With a few tweaks, the plan, dubbed 'Operation Stabiliser', was put in front of delegates at ABTA's 1965 annual conference, on the island of Jersey. It was adopted by a narrow margin, after a long and heated debate. The travel agents, who already disliked Harry because he sold his holidays direct to the public, had even more reason to dislike and distrust him – or so they thought.

For all his years as a member of ABTA, his work on its committees and councils, and his efforts to create and steer the vastly influential Tour Operators Study Group, Harry Chandler was never honoured with the presidency of the Association. This is a demonstration of the collective strength of small minds.

As the years passed, there were further massive changes in store for the UK travel trade. Of these, advances in technology, in particular the use of the Internet, transformed the scene the most. Those travel agents who regarded themselves as a vital part of the holiday selling-and-buying operation were increasingly sidelined as the public went online to buy their hotel rooms, their flights and their hire cars direct from the suppliers.

The tour operators themselves had to adapt to this change. Once upon a time, they had sent people away on weekly or fortnightly deals, with everyone flying in the same chartered plane, being transferred in a few chartered coaches and staying in the same block-booked hotel, until it was time for all of them to make the return journey. Under these controlled circumstances, the tour operator could do the sums and plan accordingly for a determined profit. However, when holidays began to break out of the package – when people chose their own dates of departure and return, travelled in couples or family groups rather than by the planeload, and hired a car or required a taxi transfer to the hotels – that was when uncertainty came into the picture.

It was mainly for this reason that Paul Chandler, son of Harry and Rene, sold the Travel Club of Upminster in 2009. The redoubtable Harry had died, aged 79, in 1992, followed by the equally redoubtable Rene, aged 95, in 2008. With them gone and with the situation so utterly changed from the halcyon days, Paul's decision was understandable. In September 2010, the Travel Club of Upminster and its subsidiary, Austria Travel, went into administration. It was a sad end to the story of one man's ambitions and hopes, but the story of how Harry Chandler struggled to achieve business success, how he influenced the post-war development of the UK travel industry and how he left his mark on that industry is what counts, not the way it ended.

I had been trained by Harry's first local representative, John Bacannello, and also, some years later, met Harry and Rene Chandler, during the ABTA Convention in Athens. Yet I was to have another curious connection with the Chandlers' Travel Club: on the company's demise, understanding its history, I bought the mailing list. This turned out to be the very list that I used in 2011 to promote the *Spirit of Chartwell* and my 'Memories of London' voyages, in advance of the vessel later being employed, in June 2012, as the royal barge on the occasion of the Queen's Diamond Jubilee celebrations.

CHAPTER 59
THE CAPTAIN

"I quite seriously maintain that Langton was the greatest man in travel since Thomas Cook – and, if you look at it in many ways, his contribution was the greater." J.E.D. Williams, avation pioneer.

INTRODUCTION

THE annals of the travel industry are filled with tales of daring initiatives and ingenious solutions. It is a business which thrives on exploration and risk-taking, and which holds up as heroes those pioneers who were the first to venture where others feared to tread. This was never truer than in the early days of organised travel. Once popular tourism had taken root in the public consciousness, it mushroomed at an astonishing rate, thanks to a succession of restless entrepreneurs who either spotted gaps in the market or else found new ways to exploit what was already there. The names of some of these people live on in one way or another, whereas others have gradually faded from memory.

One such travel innovator, who did not receive the public recognition he deserved, was 'Captain' Ted Langton, the archetypal swashbuckler-cum-businessman and the most inventive and resourceful of the early travel entrepreneurs. The mark he left on the travel business was both profound and enduring. Even his rivals acknowledge that it was he who led the way, when it came to fashioning the holiday and touring business we all recognise today.

The aviation pioneer J.E.D. Williams summed up Ted Langton's achievements in the following way: "I quite seriously maintain that Langton was the greatest man in travel since Thomas Cook – and, if you look at it in many ways, his contribution was the greater." Cook, he pointed out, may have been the first to charter a train as a middleman, but he had, in time, moved away from the chartering concept. By contrast, Langton single-handedly developed the formula for the all-inclusive travel business that we know today. All this against the background of two World Wars, the Wall Street Crash, currency restrictions, anti-competitive regulatory regimes, the Great Depression and the general strike of 1926.

Possibly because he had always kept things close to his chest, outsiders often thought Ted Langton a bit of an enigma. As well as being considered something of a recluse, he was known for the relentless chiselling-down of hotel and airlines rates, which was the basis of his success. The reality, however, was somewhat different: Andy Sawicki (who later became my boss) worked as a hotel negotiator for Ted during the early days of Skytours, and he recalls the Captain as a tough but fair negotiator, with an intuitive sense both of what represented value for money and of the rate that would produce the best results for the supplier.

It was Ted's belief that, if he could guarantee hoteliers (as well as coach operators and airlines) a long season – whereas before, many had been getting by with just 10 weeks during summer – plus a high rate of occupancy, then this would translate into both lower prices and better standards for the customer. It was a virtuous circle in which everyone could potentially benefit: travellers, hoteliers, coach operators, airlines and, of course, the Captain himself. However, it was also a daring high-wire act that could have gone spectacularly wrong at any point.

In exchange for an advantageous tariff, Ted was now guaranteeing suppliers a minimum level of occupancy much higher than what they were used to, thereby gaining a price advantage over his competitors. It was a negotiating/marketing device he had used earlier with his various coach tour operations, and it had worked – not unnaturally, then, he applied the same technique to air travel.

In 1953 he founded Skytours, again using his trusted formula, and it became an immediate and resounding success, so much so that Skytours customers could regularly be seen queuing around the block, in anticipation of the publication of the company's new holiday brochure. It didn't stop there, either: Ted advanced large sums to hoteliers to improve their establishments by, for example, installing en-suite facilities, building swimming pools and even demolishing existing hotels with a view to rebuilding them (often to his precise specifications). To cap it all, he formed his own airline, Britannia Airways, despite knowing nothing about aviation, other than that most independent airline operators were hopelessly unreliable, and often unsafe.

In essence, what Ted Langton built in Skytours was nothing less than the first vertically integrated tour operator, controlling sales, coaches, aeroplanes and hotels. It was surprising then, that, just as everything seemed to be coming good, Langton agreed to sell his business, in 1965, to the Thomson group, for a price that turned out to be lower than the following year's annual profit. He had, in effect, given Skytours to Thomson for free, with a little surplus on top. Why?

Perhaps the answer to this question goes back to Ted's very beginnings, to his character and acute, if not astute, understanding of his own limitations. His passion was to build things, to create them from scratch; he took little pleasure from actually running operations or fronting them up, at least for any length of time. What's more, he shunned publicity like the plague and was always itching to start the next big project.

As with most entrepreneurs, Ted kept the essentials of running his businesses in his head and wrote little down, yet he had an uncanny knack of gathering some very able people around him. What's more, the decision-making process was quick and efficient, without the Thomson-like committees. In short, a clash of cultures was inevitable. Ted felt that he had been steamrollered by his new bosses, who, having run the slide rule over his businesses with a phalanx of advisers, lawyers and accountants, had come to the (incorrect) conclusion that most of them were losing money and without any form of corporate structure recognised by Thomson.

The process of due diligence is always unnerving for the seller, with the buyer not unnaturally focused on getting the lowest price and having no interest in talking up underlying values. It seems possible that Ted was bamboozled into somewhat believing what he was hearing, with regards to the underlying value of the companies, besides simply being caught up in the wooing process. There seems to be no other rational explanation as to why he sold the companies for the price he did, given that he was in good health.

For Langton, then, the relationship ended badly. For Thomson, it was quite the reverse. Some 35 years later, they sold, for £1.7 billion, a travel business that had essentially cost them nothing. Tragically, the Captain later revealed that he had shaken hands on the deal during an alcohol-fuelled restaurant meal. Even though he was subsequently racked with doubt, he felt that, having given his word, he was duty-bound to honour it. Thus, the sale went ahead.

THE BEGINNINGS

Ted Langton's story starts at the beginning of the 20th century, in the tiny, coastal village of Churchtown, a mile or two from the genteel Victorian seaside resort of Southport and just a short train ride away from the bustling port city of Liverpool.

Thomas Edwin David Langton was born on 16 April 1904, to a father, Ernest, engaged in the business of livestock, first as a pork butcher and then as a butchery manager. Ernest Langton eventually became a well-known visitor to livestock markets across the length and breadth of the Midlands and Northern England, not only in his professed trade of butchery, but also as a promoter of the benefits of the 'humane killer', a stun-gun device for the slaughter of pigs, cattle and horses, designed to replace the traditional mallet and rivet.

At the outbreak of World War I in 1914, the now 10-year-old blond, curly haired Ted Langton had already spotted a market opportunity by selling lockets of his hair for a penny; he also organised other boys to collect horse manure from the streets which he then sold to the larger houses in the area. Then, in 1916, two years into World War I and in response to high casualty rates, the rules for military enlistment suddenly changed. Until that point, only unmarried men had been obliged to enlist, but now the scope was widened to include married men as well, which must have come as a profound shock to Ted's middle-aged father. What's more, after barely a year in the army, Ernest became listed as a wartime deserter, a crime punishable by death.

From that point on, Ted's father never returned home – presumably, he had to change his name in order to survive. As a result, the family now consisted of Mrs Hannah Langton and her three children, and they had to get by as best they could, while living with the stigma that would have been attached to their father's absence and the reasons for it.

When the war ended, in 1918, Ted turned 14 and needed to start earning his keep. His first job was with Galleon Shipping Agents at Liverpool Docks; each morning, he would board the first train from Southport in order to reach their offices by 6.30am. In those days there were still few emigration restrictions on entry into the US, and Liverpool had become a transit point for many thousands of Irish citizens seeking a new life in the New World. First they would sail to Liverpool, from where they would embark on one of many cramped ocean liners headed for Ellis Island, New York. It was a lucrative time for ship owners, boarding-house keepers and shipping agents alike. Ted's job was to meet the Irish passengers arriving from Dublin and Belfast, issue them with onward tickets and ensure that they settled any outstanding accounts.

From 1921, however, the US began to impose restrictions on entry, introducing a strict quota policy that was further tightened in 1924, with the implementation of the Johnson-Reed Act. The effect was to turn a profitable transatlantic trade into an ever-dwindling trickle of customers. Thus Ted was soon on the move, securing a position on the foreign exchange desk of Messrs Thomas Cook & Son, of 75 Church Street, Liverpool, followed by another with Messrs Dean & Dawson, a firm of general travel agents at 26 North John Street, Liverpool. There then followed a sequence of events that are, even now, still clouded in mystery, as it was while working at Dean & Dawson that Ted somehow got his first break in the travel business. In 1927, together with his wife, Dorothy, he headed for London.

A Story in Brief

THE LANGTON CENTRE: 'The co-founder of The (Captain) Langton Adventure Centre was Rev. John Thursfield. He had been the vicar of Ross-on-Wye for many years, but his first parish was the tiny village of Yarlington in Somerset, where my parents lived (although Father was only there at weekends). As time went by, John became a very good friend of the family, and always bearded Father in his den when he visited London. The centre was John's idea, but while Father was prepared to provide the capital, he was adamant that once the centre was set up it had to pay its own running costs, although he would usually help out with improvements etc. John was always very keen to assist young lads who needed help, and while Father had a generous streak and did help several people, he always shunned publicity. And, as it happens, the adventure centre is still going strong to this day'. June Langton. **IMAGE COURTESY: JUNE LANGTON.**

THE SPANISH TRAVEL BUREAU

Spain was the country that marked both the beginning of Ted's career and, poignantly, its end. In later life he always claimed that his affection for all things Spanish had originated in the folklore of the area in which he grew up: it was believed that a ship from the Spanish Armada had washed up on the nearby coast and the captured sailors had stayed on, marrying local girls. The story stems from the English Civil War, when that part of Lancashire was on the side of the Royalists. In 1643, a Spanish frigate, the *Santa Ana*, was washed up in the Wyre Estuary by a storm; she weighed 600 tones and boasted 25 guns plus a crew of 300. The ship itself was burnt by locals to save it from falling into the hands of the Roundheads and, instead of going back to Spain, many of the crew settled in the area and did indeed marry local girls. This led to many a local, including Ted, speculating that they had a bit of Spanish blood running through their veins.

The Spanish Travel Bureau had its offices at 87 Regent Street, London, and, in common with many overseas enterprises connected with Spain at the time, there was an element of royal patronage, to the extent that King Alphonse XIII had a particular interest in tourism. Somehow – and no one quite knows how – Langton had secured himself, at the age of just 23, a plum managing role with what was essentially the forerunner of the Spanish National Tourist Office in London.

In its guise as a travel agent, the most important function for the Spanish Tourist Bureau appears to have been the promotion of Compañía Trasatlántica Española's (CTE's) passenger shipping services between Marseille, Barcelona and Alicante. To grasp the importance of this service, you have to understand that these were the days when there were no regular and reliable air services between the UK and Spain; what's more, due to poor roads, the overland route was likewise a less than satisfactory option. This meant that the quickest, most convenient and most comfortable way of getting there was to take an overnight wagon-lit (sleeper) train to Marseille, from which point a CTE ship would carry the traveller, in great comfort, to either Barcelona or Alicante, whereupon connecting coach services would be available to ferry travellers into the interior of the country, including the capital, Madrid.

It was at the time of the 1929 Barcelona International Exposition that the young Ted Langton was given the job of making the travel and other arrangements (at a fee of £1,000) for Bolton Wanderers to play Catalan XI in Barcelona (Bolton lost 0-4), and for Jack Hylton and his 27-piece orchestra to perform three sell-out performances, along with the full cast and props, of the West End review *Wake Up and Dream*. For the next four years Langton ran this little bit of Spain in London, during which time he was a frequent visitor to Barcelona and Seville and became involved in a number of ventures aimed at building relations between Spain and Britain.

All this changed in 1931, however, when the Spanish Royal Family abdicated and went to Rome in exile. CTE's ships were either given less royal-sounding names or, in the case of the flagship, the *Reina Maria Cristina*, scrapped altogether. It was also around this time that King Alphonse XIII's eldest son, Juan (the father of the present King, Juan Carlos), had enlisted at the Britannia Royal Naval College in Dartmouth, despite being older than most of the other cadets. Ted, presumably at the King's behest, was given the task of keeping the young pretender supplied with pocket money.

ON HIS OWN ACCOUNT

Towards the end of 1931, it became clear that the affairs of the Spanish Tourist Bureau were in a state of flux, with the royal patronage now more a hindrance than anything else. So Ted, together with his young family (June had been born in 1928 and Norma in 1930), decided to head back north to Southport, to live with an aunt. Once there, he lost no time in opening a travel agency on Southport's fashionable Lord Street (at No. 96c), but before long he was back in London, marketing a series of coach tours under the name 'Happiway'. These tours focused largely on the West Country and the Isle of Wight, and presumably made use of both the coach licences and offices of the General Travel Agency (London) Limited, who he knew from the Spanish Tourist Bureau days. The agency had its headquarters at Woburn Place, Euston, just 200 yards from Mabledon Place, where years later Ted was to open his own, much bigger offices and coach service bays for Skytours.

For the time being, though, Happiway was a huge success and marked the point at which Langton went into business on his own. He followed up the domestic coach venture with a series of short trips to the Continent, for which he needed to join up with an operator in Belgium. Presumably, this was how he came into contact with a certain Constant Claes, the owner of Les Cars Bleu S.A., in Brussels.

BLUE CARS

In 1933-34, Ted sold his Happiway coach tour business and, in 1935, began operating from prestigious offices and showrooms at 224 Shaftesbury Avenue, in the West End. He had joined up with Constant Claes to market a series of Continental coach tours in London, under the 'Blue Cars' brand name. In due course, Langton bought out Claes and found himself owning not just a travel company in London, but a coach company in Belgium too. What's more, the enterprise was a huge success: before long, he had opened offices in Milan and

Paris, as well as sharing an office with Frames Tours in New York.

The success of Blue Cars was built on the back of brilliantly worked itineraries, attractive prices and original brochure layout designs. At the same time, Ted ensured that he emphasised what differentiated him from his rivals: the quality of his motor coaches, the standard of his selected hotels and the expertise of his guides. Great importance was placed on the fact that his coach tours did not begin with a train trip to the coast and then continue on a foreign-based coach, as was the case with his rivals. Rather, Blue Car passengers travelled in reserved-armchair comfort on a British-built coach – usually a Leyland Tiger – from the moment they left London and until they returned.

Next, the Captain took to the skies. In 1936, he chartered four de Havilland Dragon Rapide aircraft to fly from Lympne Airport, in Kent, to Le Touquet, in Northern France, where he had stationed three coaches for the purpose of carrying passengers to Brittany, the South of France and on to Spain. The business expanded exponentially; soon, however, World War II was to intervene and call a halt to all his operations.

WORLD WAR II

There was a period after September 1939, following the declaration of war with Germany, when calamity was expected but not much seemed to be happening (in Western Europe, at least). It was referred to colloquially as the 'phoney war'; some evacuees even started to return home. Nonetheless, the mere threat of war was enough to stop organised tourism in its tracks, as were the numerous government warnings that citizens should not travel. All Ted Langton could do was mothball his operations and hope that the war would be a short one.

He had married Dorothy Heaps, the daughter of a successful Liverpool poulterer and feather importer, on 1 June 1927, when he was 23 and she was 21. They had both wanted to marry earlier, but Ted was not quite the suitor that George Heaps had in mind for his daughter, so Dorothy had to wait until she was 21 and no longer required her father's consent.

As things turned out, this didn't seem to cause any lasting discord between George and Ted – if anything, George's initial disapproval may well have spurred Ted on to prove himself in the eyes of his father-in-law and of other people. George was one of those restless souls who worked all hours to, when he could, live extravagantly. His penchant was travel of the posh, adventuresome kind, and he was forever reserving passages on the great ocean liners of the day. He would sail to the Far East and Australia, always taking his motor car with him so that he could explore the interior of whichever country he was visiting.

One of George's favoured destinations was the French Riviera (either Nice or

Monte Carlo) in springtime, and the spring of 1940, war notwithstanding, was to be no different, except that this time Ted, Dorothy and their two daughters would join George and his wife, Adrienne. At the outbreak of war, Ted had volunteered to enlist with the Royal Engineers but failed the medical, and so, at a loose end and with no business to run, a trip to the Riviera seemed a good idea.

Normally, George and Adrienne travelled to the Riviera in the sumptuous splendour of the 'Le Train Bleu'. Whereas this time, the expanded group decided to drive down in two cars. The holiday was not to end smoothly, however: in May, fearing they might get trapped in a pincer movement by the Italians from the east and the Germans from the north, Ted and his family decided to make a dash from Nice for the Channel, reaching Saint-Malo just in time to catch one of the last sailings to Southampton, on which they travelled as foot passengers.

Unfortunately, it wasn't just Ted's Jaguar that had to remain behind: George had been taken ill in Nice and was now in the English Hospital, being tended by Adrienne. The story of George and Adrienne's eventful return journey is recalled by their granddaughter June (Ted Langton's eldest daughter):

'It was a warm sunny day in Nice when the driver drew up outside the hotel, on the Promenade des Anglais, to collect his passengers and drive them to England. Routine, one might think, but not quite – it was early June 1940 and the 'phoney war', which had lulled so many into a false sense of security, had ended.

The German Army was on the march; April had seen Hitler invading and occupying Norway and Sweden, to secure his route for Swedish ore and to establish a Norwegian base to break the British blockade of Germany. Then, in early May, they swept through the neutral countries of Holland and Belgium, bursting rapidly through the Ardennes. Turning to the north, towards the coast, they successfully trapped the British Expeditionary Force in a pocket around Dunkirk. There then followed the epic evacuation of Dunkirk.

Whilst all this was happening, George Heaps and his wife, Adrienne, were also trapped by circumstances they had not foreseen. George was a man of great determination, inclined to stubbornness: Germans and war would not stop him taking his usual spring holiday. The way was clear; ferries were still running across the Channel. So, taking their car, they had set out blithely for France sometime in early April.

Their daughter, Dorothy, and her husband [Ted Langton] had also driven out with their two children and joined them on the Riviera. Life there continued as usual, with only a watchful eye towards Italy, in case the Italians decided to join Hitler. In the middle of May, though, as news of the German advance filtered through, George was rushed to the English Hospital for an emergency appendicitis operation. Once he was out of danger, his daughter and family left for home, but

George was still in hospital and would not be able to drive for at least four weeks.

For the time being, they were alright. The fighting was all in the North, but, by now, anyone living on the Mediterranean coast was increasingly aware of the threat posed by Italy if they declared war on France and on her allies, which, of course, they did, on June 11. Meanwhile Tom, their eldest son, waited anxiously in England, to hear when his father would be thought fit enough to make the journey home. Through the Automobile Association, he managed to arrange for a driver to bring them back to England, with their car. It was a traumatic journey for them, and for their family awaiting news of them. Keeping to minor roads on the western side of France, they avoided the main roads, which were thronged by hordes of evacuees fleeing the north-eastern areas.

But make it back they did, having taken what is thought to have been the last sailing across the Channel. Meanwhile, back home and living in Liverpool, Ted reapplied to join the army and, this time, he was accepted and assigned to the Royal Pay Corps in Manchester. His prowess in the job proved to be his undoing; so much so that, when he applied for a transfer to the Royal Engineers, his Colonel refused to sanction it.

In the end, it was compassionate leave (to look after his sick wife) that enabled Ted to leave the Royal Pay Corps and join the Royal Engineers in Liverpool. Here, he was again given a job he knew something about; he was appointed Embarkation Officer, arranging troop movements and the like through Liverpool Docks, and eventually rising to the rank of captain. In 1945, the war came to an end. Ted was de-mobbed and turned his attentions not just to his Blue Cars, but to affairs at home.'

BLUE CARS – AFTER THE WAR

George Heaps died in 1942, just two years after returning from that eventful wartime journey from France. He left Dorothy and the rest of his six children each a small inheritance, which Dorothy, at Ted's behest, spent on purchasing the lease of the Red Lion Hotel, in Uttoxeter, soon to be followed by the lease of the Hotel Bradford, opposite the Liverpool Royal Exchange.

However, Dorothy and Ted's marriage was going through a difficult patch. By the end of the war the couple decided to separate, and when it came to the businesses, Dorothy took the Red Lion under her wing while Ted got the Bradford. He subsequently acquired the Lamb, in Ely, as well as hotels in Farnborough and Bodmin.

Ted now had to pick up the pieces of his former businesses: the Blue Cars emporium in Shaftesbury Avenue and the coach division in Belgium and France. The bad news was that his coaches in France had completely disappeared; the good news was that his fleet in Belgium was more or less intact. The task now was to continue with Blue Cars in much the same way as he had done before the war – easier said than done, not least because of the post-war restrictions on currency and travel. Nevertheless, by 1946 he was already planning the re-launch of Blue Cars, which, in due course, was to become one of the most important Continental touring companies not only in the UK, but in the US also.

In 1947-48, Ted entered into a partnership with US-based Percival Tours, who acted as general sales agents for 'Blue Cars Continental Coach Cruises', as Langton was now calling his operation. It was around this time that he also acquired the George Hotel in Colchester, which henceforth was to serve as his base for many years. He soon acquired other hotels, including Yarlington Manor in Somerset and a number of coaching inns that were run by his brother and sister.

By 1950, Ted was making a significant input into the design and manufacture of the vehicles that served as his Blue Car coaches, particularly the Leyland Royal Tiger. Indeed, one aspect of his coach operations was reviewed in the November 1950 edition of the *Coaching and Bus Review*. This told the story of how Langton was to take one of his re-designed coaches on a 12,000-mile tour of Canada and the US, as part of a promotional trip arranged in conjunction with Percival Tours. The journey culminated with the coach's arrival in Washington, in time for that year's ASTA Convention, and the headline of the article read: 'All Out for the Dollar Trade: Blue Cars' 12,000-mile Pilgrimage across the USA and Canada'.

By 1953, Ted owned hotels, coaching inns, a restaurant on the Brighton Road, a successful travel business and a coach company in Belgium. Yet, he decided to accept an offer of £145,000 for his travel business from the British Electric Traction (BET) company. It was a baffling decision, but there it was; Ted obviously had something else in mind. Perhaps he was fearful as to how the advent of affordable, reliable air travel might impact his coach-tour businesses – perhaps, too, he was already nurturing the idea of setting up his own air-travel arrangements.

Within a year of the sale, Ted had launched a new company, which he called 'Universal Sky Tours' (later Skytours). No sooner had the company's first brochure appeared, however, than BET applied for an injunction to stop it trading, arguing that Langton had breached the seven-year non-compete clause attached to his sale of Blue Cars (something that, today, would most certainly be classed as a restraint of trade).

In defence, Ted argued, quite rationally, that Blue Cars was concerned with the business of coach tours, whereas Universal Sky Tours, as the name implied, was in the business of air travel. It didn't wash with the judge, however, and although the injunction was lifted, BET were awarded damages amounting to £50,000.

THE PHILANTHROPIST & IMPRESARIO

Langton might have been a chain-smoker (not uncommon in those pre-health-conscious times), but, as Andy Sawicki recalls, he was always impeccably dressed, well-mannered and extremely kind to people he liked. Once, when he was staying at the Grand Hotel in Paris in 1945, Ted suddenly took a shine to two commis waiters. So impressed was he that he went on to sponsor them both at the renowned Lausanne Hotel School, the best in the world at the time. He also helped one of the waiters (Gerard – surname unknown) to buy his own hotel, at St Raphael on the French Riviera, and the other (Léo Roupioz) to set up his own travel company.

While visiting New York in 1957, Ted gave Richard Day $10,000 to open a company in the US, with the instruction that it should be called 'Universal Tours'. It just so happened that that particular name was already taken, so 'Unitours' was settled upon instead. Unitours later established offices in a number of countries and became one of the biggest operators of pilgrimages to the Holy Land.

Also at that New York meeting was the erstwhile waiter Léo Roupioz, who had earlier helped Ted on signing-up hotels for his various travel programmes. He too was given $10,000, and instructed to open a travel business in Paris likewise called Universal Tours, which he duly did. Tragically, Léo was to meet an untimely end in 1997, when a disgruntled ex-employee murdered him and his wife in their bed at the Grand Hotel Saint-Quentin, which Léo had owned and run together with another local hotel and three restaurants.

By 1970, the 'Langton Adventure Centre' had opened in the Lake District. Its stated aim was 'to be used as an adventure centre for character training, to help boys, girls and young people through their leisure-time activities, to develop their physical, mental and spiritual capacities so that they may grow to full maturity as individuals and members of society.' It came into being after Langton found himself being button-holed at his desk by a priest, Canon John Thursfield, who insisted that Ted should be the sponsor of this centre and who left, some hours later, with a large cheque. What's more, the Langton Adventure Centre is still going strong and still fulfilling its original aspirations.

Another example of Langton's largesse was when Andy Sawicki, Sid Silver and Julian Waterman left Thomson to form their own travel company, 4S. Ted offered up his own Mayfair office, on Conduit Street, charging only a peppercorn rent and finding a much smaller office for himself elsewhere.

Flushed with success, Ted was also something of an impresario. In the mid-1950s he had opened Winston's nightclub on Clifford Street, just across the road from one of his Sky Tours offices. The club became a well-known part of the

London nightlife scene, especially after Danny La Rue was lured from nearby Churchill's for a residency that lasted seven years and helped establish the careers of many other well-known performers, including Barbara Windsor, Ronnie Corbett and Barry Cryer.

The wider Langton family were deeply involved with their first love, horses, and this applied especially to Ted's daughters, now grown up and living in Somerset. Ted's interest in racehorses was kindled by a son-in-law owning a successful racehorse called Fighter Command, which, with the assistance of certain jockey named Sir Gordon Richards, went on to win a large number of races.

From the 1950s Ted also took to the seas, buying a yacht in Ramsgate which was later replaced by a converted German E-Boat, dubbed the *Pacemaker*. In the mid-'60s he bought the luxury eight-berth yacht, the *Glorongay*, in which his family regularly sailed along the Italian and Adriatic coasts. Ted, however, could rarely spare the time to enjoy his acquisitions and never once slept on board.

In 1965, the *Glorongay* wintered in Malta, a spot that Ted had always considered to be the ideal victualing location for what would become his Sovereign Cruises. Indeed, it was there that Ted cemented the deal that produced the Mellieha Bay Hotel. As for the *Glorongay*, she was sold, next heard of in Somalia, and ended up in Tanzania, where she sank and became a popular Indian Ocean scuba-diving site.

UNIVERSAL SKY TOURS

Right from the start, it became clear that being in charge of a company involved in international aviation was going to be a lot more complicated than just running coach tours. Anything to do with flights, including charter flights, was under tight government control, whether in the interests of safety or, as sometimes seemed to be the case, commercial protectionism. The jet age was in its infancy, and so far it had been a troubled childhood, with three de Havilland Comets crashing in the space of eight months between 1953 and 1954. As a result, anyone wanting to start operating air flights was required to jump through a number of bureaucratic hoops.

First, a licence was required. Applications had to be submitted months before the annual hearings of the Air Transport Licensing Board, whose main objective appeared to be to safeguard the routes operated by BEA and BOAC, the state-owned forerunners of British Airways.

As an added complication, the organisations that had to apply for the licence were not the operators but the airlines, who, in order to avoid the all-but-inevitable refusal, expressed a preference for routes to apparently minor destinations unwanted by the major airlines: Perpignan for Barcelona, Alicante for Valencia and Rimini (a military airport) for the Adriatic, in addition to a variety of small airports in Italy, Yugoslavia, Austria, Belgium and France. Similarly, applicants had to avoid the major British air hubs, with the result that smaller airports such as Croydon, Blackbush, Luton, Gatwick, Southend and Manston became essential to the success of any application.

Then there was the question of what constituted an airline. Once the war was over, an abundance of obsolete aircraft suddenly came onto the market, along with the men who had flown and repaired them. Some 400 airlines, mostly one- or two-aircraft operations without any money behind them, were created in a very short space of time. Once these outfits had fought off objections from the national carriers to obtain a licence, they too became fiercely protective of what they now considered to be their exclusive routes.

It was an unedifying display of double standards, but those operators who were unable to get an airline licence and couldn't employ a lawyer to fight their case found that they had only two alternatives. One was to use foreign airlines, which were usually more expensive, and which operated flight patterns unsuitable for the home market. The second was to buy up seats on aircraft chartered by other, successful applicants, which would naturally have to be sold at premium prices. This was the situation in which Langton found himself in 1953. He had set up an extensive programme for Skytours' debut season, and it would require all his ingenuity to get around the various obstacles in his way.

Ted got around this potential problem by commencing operations out of Blackbushe Airport, in Hampshire instead, but this required a lengthy coach journey out of London, on top of which very few airlines were inclined to fly from there. At the same time, he had failed, despite repeated attempts, to get a licence to fly to Palma, Mallorca. Refusing to abandon the idea, he came up with the idea of flying from Manston, in Kent, to Maastricht, from where he could take off again to Palma.

The way he set about securing more licences was to team up with the legendary Captain Marian Kozuba-Kozubski, a much decorated ex-Polish-Bomber Command pilot, and create a firm called Independent Air Travel (IAT), at first flying a single Douglas C-47 Dakota (the military version of the DC-3) out of Croydon Airport and, later, from Blackbushe.

However, Kozubski's operations were questionable to say the least, and before long the licensing board took away his operating licence. Undeterred, Kozubski simply painted the plane in a different livery, calling it Falcon Airways, and proceeded to conjure the same illusion over the following years, with the name Blue Sky and a variety of other surrogates. It was a device that kept the Dakota and his other aircraft in the air, of that there is no doubt. However, this eventually wore thin even in the eyes of Langton, who realised that his continuing association with Kozubski would mean only perpetual conflict with the authorities.

Ted began to look elsewhere for aviators and decided to try and set up his own airline. Through J.E.D. Williams, a former BOAC pilot-turned-consultant, he made contact with the Israeli state airline, El Al, which, he understood, was selling three of its Lockheed Constellations. The purchase of these aircraft marked the birth of the airline initially known as Euravia. With the addition of five more Constellations obtained from Skyways, a long established operator then in decline, Ted based a substantial fleet at Luton's fledgling airport – the first tour operator to do so.

On 5 May 1962, the first Constellation filled with Skytours' passengers took off from the UK. In those days, aircraft costings were based on the principle of direct operational costs, which took into consideration the fact that the planes only flew at weekends, from Friday midday to Sunday night – i.e., the times that the vast majority of package-tour passengers could manage. This rendered the planes redundant for the rest of the week, and so Langton's next priority was to find a way of making use of them then.

A man named Peter Sinclair, owner of a small Southampton-based company called Flightways, first recognised the advantage of midweek flying: low aircraft costs, no deposits and no contract penalties. He set up a 10- and 11-day holiday operation, flying into Madrid and then taking passengers by coach on to Malaga or Tangier. Back then, however, these were still obscure destinations and the programme failed miserably. Nonetheless, Langton saw that the basic idea was sound – what had let it down was the combination of remote destinations, high ticket prices and the gruellingly long coach journey. He spent the next few months tinkering with the component parts and, the very next year, launched his own 11- and 12-day programmes to the Costa Brava.

These proved to be tremendously popular and were soon oversubscribed, encouraging Ted to expand the principle to Mallorca and other resorts, thereby making maximum use of his aircraft and allowing him to reduce his weekend prices while increasing profits. Other operators flocked to follow his example, and in next to no time midweek travel became an established business practice.

Meanwhile, as the company grew, so did the need for aircraft to replace the Constellations, and Langton discovered that BOAC had mothballed six of its Bristol Britannia 102s at Cambridge Airport, in order to make way for new aircraft. He not only bought five of these planes, but also, in 1964, changed the name of the airline from Euravia to the altogether more patriotic and glamorous-sounding Britannia Airways.

By this time, the 'Captain' was no longer a young man, having entered his seventh decade. In April 1965, he sold Skytours and Britannia Airways lock, stock and barrel to the Thomson group, who were looking to invest in a business unrelated to media. It was not a smooth transaction by any means: the Thomson hierarchy, for whom Ted had nothing but contempt, found him unhelpful and uncooperative. Still, the sale went ahead, even though the auditors maintained that profitability was minimal and management almost non-existent, with almost every decision, no matter how small, being made by Ted.

His only regret was to have sold Skytours too cheaply. The deal was based on a lump sum in advance and the rest, limited to £700,000, was to be related to performance under the stewardship of Thomson, who in their first year of operation made a profit of over £1 million. Perhaps predictably, the relationship ended sourly, with the Captain returning one day to find that the new owners had changed the locks to his office.

SOVEREIGN CRUISES

Ted's last solo venture was to resuscitate a cruise programme that had been side-lined at the time of the sale to Thomson, involving hiring the *Queen Frederica* from the Chandris Line. Like Langton's other enterprises, it proved a huge success. Ideally though, Ted wanted to own his own ships, so, in 1969, he bought the French passenger vessel *Floriana*. Once she was in dry-dock, however, the stripping-out process revealed that refurbishment would be uneconomical, and so he sold her for scrap.

Soon after came the *Galaxy Queen* – which eventually was to let everyone down (after having been delayed by many weeks coming into service, she continually broke down – in the end both the programme and the ship were abandoned – having cost both Langton and his partner Sergio Mantegazza of Cosmos a small fortune) – and, lastly, the Bulgarian passenger ship *Varna*, for a programme of Sovereign back-to-back fly-cruises. But although these sold extremely well, the bad experience of the *Galaxy Queen*, together with the 1973 oil price shock, finally convinced him to suspend passenger cruise operations until more propitious times.

THE FINAL YEARS

One of Langton's restaurants of choice was The French Horn, overlooking the Thames at Sonning. He had got to know the owner fairly well and once tried to buy it, but it was not for sale. So, in 1959, he looked around for another property and found a little pub at Bray in an idyllic location, again on the Thames, complete with a huge weeping willow sweeping over the water. Langton extensively transformed the property and renamed it The Waterside. In 1970 he sold it on to the Roux Brothers, who changed the name to what is now the famed Waterside Inn.

Langton then retired to Mallorca and bought a property, Casa Lynne, in Son Vida. An exclusive, country club-type development (all golf and cocktail parties), it wasn't to his liking, so he moved to a villa in San Agustin. Ultimately, unable to resist the temptation, he bought the small Hotel Morocco in Palma Nova, where, in his latter days, he could be found passing the time of day, accompanied by his dog, Zek.

Suddenly but peacefully, in his sleep, Thomas Edwin David Langton died in Mallorca on 6 July 1978, at the age of 74: a bright and leading light in the business of travel had finally gone out. Ted may have started out by selling lockets of his hair for a penny, but he ended up laying the foundations of a company that is arguably the most important travel business in the world: Thomson Holidays.

The Captain's final journey was to be one he hadn't planned, however. After plenty of ups and downs – after their divorce, they got back together much later in life and even remarried – Ted and Dorothy Langton were once again living apart at the time of Ted's death. Twenty years later, in 1998, their two daughters resolved that Ted should be brought back home to England, to the small village church at Long Load in Somerset, in order to be reunited with, and laid to rest alongside, his wife, Dorothy. It was a poignant moment.

FOOTNOTE: Although he was christened 'Thomas', no one ever called the Captain by that name. To people within the travel business, he was known as Ted. To his family, he was always known as Edwin.

THE SHIP SAILS ON

In addition to acquiring Skytours (and Britannia Airways) from Ted Langton, Lord Thomson also purchased Riviera Holidays from Aubrey Morris, a former taxi driver, along with two other companies, Luxitours and Gaytours, from Norman Corkhill. The result was what can only be described as a gallimaufry of travel companies, each located in a different part of the country and specialising in different spheres of activity.

In retrospect, Langton was probably right: Thomson did not know what they were doing, at least to start with. At first, these separate companies were allowed to develop as they had under their original ownership, but it wasn't long before some parts of this disjointed empire began to falter, not helped by Thomson using managers with no experience of the travel trade.

Soon, other companies like Clarksons and Court Line were romping away, leaving the Thomson group of companies to flounder in their wake, both in terms of product spread and overall passenger numbers.

A PASSAGE TO MESSINA

In the late '60s, I had been sent by Skytours to Tunisia, both to evaluate the country as a possible tourist destination and to travel on board Captain Langton's ship, the *Queen Federica*, to Malta, where Skytours were building a hotel. I travelled with a gentleman of unknown Middle Eastern origin who was slightly podgy, had greased and flattened black hair and always wore the nattiest of suits, whatever climate he found himself in. His name was Maurice Sakal and he had been with Langton from the very earliest days; in fact, he had been the manager of Ted's George Hotel in Colchester at one point, but was now working for the company's hotel-owning-and-managing arm, which comprised the Arenal Park in Mallorca and the soon-to-be completed Mellieha Bay Hotel in Malta.

On arrival in Tunis, it was raining cats and dogs. The area was experiencing some of the worst floods in its history, and our first impression was: 'Some tourist destination, this!' Thankfully, our hotel was located on higher ground and, later that day, in the bar, I came to appreciate the full range of Maurice's hotel management skills.

During the course of the evening, he suddenly announced that, in his opinion, the barman was 'on the fiddle'. When I asked why he thought that, he pointed to the array of various spirits on the back-bar and replied: "You see that bottle of vodka? It has been watered down." Clearly intent on showing this novice (i.e., me) the full extent of the Byzantine and myriad methods of bar-fiddling, he then asked the sheepish barman to hand him the suspect bottle.

Taking the bottle in hand, Maurice turned it upside down and a distinct line appeared at once, showing where the water had separated the vodka. What's more, once the bottle had been shaken up, you could see a dead mosquito floating inside it. Maurice's observations were clearly spot-on: there was no mistaking the curled-lip snarl with which the barman put the bottle back in its place.

On turning in for bed that night, Maurice, who was definitely from the old-fashioned, gentlemanly school of travel, took his shoes off and left them outside his bedroom door, expecting some lackey to come and clean them. Unfortunately, however, this shoe-cleaning custom had fallen into disuse in this particular Tunisian outpost of would-be civilisation and, next morning, I found Maurice wandering around the reception on his stockinged feet, ranting that someone had pinched his shoes.

No one was owning up to this dastardly deed, but I couldn't help suspecting that the barman had been involved in some way. Before driving to the quay and boarding the *Queen Federica*, we stopped at a nearby souk, where Maurice bought a pair of flip-flops that looked rather at odds with his pin-striped suit.

On boarding the ship, I was reminded of the brain-teaser, 'Why are sardines packed so tightly?' Answer: 'Because the oil is much more expensive than the actual fish.' The fact was, with its seemingly never-ending, narrow corridors, the *Queen Federica* had all the appearance of a sardine tin, and without the oil excuse either – clearly, Captain Langton considered the experience of being on the ocean compensation enough for his customers.

Throughout my time on that vessel, I cannot remember finding anything resembling what might have been the lounge – I was permanently lost. What I can remember, though, is the weather. The storm that had raged over Tunisia was now sitting squarely over Malta and, without bow thrusters, the *Queen Federica* made several valiant attempts to enter the narrow harbour entrance at Valletta before diverting to Messina, Sicily, where I disembarked and made my own rather circuitous journey back to Malta.

POTALA PALACE, LHASA, TIBET BY ALISON MUSKER

A Story in Brief:

THE LONE WOLF: 'Our father (Captain Langton – Skytours) was not a Chamber of Commerce man or anything like that, much more of a lone wolf. When it came to building up a business, he was the management, there was no management structure, and all decisions were taken by him. And when the whole thing got too big, he would become receptive to offers, and his mind would move on to other ideas. Someone in the travel trade once remarked "Where Langton goes – the rest follow". Although some thought he was a risk taker he would not have agreed. He knew he could always make his ideas work'. June Langton.
IMAGE COURTESY: ALISON MUSKER/VJV.

CHAPTER 60
COMETH THE HOUR

Morale was low but, thanks to Bryan Llewellyn, all the fractious parts
were joined into a united fighting force to be reckoned with. Before
long, we were in a fit state to take on all comers.

BY the time Bryan Llewellyn arrived in late 1969, some five years had
elapsed since the Thomson group had bought a disparate bunch of tour
operators and, in the interim, there had been five different managing
directors appointed to run the travel division, all of whom had failed miserably
to meld the tour operators into a coherent whole.

Meanwhile, Clarksons Holidays, run by ex-naval officer Tom Gullick, were
out-gunning us in every department. Morale was low but, thanks to the appointment of Llewellyn, all the fractious parts were joined into a united fighting force
to be reckoned with. Before long, we were in a fit state to take on all comers, and
we would eventually see off Clarksons, turning ourselves from a basket case into
an outfit that would end up being sold for £1.7 billion pounds.

One thing that everyone could agree on was that without Bryan Llewellyn,
there would most definitely not have been such a happy ending for Thomson
Holidays. However, despite being one of the most successful and prolific pioneers
of mass tourism, a recent interview with Bryan revealed that he held no lofty
notions about how he came into the business:

"I joined around about the time when Roy [Lord Thomson] had just sold off
Scottish Television and the Thomson Organisation's managing director, Gordon
Brunton, was looking for another 'cash cow'.

What had attracted Thomson to the travel industry was the fact that customers had to pay up long before they actually went on holiday. The trouble was,
they needed someone who could knit those different firms together and, at the
start, they had problems finding the right person for the job. I was the fifth

managing director in the space of 18 months, and I found out later that people in the building were running a book on how long I would last.

I knew nothing about travel, but I did have experience of management, and that, in my view, is a skill which is infinitely transferrable. No matter what your business, you need to find answers to the same three questions: what's your market; how do you cater for it at the least cost; and what staff do you need to help you get there?

The fourth question is: what do you call your company? The decision was taken to bring all the newly acquired firms under a single Thomson banner. As for the logo, the team alighted upon a seagull, on the grounds that it symbolised escape, the seaside and a certain soaring, independent quality.

Next the hard work started, in spreading the word around the nation's estate agents. To this end a short promotional film was put together, aiming to encapsulate the whole notion of a holiday; it began with blue sky, the sound of an aircraft engine and a cheery, capable pilot turning round in his seat to welcome you, the viewer, on board.

The film went out on the road and was shown at drinks receptions, not just to the bosses of travel agencies, but also to all their frontline counter staff, who would be handling the bookings when they came in. And those bookings did come in, in their hundreds of thousands. Key to this success was price.

We were going for the broad mass market, where the cost of the holiday is everything. We discovered that, for every one per cent you discounted, your sales volume went up one per cent accordingly. We were, at that time, in head-to-head competition with our rivals, Clarksons, who were a real nuisance. The fact was that the public didn't care which firm they booked through; they only cared about the price.

So, I went to Gordon Brunton and told him that I was going to chop our prices by 10 per cent, which would create a massive loss in the short term, but would have far greater, larger benefits in the long term. To his credit, he got this straight away, and said: 'OK, I'll present this as us investing half a million pounds, rather than losing half a million pounds.'

And it worked. Pretty much from the moment our brochure came out, with our reduced prices, the Clarksons' death warrant was on the table. We had taken them completely by surprise. They were shocked and they crumbled – they simply didn't have our back-up resources. Before long, they had collapsed and Court Line, their airline, had gone down with them in January 1974.

Prior to that, I had actually had discussions with Tom Gullick, Clarksons' managing director, with a view to our two companies joining forces. It was a very long lunch – 13 hours, as I recall – but, at the end of it, we decided to go our

A Story in Brief

ON AND OFF THE MAURITANIA: 'Both Norma and I had bad reactions to the jab – a requirement for getting into the States at the time, and felt so bad during the first week we are both very hazy about the whole visit. As I recall, sometime in 1948 Mr Percival (of Percival Tours) met us in New York, where we stayed for a couple of days, before travelling by car down to Miami. We had two stops on the way, the second one in Washington, where Percival had arranged some publicity; I remember coming out of some large building and being greeted by flashing cameras, which I don't think Father (Captain Langton) was happy about. In Miami, we found large hotels and very few people, as it was out of season; all of which meant that 24 hours was enough for Father, and he decided to fly back to New York. On finding that the *Mauritania* was due to sail the next day, he managed to get berths for us. He never went back to America'. June Langton. **IMAGE COURTESY: BRYAN LLEWELLYN.**

separate ways.

Coincidentally, Brunton and I were having lunch with Tom and his wife, at their exquisite house in Regents Park, when the phone started ringing, with news that Clarksons was in serious trouble. Tom, who was a charming man, an ex-naval officer, found himself being increasingly drawn away from the cold salmon by all these phone calls and, at one point, he came back and said: "They've pulled the plug on us."

Having won the war, we then set about winning the peace, taking on more and more aeroplanes, pushing up passenger volumes and building more and more hotels, mainly in Spain (one or two looked OK, but most were hideous). Keen to hone this holiday product ever more closely to his customers' specifications, we began to introduce the kind of marketing methods not hitherto seen within the travel industry. One of the first things we identified was that large numbers of our holidaymakers were travelling with young children, as a result of which Thomson developed packages that would include not just things for the children to do, but staff to look after them too.

Next came the questionnaires, which all returning passengers were asked to fill in and hand back to the stewardesses when they got off the plane. I can't stress too strongly how fundamental these questionnaires were to our operation. If someone told us, for example, that there was an open sewer next to the hotel where they had stayed, we would leap on it straight away and sort it out.

The other big improvement was the setting up of our 'real time' computer booking system instead of what we had before which amounted not much more than to a rather large accounting register, but a lot less efficient to boot. It took longer than we had hoped to get up and running, but eventually it meant that, instead of having to ring us, travel agents could call up available holidays on screen, at the touch of a button, and book them on the spot. We had these massive IBM computers, powered by a huge diesel generator in the basement that would keep the system running in the event of power cuts – of which we had quite a few, in those days.

We also started up three- and four-night holidays in Moscow and Leningrad. I remember taking a press trip to Red Square, in the course of which the novelist, Jilly Cooper, went up to this great big Russian guard and started kissing him. That went quite well in the end, but, three weeks before the flights were due to start, I got a very worrying phone call. There had been a bit of a spying row and Britain had just got rid of a lot of people from the Soviet Embassy in London; suddenly, there was this Russian man on the phone, telling me, in a rather sinister voice, that, unless the British authorities reneged on these decisions, our planes would not be taking off.

Straight away, I rang the Foreign Office and said: 'Look, I'm out of my depth here, we've got a lot of people booked on these planes.' To my astonishment, the person at the other end said, in a very calm voice, that they already knew about the phone call and that I was to go ahead with the flights, as planned. I have to say, I found it all rather unnerving. It was as if someone had lifted the floorboards and I'd got a glimpse into the workings of a different world."

Given that Thomson Holidays was very much Llewellyn's baby, and a vastly bigger and higher-earning baby than it had been when he took over, it seems surprising that he should have been among the first to suggest that the division be sold off. But to him, ever the businessman, it was only logical: I said, "Look, this is a high-risk industry; we should think about selling up and getting out." In terms of finding buyers, I had a meeting with Jimmy [Sir James] Goldsmith, who turned up in his Rolls-Royce, and I flew out to New York for a week, for discussions with American Express. In the end, the eventual sale of Thomson Holidays, to TUI for £1.7 billion in 2000, happened decades after Llewellyn had left, having been summarily shifted to the publishing wing of Thomson following the sudden death of his predecessor from a heart attack:

"I asked if I had a choice, and was told that I wasn't in an Eastern bazaar now, and that negotiating wasn't an option. I did run the publishing companies for two years, but then left.

Looking back, I can see that the travel business in those days was very different from what it is today. Yes, Clarksons were our biggest competitors, but we respected them, and, at the height of our rivalry, in 1970, when a plane of theirs crashed into the Pyrenees (112 passengers and crew killed), we sent a note straight away, saying: 'What do you want? How can we help? Tell us, and we'll provide it.' I remember another occasion, when we were building a new hotel in Corfu and Clarksons' boss, Tom Gullick, sent us a cardboard box. Inside was a tiny tortoise he had picked up, which had been displaced by our construction work! As I say, different times."

There is no doubt in my mind that, wherever the head office of Thomson Holidays is now, there should be two plaques displayed, bearing the names of Bryan Llewellyn and 'Captain' Ted Langton respectively.

CHAPTER 61
THE WANDERING MONK

I knew for certain that I would move on from being a monk to
vocation number two (a resort representative) and I asked the
monastery to apply to Rome for me to be laicised.

H E rose to become overseas director of Thomson Holidays, but Paul Diggins
began his life as a Benedictine monk in Belgium. Here he looks back over
his unusual journey:

"I came from a family of six children; the first three of us were born during
the war, and the second three in post-war and deprived England. For a substantial
part of the war, my father was with Earl Mountbatten and General Slim fighting
in Burma. It was a dreadful war arena: the Japanese enemy was determined and
fearless and the Burmese, after years of British oppression, were looking for
liberation. Battles were relentless and the British were holed up in the jungle, an
unkind terrain and one the British were not trained to conquer. The Battle of the
Admin Box was a tragedy, with the Japanese setting a square mile of fire in the
jungle surrounding the British 'administrative area'. My father was inside. Few
survived!

Following VJ day my father, with the remnants of his platoon, was relocated
to Siam. Because of its co-operation with the Japanese, Siam was occupied by
Britain for some months after the war. I was almost six before my father returned
to the UK and saw me for the first time.

I was born in Suffolk and for the first six years of my life had been brought
up by my mother and her sisters in 'The Old Manse' in Rendham, an idyllic house
full of Victorian character – children playing in all rooms, in the outhouses, in
the gardens and at the stream, blissfully unaware of the London blitz. Schooling
was basic and at the local village school where my mother and her sisters had all
been pupils 30 years before. Eventually we returned to London and to reality and

to meet with my father. We moved to Cockfosters.

My father was Irish, an Irish Catholic, but it was my Anglican mother who was mainly responsible for religious discipline within the family. Every Sunday, we would go twice, or sometimes three times, to church. We had no car and had to walk some distance to get there in the early morning – there were some wicked, cold and foggy winters in those post-war years. Later on, mass became an almost daily activity for me, slotted in at six o'clock in the morning before returning home for breakfast and running to catch the eight o' clock school bus.

I was a grammar-school boy and attended nearby Finchley Catholic Grammar, founded between the wars by Cannon Parsons and later run by him and several secular priests. I well remember early discussions with my mother about my Latin and Classics studies. Much of our church and school lives depended on Latin, the vernacular only coming into common usage after the Second Vatican Council. From quite early on, it was evident – perhaps inevitable – that I would become religious.

Our Catholic parish in Cockfosters was run by a group of Benedictine monks. The order had its origins in Sienna, in Italy, and the monks were variously from Belgium and Holland, Ireland and England and the abbot was an Italian. At the age of 18, I chose to join this community and become a Benedictine myself. They were unusual: they were white-robed Benedictines and had their study house near Leuven (Louvain) in Belgium, seat of the largest Catholic university in northern Europe. I was intrigued by the international mélange and the make-up of the community.

The study house, which was situated 12 kilometres from Leuven, was in a small village called Gelrode, near Aarscott. Lectures were in French, but within the house we also spoke Flemish and some English. We had to work, of course, as well as study. I chose to work in the kitchens, which was less arduous than being out in the fields and, as we were assisted by several kitchen workers from the nearby village, also enabled me to learn and then improve my Flemish.

At the end of my studies I was transferred to London and was very unhappy. I was cut off from my monastic community, almost alone and isolated. I was sad and lonely and began thinking about the rest of my life. I was 24 and started to have doubts about my monastic stamina – could I do this for the rest of my life?

I returned to Belgium to discuss my future with the Abbot. We discussed various options and decided to apply for temporary exclaustration; this meant living outside the study house, having to support myself, and to remain in Belgium so I could make regular visits to the mother house.

So I needed a job, a means of support, a place to live and a new structure to my life. I spoke languages and my brother told me he had recently been on a

A Story in Brief

NEVER ON SUNDAY: *The Boys from Piraeus* is a 1960 Greek black-and-white film, and it's a variation on George Bernard Shaw's play *Pygmalion*. It tells the story of two people. Firstly, Ilya, a self-employed, free-spirited prostitute who lives in the port of Piraeus in Greece. And secondly Homer, an American tourist from Middletown, Connecticut, a classical scholar in love with all things Greek. Feeling that Ilya's lifestyle typifies the degradation of Greek classical culture, he tries to steer her back onto the path of morality. The film stars Melina Mercouri (later Minister of Culture) and Jules Dassin, and it gently submerges the viewer into Greek culture, including dance, music, and language. The signature song, *Never On Sunday,* and the bouzouki theme of the film became big hits in the 1960s, and won the composer, Manos Hadjidakis, an Academy Award. The film harks back to a kinder, gentler, perhaps more naive Greece of the popular imagination – and one that certainly influenced me. IMAGE COURTESY: PAUL DIGGINS.

package holiday and was looked after by an English tour guide. It was a summer season-only position but it seemed ideal for me. I applied and got a job with a small London-based tour company called Riviera Holidays. Founded, owned and run by a tour-operating pioneer, Aubrey Morris, Riviera Holidays was a friendly organisation, everyone on first name terms and so much kissing. You kissed when you met, you kissed again when you said goodbye and there might be several other kisses in between.

For a prim Irish Catholic, recently out from his monastery, this all made a great impression. I enjoyed the work immensely, seemed to fit in so easily and although initially daunted by the prospects of being out there alone, I was definitely a survivor. During that first summer season Aubrey sold his company to The Thomson Organisation. I had no understanding in 1966 just what impact that would have on my life.

It was a seasonal job, with no long-term prospects for most, but I was already institutionalised, liked living in hotels, was a comfortable team player and was happy and successful. I understood that life outside the monastery could also be fun!

By the end of that summer, I knew for certain that I would move on to vocation number two and I asked the monastery to apply to Rome for me to be laicised, returning me to my original lay status. I went to America for the winter and waited for the process to complete. The following spring Thomson asked me to return and work for them in Tangier, Morocco, till recently an international town, full of intrigue and mystery and the complete antithesis of everything I knew. I stayed in North Africa for five years.

It was so very different, to say the least, from my life in the monastery. At that time, Tangier was a most unusual and unconventional place. It was where the underworld took its holiday, where the unconventional scions of aristocratic families were sent into exile, where the rich and famous came to indulge and hide. It was hedonism from morning to night.

My workday started at 7.30am with early-excursion coach departures to places like Tetouan and Asilah, Gibraltar and Seuta. I would then visit clients in their hotels, attend to finance and paper work, go to the airport to collect new arrivals and eventually, tired in the evening, go to one of the town's watering holes. My favourite was El Piano, run by two wonderful characters from Yorkshire called Syd and Dennis.

Then, Tangier was a haven for the gay community, for those attracted to 'wacky backy', shisha and other Oriental delights. There were at least 30 gay bars in town, all run by expat men and women and situated either on the beach for daytime amusement or in town for evening and night entertainment. The El Piano cabaret bar was different. It had previously been the cabaret spot for the French community and loosely attached to the Embassy, whereas much of the property in that part of town was owned by the Bute Estate, the Scottish-Catholic family from the Isle of Bute. But what really distinguished the El Piano was that Dennis, without being able to read a note of music, could play on the piano almost anything from Noël Coward to Winifred Attwell, from Bach to Mrs Mills. Meanwhile Syd held court at the bar with banter and chat, wit and repartee. It was a good place to recommend to my holiday-makers; they always had fun there and might even meet Kenneth Williams or Joe Orton, Stanley Baxter, Rita Tushingham or James Coburn at the bar.

Tangier was so different then. A small port town, set along Mediterranean and Atlantic beaches, with a population of some 140,000, more than 50,000 of them Spanish. It had just started to adjust from its earlier international status to the small city it is today, with over one and a half million Moroccan nationals. Islam now has a greater influence, almost all of the bars have disappeared, the cabaret spots proscribed, the international restaurants and shops replaced with hamburger bars and mobile-phone shops. Those people from the Rif Mountains and Tétouan, together with the native 'Tangerines', have recolonised their own city. The smuggling and intrigue has long gone and has, reputedly, been replaced with people-trafficking from Africa to Europe.

Philip and I first met in Tangier where I arrived by way of Belgium and he from Benidorm. Then came the great Greek adventure. Thomson opened up their first air programme to Greece in 1970 and I was asked to transfer to this new destination. I left North Africa in tears; I so wanted my new life of hedonism and freedom to go on and on. But it was not to be: although the early Greek programme was insignificant in size, the country had been identified and highlighted as the next boom destination.

In our first year we started with a humble capacity of 3,500 passengers into Athens, and 20 years later had grown the business to almost 900,000, featuring all major destinations including Corfu, Crete, Rhodes, Kos and Halkidiki and many lesser-known islands as well. What started as a short season into Athens finally became a March-through-to-November operation and second only to Spain by volume.

In 1972 I became resort manager for Athens, later regional manager for the whole of Greece and eventually general manger for all beach destinations outside of Spain. Without realising it, I was on my way back to London!

I was amazed at how quickly I adapted to life in Greece. I was a vegetarian and therefore loved the diet, I loved the sea and island life, I had a partner – he was Greek and spoke little English, so I was soon able to express myself in the language. I was so very comfortable, I made that world my own, and soon became synonymous with Thomson Greece.

The Greek people were no doubt the best friends you could ever have, but woe betide you if you crossed them, as they were implacable and the worst of enemies. They had a code of honour, particularly toward strangers (xenos): they were hospitable, friendly; they would take you in and look after you, feed and clothe you. As a foreigner, you were their guest, so very unlike the Britain I knew, the land I had grown up in. However, there were some extraordinary times. For a period Greece became the battleground of the Palestinian conflict. One afternoon in 1973, we had taken clients to Athens airport, for their return to the UK, when they became embroiled in a highjack attempt at the airport. There were grenade explosions and gunshots fired in the lower departure lounge where departing passengers were assembled.

Two young Palestinians were in the building attempting to highjack a flight, firing machine guns and throwing grenades across the floor. It was carnage and horror. It was a total nightmare. All flights were diverted and the Palestinians held a group of hostages for several hours. Luckily none of our clients was killed, though some were badly injured. Finally the attackers surrendered to the police, and we were able to gather up our clients, who had fled throughout the terminal and onto the tarmac, all their possessions abandoned.

Several months later two more Palestinians took a group of tourists hostage inside a large hotel on Syntagma Square. Then a TWA flight carrying Demis Roussos was hijacked from Athens, diverted to Jordan and, fortunately after all the passengers had been released, blown to pieces on an isolated airfield. Finally another TWA flight overhead Greece was punctured in the side of its fuselage when a bomb exploded in the cargo hold, though the captain valiantly made it safely to Athens airport.

In 1974 there was the Cyprus crisis, when the Greek junta tried to annex Cyprus and moved against Archbishop Makarios and the Cyprus government, threatening the fine balance of power on the island and alarming the Turkish minority. There were several months of conflict and so we had to evacuate our clients in both Greece and Cyprus and reposition our staff – a logistical nightmare, as all Greek airports except Crete and Rhodes were closed. In Cyprus we used the British airbase facilities at Akrotiri; in Greece we bussed holidaymakers to Patras and then took them by ferry to Brindisi, where they were airlifted by a special fleet from Britannia Airways.

This military-style operation had to be arranged from our office in Athens. We were only three people, phone connections with the outside world were poor – they were not automatic and went through an operator – and we often had to rely on the telex, again not a very robust communication system. But eventually all passengers were repatriated and staff were repositioned to Tunisia, Malta and Sicily.

My Greek went from strength to strength and by this time I had acquired the epithet digginopoulos. Most Greeks assumed I was of Greek origin, perhaps a Greek from abroad, but I was not! I would count in Greek, would often dream in Greek and developed 'Greek' solutions to many a Greek problem: small problems needed a small gift, and larger problems might mean a return flight to London or an unusual holiday. London was always very supportive, very understanding.

After the Cyprus crisis we restarted programmes to Greece and in the winter added exotic 'bolt-on' destinations from Athens. We twinned Athens with Damascus, with Baghdad, with Amman and with Cairo. They were all good fun to arrange and, like the curate's egg, good in parts. The 20-seats-per-week Cairo bolt-on has now evolved into an enormous Thomson presence in Egypt of more than a quarter-million passengers each year.

Then we did China. Philip and I went to China soon after the time when Mao Zedong was in power. The Gang of Four were being investigated, Beijing was full of bicycles and the obligatory Mao suits came in two colours only, navy blue and khaki/olive green. It was a time of the Friendship stores, the Underground City, the Peking Hotel, the Summer Palace and the Forbidden City, recently opened to non-Chinese nationals. It was exciting and, in retrospect, quite a brave thing to do.

In 1988 I was asked for the second time to relocate to London. Michaeli and I and the two dogs, the furniture, pans and pictures were all transferred to London and within weeks I was offered the position of Overseas Director. It was an enormous task, a great responsibility: over 2,500 employees working throughout many holiday destinations, buying beds and services for over five million passengers, with a purchasing budget of almost £1 billion and delivering a quality, value-for-money holiday experience. It was so very critical to get the purchasing and delivery in balance. I enjoyed it immensely – the challenge, the kudos, the status – and did the job for six years. These were happy professional years but sadly overshadowed by Michaeli's health issues. He died from cancer in 1993.

It was my cathartic moment, and shortly after I decided to leave Thomson after almost 30 years of service and leave England for another land. I considered a move to either Istanbul or Cairo and eventually chose Egypt for its milder winters. Another land, another language and another experience. After several years there, Philip recommended me for a position in Sub-Saharan Africa and so I worked for six years in Zimbabwe, Kenya, South Africa, Zambia and Tanzania, until the group was broken up and sold to local indigenous organisations.

I look back to my early life in Rendham, Suffolk, home to George Crabbe, Thomas Churchyard and Edward Fitzgerald, and muse on what might have been.'

CHAPTER 62
LIFE BEYOND THE ANJOU CLUB

Once de-mobbed, Aubrey Morris became a taxi driver, earning himself
the nickname 'Red' due to his lifelong socialist views.

BORN into a tight-knit Jewish community in the East End of London in 1919, Aubrey Morris left school at the age of 14 and began work as a van driver, delivering the bagels his father baked.

His grandparents had fled to London to escape the persecution of Jews at the hands of the Russian Tsars and, in the 1930s, Aubrey found himself involved in street battles against the anti-Semitic followers of home-grown British fascist leader Oswald Mosley. Later, after joining up at the start of World War II, he then found himself fighting the advancing Nazis, during the course of which he was evacuated from Dunkirk.

Once de-mobbed, Aubrey became a taxi driver, earning himself the nickname 'Red' due to his lifelong socialist views. It was only when he came back from a Mediterranean holiday that he alighted upon the career that was eventually to make him wealthy. Together with his school friend, Joe Morrison, Aubrey set up a travel agency called Riviera Holidays, which took off when the pair of them started booking group holidays to the Continent, first for a football team (Bedford & Kempsford Rovers), then for workers at the Sainsbury's sausage factory and, most spectacularly of all, for supporters of the great Tottenham Hotspur football team of the early 1960s.

In December 1960, Aubrey officially gave up cab-driving. By the following March, he had arranged the first-ever air charter operation for football fans, flying some 2,500 Spurs supporters (of whom he was one) to an away match in Rotterdam. There then followed many similar nights of European football, as the all-conquering Tottenham team, captained by Danny Blanchflower, travelled across the Continent, taking on Europe's best.

In his autobiography, Aubrey recalls a match played in Lisbon against the mighty S.L. Benfica team:

'The game was played under floodlights, on a beautiful warm evening, with kick-off at 9.00pm. By far, the majority of those who travelled with us had never before experienced the all-embracing warmth of the southern (sic) hemisphere.'

It wasn't just football fans to whom Aubrey gave a first taste of the Mediterranean. Soon, Riviera Holidays were taking planeload after planeload of British holidaymakers out to sample the sun – the more people that travelled with them, the more popular the package holiday became.

'Building Riviera Holidays necessitated an ever-extending programme and, soon, it was Benidorm on the Costa Blanca and Fuengirola, Torremolinos and Marbella on the Andalusian coast,' Aubrey records. 'Everywhere, hotels were being erected, larger and larger, with more and more beds, to satisfy the exponential demands of the holidaymakers. We were forever seeking new countries, resorts, hotels and, occasionally, modes of transport. Within a short time, we had extended to Yugoslavia, Ibiza, Sorrento, the Venetian Riviera, Morocco and Greece.'

It was a time of non-stop growth and high excitement. Aubrey talks of how tour reps were selected by a primitive process whereby appointments were made less on qualifications than on 'intuition and need'. He also observes how the tourist industry sent ripples across Spain's hitherto rigid class system:

'According to the Spanish custom of primogeniture, the eldest son was entitled to the major assets of an estate, while the others were treated with diminishing rewards. Now, Spain at that time was an agricultural country and, consequently, the land was split between the sons accordingly. The youngest had always inherited land nearest the sea and, up until the advent of tourism, there was little he could do with it. Then came tourism and, suddenly, the land nearest the beach carried the greater value and the greater number of possibilities.'

All of a sudden, however, the adventure came to an abrupt halt for Aubrey, when in 1965 his business partner, Joe Morrison, announced that he wanted to sell up and leave the company, and that he had lined up a company willing to buy it: the Thomson group, who were already in the process of snapping up rival firms Skytours and Britannia Airways.

A lunch was held to discuss the deal and was attended by the two Riviera founders, Horizon boss Vladimir Raitz and Thomson Organisation's joint managing director Gordon Brunton. It was, writes Aubrey, a gloomy experience:

'It was obvious that everything had been agreed earlier between them, with the exception being that Brunton insisted I remained in the business, under a contract which forbade me from setting up as a tour operator for a number of years. I spent that evening with my family, a few colleagues and friends, with a

A Story in Brief

THE GAY HUSSAR: This is the Soho restaurant that for many years was a home-from-home for left-wing politicians. It all began in the 1950s, when Aneurin Bevan began to dine there, followed by other Labour MPs such as Barbara Castle and Ian Mikardo. It's here that Labour Party chairman Tom Driberg is said to have tried (unsuccessfully) to get Mick Jagger to stand as a Labour candidate, and it's also here that Tony Blair was persuaded (successfully, this time, by Tom Pendry) to run for Prime Minister. The restaurant was also the haunt of Aubrey Morris, the former East End cab driver and founder of Riviera Holidays, who moved the meetings of his left-wing Anjou Lunch Club to the Gay Hussar. Unaware of his political leanings (he was nicknamed Red Aubrey), I once referred to what I thought was agent provocateur as being a possible Communist, following a newspaper story about one of our Yugoslavian tour guides being repeatedly refused entry to the UK. He was not amused.
IMAGE COURTESY: MICHAEL MAYNARD.

cheque in my hands for a sum of money I had never imagined I would see, let alone possess. Yet we were all of us in tears. This was not the way it was supposed to be.'

Nor were the coming years at Thomson, where Aubrey found he had walked into the middle of some bitter personal and inter-departmental battles, the way they were supposed to be. Before long, he found himself missing the old hands-on, manageable nature of Riviera:

'The idea of long-distance control of such a vast organisation was anathema to me. I had established a chain of control at Riviera, and had a deep knowledge of individual responsibilities. The company consisted of a tight group in a small building in Bishopsgate, close to the Bishopsgate Institute, with additional accommodation some 50 yards away. In contrast, Britannia's offices were at Luton Airport, and Thomson's were in a building on Gray's Inn Road. I had no clue about Skytours, and even less about the two Manchester companies.'

Things finally came to a head when, soon after returning to London from presenting an award to hoteliers in Mallorca, Aubrey was tipped off that he was to be fired within the next hour. Unsurprisingly, the news sparked outrage amongst the firm's employees:

'I had always made it my business to walk round each of the departments, to see how they were coping with the chaotic conditions, and had tried to explain away the obvious inadequacies. That said, I was surprised at the reaction from a large section of the employees, who organised a day of disruption and disaffection. The external communication through the switchboard was disconnected, and files were scattered.'

After leaving Thomson, Aubrey continued to direct his finances towards artistic, theatrical and left-wing ventures, most notably the Anjou Lunch Club, the socialist discussion forum he founded in 1989 and whose regular meeting-place, after it moved from the eponymous north London restaurant, was the famous Gay Hussar restaurant in Soho.

Although Aubrey was in the travel business for less than a decade, it is widely agreed that there have been few people, before or since, who have left such a lasting mark upon the industry.

CHAPTER 63
LORD THOMSON OF FLEET

He began his business career selling radio sets in Northern Ontario,
but had difficulty finding customers: reception was patchy, so he
bought a transmitter and a licence and set up his own radio station.

ROY Herbert Thomson was born on 5 June 1894 in Toronto, Canada. He was the son of Herbert Thomson, a barber, and the English-born Alice Coombs. During World War I Roy was barred from joining the army, on the grounds of his poor eyesight.

He began his business career selling radio sets in Northern Ontario, but had difficulty finding customers: the nearest stations were a long way away and reception was patchy. To overcome this problem, he bought a transmitter and a licence and set up his own radio station, in 1931.

In 1934 Roy moved into newspapers, buying a local Ontario publication called the *Timmins Citizen* and re-launching it as the *Timmins Press*. The paper started as out as a weekly, then it became a twice-weekly and, eventually, a daily. By the mid-1950s, Roy Thomson owned 19 different newspapers, a variety of radio stations, a chain of hairdressing salons, a fitted-kitchen factory and a firm manufacturing ice cream cones.

He was duly elected Chairman of the Canadian Press, but in January 1952 his wife Edna died, after a brief illness. He later wrote: 'At such a time, a man realises what he has sacrificed and neglected, while he went, in blinkers, about his business.'

In 1953, at the age of 59, Roy flew to Scotland and bought control of Edinburgh's failing *Scotsman* newspaper. One of the conditions of the sale was that he should not sell the paper, at a later date, to an Englishman. Roy himself had Scottish ancestry: his great-grandfather had been brought up in Dumfriesshire and, in 1773, had been one of the first Scots to settle in Canada. Roy Thomson was initially cold-

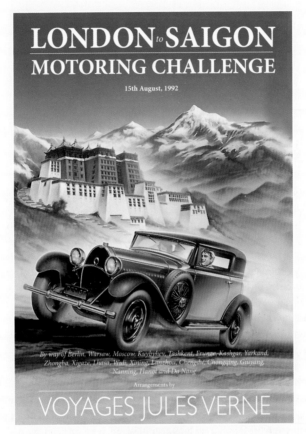

A Story in Brief

A BOOK BY ITS COVER: It was to David Scutt that we at VJV turned, for our iconic Motor Challenge posters : London to Peking, Saigon and New York. There's no doubt in my mind that he is one of the finest illustrators of his generation. Just look at his record: he's worked for television (on *The Two Ronnies* and *Jackanory*), he became art director at DJM Music (covers for Elton John, among others), and he's renowned for his film-making and animation (*Brazil* and *Absolute Beginners*). At the same time, he's created jacket covers, he has illustrated for some of the world's most famous authors: Tom Clancy, James Ellroy, Robert Ludlum, Bernard Cornwell, Jeffrey Archer, Mario Puzo, Ian Fleming, Philip Pullman amongst many others. And the series of front covers he did for the Coronet-published James Bond novels (T*omorrow Never Dies, The World Is Not Enough, Goldeneye*) are considered classics to this day.

IMAGE COURTESY: DAVID SCUTT/VOYAGES JULES VERNE.

shouldered by the Edinburgh establishment, who disliked his brashness and red socks, as well as his plans for reviving the Scotsman's fortunes (including, among other things, taking small ads off the front page).

In 1957 he won the franchise to run Scottish Television. It was, he famously said, 'a licence to print money'. In 1959 he bought *The Sunday Times* from Lord Kemsley, of Kemsley Newspapers. In 1962 he started up *The Sunday Times Magazine*. In the New Year Honours list of 1964, Roy Thomson was named a hereditary baron and, as his title, he chose 'Lord Thomson of Fleet'. In 1965 his company expanded into the package holiday business, and in so doing they freed whole generations from shivering bucket-and-spade holidays in Britain and opened up the possibility of sunshine and overseas adventure.

Lord Thomson best described the new vacation-industry philosophy in his autobiography, *After I Was Sixty*:

'If you made a business of it and organised everything well in advance, if you chartered aircraft, booking thousands of seats, and reserved blocks of bedrooms, if not entire hotels, and if you put clever advertisements in the way of people who had never thought of going abroad, you could sell them a fortnight on the Mediterranean, including aircraft, all meals and hotel, for less than the cost of the scheduled air fare to that particular spot. In cost terms, they could have a holiday in the Mediterranean sun, in a comparatively high-quality hotel, for less than they would be asked to sit and watch the rain from a Blackpool boarding house.'

In 1966 Lord Thomson bought *The Times* from the aristocratic Astor family. By that stage, he owned some 200 newspapers worldwide. Later, in March 1971, he joined a consortium to search for oil in the North Sea. They struck oil in the third place they drilled, but Lord Thomson shrugged off the suggestion that this had been merely a lucky gamble: 'My idea of luck is that it is an opportunity seized. You go through life looking for opportunities and, because you have managed to seize quite a few of them, you will be called lucky by your friends.'

During the course of his working life, Lord Thomson met a wide range of world leaders, including Khrushchev, Tito, Nehru, Golda Meir, the Shah of Iran, Haile Selassie and Zhou Enlai. 'What prime ministers liked about me,' he reflected, 'was that I had no axe to grind.'

After a lengthy period of industrial unrest and closure that lasted nearly a year (December 1978 to November 1979), the Thomson group sold *The Times* and *The Sunday Times* to Rupert Murdoch's News International.

Lord Thomson died on 4 August 1976, aged 82, following an illustrious career based on the rationale: 'I have got to be doing some sort of work, and, of course, I wouldn't enjoy it unless it was profitable.'

CHAPTER 64
MEET GORDON BRUNTON

He needed to find an industry that was still growing, and
where there were opportunities still waiting to be taken. Travel
was an obvious area.

AS with so many millions of people, World War II got in the way of Gordon Brunton's career: no sooner had he started his degree at the London School of Economics than he was sent abroad to fight in the Far East. He found himself being shipped out to Burma in 1941, as a 19-year-old second lieutenant with the Royal Artillery. When he returned to Britain five years later, not only was he married, but also his wife was soon after to expect their first child.

As he recalls during an interview in 2013: "I began my working life earning £8 a week, going round knocking on companies' doors, trying to sell them advertising,". "Did I mind? That wasn't really a relevant question, since I had a wife and a young baby, and needed to make a living to support them. The fact was, after four and a half years in the Army, the total sum of my worldly wealth was £105. I just had to get on with it. So, I began in publishing at the very bottom, selling advertising space in *Crown Colonist and Industrial Chemist*."

It wasn't long, though, before Gordon began to rise up the ranks and, in 1956, he was appointed advertising manager of a firm called Tothill Press (formerly Transport 1910), from where he went on to a slightly shakier outfit, Tower Press, before joining the altogether more reliable Odham's Publishing. In his own words:

"It was while I was with Odham's that Lord Thomson asked me to join his organisation. In some ways, I took a hell of a risk and certainly a substantial salary cut: instead of £6,000 a year at Odham's, I was only getting £5,000 with Thomson.

That said, it turned out to be the most edifying period of my working life. Lord Thomson regarded me more as a son; he and I really hit it off. I was 39 when he took me on, and he was already well into his 60s. Although our business relationship encompassed a large number of disagreements, we never fell out over them. I remember, for example, in 1967-68, I took over as managing director and, after a fortnight, I managed to see the salaries of the directors, and they were, to my mind, deplorably low. I went to Lord Thomson and told him that this had to be put right. We had a blazing row, in which he said he didn't believe in paying pensions, and that it was up to individual people to save up for their retirement. He told me, in no uncertain terms, that he hadn't made me managing director to go round spending all his money.

That night, at home, it struck me that I was going to be the shortest-lived chief executive in British business history. However, I was wrong. Most days, I got into the office at around 8.30am and Lord Thomson came in at 9.30am. On the morning after our argument, though, he was already at work when I arrived. He said, "Come on into my office," and told me he hadn't slept the previous night. "I know you're right," he told me. "It's just that I can't stand spending money if I don't absolutely have to. I want you to adjust the payments as you see right; I won't interfere." That was Roy all over. He was a big man, a man of total integrity. Being him, though, he couldn't resist taking a look, a few weeks later, at the changes I had made."

The reason Brunton was employed by Thomson was to diversify. The company's main profit centre at the time was Scottish Television, but with a Labour government that was hostile to individual ownership of newspapers and television stations, it was felt that this income stream would be susceptible to political interference. Enter Brunton and, within nine years, the company had sprouted all sorts of wings, buying up 100-or-so magazines, setting up the Yellow Pages phone directories and snapping up a number of well-known publishing companies (Hamish Hamilton, Michael Joseph, etc.). Before long, the company was achieving a 30 per cent compound profit growth, year on year.

Then, of course, there was the travel business, as Gordon recalls:

"I needed to find an industry that was still growing, and where there were adventures and opportunities still waiting to be taken. Travel was an obvious area; even in the 1960s, going overseas on an airplane was seen as something almost exclusively for the elite. As it happened, I had shared a flat at university with Vladimir Raitz, at the beginning of the war, when the London School of Economics was transferred to Cambridge, in order to escape the Blitz.

Later, Vladimir went on to start up the tour company Horizon Holidays; he had the quality, more affluent market, while Captain Ted Langton set up Skytours, which was less expensive. Vladimir helped us find companies that we could buy and, together, he and Langton were the founders of what we know as the modern travel businesses."

It was a business that Brunton was to witness at close quarters, as the Thomson group went about buying up some of the biggest names in the travel world: Gaytours, Luxitours, Rivera Holidays and (from Langton) both Skytours and Britannia Airways. The latter relationship, however, was never harmonious. It got off to a bad start when, having sold Skytours for just £700,000, following a damning auditors' report on Skytours' haphazard financial management, Langton saw the firm make a £1 million profit in its very first year with Thomson.

When Langton's demands for further payment received a frosty reception from Thomson, he played his trump card, threatening to withhold details of the next season's Skytours brochure, to which only he had access. "I asked Langton to my office, to discuss his threat," says Brunton. "While we were negotiating, my PA went to his offices, forced open the lock and came away with all the brochure 'dummies'. With great difficulty, we managed to produce the brochure, and Langton was fired."

By contrast, one appointment that did bear fruit was that of Bryan Llewellyn, as head of the travel division. "I wouldn't call Bryan a businessman, but he was exactly what we needed at the time, which was an excellent marketing brain," says Brunton. "No doubt about it, he can take a lot of the credit for the success of Thomson Holidays."

Not that Brunton and Llewellyn had the field to themselves, by any means. More and more companies began to realise the commercial opportunities that the travel business offered, and it was only thanks to Lord Thomson himself, with support from Brunton, that the travel division did not get sold off altogether. This turned out to be a far-sighted decision: "In 1975, a profit of £6.375 million was achieved, against the previous year's loss of £850,000," notes Brunton. "40 years later, Thomson Travel was sold to a German consortium (TUI) for £1.7 billion."

Indeed, while Brunton remained committed to fair business practice – witness the time he and Lord Thomson offered more for a publishing company than its recently bereaved female owner was asking – he was prepared to court unpopularity with his business decisions. One notable occasion was when he opted to buy American-built Boeing 737 jet planes, rather than the British-made BAC 1-11s: "I came in for some criticism for not buying British. My response was robust. I stated that, in anything but the shortest term, it was not in British industry's advantage to be featherbedded. If we were to be a world player in the aviation or any other industry, we had to be competitive."

A glance at the group's 1976 balance sheet shows that the Thomson travel division was the most profitable in the whole company, making a profit of £7.304m, as against its publications (£6.559m), regional newspapers (£5.584m) and national newspapers (-£1.47m).

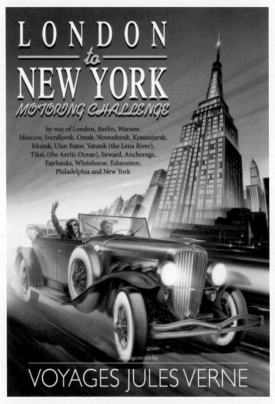

A Story in Brief

THE CHALLENGES OF A CHALLENGE/THAT MAN AND HIS VALET: Asked what it's like to organise a Motor Challenge, I would say 'exhausting'. The main problem is that your average Challenger is used to giving orders, and not following them. Of course, some of the participants were a delight. Under this heading, I include the Portuguese Challenger who brought his two Argentinian guitarists, the ESPN film crew who captured all the action, and the four Americans who turned up with the first public version of the Hummer. Then there was the American who brought along his valet, only the pair fell out and the valet was sent back home. In short, arranging a motor challenge calls on all the logistical skills you can imagine. There are meal stops, hotel reservations, escorts, permissions, egos, sponsors, arranging of fuel dumps in remote, sometimes desert locations. For me, though, everything pales into insignificance compared to arranging insurance, at a time when no policy existed covering both the Soviet Union and China.

IMAGE COURTESY: DAVID SCUTT/VOYAGES JULES VERNE.

This wasn't the end of the Brunton story. Gordon was an instrumental part in the company moving into the North Sea oil business and was the lynchpin of negotiations that resulted in the sale of *The Times* and *The Sunday Times* to Rupert Murdoch. Of Murdoch, Brunton states: "It's true that Rupert Murdoch and I had very little in common, when it came to our views on what newspapers should do. That said, he was a man who absolutely kept his word in business; he was always extremely reliable in that way."

As for Brunton's years with the Thomson Organisation (which he left in 1985), he describes them as "the busiest, happiest and most successful... of my life," adding: "The time I spent with Roy Thomson was particularly memorable. The fact he was the majority shareholder in the business meant that one particularly gratifying result of working with him was that he was able to make decisions quickly and positively. His ability to take the long view was very much the key to our success."

Brunton's post-Thomson life has been spent in a wide range of commercial, voluntary and horseracing-related roles (he was the proud owner of Indian Queen, winner of the 1991 Ascot Gold Cup). Throughout it all, though, he has carried two invaluable pieces of advice:

"The first was from Lord Thomson. The one great lesson I learnt from him, though I don't think many people would agree with it, was not to go in for a lot of haggling. If I was buying a business that I thought would give us a fair return, then I would offer a fair price. A lot of businessmen go in for bargaining, because they think it's macho and will make them look like tough guys. I think Lord Thomson's way is better."

The other big lesson I learnt was in the Army, and it also stood me in good stead throughout my business life. I was being trained by a sergeant major, who asked me what I would do if I was in charge of a platoon and came under fire from two machine gun positions. After I had spent some time replying and weighing up the options, he said to me: "The only wrong option, Brunton, is to dither. Be decisive and, whatever you decide, carry it out with energy and determination." I discovered, in the years ahead, how right this was.

CHAPTER 65
THE MAN FROM SUN STREET

In 1974, the whole edifice did indeed come tumbling down. Clarksons, Horizon and Court Line all went down together, at the height of the summer season, with some 40,000 customers on holiday at the time.

TOM Gullick joined the Navy at 17, built Clarksons into one of the most powerful tour companies in the world and then went back to bird watching, when the firm folded. No doubt about it, Tom Gullick was always destined for a career in the Royal Navy. At the age of just 13 he entered the Britannia Royal Naval College, Dartmouth, as a cadet, and at 17 he became a midshipman. He served on sub-marines, becoming an assistant operations officer with the reserve fleet on the River Clyde, and was appointed flag officer to the commander-in-chief of the home fleet.

All of this meant that when he left the service in 1958, in his late 20s, having wined and dined with not just admirals but visiting heads of state too, there were few challenges that Tom didn't feel ready to face. He entered the travel business when he got a job running a small travel agency called 'Clarksons Air and Shipping Service'. He started out by organising trips to the 1958 Brussels World's Fair, as well as tours of the Dutch tulip fields for branches of the Women's Institute.

Growth was as dynamic as it was rapid. Soon, the firm was taking travellers to Copenhagen, down the Rhine, and through the vineyards of Burgundy. Realising his customers wanted to buy gifts to remind them of their trip, Tom built a huge Clarksons shopping hangar and piled its shelves high with souvenirs.

The real breakthrough came in 1965, when Clarksons not so much entered as stormed the Spanish summer-holiday market. Their brochures offered all-in breaks of 8-15 days' duration with prices starting at just 26-and-a-half guineas (around £28), some 20-30 per cent less than what their competitors were charging.

Within four years of entering the mainstream summer package-holiday business, Clarksons were the number one firm in the field – Gullick claimed their chartered aircraft were never less than 95 per cent full. He pioneered the policy whereby potential customers could call the company's reservation centre free of charge after 6.00pm.

In addition to encouraging hoteliers, especially in Benidorm, to enlarge and expand their establishments, Clarksons built eight hotels of their own, each with a 600-800 bed capacity. Margins, however, were tight: so cheap were the holidays, an estimated 85 out of every 100 plane seats had to be filled before the company made a profit. All of a sudden, the name of the game was bulk: the era of mass travel had arrived.

To this end, the ever-determined Gullick set about paying large advances to hoteliers in the most popular resorts, in order to block-book their beds for Clarksons customers. Secondly, he trimmed his already lean prices still closer to the bone and joined up with an airline named Court Line, whose Lockheed TriStars had up to 400 seats, compared to the 130-or-so on the Boeing 737s used by many of the firm's rivals.

In February 1971, in response to the government relaxing minimum price levels for holidays of seven nights or less, Clarksons started offering long weekends in Benidorm for just £15; within a week they had sold 200,000 of these ultra-bargain breaks. The estimated profit on each holiday was tiny (about £1.50 per person), but the firm counted on making a further £5 profit per person by selling them excursions while they were at the resort.

This formula proved a big hit with holidaymakers; in 1970, to a great fanfare of publicity, Clarksons announced they were carrying their one-millionth passenger. But while they may have been successful, they were not popular with their competitors. During the 1970s, rumours were constantly being circulated to the effect that Clarksons were losing money. Nonetheless other UK tour firms had no option but to lower their prices too, since it was clear that the travelling public cared less about brand loyalty and more about the bottom line. As the price war heated up, smaller firms went out of business, and even the mighty Thomson Holidays was losing money (although as part of Lord Thomson's business empire, it had deep pockets).

It was the oil crisis of 1973 that really did it for the travel firms, when Arab states in the Middle East increased oil prices by 70 per cent in retaliation for the US's support of Israel. Faced with massively inflated fuel bills, widespread strikes, the Three-Day Week and constant electricity cuts, travel giant Horizon Holidays gave up the unequal struggle and, having been forced into receivership, was taken under the corporate wing of Court Line in 1974. In the mind of Horizon boss Vladimir Raitz, there was no question of where the blame lay: 'Tom Gullick's price

A Story in Brief

THE GREAT ESCAPE: In 1981, aeronautical engineer Frank Skinner (late of Independent Air Transport; one of its engineers at the time of the Southall Air crash) was working for Iran Air, in Teheran, and helped a friend flee the country, by hiding him in an aircraft void below the cockpit. Trouble was, that on arrival in Heathrow, the lucky escapee started making a big song and dance about how he had got out. Which was when the Ayatollah's men came knocking at Frank's door. He was slung into the notorious Evin prison, except that no one quite knew what to do with him. Having been given a meal of eggs, and plied with cigarettes, Frank was invited by the guards to watch a film – *The Great Escape*! After nearly a year in prison, he and his Iranian wife left Teheran in an Iran Air aircraft to London. However, fearful that the aircraft might suddenly still be ordered to return, Frank decided to disembark in Athens, where he went straight to the bar and spent all the money he had – a 20 dollar bill! IMAGE COURTESY: MICHAEL MILLS/DOMINQUE WEST.

war tactics had even brought their own organisation to the brink of ruin.'

In 1974, the whole edifice did indeed come tumbling down. Clarksons, Horizon and Court Line all went down together, at the height of the summer season, with some 40,000 customers on holiday at the time, spread across 75 different resorts. As for those customers who had not yet gone on holiday (but had paid their money), they besieged the Clarksons office near Liverpool Street Station, where staff members were advised to move to the rear of the building in case the angry customers started smashing windows.

Looking back on it all now, some 40 years later, Tom Gullick speaks not as a package tour mogul, but as someone who is as committed to bird watching – and as determined to succeed – as he was back in his Clarksons days. Indeed, at the age of 81, he was officially named as the first person in the world to have seen 9,000 different species of bird.

A SYMPHONY OF COLOUR POSTER BY ALISON MUSKER

A Story in Brief:

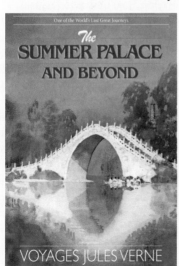

IMAGE COURTESY: ALISON MUSKER/VJV.

Chinese gardens with their buildings, landscaping and different kind of flowers and trees, are integrated works of art, lyrical and picturesque. That is how they are seen through the eye of the traditional Chinese. It is a view of the garden that is in marked contrast to the one held by an Englishman, for whom a traditional garden is at its best when seemingly free of artifice, rich in colour and organised as a sort of contained wilderness – a symphony rather than a poem or a painting. Yet the Chinese interpretation of the word 'artifice' is evidently different, for one of several aims of Chinese landscaping is to be a close to nature as possible. A garden which fails to convey a feeling of naturalness is a failure. Part of the reason for this contradiction in conception must be spatial considerations. China, with some exceptions, has always had a shortage of room.

CHAPTER 66
THE POLISH FALCON

Had MKK's past exploits and legendary bouts of rule-bending gone
before him, and convinced people that blame should be laid at his
door? Or had he and his airline been the victims of circumstance?

PRETTY much everyone has heard of Sir Freddie Laker and Sir Richard
Branson. A rather less well-known name, I suspect, is that of Captain
Marian Kozuba-Kozubski. And yet many people believe that the modern,
all-inclusive tour business was built almost entirely on his aviation exploits.

The year it all began was 1954, when Kozuba-Kozubski (or 'MKK') bought a
travel business then formed an airline called Independent Air Travel (IAT), later
Independent Air Transport. Somehow, MKK had teamed up with 'Captain' Ted
Langton at around the same time as Langton was beginning tour operations under
the Universal Sky Tours brand. In fact, Langton became a director of MKK's
fledgling airline, and used both it and its various surrogates (Blue-Air and Falcon
Airways) to fly the bulk of his passengers to the costas of Spain and elsewhere.
Which was how things remained until 1961, when, after MKK had lost his air
operator's licence, Langton went on to set up his own airline, Euravia (later
Britannia Airways).

Was MKK daunted by this setback? Not at all. He went on either to operate
or work for airlines in Holland, Austria, Yemen and Kenya before ending up flying
in the Biafran conflict of 1967-70. That war did not end well for him, however: he
was badly shot-up, and returned to the UK in 1971 a somewhat broken man. In
urgent need of a job, he wrote to all his former airline associates and others but
was shunned by them all, and, beset by drink and depression, died before his time
at the age of just 61. No one, it seemed, wanted to be associated with him, and his
ashes were scattered over the English Channel.

It was a sad end to an amazing life that had begun in Poland in 1918 and deserves an account here. We pick up the story of MKK's life at the outbreak of the Second World War, in 1939. He fled Poland first for Hungary, Serbia, Croatia, then Switzerland and, following a spell with the Free French, worked his way across the length of Spain to Gibraltar, where he boarded a troop ship and arrived in Britain in 1942. He joined the Polish Squadron of Bomber Command at Faldingworth (later Transport Command), in Lincolnshire, and learnt to fly Lancaster bombers. MKK subsequently launched numerous daring bombing raids over Germany, and his exploits became the stuff of legend (he was awarded both the Polish equivalent of the Victoria Cross and the French Croix de Guerre).

His adventures didn't stop once the war was over, either. In 1947 he helped evacuate hapless refugees at the time of the India partition, and in 1949, along with the likes of Freddie Laker, he was one of many pilots who took part in the Berlin Airlift. He even entered and drove his own car in the Monte Carlo Rally, which only bolstered his reputation for fearlessness – probably the quality that attracted Langton in the first place.

The thing was, while Langton clearly needed an airline to fly his passengers, he also needed someone who would do battle with the licensing authorities at a time when just about everything required prior approval. This was a time, remember, when the national carriers, BEA and BOAC, received feather-bed treatment, being afforded access to subsidised aircraft shielded from competition on the most popular routes and at the most popular airports. Every little concession, it seemed, had to be fought over, and there was no better man for this task than MKK.

It got to the point that some private airlines were driven to the margins of viable operation: not only were they were flying aircraft that had passed through many hands, but they were also obliged to fly them into and out of airports that were short of facilities. In many ways, it was a kind of state-sponsored uneven playing field, and it had consequences which, while unintended, were later exposed for all to see during the inquiry into the 1958 Southall air crash, in which seven people (four of them on the ground) were killed when a plane operated by MKK's Independent Air Travel crashed into a row of houses in west London.

Had MKK's past exploits and legendary bouts of rule-bending gone before him, and convinced people that blame should be laid at his door? Or on the contrary, had he and his airline been the victims of circumstance, vested interests or simple pilot error? Opinions were divided, but one thing was certain: the crash was the beginning of the end for MKK. That was the bad news; the good news was that the disaster marked the start of a fairer, and therefore safer and more viable, private commercial airline environment.

The revealing story of the Southall air crash is recalled here by Thomas Ovans:

THE SOUTHALL AIR CRASH

On the morning of 2 September 1958 I had arranged to go on a cycle ride with a few school friends – probably our last excursion of the summer holidays. As we gathered at around 9.00am, one of our group arrived with the news that there had been a plane crash in Southall, only a few miles away. He may even have claimed to have heard the sound of the aircraft coming down.

Being schoolboys, I suspect we all felt a shiver of excitement that something dramatic and shocking had come so close to our ordered, suburban lives. I don't recall being tempted, however, to go and see the scene of the accident. Instead we set off, as planned, for a ride in the Surrey countryside; and I suspect that, by lunchtime, we had forgotten about the Southall crash. It is perhaps significant, though, that during the afternoon we had the idea of staging and photographing a mock accident involving a heap of bicycles and several of our arms and legs protruding from the hedge and ditch.

In the days that followed I was oddly incurious about details of the crash. I think I assumed there had been a sudden loss of control after take-off from nearby Heathrow; hence I pictured the aircraft coming down from a fairly steep angle with very little warning. It was only recently – over 50 years after the incident – that I thought of using the Internet to try and find out more about what happened. It was surprisingly easy to get some basic information, which showed that my assumptions had been wrong. But it has proved much more difficult to discover an adequate explanation for that morning's events. What I did uncover, however, were some commercial and political attitudes and behaviours that do not seem to have changed much since 1958.

Some essential facts of the story can be gleaned. At 05:54 GMT on 2 September, a twin-engine Vickers Viking aircraft, call sign Juliet-Echo, took off from Heathrow airport with a crew of three, carrying freight bound for Tel Aviv. It was operated by Independent Air Travel. After 15 minutes, when the aircraft was about 7,000 feet high over the Horsham area) the captain reported engine trouble and asked for air traffic clearance to land at Blackbushe airport, on the border of Surrey and Hampshire.

At this stage both engines were still running but the starboard one was throttled back. A few minutes later, however, the pilot said the starboard engine was stopped and 'feathered' (i.e. its propeller blades had been set to a minimum-drag position).

At about the time of this second message, Juliet-Echo began steadily losing height. Even as the pilot was striving to coax the aircraft as far as Blackbushe, it was slowly falling out of the sky at about 200 feet a minute; and with an awful and tragic inevitability, it ploughed into houses on Kelvin Gardens, Southall, at about 06:30 GMT. All three crewmembers died in the crash, together with four people on the ground.

The aircraft seems to have hit the ground at quite a shallow angle, and the commentator makes the poignant observation that in the last seconds the captain was seen leaning out of his cockpit window, shouting and waving in a desperate and probably futile attempt to warn people in the street.

Two questions immediately presented themselves to the accident investigators. Firstly, why was the aircraft unable to maintain height? The Viking was designed to fly safely with one motor stopped; indeed, Juliet-Echo had very recently been shown to be capable of climbing at better than 600 feet per minute on a single engine. Secondly, why was the aircraft anywhere near Southall? To reach Blackbushe from Horsham the aircraft should have flown north-west, but Southall is to the north of Horsham and some 20 miles east of Blackbushe.

The public inquiry into the accident concluded that part of the answer to the first question lay in the fact that the aircraft had been 400kg above its maximum takeoff weight when it left Heathrow. (The flight test showing that the aircraft could maintain height with one engine stopped had been performed under light load conditions.) This 400kg overloading was due to extra fuel having been taken on – perhaps to enable one of the refuelling stops to be avoided.

The inquiry also felt that an explanation of Juliet-Echo's inadequate single-engine performance might lie in some strange events that took place before the flight left Heathrow. On 1 September, the day before the accident, the aircraft made a short positioning flight from Blackbushe (its maintenance base) to Heathrow (to take on its cargo). On arrival at Heathrow, a loss of oil from the starboard engine was noted and members of the flight crew decided to do a partial strip-down and rebuild of the propeller unit in order to try to find and fix the leak. It was of course both unusual and entirely contrary to air transport regulations for them to attempt such a task, which was a job for a licensed engineer. It was even more unusual for it to done at night and in the open air.

Examination of the wreckage yielded no evidence that the propeller unit had been incorrectly re-assembled; nevertheless the public inquiry concluded, on the basis of this incident and also a number of others, that there was a generally cavalier attitude towards proper maintenance procedures within Independent Air Transport. This observation cast doubt upon the overall serviceability of the aircraft and might account for its poor single-engine performance. The inquiry report includes the damning comment that 'the policy of this company was to keep its aircraft flying at all costs and without any real regard for the requirements of maintenance.'

As to why Juliet-Echo was heading in the wrong direction, the inquiry could only conjecture that the pilot had been homing in on the wrong radio beacon. The last few messages from the aircraft showed that the crew believed they were within five miles of Blackbushe when in fact they were more than 20 miles away. Their outward journey had overflown beacons at Epsom and Dunsfold; after turning back, the pilot was told to return to Dunsfold and then tune his direction finder to the Blackbushe frequency. However, the subsequent flight-path suggested that one of the pilots might have mistakenly re-tuned to the Epsom signal that had guided them on their outward route.

This use of the wrong beacon probably meant that, until the last few minutes, the crew were not aware of being in much danger. The persistent loss of height would have been worrying, but if they believed they were getting nearer to Blackbushe they must have expected they could stay in the air long enough to make a safe landing. It would have been a sudden and terrible shock, then, to realise that the landscape below them did not match the familiar approach to the Blackbushe runway. This would explain why they did not broadcast a 'mayday' distress call until just before the crash.

To make such a navigational mistake – and to persist in it, in spite of counter-evidence such as the position of the sun – would of course constitute pilot error. And pilot error could also have accounted for the aircraft failing to stay in the air – if, for instance, its airspeed had been allowed to get too low. But, when commenting on the crew's responsibility, the inquiry had to take into account the possibility of severe fatigue.

There was evidence that during 30-31 August the aircraft's captain was effectively on duty for 31.5 hours. (The maximum permitted time without rest was 16 hours, but long periods of duty were not technically illegal owing to a loophole in regulations which allowed pilots to fly during 'rest' time provided they were not carrying passengers or cargo.) It also emerged that on 1 September, the day before the crash, the captain was again on duty from 13:25 until at least 20:00 and that he then returned to the airport at about 04:00 on 2 September in order to prepare for the fatal flight. 'In short,' the inquiry report states, 'this crew had not had the rest desirable, and to which they were entitled... before taking off in an overloaded aircraft whose condition was suspect.'

The inquiry report makes further criticisms of the way Independent Air Transport carried out routine proficiency checks on their pilots. The most recent such check on Juliet-Echo's captain was found to have been 'perfunctory'. Crucially, 'a true stoppage of an engine and single-engine landing both by day and by night were not carried out'. Hence there had been 'no sufficient check on the captain's ability to fly and land the aircraft with one engine inoperative'. In view of

A Story in Brief

AN ENEMY FOR LIFE: When Marian Kozubski turned down Freddie Laker's offer for his airline Independent Air Transport, his decision did not go down well. As became clear in 1958, when an Independent flight crashed at Southall, with the loss of all the crew. As Marian's wife recorded in her diary: 'There was an inquest, then an inquiry. Everyone – but everyone – was anti Marian and anti-Independent; it was a dreadful time. Things were twisted round to make it appear that Marian was negligent.' With the collapse of his airline, Kozubski ended up as a pilot in the Biafran conflict, but came back a broken man. On 13 February 1966, he wrote to Laker, asking for a job. The reply he received read as follows: 'Thank you for your letter applying for a position with Laker Airways. At this early stage we have no suitable vacancy to offer you, but your application has been filed for future reference.' I guess as John Bloom had found: when you have a million, you have a million friends.

IMAGE COURTESY: JOANNA KOZUBSKA.

463

these less-than-rigorous crew-training procedures – on top of suspected lax maintenance and long working schedules – the inquiry decided that the captain 'was put in a situation which no pilot should be required to face, and it is dangerous to criticise his handling of it'.

The inquiry also commented that 'The attitude of the company was remarkable. Those directors who gave evidence put the whole blame for this accident on the captain. It was said that the loading responsibility was his, and his the responsibility for taking-off in the aircraft... It is not difficult for employers who are not unduly concerned to observe the regulations, to drive their employees... to disregard the regulations designed to ensure safety in the air.'

The impression given by the inquiry report is that Independent Air Transport was operating as a ruthlessly cost-cutting business. Its managing director – himself a pilot – came across as a rather swashbuckling figure when interviewed. As the name of his company suggests, he seemed to enjoy competing aggressively with the larger nationalised airlines. One suspects that certain aspects of his business model would be looked at favourably by some of today's entrepreneurs who like to boast about leanness and efficiency and the importance of risk-taking. Of course, I do not accuse any present-day organisations of setting out to break the law. But, for any business manager who takes pride in cost-saving measures, the words of the Southall inquiry are still relevant: 'It is not difficult for employers... to drive their employees... to disregard the regulations...'

In view of the inquiry's findings it might have been expected that Independent Air Transport would have faced prosecution – perhaps even for manslaughter, but at least for failures in operating procedures. The fact that this did not happen led to some acrimonious exchanges in Parliament over the subsequent two or three years. And if a narrative about unintended consequences of cost-cutting is one which sounds both familiar and plausible in 2014, then so also is a narrative involving accusations of ministerial incompetence or even complicity in questionable business dealings.

Of a civil aviation debate on 20 July 1959, Hansard reports suggestions by opposition MPs that the Ministry of Transport and Civil Aviation had been too light-touch in regulating the airline industry – not policing maintenance requirements tightly enough, and not closing the legal loophole which allowed pilots to continue flying during rest periods. These allegations were of course refuted. In particular, a long statement was made by the MP in whose constituency Independent Air Travel's headquarters were located. This statement sought to cast doubt on the Southall inquiry's findings.

The constituency MP argued, for instance, that Juliet-Echo's overloading was not a significant factor in the accident, likening it to driving at 32 mph in a 30 mph area. This seems an arguable point; but he then went further and questioned the evidence for crew fatigue, stating that the captain had been heard to say he felt 'very fit' on the day before the crash. The MP also claimed it had been entirely the captain's decision to leave Heathrow at around 6.00am on 2 September – the company's schedule for the round trip to Tel Aviv meant that he could have left later in the day if he had indeed felt tired. (It is hard, however, to square this claim with the fact that the crew had felt it necessary to do emergency repairs the night before, instead of waiting for a qualified mechanic.) Finally he said he had listened to tape recordings of the crew's last messages in which their voices showed 'no trace of tiredness'. (In a tense situation, surely adrenaline would have temporarily compensated for fatigue.)

It should be said that the MP had very properly preceded his statement by declaring his interest in the matter – namely, that he had for many years been a friend of the managing director of Independent Air Transport and, moreover, that he had recently become a director of Falcon Airways, a new company founded by the very same managing director.

Hansard also reports that on 21 December 1961 – over three years after the accident – the Attorney General was asked why there had been no prosecution of Independent Air Transport. Suspicions were voiced that delaying tactics might have been employed within the Department of Public Prosecutions (DPP) to prevent such a prosecution taking place. Such suspicions were based, in part, on the fact that a former employee of the DPP had subsequently gone to work for Falcon Airways. Naturally the Attorney General strongly resisted any implication of wrongdoing; but he also went further towards undermining the Southall inquiry by drawing attention to a conflict of evidence about the aircraft's over-loading which would have made it hard to achieve the standard of proof needed for a conviction, even if a prosecution had been brought.

So, three years after the accident, we find a swirl of accusation and counter-accusation. By 1961 Independent Air Transport had ceased to exist, after briefly rebranding itself as Blue-Air. Its former managing director had resigned in 1959 – insisting his departure had 'nothing whatsoever to do with the accident' – in order to start up Falcon Airways, which itself ceased operating in 1961 amid concerns about its safety record.

Many of the questions raised in 1958 remain unresolved. Were the crew (and the occupants of 6 Kelvin Gardens) victims of an unscrupulous company that insisted on over-long hours being flown in unsafe aircraft? Was the government complicit in this by weak regulation and weak enforcement? Was the lack of a subsequent prosecution partly a cover-up of government mistakes with a touch of conspiracy or corruption thrown in? We may be inclined to believe 'yes' could be the answer to any or all of these questions. And yet it may equally be the case that the crew of Juliet-Echo simply made some fatal mistakes.

The possibility of pilot error arises again because of a puzzling claim in the Hansard report. The MP defending Independent Air Transport mentions something that, he says, was omitted from the inquiry report – namely, that no fault was found in Juliet-Echo's starboard engine. But if this is true, then why did the crew report an engine problem and abort the flight? Did this accident prefigure the January 1989 Kegworth disaster, which was caused by pilots shutting down a correctly operating power plant by mistake?

Pre-flight doubts about the starboard engine (which had prompted last-minute repairs the night before) centered on the propeller unit rather than the power plant itself. Problems of 'surging' had previously been reported in the constant speed unit (CSU), which automatically adjusts the propeller blades during flight. In one of his last messages, Juliet-Echo's pilot stated: "I have one engine feathered and don't seem to be able to unfeather it at the moment."

As mentioned earlier, a 'feathered' propeller has its blades set to reduce air resistance when an engine is stopped. But the pilot's remark suggests that he wanted to unfeather the propeller – perhaps in order to start the engine again. Could the starboard CSU have had an intermittent fault that allowed the propeller blades to become feathered while the engine was running? This might have caused erratic or asymmetric application of thrust, and compelled the pilot to shut down a perfectly good engine. But this is guesswork and, among the many possible contributing factors to the accident, even the root mechanical cause for Juliet-Echo turning back remains unclear.

The Hansard report also describes how features of the air traffic control system had thwarted one last chance of preventing the disaster. Because of the navigation error, Juliet-Echo was actually quite close to Heathrow when it crashed and it might have been guided to a safe landing there if communication with Heathrow control had been possible. But because Juliet-Echo's crew were in radio contact with Blackbushe, the Heathrow control tower could not speak to them.

Paradoxically, Heathrow's radar could follow the Juliet-Echo's progress, while the smaller airport at Blackbushe did not have the radar to detect that the aircraft was off-course. Hansard aptly sums up this tragic conflict of partial information: 'London could see the Viking but could not speak to it. Blackbushe could speak to the Viking but could not see it. London knew its position but not its height. Blackbushe knew its height but not its position. If either airport had known both facts together the aircraft could have been taken over by London Airport and safely landed.' Among these mutual contradictions, the last hope vanished for the crew of Juliet-Echo to escape the consequences of a sequence of tragic errors (however they occurred and whoever was to blame for them).

It has been interesting but distressing to discover that muddled and unsatisfactory conclusions could result from parliamentary debates and public inquiries back in 1958, in just the same way as they have done in more recent times. Contemporary discontent with politicians (and their interactions with business and the media) may tempt us to believe there was a slightly-more-golden age 50 years ago, when straight-talking politicians and clear-thinking commentators joined forces in the interests of perfect transparency. Evidently this was not the case.

As I said earlier, I have always felt 'close' to the Southall disaster even though I knew little about it. My quite unjustifiable sense of somehow being involved with its mysteries has continued throughout my belated gathering of the available and contradictory facts. In fact, I experienced a small extra frisson when I discovered for the first time that Juliet-Echo had been trying to reach Blackbushe airport because, coincidentally, we went quite near there on our cycle ride later that fateful day. However, my Internet search produced one last 'hit' to remind me of the insignificance of my activities on 2 September 1958 compared with those of another 14-year-old. A short newsreel clip of 1959 records the presentation of a Carnegie medal to a Southall schoolboy for saving his five-year-old nephew from the fire that followed the crash of Juliet-Echo on Kelvin Gardens.

FOOTNOTE: Another possible explanation as to why no prosecution of the airline and its directors followed is perhaps contained within the unpublished memoirs of Mrs. Kozuba-Kozubska, who recalls that the Heathrow air traffic control facility at the time of the accident was defective. Air traffic control was of course the responsibility of the Transport Minister, and if the facility had indeed been sub-par, then it is reasonable to assume that more would have been revealed as the state's culpability in the event of a prosecution.

Shortly after the accident, MKK was keen to get his own back against an establishment that was now seemingly set against him. The Southall coroner, who had also been damning of the airline in his report, had booked a family skiing holiday that, as it happened, commenced with a flight onboard one of MKK's aircraft. Having got wind of this heaven-sent piece of PR, MKK promptly arranged for the ranks of the national press to assemble and record this moment of maximum embarrassment, no doubt mentally captioning as he did so: 'If the airline had been unsafe in its practices as alleged, why, then, are you now entrusting your lives with us?'

CHAPTER 67
FROM COLVILLE TO CLIVEDEN

Though to be honest I cannot recall him ever being other than straightforward, to this day though his name lives on in the English language as a byword for all that is bad about landlords.

URING the early 1960s I lived with the Garro family in a rooming house on Colville Terrace, Notting Hill. The reference to 'Cliveden' relates to where, 45 years after leaving Colville Terrace, I was to operate the sister vessel to the *Spirit of Chartwell* (a.k.a. Royal Barge), the good ship *Passepartout*.

The rooming house was owned by Peter Rachman. Though to be honest I cannot recall him ever being other than straightforward, to this day his name lives on in the English language as a byword for all that is bad about landlords. Open the Collins English Dictionary, and the definition of 'Rachmanism' is given as 'extortion or exploitation by a landlord of tenants of dilapidated or slum property, especially when using intimidation or racial fears to drive out sitting tenants whose rent is fixed at a low rate'.

Peter Rachman was born in Poland in 1919, imprisoned by both the Germans and the Russians during World War II, and died in 1962, at the age of just 43. It has been fully half a century since his death, yet this tubby, balding, bespectacled figure is still demonised for the slum empire he built up in Notting Hill during the period between his arrival in Britain, in 1948, and his death only 14 years later.

Just like the damp that used to permeate the walls of the properties he let out, his shadow still hangs over the streets of London W11, even though the houses have, in the intervening years, been transformed from tenements for the poor and exploited into high-priced homes for the fashionably well heeled.

His speciality, so the stories go, was to frighten away existing tenants, through measures that involved everything from physical intimidation to dumping dead rats in their beds. He would then rent out the vacant properties, at hugely inflated rates, to newly-arrived immigrants from the West Indies, who were often unable to find accommodation elsewhere, or else to prostitutes who needed a room in which to ply their trade (the railings along the Bayswater Road were a popular soliciting point during the 1960s).

To later generations, then, the name 'Rachman' has come to mean the worst kind of urban bully, surrounded by an equally unappealing crowd of heavies and henchmen. It comes as something of a surprise, therefore, to discover that despite being accused of everything from intimidation to living off immoral earnings, Peter (born Perec) Rachman was only ever found guilty of one crime in the UK, and that was parking his car without the headlights on.

What's more, although well known in Notting Hill, he did not achieve nation-wide notoriety until after his death. And even then, this was due not to the discovery of some brutal misdeed, but to his relationship with a young, blonde model from Solihull by the name of Mandy Rice-Davies. It was Rachman's fate – or good fortune, depending on which way you look at it – to have been involved not just with the cheeky, blonde Mandy, but also with her sultry and seductive counterpart, Christine Keeler.

Both had been his mistresses at some stage, and it was at a Marylebone mews house owned by their mutual friend Stephen Ward, a high-society osteopath with a taste for the low life, that an incident occurred which, though seemingly small at the time, was to shake the British political establishment to its very foundations.

It stemmed from a fight that had taken place in a Soho nightclub, in October 1962, between Keeler's then boyfriend, Johnny Edgecombe, and one of her previous lovers, a musician who went by the name of Lucky Gordon. The fight came about when Keeler told Edgecombe that Gordon had attacked her after she ended their relationship, upon which Edgecombe cut his rival across the face, inflicting a wound that needed 17 stitches.

Things took an even uglier turn a few weeks later, when Keeler not only split up with Edgecombe but also threatened to give evidence against him to the police. In a fit of rage, her scorned lover pursued her in a cab to Stephen Ward's flat and, on being refused entry, fired seven shots at the front door.

From that point on, events moved swiftly. First, Edgecombe was arrested. This prompted Keeler to seek legal advice, in the course of which she let it be known that, in 1961, she had embarked on affairs both with the Secretary of State for War, John Profumo, and with a Russian naval attaché (and spy) called Yevgeny Ivanov.

Her introduction to Profumo had taken place at Cliveden, the Berkshire country seat of Lord Astor, who let Stephen Ward spend weekends in one of the estate cottages. The Keeler-Profumo liaison was not a lengthy one, and failed to

A Story in Brief

A SONG OF FREEDOM: This is a Portuguese poster for *Boys' Town*, the film that mirrored our lives at Barnardo's, but nearly didn't see the light of day. Film executive Louis B. Mayer decided its themes of poverty and crime were too much a departure from the studio's musicals and glamour productions. It took a meeting with the film's stars, Spencer Tracy and Mickey Rooney, to change his mind. As Rooney recalled, decades later: "Spence and I said, 'You've got to release *Boys' Town* because our nation needs this'. Mayer replied, 'It will never sell. There's no sex. There's no songs'. And I said: 'It's a song of freedom. It's a song of rehabilitation. It's a song of youth, no matter what colour or faith you are. It's about praying. It's about living a good life." In the end, Mayer not only relented but said that, in 25 years of running the studio, *Boys' Town* was his favourite MGM movie.

survive an MI5 warning to the War Secretary that, since he was sharing Keeler with a Russian spy, it was endangering national security.

In normal circumstances, Profumo's indiscretion might have never come to light, but because of what Keeler had revealed following the Edgecombe shooting, the secret had now begun to spread.

In March 1963, in a bid to quash the rumours, Profumo stood up in the House of Commons and declared: "There was no impropriety whatsoever in my acquaintance with Miss Keeler."

Meanwhile, the press were now well onto the story. When Keeler failed to give evidence against Edgecombe at his trial for the door-shooting incident, she was attacked by Lucky Gordon, who was himself then arrested, only to be bailed with money that came via Stephen Ward.

The heat turned up another few degrees when Mandy Rice-Davies was arrested for possessing a false driving licence and sent to Holloway Prison, upon which the police started investigating the basis of her friendship with Stephen Ward, who promptly announced to both the press and the Home Secretary that he had been covering up for Profumo. Which meant that the War Secretary had no option but to admit that he had misled the House of Commons and resign.

Soon afterwards, Lucky Gordon was given a three-year sentence for attacking Keeler (Edgecombe had got a seven-year jail term for his firearms offence), and Ward was charged for allegedly living off Keeler's 'immoral earnings'. He went to trial and, on the eve of the inevitable guilty verdict, took an overdose and killed himself.

Around this time, the name of Peter Rachman started appearing in the newspapers – ironic, since he had already been dead for seven months, having succumbed to a heart attack in November the previous year. The press had shone a light into the late landlord's business dealings and come up with a treasure trove of lurid stories, helped in no small part by the fact that their corpulent quarry was no longer around to defend himself, or bring legal action. It was alleged that Rachman had built up a whole empire of crumbling Notting Hill properties, houses that today sell to well-to-do folk for millions of pounds, but which in those days were occupied by scores of 'fresh-off-the-boat' Caribbean immigrants.

What was beyond dispute was that, during the 1950s, Rachman had gradually enlarged his property portfolio in the W11 postal district. Operating from his offices at 91-93 Westbourne Grove, or alternatively from a table in the Kenya Coffee Company (later Kenco) shop on Queensway, Rachman expanded his empire into Powis Terrace, Powis Square and Powis Gardens, at the same time as buying up large parts of Colville Road and Colville Terrace.

According to his critics, he employed an unsavoury team of henchmen to drive out mostly white tenants and then replaced them with large numbers of West Indians, many of whom had been unable to find accommodation in London, due to the kind of prejudice expressed in the signs that landlords commonly displayed in their front windows: 'No blacks, no Irish, no dogs.'

All of which meant that for every person who claimed Rachman was an unscrupulous bully, there was someone else who applauded his willingness to rent property, albeit at an inflated rate, to people in whose faces other doors were being slammed shut.

A report at the time in the local *Kensington News* describes Rachman as a familiar figure in the area, colourfully dressed in white suit and dark glasses, and driving his maroon-coloured Rolls Royce, registration number PR23. The same article quotes an 86-year-old Irishwoman called Bessie King who declares herself shocked by the ugly rumours she has heard about him, and testifies: "He was always polite, and I found him a charming man. He always showed me the utmost consideration and kindness."

Meanwhile, another Notting Hill resident observed in the same article: "Peter charged exorbitant rents, but without him, a lot of black people would have slept on the streets."

As to sitting tenants being intimidated out of their homes, through rubbish being dumped on their floors or having their belongings thrown out into the street, the 1965 Milner Holland Report on housing put forward a less dramatic reason for their departure:

'Coloured people, always in some difficulty in finding accommodation in the face of shortage, made worse by racial prejudice, were welcome. Cheerful people, and given to much singing, to playing radiograms and holding parties, they were not always appreciated as neighbours by the remaining tenants in Rachman's houses. These started to move out, and what perhaps began naturally, Rachman began to exploit.'

That's not to say, of course, that London W11 was exclusively inhabited by sunnily-disposed and sweet-tempered characters. Gambling and drinking dens began to proliferate (a half-crown to get in, a half-crown to have a beer), and by 1961 the *Kensington News* was lamenting the way in which 'on Friday, Saturday and Sunday nights, the streets are lined by expensive, flashy cars, and are loud with the shouts and screams of the women and the arguments, and worse still, the fights of the men'.

As for standards of Notting Hill housing, a Kensington Council survey discovered, in the early 60s, that some 2,000 houses in the Colville and Golborne wards were beyond renovation or repair, and that in Notting Hill overall, there were more than 1,000 households with more than three people living to a room.

No one, then, is claiming that Rachman operated in an area renowned for God-fearing rectitude, adherence to the law, or respect and reverence for tenants' rights. Nevertheless, it is worth noting that his notoriety was achieved only posthumously, when he was cast in the press as a conveniently villainous supporting character in the whole, lurid Cabinet Minister-and-call-girl scandal. What's more, his death did not by any means mark the birth of a new, more scrupulous style of landlording. As the local paper again records: 'Now that smaller property kings have mushroomed up, this evil man's incredibly complex slum empire continues, under the guidance of his minions. And this in 1963 when men are being shot into space.'

To this day, debate rages over the extent to which Rachman had distanced himself, both financially and administratively, from the running and indeed the ownership of his Notting Hill properties. For while he may have posthumously earned his own entry in the English dictionary, at the end of his life the total value of his estate came to just £8,000. Had it all just been a precarious financial balancing act? Had he been constantly selling off one property in order to pay another? Or had he somehow stashed away some enormous sum, out of sight and maybe even out of the country?

All questions to which no one has ever come up with a definitive answer. It seems it's not only the name of Peter Rachman that lives on, but his legend too.

A SLICE OF SIGHTSEEING HEAVEN POSTER BY SEDELY PLACE

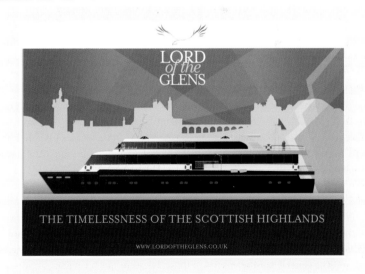

CHAPTER 68
BENNETT'S BAZAAR

Where and when did the travel business begin and who was the first to make a living out of it? The answer to the latter question would almost certainly be Thomas Cook, yet beforehand had come Thomas Bennett.

W HEN researching the origins of Jules Verne's novel *Around the World in Eighty Days*, I was so struck by the detail and accuracy of the itinerary that I felt sure it must have been based on a real-life source. And indeed, so it was. The introduction to one of George Bradshaw's *Companion* guides, written for the Victorian gentleman traveller, describes a route in which a complete circumnavigation of the globe could be accomplished in around 78-80 days. Naturally, I wanted to find out more about Bradshaw himself, but could unearth little apart from the most basic of information and the fact that in 1853, while visiting a friend, he had died and been buried in Christiania (present day Oslo).

Bradshaw's friend, it turned out, was another Englishman by the name of Thomas Bennett, who in addition to his friendship offered an invaluable fund of knowledge and travel information. Bennett, who had started his own travel agency in 1850, probably knew more about travelling around Scandinavia than any man alive, which is why Bradshaw, like numerous of his contemporaries before him, had come to visit. In fact, when Bennett later died, despite being virtually unknown in the country of his birth, he was buried in Norway as a hero.

Intrigued by this story, I decided, in 1982, to follow in Bradshaw's footsteps and visit Oslo, with two aims in mind: first, to appoint a local agent to market my China products; and second, to pay a visit to the Bennett Reisebureau (or travel agency), which was still in existence and trading under that name. In the end, I achieved both my aims in one fell swoop by appointing Bennetts as the Voyages Jules Verne general sales agents.

But what of Bennett the man? Scarcely anything has been written about him, save for a short essay by the well-known Norwegian author Christian Gierløff.

Where and when did the modern-day travel business really begin, and who was the first to make a living out of it? The answer to the latter part of the question would almost certainly be Thomas Cook, a name synonymous with organised travel and a brand that still carries commercial weight as a metaphor for reliability and knowhow.

As for the 'where and when', however, the answers are harder to find. No doubt functionaries were making travel arrangements of one sort or another far into antiquity – taxi drivers, ostlers, wheelwrights and military scouts have all, at various times, played indispensable roles in the displacement of mankind.

But that is to nitpick, as the apposite word in this context is not 'travel', but rather 'business'. The image evoked by Cook's name is a very British one – essentially Victorian, perhaps Edwardian, a refracted picture that brings to mind a sunny mosaic of parasols and straw boaters, moustaches, a Belgian detective on the Nile, archaeologists and clothing inappropriate to warm climates. A jumble of sepia reflecting the high point of an empire, just as it was embarking on its long, slow decline.

There were others, too. In 1822, Robert Smart of Bristol became the first steamship agent, booking passengers on steamers to various Bristol Channel ports and to Dublin. However, while he and Cook created excursions that made use of the rapid advances in technology, we may have to look elsewhere to find a pioneer within the actual travel agency field – that is, the provision of inclusive individual travel. We might regard all of this as a recondite, or even jejune, enquiry, were it not for the personalities of the people involved. This brings us to a certain Thomas Bennett of Oslo, who among his customers and friends could count on luminaries such as Jules Verne and the great timetable compiler George Bradshaw.

Indeed, by the 1850s Bennett had established a respected worldwide reputation as a chronicler of travel information, travel entrepreneur and arranger of travel itineraries. This in an age before mass communications and despite being based in what must have then seemed far-off and little-understood Norway, which at the time of his arrival, in 1848, could claim only the barest of infrastructure and not even a railway line.

Mention Bennett's name today in England, and there will be few who can tell you who he was. Viewed as a maverick in his lifetime, his contribution to the development of travel has been obscured by the fame of those that came after him. What's more, his family name wasn't even Bennett, nor was his first name Thomas. He was actually born Thornton Benthall in 1814, and had grown up at Benthall Hall, near Much Wenlock in Shropshire. His was an aristocratic family – motto:

Tende bene et alta pete ('Strive well and reach high') – that could trace its ancestry to before the Norman conquest of England in 1066.

Young Thornton's father, William Searle Benthall, had attended Westminster School and duly sent his son there too, to acquire an all-round education, learn the art of being a gentleman and become proficient in several languages, including French and German.

Around 1844, Thornton Benthall left England for the Continent. He travelled first to France, then on to Switzerland and Germany. He earned his keep along the way by offering tuition in English and French, before arriving in Copenhagen and becoming Thomas Bennett.

The precise reasons for his change of name are not known, but it is worth noting that it coincided with the sale (after 28 generations) of Benthall Hall, the failure of the family's wool business and his enlistment as a reservist medical assistant, on the side of the Danes, in the first Danish-German war of 1848-51. It was following his demobilisation from the Danish army that Bennett, as he was now known, boarded the paddle steamer Vixen on one of its regular sailings from Copenhagen and, on 13 November 1848, stepped ashore in Christiania for the first time.

The city that greeted him bore only a slight resemblance to the cosmopolitan capital it was eventually to become. Not surprising, as Norway's independence was still a somewhat tenuous phenomenon. From 1523, it had been part of a union with Denmark and ruled by a sovereign in Copenhagen. The Reformation, proclaimed in 1537, strengthened the King's power: all church valuables were sent to Copenhagen, the land owned by the church came under control of the King, and Danish was introduced as a written language. Power duly shifted from provincial nobles to royal administrators: district stipendiary magistrates were appointed as judges, and the sheriffs became employees of the Crown rather than of the local nobility.

In 1814, following Denmark-Norway's defeat in the Napoleonic Wars, Denmark was ceded to Sweden. This time the relationship was less restrictive, and at the time of Bennett's arrival, the move towards full independence was gathering pace. In short, Christiania was a city in transition, from provincial Hanseatic trading port to capital city with an expanding industrial base. A national identity was gradually asserting itself.

In the meantime, Bennett was short of money and needed to find a source of income. He made his way to the British Consulate-General, where he was fortunate to obtain the position of secretary almost immediately. It wasn't exactly a prestigious post: Christiania could hardly be described as a glittering jewel in the diplomatic firmament, and Bennett's tasks would have been pretty menial.

A Story in Brief

THE CASE OF THE MISSING PROPELLER: 'In 1957, Captain Marian Kozuba-Kozubski, of Independent Air Transport, was presented with a problem. He and his DC4 aircraft were stuck on the ground at Frankfurt Airport: one of the aircraft's four engines was not functioning and the airport commandant was adamant that it could only leave when all four engines were functioning properly. It cut no ice, either, when Kozuba-Kozubski protested that the aircraft was designed to take off with just three engines working. Determined not to be thwarted, the Captain ordered the engineer to remove the propeller from the defective engine, started up the remaining three good engines, and requested permission to take off. The tower saw nothing untoward, the reason being that it's impossible to spot a propeller revolving at high speed, but all too easy to see one standing idle. As a result, the aircraft took off without incident, and made it back to Hurn Airport just in time for its next service'. Frank Skinner – IAT engineer.

However, it wasn't long before he was entrusted with the altogether more important job of making arrangements for visiting British guests.

Much of this consisted of meeting and greeting at the dockside, in addition to booking accommodation and arranging porterage, guides and interpreters. As well as providing these standard, consular services, Bennett devised ways to supplement his meagre salary. He laid on, for an extra charge, horse carriages to transport guests about the city, while at the same time developing a thriving language-tuition business, which counted up to 300 pupils on its books, among them the great Norwegian writer Henrik Ibsen and, later, the painter Edvard Munch.

Gradually, though, the task of juggling the demands of the Consulate-General with those of his burgeoning business interests became too much, and in 1849 Bennett opened his own premises on what is now Fred Olsen Gate, at number 17. To begin with, the shop looked more like a delicatessen than a travel agency, with a whole gallimaufry of items for sale – everything from French brandy and champagne to books, British beers and locally produced souvenirs, including silverware and woodcarvings. It was not unlike a duty-free shop – little wonder that the sign outside read 'Bennett's Bazaar'. In his book *The Lottery Ticket*, Jules Verne vividly describes the scene:

"Good-morning, Mr Bennett. It is always a great pleasure to me when I have an opportunity to shake hands with you."

"And for me, professor, it is a great honour."

"Honour, pleasure – pleasure, honour," laughed the professor. "One balances the other."

"I am glad to see that your journey through Central Norway has been safely accomplished."

The following conversation scene takes place while Sylvius Hogg, the protagonist in Jules Verne's *The Lottery Ticket*, is walking through the establishment of Mr Bennett – well known in Christiania and, indeed, throughout Norway:

'It is difficult to mention an article that cannot be found in the bazaar. Travelling-carriages, carioles by the dozen, canned goods, baskets of wine, preserves of every kind, clothing and utensils for tourists and guides to conduct them to the remotest villages of Finnmark, Lapland, or even the North Pole. Nor is this all. Mr Bennett offers, to lovers of natural history, specimens of the different stones and metals found in the earth, as well as of the birds, insects and reptiles of Norway. One can find nowhere a more complete assortment of the jewellery and bric-à-brac of the country than in his show-cases'.

This gentleman is consequently the good angel of all tourists desirous of exploring the Scandinavian Peninsula, and a man Christiania could scarcely do without. "By the way, you found the carriage you had ordered waiting for you at

Tinnoset, did you not, professor?" he asked. "Yes. Having ordered it through you, Mr Bennett, I felt sure that it would be there at the appointed time."

It wasn't long before more, real-life travellers were obliged to Mr Bennett for his services, too. By 1851 he had acquired the scheduled carriage routes from Christiania to Eidsvoll and Fredrikstad, in addition to the establishment of an entirely new service from the capital to Drammen, all operated using imported British carriages manufactured to his bespoke design.

As things turned out, Norway was not quite ready for this kind of transportation system: Bennett's carriage services went out of business, as did the taxi dispatch service he inaugurated in Christiania itself. To his credit, though, he was undaunted by these setbacks. Perhaps he understood that, because the country was on the brink of change, success would be a question of timing and patience.

It wasn't long before he was able to take advantage of new opportunities. Things were certainly moving fast, when it came to transport. Around 1850, the British steamboat company Wilson & Co. began regular sailings from Hull to Christiania. And whereas in 1847 there had only been 22 standard carriage routes, by 1854 there were over 200.

1854 also saw the opening of the first railway in Norway, a 60-kilometre line linking Christiania with Eidsvoll (which brought within reach the possibility of steamboat cruises on Mjøsa, Norway's largest lake). Then, in the 1860s, the typical British gentleman's obsession with travel to the south of France began to wane, and he started seeking out majestic scenery, along with adventure, trekking, exploration and salmon fishing.

All of which Norway – through the estimable Mr Bennett – could provide in abundance. Before long, travellers were arriving in their hundreds, then in their thousands. As there was no existing transportation network across Scandinavia, it fell to Bennett to traverse the length and breadth of the region, from Copenhagen to the Arctic Circle, establishing new carriage routes, stabling for horses, guides and inns. Hitherto, currency exchange and payment for services in remote areas had been a problem, but Bennett triumphantly overcame this hurdle through an innovative system of coupons and vouchers – an early forerunner of traveller's cheques and credit cards.

In short, Thomas Bennett had built up a travel business from scratch, at the same time as a nation was opening up and being reborn. Luck played a role, but, as always, luck is what you make of it, and Bennett made rather a lot: he established his own carriage network throughout Norway and came to know the geography of Scandinavia probably better than any living person – accomplishments which encouraged the cream of European society to beat a path to his door.

What's more, to his great advantage, he could speak the languages of the area.

Nor did he keep all this knowledge to himself: he collated it in the form of brochures, posters, phrasebooks and, in particular, his ground-breaking *Handbook for Norway*, a volume that would be imitated by the burgeoning ranks of travel agents all round the globe.

It was no surprise, then, when, in August of 1853, George Bradshaw of Salford, the great compiler of timetables and handbooks for travellers, came to visit his friend in Christiania. What had not been foreseen though, was Bradshaw's sudden death from cholera, just a few hours after the first appearance of symptoms. He was buried in a cemetery next to Oslo Cathedral.

Eight years later, in 1861, Jules Verne also called in on Bennett, in search of inspiration for new, adventurous themes for his books. It is poignant that all three of these men – who, in their different ways, made significant contributions to the discovery of the world – are linked through their connection with the Norwegian capital.'

THOMAS BENNETT – A MAN WITH CONNECTIONS

Thomas Bennett died in Christiania in 1898, at the age of 84, and is buried at the Cemetery of Our Saviour in Oslo. His business, Bennett Reisebureau, continued operating under the same name until the mid-1990s, when it was taken over by a cruise company.

All those in the business of travel owe him a great debt for the pathways he either uncovered or laid down for others to follow. In addition to Jules Verne and George Bradshaw, Thomas Bennett was able to reflect upon the fact that, among his many illustrious guests, he could count some of the most eminent Europeans of the era: Henrik Ibsen; Lord Randolph Churchill; Knut Hamsun; Karen Blixen; Edvard Grieg; Roald Amundsen; the Archbishop of Canterbury; Sir Arthur Conan Doyle; Coco Chanel; Queens Wilhelmina and Juliana of the Netherlands; Emperor Wilhelm II of Germany; King Oscar II of Sweden-Norway; Queen Maud and King Haakon VII of Norway; Crown Princess Märtha and King Olav V of Norway.

CHAPTER 69
ARISTOCRATS ONLY BY NAME

The 'Princess Alice' pleasure steamer with some 800 Londoners enjoying the last few minutes of their day excursion to Gravesend and back – it ended tragically.

I N May 2011, when the *Spirit of Chartwell* arrived on the Thames for the first time, it became immediately clear to me that the regularity authorities were still chastened by the events of 28 August 1989 – the *Marchioness* disaster. In fact, they were freely quoting from Lord Justice Clarke's inquiry, this being but one reason why I could not fulfil my long-cherished dream of creating on the Thames a cruise operation of a standard I thought fit for this great river. But much earlier there was the fate that befell the Thames river cruiser *Princess Alice*, a disaster that remains still Britain's largest peacetime loss of life.

It was 7.30pm on a balmy September's evening in 1878 and, on the convivially crowded decks of the *Princess Alice* pleasure steamer, some 800 Londoners were enjoying the last few minutes of their day excursion to Gravesend and back. For most of them, it was also to be the last few minutes of their lives. Not that they had any inkling of what was to come – indeed, to those on the top deck, the approach of a large, grimy collier ship at Woolwich seemed no cause for alarm: it was just like lots of other outsized working boats they had seen earlier in the day, and a small adjustment in the *Princess Alice*'s course seemed to ensure that the two vessels would pass each other with plenty of room to spare: the pleasure steamer taking the north side of the river and the coal-bearing ship, whose name could now be made out on its giant hull (SS *Bywell Castle*), taking the south side.

Right up until the last few seconds, the two boats observed the informal drive-on-the-right rule that applied in the capital's busy waters, the *Princess Alice* on its way into town and the *Bywell Castle* on its way out into the Thames Estuary. Suddenly and disastrously, however, Captain William Grinstead, of the *Princess*

Alice, chose to make a sudden turn to port (left), taking his boat into the path of the oncoming leviathan.

If this was a misjudgement, it was of the most monumentally catastrophic kind. Unable to either slow down or take evasive action, the 890-ton, solid-iron *Bywell Castle* ploughed into the 250-ton *Princess Alice* with all its force, splitting the smaller vessel in two, as if it were no more than a brittle matchbox. Men and women, who, seconds earlier, had been chatting and laughing, now found themselves frantically fighting for their lives.

Those who could not get out from the packed lower decks ending up drowning in a solid human mass, wedged up against their neighbours. Those who escaped into the water found themselves not just struggling against capricious and powerful river currents, but also choking and spluttering in water recently augmented by 75 million gallons of raw sewage, released an hour previously from the sewer outfalls at Crossness and Barking.

For days afterwards, corpses of the victims were washed up along the Thames, as far downriver as Rainham and Dagenham. A final death toll was never confirmed, but it is thought that 650 people died: the biggest loss of life ever to have taken place on the Thames, and the largest-ever civilian death toll in British territorial waters.

Of the passengers who were saved, many told tales of incredible good fortune. One man stepped off the skyward-pointing prow of the stricken *Princess Alice* and straight onto the deck of the *Bywell Castle*, while a member of the onboard musical band floated to safety by clinging on to a double bass. They, however, were the lucky ones. A reporter at the time, W.T. Vincent, recorded the pitiful scene at the steamboat company's offices, which had been requisitioned as a makeshift mortuary: 'The lifeless frames of men and women lay about and on the balcony. It was sight to wring tears of blood from the eyes of any beholder. A row of little innocents, plump and pretty; well-dressed children, all dead and cold.'

Over the coming weeks, funeral processions became a common sight in the streets of East London. A mass grave was dug in Woolwich Old Cemetery for 120 of the victims. Members of the public donated sixpences in their thousands to a fund for the erection of a memorial.

When it came to allocating responsibility for the crash, the Board of Trade inquiry had no doubts as to where the blame lay. It produced its final report on 6 November 1878, just a month before the death of Queen Victoria's third daughter, Princess Alice, after whom the ill-fated boat had been named. (Princess Alice was 35 when she died of diphtheria, contracted when she kissed her young son Ernst, who had the disease but survived it.) 'The *Princess Alice* was not properly and efficiently manned,' the report concluded. 'In addition, the number of persons

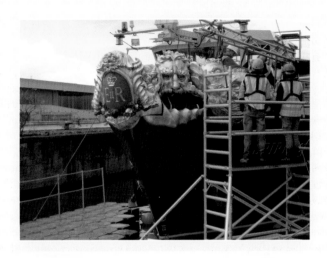

A Story in Brief

RIVIERA/THE COMFORT OF THE COTE D'AZUR: *The Côte d'Azur Pullman Express* was the deluxe French train which ran for 10 years, from 1929 to 1939, and was operated by the Compagnie Internationale des Wagons-Lits and the Compagnie des Chemins de Fer de Paris à Lyon et à la Méditerranée (known as the PLM). Only 612 of the train's original Riviera dining armchairs were ever made, and when 33 of them were rescued from derelict Wagons-Lits carriages, in Normandy, I decided to buy just one of these sumptuous pieces of furniture, and then replicate it, for use on board the *Spirit of Chartwell*. Unfortunately, the wily M.Frederic saw me coming, and insisted that I either buy them all – or none. IMAGE COURTESY: MARKO MILASEVIC.

aboard was more than was prudent, and the means of saving life inadequate for a vessel of her class.'

Captain Grinstead was not alive to hear this verdict. He had been lost with his ship, as had his son, his elder brother and his wife. Meanwhile Captain Harrison, the master of the *Bywell Castle*, did not fare much better: although he survived the disaster, his health suffered as a result, and he was never put to sea again. Even the coroner, a Mr C.J. Carter, was badly affected; already suffering from heart disease beforehand, he never recovered from the trauma of the inquest and died soon afterwards.

Indeed, the impact of the *Princess Alice* tragedy was felt throughout the country. 'It shook Great Britain like an earthquake,' wrote one columnist. 'It sent a shudder vibrating through the world.' It also galvanised the authorities into implementing stricter safety procedures on the Thames. Instead of rowing boats, the Marine Police Force at Wapping was issued with steam launches with which to attend emergencies. Measures were introduced to dispose of sewage farther out to sea (some of the passengers who survived the crash had died of diseases contracted from the filthy water). New rules were also introduced regarding the maximum number of passengers that any vessel could take, while the provision of lifebelts and rafts was made both mandatory and subject to annual inspection. Crucially, the convention of ships keeping to the right-hand side of the river was upgraded from an unwritten rule into a codified requirement.

The waters of the Thames had, in recent years, become both crowded and dangerous, the only cast-iron rule being that smaller ships had to get out of the way of bigger ones. Only days after the disaster, an aggrieved father wrote to a newspaper, complaining about the way in which, just a few days before the accident, the *Princess Alice* had ploughed through a rowing skiff containing his son and friends. Far from stopping to help the stricken craft, its crew had thrown a lifebelt in the water and proceeded on their way.

Without a doubt, the changes introduced after the *Princess Alice* disaster helped do away with the old culture of large ships bullying smaller ones. The system was not fool proof, however, as demonstrated some 111 years later, just a few miles up-river at Southwark. This time the tragedy involved a much smaller pleasure boat, the *Marchioness* (46 tons), being sunk by a massive working boat, the dredger *Bowbelle* (1,880 tons), and the two boats were travelling in the same direction, rather than the opposite direction. At 1.46am on 20 August 1989, the bigger ship ploughed into the rear of the little vessel, on which 127 young people were celebrating their host's 26th birthday party.

The moment the *Bowbelle* struck was described, 20 years later, by one of the passengers who survived: "I looked up and saw a monster," Andrew Sutton told the *Daily Mail*. "The boat that hit us was a big, black ship above me, and it looked like it had eyes."

If it did have eyes, then they must have been shut. Within 30 seconds of the collision, the *Marchioness* had sunk – or rather, had been literally pushed underwater by the *Bowbelle* – trapping groups of guests below deck. Survival was purely a matter of chance: 80 survivors were pulled from the water, while the bodies of 24 people were found inside the ship and 27 others washed up along the Thames in the days following the accident. Among the dead was Antonio de Vasconcellos, the successful young banker who had been giving the party, and 19-year-old Francesca Dallaglio, sister of the future England rugby union captain Lawrence Dallaglio.

How could Douglas Henderson, skipper of the *Bowbelle*, not have seen the *Marchioness*? That was the question put forward again and again at not just one, but two court trials. On both occasions, however, Henderson was acquitted of the charge of not keeping a proper look-out.

It wasn't until six years after the disaster that bereaved relatives secured what they felt was the rightful verdict, when a coroner's inquest ruled that the 51 victims had been unlawfully killed. The single most influential factor in causing the accident, it emerged, was poor visibility from the wheelhouses of both ships. Not only was the view ahead from the *Bowbelle* impeded, but so too was the view to the rear from the *Marchioness*. Added to this, the lights on both vessels were found to be inadequate, and neither radio nor shouted communications proved sufficiently audible over the noise of engines and amplified party music.

Again, as in the aftermath of the *Princess Alice* disaster, a whole new set of safety regulations was introduced. Evacuation and emergency training was made obligatory for bar staff and crew, and a rule was brought in requiring all furniture over five kilograms in weight to be secured to the spot – when the *Marchioness* had tilted post-crash, all the tables and chairs had slid to one side, blocking the exit. In addition, new rules were brought in to improve visibility: as well as better lighting, all boats were required to have a reflective yellow square on their rear, and all Thames bridges were to be illuminated from below, thus ensuring that ships passing underneath would be spot lit, rather than shrouded in darkness.

Most significantly of all, four lifeboat stations were set up along the river (at Gravesend, Tower Pier, Chiswick and Teddington), thereby ensuring the presence of motorised rescue launches within minutes of any future emergency. Too late, of course, for the victims of the *Marchioness* disaster, let alone those who perished aboard the *Princess Alice*, but without a doubt, the safety improvements resulting from these twin tragedies have made the Thames a less hazardous river to navigate.

Although separated by more than a century, these two disasters are joined together by strange and ironic postscripts. In 1883, just five years after that fateful evening in Woolwich, the *Bywell Castle* went down, with all 22 hands, in the Bay of Biscay. Similarly, the *Bowbelle*, under its new name *Bom Rei*, sank off the coast of Madeira in 1996. All four of the ships involved in these catastrophes are thus no more. While the final resting places of the two large ships are both out at sea, the sites of the *Princess Alice* and *Marchioness* disasters remain within view of any Londoner who looks out onto the Thames. This brings to mind the lines written just after the *Princess Alice* tragedy:

'And the dark river's muddy waves – now roll o'er many a hundred graves.

'LORD OF THE GLENS' CROSSING LOCH NESS POSTER BY ROBERT SCURRAH

A Story in Brief:

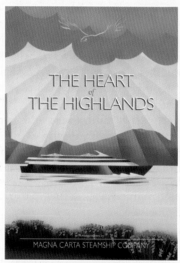

IMAGE COURTESY: ROBERT SCURRAH.

GERARD BLITZ: There aren't many people who can claim to have been an international water polo player, a trained yogi, and a member of the French Resistance. Step forward Belgian-born Gérard Blitz, who can lay claim not only to those three distinctions, but to having founded the now world-famous organisation Club Méditerranée. At the same time as the club's first holiday resort was being opened on the island of Mallorca, Gérard Blitz was busy promoting yoga practice; indeed, he remained secretary and then president of the European Union of Yoga from 1974 right up until his death in Paris, in 1990. The original Club Medi-terranée villages were a lot simpler than their modern-day counterparts: members stayed in unlit straw huts on a beach front; instead of having en suite bathrooms, they all shared communal washing facilities.

CHAPTER 70
RED STAR OVER CHINA

Anyone who was contemplating a visit to China in the early years of
the 'open-door policy', Edgar Snow's 'Red Star Over China' was
considered essential reading.

I N 1974 I had hitched a lift on a Neckermann charter flight to Hong Kong. While there, I took the obligatory excursion to the Chinese border, close to the railway station at Lo Wu, and was immediately captivated with the idea of getting in. At Kai Tak Airport, before boarding the return flight home, I bought a copy of Edgar Snow's *Red Star Over China* and read it cover to cover, after which I was more determined than ever to get into China.

For anyone from the West with an interest in the China of the 1930s, when Mao Zedong was still a guerrilla leader, or who was contemplating a visit to China during the early stages of its 'open-door policy' of the late 1970s and early 1980s, *Red Star Over China* was considered essential reading. Today, now that China has changed so much so quickly, and with the publication of more realistic appraisals of the events of the Chinese Revolution, Snow's book has lost its lustre. Yet for many years, his early history of the Chinese Communist Party and reportage of the Long March piqued a fascination with the People's Republic of China, a romantic view of a country that had long been considered mysterious and unknowable.

Edgar Snow was an American and is believed to have been the first Western journalist to interview Mao Zedong. Born in 1905, he studied journalism and made money on the stock market, selling out prior to the Wall Street Crash of 1929. Now well set up financially, he embarked on an around-the-world tour, but when he reached Shanghai he was bitten by the China bug and decided to stay. He remained in the country until 1941.

Shanghai, essentially run by the Western powers of the time – France, the

United States and Great Britain – was a vast, seething melting pot of a city, characterised by a collision of political and criminal intrigue with big money and dire poverty which produced a bewitching, desperate glamour.

Snow was taken on by the English-language *China Weekly Review* as assistant advertising manager, and then, in 1932, he married Helen Foster Snow, an aspiring journalist working in the American Consulate. The newlyweds moved to Peking, where Snow worked as a part-time lecturer in journalism at Yenching University and where, through students who were at the forefront of Chinese radical politics, he acquired a taste for the revolutionary movements that were a feature of China in the 1930s.

In this era, China was a country beset by calamity: there was a civil war between Chiang Kai-shek's nationalist Kuomintang (KMT) and Mao's Communist Party, and this had created a breach which was seized upon by an invading Japanese army.

Chiang Kai-shek's apparent indifference to the danger posed by the Japanese caused Snow to become disenchanted with the man he had initially admired. Through contact with the underground Communist network, Snow was invited to visit Mao Zedong's headquarters in Bao'an, the town in the arid province of Shaanxi where Mao had settled his army following the Long March. In June 1936, Snow – together with his friend George Hatem, a doctor who had moved to China from the US to help the poor – went to Xi'an and, from there, to Bao'an, where he was to spend three months and which he described as follows:

'Bao'an was once a frontier stronghold. Remains of its fortifications, flame-struck in that afternoon sun, could be seen flanking the narrow pass through which once emptied into this valley the conquering legions of the Mongols. There was an inner city, still, where the garrisons were once quartered, and a high defensive masonry, lately improved by the Reds, embraced about a square mile, in which the present town was located.'

Snow had wanted to write a book on the Communist movement in China, but *Red Star Over China*, first published in London in 1937, was given credit for introducing both Chinese and foreign readers not so much to the Communist Party, which was already reasonably well known, but to Mao Zedong, whom Snow described as a political reformer, rather than the purely radical revolutionary he had been during the 1920s.

Red Star Over China, together with Pearl S. Buck's *The Good Earth*, was the most influential book on the Western understanding of China in the 1930s. Whereas Buck's book helped win her the Nobel Prize in Literature 'for her rich and truly epic descriptions of peasant life in China', Snow uses his extensive interviews with Mao and the other leaders of the Chinese Communist movement (among them Zhou Enlai, Peng Dehuai and Lin Biao) to portray vivid descriptions of the Long March as well as Mao Zedong's life story.

At the time, there were no reliable reports reaching the West of what was going on in the Communist-controlled areas of the country. China was then regarded by most outsiders with a mixture of suspicion and fear based on profound ignorance. Hong Kong, Shanghai and Peking were familiar names, but beyond the confines of these fairy-tale cities there was, most Westerners imagined, nothing but unrelenting poverty.

Snow, too, was all but unknown, and this was his strength. With no history of political sympathies, his book seemed authentic and authoritative and written from direct personal experience, thereby arousing a latent curiosity in readers around the world. His portrayal of life amongst the soldiers of the Red Army in remote Shaanxi inspired admiration for their feats of endurance and for their unstinting dedication to their cause. Liberal Westerners were gratified and relieved, while even sceptics, who associated communism with the excesses of the Soviet Union, were won over by the romance of the story.

Snow conveyed a seriousness of intent on the part of Mao, causing people to believe in his integrity, in marked contrast with the apparent corruption of Chiang Kai-shek's KMT government. Furthermore, much was made of Mao's United Front policy, which perceptively forsook class struggle in favour of an alliance between all parties against the common threat posed by the Japanese invaders.

Not only foreigners learned more about Mao through Snow's book – many Chinese did too, and it is possible that the cult of Mao really began with the translation of *Red Star Over China* into Chinese. The book, one of the great journalistic scoops of the 20th century, certainly played a role in swaying Western and Chinese opinion in favour of Mao. Indeed, Mao commented that the book 'had merit no less than Great Yu [a legendary ruler in ancient China, famed for his introduction of flood controls] controlling the floods'.

Many decades on, with Chairman Mao dead and out of favour and the Communist Party of China only nominally communist, the merits of *Red Star Over China* are debatable to say the least. But of course, the 1930s were a long time ago, and it is perhaps too easy to scoff at those who should have known better, but who were swept along on the revolutionary tide.

For example, back then there were plenty of liberal intellectuals who were ready to turn a blind eye to the brutality of Stalin and who suggested to Snow, who had little time for the Soviet leader, that he tone down his criticisms of Soviet policy – indeed, it appears that Snow submitted transcripts of his interviews to be edited and approved by Communist Party officials.

Nonetheless, many would now claim that Snow, who was aware of Mao's

A Story in Brief

BEAUTY & THE BEAST: The last time I had set foot in the building was in 1965, for a job with Horizon Holidays which I didn't get. Now, in 1979, this was the headquarters of Vogue magazine and they wanted to be the first fashion magazine to do a photo-shoot in China. I suggested the northern city of Datong, where the Chinese were still building steam locomotives, and where there would be the right combination of revolutionary Mao-suited workers, steam and grime, contrasting with the free-flowing haute couture garb of the Vogue models. The Chinese Ministry of Culture were initially reluctant to agree to this assignment, having earlier turned down our requests on behalf of American singer Glenn Campbell and UK musician Mike Oldfield (though we were luckier with a Harrow School group which included Solzhenitsyn's son). The Vogue China number appeared to great media acclaim in September 1979, and is still considered one of Vogue's most iconic and sought-after issues. **IMAGE COURTESY: VOGUE MAGAZINE.**

intention to govern China, contrived to convey a more benevolent assessment of Mao than was his due. Certainly many readers concluded, after reading *Red Star Over China*, that Mao's followers were really only concerned with improving conditions on the land – a terrible irony, considering the famines that later benighted China as a result of policies like the Great Leap Forward. Whether Mao was already a monster in 1937 or grew into one once he became the 'Great Helmsman' is a moot point. Many commentators reckon the former and believe that Snow, although sincere, was taken in by Mao's cunning.

In later years, when accused of having sympathised with undemocratic governments during World War II, Snow retorted: "In this international cataclysm, brought on by fascists, it is no more possible for any people to remain neutral than it is for a man surrounded by bubonic plague to remain 'neutral' towards the rat population. Whether you like it or not, your life as a force is bound either to help the rats or hinder them. Nobody can be immunised against the germs of history."

Snow's heart was in the right place, but although he made an intellectual case for his beliefs, they ultimately fell foul of the old enemy of ideology: facts.

VOGUE MODEL AT THE DATONG LOCOMOTIVE FACTORY 1979

CHAPTER 71
SHANGHAI – LIFE ITSELF

Its metaphor for debauched living, lingers on. Two of the various epithets that were popularly attached to it – the 'Whore of the Orient' and the 'Paris of the East' – convey depravity and a certain risqué stylishness.

O N my first visit to China in 1977, the itinerary provided for visits to both Peking and Shanghai. Shanghai proved the more revealing of the two cities – if eerily so, because of the darkened streets – and certainly the local people's reactions were much more conservative than had I encountered in the capital, Peking. Two things stood out for me in Shanghai: the delicious Western cuisine that was still being served up at the Red House Restaurant and, perhaps more amazingly still, the jazz band that was still playing at Victor Sassoon's old Cathay Hotel on the Bund. It was also in there that I received the fateful call that my apartment had been badly damaged by a fire that had started during a fireman's strike.

Some place names evoke an image instantly – or, if not an image, a specific association, no matter how threadbare, which lodges permanently in the human imagination. Such is Shanghai. The name, as a metaphor for debauched living, lingers on. Two of the various epithets that were popularly attached to it, the 'Whore of the Orient' and the 'Paris of the East', convey exactly the reputation for depravity and a certain risqué stylishness that prevailed during its heyday, in the first half of the 20th century.

The transformation from a Chinese port of moderate significance to a metropolis that attracted, by the million, the famous and the rich, seekers of fame and fortune and refugees from revolution and poverty was the outcome of a curious form of political compromise.

Shanghai's modern history begins in the mid-19th century, when the British Empire clashed with Imperial China over the importation of opium. The British, in an effort to find a way around the strict limitations imposed by the Chinese on trade between China and Western powers (and thus reduce their trade deficit), came up with the idea of exporting opium from their unprofitable colony in India and importing it into China.

The Chinese government naturally took exception to this, if only because of the ensuing loss of revenue. A period of political skirmishing led to military conflict and a defeat for the weaker Chinese forces. Victorious, the British now demanded unlimited trading rights, which would no longer be confined to Canton (until then, the only port accessible to foreigners) but extended to other ports, including Shanghai, along the eastern Chinese seaboard.

Within these ports, Britain and the other Western powers were to be allocated special areas, known as 'concessions', situated beyond the city purlieus in which they were to obtain the privilege of 'extraterritoriality', a form of exemption from Chinese law. Over the years, even as the boundaries between the concessions and neighbouring Chinese areas blurred, the character of these ports – distorted reflections of sedate suburbia in faraway countries, quite at odds with the hubbub of local life – became defined by their foreignness. What was unexceptional in Paris and London looked exotic and almost fabulous built around a walled city in far Cathay.

Of all the concession ports, Shanghai prospered the most. Its location, right in the middle of China's long coastline and on the Huangpu, a wide and deep river both navigable for large ships and feeding into the mouth of the mighty Yangtse just a few miles downstream, was greatly to its advantage. Although placed at the lowest administrative level in the political hierarchy, in terms of commerce, Shanghai had, even before the arrival of the Western powers, established itself as the major entrepôt for the lower Yangtse River region.

By the 1920s, Shanghai had become the richest city in the world. Its success was attributable to a combination of factors: river access to the heart of the country; cheap labour arising from a continuous flow of Chinese fugitives, both from poverty and the weak, unstable Chinese government; international events, including World War I and the Russian Revolution (and later, Nazi persecu-tion), which propelled waves of international refugees into a place that was neither colony nor state and to which they would not be refused entry; the opium trade; and entrepreneurial flair.

Good organisation, together with a large amount of circulating money and a large pinch of desperation, is a good recipe for business and, for those wanting it, riotous living. As a guidebook of the era stated: 'There are three kinds of club in Shanghai – high class, low class and no class.'

For those that made it, Shanghai was a world within a world, not merely a city but, as was sometimes said, 'life itself', for everything was available at the right price. In the end, Shanghai was all about money – making it and spending it, or, for the poor, trying to live without it. This was a city that had a racecourse not at its fringes, not in the neighbouring countryside, but right in the very centre of the International Settlement (a later combination of the British and American concessions), immediately adjacent to Shanghai's busiest shopping street, Nanking Road. Work, shop, visit a club and go to the races – all within an easy rickshaw ride of each other.

This set-up would not have been possible were it not for a fundamentally well-organised administration. There were some anomalies – the International Settlement and the French Concession had, for example, different electrical systems – but, on the whole, Shanghai worked.

Had it been only a free-for-all, then the entire city, and not just part of it, would have been run by the likes of 'Pockmarked Huang' and 'Big-Eared Du', gangsters who controlled much of the criminal underworld and all that went with it (and, in the case of Huang, worked as a detective for the French Concession Police). As it was, their activities were sufficiently contained for more traditional entrepreneurs to ply their various trades within the liberal business constraints of laissez-faire Shanghai.

Among these men of business were some remarkable individuals, several of whom emanated from the same community, that of Iraqi, Sephardic Jewry: a name given to all Jews who use a Sephardic style of liturgy, which had its origins in the Jewish community of the Iberian Peninsula. Most Sephardic Jews were expelled from Spain in 1492, and eventually settled in various parts of the Levant, including Baghdad, then part of the Ottoman Empire. Life eventually became difficult there, too, and families looked elsewhere to make their fortunes.

The Sassoons moved to Bombay and did well. When Shanghai became available, they were quick in spotting a good opportunity and did well there, too. Eventually they forsook Bombay for Shanghai entirely, and by the time Victor Sassoon inherited the business, his family had been there for four generations. It was Victor who built one of the great Shanghai landmarks, the Cathay Hotel (now the Peace Hotel), overlooking the river on the Bund waterfront. There Noel Coward wrote *Private Lives*, and there too would the beneficiaries of China's re-admittance of foreign visitors from the late 1970s onwards have found ageing members of the old house jazz band, pumping out pre-war swing standards with something short of pre-war gusto.

One of Sassoon's acolytes was a fellow Jew from Baghdad, Silas Hardoon, who became the wealthiest man in Asia and whose mansion occupied 26 acres of prime real estate plumb in the centre of the city. After Silas died, squabbles over his will

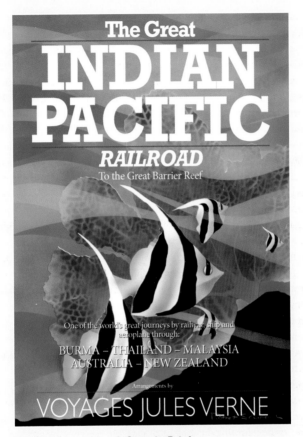

A Story in Brief

THE DATONG LOCOMOTIVE FACTORY: In 1979, this was one of the last places on the planet still making steam trains. It was a Mecca for locomotive buffs, which meant it wasn't just Vogue fashion photographers who wanted to go there: steam train enthusiasts used to beat a path to our door, in order to set up visits to Datong, in Shanxi Province. The factory was founded in 1954, as part of the first Chinese five-year plan for economic development, and it produced its first locomotive in 1959. By 1988, the factory had produced over 5,000 steam engines, and proceeded to turn them out at a rate of 250-300 per year. Production at Datong was a vertically integrated process, starting from raw steel, and ending with the finished, glistening locomotive. The factory's last steam locomotive was manufactured on 21 December 1988. From which point on, the place produced diesels.

IMAGE COURTESY: ROBERT SCURRAH/VOYAGES JULES VERNE.

continued into the 1950s, and today there is nothing left of Hardoon Gardens: its foundations are concealed by the massive Shanghai Exhibition Centre, a gift to China from the Soviet Union in the days when the two countries were theoretically united by ideology.

Silas, in his time, was the classic rich and eccentric recluse. Of all the celebrated Shanghai Jewish families, it is only the more sober Kadoories who have continued to prosper. They, too, ended up in Shanghai by way of Bombay but, shrewdly, also had major business interests in Hong Kong which they continue to run today. Indeed, Horace Kadoorie was the first man from Hong Kong to sit in the House of Lords. The palatial Kadoorie residence in Shanghai, known as 'Marble Hall', on the former Bubbling Well Road, is still there; it is now the Shanghai Children's Palace.

After 1949, with the exception of a few misguided optimists who thought that life in Shanghai would go on as before, notwithstanding the triumph of the Communists and the loss of extraterritoriality, most people realised that the game was up. As the ever-sanguine Victor Sassoon allegedly commented at the time: "Well, I gave up India, and China gave me up."

In one sense, Shanghai did not change for a further 40 years. Once all the 'sing-song girls' (courtesans) and mobsters had been subjected to 're-education', in order to turn them from objects of exploitation into model Maoists, the neon lights went out. The city itself, with its acres of leafy avenues flanked by suburban villas and its monumental Western architecture that appeared to have been lifted directly from London, Liverpool or New York, did not change.

Single houses were divided into flats, former dance halls and clubs became offices, synagogues and churches became storage depots and streets were given names more in keeping with the revolutionary spirit that pervaded the land. However, in the following decades, until the Chinese economy accelerated from about 1990, nothing was removed and little was added. Someone leaving Shanghai in 1949 and returning in 1981 would have discovered the city looking much as it had been left, only etiolated.

On the streets, ageing Chinese who, before 1949, had worked in the concessions would approach foreigners in perfect English or French and hand over their written credentials, in the hope of finding work abroad. Gardeners, their pride in the individual character of their city undimmed, maintained the lawns and flowerbeds of the former consulates and mansions, just as in the old days. Hotels still produced cruets, teapots and sugar tongs at breakfast. Bellhops in the Peace Hotel still wore the uniforms of the 1930s and, along the corridors, brass fire-extinguishers made in San Francisco gleamed dully beneath art-deco lamps.

However, daily life, in a country still recovering from the Cultural Revolution (largely spawned, ironically, in Shanghai), was very different from how it had once been. Yet somehow, one or two old Shanghai institutions still functioned, miraculous survivors of political reform and anti-foreignness. The Red House, as it was now called in accordance with political correctness, had been established in 1935, on what was then Avenue Joffre, in the French Concession, as 'Chez Revere'. For early visitors to post-Mao China, desperate for food that was not Chinese, the Red House was almost a rite of passage. The food on offer was poor, but at least you were able to sink your teeth into a steak au poivre or a chocolate soufflé (in name at least) and use a knife and fork.

Shanghai is now, once again, a major international trading centre, with the major difference that Western influence today is purely based on commerce. Its wonderfully unsavoury past is commemorated only in a few evocative names, some impressive early Sino-Western art-nouveau and art-deco architecture, and an attempt to maintain its reputation as the crucible of Chinese style.

It still has something, but Blood Alley and the opium dens are all long gone.

THE SILK ROAD REVISITED POSTER BY VOYAGES JULES VERNE

A Story in Brief:

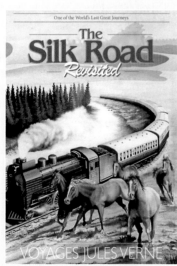

IMAGE COURTESY: VOYAGES JULES VERNE.

THE EARLY DAYS: 'Father's (Captain Langton) original venture was to run coach holidays from the North West down to Bournemouth and Torquay at very reasonable cost; thereby making holiday travel affordable for many workers in that area. As he had worked previously for a firm of travel agents, he knew of the difficulties coach and hotel business were experiencing due to the depression of the late 20s; at the same time, though, he knew that customers could be found, if firms could be persuaded to cut prices to a minimum. And it worked! Operating under various surrogates such as Happiway, Universal and Iberian Travel, these coach operations were transmogrified into what became Blue Cars. One thing I always remember, though, which is that my father always played business matters close to his chest and, once he began to get established, he never brought his work home with him.' June Langton.

CHAPTER 72
THE MAN WHO BOUGHT ME

He is considered by many to have pioneered affordable, long-haul travel. Spotting the large number of planes lying idle during the winter months, he re-deployed them to all four corners of the globe.

IT was in 1966, the year England won the World Cup, that 24-year-old Peter Diethelm came to London, to set up a UK operation on behalf of Kuoni, the Swiss travel firm that was celebrating its 60th anniversary that year. There wasn't, he admits, much competition for the job, which had been created following Kuoni's takeover of travel firm Challis and Benson. To be honest, not many people in the UK had heard of the name Kuoni, but, under Peter's direction, all that was to change.

Peter is considered by many to have pioneered the introduction of affordable long-haul travel. Spotting the large number of planes lying idle during the winter months, he re-deployed them to all four corners of the globe. Thanks to him, travellers could book a week's 'all-in' package holiday in Mombasa, Kenya, for just £199 (roughly half the price of the standard scheduled airfare), or a week in Luxor, Egypt, for the same price as a single night in a Caribbean luxury hotel.

Not only that, Peter introduced a seven-day-a-week, 8.00am-8.00pm telephone bookings line and oversaw the introduction of a computer system (Kudos) which allowed customers far greater flexibility when it came to choosing dates, times, hotels and flights. He also moved the firm from cramped premises in New Bond Street to far more spacious (and cheaper) headquarters in Dorking, where office space cost £1.90 per square foot, as opposed to £8.90 per square foot in central London.

It wasn't just the Kuoni customers who benefited, either. "We explained to travel agents that if we popularised long-haul travel, then it would be as easy for them to sell a holiday to Thailand and earn 10 per cent commission as it would be to sell a holiday to Spain and earn just £10-£15 in commission," recalls Diethelm, who won a reputation for taking high risks but charging low prices. "My argument was always that I created more opportunity, without hitting anyone in the pocket."

That said, some of his initiatives earned him a degree of unpopularity within the travel industry, particularly his weekend phone-line policy. Some agents even threatened to take Kuoni brochures off their racks, but Peter was never afraid of taking bold decisions. At one point, for example, he shut down the whole Kuoni chartered travel operation. He explains: "Boeing had introduced the 747, which doubled the capacity of the old 707, and meant we just could not compete with scheduled airlines, so we shut the whole chartered side down and only re-opened it in the 1980s, when there was a shortage of capacity.

"We pretty much trod a permanent tightrope between chartered and scheduled flights, but I made sure we had the flexibility to do so. I would point out, in our defence, that we won the 'Best Tour Operator' award for some 25 years, and that the people who voted for us were the travel agents, who often kicked and screamed over things we did, but who respected us nonetheless."

Whatever the travel industry thought about Diethelm, the travelling public were fully for what Kuoni had to offer. There may not have been any online Trip-Advisor or Expedia recommendations in those days, but there was plenty of word-of-mouth promotion. "Back in the 1960s, travelling to South America, Kenya or Thailand said something about you," says Diethelm. "You really were someone if you had been to those places, and there was a kind of cocktail party effect: people who had the money to go on safari to Kenya really wanted to tell others about it."

A strategy Diethelm made full use of was inviting past clients to give drinks parties (with £15 worth of booze provided by Kuoni), at which guests would be given a slide show of their host's holiday and a glossy Kuoni brochure to take home. "It was one of the cheapest, but most effective, forms of promotion you could imagine," he says. "We were a small company, but we had a huge profile and we were making money, too: 10 per cent profit, whereas most firms were making two per cent."

He also kept an eye out for other companies to acquire and, in 1998, launched a successful bid for Voyages Jules Verne. "I had followed VJV for some time and I had the greatest admiration for Philip Morrell," Diethelm recalls. "He took the firm from being a China specialist to an Egypt specialist, and it seemed to me that he had this talent both for taking risks and for morphing when circumstances dictated – the bigger the disaster, the bigger the recovery. Also, VJV had a product that was an absolute fit for Kuoni. At a stroke, we bought a company with a £50

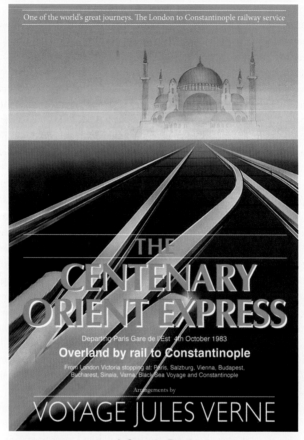

One of the world's great journeys. The London to Constantinople railway service

THE CENTENARY ORIENT EXPRESS

Departing Paris Gare de l'Est 4th October 1983

Overland by rail to Constantinople

From London Victoria stopping at: Paris, Salzburg, Vienna, Budapest, Bucharest, Sinaia, Varna, Black Sea Voyage and Constantinople

Arrangements by

VOYAGE JULES VERNE

A Story in Brief

A FAMILY FIRM/SAWDUST IN THE BLOOD: They designed and crafted the marquetry for the *Titanic*, the *Mauritania*, the *Aquitania*, the *Lusitania*, the *Queen Mary* and the *Queen Elizabeth*, as well as the luxury carriages of the Wagon-Lits company. Not to mention our own royal barge, the *Spirit of Chartwell*. The firm of Dunn and Son, at Chelmsford, in Essex, was founded in 1895 by Mr Albert Dunn, after serving a seven-year apprenticeship with a French firm, based in London. In more recent years, Dunn and Son have produced panelling for the Pullman cars of the *Venice Simplon Orient Express* and the *Northern Belle*, as well as carrying out restoration work at Buckingham Palace, and on The Queen's Doll House, in Windsor Castle. The business today is still carried on by a Dunn: Albert's great-grand-daughter Cheryl.

IMAGE COURTESY: ROBERT SCURRAH/VOYAGES JULES VERNE.

million sales turnover, which put us in a different league."

The growth in Kuoni sales had been pretty phenomenal anyway, rising from £6 million per year in the 1960s to £369 million in 2000. Figures like this ensured that Kuoni did everything in their power to keep their high-flying UK manager on board. "I got many proposals from outside companies, but I was very well looked-after by Kuoni," says Diethelm. "They gave my own share options and, just as importantly, they took the attitude, organisationally, that, if I asked for something, then I got it. I reported directly to the company's CEO, and to be honest, most people in the UK thought Kuoni was my own company anyway."

The level of respect that Diethelm got from HQ was matched by his pay packet. Today he has his own farm in the Surrey countryside, in addition to a ranch in California, and makes regular visits back to his native Switzerland, especially during the skiing season. He also runs his own charity, the PD Foundation, helping disadvantaged communities in Thailand, Sri Lanka, Kenya and Egypt.

The question is, could someone today rise, as both he and I did, from tour guide or tour rep to managing director? Diethelm shakes his head: "You know, I don't think the same thing would happen now; you wouldn't just go from being a tour leader to running an office. That said, I think it was my time as a tour leader that helped me get to know our future customers and see how much our products meant to them. Once you've seen that at first hand, you never forget it."

CHAPTER 73
PASSPORT TO ANYWHERE

Lars-Eric Lindblad was a Swedish-American entrepreneur and explorer, who pioneered tourism to many remote and exotic parts of the world including the first tourist expedition to Antarctica in 1966.

LARS-ERIC Lindblad once confided in me the secret as to how he got Lindblad Expeditions into China ahead of any other American company. Since Lars-Eric held dual Swedish and American nationality, when he approached the Chinese he naturally emphasised his Swedish credentials, given that the Chinese were then not disposed to direct dealings with American companies. Wan Fu, my contact in China and the man who had given me my first break, had, it turned out, given Lars my hard-sought-after entry visas once Thomson had axed the China programme – in the process no doubt saving a little face.

Lindblad was born in 1927 in Solna, just north of Stockholm, and emigrated to the United States in 1951, later becoming an American citizen and establishing Lindblad Travel in 1958. An entrepreneur and explorer, he pioneered tourism to many remote and exotic parts of the world – for example, the Arctic and Antarctic regions, Tierra del Fuego, the Falkland Islands, the Galápagos Islands, Easter Island, the Seychelles, Bhutan and the islands east of Bali. He led the first tourist expedition to Antarctica in 1966 – on a chartered Argentine navy ship – and for many years thereafter operated his own vessel in the region, the MS *Lindblad Explorer*. Observers point to the *Lindblad Explorer*'s 1969 expeditionary cruise to Antarctica as perhaps the frontrunner to today's sea-based tourism there. In 1984 he led the first voyage by a tourist ship through the Northwest Passage, from Newfoundland, Canada, over the top of the American continent and via the Bering Strait to Yokohama, Japan. The voyage took 40 days, over a distance of 8,920 nautical miles (16,520 km), and was covered by most news media in North America and Europe at the time.

Lindblad was president and chief executive officer of Lindblad Travel in Westport, Connecticut, for more than 30 years. Lindblad Travel ceased operations in 1989, the same year it was fined more than $75,000 for violating US trade embargoes against Vietnam and Cambodia by offering tours there. Lars-Eric later said the penalties and legal fees incurred in his dispute with the US Government had contributed to the company going out of business. In an interview in the *New York Times* when the penalties were levied, he admitted to intentionally violating the sanctions and was unrepentant: "I would do it again. Travel, in my opinion, is not ordinary trade. Travel is a way of communication. To embargo travel is like burning books or imprisoning journalists." Just three years later, in 1992, the embargo against Cambodia was lifted by President George H. W. Bush, while in February 1994 President Bill Clinton lifted the trade embargo against Vietnam, resulting in a number of American companies starting to offer tours there.

Lindblad was also a noted environmentalist who believed tourism had been responsible for saving many threatened areas. In opening remote and exotic areas of the world to tourism, he became widely recognised as a prominent figure of ecotourism. He was awarded the Order of the Golden Ark by the Netherlands, for services to wildlife conservation, and was made a Knight of the Polar Star by the King of Sweden.

He also received a number of environmental and cultural awards, served on the council of the World Wildlife Fund and African Wildlife Foundation, and was elected to the Hall of Fame of the American Society of Travel Agents. In 1993, *Travel + Leisure* magazine named him one of the top 20 explorers of all time. His autobiography, *Passport to Anywhere*, with an introduction by the ornithologist Roger Tory Peterson, describes his many adventurous travel experiences.

At one point, Lindblad sold a controlling interest in his company to a Hong Kong entrepreneur, and it was this gentleman that I was to go on to meet, with a view to possibly acquiring Lindblad Travel. I already knew Lars-Eric personally and our paths were to cross many times in both Connecticut and London, as we explored if and how Voyages Jules Verne and Lindblad could co-operate.

Indeed, my connection with Lars-Eric had started much earlier, due to his work on opening up China for travel, for which he was given the accolade of an appearance on the front cover on *Time* magazine. In 1977 I had established contact with the Chinese, and at the time Great Britain was considered an 'old friend of the Chinese people'. This epithet most certainly did not extend to Americans; in fact, the Chinese had an aversion to anything American, especially American Express, for some unknown reason.

By the time I had found my way to Lindblad's office in Connecticut, with the idea of possibly buying Lindblad Travel, it was clear that the original drive and inspiration of the man that had created this amazing company had not survived the emotional drain of having passed ownership of his 'baby' to another – and I could see that, without that spark, it would have been futile to proceed with the acquisition.

Lars-Eric died suddenly of a heart attack in 1994, while on holiday in Stockholm. The company was to live on, however, rekindled as Lindblad Expeditions by his son, Sven-Olof Lindblad, who later entered into co-operation with National Geographic, thus continuing his father's tradition of pioneering and expedition voyaging.

My Lindblad connection lives on, too: my Scottish Highland exploration vessel, *Lord of the Glens*, is a regular part of the Lindblad / National Geographic offerings. As for my vessel *Lord of the Highlands*, it was bought by Lindblad Expeditions, renamed the *National Geographic Islander*, and is now happily plying its trade for them among the Galapagos Islands.

A Story in Brief

'BANNING TRAVEL IS LIKE BURNING BOOKS': The moment you met this Explorer Extraordinaire, he made you feel you'd known him for years. He was as charismatic a character as you could hope to find, and he just loved being among people. What's more, he had this capacity for attracting immensely talented people to work for him. Not just established experts in their fields, such as the ornithologists and conservationists Roger Tory Peterson and Sir Peter Scott, but young people he'd just met; he would have this hunch that they would do well. In the words of naturalist Tom Ritchie, who worked for him for many years, Lars-Eric was "larger than life, outgoing, creative, effervescent, talkative, enthusiastic, knowledgeable, experienced, extremely likeable, and a true trailblazer in the travel industry". To my knowledge, Lars was the only tour operator ever to have made it onto the front cover of *Time* magazine.   IMAGE COURTESY: RALPH HAMMELBACHER/LINDBLAD.

CHAPTER 74
DEATH ON THE NILE

Speaking of Hercule Poirot, Mr Gaafar was responsible for some of the arrangements for the making of 'Death on the Nile', the film of the Agatha Christie novel, starring Peter Ustinov as Hercule Poirot.

I N all the areas where Thomson and Voyages Jules Verne operated, it was the usual practice to appoint a local agent, and nowhere was this as important as in Egypt, where the Byzantine blind alleys could all too easily catch out the unwary tour operator. In Thomson, we used the long-established Eastmar company, and for good reason, since they had both the political clout and the tourist hardware that most operators needed – namely, coaches, guides and, above all, Nile steamers.

The owner of Eastmar was Youssef Gaafar, who, in 1971, somehow managed to get Thomson permission to bring direct flights into Cairo, in the teeth of outright opposition from the national carrier, Egyptair. (These flights were halted by the Yom Kippur War of 1973; ironically, we started flights soon after to Tel Aviv.) At the time, we were keen to get into the Nile cruise market, but were ultimately unsuccessful because although Youssef Gaafar owned and operated the few traditional vessels on the river, these were all chartered out to Swan Hellenic, Bales Tours or Club Méditerannée.

Nevertheless, I kept in touch with Youssef after I left Thomson in 1978, and it so happened that he was one of the first people to cross the threshold of my Glentworth Street office. Once Voyages Jules Verne had decided to go into the Egyptian market, he was my natural choice as local agent.

Given that we were carrying more than 900 travellers a week into the country, we needed to charter a whole host of different vessels. We especially sought those with a bit of history attached so that we could work up a suitably nostalgic theme, as we did with King Farouk's private Nile steamer, *Karim*, which had originally been sent from London in kit form and re-assembled on the Nile in 1917.

The *Karim* was a bestseller for us from day one. She had, in her time, carried most of the Egyptian royalty on board, having been reserved for the exclusive use first of King Fuad and then of his son King Farouk. Following the 1952 revolution, she had been taken over by the Egyptian state, hosting President Gamal Abdel Nasser and, later on, President Anwar el-Sadat and his wife, Gihan. In short, this was precisely the kind of combination I was after. (Amazingly, the *Karim* is still going today, powered by her original 1917 steam engine and stern quarter-wheel paddles, combining the comfort of the 21st century with the grandeur of the bygone past.)

Although the *Karim* wasn't one of Youssef Gaafar's vessels, it might as well have been, since he was unquestionably the modern-day father of Nile cruising. Not that you often got to meet the man himself. Such were the complexities and confidentialities of his business arrangements that he employed a small number of trusted lieutenants, all under the Eastmar banner. He erected around himself a sort of Chinese wall, whereby he would allocate a particular lieutenant to deal with a particular tour operator, and often that lieutenant would be competing against another of Youssef's trusties, to try and get the best deals.

When I was at Thomson, my allocated lieutenant was Hisham Imam, and when I was at Voyages Jules Verne, I was allocated his equally able brother, Tarek. It was their job to respond to my insatiable demands for more vessels and new product ideas – and, every so often, to be the bearers of bad news.

There was no question, though, that the man in charge was Youssef, who in 1991 recorded his reflections on the rise of the Nile cruise:

'Touring beyond the confines of Europe is something that does not date much before the late 19th century; the 'Grand Tour' of Italy and France, an 18th-century phenomenon, was one thing, but to venture into Africa was quite another. Archaeological discoveries, however, began to excite an interest in the Egypt of the Pharaohs and in their cities along the banks of the Nile. So, the Nile cruise was born.

This phenomenon began at the end of the 19th-century, with Thomas Cook and, inevitably, another lesser-known company that no longer exists, the Anglo-American Line. Both ran cruises until just before the Second World War: the basic route, Cairo to Aswan, or Luxor to Aswan, was the same as today.

These are the most interesting parts of the river for aficionados of Egyptian civilisation, then as now, but to continue further south, into Sudan, has always been a problem, as any account of the early explorers will tell you. The main obstacles to such a journey are either the cataracts, of which there are several of varying difficulty, or, more recently, dams – of which there are two, the newer one

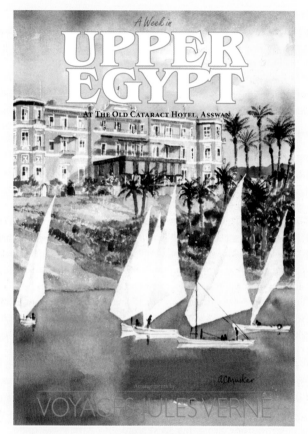

A Story in Brief

THE DRAMATIC ARTIST: Watercolour painter Alison Musker made an interesting discovery, while tuned in to BBC's Radio Four. "I found that, when painting, if I was listening to an exciting play, and the action was repeated at a later date, the exact point of thought in the painting could be clearly remembered." Along with Sir Hugh Casson, Alison was responsible for the majority of the water-colours that featured either in the Voyages Jules Verne or Serenissima brochures. She is a member of The Small Paintings Group, the Chelsea Art Society and the Reading Guild, and is both an Associate and a Full Member of the Royal Watercolour Society. She has had five solo exhibitions, mainly in London but also in Italy and Albania, and her work has featured in the collections both of The Queen Mother and Prince of Wales. The example here of the Old Cataract Hotel in Aswan is also by Alison Musker.

IMAGE COURTESY: ALISON MUSKER/VOYAGES JULES VERNE.

built, with the help of the Russians, in the 1960s.

In fact, even the old dam could allow only small craft to pass through. For anyone wishing to proceed into Sudan, it was a question of leaving the leisurely comfort of Egyptian cruise vessels and boarding the rather more utilitarian facilities offered by Sudanese steamers, then operating between Aswan and Wadi Halfa.

The level of comfort offered by early steamers on the Egyptian Nile differed from today's vessels only in that they reflected the lifestyles and technical possibilities of the time. There were fewer people, fewer cabins and larger sun decks. We tend to think that the early tourists were rather more cosseted than they are today; seemingly, they were just more relaxed – that's all.

Today's Nile steamers are, of course, supposed to be more luxurious than ever before. There is air-conditioning, for example, and although in the past some of the cabins might have been larger, they were certainly rather basic in other ways. Overall, there are surprisingly few differences between the two experiences.

After World War II, there was little, if any, cruise traffic on the Nile until 1954, when Eastmar decided the time had come to re-establish the Nile cruise as one of the world's great journeys. The company leased a steamer from the Egyptian government that had previously been operated by Thomas Cook and was called the *Sudan*. In 1992, it was sold to the family that had originally owned the vessel, and in which Eastmar had retained a shareholding in the owning company.

Eastmar also leased from the government one of King Farouk's gorgeous private Nile steamers, the *Khassed Kheir*, which had just two en-suite cabins, plus a few separate cabins for the royal princes and princesses. In 1960, the vessel was transformed into a yacht, designed to carry upwards of 75 guests in some style, but its life came to an end when it was requisitioned by the government, leased to Club Méditerannée and completely destroyed in a fire.

Eastmar then decided to build the *Memphis*, the first cruiser that it had owned outright. At the same time, other companies had spotted the growth in cruising on the Nile and two spanking, new super-luxury cruise vessels were built in Germany – still operating to this day under the auspices of the Cairo Hilton Hotel.

It was the beginning of a Nile cruise boom that is still going today. Presently, there are something like 300 Nile steamers plying different sections of the river. Most of these were built in Egypt, but Eastmar, by contrast, decided to build two Nile cruisers in Hull, in England, of all places: they were called *Ra I* and *Ra II*, and were the first to have balconies, of a sort.

At the time, British shipyards were in the doldrums and desperate for the work, which meant that the prices were super keen. On the other hand, the job of transporting the vessels to the Nile proved both costly and complicated, given that it is only possible, on rare occasions, when the sea conditions are just right, for vessels to make their way through the Delta and onto the Nile proper.

Of course, the biggest change to have taken place on the river, in this Nile cruise period, is the building of the new dam. As soon as it became clear that some of the monuments were going to be lost to the rising waters and others would be moved to higher ground, Eastmar began a steamer service to Abu Simbel, which ran for two years, until the Aswan Dam had been completed.

These cruises were enormously popular; as can be imagined, visitors were clamouring for a chance to see, possibly for the last time, these ancient monuments in their original locations. In the end, these astonishing statues were levered out of the water for safe keeping and re-arranged precisely as they were and, remarkably, this has been the only serious change in the scenery since Thomas Cook started their cruises over a century ago.

Otherwise, as you look over the rails across the tranquil waters of the Nile, everything is pretty much the same – feluccas, egrets, date palms and a timeless atmosphere. The journey and days slip noiselessly by, just like the river.

A hundred years ago, the only difference was that visitors would have taken things at an even more leisurely pace. If they had come from England (and most probably did, the majority of visitors being American or British), they would most likely have travelled by ship to Alexandria. From there, they would have travelled to Cairo and spent some time there, before boarding the Nile steamer and visiting the various archaeological sites up until Aswan, sleeping, as today, on board.

The visits to the West Bank and the Valley of the Kings would have required a whole day, rather than a half-day, as now, and this was the same until as recently as 20 years ago. Today, there are coaches to carry visitors from the shore to the sites, whereas before there were only horses and carriages.

Once in Aswan, the visitors of yesteryear would probably have stayed in the Old Cataract Hotel for a few weeks, before making the return journey back north by train. Some (Egyptians, as well as foreigners) might spend up to two months basking in the winter warmth beneath clear, azure skies and enjoying the hotel's excellent amenities.

The main difference, therefore, was the time factor. For the traveller of yore, an abundance of time was the main prerequisite for a visit to Egypt. In order to make it worthwhile, bearing in mind the length of the return journey to England, the whole of the winter season would have to be put aside for the trip, and that usually implied having the money to do it. The sort of people with complicated histories who end up under the suspicious gaze of a certain Belgian gentleman with waxed moustache and silver-topped cane, perhaps?'

Speaking of Hercule Poirot, Gaafar was responsible for some of the arrangements for the making of *Death on the Nile*, the film adaptation of the Agatha Christie novel starring Peter Ustinov as Poirot. The steamer used was the *Memnon*, sadly no longer in operation, which at the time was also chartered by Club Méditerannée.

The film was produced by John Brabourne, the son-in-law of Lord Mountbatten, who needed to shoot on certain dates in order to have all the actors in the right place at the right time. Fortunately, on those dates Club Mediterannée did not require the ship.

Although the exterior of the *Memnon* might have looked the part, which is why the production company wanted it, the ship itself was not that luxurious a vessel at all. And for the record, there has never been a murder on board any of the Nile steamers. Nor, I would suggest, is there ever likely to be, since the comfort of the newest vessels, allied to the gentle pace at which they proceed through the unchanged landscape, allows for nothing but the most peaceful thoughts.

JOHN BLOOM ON THE SHORES OF LOCH NESS 2013

A Story in Brief:

THE FACE OF WONDERBRA: One of my most memorable encounters was with glamorous grandmother Pearl Read. I met her at the Pomodoro Restaurant, in Knightsbridge; I had been invited there by that ever-newsworthy businessman John Bloom, and it turned out Pearl had a history every bit as interesting as John's. Telling her life story to the *Daily Mirror*, Pearl chronicled her marriages to gangland boss Joe Wilkins (who went on to own Captain Langton's nightclub Winston's), to former Queen's Park Rangers chairman David Bulstrode, and to horse trainer Brian Dye. When she was picked as a model for the organisation Age Concern, wearing a form-hugging (36-24-36) outfit, a spokesman pointed out: "Pearl was picked for her image, not her background." Her comment was: "I may have had a strange past, but I have come through smiling."

CHAPTER 75
ME AND THE TRAIN BLEU

Each night, this deluxe train left Nice for Paris and I decided, there and then, to risk the wrath of my employers, who were famed for counting every last centime of expenses, and buy myself a ticket.

THE Route Napoléon is a beautiful, 200-mile-long section of France's route nationale 85 that takes you from the Côte d'Azur to the foothills of the Alps, at Grenoble. It owes its name to the fact that it was down this road, in 1815, that Napoléon Bonaparte marched his troops, having returned from Elba to confront Louis XVII. It was 150 years later, in 1965, when I was asked to escort a party of Cosmos coach passengers along the Route Napoléon, albeit in the opposite direction to which Bonaparte and his troops had travelled.

Our journey was to take us from Ostend, via Paris, to Grenoble and then back up to the Côte d'Azur. My instructions from head office were precise: I should escort the group only until we arrived in Nice, where I was to hand over to another courier and return immediately to Ostend by train, on a second-class ticket. My orders were clear enough. However, I had been captivated by what I had seen on the journey: the snow-clad Alps, the mountain passes, the clarity of the light, the blueness of the sea and the vibrancy of the colours of Nice itself. It was all in such stark contrast to the London greyness that I had left behind, that I really did have half a mind to stay.

After some serious reflection, however, I came to the conclusion that, given the precariousness of my position as a stand-in tour courier, and a probationary stand-in at that, going back to London was probably the better option. Still, the prospect of staying in Nice was an enchanting one. It had not gone unnoticed by me that the more well-to-do, non-Cosmos British tourists were living the true Belle Époque life there on the Côte d'Azur. No second-class sleeper back to London for them: they would have reservations on the celebrated 'Train Bleu'

A Story in Brief

APRIL FOOLS: In 1972, the London *Times* ran an article on the centenary of Thomas Cook's first round-the-world tour, noting that in 1872 it had cost the participants only 210 guineas. Meanwhile, in another part of the paper, a piece appeared reporting that Thomas Cook was offering people the chance to buy a similar tour at 1872 prices. The first 1,000 applicants to write to 'Miss Avril Foley,' would be able to take advantage of this special offer. Unsurprisingly, the public response to the offer was overwhelming, and long queues quickly formed outside the Thomas Cook offices. It was only later that the (Thomson-owned) *Times* revealed the offer was an April fool's joke. The people who had waited for hours were not amused, and John Carter, the author of the article, was fired. Late, though, he was reinstated, and went on to become a successful travel writer and broadcaster.

IMAGE COURTESY: ROBERT SCURRAH/VOYAGES JULES VERNE.

(Calais-Méditerranée Express), with its distinctive blue-and-gold edged livery and smartly uniformed wagon-lits conductors. Best of all was the restaurant car, with its elegant hardwood finishes, crisp white-linen table settings, Lalique glass panels, shaded table lamps and plushly sprung Riviera armchairs.

Each night, this deluxe train left Nice for Paris, so I decided to risk the wrath of my employers, who were famed for counting every last centime of expenses, and buy myself a ticket. Sure enough, on my return to London, I was reprimanded for my profligacy. (I gave the somewhat weak excuse that all the other trains had been full.) But it had been worth it. From that time onwards, the sheer sumptuousness of the Train Bleu experience never left me. In fact, there's a little bit of it in all the posters, plus the Train Bleu was the central design theme of the *Spirit of Chartwell*.

IDYLLIC ISLANDS OF THE CARIBBEAN COVER BY ROBERT SCURRAH

A Story in Brief:

One of the World's Last Great Journeys

IDYLLIC ISLANDS
of
THE CARIBBEAN

Arrangements by

VOYAGES JULES VERNE

IMAGE COURTESY: ROBERT SCURRAH/VJV.

A CIRCLE JOINED: In 1957, Captain Langton gave Richard Day $10,000 to open an office in New York, which, in due course, became Unitours, spawning offices and affiliate companies throughout the USA and overseas, including London. All of which, thanks to the Captain's generosity, eventually reverted to the ownership of local operators. One such affiliate, called Club Universe, was based in Los Angeles, and was bought by Thomson Holidays (from Mike Alford) in 1980. Thus a company (i.e., Thomson) which owed its origins to Captain Langton, also came to buy another company that owed it origins to – Captain Langton. Not only that, but Club Universe were to go on to represent my company, Voyages Jules Verne, on the west coast of the States. A case of travel-industry wheels within wheels.

CHAPTER 76
WHERE SHIPS GO WHEN THEY DIE

A vessel that arrives as a 1,000-foot-long giant ends up leaving in small, skillfully-detached pieces. Everything, but everything, is removed.

THERE is a strange and particular place, on the coast of Gujarat in Northern India, 30 miles south-east of the city of Bhavnagar, where half the world's ships go to die. It's called Alang Bay, and it's the global capital of the marine recycling industry. Once a ship has beached here, be it an elegant cruise liner or a workaday cargo tanker, the dismantling process begins, and doesn't stop for at least the next six months.

A vessel that arrives as a 1,000-foot-long giant ends up leaving in small, skillfully detached pieces. Everything, but everything, is dismantled, removed and resold – the propeller, the engines, the wooden decks, the chairs, the washbasins, the crockery, the electrical equipment, the metal cables, the hull, even the light bulbs and beds.

"I bought up 300 original bunk beds off an ocean liner just the other day," says Mark Jameson, who with his father, Roger, runs Trinity Marine, a UK firm specialising in salvaging architectural and design treasures from de-commissioned ships, and which has supplied my *Lord of the Glens* and *Spirit of Chartwell* with pieces that once adorned the handsome ocean liners of the 1950s. The items that have come to me via Trinity include portholes, bar stools, coat hooks and assorted deck furniture from the RMS *Windsor Castle*, along with brass friezes from her sister ship, the RMS *Kenya Castle*, both of which belonged to the celebrated Union-Castle cruise line.

"In many ways, Philip was ahead of the game when he first came to us, for pieces that would complement those ships," says Jameson. "Since then, demand for marine collectables has just taken off – chandlery, fittings, décor, you name it. Particularly from ships launched pre-1960. Things were built so solidly and permanently in those days." Responsible for these beautifully appointed ships – up until around 1960, that is – were the great British shipyards, among them Harland and Wolff (Belfast), Cammell Laird (Birkenhead) and Alexander Stephen and Sons (Glasgow).

"From that point onward, aluminium started to replace brass, and then Bakelite replaced aluminium," explains Jameson. "Out went the intricate marquetry, out went the exotic woods; basically, the quality and durability just went downhill. That said, however, you can find some lovely furniture on BP oil tankers of around 1965. There's always some good-quality stuff in the captain's cabin."

Although Trinity Marine is based in the Teign Valley, on the edge of Dartmoor, the Jamesons are frequent visitors to Alang Bay, some 4,500 miles away in India. "I get notification that a ship is going to be beached and broken up there, so I don't mess around, I get out there pretty quick," says Mark Jameson. "I'm usually there on the beach, waiting for it to arrive, and I'll be one of the first people climbing the 100-foot ladder up the side of the ship, once it's come to a halt.

"Sometimes, a cruise liner can't get right up onto the beach, so you have to wade out into the water until you reach it. Once we're on board, we go round making notes and taking photos of all the things we want, putting those pictures on iPads so we can remember what we've got our eye on.

"We won't be the only ones, either. Quite often, there will be some other European guys there, in suits, who are putting in bids for the really mundane, specialist, unexciting bits of kit. The way we operate, though – and the way we compete, I guess – is that we don't cherry-pick: we don't just bid for the nice bits of furniture; we put our hand up for enormous amounts of stuff, which gives us a much better chance of getting what we want. We're only spending pocket money, really, compared to what the whole ship is worth, so we're prepared to take some wheat with the chaff."

Then comes the tricky part: the bargaining. Here, the Jamesons adopt a strategy that runs counter to the slow-paced traditional, Eastern way of doing business. Rather than spending a week or so gradually beating the price down, they go through the process at a rate of knots, on the basis that they have to get back to Britain, and therefore can't devote day after day to the process of haggling.

"I allow myself 10 minutes maximum," says Mark. "I offer £6,000, they ask £16,000, and we end up doing the deal for £10,000. Mind you, it takes a bit of nerve, once you've agreed the price, handing over £50,000-£100,000 to the person

A Story in Brief

RMS WINDSOR CASTLE: To huge excitement, this handsome ocean liner was launched live on television, on 23 June 1959 by the Queen Mother. But things didn't go quite as smoothly as planned. The ceremony was due to take place at 1.30pm, but with only a short time to go, the Queen Mother had a severe nosebleed which threatened to delay the event. Drawing on all her royal sangfroid, however, she rallied from this setback and managed to carry out the vessel-christening a mere one minute past the scheduled hour. Forty-six years later, on 11 May 2005, the *Windsor Castle* was the centre of a rather less well-attended event, when it made its final journey to Alang Bay, in India. Here, it it was hauled onto the beach and broken up. But not before a large number of items were saved, including a number which adorned the royal barge *Spirit of Chartwell*, on the day of Queen Elizabeth II's Diamond Jubilee Flotilla. IMAGE COURTESY: TRINITY MARINE.

you're buying from and then going home. The goods you've bought won't end up getting delivered for weeks, and even when the container does arrive, there are usually 20 per cent of the headaches waiting for you when you open it up. You'll have bought 100 original lights, for example, and you'll find 10 or so of them are modern copies that have been substituted. So you raise this with the vendors, and they say, 'OK, we won't re-fund you the money, but we will make it up to you in the next container-load.' And to a large extent they do, though you've got to take the attitude that this is a long-term business relationship. You can't go over to Alang, put your foot on the boss's chair and start making demands; you'll get eaten for breakfast. All of which means that each time you open up a container, it's a bit like Christmas: you never quite know what you're going to get. Rough rule of thumb is, the longer you've been dealing with the people at Alang, the better you'll be treated."

And it's not just in the Subcontinent that the Jamesons do their best buying. They have worked with the Ministry of Defence for many years, selling off equipment surplus to armed forces requirements. "We've got rotating gun emplacements that don't have any guns attached; we've got miniature yellow submarines that we sell off for £850 a time, and which will probably end up in beach bars, in places like the Gulf."

"Of course," Mark continues, "you have to make sure that what you're buying is a genuine original. For example, I can make a porthole that looks old, costs £50 to manufacture, and I'll sell it for £80. There are other people, though, who do the same and sell it for £350 [as an original].

"By and large, we charge the same sort of price for an item, no matter what vessel it has come off. We tend not to feel that sentimental about the ships we work on – this is a business, after all, and we don't get too excited about the history. That said, there is a good chance we're going to be working on the breaking-up and sale of fittings off the old *Ark Royal* aircraft carrier. I don't know if I'm getting soft or something, but I have to admit, just thinking about that does give me a definite twinge!"

CHAPTER 77
ROHAN VOS AND THE 'PRIDE OF AFRICA'

Sitting at home in South Africa, staring financial ruin in the face. Four years earlier, Rohan Vos had launched what was, at that time, an unheard-of venture in this part of the world: a luxury, vintage train.

I N the mid-1980s (and probably still now), African countries were fiercely protective of the interests of their national airline carriers such that charter flights were discouraged – nowhere more so than in Zimbabwe, especially around Victoria Falls. The solution I found was to fly my passengers instead to Kilimanjaro, in Tanzania, and thereafter have them ferried by an armada of very small local aircraft to Victoria Falls. From Kilimanjaro, I was able to arrange additional onward travel to Botswana, Zambia and Mauritius. It was also at this time that I was able to convince Rohan Vos to start his train service, *Pride of Africa*, from Victoria Falls rather than Pretoria on its runs to Cape Town.

The year was 1993, and Rohan Vos was sitting at home in South Africa, staring financial ruin in the face. Four years earlier, he had launched what was, at that time, an unheard-of venture in this part of the world: a luxury, vintage train taking passengers through some of the world's most breath-taking scenery. Trouble was, he wasn't breaking even. Not to put too fine a point on it, he was going broke fast. Instead of coal, he might as well have been feeding shovel-loads of cash into his steam train's firebox.

"To keep the railway going, I had sold various cash-generating businesses in and around the town of Witbank, mostly to my management partners," he recalls. "Just prior to the train launch, I sold my motor spares businesses to a public company. I accepted shares for the transaction and these were lodged with the bank as security for the overdraft to finance the train operation. Then the public company went insolvent, and my shares became valueless.

"My bankers, of course, were not amused. With the first democratic elections coming in 1994, and confidence in the business future of South Africa tumbling to an all-time low, they put pressure on me to repay the overdraft. Although I was of the opinion that they were well enough secured and that I could service the account, they were not interested and proceeded to summons me for the outstanding amount in late 1993.

"I was furious with them, really outspoken. I was a long-time customer who had never let them down, never written a bad cheque, yet they were pulling the rug from under my feet at the first opportunity. I remember banging my fist on the manager's desk, I was so incensed.

"At that point, I would have done anything to get myself out of the hole I was in. There I was, at the age of 40, being told I was going to have to sell my business, being told my house wasn't worth what I thought it was worth, and being told by everyone what I ought to be doing and what I ought to have done."

It was with a sense of growing desperation, then, that Rohan came to London that year, to the London World Travel Market. At this point, however, fate intervened – in the form of me. At the 11th hour, Rohan and I hatched an ambitious plan to run the *Pride of Africa* from Cape Town to Victoria Falls. The package was quickly advertised in the *Sunday Telegraph*, and on 30 December I placed a call to Rohan that he had been both anticipating and dreading.

"Personally, I couldn't see how anyone was going to take much notice of an advertisement over the Christmas period, when they would all be drinking and making merry," says Rohan. "To my complete and utter relief and astonishment, though, Philip said that sales were going extremely well and nearly four train loads had been booked. My answer, after a suitably stunned silence, was, 'Send cash.' Bankruptcy was avoided by a nose, and so dramatic was the turnaround that a year later I purchased 38 redundant carriages from South African Railways.

"Since then, we have never looked back, although the scars of battle are always there, reminding me never to relax. It made me age prematurely, that's for sure." Which means that instead of the spreading waistline you might expect in a successful businessman, Rohan remains as lean, trim and industrious a figure as he was in his 20s.

Even when he started up his motor spares business, in the mining town of Witbank, 100 kilometres east of Johannesburg, he was constantly on duty, staying open from 7.00am to 7.00pm and even running an out-of-hours breakdown service. The latter got him into trouble with the local magistrates, since staying open after normal working hours was, at that time, illegal in South Africa.

But Rohan was not to be deterred or deflected. When the town's authorities built a smart, new shopping centre across the road, he duly moved his business over there. A few years later, he bought the whole shopping centre – all 26 units – and started up a self-service car spares supermarket, working seven days a week. Soon he began opening branches in neighbouring towns.

After that, he went into the film distribution business, buying and showing movies all-round the region, often at the local coal mines. When 32mm film gave way to videotapes, he had no hesitation in throwing out all his old equipment and starting afresh.

Then, one day, trains entered his life. Up until then, his relationship with railways had been at arm's length; his introduction to steam trains had been as a boy going back and forth to boarding school in the 1950s, when the engines would spew steam everywhere and he and his friends would get smuts on their nice, clean white shirts.

Now, though, Rohan was set to immerse himself in the world of oily, gritty, grimy engines. "One of my employees had started a steam preservation society, and I thought it might be good to have a carriage on which my four kids, dogs and cats could play," he says. (In the intervening years he had met and married his wife, Anthea.) "The first carriage I bought was a caboose; I can remember the number to this day – it was 1713. Next I bought a second-class, wooden sleeper carriage from the 1930s, and before long, having got hold of a copy of a book called *Dining Cars of South Africa*, I was hooked. These carriages just oozed history, and gave me the idea of creating a train that harked back to the 1920s."

"Rohan has always been obsessed with things mechanical," continues Anthea. "In fact, he started his first business with the capital derived from the sale of a 1940 Packard and a 1928 Austin that he had rebuilt. Rohan was involved in so many ventures, but I didn't see this one coming."

In 1985, the couple took up a last-minute invitation on a Magaliesberg train trip for business suppliers, and their fate was sealed. "I became a train widow on that day," sighs Anthea. "I sat all dressed up by myself; Rohan spent most of the time in the engine with the driver. The irony was that we should have seen then how difficult it would be – the train broke down and we were bussed back to town."

The damage was done, though, and over the coming months Rohan accumulated more and more coaches, which he transported to the Railway Preservation Society yards in Witbank. However, the complications of working with the South African Transport Services administration soon convinced him of the need for self-sufficiency, and as a result, he bought a 1938 Class 19D locomotive from Lowenthal's Scrap Metal in Johannesburg. It was rebuilt and named *Bianca*, after one of his daughters.

Initially, Rohan's intention was just to run the train as a sort of family caravan.

A Story in Brief

NOT QUITE THE END OF THE LINE: The idea of a railway connecting Alma Ata, in Kazakhstan, and Urumchi in Chinese Xinjiang, was first thought of in the 1950s, but was later abandoned by Krushchev; it wasn't until 1991, that the link finally became a reality. The railway that had previously run between Pingxiang, in Southern China, and Hanoi, in Vietnam, had been destroyed during the brief war between the two countries in 1978/9. However, a rapprochement between the two nations led to the re-establishment of a railway service, making it once again possible to journey by train from the Channel coast all the way to Singapore: a journey of 13,500 miles or the equivalent of travelling practically half way around the globe. It was these developments which made it possible for VJV to organise the London to Saigon Motor Challenge. **IMAGE COURTESY: ROHAN VOS.**

The price quoted by the authorities for hauling the train was forbiddingly high, but they did say that he could offset the cost by selling tickets to the paying public. All of a sudden, he was presented with the opportunity to transform what had been intended as a family hobby into a viable business.

"I remember the occasion very clearly," he recalls. "On a wintry evening, I was subsiding into a hot bath with my Red Heart rum and Coke close at hand. There'd been a power cut, so, musing by candlelight about the consequences of turning a hobby into a business, I let my imagination float around in delusions of grandeur.

"I knew that launching into the arena of tourism and trains, of which I had no experience, held many dangers. It was an uncharted course such that I had little idea where to start, let alone where to aim. However, a unique challenge was right up my street and the decision was made to go ahead. This was – unknown to me at the time – a life-changing moment, and sadly, during the next few years or so, I would have many agonising thoughts regretting the move. I could never have imagined how all-consuming the business was to become, both financially and emotionally."

Even today, nearly a quarter of a century later, he says he still bears the mental scars that were inflicted on him by his rail business. Nevertheless, on 29 April 1989, a locomotive and seven carriages, carrying four paying passengers (Rohan and Anthea can remember their names) plus friends and press, set off for Eastern Transvaal. And so Rovos Rail was born.

It was the start of a runaway train ride, and on many occasions it looked like the whole enterprise was heading for the buffers of bankruptcy. That said, it was a scenic route, with passengers treated to close-up views of Victoria Falls, the Kruger National Park and countless other breath-taking sights. On numerous occasions, too, the boss would be spectating not from inside the train, but from the very front of the engine.

"Rohan loved some of the journey so much, he would sit on the very front of the engine, on the 'cowcatcher'," says Anthea. And there, metaphorically at least, he has stayed ever since. Instead of nose-diving straight after the 1994 elections, as many had predicted, the South African tourist industry has been reborn far stronger than it ever was before.

And with it, Rovos Rail has flourished. Moving on from those dark early days, Rohan and Anthea have built up the business to a point where it can claim, with some justification, to be the most luxurious railway company in the whole world, offering journeys throughout South Africa and numerous excursions to nearby countries such as Zambia, Tanzania and Namibia.

Not that his taste for the adventure has been dimmed, as demonstrated by the occasion, in 2000, when he went over to Bolivia to buy two propeller-driven 1954 Convair 440 aircraft and then flew them, via Brazil, back across the Atlantic to Africa. Because of their limited range, they had to be refuelled mid-air, using two sets of 17 44-gallon drums of fuel that Rohan had had loaded on board.

When they landed in Liberia, it was with engines failing and in rain so driving that the pilots couldn't see out of their windscreens; the aircraft Rohan was in aquaplaned at a 90-degree angle on touchdown. Characteristically, what Rohan remembers is that of the four impoverished customs officials who came to greet them, only one of them wore shoes.

And that, it seems, is the measure of the man. The travel industry is full of bluster, full of people talking up what they do. The great thing about Rohan, though, is that what you see is what you get.

FLIGHT OF ANGELS – VICTORIA FALLS POSTER BY VOYAGES JULES VERNE

A Story in Brief:

COBHAM'S FLYING CIRCUS: 'The famous aviator Sir Alan Cobham had opened up all sorts of commercial possibilities for civil aviation. Large numbers of people had been up with Cobham's Flying Circus, which operated all over the country, and public awareness of aeroplanes had, of course been heightened by the war. And when we had a small cere-mony to launch Independent Air Transport, Sir Alan was the man who broke a bottle of champagne and wish-ed us well. No question about it; there was a lot of interest, both in Independent as a new venture, and in Marian himself, because he was quite well known by then.' Mrs Kozub-ska, from her unpublished memoirs.

IMAGE COURTESY: VOYAGES JULES VERNE.

CHAPTER 78
A MOVING MOMENT

There had been one other attempt at moving a vessel from the Nile onto Lake Nasser. This by means of a series of giant inflated cushions. It ended in failure.

THERE had been one previous attempt at manoeuvring a vessel from the Nile onto Lake Nasser and that had ended in failure, when the vessel, while being dragged up and around the obstacle of the Aswan High Dam via a series of inflated cushions, promptly split into two. To overcome the Nile-to-Lake Nasser problem, Mostafa el-Gendy created his very own miniature shipyard on the lake's shoreline, where he was to build the MS *Eugenie*. And it was Voyages Jules Verne's passengers that were on board when the *Eugenie* was first launched, the travel company having by then commenced direct flights to Aswan from London.

The first Aswan dam (the 'Low Dam'), completed in 1902, had had dramatic effects on the irrigation and agriculture of the Nile region, but as the years passed, it had proved insufficient for the burgeoning needs of Egypt. The yearly floods had not been fully harnessed, and a considerable amount of water was merely running off into the Mediterranean while low Nile levels could not be supplemented by stored reserves. However, the overriding factor that led to the decision to improve the water situation was Egypt's population explosion.

The growing population could realistically no longer survive exclusively on agriculture. The power for industrialisation could only come from a cheap and plentiful source, and the obvious solution was hydroelectricity. At that time, it should be remembered, nuclear power was not available and little oil had been discovered in Egyptian territory. After painstaking research and argument, for there were many disadvantages as well as benefits, the decision was taken to proceed with a 'High Dam' seven kilometres south of Aswan, with work officially starting on 9 January 1960.

It was, of course, evident well before this time that the flooding of the Nile Valley through Lower Nubia and up to the Dal Cataract, in Sudan, would have disastrous effects on the surrounding ancient monuments and antiquities. The Egyptian Supreme Council of Antiquities, directed at that time by Mostafa Amer, had published a report in 1955 and distributed it as widely as possible in an attempt to awaken public opinion and attract international support and co-operation for the rescue of the monuments.

It was the United Nations Educational and Cultural Organisation (UNESCO) that responded under the terms of their constitution: 'the conservation and protection of the world's inheritance.' In turn, UNESCO appealed to the governments of the world for technical and financial contributions to save the monuments and temples from certain destruction. With only three exceptions – where only fragments could be removed – the monuments would all be dismantled or carved up, moved to another site and re-assembled into six groups. One of these was Abu Simbel.

In their original position, the temples of Abu Simbel had by no means been the most important or popularly visited monuments in Egypt. However, between 1960 and 1963 a veritable flood of tourists was drawn to see them by the debate over their fate. This provoked a plethora of suggestions, from laymen and experts alike, on how they should be saved, some practical and well thought-out, some born of sheer fantasy.

A selection of the more spectacular proposals included: a Polish engineer's suggestion to construct reinforced concrete domes over the temples, making them accessible to visitors by means of lifts operating in vertical shafts; an American's idea of building concrete barges under and around the temples, so that when the reservoir water level rose, the temples would float up; a suggestion from a Briton to allow the temples to be submerged while sealing off their interior chambers, making them accessible from above. In addition, a revolutionary membrane would separate the muddy waters of the reservoir from clear, filtered water inside, allowing the temples to be viewed as if in an aquarium.

It was in fact four years before the Egyptian government decided upon a course of rescue. Much time had been lost undertaking unrealistic exercises and following up spurious proposals, and therefore, by November 1963, when the plan was signed off, a race had begun between the rising waters of the reservoir and the money and pledges necessary to finance the rescue project.

The original 'final' choice of scheme was one from Italy that involved lifting the temples in their entirety with hydraulic jacks and then moving them to higher ground. At this stage an engineering company, Vattenbyggnadsbryån (VBB) of Stockholm, was brought in to carry out the technical supervision of the work and

A Story in Brief

PRISSE D'AVENNES: British by blood, French by birth, Muslim by choice, scholar by avocation. He was in many ways a paradox. An artist of consummate skill, he was also a writer, scientist, scholar, engineer and linguist, a genius who spent much of his life among the illiterate. French to the bone, he was of British blood; a European, he embraced Islam and took the name Edris-Effendi. By nature contentious, he alienated colleagues, yet succoured the sick and the poor. Of the hundreds of Orientalists – those western artists, scholars and writers who gravitated to the Islamic world following Napoleon's invasion of Egypt in 1798 – few possessed so prodigious an intellect, such a trove of talents, so insatiable a curiosity and so passionate a commitment to record the historical and artistic patrimony of ancient Egypt and medieval Islam. He succeeded brilliantly, yet failed to achieve the stature to which his successes entitled him, both during his lifetime and the years since his death.

IMAGE COURTESY: VOYAGES JULES VERNE.

prepare a detailed study. It was discovered that the lifting scheme would be too expensive, at $55 million, in relation to the international contributions, so the Egyptian government decided to adopt a cutting scheme that VBB determined would cost only $36 million.

This alternative scheme required that the sculpted and decorated surfaces of the external cliffs and internal rooms be cut from the rock in blocks, to a size suitable for handling. The blocks would then be moved to a holding area for cataloguing and repair, in preparation for reassembly some 65 metres higher up the same cliff face. Not only that, the plan was to provide for a similar setting for the temples by cutting entire sections of the original cliff face adjacent to the facades and use them to cover an artificial hill on top of the cliff.

The construction of the High Dam had not waited for the rescue schemes to be finalised, and in August 1964 the level of the Nile had begun to rise. For this reason, one of the first tasks of the rescue team was to build their own dam against the primary floods caused by the High Dam. The construction of this cofferdam was in itself a great achievement, only completed after a dramatic race against time. Its height was 27 metres and the length of its crest 370 metres; the total volume of the rock-fill and sand used to fill the dam was 380,000 cubic metres.

Having bought themselves time by temporarily protecting the site, their next step was to remove the uncarved rock facade directly above the massive figures. The use of explosives was prohibited, so some 150 cubic metres of rock had to be removed by rippers, pneumatic tools and bulldozers. The front facades of the temples had been sand-filled, and the inner chambers supported by steel scaffolding, to afford some protection while this work was carried out.

The final stages of this part of the excavation stopped just short of the facades, above and to the sides. Then the rock sections that formed the statues, walls and roofs of the temples were cut into blocks of a suitable size for lifting and transportation. These blocks measured approximately 0.8 metres deep, three metres high and up to five metres long. They weighed around 20 tons each, while some of the more compact parts of the columns weighed up to 30 tons.

It was all too easy to fracture the sandstone from which the figures had been hewn; consequently, careful attention had to be paid to strengthening the weaker blocks that were cut and removed. This was done by means of drilling and inserting steel reinforcing bars into the blocks and then cementing the entire block together using epoxy resin mortar.

The cutting itself was done by saws of various kinds – many different tools and methods had to be tried. The saws themselves were subjected to incredible strains and wear and tear, and had to be armed with especially hard steel teeth. The main cuts at the back were made by large motor-driven chainsaws, while for more intimate cuts, specially designed handsaws were devised to minimise the effect on the sculpted surfaces. Other methods of cutting the sandstone blocks were used, such as line drilling with wedges and wire cutting, but the saws did the majority of the work.

Having divided the temples into blocks, the next stage was to lift and transport the 1,042 blocks of sandstone that made up the temples' facades. Again, great care had to be taken not to damage the fragile surfaces. Special yokes were used to cradle the blocks as they were lifted by large cranes ranged over the entire working area. Having thus been loaded onto sand beds on low loaders, they were then moved to a storage area on the desert plateau.

The storage area was more than just a holding point before reassembly. At this juncture specialists from the Supreme Council of Antiquities took the opportunity to inspect all the material and restore worn or damaged stone. In preparation for re-erection, the blocks had their rear sides fitted with steel anchor bars and their surfaces waterproofed by impregnation with resin.

Before the blocks were re-erected, the new site, at the top of the same hill into which the temples had originally been carved, had to be prepared. A suitable foundation was necessary on which to base the temples and the massive domes that were to be constructed over them. Indeed, the area in front of the temples also needed extensive excavation and levelling to form a flat foreground.

The final position of the temples – in relation both to each other and the exact direction they would face – was of great importance, as their original architects had, many thousands of years ago, especially lined up the statues and entrances to the inner chambers to catch the first rays of the morning sun.

For the facades of the statues, supporting frameworks were first erected, then the blocks were placed against the framework and set in concrete. The temple rooms, by contrast, were re-erected by placing them in position and then casting a supporting concrete structure behind and over them.

To encompass the reassembled temples and to complete the new site, two enormous concrete domes were built, one over each temple. These domes were effectively used as an elevated base for carrying the weight of the artificial hills that were to be formed over and around the temples. The dome built over the Great Temple is in itself a great feat of engineering: it has a span of 60 metres, a height of 25 metres and a width of 45 metres, and carries a load ranging from 20 tons per square metre at the crown to 70 tons per square metre at the footing. The artificial hills were, effectively, thousands of tons of hard-core and sandstone blocks taken from the surface of the original cliff at its lower levels and landscaped over the domes. In this way the picture was completed.

To undertake the work, some 1,700 workmen and 200 staff members were employed on the site; when they were joined by their families, a thriving community of over 3,000 lived there. But lived where? Abu Simbel was in a desert 300 kilometres south of Aswan, with no notable roads or communication links. So when work started, all the personnel had to live in the desert in tents, sheds or houseboats on the Nile itself. Conditions were not ideal, especially when the summer season temperature exceeded 45°C in the shade. Early plans had included a township, but the construction of the cofferdam had taken precedence in view of the rising waters. In the end, however, a township was built which boasted houses and offices, a mosque, a police station, a hotel, a mess room, shops and even limited sports facilities.

The whole salvage operation was to last four and a half years and was completed by the autumn of 1968, about 20 months ahead of schedule. And so when it came to the inauguration on 22 September 1968, there were many who were justly proud of their achievements. For those who had carried the burden of the project – planners, masons, engineers, labourers and executing contractors – it was a day of deep satisfaction.

No greater testimony to the success of the Abu Simbel operation was made than the innocent query from a journalist who was present at the inauguration: "Everything looks exactly like it was before! What have you done with the 40 million dollars?"

CHAPTER 79
THE PRICE OF TIMETABLES

I had 'nicked' Herbert Harrison's copy of the Thomas Cook timetable from
his desk; in fact it still had his name on it when it guided me to Benidorm
and when I came to compose the Central Kingdom Express.

UNLESS it happens to be inaccurate, a timetable is one of those things we
tend to take for granted. It is an essential tool for the traveller, for a
timetable represents organisation, optimism and confidence. Even if it
conceals a horrible lie – as passengers on certain lines in Britain know to their
cost – then at least it provides grounds for justifiable anger.

Yes, with a timetable in the hand, anything seems possible, no more so than
with the comprehensive timetables of rail, road and shipping services published
by Thomas Cook, as popular as ever after almost 120 years. There are two: the
monthly *European Timetable* and the quarterly *Overseas Timetable* (for outside
Europe). The journey to this point has been a long one.

The need for a timetable omnibus was recognised in the early days of popular
travel: George Bradshaw began publishing his railway guides in 1839. Then John
Bredall, one of the earliest employees of Thomas Cook, noting that the vast
amount of advertising within the Bradshaw guides rendered them impracticable,
pondered the idea of producing a comprehensive timetable of Continental services
that was portable as well as informative.

Bredall put his suggestion to the board; he was given a cautious go-ahead and
produced, in his spare time, Cook's snappily titled *Cheap, Concise and Simple
Guide to All the Principal Lines of Railway, Steamers and Diligences on the
Continent of Europe*. An edition was distributed to seek out comment in March
1873. Bredall was to be paid a penny for each copy sold, Cooks having purchased
the copyright for £25.

Reaction was favourable – so favourable that the following edition was filled
with quotes extolling its virtues. Initially it appeared quarterly, but by 1883 the

guide was appearing every month. Over the years changes were made to the cover – updating the locomotives, replacing a camel with a Rhine steamer – though, remarkably, it proved possible to keep to the original price of one shilling until 1919, when it increased to half a crown.

Bredall, meanwhile, retired as editor in 1914, to be succeeded by Clarence H. Davies, who contrived to continue publication throughout World War I. Editions of the period noted, with English propriety, that for certain countries – Germany and the Balkans, for example – the services shown were those in force prior to the outbreak of war. Simultaneously it became a world shipping guide, thus extending its horizons beyond Europe.

The other important change concerned the timetables themselves, for from December 1919 they were to be based on the 24-hour clock – British timetables, unlike those of her Continental counterparts, still used the 12-hour clock, whereas Italian 24-hour timetables had been in operation since 1898. Thomas Cook went ahead with this momentous innovation, if only to create more space by disposing of the a.m. and p.m., while Bradshaw, with characteristic British resistance to change, followed some time later. Nonetheless, competition between the two remained strong, and in fact the Thomas Cook publications operated at a loss for some years during the 1930s, despite an increase in price in 1937 to three shillings.

Upon the outbreak of World War II, publication ceased for the first time in 67 years. Most of the staff joined up, many finding themselves, appropriately enough, serving as Rail Transportation Officers (RTOs), who were sort of travel agents to the military. Publication resumed only in July 1946, under the editorship of H. V. Francis, who is still alive, though long retired. The new timetable, at five shillings, was somewhat larger in format than its predecessor, and more suitable for displaying the timings of trains making a long run across Europe. Only then were the 1930 international timetable symbols adopted – the bed, the crossed knife and fork, and so on.

The pre-war editions had been bulky with superfluous information – superfluous, at any rate, to the austerity of post-war Europe – so the new ones jettisoned information about golf links, suitable travel clothing, etc., and were filled instead with warnings about the need to obtain permits for certain regions of Europe. Bradshaw, meanwhile, eschewed trains for aeroplanes but, unable to complete with the ABC guides, folded in 1961.

John Price, who was editor at Thomas Cook until 1988 and who remains a consultant editor to this day, joined the company in early 1948. Around this time, H. V. Francis moved to higher management, and so, at the exceptionally young age of 26, Price took his place. There were several new developments; for example, Price immediately rejected the old engraved geographical maps in favour of the

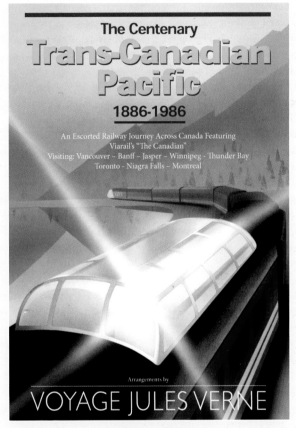

A Story in Brief

AN ARTIST AT WORK: "Before Thomson, where I was Art Director in the commercial department overseeing design projects for the Hotels that were owned and operated by Thomson, I had been in Bermuda, firstly as Art Director for a printing company and secondly a co-owner of a design studio (Omni Graphics) dealing with hotel projects. My interest in air brush work started back in the mid 60s when I worked for a London Advertising Agency (Saward Baker). It was my first job after leaving Art School. They sent me on a day release to The London College of Printing to study it. My design influences were probably from the Art Deco era and artists of that time i.e., Cassandre, Roger Broders, Tamara de Lempicka. At the moment I work mainly in photography and digital art work/design." Robert Scurrah now lives in Tenerife. IMAGE COURTESY: ROBERT SCURRAH/VOYAGES JULES VERNE.

simpler, monochrome line maps you see today, thus saving a day of production.

Furthermore, as the war receded towards the past, travel in Europe began to pick up, bringing significant changes in the rail systems of the Continent, such as the adoption of a two-class system and the inauguration of the TSE network. The service supplements at the back of certain editions, with a summary of expected changes in future timetables, were introduced in 1955. The Trans-Siberian reopened to Westerners in 1956, and Continental sleeper-trains were introduced in 1958; these events required additional pages in the guide.

This was also the era of the aeroplane, which by the mid-1960s had displaced the train and the ship as the principal means of transportation in the developed world. Yet the timetables remained as popular as ever, assuming a new relevance as a source of information on feeder lines to and from airports and for a new generation of foreign visitors to Europe who preferred to cling to the old for the time being.

In 1976 came the introduction of the separate *Overseas Timetable*. Price had wanted to experiment with the timetables of the world beyond the frontiers of Europe as early as 1963, but he had been unable to prove that there was sufficient demand for such an enterprise (the French publisher Chaix had tried with *Chaix Mondial* in 1949, but folded after only two issues). It was the Americans that finally led to its introduction by Thomas Cook. The state-owned railway company Amtrak had been formed in 1971. Eager to obtain agents' business in Great Britain and elsewhere, they purchased space in the guide. This prompted requests for information on other countries, and an effort was made to condense it into a mere 80 pages, the *Continental Timetable* metamorphosing in 1976 as the *International Timetable*.

Soon, however, it became clear that the rest of the world could not be squeezed into 80 pages. Thus the *International Timetable* was split into two, the *European* and the *Overseas*, the pilot of which was published in Autumn 1980, with full production starting in January the following year. This proved to be an astute move, for although many of the sales are to travel agents and to the business world, in recent years a new market has sprung up among Interrailers and Eurorail pass-holders. The largest overseas market is that of Japan, and in fact the only foreign-language edition is in Japanese.

It might be imagined that the collation of the world's timetables would have become easier in modern times with the introduction of fax machines and other modern paraphernalia. Yet while these have made a difference – one of the difficulties in the past had been to condense all the data in a manageable form, whereas a computer allows almost limitless condensation – in other respects the improvement is barely discernable, for the other major problem, the simple acquisition of basic information, depends ultimately on human beings.

For every component timetable, there has to be someone in each country making the decision to send a fax, and such an action is far from automatic, even in Western Europe. Information on Europe's international services is fairly easily obtained – albeit in a mixture of languages – from the minute book of the annual International Timetable Conference, but the timetables of internal services have to be provided separately, and some railway systems, notably the Spanish, are extraordinarily remiss about this.

The problem is even more acute for the *Overseas Timetable*. How do you deal with the former USSR, which seems to have given up publishing timetables altogether? From where may information about the bus services of North Korea be gleaned? Only six companies around the world send new timetables as a matter of course. Anecdotal information is much appreciated, although it remains anecdotal until there is documentary proof. And even then…

Despite all the changes over the years, an element of continuity is a striking feature of the history of Thomas Cook timetables. They have been using the same printer, Albert Gate, since the 1950s, an impressive feat of longevity in an era of impatient change; in fact, that same company has been printing vouchers and stationery for Cooks since 1872.

The feeling of permanence extends to their offices, where there is patently a deep interest in the work – a sort of mission. John Price, the former editor, remains a regular visitor and clearly is a veritable font of knowledge. All the information, one suspects, is in his head. And so it proves: when asked whether he can remember things off the top of his head, a delighted smile appears. "Go on, try me!" he challenges, and the proposal "Zagreb-Trieste?" elicits a torrent of possibilities.

But he always carries a copy of the timetables on his travels, because the moment you produce it people are drawn into conversation, fascinated by its comprehensiveness, like an atlas or a dictionary.

The current editor of the *Overseas Timetable*, Peter Tremlett, reckons that it is possible to obtain a pretty accurate picture of the state of a country through its transportation services. A newspaper, wishing to demonstrate the state of anarchy in a country shredded by war, may affirm that cross-border train services have been cut, which immediately suggests chaos and isolation. But the truth turns out to be that a vital bridge was blown up and a bus service has been established instead between the bridgeheads – business as usual, then.

Clearly, these timetables are not just compilations of figures and symbols, not only travel companions – telling you, in the European versions, the scenic train routes and the particular favourites of the editor, Brendan Fox, or the location of the main stations of Moscow – but also reflections of the world.

CHAPTER 80
A LINE IN THE SAND

The modern-day package holiday business is such
a multi-million-pound industry, it's hard to believe that
its roots lie deep in socialist soil.

THE modern-day package holiday business is such a multi-million pound industry, it's hard to believe that its roots lie deep in socialist soil. Yet the organisation that was the forerunner of today's sun-sea-and-sand giants was in fact the Workers' Travel Association (WTA).

The WTA first convened at Toynbee Hall, in Whitechapel, east London, a meeting place with a long history of nurturing radical, left-wing thinkers. The date was the 25 November 1921, and the records show that barely half a dozen people attended the meeting; nonetheless, thanks to the decisions made there, millions of ordinary people now have the opportunity to take cheap holidays in foreign countries.

The driving force behind the WTA was Cecil Rogerson, an idealistic, occasionally disorganised man who pioneered the vision of workers from different countries having the opportunity to visit their overseas counterparts, without spending a fortune in the process.

The plan was to begin, in 1922, with Easter tours to the Belgian battlefields of World War I followed by summer tours to half a dozen European countries – all for just £5 per week (£8 for two weeks), including fares, accommodation, meals and excursions.

As it happened, however, the inaugural tour involved a trip to a chateau in Normandy which bore all the hallmarks of Rogerson's somewhat hare-brained approach to administration. The unfortunate travellers got to France and found themselves stranded 17 miles from their destination, without food or transport. Finally they paid a local farmer to pile their luggage onto a cart and take it to the chateau, where, instead of staying in private bedrooms, they were put up in a stable-block dormitory and fed on black bread and bean soup.

Other early WTA excursions ran into similar problems: luggage went missing, meals failed to materialise, and guests complained about everything from overcrowded conditions to food riots in places like Berlin. 'But despite all the things that went wrong, most of the WTA travellers did manage to enjoy *themselves*,' records historian Francis Williams, in his book *Journey into Adventure: The Story of the Workers Travel Association.* 'The organisation had discovered a genuine demand. It had taken the first, faltering steps in a revolution in holiday-making that was to take thousands of ordinary people abroad, and show that even for those with very little money, and no knowledge of foreign ways or tongues, the world need not end at the cliffs of Dover.'

Mind you, from Rogerson's point of view, the main purpose of their going abroad was not so much to have fun as to spread international goodwill and solidarity. Before leaving the UK, anyone who had booked a WTA holiday was handed a leaflet bearing the following instructions: 'Bear in mind that English people have not a great reputation for courtesy and civility, and try to improve this feeling towards our nation. The honour of the WTA, and in a small way that of our nation, depends on you. Realise that even light wines and beer can make a fool of you if you take too much; help others to keep straight so that all others may have a good time.'

It is advice that could usefully be directed to the British holidaymakers who today fly off, in their hundreds of thousands, for booze-filled fortnights in foreign climes. Back then, though, the UK 'invasion' of Europe amounted to just several hundred hardy souls, many of them led by volunteer tour leaders who, in daily life, worked as teachers, students and trade union officials.

As more and more people returned with tales of overseas adventure, so the demand for WTA holidays increased. In the first year, 700 holidaymakers booked a WTA trip, but next year that figure went up to 1,996, and receipts shot up to £45,000. Whereas previously, going abroad for a holiday had been the sole province of the upper and professional classes, now it was a privilege that was within reach, if not of everyone, then at least of those who had a modest amount of money to spend.

Nor was it all just one-way traffic. In 1924, having indicated that they wanted to encourage Russian workers to come to London, the WTA found themselves in the position of having to accommodate 25 young Soviet engineers, who had come to the UK for a month, with £100 between them, having been told to report to the WTA when they arrived.

Conversely, when an unworldly Scottish gardener went on a WTA tour of

Europe carrying not a passport but only a passport application form, the tour leader managed to persuade the border authorities of several countries that this was documentation enough.

Trouble was, though, that while many WTA travellers had problem-free holidays, a significant number found themselves enduring a lack of food, sub-standard hotels and lost luggage. And the blame fell on one man: Rogerson. On the grounds that these botched arrangements were doing harm to the reputation of the labour movement, the WTA's founding father was asked to resign. While this was painful for him, it was felt to be a necessary step, if the organisation was not to disappear under a mass of complaints and claims for re-imbursement. A farewell payment of £500 did little, it is said, to soothe Rogerson's feelings of resentment at having been removed from the organisation he had not only visualised, but also helped create.

A few years later, Rogerson died; ironically, while on holiday in Switzerland, he fell from a mountain near Lake Lucerne where he had been picking wild flowers. Meanwhile, the man who had stepped into his shoes was the altogether more level-headed Ernest Wimble, under whose leadership the WTA opened their first UK residential holiday centre, at Heacham in Norfolk.

Despite the General Strike of 1926, the WTA recorded a £100,000 turnover for 1927. Soon, the association began adding new holiday centres all round the country, at locations as far apart as Rhyl and the Isle of Wight. In 1930 they launched their first cruise holiday, charging passengers £12 for a fortnight's ocean-going on board the good ship *Esperance Bay*, setting off from Southampton and visiting Gibraltar, Algiers and Lisbon. (In characteristically egalitarian fashion, voyagers were only able to travel in one class.) Eventually, there was even a 'Round the World Tour', which lasted four months and cost 185 guineas.

From 1922 to 1939, the WTA organised some 230,000 overseas holidays abroad. But with the outbreak of World War II, the time for holidaymaking came to an end. With the fall of European country after European country to the Nazis, so the WTA's annual turnover plummeted from £595,000 in 1939 to just £94,000 in 1940 (yes, 12,500 determined people still went on holiday that year, in the hope that the 'phoney war' would continue).

The destruction of World War II was a blow from which the WTA never fully recovered. Nevertheless, with their holiday centres requisitioned for government use, they still did their bit by helping to house munitions workers and harvest volunteers in rural camps and hostels.

Once hostilities were over, it was clear that the organisation needed a firmer financial footing than they had had in the past, and to this end they began raising capital through share issues. This began to blur the differences between

A passage across the
Indian Subcontinent
on the

RAJ
RESS

Stopping at:
Rawalpindi (Pakistan) –
the Khyber Pass (Peshawar) –
Lahore – Amritsar (India) – Delhi –
Darjeeling – Calcutta – Agra –
Jaipur – Udaipur – Bombay –
Madras – Mysore –
Ootacamund Hill Station –
Cochin – Trani – Colombo –
(Sri Lanka) – MOunt Lavinia –
Nuwara Eliya –

Arrangements by
VOYAGES JULES VERNE
one of the World's last great journeys

A Story in Brief

COX & KINGS: In 1986 Voyages Jules Verne briefly absorbed the long-established travel firm Cox & Kings. The association didn't last perhaps much more than a year, following which Cox & Kings were to go onto much greater things with Peter Kerkar, son of Ajit Kerkar, who in turn had run the Taj group of hotels in India. The long, illustrious history of Cox & Kings was told in one of our quarterly newsletters. Cox & Kings, it said, is the oldest travel company in the land (though some might quibble as to the term 'travel company' in this context). The history is fascinating. It was in 1758 that Cox & Kings began, with the appointment, by Lord Ligonier, Colonel of the Foot Guards (Grenadier Guards), and Richard Cox as regimental agent. An agent was a civilian attached to each regiment responsible for regimental affairs, including the pay of its officers when they were serving overseas. Richard Cox soon established himself as one of the army's best, and subsequently added many other famous regiments to his books which in turn brought forth Cox & Co. By 1875, Cox & Co. were agents and bankers to the entire Household Brigade, and nearly all the Cavalry and Infantry regiments, the Royal Artillery and the Royal Wagon Train.
IMAGE COURTESY: ROBERT SCURRAH/VOYAGES JULES VERNE.

the once left-leaning WTA and other, less idealistic organisations now entering the holiday market.

Soon, the pressures of post-war competition forced the WTA to start sharing charter trains, boats and airplanes with commercial competitors, who in turn required them to stick to agreements on pricing.

What's more, the average British holidaymaker started to see the word 'Workers' not as a badge of working-class honour, but as a bit of an unglamorous tag, especially when it was attached to their suitcases in the form of a big WTA label.

The image problem was not helped, either, by the WTA's focus on British, rather than foreign, holidays, in camps where everyone was expected to 'join in'. In short, the end was in sight, though it was not until 1966 that the WTA was renamed Galleon Travel (the WTA logo had been a ship in full sail), and not until 1984 that the organisation was taken over first by travel operators Kennedy Brookes, and then by Trusthouse Forte, before quietly disappearing forever.

Still, there is no question that the WTA laid the ground for the modern-day package holiday, and in the process opened the British public's eyes to the joys of foreign travel. 'In its short history,' concludes WTA biographer, Francis Williams, 'the WTA succeeded in adding to the pleasure and happiness of so many.'

CHAPTER 81
THE SHOP WINDOW

When it came to evoking the Golden Age of travel – portraying the romance and magic of an excursion into the unknown – the acknowledged master was the French artist Adolphe Mouron.

R IGHT from the very earliest days of Voyages Jules Verne, I took the view that in order to capture the spirit and essence of a journey, a mere photograph was not enough. Only an illustration would do. And when it came to evoking the golden age of travel – portraying the romance and magic of an excursion into the unknown – the acknowledged master was French artist Adolphe Mouron, otherwise known by his pseudonym Cassandre.

He was born to French parents in Kharkov, Ukraine, in 1901. When World War I came to an end, his family re-located to Paris, where the young Adolphe studied at a number of well-known art schools, including the École des Beaux-Arts.

It was around this time that he began working for a printing company called Hachard et Compagnie, and it was there that he developed his skills as designer of posters. His first eye-catching creation, at the age of 22, was an advertisement for the Parisian furniture store Au Bucheron, on the Rue de Rivoli, depicting the dramatically illuminated image of a muscly, axe-wielding wood-cutter (bucheron, in French) cleaving a tree trunk in two. It was signed 'Adolphe Mouron Cassandre', and the boldness not just of the image but also of the typeface announced the young man's arrival in the art world.

Such was the impact of this one poster that Hachard secured a deal for exclusive rights to publish Cassandre's work. Over the next five years, he produced some of his most memorable designs, many of them capturing the excitement and glamour of travel. In Cassandre's hands, the great ocean liner SS *Normandie* was portrayed as a vessel blessed with both overwhelming grandeur and exquisite elegance. Even a steam train became a thing of beauty: the express train *Etoile du*

Nord is showing flying along pristine rail tracks that stretch far ahead and culminate in a glorious, if distant, white star.

A contemporary writer, Maximilien Vox, described Cassandre as "a thinker and an engineer, a lover of nature and a reader of books. A puritan in our midst, a worshipper of all things beautiful".

True enough, Cassandre's posters captured at once the man-made magnificence and the more intangible aesthetic beauty of the ocean liner or steam train. He never forgot, though, that his job was to do more than merely please the eye. Central to his philosophy was the notion that a poster had not just to appeal to the visual senses, but also to generate sales.

'Poster work demands of the painter complete renunciation,' he wrote. 'He cannot express himself that way; even if he could, he has no right to do so. Painting is a self-sufficient proposition, but not so the poster. It is a means, a short cut between the trade and the prospective buyer. A kind of telegraph. The poster artist is an operator, he does not issue a message, he merely passes it on. No one asks for his opinion. He is only expected to establish a connection – clear, powerful, accurate.'

And one of the ways in which Cassandre established that connection was through his use of bold lettering, which spelt out the sales message in a way that was both businesslike and beguiling. To this end, he developed a number of new typefaces: Bifur (1929), Steel (1930), Acier Noir (1935) and Peignot (1937).

In the 1930s he opened his own advertising agency, Alliance Graphique, and pioneered the production of poster images that were eye-catching and legible from a moving car. The outbreak of World War II brought an end to this enterprise, but still he managed to keep busy, designing stage sets and costumes for the theatre, teaching and lecturing at the École des Arts Decoratifs, and even designing the logo for the fashion house Yves Saint Laurent in 1963.

Unquestionably, Cassandre's work had an influence on Robert Scurrah, the man responsible for many of Voyages Jules Verne's illustrations and poster designs. Scurrah's interest in airbrush work began in the mid-1960s, when, having just graduated from art school, he was working for London advertising agency Saward Baker. He then went on to work as art director for a printing company in Bermuda, and later for the commercial department at Thomson Holidays.

So memorable were Robert's illustrations that, to this day, we still have demand for his limited edition prints of his two most enduring works. One shows a classic green-liveried steam train merging imperceptibly with a VJV classic ocean liner; the other, entitled 'News from Tartary', shows a small herd of camels making their way across a desert alive with shifting shapes and sand dunes.

Of course, the other pioneering poster designer who helped shape the look of our promotional material was the German artist Ludwig Hohlwein (1874-1949). Rather than going down the stylised route that Cassandre took, Hohlwein preferred a looser, altogether jollier format, usually involving human beings. 'His figures are full of touches of colour,' writes poster historian Alan Weill. 'A play of light and shade brings them out of their background and gives them substance.'

Nowhere can you see Hohlwein's influence more clearly than in the series of 'Motor Challenge' posters created for us by artist David Scutt, whose other claim to fame is that he designed the covers of the latter-day James Bond books.

Yes, the people who inspired the various Voyages Jules Verne journeys may have been writers: Peter Fleming (*News from Tartary*), Fitzroy Maclean (*Eastern Approaches*) and Paul Theroux (*The Great Train Bazaar*). But it was our artists and illustrators who bottled and distilled the magic, so to speak – none more so than Sir Hugh Casson, from whom we commissioned a number of beautiful watercolours.

Not that painting was by any means the beginning or the end of Casson's talents. In 1948, at the age of just 38, he was appointed director of architecture for the Festival of Britain, receiving a knighthood for his work and never leaving the public eye from that point on. His architectural practice, Casson Conder, was responsible for a whole host of distinguished and groundbreaking buildings, including Cambridge University's Sidgwick Avenue arts faculty buildings and the landmark Elephant House at London Zoo.

Casson designed stage sets for the theatre and the Glyndebourne Opera, and at the same time created and ran the School of Interior Design at the Royal College of Art. He also designed interiors for Buckingham Palace, Windsor Castle and the royal yacht *Britannia*.

It is for his watercolour work, however, that he is most fondly remembered. Somehow, he managed to capture the character of a place not so much in the form of broad brushstrokes, but by identifying and celebrating the minutiae of the surroundings. That is what conveyed to would-be Voyages Jules Verne/Serenissima customers, as they leafed through our brochures, not just the look of a place, but also – crucially – the feel.

The same applied to Alison Musker, the other distinguished watercolourist who provided illustrations for us. No need for her to paint dramatic mountain ranges or soaring temples; her paintings of atmospheric, old doorways somehow told you everything you wanted to know about what it would be like to visit that particular, dusty corner of France, Italy or Morocco.

As befitted my Emporium of Travel, I wanted to entice my customers through sights as well as words. We couldn't actually provide the heat, scents and sounds of foreign adventure, but with our illustrations, we did the next best thing.

A Story in Brief

SARTORIAL SPLENDOUR: The world's most famous street for sartorial splendour for the gentleman about London town. Built (1731 to 1735) by 'the architect Earl' (the Earl of Burlington), he named the street after his wife Lady Dorothy Savile. Poole & Co in the person of Henry Poole was the favoured tailor of the Prince of Wales, which elevated the status of the street. Poole is credited with introducing both the dinner (tuxedo) and smoking jacket. It was also to Savile Row that the higher ranked military officer would turn for their uniforms – a legacy that remains to this day. When Tommy Nutter and Edward Sexton set up Nutters of Savile Row in 1969, suiting became cool. Nutter was known as the 'maverick tailor' – the godfather of the modern Savile Row suit. He dressed all the celebrities of the time; three of the four suits worn by the Beatles on their iconic Abbey Road album cover were tailored by him.

CHAPTER 82
LIFE IMITATING ART

After yet another performance of the West End musical 'My Fair Lady'.
It is a case of life imitating art as theatregoers stream out past Covent
Garden Market, the setting for so much of what they've just seen.

I had learnt to cut hair when Barnardo's had assigned me to a firm of barbers that were located at the gates of the Ford Motor Company in Dagenham. In fact it was more akin to a hair cutting factory than a barber shop where the accent was not on coiffeur's skill but on speed. Sometime later, having been on a merry-go-round of other jobs, I got another in a barber shop in Bayswater. It was while working there and cutting the hair of the principal stand-in for the male lead part in *My Fair Lady*, I got my first break. I was never to pick up the scissors and shears again – I had now gotten a job as a dresser with the Male Chorus on the Drury Lane production (in the evenings) and during the day a job working in the old Covent Garden flower market; such in my case at least, life indeed was imitating art nicely captured in the story below:

It's half past ten at night, on 18 June 1963, and the audience is spilling out of the Theatre Royal in Drury Lane, after yet another performance of the record-breaking West End musical *My Fair Lady*. It is a case of life imitating art as the homebound theatregoers stream out past Covent Garden Market, the setting for so much of the action in the show they've just seen.

It's here that the spirited young Cockney flower-seller, Eliza Doolittle (played by Julie Andrews), first encounters Henry Higgins (Rex Harrison), the professor of phonetics, who is going to turn her life upside down. Henry is amongst a crowd of silk-scarved opera-goers hailing taxis for the journey back to Belgravia or Mayfair, while Eliza is busy trying to sell her bunches of violets to the top-hatted toffs. Unlike the professor and his friend, Colonel Pickering, Eliza does not come from a well-to-do part of London, but from nearby Lisson Grove, in Paddington, where she has, until recently, been paying 4/6d rent per week 'for a room that wasn't fit for a pig to live in'.

As to what happens next, we all know the story of how Professor Higgins takes Eliza on as a sort of human experiment, boasting of how he will raise her from the 'gutter' and will teach her to talk like a lady. Professor Higgins only realises too late that he has fallen in love with Eliza.

The tale is set a good fifty years earlier, in Edwardian times, and is based on the George Bernard Shaw play *Pygmalion*, yet both the Covent Garden Market and the life of the people who work there are not much different in 1963 than in 1913.

There are still another eleven years to go before the market will be uprooted from its home in the heart of theatreland, to its soulless new location at Nine Elms, south of the river. The age of the juggernaut has yet to dawn and boxes of cauliflowers and cabbages are still hauled along the bumpy streets on handcarts, many of them pulled by men whose fathers and grandfathers did the same job in generations before.

As couples stroll hand-in-hand past the vast, slumbering market hall, humming songs from the show (perhaps 'The Street Where You Live', or 'I Could Have Danced All Night'), there is nothing to see but the closed-up shop frontages of the fruit-and-veg traders, along with rows of long-handled barrows, tied up and awaiting the coming day's work.

In another four hours' time, however, the scene will be transformed beyond recognition. As the area drains of playgoers and restaurant diners and the dinner-jacketed gentlemen and stiletto-wearing ladies drift off home, this cobbled kingdom begins to fill up with folk in altogether more workaday footwear. To begin with, they arrive in ones and twos, opening up the little wooden booths that serve as headquarters for the different market firms. By midnight, there are tens of people, yet, by 3.00am, there are hundreds: a teeming mass of porters, traders, farmers and greengrocers, weaving in and out of the rows of haphazardly-parked trucks.

Talk on the morning of 19 June is all about the fight the previous night at Wembley Stadium, in which the nation's favourite heavyweight, Henry Cooper, managed to floor world champion Cassius Clay (later Muhammad Ali) with his trademark left hook ('Our 'Enery's 'Ammer', as it was called). Cooper is not just popular amongst the housewives – in addition to being Britain's best-known professional boxer, he's a fruit-and-veg man, too: he and his twin brother, George, run a greengrocer's shop in Wembley High Road, and the champion is as likely to be found bagging up sprouts as he is training in the gym.

This makes him an honorary Covent Garden Market man. The world-famous ballerina, Dame Margot Fonteyn, may be popular among the stallholders (she often stops for a chat on her way to and from performances at the Royal Opera House next-door), but it's the unassuming Cooper whom they consider as one of their own. The only trouble, they say, is that, when you hit him, he bleeds like a beetroot; last night, again, the fight with Clay had to be stopped, due to a cut over Henry's legendarily vulnerable left eye.

A crying shame, agree the porters. If only the knockdown hadn't been at the end of the round, then Henry could have finished the job and he'd be world champion this morning. If only there hadn't been that extra delay, in which Clay's damaged gloves were changed, giving him yet more time to recover. Ah well, it wasn't to be, and everyone in the Market agrees that Cockney hero Cooper, gracious and blood-spattered, did them proud. Meanwhile, of course, the daily life of the Market goes on, in pretty much the same way it has done for the past 130 years.

To the outside observer, the scene looks chaotic and disordered. Lorries seem to be parked with no particular regard to logic, handcart-carriers criss-cross haphazardly and everywhere there is the sound of shouting, negotiating and requests to fellow-toilers (often impolitely phrased) to get out of the way.

However, like any beehive, there is a structure and a status quo. At the bottom of the pile, in terms of status, are the 'Empties' boys: the youngsters whose job it is to stack up the piles of boxes that are brought in. In the middle are the porters, who pride themselves on their ability to pilot a barrow load of parsnips, at speed, through the crowd. At the top of the tree are the salesmen, with their trilbies and cigarettes and the bulging wads of banknotes stuffed inside their jacket pockets.

Nowhere is the spirit of the old market kept fresher than in the collection of images and recollections put together by photographer Clive Boursnell, in his book *Covent Garden*, published by Frances Lincoln. Over a period of five years, Boursnell captured the likenesses of countless Market characters, such as colourful Alfie Marks, from Brick Lane, and Portobello Rosie, the greengrocer who would take her fruit and veg back to Notting Hill by horse and cart. Boursnell recorded his observations of the salesmen on paper:

'Some thin, some portly, rocking from heel to toe, surveying the street, puffing on cigars, the salesmen watched over their goods as if they were a flock of sheep.

A wave of a cigar to a porter would bring a barrow to the pavement or road and then, from the back of a shop, would appear boxes of oranges; apples; pears; cauliflowers; beans; carrots, still with their green hats on; sacks of onions; potatoes; greens; cabbages; delicate trays of peaches; cherries; the first raspberries and early grapes.'

One of the World's Last Great Journeys

JOURNEY ACROSS TOP OF THE WORLD

Arrangements by

VOYAGES JULES VERNE

A Story in Brief

MAKING POLAR HISTORY – ALMOST: In May 1991, Voyages Jules Verne announced, via a full page advertisement in *The Times*, that the the company would be sending a party to Murmansk to board the nuclear icebreaker *Sovetskiy Soyuz*. The party would then be undertaking a 21-day voyage, via the Arctic Sea and Franz Josef Land, to the North Pole, thereafter continuing to Nome, in Alaska. By anyone's standards, this was going to be an epic expedition, both geographically and politically. After all, submarines had sailed beneath the North Pole, but only three ships had ever sailed there, and they had all happened to be the three identical sister ships of the *Sovetskiy Soyuz*. Sadly, though, this historic adventure never took place; the American government refused the operating company permission to enter their waters, and the itinerary had to be changed. IMAGE COURTESY: VOYAGES JULES VERNE.

The presence of fruit and veg on this patch of land was nothing new, although, in the fourteenth century, the produce was not so much sold here, as grown. Back then, the area was known as Convent Garden, a 40-acre site which served as kitchen garden for the Abbey and Convent of St Peter at Westminster.

It wasn't until the seventeenth century that the owner of the land, the Fourth Duke of Bedford, commissioned architect Inigo Jones to build the church (St Paul's, finished in 1638) that still stands there today. Also, part of Jones' brief was to design and construct houses that were 'fit for the habitations of gentlemen', which he duly did, taking care to name the streets after the monarch of the time; witness King Street, Charles Street and Henrietta (the name of King Charles I's wife) Street.

The architect's most significant contribution was the creation of the Piazza, the great, open cobblestoned area in front of St Paul's Church. It was the perfect spot for a market and, after the Great Fire of London had obliterated most of the other marketplaces in the City, King Charles II issued, in 1670, a grant to the Duke of Bedford, to hold a market in Covent Garden's Piazza 'on every day of the year except Sundays and Christmas Day, for buying and selling all manner of fruit, flowers, roots and herbs'.

The year 1830 saw the opening of the market buildings that still stand on the site today, and, in 1870, a glass roof was added to the main market hall. By this point, Rules Restaurant, in Maiden Lane (founded 1798, still in operation today) had been serving game and oysters for nearly three-quarters of a century. It wasn't just the capital's oldest restaurant that first opened its doors in this area, either. The outfitters Moss Bros, the auctioneers Sotheby's and the grocery store Sainsbury's also chose Covent Garden as the launching-point for their businesses.

Not that the supermarket-bought sandwich had yet become a lunchtime staple. Back in 1963, the Covent Garden porters ate and drank at the pubs which proliferated throughout the area, and which remained open from the small hours of the morning onwards. Many a cart-puller would duck into the Nag's Head, The Market House, the Marquis of Anglesey or the Essex Serpent for a quick pint in between jobs. Those with a bit more time to spare would tuck into a filling plate of either Baby's Head (steak and kidney pie with a white, round top) or Airships in the Clouds, a pair of sausages wedged into a mound of mashed potato, often before dawn had broken.

Back then, most of the market traders were family-run firms (Howgeggo and Company, Chas J Smith, Joseph I Emmanuel) and most of the porters they employed had family connections with the market, too: Clive Boursnell recalls that, at one point, there were five different members of the Sullivan family earning their living on the handcarts. Despite the fact that everyone was working for various and often quite small companies, a clannish feeling still existed amongst the market folk.

When one of their number died, there would be a substantial turnout for the funeral; most burials took place at the Kensal Green Cemetery, just north of Paddington, and mourners traditionally stopped en route at the Halfway House pub, on the Harrow Road, to drink a toast to the departed.

In contrast with today's altogether more anonymous corporate culture, the market thrived on individuals, many of whom had been around since anyone could remember. There was 'Old Nell', the elderly cart-minder who would guard porters' barrows while they were in the Nag's Head, perhaps discussing the latest snakes and scorpions to have been found among the bananas (such hazards meant that porters got paid more for handling fruit shipped from the tropics).

Then there was the famously grumpy Peter Hicks, a Sussex farmer who delivered convoys of produce each day to the market and came up with an ingenious way of avoiding parking tickets. He didn't just write a 'Back Soon' notice and leave it on the dashboard of his lorries: instead, he rigged up a formidable device that gave an electric shock to any traffic warden who touched his vehicle.

"The wardens come regularly and do the whole lot of lorries," he complained to a BBC reporter. "It costs me £20 to £30 a week, so I'm using a machine that is intended for keeping cattle away from a fence. I park the lorries right up next to each other, so that they are touching, which means that, once I activate the machine, the whole lot are electrified. It's a jolly good device and I shall keep up my private war until someone tells me what law I am breaking."

As it happens, no one could tell Mr Hicks what law he was breaking. The police did confiscate his patented, warden-jolting device, but returned it to him nine months later, announcing that they would not be seeking a prosecution.

Today, one cannot imagine the authorities being quite as lenient, but, then again, it's hard to imagine today's Covent Garden, with its well-groomed wine bars and upmarket boutiques, as a rough-and-ready fruit-and-veg market, jammed up with carthorses and haphazardly-parked lorries.

It is no wonder that, when the film *My Fair Lady* came to be made in 1964 (with Rex Harrison still playing Professor Higgins, but Audrey Hepburn playing Eliza, rather than Julie Andrews), the producers chose not to make the movie on location in London WC2, but in the altogether more controllable environment of the Burbank Studios, in California.

In 1974, the market moved, in its entirety, to the more spacious, if less characterful, patch of concrete at Nine Elms, just the other side of Vauxhall Bridge. Although the waft of over-ripe cabbage can no longer be detected in the Covent Garden air, what with all the sweet-smelling odours emerging from the perfume and body lotion emporiums, the memory of the old market still lingers on, in the form of a small ritual performed once every year.

If you find yourself on the cobblestones of Covent Garden around the end of June, you might see a strange little procession taking place. Taking part are members of the Covent Garden Area Trust, the body set up in 1988 to conserve the area's heritage. They have been granted, by government decree, a 150-year lease on what is known as the 'Protected Lands', a chunk of central Covent Garden that incorporates the central market and a number of surrounding buildings.

Normally, the rent payable for such prime properties would amount to millions, but, instead of handing over a large cheque at the end of their procession, the Trust members simply give their landlords one red apple and one simple posy of flowers.

Yes the old market may have gone, but its roots still lie deep in the Covent Garden cobblestones.

BACKSTAGE

On the evening of 18 June 1963, I was backstage at Drury Lane, caring for the male chorus as they were changing into their Ascot scene finery (costumes designed by Cecil Beaton).

I know this because, in between scene sequences, they (and I) were rushing back to the dressing room, to listen to the bout between Henry Cooper and Cassius Clay on the radio. By the time I joined the *My Fair Lady* outfit, the production had already been running for a number of years, and backstage was more akin to a gentleman's lounge than a theatre, especially for the 'leads', with their comfy armchairs and TVs. They seemed to be able to rise effortlessly and, on signal, do their piece on stage, then return to their sedentary position to watch, say, an episode of Morecambe & Wise.

I myself never got to see My Fair Lady as a punter until many years later and, when I refer to 'male' chorus, most of them were actually raving queens – interesting in 1963, given that it was still illegal to be openly gay. Post-theatre, I got a glimpse of their secret Soho venues and clandestine parties.

I had also previously worked around the corner from the Theatre Royal, Drury Lane, at the Golden Egg, as a sort of chef (in reality, just cracking the eggs for the omelettes). After that, I had got a job in Covent Garden Flower Market, working for a florist supplier named Cocquorrelles. My job was to make up the signage for the wreaths, which I had then to dip in glitter – I shudder to think of my attempts at spelling.

My other memories of that time are of the all-day opening of the Covent Garden pubs, the lunch time jive sessions at the nearby Lyceum Ballroom, and the pavement artists that, alas, are no more.

When I got the job at the theatre, I didn't miss the early-morning starts at the flower market; not because I had to start work at 4.00am, but because I finished work at 2.00pm, leaving the afternoon void of things to do and no one to interact with, since everyone else was at work. That said, I was glad when I didn't have to drive my hire-purchase Lambretta, untaxed and barely insured, through the empty streets at 3.00am. Time after time, I was stopped by the police, as, at that hour, there was just no one else on the road.'

'LORD OF THE HIGHLANDS' – GAIRLOCH

A Story in Brief

PLAN 'B': Following the Gulf War, VJV were anxious to create alternative pro-grammes to perceived 'safe' destinations – and what could be safer than an around Britain cruise we pondered. The 1992 *Travel Review* set the scene as follows: 'How well do you know your own shores? Many of us may be made uncomfortable by such a question having spent many of our holidays in far flung places in preference to exploring our own lands. There is no doubt that as the nation's motorways be-come more crowded each year, making long journeys tedious and uncomfortable, the desire to explore the remoter regions of Scotland, Ireland and Wales has for many of us dwindled. Now, we believe we have found the perfect solution. Our comprehensive seven-night cruise between Avonmouth and Edinburgh offers a carefully planned itinerary providing an excellent balance of some of these islands' most beautiful scenery and historic houses and gardens'. The image above shows the *Lord of the Highlands* at Gairloch with the Torridon mountains beyond. She is now the *National Geographic Islander* cruising the Galapagos Islands.

CHAPTER 83
THE VIEW FROM
CONSTITUTION HILL

In the second half of the 1940s the first stop for travellers heading towards Cairo, Durban, Calcutta or Hong Kong would be a night at the Harbour Heights Hotel, Poole.

D R Barnardo's Homes once ran a sea-training school to prepare us boys for a healthy outdoor life at sea. It was located at Parkstone, near Poole in Dorset, and I stayed there three years, from the ages of 12 to 15, after which I left the homes for good. Close to the school was Constitution Hill, a local beauty spot where on most Sunday afternoons I would idle away my time, observing the tourist-coach guides describing the idyllic panorama of Poole Harbour below. It was in these moments, as if in a trance, that I knew what I wanted to be next: a tourist guide, and that is what I eventually became. The following perfectly conjures the sights, sounds and history that enthralled me then, and endured with me for the rest of my life in the business of travel:

Stand on the quayside at Poole Harbour today and you'll see a teeming, churning panorama of maritime life. Pleasure boats, ferry boats, rowing and motor boats, all travelling to-and-fro, between the various islands and headlands. It is hard to imagine that, 70 years ago, this whole area was not just a waterway, but an airport runway too, home to the country's biggest and busiest fleet of flying boats, which would set off for all kinds of far-flung and exotic destinations.

Today, if you were flying to Africa, Asia or Australia, your starting point would be Heathrow or Gatwick. In the second half of the 1940s, however, the first stop for travellers heading towards Cairo, Durban, Calcutta or Hong Kong would be a night at the Harbour Heights Hotel, Poole. They were then ferried out onto the water next morning, to their waiting seaplane.

At the height of its operations here, the British Overseas Airways Corporation (BOAC, formerly Imperial Airways Limited, later British Airways) employed some 650 local people in roles such as pilots, stewards, engineers and the boatmen (and boatwomen) who transferred passengers from shore to plane and vice versa.

Everyone who was anyone flew into or out of Poole on one of those famous flying boats: General de Gaulle; Field Marshal Montgomery; Lord Mountbatten; Anthony Eden; the entertainer George 'When I'm Cleaning Windows' Formby; the author Francis Durbridge (creator of fictional sleuth Paul Temple); and even the official hangman, Albert Pierrepoint, en route to execute a couple of spies in Gibraltar.

When working to full capacity, the harbour boasted five active seaplane runways, most of them three-quarters of a nautical mile long. It was no problem accommodating such a high volume of traffic, either: there is only one natural harbour in the entire world which is bigger, and that's Sydney harbour, in Australia.

Despite its God-given attributes and all the illustrious travellers landing and taking off in its waters, Poole's pre-eminence in the world of post-war air travel turned out to be short-lived. In 1948, the whole flying-boat operation was closed down and moved to Southampton – precisely where it had been moved from in 1939, at the start of World War II. It had been felt that Poole would be a safer place for the seaplanes, as it wasn't surrounded by the same industrial and strategic targets as Southampton, yet it was still accessible, by train, from London.

During the war, the authorities even did their bit to fool the German Luftwaffe by lighting lots of fires each night on Brownsea, the uninhabited island that sits in the middle of the harbour (and where Lord Baden Powell began the Scout movement). The idea was that the enemy planes would take the lights to be Poole itself, and either waste ammunition by launching an attack, or else re-plot their course based on this erroneous assumption. Either way, the outbreak of hostilities with Germany meant that every building around the harbour was pressed into active service, even the celebrated Poole Pottery.

The Fleet Air Arm took up residence on the Sandbanks peninsula (famed today for its multi-million-pound mansions), while the RAF set up a base just across the water, at RAF Hamworthy. A fleet of some 14 fast launches, maintained by the British Power Boat Company, marked out the runways and kept them clear, while a mass of smaller boats known as 'pinnaces' served as small tugs, pulling the flying boats from their moorings to the runways prior to take-off, and reversing the process once they'd landed.

The type of flying boat most commonly used for wartime duty was the Sunderland, made by Short Brothers in Rochester, on the River Medway. It was used for escorting Allied convoys, attacking U-boats (with depth charges) and carrying out air-sea rescue missions, mainly in the Bay of Biscay and the Atlantic. According to Peter London, author of the definitive book British Flying Boats, the Sunderland was extremely well-suited to the tasks required of it, combining reliability and durability with both offensive strike power and defensive capability. 'It was one of the finest seaplanes ever,' he concludes, 'the queen of flying boats.'

It was readily apparent that the Sunderland was not as noisy as its counterpart, the Walrus, made by Supermarine Aviation Works, creators of the Spitfire. Whenever one of these monsters flew overhead, teachers in the surrounding schools would have to stop their lessons until the roaring had died away. These great airborne whales did not just make their mark on children, either: the author Enid Blyton, a resident of the nearby Isle of Purbeck, worked them into the very first set of stories she wrote about her young heroes, The Adventurous Four.

It was hardly surprising that the seaplanes should fire the imaginations of all who witnessed them, as the missions they were engaged in were frequently of the truly daring and heroic kind – a rescue mission in a far-off land, for instance. The great virtue of all the flying boats, regardless of make, was that on overseas missions they could be landed offshore, thereby avoiding the need to use conventional airports or landing strips, which would be guarded and heavily defended by enemy guns.

When it came to evacuation work, this came in very useful. Throughout the course of World War II, Poole-based Sunderlands airlifted, from countries invaded by the Nazis, not just military and political leaders, but royalty too (for example, King Petar II of Yugoslavia and King George II of Greece). It also brought less grandiose figures to these shores, including (after the war) many British servicemen who had been held as prisoners-of-war by the Japanese and who were returning to Britain in a bad way.

"They flew the seriously ill ones home; I will never forget it," says Eileen Armstrong, one of the many women who served as members of the Poole Harbour launch-craft crew, taking pilots, engineers and passengers out to the flying boats. "There was this poor boy, who was a skeleton, really. We carried him out of the plane and put him on the engine cover, on the slipway. He said, 'Oh, it's lovely to be home,' and died."

Once the war was over, it wasn't long before the harbour waters began to be used for tourism as well as naval and military purposes. In only a short space of time, the flying boats were stripped of their military hardware and bomb hatches and kitted out as passenger planes instead. Gradually, the Sunderlands were replaced by a more civilian-friendly model, the Sandringham (also made by Short Brothers), and the world witnessed the birth of international air travel for the purpose not of dropping bombs on overseas lands, but for visiting them.

A Story in Brief

THE HOLY LAND IN PICTURES: David Roberts was a Scottish-born painter, who travelled to the Holy Land in 1838, with lithographer Louis Haghe, to produce a series of lavish illustrations, entitled Sketches in the Holy Land and Syria and Egypt and Nubia. The scenery and monuments of Egypt and the Holy Land were considered fashionable subjects, but had rarely been portrayed by British artists. So when Roberts announced that he would fund the trip through advance subscriptions, he accumulated 400 takers, with Queen Victoria being subscriber number one. More than a century later, I found my own collection of David Roberts' original, hand-painted lithographs whilst rummaging in the market stalls of Church Street Market. They were used extensively on advertisements in the eighties and nineties, and the originals are now in Scotland, adorning the restaurant walls on board the *Lord of the Glens*.   IMAGE COURTESY: VOYAGES JULES VERNE.

Admittedly, BOAC still used the same logo (a stylised skybird) that it had sported during the war years, but now it made use of the flying boats' workhorse-like qualities in an entirely peaceful way. Global hostilities had barely ceased when Poole Harbour became the launching pad for travellers keen to experience the world.

The immediate post-war years saw the start of numerous different services, including the 'Dragon Route' to Hong Kong and the 'Kangaroo Route' to Australia. These were not direct flights, by any means. The journey to Sydney, for example, took 12 days in all, with stops every 500-700 miles for refuelling. Take a BOAC plane to Karachi, and you would call in at 11 different locations on the way, including Marseilles, Brindisi, Athens, Alexandria, Basra and Bahrain.

The service was a lot more personal and less mass-market than the average air flight today. The flying boats took a maximum of 24 passengers for daytime flights, and that figure was reduced to 16 if there were to be overnight flights and sleeping accommodation was required. Furthermore, instead of eating out of polystyrene trays with plastic cutlery, passengers could expect silver service from attentive stewards.

Some passengers who went on flying boats even got a special certificate for crossing the Equator which declared: 'Having this day flown over the Equator and having been cleansed, by flying through the Heavens of all offences and malice and the evils associated with Demons, Gremlins, Poltergeists and other Devils of the middle air, this person has become acceptable as a liege and loyal Member of our Royal Demesne (Aerial Division).' It was signed, 'King Neptune, Omnium Rex (King of All Things).'

For some people, especially the pilots, the charm of flying a Sunderland never wore off. One such aviator was the dashing Captain Charles Blair, an American-born flying-boat pilot who, as well as touching down at Poole, had the distinction of being the first person to fly solo over the North Pole. To add to the glamour of the story, he not only soared through the heavens but, in 1944, also married a movie star, the actress Maureen O'Hara, who had played leading roles in many a big Hollywood blockbuster, including The Hunchback of Notre Dame and The Quiet Man. The love of flying boats must have been catching: when Captain Blair was killed in an air accident over the Caribbean, O'Hara took over the running of the aviation business her husband had set up during his lifetime.

Of course, for most people, flying in a Sunderland just once was excitement enough. Accounts written at the time testify that taking to the skies in one of these conveyances was an experience never to be forgotten. 'At first, as it gathered speed, the tail would drop into the water for a few seconds, which would rush by in a mass of foam,' recalls airline employee Norman Hull. 'As the nose took to the air, the whole aircraft would detach itself from one element, the sea, and become part of another, the air. Touching down, the pilot had no need to lower any landing gear; the very design of the flying boat made it natural to adapt from one element to the other, with the grace of a swan.'

All too soon, of course, these swans upped and flew away from Poole for good, leaving only a fading echo in the minds and ears of the people for whom they were once part of daily life. There's little left now to mark the flying boats' presence, other than the sign on the boatshed wall at the Royal Motor Yacht Club, one of many buildings around the harbour that were requisitioned for war use. It reads, simply, 'Instructions for the Stowage of Seaplanes'. Thereby, of course, hangs a tale, not just of the glamorous early days of international air travel, but also of the many brave wartime pilots and aircrew who took off from Poole but never came back.

Yes, the fuselages of the Sunderlands were treated so that they would not be corroded by contact with seawater, but they could still be pierced by the enemy's shells and bullets. In order to highlight the existence of the seaplanes and the valiance and sacrifice of the people who flew them, a local organisation called the Poole Flying Boats Celebration (PFBC) has been formed.

'The story of the Sunderlands and Sandringhams is, in many ways, an adventure of epic proportions,' says the introduction to the PFBC website. 'It encompasses heroism, courage and an engaging human spirit, a wealth of experience, expertise and a dedication to duty which transcended national boundaries, to reach the farthest horizons attainable in their day.'

CHAPTER 84
BROWNSEA ISLAND
REVISITED

*Folklore had it that the island was inhabited by a wicked witch of a
lady who repelled anyone whosoever even attempted to set foot.
Ironic, then, that many years later, I should commission this article.*

P ART of the seamanship lessons at Barnardo's Sea Training School at
Parkstone involved rowing a whaler, under the tutelage of Mr Busby, close
to mysterious Brownsea Island in Poole Harbour, never once being allowed
to land – folklore had it that the island was inhabited by a wicked witch of a lady
who repelled anyone whosoever even attempted to set foot. Ironic, then, that many
years later, having entered a marketing arrangement with the National Trust (who
now own the property), I should commission this article for the Voyages Jules
Verne quarterly *Travel Review* which is retold below:

'The island, which from afar looks to be covered in vegetation of tropical
density and greenness, is a 20-minute journey from Poole quay: a short cruise
among the hundreds of craft that are moored in the harbour, their spindly masts
erect like plantation trees. Occasionally they rock in the looming shadow of a
Truckline ferry on its way to Cherbourg, or are tickled by the lapping ripples from
a windsurfer skimming in their midst.

It is an invigorating marine scene, although quieter this year than usual. The
taxi driver said that it had been a bad summer, which, judging by the crowds along
Poole High Street, was perhaps not altogether a bad thing. The head warden at
Brownsea, supported by an excellent staff of wardens and helpers, is Barry Guest.
Highly approachable, you cannot miss him because his constant company is a
crackling walkie-talkie which is inclined to interrupt him, mid-flow, to reveal the
latest conundrum requiring his attention.

Barry is a Poole man originally. He was trained as a marine engineer and spent some years at sea on a coaster before returning, between jobs, to work in the employ of the last private owner of the property, Mary Bonham-Christie, just six months before she died. He was in Kent at the time, and although the letter she wrote to him appeared to offer a job, the proposal was less certain when he showed up with his suitcase. Anyway she installed him in one of the cottages, and there he remained until the coming of the National Trust.

By the time of Barry's arrival, Mrs Bonham-Christie had become a rather eccentric woman. She was probably in her 90s and apparently bore a considerable resemblance to Queen Victoria in her old age, plump and severe. The scion of an eminent family and formerly the mistress of a 3,000 acre estate in Somerset where she had earned a reputation for formidableness, she had retired into seclusion on Brownsea, occupying little more than a single room where she would cook her own food on a paraffin stove.

Although her eyesight had been ruined following a youthful fall from a horse that had rolled on her twice, she was a stalwart woman. Years later, when offered a pain-killing injection for a broken arm, she informed the doctor that as animals had suffered in the cause of medical experiments, she preferred to pass the night in pain.

On purchasing the island, Mrs Bonham-Christie had instructed the last remaining residents to return to the mainland, thereby allowing her property to resume its wild and untamed state.

Of course, the history of Brownsea reaches back long before the time of Mrs Bonham-Christie, to at least 500 BC. But its modern history really begins with the establishment, in the 6th century AD, of a chapel dedicated to St Andrew (the patron saint of fishermen), the custodian of which was a hermit who cared for the spiritual lives of local seafarers.

The name 'Brownsea' – the most modern variant of an older name, variously Bruncksey, Brouneksey, Brankesey and Branksea – apparently derives from a 'Bruno' who ruled the area at the time of the Norman Conquest. The island seems to have then been considered of little importance, although there is evidence of a small community, perhaps making a living by fishing or salt production. From what it is possible to glean about Brownsea, it seems fair to say that life was on the quiet side for quite some time, until the religious policies of Henry VIII prompted the construction of new coastal defences along the south coast.

Poole was by then a port of some importance, and when its merchants petitioned Henry for the building of a new fort, a blockhouse was duly built. The inhabitants of Poole were less keen on manning the fort, preferring instead to pay a fine for not doing so and hiring a crew of six to act as wards all year round.

As the threat from the Catholic states of Europe appeared to recede, the island lost its strategic importance for the time being, and became instead a repository for the booty of smugglers who had made Studland their main area of operation. Its next legitimate activity was the production of copperas, a green vitriol used in the manufacture of ink.

In 1765 Sir Humphrey Sturt, MP, land owner and dedicated follower of the Enlightenment, which had evolved a number of new theories about cultivation and landscaping, added four stories to the remains of the blockhouse as well as a pair of wings and an extension – the blockhouse had now become a castle. He laid out gardens and planted 'to the quantity of a million trees', while his successors added pineries, a pheasantry and some ornamental cottages.

Since smuggling remained a problem in the area, the island was also used as a base for the Preventive Service, quarters being built near the castle for its officers. By 1842, a complete coastguard station had been built on the quay.

Life on Brownsea took a significant turn in 1852, when the island was purchased by a Colonel Waugh of the Indian Army who, in true Victorian spirit, entertained ideas of turning it into a money-spinner. The story goes that his wife's parasol, having pierced the earth on the island, was seen to be tipped with a fine China clay. An ambitious woman, she instantly visualised an industry devoted to the production of fine porcelain, her ideas given weight by the opinion of an eminent geologist.

As a result, the Colonel borrowed heavily from the bank in order to finance the construction of the most modern factory possible for the production of both sanitary ware and ornamental terracotta. A railway, its cars drawn by horse, was constructed for the transportation of the clay across the island and of the finished product to Potter Pier. A village, named Maryland in honour of the Colonel's wife, was built for the workers and the church of St Mary the Virgin consecrated to give thanks for the foundation of this new community.

The only problem was the discovery that the clay was not of the required quality after all, fit only for sanitary ware and nothing more. Then, when a deputation of local worthies arrived to ask the Colonel to stand for Parliament, his wife misunderstood and pleaded for more time to pay the bills. Confidence was undermined and the whole project fell to pieces. The island was sold, with pottery production finally ceasing in 1887.

After half a century of disappointment, the new owners of Brownsea were to usher in its golden age. The Van Raaltes had acquired their wealth through jute and tobacco and entertained with spectacular lavishness. A golf course was built near the house, and the gifted, the wealthy and the well-born of Europe were regular visitors. Such was the hubbub that the residents of the island were able to find employment in the castle. After Charles van Raalte's death in 1908, his widow, Florence, continued to entertain at the same level until she left the island in 1925, and in the meantime even set up an industry for the cultivation of daffodils.

Her place was taken in 1927 by Mrs Bonham-Christie. Such was the latter's reclusiveness that the island, following a massive fire in 1934, became a mystery to even the locals, who were forbidden to land there. During the war, of course, it was impossible for her to remain quite so isolated from the world, and the island was used to house refugees from Holland and Belgium.

A story tells of how a British spy was travelling on a train in Italy and overheard enemy officers discussing a secret radio beam for directing bombs with great accuracy. When the agent sent back his report, it was decided that to counteract this new weapon certain places, Brownsea among them, would have to act as decoy areas to deflect bombing from the mainland.

The net result of all this was that, by the time the National Trust took the island over, it was in something of a mess, in places an almost impenetrable one. Confrontation with untrammelled nature is always a problem. Decisions have to be made: how much to leave as is, and how much to dispose of and recreate. After all, the island had been through so many changes in the course of its history that it had no clearly defined character.

In general, it has returned to what is has always excelled at, being a sort of island estate with the feel of a rustic hamlet in the shadow of a castle. Although the cries of peacocks can be heard all over, the land becomes wilder and more sylvan as you amble along the tracks, most of which reappeared as the island was cleared after the death of Mrs Bonham-Christie.

A walk of just over three miles will take you from Colonel Waugh's church 'of beautiful design', as it was described by the Illustrated London News on 28 October 1854, across the site of the old daffodil orchards to the secluded strands on the other side of the island. Some things have gone, like the old cottages, but enough material traces of the past remain to engender a feeling of the island's history. At one of the (surprisingly high) higher points of the island there are enchanting views towards the south-west and other islands that are seemingly uninhabited, like some South Sea archipelago.

Barry Guest had almost decided to go back to sea when the National Trust took on the property – he had been offered a post on a deep-sea oil tanker – but in the event he stayed on to become head warden and to marry, which means that he has been a resident of Brownsea for nigh on 30 years.

He is not alone, of course, for some 30 people work on the island in one capacity of other, either for the National Trust; on the nature reserve, which is run by the Dorset Trust for Nature Conservation; or in castle, which is leased to the

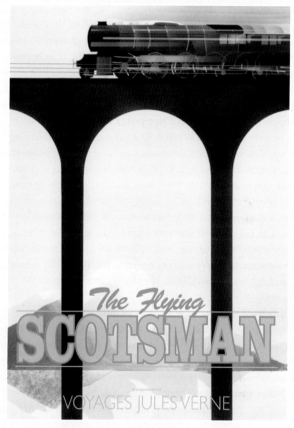

A Story in Brief

THE KING OF CARNABY STREET: I was in the La Siesta coffee bar, when I noticed the shop next door had been having a clear-out, and had left out a gigantic, blow-up image of a male model with the rubbish. I couldn't help thinking this outsize cut-out might make my drab bedsit look a bit more hip. So I went into the shop to ask if I could take the thing away, and it was here that I met John Stephen, who readily agreed, clearly bewildered that anyone in their right minds would want this piece of trash. His nickname, at the time, was the King of Carnaby Street; he was the first in the UK to sell mass-market, disposable fashion menswear, and by 1967, together with his boyfriend Bill Franks, he owned 15 shops on Carnaby Street, the very epicentre of Swinging London. "Carnaby is my creation", Stephen said in 1967. "I feel about it the same way Michelangelo felt about the beautiful statues he created."
IMAGE COURTESY: ROBERT SCURRAH/VOYAGES JULES VERNE.

John Lewis Partnership. The population varies with the comings and goings of offspring and the mainland-based staff who work in the shops and café, nonetheless the island functions rather like a small village with all that entails. If the community differs from any other of similar size, it is in that everyone is engaged in work that is broadly related.

For Barry, the days are long and absorbing. Brownsea's insular character distinguishes it from most of the other National Trust properties and brings with it some peculiar problems. The island has its own sewerage arrangements, for example, and its own water supply, both of which require a good deal of attention, never more so than when new EC regulations decree that the quality of the water is inadequate – a succession of long nights have recently been necessary to effect the required changes.

The weather, too, should not be under-estimated, for although the island is sheltered to a certain degree by its position, wild weather can make the use of boats difficult, to put it mildly, and were it not for the sea wall that creates a lagoon just beyond the quay, the sea water would regularly lap the old castle walls (a small red strip marks the sea's most daring encroachment). In fact, one of the most pressing problems for the island is the repair of this wall, which is old and, in part, crumbling away.

The daily challenge is of course reconciling the needs of the public with the demands of the island. On the one hand, it must remain accessible; on the other, it must retain as much as possible its identity as a piece of unspoilt countryside. During the summer months the two ideals may conflict a little, when, for example, a gashed knee takes precedence over daily maintenance. Occurrences of this nature, however, are all part of life on the island and are accepted as such, for the wellbeing of the paying public and the custodianship of the island are interdependent. Visitors to the island on the whole tend to respect the Trust's aims: the worst offenders may be lads chasing the peacocks (there are plenty of feathers lying about, anyway) or yachtsmen not paying their landing fee on the southern, pottery-littered shore. In the case of the latter they will be politely asked to pay up by Dennis, the genial Welshman who patrols the beaches.

Then there is the open-air theatre. Every summer performances are given on the equivalent of the village green, just by the church, and are regularly sold out. Come the winter, however, and seasonal closure, it is possible to give undivided attention to the welfare of the island itself.

A walk across the island is a delight, for as well as the superb views across the water there is an abundance of flora and fauna. Along with the Isle of Wight, Brownsea is the last bastion in Britain of the red squirrel, of which it is reckoned there are at least 100 healthy individuals making use of the pine trees. Rabbits and sika deer are pretty but voracious destroyers of vegetation, and a careful eye has to be kept on their depredations.

On the sea shore are stalking oystercatchers and scuttling redshanks and sandpipers; inland dart siskins, reed buntings, goldfinches, kingfishers and a host of other birds which haunt the woodland, lakes, marsh and lagoon. The island is rich in butterflies, including the rare White Admiral, which can flutter at peace amid 60 species of tree including plenty of native hardwoods.

For Barry Guest the island and challenge of preserving its unique, indefinable character has become his life. When ships ease past Brownsea on their way to who-knows-where, he must wonder, sometimes, where he might have gone had he accepted that original job offer. As it is, he and his colleagues have created their own world on Brownsea, every bit as varied, in its way, as the wider world itself.'

PASSAGE TO AMERICA LATINA COVER BY ROBERT SCURRAH

A Story in Brief:

IMAGE COURTESY: ROBERT SCURRAH/VJV.

DESTINATION LOURDES: In 1956, Independent Air Transport was asked to fly a group of 40 nuns from Dublin to Lourdes. Everything went smoothly, and the plane took off on time, but not long out of Dublin, the aircraft developed a generator problem, and the pilot decided to divert to the airline's technical base at Bournemouth Hurn Airport. Once they had landed, it became clear that fixing the faulty generator was not going to be a quick job. In response to the question of how to keep the sisters occupied, the engineer was instructed to arrange for them to go on an excursion around the New Forest. After several hours, the excursion coach returned, by which time all the nuns were drunk as lords. In which state, they took off once more for their original destination.

CHAPTER 85
CHINA'S MANY FACES

The Confucian Gentleman is humane, loyal, righteous and considerate in all his dealings; his prime motive is not profit. Confucius lived 2,500 years ago and his ideas have flowed through Chinese thought ever since.

WHAT do people mean when they talk about the importance of 'face' in China? On one level, it is simply common courtesy. It is bad manners to do or say something that will embarrass other people in public, especially those who are close to you or whom you should respect. This has its origins in the social philosophy of Confucius and the principle that every member of society or a family has their own place, duties and responsibilities, as in the relationship between the Emperor and his minister, father and son, husband and wife, and so on. The emphasis is on respect for your ancestors and respect for your parents – filial piety.

The Confucian junzi (gentleman) is humane, loyal, righteous, considerate and polite in all his dealings; his prime motive is not profit. Confucius lived 2,500 years ago, and his ideas have flowed through Chinese thought and life almost continuously since. They were reinvigorated by the renowned Neo-Confucian scholar Zhu Xi during the Song dynasty, in the 12th century.

However, post-1949, when the Chinese Communist Party came to power, this traditional way of thinking and behaving began to be questioned. Confucian values were regarded as conservative and regressive by the Party. During the 10 years of the Cultural Revolution (1966-76), the old natural order was overturned, and now people found themselves having to defer to fierce young Red Guards or the local Communist Party boss, who may have previously been a farmer from the countryside.

Teachers, artists and intellectuals were regarded with suspicion and sent to remote, rural corners of China to work. The correct political background – worker,

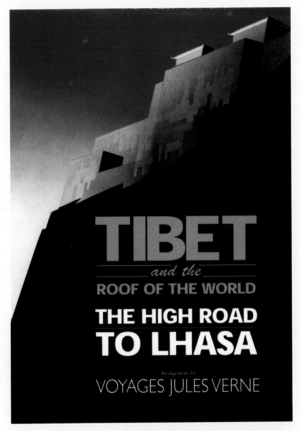

A Story in Brief

CURFEW ON THE CASPIAN: On arrival in Baku, we learnt that the town was under dusk-to-dawn curfew. Undaunted, the two Argentinian guitarists who had travelled with us, and had played for us in each location, decided they were going to play in Baku, as well. We all repaired to a charming al fresco location just outside the city, where much raki was downed and many stirring flamenco rhythms played. Unfortunately, by the time darkness descended, we had completely forgotten about the curfew; and by that time of night, public transport had long since stopped. It was rather gingerly, then, that we began the walk back to town, bumping en route into militias guarding the intersections, who gave up on us once we murmured something in English. All of a sudden, we spotted an empty bus, piled into it, and pleaded with the driver to take us to our hotel, which he did, albeit under a police escort. Panic over. **IMAGE COURTESY: ROBERT SCURRAH/VOYAGES JULES VERNE.**

peasant or soldier – was key to one's position in society. This was an era when China was inward looking; contact with foreigners was limited, and an interest in overseas affairs was dangerous.

Culturally, only certain works of music, art and literature were approved by the Party. The 1973-74 political campaign to criticise Lin Biao and Confucius was yet another signal that the old ways were wrong and people learnt, under great duress, to say the right thing, using certain political phrases, or to say as little as possible and trust no-one.

Soon after the death of Chairman Mao, in September 1976, Hua Guofeng, Mao's chosen successor, became Premier. Mao's core of supporters – the 'Gang of Four' led by his widow, Jiang Qing – were blamed for the excesses of the Cultural Revolution, publicly ousted, put on trial and sentenced. Meanwhile, behind the scenes, Deng Xiaoping was working to put in place a more open economic policy, in order to create a climate of enterprise and modernisation and to rehabilitate the experts and entrepreneurs who were essential to this process. The Chinese people, by now experts in reading political signs, breathed a collective sigh of relief. New business links began to be established with overseas Chinese in the Special Economic Zones of the south-east and, of course, in enterprises that would bring in foreign currency, such as tourism.

To those of us who became involved in the early days of dealing with Chinese organisations, what soon became apparent was that the forum for putting forward such things as new ideas or requests for extra capacity was not the formal meeting over green tea with the department head, his number two and English-speaking interpreters in large reception rooms, where the stock reply would be, "We'll let you know."

Rather, these matters – and their details – had to be dealt with informally, perhaps walking back from a theatre performance, over a cup of tea in the hotel lobby or in conversation with an assistant. This would then be discussed back at the office, probably with a Party representative, and a further formal meeting would be held in which the department head would indicate their approval.

More than 30 years have passed and China has progressed economically in an astonishing way. Within the Communist Party, there has even been talk of creating a civil society and a return to Confucian values. In 2005 Hu Jintao, as General Secretary, introduced the concept of a 'harmonious society', while in 2008 there was a very popular series of programmes on China Central Television entitled *The 100 Schools Lectures*, in which the Analects (sayings and ideas attributed to Confucius) were analysed and applied to contemporary life in China.

In many ways, then, there has been a restoration of the old values and the unspoken language of 'face'. Everybody knows their place again, both at work and within the family. When a Chinese business group or delegation travels abroad, its leader is accorded due respect; their views are listened to and sought at the table, and they do not become involved in discussions over arrangements or money.

A woman must be careful not to show that she can do something better than a man, and a prospective businessperson in China has to learn to recognise who is in charge when he or she walks into a meeting. They must remember not to put the leader on the spot with an awkward question, but rather to raise any such issues outside the meeting with a person who has a more operational role.

JOURNEYS OF DISCOVERY COVER BY ROBERT SCURRAH

A Story in Brief

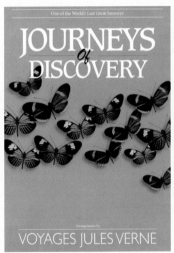

IMAGE COURTESY: ROBERT SCURRAH/VJV.

NORWEGIAN WOOD: I remember travelling with Adele Biss on a business trip to Norway, in 1973. We were keen to compete with Clarksons in the Lakes and Mountains area, so we went round signing up hotels on the spot, for an instant Norway programme. At that time, she was a Thomson director, and following Bryan Llewellyn's departure, her husband Roger Davies became managing director. Of course, Adele's time at Thomson was just the start. She went on to found and run her own PR business and consultancy, become chairman of both the English Tourist Board and British Tourist Authority, a governor of Middlesex University, and a Council Member of University College London (UCL). And in 2010, she was appointed to the Civil Service Commission, the body that evaluates applications for all the top posts.

CHAPTER 86
MEMORIES OF LONDON

William Wordsworth wrote 'the river glideth at his own sweet will: Dear
God! The very houses seem asleep; And all that mighty heart is lying still'.
He was standing on Westminster Bridge at dawn at the time.

HERE follow two examples of advertorial-style advertisements applied to voyages along the Thames, on board the *Spirit of Chartwell*, and in the Scottish Highlands, on board the *Lord of the Glens*. It was also the application of this advertorial style of advertisement, where the whole deal is explained on the page, that enabled me to react quickly to geo-political events such as the Gulf War and the Tiananmen Square incident.

When, in 1803, William Wordsworth wrote, 'the river glideth at his own sweet will: / Dear God! The very houses seem asleep; And all that mighty heart is lying still,' he was standing on Westminster Bridge at dawn, looking along the Thames as it rippled through one of the great cities of the world at the only moment in the day when it lay motionless.

For London, by then, was the hub of a great empire and the Thames, as later described by the politician John Burns, was 'liquid history'. The capital's history is, of course, intimately linked with the river that flows serenely through its centre. Reflected in its waters are all the great buildings and projects that have arisen throughout the 2,000 years since the Romans made London their British capital and principal port.

No doubt about it, London's history is, to a great extent, Britain's history and, it could even be said, the history of the modern world. There is the Tower of London, a solid reminder of the last time Britain was invaded, and the Houses of Parliament, within which were laid the foundation of liberal democracy. There are scientific advances and military power at Greenwich, an elegant example of the happy coincidence of art and utility, and the majestic, massive presence of St Paul's Cathedral, not to mention Shakespeare's Globe and the London Eye. All of them on or near the banks of the River Thames, as the river and the city it cleaves have always been one and the same. All of them built to be used and appreciated with the river in mind. Always the river. Liquid history indeed.

London has grown into one of the most significant cultural and financial capitals of the world, and yet its river, the source of its greatness, is oddly underused. Once, the Thames was London's single most important transportation conduit, only to be supplanted by the railway and the road. The road has become impossible and the train shows you nothing of London, unless your interest lies in the suburbs. From the river you see everything and, on a luxurious ship, you can gaze out at the landmarks of London, unhurried and in comfort. Just as it is traditional to cruise the Nile in order to see the best that Egypt has to offer, so too should it be possible in London.

Now, it is. On Monday 11 April, 2011, on a voyage called 'Memories of London', the MV *Spirit of Chartwell*, flagship of the Magna Carta Steamship Company, made her maiden passenger voyage along the Thames, carrying no more than 70 fortunate travellers for a day of civilised relaxation and cultural appreciation, fine dining and pampered luxury, and the best views in town.

To call the *Spirit of Chartwell* a pleasure cruiser is akin to referring to the *Queen Mary* as a ferry. At 210 feet, she is as long as Nelson's *Victory*, and yet can turn on a sixpence. It is the luxury of her appointments, however, that appeal to most passengers. 'Coach-built' does not begin to describe her. Take the distinctive chocolate and cream livery – if it calls to mind the great days of Pullman train travel, this is no accident, because the design of the public spaces on board have been inspired by the René Lalique Pullman car 'Côte d'Azur', which was operated by the Compagnie Internationale des Wagons-Lits and, later, by the Compagnie Des Chemins de Fer Paris à Lyon et à la Mediterannée.

Amazingly, the Magna Carta Steamship Company has discovered authentic pieces of Lalique's carriage, the highlight of which is a series of exquisite glass panels featuring classical figures. These, together with 33 original 'Riviera' armchairs, have been painstakingly restored and integrated into the new vessel.

Furthermore, genuine pieces from the great ocean liners establish a vital connection with another branch of the age of luxury travel. There are two magnificent portholes in the main lounge, bathroom fittings, bar stools and fine brass friezes that formerly graced the RMS *Windsor Castle*, the last flagship of the Union-Castle Line, while most of the 20 staterooms are illuminated by wall lights from the SS *France*, once the longest passenger vessel afloat.

Indeed, links with the golden age of travel have been preserved throughout.

The main restaurant and lounge commemorates George Bradshaw, a real-life founding father of modern travel, whose railways and shipping timetables – items we now regard as indispensable – provided both the inspiration and the practical information for perhaps the greatest of travel adventure books, *Around the World in Eighty Days*.

On the *Spirit of Chartwell*, today's voyagers can experience all the charm and elegance of what travellers once took for granted, combined with the comforts and conveniences of modern life. Panoramic windows offer unrivalled views, while inside, rich hardwood finishes and flooring, intricate marquetry-work, glittering table-settings and the gorgeous Lalique glass panels are as fascinating to the eye as the views outside, as the city slips by.

The George Bradshaw Restaurant and Lounge and the adjoining Somerset Maugham Piano Bar occupy the entire central passenger deck. Above is the London Observation Deck, where both open and covered spaces provide uninterrupted views and al fresco dining.

The cruise begins and ends at the *Spirit of Chartwell*'s home berth, in the heart of London's historic docklands. Following a champagne reception, the cruise heads downstream towards the estuary at Gravesend, passing the O2 Arena, Tilbury (where Elizabeth I delivered her speech to the troops, before the attempted invasion by the Spanish Armada) and the Thames Barrier. A three-course lunch will then be served aboard as the voyage continues upstream to Greenwich, where passengers disembark to visit the National Maritime Museum, in the Old Royal Naval College.

As the ship passes the Tower of London, HMS *Belfast* and the Globe, high tea is taken, before a stop to visit the Tate Modern gallery. Then it's back on board to see St Paul's Cathedral, the London Eye, Lambeth Palace and Chelsea, and to enjoy a five-course gala dinner as one after another of London's pearls drift by.

The high-quality cuisine is prepared on board by chefs at the peak of their profession, using fresh local produce. It is served by highly trained, liveried stewards. There are three dining options: the Commodore's Table, where travellers may eat with their fellow guests, window tables for four or five diners and intimate window tables for two.

Sunday departures in April and May will feature guest speakers, among them eminent journalists like Martin Bell (doyenne of war correspondents) and Michael Nicholson (*Welcome to Sarajevo*), as well as academics and historians such as Mary Dicken (Tudor and Stuart specialist). The following months will feature other equally entertaining speakers.

After the voyage, guests may like to book a one- or two-night stay in one of the 20 luxurious twin or double staterooms. All are finished in rich cream and

A Story in Brief

MEMORIES OF CHINA – AND KENNETH LO: Despite his gentle, unassuming manner, Kenneth Lo was a man of drive and erudition, who could have succeeded in any number of fields. By the time he wrote the first of his 40 Chinese cookbooks, in 1953, he was already a tennis champion, a Cambridge graduate, a former diplomat and an importer of modern Chinese art. If he sometimes gave the impression of being the perfect English gentleman, that was hardly surprising. Strange though it may seem, it was the one thing he was born to be. Kenneth was one of VJV's first guests, escorting two explorations to China for both himself and his friends. When his restaurant in Ebury Street first opened he invited me over; it was empty of both customers and staff, so he cooked the meal himself. The restaurant was called Memories of China; no secret, then, as to where 'Memories of London', the title of the *Spirit of Chartwell*'s London voyages, came from.

mahogany and adorned with perfectly restored antiques with a naval flavour. All have en-suite bathrooms and satellite television. Accommodation on board the ship is an excellent, unusual and a good-value alternative to conventional hotels.

Passengers may also like to consider a voyage aboard the Magna Carta Steamship Company's smaller vessel, the MV *Passepartout*. 'A Passage to Cliveden' plies the serene upper reaches of the Thames from Runnymede, where the Magna Carta was signed, passing Eton, Windsor and Maidenhead and finishing at Cliveden, the former home of the Astor family, with its wonderful gardens

THE LONDON TO SYDNEY MOTOR RALLY

A Story in Brief

No question about it, the 1968 London-Sydney Marathon Car Rally really captured the public's imagination. The idea had been dreamt up over a roast-beef lunch in the Savoy Grill, by three *Daily Express* executives, Sir Max Aitken, Tommy Sopwith, and Jocelyn Stevens. The challenge was to drive 10,000 miles in 10 days; the prize was £10,000 – a pound a mile. It was not perhaps as tough or demanding as some of the follow-up events, but it was clearly a dramatic test of both motor car and driver endurance. 'A race half way round the globe for ordinary showroom cars would be a beacon, and an ideal show-case as to what the British motor-industry is made of', declared the *Express* management. As a result of which, more than half a million people packed in to Crystal Palace to see the start of the marathon, with several million more lining the route to Dover.

CHAPTER 87
A SLICE OF SIGHTSEEING HEAVEN

In 1873, there was no bigger name in Britain than Queen Victoria. So, when the monarch and her entourage took an early autumn trip along the Caledonian Canal, it established this waterway as the 'Royal Route'.

A celebrity endorsement never harms, as we all know, and, back in 1873, there was no bigger name in Britain than Queen Victoria. So, when the monarch and her entourage took an early autumn trip along the Caledonian Canal, in September of that year, it not only established this Highland waterway as a tourist attraction; it ensured that, henceforth, it would be known as the 'Royal Route'.

A boat journey along the canal is, indeed, a regal 62-mile glide, taking the traveller from Inverness southwards to Fort William, through four different lochs (Dochfour, Ness, Oich and Lochy) and past an array of mountains described as 'considerable protuberances' by the celebrated author Doctor Samuel Johnson when he visited the area in 1773 (accompanied, of course, by his biographer, Boswell).

By the end of the 19th century, this part of the world had come to be seen as a slice of sightseeing heaven, but it hadn't started out that way, 100 years earlier. Initial thinking, circa 1800, was to create a workaday conduit, making use of this water-filled geological fault that ran diagonally down from north-east to south-west Scotland, and joining up the naturally occurring lochs with lengths of artificial watercourse (only one-third of the canal's length is actually man-made).

Far from viewing the project as a means of boosting visitor numbers, the authorities intended that it should serve three rather sterner purposes. Firstly, as a commercial shipping lane, providing cargo-bearing vessels with a safer and

A Story in Brief

IONA: 'At mid-summer when night scarcely touches day on the west coast of Scotland, the highlands and islands of Argyll weave their magic spell upon the traveller. The breath-taking expanse of sky vaults the clear green-blue seas which are peppered with small islands and inlets and the granite hills swathed in purple heather tumble down to the white strands of shore-line where seals play and the shag duck fish. It was to this earthly paradise that St Columba came from Ireland to set up the first Christian outpost in this country. Some thirty years before St Augustine arrived at Canterbury. The mythology goes that Columba was exiled from Ireland and set sail with a small band of monks to find a new home. They searched until they found somewhere from which Ireland could no longer be seen. Whether this is true or not they discovered fertile land, spring water and a safe haven on Iona from which they were to travel out across Britain.' **VJV TRAVEL REVIEW.**

quicker alternative to circumnavigating the perilous northern coast of Scotland. Instead of having to negotiate two shipwreck black spots (Pentland Firth in the north-east and Cape Wrath in the north-west), skippers could take a handy little cut-through, which would transport them from the Atlantic Ocean to the North Sea, with no risk and in less than half the time.

Secondly, the canal would fulfil a vital military role, providing a secure and quicker passage to British warships and supply frigates engaged in naval confrontation with our old enemy, Napoleon. Thirdly, the construction of a canal would bring not just employment, but also people, back to an area which had been denuded of population, thanks to the notorious Highland Clearances, whereby humans had been forcibly removed in order to make way for (altogether more profitable) sheep.

It was with this three-fold brief in mind that the renowned Dumfriesshire-born engineer, Thomas Telford, paid a couple of visits to the Highlands, along with his colleague, James Jessop, in 1801, and again in 1802. Having already had success with his construction of the Ellesmere Canal, in Shropshire, and the re-building of London Bridge, he now came up with the idea of creating a link between Inverness and Fort William.

This was easier said than done, as things turned out. Having got the go-ahead to construct the canal in 1803, Telford and Jessop estimated that it would take seven years to complete, and would cost around £475,000. However, problems with constructing the locks (unstable, muddy foundations) and worker absenteeism during the potato harvest and peat-cutting seasons meant that work didn't finish until 1822, some 12 years behind schedule and roughly £440,000 over budget.

In the meantime, the world had moved on. With the final defeat of Napoleon at Waterloo, in 1815, the military and strategic significance of the canal disappeared. What's more, the finished canal was now too small to accommodate the larger breed of steam-powered, iron-hulled ships that had started to replace their wooden forbears. In short, the scheme was not a financial success. It is recorded that, throughout the course of one entire year (1839), just 544 vessels used the new waterway. Enter, wearing a crown, the Caledonian Canal's royal saviour.

The date was 16 September 1873, and the vessel that bore Queen Victoria from Banavie (at the Fort William end, in the shadow of Ben Nevis) to her disembarkation point at Dochgarroch was the Glasgow-registered paddle steamer *Gondolier*. It was a journey of just 52 miles, but the publicity resulting from this day trip launched the Caledonian Canal as a tourist destination. All of a sudden, a voyage through its waters took on the status of a sort of UK Grand Tour (the continental-Europe version having been curtailed by the Napoleonic Wars).

Before long, other travellers followed, including the celebrated explorer Jules Verne, who, in 1880, is said to have piloted his yacht, *St Michel III*, along the canal, on a voyage which also took in Ireland and the Baltic. Not surprisingly, the new breed of tourist wanted a level of comfort rather greater than that experienced by Messrs Johnson and Boswell, when they embarked on their horseback tour of the area in 1773 (during the course of which Boswell coined the word 'equitation').

Instead of the comforts a monarch might expect, the pair of adventurers spent their nights in humble, even squalid, lodgings, which, in some cases, they shared with mice and rats. One particularly humble home was described by Boswell as follows:

'It was a wretched little hovel of earth only, I think, and, for a window, had just a hole, which was stopped with a piece of turf, which could be taken out to let in light. In the middle of the room (or space which we entered) was a fire of peat, the smoke going out at a hole in the roof. The woman who lived there had a pot upon it, with goat's flesh boiling. She had at one end, under the same roof but divided with a kind of partition made of wands, a pen or fold, in which we saw a good many kids.

Mr Johnson would not hurt her delicacy by insisting to see her bedchamber, but I was of a more ardent curiosity, so I lighted a piece of paper and went into the place where the bed was. There was a little partition of wicker, rather more neatly done than the one for the fold, and close by the wall was a kind of bedstead of wood, with heath upon it for a bed. At the foot of it, I saw some sort of blankets or covering, rolled up in a heap.

The woman's husband was a man of eighty, and Mr Fraser of Balnain allows him to live in this hut and to keep sixty goats, for taking care of his wood. He was then in the wood. They had five children, the oldest only thirteen. Two were gone to Inverness to buy meal. The rest were looking after the goats. She had four stacks of barley, twenty-four sheaves in each. They had a few fowls. They will live all the spring without meal upon milk and curd, etc., alone. What they get for their goats, kids, and hens maintains them. I did not observe how the children lay.

She asked us to sit down and take a dram. I saw one chair. She said she was as happy as any woman in Scotland. She could hardly speak any English, just detached words. Mr Johnson was pleased at seeing, for the first time, such a state of human life. She asked for snuff. It is her luxury. She uses a great deal. We had none, but gave her sixpence apiece. She then brought out her whisky bottle. I tasted it, and Joseph and our guides had some. So I gave her sixpence more.'

Fast-forward to the 21st century; a trip to this part of the world involves not sinking down into the depths of deprivation, but cruising along in the lap of luxury. Not aboard the vessel which bore Queen Victoria, however. At the end of its working life on the Caledonian Canal, the steam ship *Gondolier* rendered one final service to King and Country when, in 1939, it was deliberately sunk near the Orkney Islands, in order to form a barrier against German ships attempting to attack the Allied naval base at Scapa Flow.

However, while one lovely old vessel now resides beneath the waves, another beautiful new boat has risen up to replace it. In August 2000, the Caledonian Canal witnessed the arrival of the most lavishly appointed craft ever to have cruised its waters: the *Lord of the Glens*. Constructed by Spanish craftsmen to exacting standards, both in terms of visual impact and technical capability, this aristocrat of the water is blessed with propulsion systems that enable it to cope with the rigours of the open sea and, at the same time, navigate the intricate confines of the Caledonian Canal.

'Confines' is an apt word. The first test any vessel on this stretch of water must face is whether it can fit inside the 36 locks along its banks. Each lock has a maximum dimension of 150 feet in length and 34 feet in width, with a depth of no more than 12 feet. Due to the meandering nature of the waterway, dual propulsion systems and bow-thrusters are required to be controlled not only from the bridge, but also from the side-wings of the vessel. This is so that the Master can manoeuvre the ship into the impossibly tight locks and around the many tortuous bends.

So much for the science. When it comes to aesthetics, it's the royal yacht *Britannia* that comes to mind: witness the 'Mauritius' deep-blue hull, complemented by the all-round golden band and eagle motifs, plus the brilliant white superstructure. Inside, the decor does not scream modern, urban chic, but embraces a classical, timeless style that is in sympathy with the lovely landscape outside. On stepping aboard, the weary traveller is greeted by a sumptuous, even colonial look: rich, hardwood finishes offset by cream panelling, very much reminiscent of the ancient deluxe British Pullman carriage.

As for the boat's fixtures, fittings and furnishings, they come not from 21st-century conveyor belts, but are individually chosen, historic pieces sometimes originating from the grand steam-train expresses and ocean liners of yesteryear. Of special note are the original 1929 'Riviera' armchairs (PLM Orient), the hand-painted David Roberts lithographs, the light-fittings from the liners SS *France* and *Nord Norge*, plus restaurant chairs, overhead glass panelling and deck furniture from the RMS *Windsor Castle* and lovely brass friezes from the RMS *Kenya Castle*.

Look around, and there are fascinating scale models of locomotives and ocean-going ships. Look downwards and underfoot, and you'll find plush carpeting by Brinton's, along with hardwood flooring, into which compass motifs have been skilfully inlaid. Guests on the *Lord of the Glens* step aboard at the

Reception level, location not just for the Robert Louis Stevenson restaurant and the six top-deck State Cabins, but also for the bridge, where you are free to wander and chat to the mariners on duty (all the officers are Brits, while all crew members are European).

A short flight of stairs then brings guests to the splendid Upper Deck and the David Livingstone lounge bar, again richly decorated in hardwood finishes. Cleverly, this is divided into an aft area for drinking and relaxing, as well as a stern-facing viewing deck. There is also a forward area, reserved for quieter contemplation through the all-round panoramic windows; in or out, the weather can't spoil your day. When the temperature is hot, there is air-conditioning, and for when it's cold, there's toasty-warm, built-in heating.

In all, there are 27 State Cabins spread over three decks, all facing outwards (no views of corridors) and all named after well-known Scots (for example, the inventor Alexander Graham Bell, the painter David Roberts, and, of course, Thomas Telford himself). Each cabin boasts rich hardwood finishes, plush carpeting, a dressing table, a stool, a wardrobe, an internal telephone, satellite TV and en-suite facilities, with shower, WC and washbasin. All have heating and air-conditioning and, while the top and middle-deck cabins have a picture window, their lower-deck counterparts have two portholes each. Meals are freshly prepared on board by a loyal and long-serving brigade of chefs, using locally sourced produce, and nowhere is this more evident than in the sumptuous Scottish breakfast served each morning.

This is not mass-market, production-line tourism, but tailor-made travel of the old-fashioned variety. Unlike the standard, modern-day ocean cruise, the maximum number of passengers is 54, rather than 2,054, and emphasis is not on speed, but on style. At all times, progress is serene-to-steady, rather than rushed, which means the view through the windows remains beautiful, rather than blurred.

Even when the *Lord of the Glens* does put into harbour, be it for you to amble round the shops at Fort Augustus or to explore the marvel that is Neptune's Staircase (a flight of eight successive locks at the Fort William end of the canal), you are not so much an invading force as a group of handpicked invitees.

In short, then, you are travelling on a Lord and feel like a King or Queen.

CHAPTER 88
IMPORTING THE SCENERY

One neat travel solution was instead to bring the sights and sounds of say Venice and Constantinople to London at venerable venues such as Olympia, Earls Court and White City.

AGED 15, my half-sister June took a job as a 'nippy' (waitress) with J. Lyons & Co. at their Teashop located on Hammersmith Broadway in London. She was later to work at the firm's confectionary factory at Cadby Hall, where among other things Lyons produced their jam tarts – ironic, then, that a significant contingent of the influential marketing people who were later to confection what we now know as Thomson Holidays should have also served their time at Cadby Hall (though presumably, unlike my half-sister, not making jam tarts).

In the days when overseas journeys were beyond the reach of the common man, one neat solution was instead to bring the sights and sounds of, say, Venice or Constantinople to London, at venerable venues such as Olympia, Earls Court and White City. And it was the impresario extraordinaire Imre Kiralfy who did it (and J. Lyons to whom he turned for the catering). Meet the turn of-the-century showman who enabled Britons to experience the thrill of foreign travel without having to leave these shores.

These days overseas holidays are an affordable pleasure, but at the end of the 19th century they were out of most people's reach: that's where Hungarian-born Imre Kiralfy came in. He was described by *The Strand* magazine as 'by far the greatest living figure in the domain of public spectacle and mammoth entertainment,' and not without good reason. This, after all, was the man who, in 1892, re-created a working model of Venice, complete with canals and gondolas, inside the Olympia exhibition hall, in west London.

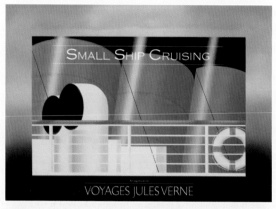

A Story in Brief

FROM SAILS TO SATELLITES: His name is not as well-known as it once was, but J.E.D. Williams is the aviation pioneer who was influential in the formation first of El Al, then Euravia and Britannia Airways. In his book *From Sails to Satellites*, he traces the history of navigational science, from primitive reckoning systems to the ultra-modern guidance devices used by planes, ships, and missiles. He also chronicles the 200-year-long pursuit of longitude. This began when King Philip III of Spain offered lavish prizes for whoever uncovered its mysteries, and entered a new era, first with the invention of the marine chronometer, built by Yorkshire carpenter-turned-clock-maker John Harrison, and then with the development of the sextant, the first practical way to measure longitude. Williams also discusses the development, in the 19th century, of the pivoted needle compass, but it was not until the emergence of the Wright Brothers, and aeroplanes, that navigation once again moved into the front line of science.   IMAGE COURTESY: ROBERT SCURRAH/VOYAGES JULES VERNE.

He capped this feat 16 years later, when, for the great Franco-British Exhibition of 1908, he created a life-sized model metropolis at Shepherds Bush, on a patch of land that was re-named White City because of the brilliant alabaster colour of the marble-clad buildings. Instead of having to go to the expense, inconvenience and discomfort of visiting foreign countries, Brits could take a bus ride to west London and witness for themselves the magic of Venice's Grand Canal or the towers of Notre Dame de Paris.

'One night,' recalled Kiralfy in his memoirs, 'I lay awake in bed and, as if by magic, I saw, sketched out in my mind's eye, an imposing city of places, domes and towers, set in cool, green spaces and intersected by many bridged canals.' Amazingly, he would sketch out the plans for these visions not on some outsized architectural chart, but on the back of a small envelope.

Other triumphs included a host of similarly spectacular presentations, such as 'Empire of India' (1895), 'India and Ceylon' (1896) and 'Paris in London' (1902), all of which took place at the Earls Court Exhibition Centre. He had perfected his art in America, where he had spent some 25 years staging similar extravaganzas – 'The Fall of Babylon', 'Nero and the Burning of Rome', a larger-than-life representation of Jules Verne's *Around the World in Eighty Days*, etc.

'I saw instantly that the great popular want in America was spectacle,' he said – and spectacle is what he gave them. For while his buildings were made of wood, canvas and plaster, the costumed characters within those structures would be real-life, flesh-and-blood humans; quite often, his cast would number 1,000 or more.

Not that Kiralfy had set out to be a big-time entertainer. As a young boy, he was something of an infant prodigy when it came to opera singing, and he even spent time in Venice in an apartment across the way from the celebrated Italian composer Verdi, listening as the great man's compositions wafted in through his window.

But it was through putting on shows, rather than starring in them, that he was to make his name and his fortune. 'I envied the Romans their Coliseum and their free, wide amphitheatres,' said Kiralfy, who in a sense was a forerunner of the modern-day travel agent – only instead of taking the people to the Coliseum, he brought the Coliseum to the people.

CHAPTER 89
THE LOCKSMITH

The narrowness of the Douro was one of the major headaches of the project, for there was very little room on the banks to expand beyond the natural limits of the river and no possibility of building a separate canal.

THE Douro River winds sinuously across northern Portugal from the Spanish sierras, cutting a deep gorge in the schistous rock of the region. On either side of it grow the wines that produce the famous port wines, which for centuries were brought downriver in rabelos, shallow bottomed boats gently tapered for the accommodation of barrels or pipes. Once in Oporto, the wine was allowed to mature in the cool cellars of the great port-producing houses, such as Dows and Warres.

The voyage was no mean undertaking. The waters of the Douro are naturally shallow, and rapids were a constant threat to the safety of the ships, which brought the port downriver early in the year, riding the spring waters before the river dried to a trickle in the summer. The Douro was therefore only of the most limited value, but as Senhor Pinto da Silva, head of the Douro Navigation Bureau, explains, "It was a dream from olden times to make the Douro navigable," to feed the great port of Oporto and to enable goods to be shipped more easily inland.

Of course, for many centuries the technical skills necessary for such a project simply did not exist, but at the end of the 19th nineteenth century a company did try, by means of walls, to channel the river at certain points with the aim of concentrating its flow. For political reasons, however, the project, similar to one that had been mooted for the Rhone in France, was never realised.

Then, in the 1920s, a plan was devised to build a dam near to where the Carrapatelo dam is now, and to use a series of three step locks to open it to shipping; but this came to nothing when it was discovered that the chosen site was geologically unsuitable.

In the end, it was not until 1960 that a decision was taken to make a start on the design of a series of dams along the length of the Douro, including the part of it that coincides with the Portuguese-Spanish border. The principal reason behind the decision was the need to exploit the resources of the Douro to produce hydroelectric power, but the old dream of rendering the river navigable had not been forgotten.

Senhor Pinto da Silva is unmistakably a Southern European. This is evident less from his colouring than from his dignified bearing, high, receding brow and waves of crinkling, silver hair. It is also evident from the enthusiasm with which he talks about the navigability project and his previous work tapping the river's hydroelectric potential.

At first he had not wanted to accept the new post that was being offered to him, because he was perfectly happy in his job with the electricity board. But the hydroelectric dam project on the Douro had become so much a part of his life that he felt loath to abandon to others what he had come to feel was in some respects his child, one that he had watched grow 'with passion'.

Like all parents, he felt uneasy when his child was in the care of strangers, and so he decided to accept this new challenge. He presumed that the work would be a matter of only a few years, four or five at most, but "it is now 12 years and I am still here". Indeed, for the first few years he continued to work for both the electricity company and the newly created Douro Navigation Bureau – "morning here, afternoon there" – until he found that there was no room for both. His work with the Navigation Bureau henceforth became full time.

It was, however, the early years – the challenge of designing the locks, "to see what would not work and why" – that Senhor da Silva found the most absorbing part of the project. For the most part a similar project on the River Rhone in France was used as the model, and Senhor da Silva and his team tried to learn from their forebears' mistakes, for there had been several problems there connected with the larger locks.

They were right to do so, for the locks have been a success. Senhor da Silva is particularly proud of the lock at the Carrapatelo dam, the second one you might meet going east from Oporto, which at 36 metres is one of the deepest locks in the world, easily eclipsing the 26 metres of the deepest lock on the Rhone, which itself had been a constant conundrum for its designers.

One of the problems with locks of this size is the business of designing a mechanism that can cope with the filling process in a manner that is at once reasonably quick and reliably constant. In the end, it was discovered that the solution was to allow the filling process to take 20 minutes rather than the normal 10.

All in all, there are an astounding 10 dams along the length of the Douro:

five where the river flows through purely Portuguese territory and a further five, of which two were built by the Spanish authorities, along the section where it marks the border with Spain. Most of the dams in the border area do not have locks and are therefore closed to ships; one of the Spanish dams, for example, is built at a very narrow point where there is little water and where there is only a spillway.

In fact, the general narrowness of the Douro was one of the major headaches of the project, for there was very little room on the banks to expand beyond the natural limits of the river and therefore no possibility of building a separate canal, as on the Rhone.

The gradient of the river is also rather steep, falling 125 metres over a distance of 200 kilometres, and although the current is reasonably, although not exceptionally, fast, the basic problem is the depth of the water – or, rather, the lack of it. While the dams and their attendant locks had been designed to cope with all these puzzles, the aim was simultaneously to avoid drowning too much of the surrounding countryside. In the event, the water level had to be prevented from rising too much anyway, because this would have necessitated the (prohibitively expensive) construction of another road and another railway line.

There was also, of course, the welfare of the local people to be considered, but fortunately there were very few living at the water's edge, and hardly anybody had to be removed.

Remarkably, there were almost no hiccups in the actual construction of the dams and the locks – once the challenges presented by the peculiar nature of the river had been ironed out at the design stage, the process of realising the plans went almost without a hitch. The dams were not built simultaneously, but one at a time, work on another beginning just as work on its predecessor was coming to a close, each dam requiring about three years to complete.

There were a number of reasons for this process. An important one, of course, was the question of money: although the government was financing the enterprise, with the help of the World Bank, funds were not limitless. Another reason was expertise, for clearly it was a great advantage to have the same people working on the construction of each dam and lock, accumulating experience all the while. Working this way was also an enormous help to the administration, which may have found the complexity of organising several undertakings too much to handle efficiently.

The locks were built as the dams were under construction, which of course rendered Senhor da Silva's task rather easier in that the challenge of working in swirling currents was largely taken out of the equation. The technique for the construction of dry working areas surrounded by flowing water would seem to be

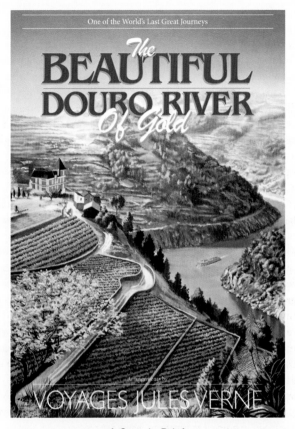

A Story in Brief

A FAIR EXCHANGE: In 1993 *Travel Review* went to talk to Paul Symington, one of the family firm who own some of the greatest names in Port – Dow's, Graham's, and Warre's amongst others. 'The English always claimed to have invented Port but it is not actually quite like that. Wine was being made in the region around Regua way back in the Bronze Age, for which there is historical proof. But the English and Scottish merchants were the first to export it. There were British merchants in Oporto since the early 1600s basically selling cod, which was fished in more northern waters – they used to sell it on the northern coast of Portugal, in Viana and Oporto (which explains why salt cod, or baccala, is a much loved dish in Portugal to this very day): rather than take the ships back empty they loaded up with Port, and so a two-way trade started which was the origin of the export of the wine.'

IMAGE COURTESY: ALISON MUSKER/VOYAGES JULES VERNE.

extremely delicate, but the method, in layman's terms at least, is relatively simple: a dry, or comparatively dry part of the river area is selected and a sort of miniature dam built around it; the area is dredged so that when the work is completed it may be filled with water, after which the work moves on to another site.

Despite the project's dangers, even with modern-day tools and procedures, there was no loss of life during the work. Or rather, there was a single fatality, but it was linked to the work in only the most tenuous way. It happened on the border section of the river, and as Senhor da Silva says lugubriously, "it was a joke almost, a sad joke" – a story of romance and gallantry, as is only natural in this part of the world. A cable had been slung across the river at one point of the river and was controlled by a crane in the middle. Being a Sunday, the crane was not in operation but a swain, anxious to visit his beloved on the other side of the river, decided to make his way across by hand. The width of the river was about 100 metres at this point; he began buoyantly enough, but soon became exhausted, lost his grip and fell to his death.

In contrast with this tragic tale of rural love, the only other surprise was rather prosaic and concerned the buoys that are used to mark the channels. Again, the technological niceties of this area are rather abstruse, but in essence it seems that the buoys were too large. At a metre and a half in diameter, they were perfect from the point of view of being seen, but their great weight, some two and a half tons, had the unexpected effect of allowing the sand around them to be swept away, and with it the buoys themselves. They have since been replaced with lighter ones of a mere 400 kilograms. Says Senhor da Silva, "I hope now that if there is a flood they will remain – or if not all of them, at least most of them!"

Though the traffic now using the river is fairly variable, most of it comprises ships carrying stone that will be exported for use as pavement kerbing, or compacted wood to be used in furniture. There are river cruisers able to make the journey almost as far as the border, but sea-going vessels of up to 1,500 tons and a length of 86 metres are able to pass through the locks only as far as Régua, beyond which the channels that will enable the passage of bigger vessels have yet to be completed. For large ships to make the journey regularly, it is also essential to keep the mouth of the river open at Oporto – it has a tendency to become clogged with sand, and dredgers are constantly to be seen at work there.

On average it takes about 12 minutes for a lock to fill with water, but generally speaking a ship needs about half an hour to pass through, given the time it takes to manoeuvre into the lock and tie up before the water is released. Everything is water driven, of course, but navigation is permitted in the hours of daylight only. Weekends are particularly busy, for a lot of smaller craft join the throng, and everyone has to wait their turn. "Upstream you may see a canoe paddling for dear life, closely followed by one of the big ships!" laughs Senhor da Silva.

Although the Douro lock and dam system is one of the most important technological achievements in Europe, the scheme is noteworthy in other respects. First, the essential beauty of the region has not been harmed, and indeed in some ways has been enhanced – the worst that can be said is that at some points there is a different splendour. Then there is the aspect about wish Senhor da Silva feels as passionately as he does about the project itself, for there is now some hope that the region will not die out, both economically and demographically. The hydroelectric scheme needs a certain amount of maintenance and provides some work for the people of the area; but above all, it is hoped that the possibilities offered by the opening up of the river to traffic will encourage more visitors and greater use of the river, thereby persuading local people to stay in their native countryside.

PASSAGE TO CHINA & JAPAN COVER BY ROBERT SCURRAH

A Story in Brief:

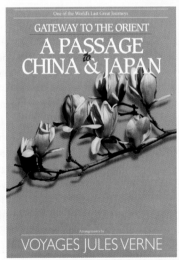

IMAGE COURTESY: ROBERT SCURRAH/VJV.

A SMALL SIP: It's a little-known fact, but in the early 70s, celebrated wine writer Jancis Robinson OBE began her working life with Thomson Travel, at Greater London House, in Camden Town. Having studied for a degree in maths and philosophy at Oxford University, she was one of four graduates hired by the company that year. She started out in the tour reps section at Greater London House, spent a week in Majorca with the Continental Section, and worked for a variety of different departments during her first year with the firm. When interviewed for the in-house newspaper, she said she enjoyed "the friendly, relaxed atmosphere of the company, the use of Christian names, and the freedom to wear whatever clothes I like". In 1975, she became assistant editor for the trade magazine *Wine & Spirit*. As well as writing a whole cluster of definitive wine guides, she has worked as wine consultant both to British Airways and The Queen.

CHAPTER 90
A SCOTSMAN ABROAD

As an alternative to travel posters (for destinations in the Holy Land and Egypt), I used the lithographs of David Roberts bought from a stall at Church Street Market.

A S an alternative to travel posters, for destinations in the Holy Land and Egypt I used the lithographs of David Roberts, bought from a stall at Church Street Market – the originals of which are now on board the *Lord of the Glens*, where even one of the decks is named after him.

Much has changed in the Near and Middle East over the last 150 years, but much remains the same too, as it was when British artists such as William Holman Hunt and John Frederick Lewis first went there. Some of the landmarks and celebrated features of the region were only discovered shortly before these artists arrived, and so, to understand the true context of their work, we must imagine ourselves glimpsing for the first time a magnificent and 'alien' world. Just what was it like for these artistic explorers?

Far and away the most successful topographical artist to ever visit the region was David Roberts. Born in Edinburgh in 1796, he was often referred to as the 'Scottish Canaletto' and became famous after his move to London, in 1822, for pictures which celebrated the architectural beauty and intricacy of so many of the capital's buildings. However, it was not until he began to look further afield, crossing the Channel to explore Europe and the Mediterranean basin, that he realised his ability as a truly innovative and accomplished painter.

In France and Spain, Roberts amassed a body of work which, when presented to viewers back in London, was received with great enthusiasm. Spurred by this reception, he embarked upon his greatest project, an expedition to the Near East. The arts at this time in Victorian England were viewed as not just an 'ornament of the diadem' but, as Francis Graham Moon was to write to Queen Victoria, 'an essential instrument of England's intellectual supremacy'.

Moon was the publisher of Robert's lithographic prints of Syria, Idumea, Arabia, Egypt and Nubia. Never before had the British glimpsed such scenes in art. Today we know of them intimately, through our own expeditions and trips as well as the screens of our television sets. Back then, however, such places were known through probably one source alone: the Holy Bible. Roberts knew this and in many senses exploited it to enhance his reputation. He had found a virgin subject, touched on only in passing by two or three Continental artists.

In his dedication to the Queen which accompanied the portfolio of prints, Moon wrote that these prints were 'illustrative of scenes once hallowed by the steps of the prophet and the apostle, possessing in all ages the highest interest for the scholar and the philosopher, and now opening the most sacred contemplations and most glowing prospects to the philanthropist and Christian'. Before he went, Roberts had known that if he really could offer something to all these figures, then he would be celebrated as the finest topographical artist ever. The expedition was, as his friend James Ballantyne said, "the dream of his life from boyhood" and the "great central episode of his artistic life". In 1838, Roberts set sail for Egypt.

He had, before departure, furnished himself with as many guide books as he could find about the region. He had become fully acquainted with the landscape and the customs of its people before he had even set eyes on them. The journey, which by the 1830s had become somewhat easier, took just under one month, arriving in Alexandria on 24 September.

There he made a pre-arranged rendezvous with a Colonel Campbell, who saw to it that Roberts was made quite comfortable. Campbell was the British Consul in Egypt and Syria, and with his help Roberts was able to organise quickly the first leg of his expedition, travelling the Nile to Cairo. Colonel Campbell saw to it that Roberts was in possession of introductions to those who would be able to aid him in Cairo, and upon arrival was issued with a personal guide to accompany him anywhere he went. As he began to busy himself, sketching, drawing and painting (he was equally proficient in water colour and oils), his guide would fend off onlookers and protect him from interruption.

Roberts' visit to the region is notable not only for the reason that he was the first to accomplish a comprehensive study of its many features, but also for the reason that he was the first Christian allowed inside a mosque – indeed, he was permitted to work inside any mosque of his choosing. This invitation carried with it certain conditions, however, the first being that he should at all times wear the dress characteristic of the indigenous population. More interestingly, as it shows that his hosts took a great interest in his methods of working and the materials that he used, he was asked to refrain from desecrating any mosque by using brushes made of hog bristle.

Regarding his depictions of Cairo, Roberts has been criticised historically for his use of figures to provide foreground colour in otherwise starkly architectural scenes. Common at the time was the debate among artists and critics as to whether it was permissible for a topographical artist to introduce imaginary incidents to add interest to their designs. Roberts quite clearly felt that this was not just permissible but essential, if those who viewed his pictures were to appreciate the scale and majesty of so many of the places that he painted, as well as to enjoy the general feeling of warmth and activity that could not be conveyed by mere faithful reproductions.

As we find in his pictures made at Petra, a little later on, he became prone even to distort the scale of people and buildings so as to impress upon the viewer the sense of grandeur that he had perceived on first glimpsing the temples and rock formations. Of this sort of practice, over-pious artists such as his contemporary William Holman Hunt scoffed at the cheek of it all.

From Cairo, Roberts ascended the Nile in a boat staffed by a crew of eight. He had provisions for three months, and during this period made a study of every edifice of the river between the Mediterranean and Wadi Halfa, at all times the Union Jack flying at the masthead. Roberts knew of places like Petra, Hebron and Gaza only from his guidebooks, and it was not until he returned to Cairo that he determined to visit them.

Notably, it was a meeting between a Monsieur Linant de Bellefonds and Roberts that did the trick. Linant de Bellefonds had been assistant and companion to Léon de Laborde, a French artist whose own brief flirtation with the region had not really been a great success, and he showed Roberts some of the preliminary sketches from their excursion. Roberts immediately began to make plans; he seems to have been struck by the mystery that tourists still talk of when visiting Petra today and the awe-inspiring magnitude of that which meets the eye.

In the 19th century, however, an excursion from Cairo to Petra was not quite as simple as it is for today's traveller. Lengthy preparations were made to cross the desert by the route of the Israelites to Mount Sinai and through the great Jordan Rift Valley. Those readers whose interest in Petra is spurred by the marvellous images that Roberts marked down on his way and the many that he made on arrival will be interested to note that for this part of his expedition the artist was accompanied by a Mr John G. Kinnear, who was to later publish a worthy account of the trip, as well as another Brit, John Pell. They must have appeared a strange group, for each assumed Arab dress, and along with three servants – not to mention 21 camels and an escort of Bedouin tribesmen – they set out with provisions, arms and art materials.

A Story in Brief

THE OLD PATAGONIAN EXPRESS: When looking for ideas for early Voyages Jules Verne adventures, I found inspiration in this marvellous book, by Paul Theroux. Starting from his home town in Massachusetts, he travels across the North American plains to Laredo, Texas, then takes a train south through Mexico to Veracruz where he comes across a woman looking for her long-lost lover. From there, he takes the train south into Guatemala, and then El Salvador, where he visits a soccer match and is amazed by the violence. He flies to Costa Rica, takes the train to Limon and Puntarenas, and ends the Central American part of his journey in Panama. Next, he proceeds to Colombia, then over the Andes and into the cold, bare heart of Patagonia, and the small town of Esquel. En route, he endures harsh climates, including the extreme altitude of Peru and the Bolivian Plateau, and meets author Jorge Luis Borges, in Buenos Aires. An amazing journey, by anyone's standards.

IMAGE COURTESY: ROBERT SCURRAH/VOYAGES JULES VERNE.

On 6 March 1839 Roberts wrote in his journal, 'We encamped in the centre of this extraordinary city; Petra. I did not expect to be much surprised at Petra after seeing Thebes. But the whole is far beyond any idea I had formed of it, in both magnitude and situation. Though the ruins of this extraordinary place are immense, they sink into insignificance when compared with these stupendous rocks. I often throw aside my pencil, in despair of being able to convey any idea of the scene.'

Later he wrote of Petra, 'The first object which meets the eye on approach is a range of red sandstone cliffs, apparently impenetrable; but the brook which flows into the centre of the city passes through a narrow cleft, hidden behind a projection of rock... The most perfect and beautiful relic of the city – the Khasne (treasury)... produces a more powerful impression than any surviving monuments of Greece or Rome.' Of Petra's theatre, he wrote that, 'Even now in all its desolation, all is beautiful. Nature has hung the rocks with prodigal and glowing vegetation; where the sculptured ornament has mouldered away, the shrub and flower have partially supplied its loss, have festooned the cliff, and coloured and tissued the ruin.'

That Roberts embraced this city so fully is clear from his paintings. But what is probably the most important thing to remember is that, as scholars agree, there still is today no better way of visiting Petra – apart from going there oneself – than looking at this body of work, the work of a virtuoso.

CHAPTER 91
TAMBURLAINE THE GREAT

*On one futile expedition I had even sent people up to find the lost site
of Kublai Khan's 'stately pleasure-dome' at Xanadu – but when they
got there they found nothing but an empty field.*

I N 1974 I, together with Kun Jaeggi, managed to get Thomson into Outer
Mongolia, something that was to prove pivotal when I was planning and then
operating the trans-Eurasian railway journey the 'Central Kingdom Express'.
Later, Voyages Jules Verne was to operate direct flights from London to Tashkent,
with feeder-service flights to the fabled cities of Samarkand, Bukhara and Khiva.
On one futile expedition I even sent people up to find the lost site of Kublai Khan's
'stately pleasure-dome' at Xanadu, in Inner Mongolia – when they got there, they
found nothing but an empty field.

In 1369 Tamburlaine, or Timur the Lame, became ruler of Samarkand. Samarkand was a wealthy oasis town on the Silk Road, part of a network of similar
towns or cities in Central Asia that had grown through the settlement of nomadic
peoples who had taken to trade as a way of life. Central Asia is a vast area, remote
from oceans, with a distinctive and arid climate, and far from the currents of
external political pressure. The Silk Road corridor runs east-west across the Asian
continent for some four thousand miles.

Samarkand had been sacked by Genghis Khan in 1223. By 1260, however,
the mighty Mongol empire was breaking up into separate khanates, between which
something of a power struggle was taking place. In 1294 the first of the Il-Khans
of the Persian khanate embraced Islam, and although the Mongols hung on, their
dreams of a conquest of the Middle East and Europe had largely evaporated. There
was to be a brief revival, however, under Tamburlaine, a leader who at least rivalled
Genghis in sheer determination.

Tamburlaine is almost a mythical figure, yet arguably he has been rather

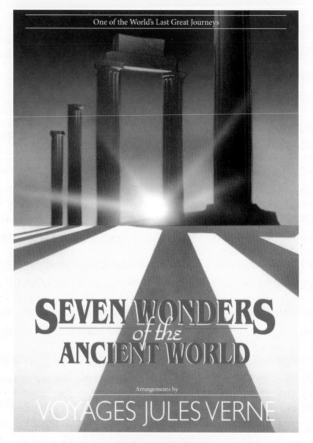

A Story in Brief

WONDERS PAST THEIR BEST-BY DATE: For some time, I entertained the notion of trying to run a tour in which we visited the sites of each of the Seven Wonders of the World. It was a nice idea, but then the Iran-Iraq war got in the way, and the plan had to be abandoned. Looking back, though, perhaps it was all for the best. The sad truth, is that all but one of the Wonders have been overcome by either time, nature, or man. An earthquake toppled the Colossus, Crusaders plundered the ruins of the Mausoleum at Halicarnassus, and only a few scattered stones are left from the once-elegant temple of Artemis. The fate of the Statue of Zeus at Olympia is unknown, and debate still continues over the site of the Hanging Gardens. Only the Pyramids have survived relatively intact, though local Egyptians did strip their outer casings to use as building materials.   IMAGE COURTESY: ROBERT SCURRAH/VOYAGES JULES VERNE under-examined by historians. Even his name has a variety of spellings (Timur Lang, Timur-i-Lenk, Tamerlane, to name but three) – the Tamburlaine used here is the same as the one used in the title of Christopher Marlowe's play *Tamburlaine the Great*, written around 1587. Tamburlaine's motives clearly exercised the minds of intellectuals from the start, and as a historical figure he has impacted the public consciousness through literature and music. Perhaps because his details are little known, or because perhaps of his fearsome reputation (timur means 'iron'), the story of his life has been founded on a single, if surprisingly accurate, image.

Born in 1336, Tamburlaine came from a noble Mongol family, through the veins of which also ran Turkish blood, his father being chieftain of the Turco-Mongol Barlas clan. His family were, in effect, the rulers of a small fiefdom to the south of Samarkand then known as Kesh and today called Shahrisabz. The journey over the hills today will reward you with a small town with an exotic, lively, market and view of what is left of Tamburlaine's White Palace, impressive if only for its ruined immensity. Kesh was his birthplace but Samarkand – 'better one look than a hundred stories' – was to be his capital.

His family owed allegiance to the Mongol Jagatai Khans who had ruled Turkestan, or the Jagatai Khanate, since the break-up of the centralised Mongol empire in the 13th century. His clansmen wielded but little power in the mosaic of Central Asian life, nonetheless by 1370 Tamburlaine had become ruler of the area called Mawarannahr, which included Samarkand, and by 1376 had driven the powerful among the Jagatai to Mongolia.

A glance at the timetable of his life is to see the tireless extension of his empire: in 1381 he invades Afghanistan and eastern Persia; in 1385 he invades western Persia; in 1391 he invades the Golden Horde, the old Mongol stronghold in Russia; in 1392 Iraq and Georgia fall to him; in 1398 he invades India and defeats the Sultan at Delhi; in 1404 he invades Syria and Anatolia; in 1405 he dies, presumably exhausted. Remarkably, he did not start his campaigns until he was more than 40.

It is remarkable, too, that he was able to accomplish all this just several generations after the unprecedented ferocity of Genghis Khan. But the 14th century was a time of turmoil throughout much of the civilised world, both in Europe and in the vast area under the influence of Islam. One of the principle causes of this chaos was the Black Death, which created not only hardship but also instability, for populations were severely reduced to the point where normal trading practices seized up.

In the Muslim world the reaction was more calm and fatalistic than in the West. Muslims fell back on to the bosom of the family and waited patiently for an improvement. Many, unable to rely on agriculture or trade, reverted to the nomadic existence that had never been far below the surface of their psychological make-up. The Central Asian economies took a long time to recover, although the region of Mawarannahr had continued to prosper.

The Jagatai Khanate comprised a vast area, however, and the mid-14th century was a period of civil war and jostling for power within its lands. It was out of this that Tamburlaine emerged.

In his youth, Tamburlaine's task had been to recover the family lands that had been lost in the various squabbles that prevailed in the area. Through these endeavours, his reputation as a leader of ability grew. He attracted a large number of soldiers to his band, and soon he was the most powerful leader in Mawarannahr, even if the Jagatai Khan, who was a descendant of the sacred khans of Mongolia, still held nominal power there, rather like a constitutional monarch.

Tamburlaine was never to be proclaimed Khan, and was even forced to have the all-but-useless Jagatai Khan sometimes accompany him on his campaigns. He did, however, have the wit to secure his own position by marrying one of the Jagatai Khan's daughters.

Once Tamburlaine had consolidated his hold over Mawarannahr, he set out on his expeditions of conquest in an attempt to emulate his forbears. His early competition came from a chieftain, Tokhtamish, from the Kipchak Khanate (the Golden Horde), which occupied the Russian steppes. The Kipchak Khanate was still a formidable power, so the fact that they were unable to make any ground amply demonstrates the ability of Tamburlaine.

The Jagatai Khanate seemed more than unlikely to produce a man of the stature of Tamburlaine – it was, after all, in many respects cleft in two. There were the grasslands of the north-east, perfect for the traditional nomadic and pastoral lifestyle of the Mongols who attempted to maintain the traditions of Genghis Khan and who tended to resist Islam. And then there was the area called Mawarannahr, where there was an established agricultural tradition around the oasis towns of Samarkand and Bukhara, home to the Jagatai aristocracy, and where the population had embraced Islam and tended to adopt an urban, Irano-Islamic lifestyle.

Furthermore, the language of the latter area, a Turkic ancestor of modern Uzbek, had developed an expressive power that would eventually be harnessed to create much fine literature. It had helped draw the Jagatai Khans from the pastures of the north-east, thereby creating what was effectively two khanates in one. Having established power in Mawarannahr, one of Tamburlaine's first aims was to bring the north-eastern steppe region under his control, even if he had little interest in the way of life there.

The further west one travelled through Asia, the more diffuse was the power of the dynasties that controlled its lands, the bitterer the rivalries between the Jalayirids of Iraq, the Mamluks of Syria, and the various local powers of Persia and Anatolia – a situation waiting to be exploited by Tamburlaine. His campaigns took him into all these territories, which he conquered with a ferocity that exceeded anything perpetrated by his illustrious forbear.

Nonetheless, he met tremendous resistance from certain among his enemies who perhaps were unaware of his brilliance as a military strategist and merciless approach to warfare. In the time of Genghis Khan, it had been understood that those who surrendered would be treated with leniency, but woe betide those who stood up to him. Whereas Tamburlaine had no time for fine distinctions, and stories abound of the delight that he took in the decimation of whole populations.

By 1387, he was in control of two of the three western khanates. Eventually he beat down the resistance of Tokhtamish and so also conquered the third. And so it went on – only when he was on his way to attempt the conquest of China did he finally expire.

Tamburlaine's savagery was legendary. After battles and massacres, he was in the habit of creating miniature mountains of skulls sealed in clay. In defeating the Sultan of Delhi, he massacred the whole population. It is thought that he deliberately razed communities along the trade routes to the north in order to force trade further south to the oasis towns of Mawarannahr, including of course Samarkand.

The governments that had arisen in the wake of the original Mongol invasions were swept aside, as was Tughluq rule in India, which had the effect of hastening the fragmentation of the Subcontinent into sultanates. The remaining Christian population of Central Asia, the Nestorians, was exterminated, notwithstanding the traditional Mongol tolerance of other religions.

Tamburlaine's invincibility had one curious side effect that was to make considerable impact on European history: by defeating the Ottomans, and so preserving Constantinople from them for a further 50 years, he unwittingly allowed time enough for Greek scholarship to make its way to Renaissance Italy. Tamburlaine differed from Genghis Khan in a number of ways. He was indisputably a great general – perhaps the greatest in history – but the interest in the other countries he took was entirely pragmatic: he conquered, took what he wanted (including craftsmen) and returned to Samarkand, which for him was his great glory. He seemed to have an idea of what he wanted to gain but no real vision of what to do with what he took, and none of the common-sense administrative skills of Genghis and his descendants, who had realised that in order to hold together an empire it was necessary to make up for the skills they did not have by recruiting men to the court who did.

Thus Tamburlaine signally failed even to emulate the non-military achievements of the khanates that had preceded him. In short, he was not a statesman. But he was a great soldier. Known for his skill at chess, which was part of the training of a Muslim leader, he was a supreme strategist, aided by the information passed on to him by a comprehensive spy network. He was the master of the indirect approach and of siege warfare, succeeding in wrestling İzmir from the finest Crusader troops. Perhaps most significant of all was his mastery of the tactical retreat, the sign of a disciplined army.

He was also adept at rather less noble tricks – for example, it was said that he would vomit boar's blood in front of visiting dignitaries in order to feign illness. Indeed, to the peoples of the western regions of Asia who had the misfortune to meet him on the field of battle, Tamburlaine was really nothing more than another barbarian from the steppes who happened to be in charge of an exceptionally efficient army that was fit for nothing more than pillage and rape.

To the sophisticated Islamic world of Persia and the Mediterranean shores, this man was not a true Muslim, but more of a pagan who had adopted some of the trappings of Islam. Yet the world from which Tamburlaine emerged was no longer truly part of the pastoral steppes that was still a part of Mongol folklore and which even, perhaps, represented a sort of idea that was simultaneously yearned for and despised. Certainly Tamburlaine showed but little obvious interest in the pastoral areas north-east of Mawarannahr, although his army was made up of soldiers from a variety of tribes and his administration, such as it was, was based on the Persian tradition.

But whereas his society was outwardly Muslim, Tamburlaine continued to observe many of the traditions of his Mongol ancestors, for if Islam was a powerful ally, then it could also be a threat. Its influence among the educated classes was considerable; but even at a more unorthodox level, there existed cults and pagan practises that had been absorbed into Islam and which were important in the spread of the Word.

Tamburlaine observed all aspects of Islam to a certain extent, presumably as a way of keeping as many people happy as possible, but it is conceivable that his fear of the more unorthodox forms of Islam was the greater – accounts of his protestations before dervishes suggest a respect for the mystical which had more in common with the traditions of his forefathers than the theology of clerical Islam. Certainly this relationship with the unorthodox was to last through the centuries in the region, and was to be one of the factors that kept it backward.

The fragility of Tamburlaine's achievements only became apparent with the squabbling among his undisciplined sons and grandsons that followed his death. (Genghis Khan's bequest, though short-lived, did at least live beyond his children.) Eventually his fourth son, Shahrukh, acceded to the throne, and under him there was a great flowering of Islamic culture. In many ways Shahrukh's was a successful reign, for he managed to hold together the principal parts of Tamburlaine's empire until just before his death, and even persuaded the weak Sayyid dynasty in Delhi to accept him as suzerain.

Samarkand, however, conceded its role as capital to Herat, for reasons that are open to conjecture. Samarkand and Mawarannahr fell to the control of Shahrukh's son Ulugh Beg, a mathematician and astronomer whose fame was great enough to attract several men eminent in the field to his court with whom he compiled an important set of astronomical tables. Ulugh Beg's observatory in Samarkand exists still. But after his death in 1449 (Shahrukh had died in 1447), the Timurid empire was reduced to the areas of Mawarannahr and Khurasan to the south-west, of which Herat was the major centre.

These areas were subsequently carved up among various relatives into appanages, according to Mongol practice. This was supposed to provide fiefdoms for all sons, not merely the eldest – a laudable aim, but one which had the effect of rendering a kingdom ever smaller and fragmenting it into bellicose princi-palities. These princes were great patrons of the arts but essentially impotent, if romantic, figures whose fecklessness was seemingly to live on for several centuries, only degenerating still further to the very depths of cruelty and barbarity. The Timurid dynasty thus came to nought, with the possible exception of Babur, a descendant of Tamburlaine who became the first Moghul emperor of India.

And so, by the beginning of the 16th century the Timurid dynasty was at an end and Samarkand in the hands of a new Turco-Mongol people, the Uzbeks. In many respects, then, the achievements of Tamburlaine were negligible, but the sheer size of his conquests, if nothing else, means that it is impossible to ignore him, and accounts for the aura of legend that attaches to him.

It may be – indeed, it is probable – that his reputation has been elevated by not only the art of Marlowe and all the other writers and composers of the West, but also by the local folklore and art that, strangely enough, given the barbarity of his acts, is the greatest legacy that he and his descendants have left to us and which can still be seen in Samarkand in the form of brilliant architecture, including the tomb of Tamburlaine himself.

A MERCHANT: We travel not for trafficking alone: By hotter winds our fiery hearts are fanned: For lust of knowing what should not be known we make the Golden Journey to Samarkand.

JAMES ELROY FLECKER

'THE GOLDEN JOURNEY TO SAMARKAND'